AF548589

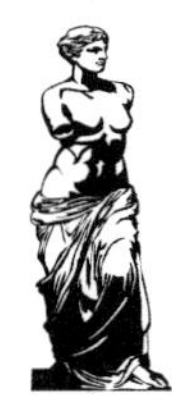

European Artists

MACMILLAN
PROFILES

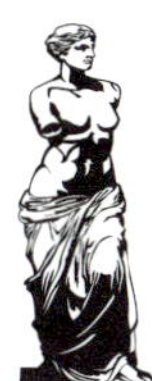

European Artists

Macmillan Reference USA
an imprint of the Gale Group
Detroit • New York • San Francisco • London • Boston • Woodbridge, CT

Macmillan Reference USA
1633 Broadway
New York, New York 10019

Gale Group
27500 Drake Rd.
Farmington Hills, MI 48331-3535

Library of Congress Catalog Card Number: 00-108562

ISBN 0-02-865500-1
Printed in Canada
10 9 8 7 6 5 4 3 2 1

Cover design by Berrian Design

Front cover, clockwise from top: Edvard Munch, Vincent van Gogh, Salvadore Dalí, Leonardo da Vinci. All photos used with the permission of Corbis.

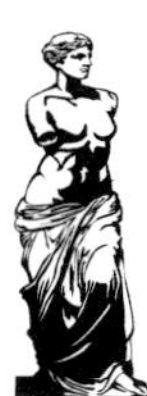

Contents

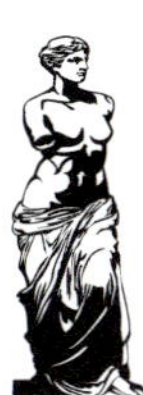

Preface

Macmillan Profiles: *European Artists* is a unique reference work featuring 125 profiles of European artists of note. The biographies of these artists, who excel in many genres of the art world, including mannerism, neoclassicism, impressionism, expressionism, surrealism, cubism, and more, provide a starting point for student research in social studies, world cultures, and history. The articles describe the struggles, triumphs, and perseverance of some of the greatest artists in history while providing information about their early years and personal development.

Art has always been an important part of European and world culture and history, and Macmillan Reference USA recognizes the need for reliable, accurate, and accessible biographies of notable figures within that framework. In *European Artists*, the vast majority of the biographies are new and were commissioned to supplement entries from original sources, which include Macmillan's award-winning reference materials for libraries across the world. In fact, it is likely that several of the encyclopedias on the shelves in this library were published by Macmillan Reference or Charles Scribner's Sons.

The goal of *European Artists* is to present an exciting introduction to the life and times of artists from European and world history who have, through hard work and talent, become the best in their field. Students will be drawn to the focused, determined nature of these talented individuals and, along the way, learn a great deal about history. Carefully researched and prepared by well-respected scholarly writers, these biographies are uplifting and informative. The article list was based on the following criteria: relevance to the curriculum, importance to history, and representation of as broad a cultural range as possible.

As we made the article selections for this volume, we were forced to make some difficult choices, but we feel that these biographies represent a broad cross-section of artists, both male and female. The article list was refined and expanded in response to advice from a lively and generous team of librarians from school and public libraries across the United States. In addition, art historian Irina Taissa Oryshkevich from Columbia University's Department of Art History helped select the artists to be included in this volume. Once the article list was finalized, we used *Webster's New Biographical Dictionary* to determine the proper name and alphabetical order for each artist.

FEATURES

European Artists is the eighteenth volume in the **Profiles Series.** To add visual appeal and enhance the usefulness of the volume, the page format was designed to include the following helpful features:

- Time Lines: Found throughout the text in the margins and also compiled in a master time line in the back of the book, time lines provide a quick reference source for dates and important events in the life and times of these artists.
- Notable Quotations: Found throughout the text in the margins, these thought-provoking quotations are drawn from interviews, speeches, and writings of the person covered in the article. Such quotations give readers a special insight into the distinctive personalities of these great men and women.
- Definitions and Glossary: Brief definitions of important terms in the main text can be found in the margins. A glossary at the end of the book provides students with an even broader list of definitions.
- Sidebars: Appearing in shaded boxes throughout the volume, these provocative asides relate to and amplify topics.
- Pull Quotes: Found throughout the text in the margin, pull quotes highlight essential facts.
- Suggested Reading: An extensive list of books and articles about the artists covered in the volume will help students who want to do further research.
- Index: A thorough index provides thousands of additional points of entry into the work.

ACKNOWLEDGMENTS:

This work would not have been possible without the hard work and creativity of our staff in New York and in Farmington Hills. We offer our sincere thanks to all who helped create this marvelous work. Special thanks go out to art historian Irina Taissa Oryshkevich for helping to select the artists in this volume.

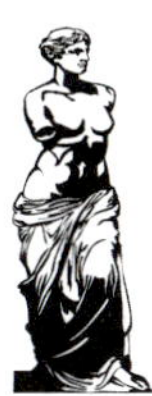

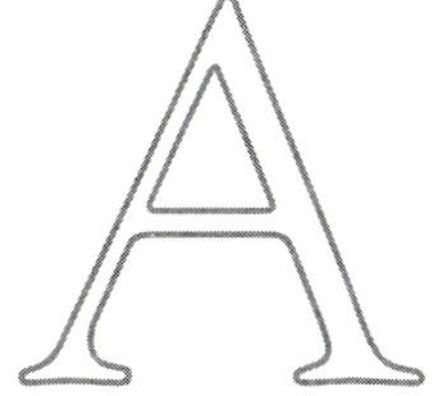

Angelico, Fra

c. 1400–February 18, 1455 ● Painter

Fra Angelico was born Guido di Pietro near Florence, where he and his brother Benedetto were trained in the manuscript industry, Fra Angelico as an **illuminator** and Benedetto as a scribe. Precisely when they began their apprenticeships is not known; but Fra Angelico was receiving commissions by 1417, and by 1425 both brothers had entered the Order of Preachers (Dominicans) at the convent of San Domenico in Fiesole. On entering the Dominicans, Guido changed his name to Fra Giovanni; but within 15 years of his death the Dominicans had already begun to call him Fra Angelico, the angelic friar.

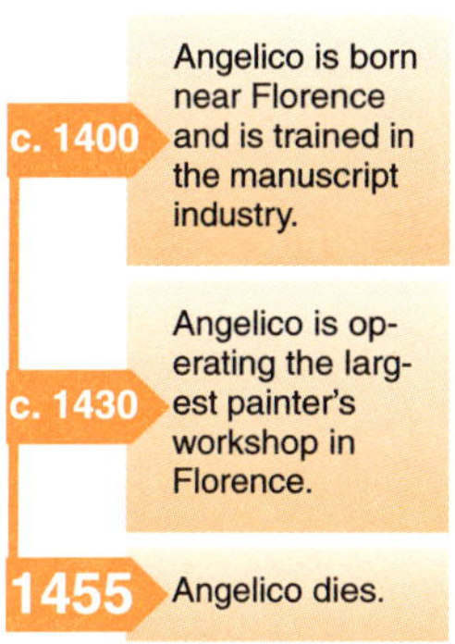

illuminator: an individual who worked as an illustrator of manuscripts and used silver, gold, and other bright colors with oftentimes elaborate decorations.

From the early 1420s until Fra Benedetto's death in 1448, the two brothers operated a large and prosperous scriptorium and painter's workshop in Fiesole. The majority of their commissions were for Dominican houses in Tuscany. However, by the early 1430s Fra Angelico had attracted the attention of the most ambitious patrons in Florence. By the late 1440s he was working in Rome for Pope Eugenius IV and then Pope Nicholas V. While there, Fra Angelico lived in the Dominican community at Santa Maria sopra Minerva, where he died and was buried.

Fra Angelico is difficult to fit among his contemporaries. He was not forward-looking like Masaccio (1401–1428); he never aligned himself with the refined, slightly classicizing taste of the Florentine upper classes, as did Fra Filippo Lippi (c. 1406–1469); nor was he willing to surrender pictorial beauty and fidelity to nature, as were Paolo Uccello (1397–1475) and Andrea del Castagno (c. 1421–1457), for the sake of endowing figures with the sculpturesque relief of chiaroscuro (the arrangement or treatment of light and dark parts) or of excavating dramatic spatial recessions with vanishing-point perspective. Although paintings such as *Coronation of the Virgin* which Fra Angelico made for San Domenico in Fiesole around 1430, make it obvious that he was thoroughly familiar with these new techniques, in that work he retained the old-fashioned allegiance to gilding, punchwork (a small repetitive pattern made with a steel punch), and brilliant pigments codified in the tradition of sacred art begun by Duccio di Buoninsegna (c. 1255–1318), Simone Martini (c. 1284–1344), and other painters of the early 14th century. Similarly, both the iconography and the radiance of Fra Angelico's *Annunciation* for San Domenico in Cortona are rooted in the traditions of 14th-century Tuscan painting.

Even so, by the mid-1430s Fra Angelico was operating the largest painter's workshop in Florence. When his workload demanded it, he seems to have employed fully trained but temporary assistants. It could be argued that some paintings from this period, such as the Linaiuoli Tabernacle and *Descent from the Cross*, include the collaboration of younger artists, such as Domenico Veneziano (d. 1461) and Piero della Francesca (c. 1420–1492), who later enjoyed great independent success.

Like every other ambitious Tuscan painter of the 15th century, however, Fra Angelico reached the pinnacle of his career working as a muralist. His largest **fresco** project is at the Dominican convent of San Marco in Florence, a commission from Cosimo de' Medici that occupied him intermittently from about 1440 until about 1450. Among other frescoes on the ground floor are *Crucifixion with Saints* in the Chapter Room and a life-size representation of St. Dominic kneeling and embracing the crucifix, on which the equally life-size figure of Jesus is still alive. This theme of an intimate colloquy between Christ and St. Dominic (and, by extension, every Dominican friar) underlies the more numerous frescoes in the second-floor dormitory. There, Fra Angelico and his shop made a fresco in each of the 48 cells as well as on three walls of the corridors. Some of these are among the greatest achievements of 15th-century painting, particularly *Annunciation* in the north corri-

fresco: a method of painting on either dry or wet plaster.

dor and *Transfiguration* in cell six. In them Fra Angelico fused the profoundly Christ-centered mysticism of the Order of Preachers with pictorial inventions of such originality that they remained largely unexplored by other painters for better than a generation.

The cells of Dominican convents were generally inaccessible to the lay public; thus Fra Angelico's professional admirers may not have seen some of his work at San Marco. In Rome, however, he worked on the monumental scale in more public spaces such as Saint Peter's, the Vatican Palace, and the cloister of Santa Maria sopra Minerva. The paintings in Saint Peter's and the Minerva cloister have disappeared. All that survives of Fra Angelico's work as a fresco painter outside Florence, are some figures in the vaults of the San Brizio Chapel in Orvieto Cathedral (1447) and a cycle of the lives of St. Stephen and St. Lawrence in the private chapel of Pope Nicholas V in the Vatican Palace (1448–1449). The pope shared his fellow humanists' keen interest in Christian, not just classical, antiquity. Thus the choice of the lives of St. Stephen and St. Lawrence bespeaks the pope's interest in the earliest period of Christian history, focused through the lives of two deacon martyrs. When Fra Angelico was working in the pope's chapel, moreover, the **humanist** architect Leon Battista Alberti was also resident at the pontifical court. Alberti may have influenced the highly classicizing design of the background architecture in Fra Angelico's scenes.

The late work of Benozzo Gozzoli (1420–1497), Fra Angelico's major assistant, gives some idea of where his thinking was leading him at the time of his death; in Benozzo's *Procession of the Magi* in San Marco, Florence, for example, one detects the impress of Fra Angelico's having studied the relief sculpture of Roman antiquity. Roman artists of a younger generation, such as Antoniazzo Romano (1452–1508), likewise furthered the friar painter's late researches. However, in the great papal building campaigns of the 16th and 17th centuries, so much early Renaissance art was destroyed that most of Fra Angelico's Roman legacy has been lost. Had it survived, one might have a very different understanding of the major fresco projects of later generations, including those of Filippino Lippi (c. 1457–1504) and perhaps even of Raphael (1483–1520) and Michelangelo (1475–1564). ◆

"Although one of the great painters of all times, [Angelico] was first and above all a Dominican friar. His calling was his life, and his life, totally devoid of external dramatic incidents, was spent in being a good Dominican, bound by his vows of poverty, chastity and obedience."

Smithsonian magazine, December 1986, on Fra Angelico's priorities in life

humanist: an individual who gives priority in their life and work to the endeavors, works, and needs of human beings rather to religious gods, symbols, or any other non-human entities.

Arp, Jean (Hans)

SEPTEMBER 16, 1887–JUNE 7, 1966 ● SCULPTOR, PAINTER, AND WRITER

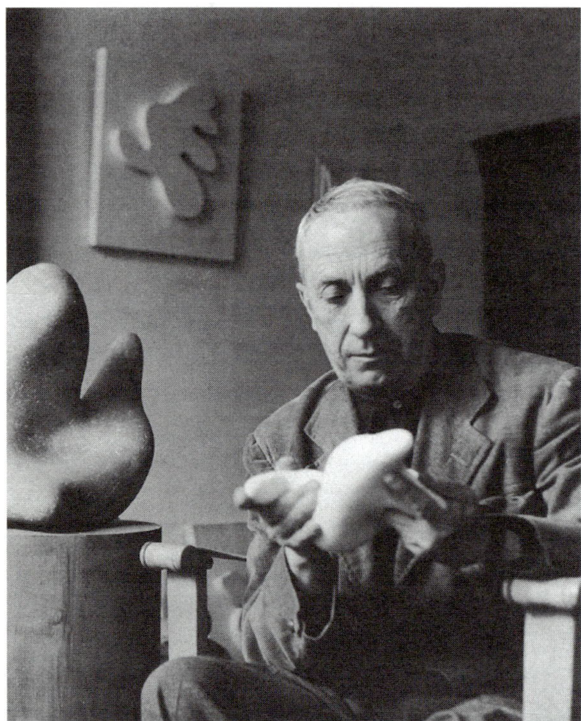

Jean Arp with several of his works.

> **"A dominant personality within Dada, Surrealism, and abstract art, his reliefs and sculptures have had a decisive influence upon the sculpture of this century."**
> *The Bullfinch Guide to Art History* on the importance of Hans Arp's work

His bi-national name bespoke the cosmopolitan aspirations of his art: he signed his essays "Jean Arp" when writing in French and "Hans Arp" when writing in German. Best known for his sculpture, Jean Arp was also an accomplished painter, collagist, printmaker, and poet. Arp was at the center of two of the most important spawning grounds of 20th-century modernism—dadaism and surrealism—both of which sought to burst the confines of traditional artistic form in order to tap the revelatory depths of the human unconscious.

Born Peter Wilhelm Arp in Strassburg, Germany, on September 16, 1887, to a French Alsatian mother and German father, Arp was attracted to art from an early age. He received his initial formal training at the Strasbourg School of Arts and Crafts (Kunstgewerbeschule) from 1900 to 1901 and then studied privately with Georges Ritleng, a local painter. In 1904 Arp moved to Weimar, Germany, to study at the Kunstschule, where he spent the following three years before enrolling at the Académie Julian in Paris, where he studied from 1908 to 1909.

Chafing under the regimentation of formal academic instruction, Arp moved to Weggis, Switzerland, to study plaster sculpture technique with Fritz Huf. Here he dabbled for the first time in abstract painting; the puzzled indifference elicited by his black-flecked gray canvases sent him temporarily back to figurative work but did not dampen his ardor for novel modes of artistic expression. His quest found its first major public expression through the Moderne Bund, a group that he cofounded in Lucerne in 1911 and that featured his work—spontaneously rendered caricatures of faces and nude females—at exhibitions in 1911 and 1913.

In 1912 Arp's encounter with Wassily Kandinsky in Munich led him to form a brief association with Die Blaue Reiter (The Blue Rider), a German expressionist movement. Under the movement's influence he produced a series of woodcuts and paintings, most notably *Bathers* (1913) and *Three Women* (1912), both of which feature rough-hewn, densely colored human figures heavily outlined in black. In 1913 his work appeared in an expressionist show in Berlin at the first Autumn Salon.

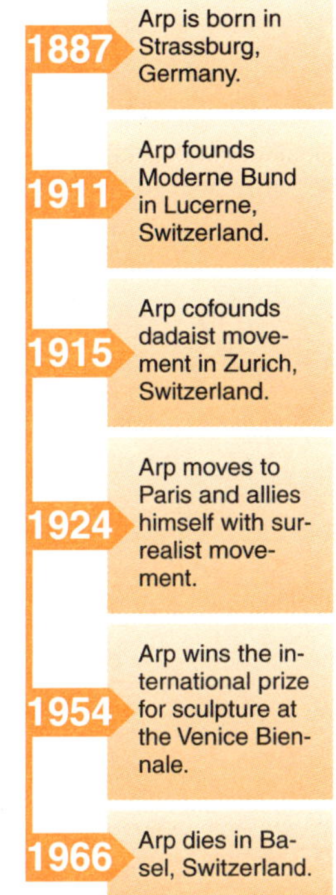

In Paris in 1914, Arp drew fresh inspiration from his meetings with the artists Modigliani, Picasso, and Delaunay and the writer/painter Max Jacob. Influences crowded into his work from both the past—ancient and primitive art and German romanticism—and the avant-garde—futurism and **cubism**—resulting in rich collages such as *Untitled* (1915) and *Wallpaper* (1915).

Despising the patriotic fervor that attended the onset of World War I, in 1915 Arp settled in Zurich, Switzerland, where his work was exhibited at Galerie Tanner. In the show's catalogue he attacked traditional academic doctrines of **perspective** and **representational naturalism,** viewing art instead as a spiritual endeavor that requires only the elemental tools of line, form, and color.

While in Zurich Arp met the painter Sophie Taeuber, whom he married in 1921. Her abstract work proved a major influence on his own, and they collaborated on a series of collages—*Duo-Collages* (1916–1918)—rendered in a striking palette of muted colors. These abstract works evinced Arp's determination to sound a spiritual depth unreachable by representation.

The artistic and literary luminaries of Zurich—including Arp, the Romanian poet Tristan Tzara, the Romanian artist Marcel Janco, and German poet Hugo Ball—met regularly at the Cabaret Voltaire to debate the proliferating aesthetic innovations of the day. Out of these passionate gatherings emerged the dadaist movement, a revolutionary challenge to traditional notions of sense and structure in art and literature. Buoyed by the dadaist whirlwind, Arp forsook his abstract formalism in favor of a free-form, curvilinear biomorphism—"moving ovals," in his words—that prefigured much of his later work. Evoking the whimsical rather than the nihilistic spirit of dada, Arp

cubism: school of art popularized by the works of Pablo Picasso and characterized by squared-off images of many different objects, animals, and people.

perspective: a technique used by artists to convey a three-dimensional illusion onto a two-dimensional surface.

representational naturalism: an art movement characterized by artists painting scenes in nature as they interpret them somewhat abstractly.

Dada

Dada (or dadaism) was an early 20th-century movement among painters, writers, and musicians, designed to question or destroy traditional views of aesthetics and morality, largely because of disillusionment at the violence of World War I. Despite the claims of its adherents to reject definitions, they had a shared taste for the shocking, absurd, and even meaningless.

According to some accounts, Romanian sound poet and essayist Tristan Tzara chose the word dada (French: "hobbyhorse") at random, to emphasize the unpredictable elements involved in creating works of art; others claim Hugo Ball coined the term. In 1916 the Cabaret Voltaire opened in Zurich. There gathered many of the central figures of the dada movement, with artists, musicians, and writers in residence, including Tzara, Hans (Jean) Arp, Emmy Hennings, Richard Huelsenbeck, and Marcel and Georges Janco.

Examples of dada art include Marcel Duchamp's bottle holder attached to a bicycle wheel; the work, which makes little sense in terms of function or form, shows the dada interest in "ready-made" objects. Also famous was Duchamp's depiction of the Mona Lisa with a mustache. Arp created collages of colored paper that were shaped and put together at random, as in his *Collage with Squares Arranged According to the Laws of Chance* (1917). Arp's colleague, Max Ernst, combined the use of collage and found objects or materials, as in the *Elephant Celebes* (1921), which is composed only of previously printed materials. Kurt Schwitters also used collage successfully, and his *Merzbau* (begun in 1923) is a classic example of dada—a largely chaotic assembling of unrelated objects, which grew to take up entire rooms.

While dada may have celebrated anarchy, it was not wholly nihilist—many of its adherents believed in the power of art to bring out an individual's good self, untainted by oppressive social structures. Its adherents could also mix shock and outrage with humor and play. Because dada was largely a reaction rather than an organized movement, however, it is not surprising that it did not last long. The movement spread to Germany, Paris, New York, and elsewhere, but by 1922 the group in Paris, comprising many of the former Zurich members, had disbanded. Many of the important dada figures interacted with artists participating in constructivism, or went on to influence the emerging surrealist movement in the 1920s.

formed collages made of pieces of colored paper strikingly arrayed on cardboard—*Collage with Squares Arranged According to the Laws of Chance* (1917).

Arp settled in Germany after the war, where he began to spread the dadaist gospel of "moral revolution" in art and reestablished his ties with avant-garde artists throughout the continent. He and Taeuber joined an experimental utopian commune, Monte Verità, in Ascona in 1918, where his work continued in a biomorphic vein in such works as *Figure* (1915) and *Madame Torso with Wavy Hat* (1916), both of which suggest the human form.

In 1924 Arp and his wife moved to Paris, where he allied himself with the burgeoning **surrealist** movement, which sought a direct path to absolute reality through the untrammeled exploration of the dream life and unconscious. Through the late 1920s he concentrated on wooden bas-reliefs and whimsical cut-cardboard pieces in which ordinary objects were endowed with human qualities or humans were reduced to mere objectivity, notably in *Clocks* (1924) and *Lips* (1926).

surrealist movement: a literary and art movement founded by writer André Breton in Paris in 1924 and practiced internationally into the 1930s. It was grounded in the psychoanalytic theories of Sigmund Freud, particularly those relating to the expression of the imagination as revealed in dreams. Using a range of styles, the surrealists, such as Salvador Dali (see entry) and René Magritte, filled their works with fantastic imagery and dream-inspired symbols.

In the early 1930s Arp turned increasingly to sculpture, first in the form of reliefs combined on a common base and then, as in *Concretions* (1930), freestanding works in plaster, wood, or stone. In the ensuing decades his sculpture, tantalizingly straddling the abstract and the figurative, always suggested a melding of human forms with their origins in a primal, mystical source of all life. Arp broke with the surrealists in 1931 to found a new movement, abstraction-creation, in conformity with the increasingly geometrical trend of his work.

Arp's deepening immersion in religious mysticism inspired no major formal departures in his later work, which tended toward variations on his longstanding biomorphic/surrealist vision, which codified as "concretions." He explained, "Concretion designates solidifaction, the mass of the stone, the plant, the animal, the man. Concretion is something that has grown."

Arp's international renown grew throughout the post-World War II era. During a visit to the United States in 1949–50, he executed a large wood and metal relief at Harvard University, and in 1958 he did a mural relief for the Unesco Building in Paris. In 1954 Arp was awarded the international prize for sculpture at the Venice Biennale.

Jean Arp died in Basel, Switzerland, in 1966. ◆

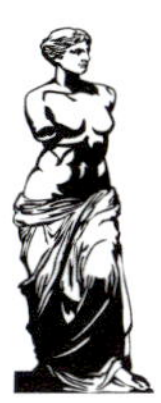

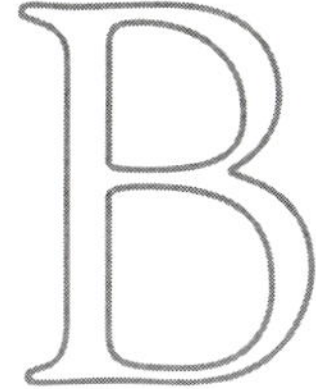

Bacon, Francis

October 28, 1909–April 28, 1992 ● Painter

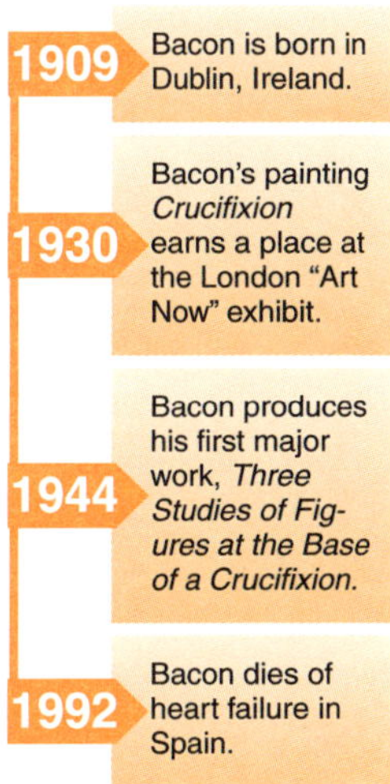

In the 1940s the painter Francis Bacon emerged from obscurity as a major artist of the postwar era, by turns acclaimed and reviled for the chilling portrayals of terror and brutality that distinguished his figurative, expressionistic canvases. Once denounced by the conservative British prime minister Margaret Thatcher as "that man who paints those dreadful pictures," Bacon defended his work as a realistic picture of the human heart. "You can't be much more horrific than life itself," he once said.

Francis Bacon was born on October 28, 1909, in Dublin, Ireland, to English parents. His father's work as a racehorse trainer kept the family on the move between England and Ireland through most of his childhood. Housebound much of the time because of severe asthma, he was educated sporadically at home by private tutors. His acrimonious relationship with his parents reached the breaking point when, at the age of 16, he was forced to leave home because of his homosexual dalliances with some of the grooms in the stables. Bacon then spent two months in Berlin, at that time a hotbed of experimentation in the arts and bohemian lifestyles. He moved on to Paris, where he spent the following 18 months soaking in the cultural life of the city, especially its art galleries and museums, where he encountered some of the surrealist work of Pablo Picasso.

Still lacking any formal training in art, Bacon moved to London in 1929 and rented a studio to launch himself as an in-

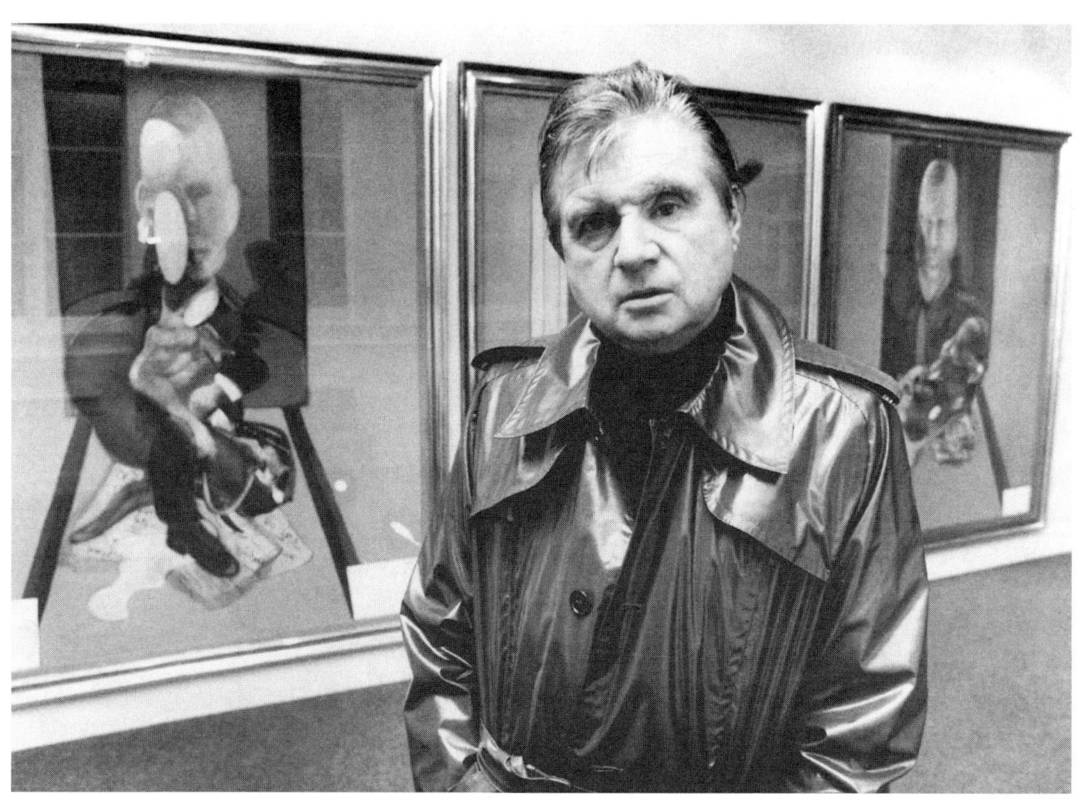

Francis Bacon, c. 1975.

terior decorator. He achieved moderate success as a designer of modernist, art deco furniture. As a sideline, he dabbled in painting. His early canvases were a melding of cubist and surrealist currents of the day, the most famous of which was *Crucifixion* (1933), which earned him a place in a 1933 show in London called "Art Now" and an appearance in Herbert Read's book of the same name. But after this encouraging moment, Bacon's progress slowed, and in the late 1930s he drifted away from painting, destroying most of his early canvases. He wandered through a series of odd jobs while yielding most of his energies to drinking and gambling.

triptych: a painting that is made up of three different parts, canvases, or panels commonly found in altarpieces during the Middle Ages and the Renaissance period.

With the onset of World War II, Bacon tried to enlist in the army but was rejected because of his asthma. By 1943, gnawed by a growing sense of emptiness and restlessness, he decided to rededicate himself to painting. After several years of labor, he produced his first major work, *Three Studies of Figures at the Base of a Crucifixion* (1944), a **triptych** that shocked audiences of the day with its juxtaposition of lasciviously rendered Greek Furies and the crucifixion of Jesus, which

Bacon—an atheist—rendered as a monument to human barbarity.

As Bacon found his painterly "voice" over the ensuing years, he turned his lack of formal training to his advantage, resisting the confines of standard aesthetic classification as he rummaged freely through the centuries of Western art for nuggets of inspiration: magazine and newspaper photographs (especially the sequential studies of human and animal movement done by Eadweard Muybridge in the 19th century), cinema, and the work of the Old Masters. He combined all three in *Head VI* (1949)—part of a series later known as The Screaming Popes. In this work, the head of a pope, patterned after a Velazquez portrait of Innocent X, is combined with a mouth agape in terror, patterned after a famous image from Eisenstein's seminal film, *Battleship Potemkin*.

As Bacon found his painterly "voice" over the ensuing years, he turned his lack of formal training to his advantage, resisting the confines of standard aesthetic classification as he rummaged freely through the centuries of Western art for nuggets of inspiration.

Through the mid-1950s Bacon remained preoccupied with the human form, using vigorous brushstrokes and jarring colors to portray it in a sequence of actions, like a Muybridge study, but dense with layers of symbolic meaning, as in *Study for a Portrait I-VIII*. Bacon said his goal in such works was to "trap reality" more compellingly than mere illustration could. Michael Kimmelman, an art critic for *The New York Times*, said of Bacon's portrayal of the human form: "His images twisted it, X-rayed it, made it bleed, transmogrify and unravel. The body became an expression of longing, exhaustion, illness, and also lust. Few artists could render flesh so palpably and voluptuously, or endow even so mundane a subject as a man turning a bathroom faucet with Michelangelesque aspirations."

Aside from a few animal paintings he did in the 1950s—for example, *Dog* (1952) and *Study of a Baboon* (1953)—the human form remained Bacon's vehicle for probing the hidden recesses of the psyche. From the mid-1950s to the early 1960s a slightly more realistic approach imparted a somewhat lighter feel to his work. Highlights of this period include *Man in Blue I-VII* (1954) and *Study for Portrait II (after the Life Mask of William Blake)* (1955). Later in the decade he painted a series of single figures—some of them nude—rendered as bulky, solid figures in quotidian settings, as in *Reclining Woman* (1961).

By the 1960s these single figures, mostly male, were often rendered with stark lighting in a cramped, prison-like, anonymous interior. He also produced a number of triptychs during this decade, many of which were unsettling variations on his own head or those of his friends (most often his close friend

George Dyer), as in *Three Studies for Head of Isabel Rawsthorne* (1965). Even at his most placid, Bacon admitted few grace notes of serenity or easy hope into his work. To the very end he was impelled to record, unflinchingly and often grotesquely, the fears and terrors of human life, as evoked in the severed nude male torso portrayed in *Study of the Human Body* (1982).

Notwithstanding the often macabre, morbid tone of his work, Bacon described himself as "an optimist, but about nothing." He told a reporter: "We live, we die, and that's it." While vacationing in Spain, Francis Bacon succumbed to heart failure on April 28, 1992. ◆

Beckmann, Max

FEBRUARY 12, 1884–DECEMBER 27, 1950 ● PAINTER

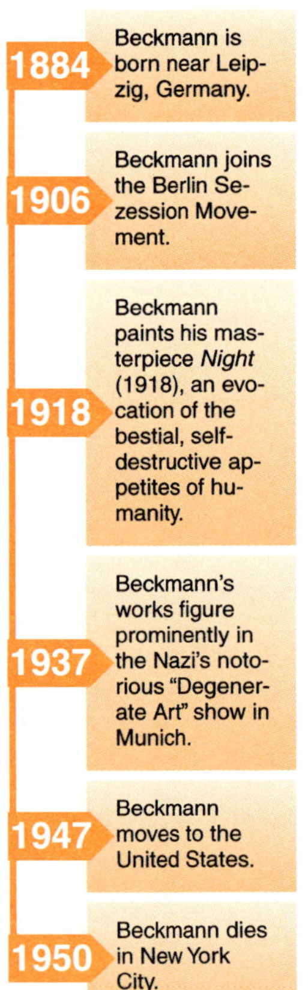

Max Beckmann's art and life are a testament to the convulsions of the 20th century—political, social, psychological, and spiritual. Often identified as an expressionist, Beckmann, a painter and printmaker, was in fact a stylistic and thematic nomad whose pressing social, ethical, and spiritual concerns were refracted through freely evolving visual idioms that strained against the expressive limits of representational art.

Beckmann was born in the agricultural Braunschweig outskirts of Leipzig, Germany, on February 12, 1884, the youngest of three children of farmers. Shortly after Max's birth, his father, Carl, moved the family to Leipzig, where he made a living as a flour merchant, real estate agent, and, later, as a laboratory technician. Only 10 when his father died, Max had already begun to show a preference for drawing over his studies, and by the age of 15 he decided to become a painter despite his mother's strenuous objections.

After failing the entrance exam for the Königliche Akademie der Bildenen Künste in Dresden, Beckmann successfully applied to the Grossherzogliche Sächsische Kunstschule in Weimar (The Weimar Art Academy). There he acquired a grounding in formal academic art from 1900 to 1903, refining his drawing skills by sketching ancient sculptures and live models. After graduating in 1903, Beckmann made his first visit to Paris, the city he regarded as the world center of art. Upon returning to

Berlin, where he spent most of his time before World War I, he turned out a series of impressionist-influenced landscapes, the most notable of which was *Young Men by the Sea* (1905).

The year 1906 was an eventful one for Beckmann. He married his fellow student and artist Minna Tube and then spent time in Italy with her, courtesy of an art fellowship. By now happily immersed in the European ferment of experimental **modernism,** he returned to Berlin and joined the Berlin Sezession (an important movement that was challenging the received conventions of academic art), where he had his first exhibition that year. There and in another 1906 show at the Kunstlerbund in Weimar, Beckmann's increasing interest in **expressionism** was reflected in several large-scale figure paintings dense with symbolic meanings, such as *Large Death Scene* (1906), an evocation of his mother's death that evinces the influence of Edvard Munch, the Norwegian expressionist painter whom he had met that year.

modernism: a school of art incorporating innovative forms of expression, integrating previous methods and techniques, and utilizing new materials and types of paint and material in creating abstract pieces as opposed to realistic representations.

expressionism: a style of art in which the artist produces a work that conveys his or her emotions, expressed through abstractions and distortions; expressionist work can be found throughout many periods of art history.

Winning the Villa Romana Prize allowed Beckmann and his wife to travel to Italy in late 1906 and early 1907. There he carefully studied the works of masters such as Michelangelo, Rubens, and Rembrandt, thereby expanding his technique for rendering the human form in supervening works such as *The Flood* (1908). Following that trip, Beckmann's social and spiritual preoccupations begin to merge. Religious themes and symbols crop up in his work, as in *Crucifixion* (1909). Despite a growing fixation on the human figure—including a number of self-portraits such as *Countess S. vom Hagen* (1908)—as a vehicle for his increasingly metaphysical broodings, Beckmann continued to produce rough-hewn seascapes and landscapes that dramatized the conflict between human artifacts and the primal forces of nature.

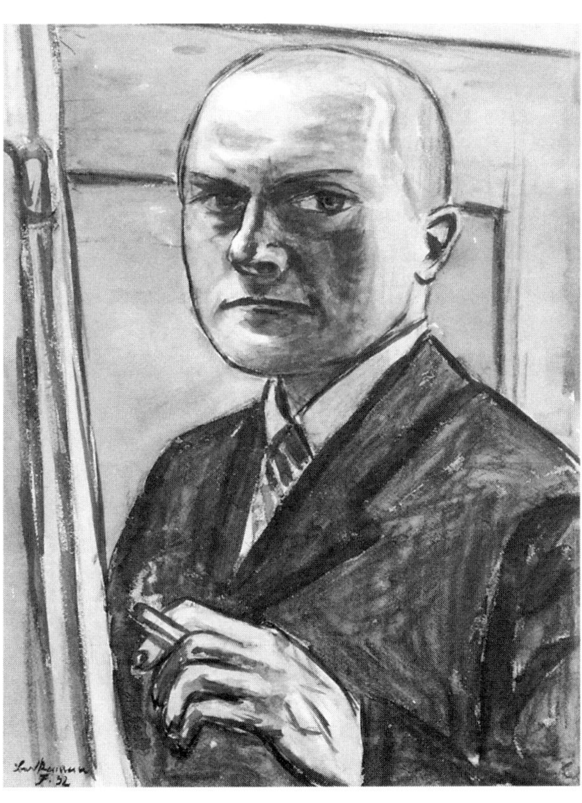

Max Beckmann, self-portrait, 1932.

Beckmann's growing renown led to his election to the executive board of the Sezession in 1910, the youngest artist ever to attain that

Max Beckmann's art and life are a testament to the convulsions of the 20th century—political, social, psychological, and spiritual.

honor. Quickly wearying of the institutional art world's distracting movements and manifestoes, he resigned from the board in 1911 to devote himself to his work, which was featured in a one-man exhibition at the Balerie Paul Cassirer in Berlin in 1913. Ranging himself against the abstractions of cubism, he publicly affirmed his commitment to "artistic objectivity toward the thing represented."

With the onset of World War I, Beckmann volunteered to join the medical corps and served on the Russian front and in a hospital in Flanders, where he was subjected to the unspeakable horrors and agonies of a wartime operating room. By the summer of 1915, he had suffered a nervous collapse and was sent to Frankfurt to recover. His sensibility was permanently transformed by the trauma of the war. When he returned to work in 1917, his paintings dispensed with the niceties of conventional proportion and perspective and took on a near-cubist angularity, compression of space, boldness of color, and angularity of line, all of which combined to evoke the tortured psyche of postwar European humanity. These post-war sensibilities are displayed in works such as *Self-Portrait with Red Scarf* (1917), as well as his signal achievement of this period, *Night* (1918), an unflinching evocation of the bestial, self-destructive appetites of humanity distilled into the claustrophobic confines of a crowded tenement room.

During the 1920s, Beckmann's work—while shedding none of its somber metaphysicality—sporadically revealed a lighter, more idyllic quality in works such as *Nice* (1921), *Landscape with Fisherman* (1924), and *Genoa Harbor* (1927). But the strain of brooding introspection and social protest persisted in other works, including *Iron Bridge* (1922), *The Martyrdom* (1919), and *The Dream* (1921). More settled in his professional life with his appointment to a professorship at the Städel Institute in 1925, he ended his first marriage and married again, this time to Mathilde von Kaulbach. His reputation steadily rising, Beckmann was the subject of major retrospectives in Mannheim in 1928 and Zurich in 1930.

Beckmann's career was thrown into turmoil by Hitler's rise to power in 1933. The Nazis regarded all variants of modernism as "degenerate" art, and they moved quickly to dismiss Beckmann from his academic post at Städel. Beckmann moved to Berlin, where he remained until 1937, when the Nazis prominently featured his works in the notorious "Degenerate Art" exhibition in Munich. Beckmann then fled with his wife and her sister to Amsterdam, where he spent the war under increasingly grim circumstances. His triptych *Blind Man's Buff* (1945) evokes the nightmare of the war years. After the Nazis were driven out of the Netherlands, there was a major exhibition of Beckmann's work in Amsterdam.

In 1947 Beckmann and his wife moved to the United States, where he spent the next three years teaching at Washington University in St. Louis, the site of a major retrospective of his work in 1948. His last major work of this period was *The Argonauts* (1949–50), the ninth of a series of triptychs he executed in the late 1940s.

In 1949 Beckmann moved to Brooklyn, New York, where he taught at the Art School of the Brooklyn Museum. He died in New York City in 1950. ◆

Bellini, Giovanni

c. 1431–May 29, 1516 ● Painter

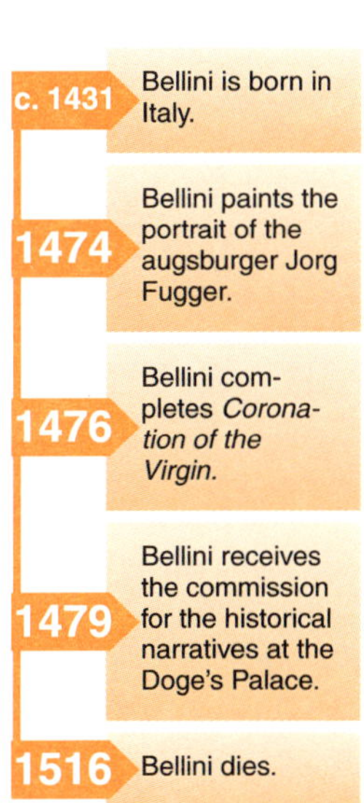

Giovanni Bellini was a member of a family of artists distinguished for their exceptional contribution to Renaissance painting in Venice. The careers of Jacopo Bellini (c. 1400–1470) and two of his sons, Gentile (c. 1429–1507) and Giovanni, represent the strength of the traditional Venetian family workshop of painters during the Renaissance. Presumably trained under Jacopo, the brothers were practicing as independent masters by the 1460s but continued to assist their father on various projects and may have shared workspace around this time. The birth dates of the brothers are unknown and subject to wide speculation. In 1453, Nicolosia Bellini, Jacopo's daughter, married the Paduan artist Andrea Mantegna. Jacopo's nephew and student Leonardo Bellini (active c. 1443–1490) was a successful manuscript painter.

Jacopo Bellini was the pupil of the renowned painter from the Marches in central Italy, Gentile da Fabriano, who was active in Venice from 1408 to 1413 and whom Jacopo is likely to have served as apprentice c.1414–1419 in Brescia.

Although few, Jacopo's preserved paintings permit assessment of him as the most advanced Venetian painter of his generation. They reflect understanding of Gentile da Fabriano's

one-point perspective: a form of linear perspective wherein all lines in the piece seem to form a horizon and meet at a single point.

experimentation in rendering the effects of light as well as the Florentine artist Leon Battista Alberti's theory of **one-point perspective.** A *Madonna and Child* of c. 1440 incorporates a diminutive kneeling figure of a donor and is allied in the drapery patterns and use of gold with the International Gothic style as embraced by Gentile da Fabrino. This panel reveals Jacopo's skill in portraiture and luminous treatment of firmly modeled flesh. It is most noteworthy for the innovative observation of the sky at dawn and the extraordinary breadth of vision in the light-bathed panoramic landscape.

Among the outstanding indexes of a Renaissance artist's inventive process are the two bound volumes of Jacopo's nearly 300 metalpoint drawings that were highly prized in the period and are now in the Louvre, Paris, and British Museum, London. These include records and fantasies of classical artifacts, some studies of nature and everyday life, and mostly religious compositions conceived as self-sufficient works of art. The Paris drawings are believed to range in date from the mid-1430s to the mid-1450s, the London drawings from the mid-1450s to the mid-1460s.

The pioneer of the Renaissance style in Venetian painting, Jacopo shared his interests in perspective and in classical form with his son-in-law Mantegna and the Florentine sculptor Donatello, resident in Padua from 1433 to 1453; reciprocal influence is assumed, Jacopo strongly influenced the next generation of Venetian painters, including Carlo Crivelli (c. 1430–c. 1494) and Cima da Conegliano (c. 1459–c. 1517). His considerable legacy to his sons is manifest in distinct ways; Gentile was to practice the mode of narrative painting indicated by Jacopo's drawings, Giovanni to carry forward his father's experimentation with landscape and the atmospheric effects of light.

"Giovanni Bellini raised Venice to a center of Renaissance art that rivaled Florence and Rome. He brought to painting a new degree of realism, a new wealth of subject matter, and a new sensuousness in form and color."

From the website, *The Web Gallery of Art,* on Giovanni Bellini's importance in the art world

Among the great innovative masters of the 15th century and one of the greatest of all Venetian painters, Giovanni Bellini revolutionized painting in Venice through his embrace of the Netherlandish oil technique, setting the stage for the accomplishments of Giorgione, Titian, and other Venetian artists in the century following. Giovanni achieved a monumental figural conception and his chiefly religious works are characterized by a profound sense of human dignity, therein comparable to the attainments of the early Renaissance Florentine masters Masaccio and Donatello. Revealing acute observation of the natural world, Giovanni Bellini portrayed landscape and changing atmospheric effects with an outstanding sense of immediacy. Well before the end of his long and productive lifetime, his works were highly prized by collectors and he was eulogized as the greatest painter in the world. The German painter Albrecht Dürer and the Tuscan artist and historian Giorgio Vasari recorded Bellini's courtesy and kindness as well as his stature in the arts.

Giovanni is first recorded in a document of 1459; a *Crucifixion* has been thought by some scholars to come from the Gattamelata altarpiece and to reflect his participation. Four triptychs for the church of Santa Maria della Carità (1461–1464) were probably commissioned from Jacopo's shop and may have been executed largely by Giovanni. Documents for his early career are sparse, but relative chronology of his numerous deeply moving devotional paintings—including many interpretations of the Madonna and Child and the Dead Christ—is established. A portrait of the Augsburger Jörg Fugger is datable to 1474, and documentation from 1476 suggests that Bellini's *Coronation of the Virgin* had been completed.

In the *Coronation*, a high altarpiece for the church of San Francesco in Pesaro, Bellini employs an aggrandized, highly plastic figural form as well as a newly rationalized and harmonious spatial system. In addition to **tempera,** he uses oil as a binding medium for pigment (as also in the Fugger portrait). This permits a greater fluidity of technique, promoting his experimentation with the unification of light and space. Apparently, Giovanni seldom left Venice, but he may have traveled to Pesaro at the time of this commission and been influenced by the Tuscan painter Piero della Francesca (c. 1420–1492)—resident in nearby Urbino—in taking these new steps. Bellini's sensitivity to the site intended for the altarpiece and to specific contemporary Franciscan devotional concerns are evident in his composition and imagery. Scenes in the predella employ motifs found in Jacopo's drawings. Bellini's great altarpieces designed for aisle locations in Venetian churches utilize a perspectival system that defines the space as a chapel-like extension of the actual space to accommodate his figures: the Madonna seated on a high throne with saints assembled below. To enhance the illusionism of these scenes, Bellini repeats the architectural ornamentation of the frame in the painted architecture.

tempera: a painting process that utilizes egg yolks to bind pigments; the artist must manufacture the substance by mixing pigment, water, and diluted egg yolk; this process was used before the availability of oil paints.

Also apparent in the Pesaro altarpiece is Bellini's experimentation with conveying recession into space in landscape using superposed planes, an innovation to be fully developed by about 1500–1502 in his *Baptism of Christ*. Bellini's explorations and mastery of landscape are further well exemplified by his *Saint Francis in Ecstasy* (1470s) and *Transfiguration* (1480s). Excelling in every category of painting, Giovanni joined Gentile in 1479 in the commission for historical narratives at the Doge's Palace. Among Giovanni's many superb portraits is the lifelike *Doge Leonardo Loredan* (c. 1501). Subsequent works bespeak an extraordinary flexibility and receptivity to new artistic currents: *The Feast of the Gods* (1514); *The Drunkenness of Noah* (c. 1514); *Nude Woman Holding Mirror* (1515).

Bellini most likely expanded his workshop circa 1479, and by around 1490, when demand for his devotional paintings had become enormous, as it remained well into the 16th century, he maintained one of the largest and best organized workshops of the Renaissance. Drawings on paper (cartoons), with contour lines pricked and sprinkled with charcoal to transfer the design (pouncing), were sometimes used for replication. Bellini trained or directed numerous painters of the next generation. Many, now referred to as "the *belliniani*," practiced his style; others—Giorgione, Titian, Sebastiano del Piombo, Lorenzo Lotto—developed distinctly personal styles and include the great pioneers of 16th-century art further realizing the potential of oil painting and enhancing the international reputation of Venetian art Giovanni Bellini had established. ◆

Bernini, Gian Lorenzo

DECEMBER 7, 1598–NOVEMBER 28, 1680 ● SCULPTOR, ARCHITECT, AND PAINTER

Baroque: a style of art in which artists sought to convey movement, emotion, and variety in their pieces; this style was at its peak in the mid-17th century mainly in Catholic nations.

The Italian sculptor, architect, and painter Gian Lorenzo Bernini was the most important European artist of the 17th century. He almost single-handedly originated the robustly ornate and emotive **baroque** style that dominated European arts until the mid-18th century. Bernini's exquisite and stunningly expressive sculpture and architecture became so emblematic of post-Renaissance Rome that his patron, Pope Urban VIII, hailed him as "a sublime artificer, born by divine disposition," who "was made for Rome, and Rome for him."

The chief sources of information on Bernini's life are two biographies: the first, by Filippo Badinucci, was issued in 1682, only two years after Bernini's death; the second, written by Bernini's son Domenico, was published in 1713. They both tell of an extraordinarily gifted boy born in Naples to an artistic calling, the son of an esteemed mannerist sculptor from Tuscany, Pietro Bernini, who was Gian Lorenzo's teacher. The family moved to Rome in about 1605. Gian Lorenzo was already a skilled marble sculptor by the age of eight, prompting his father's friend Cardinal Barberini to observe that the teacher might soon be outshone by his student. Pietro replied, "That doesn't bother me. Because, as you know, in that case the loser wins."

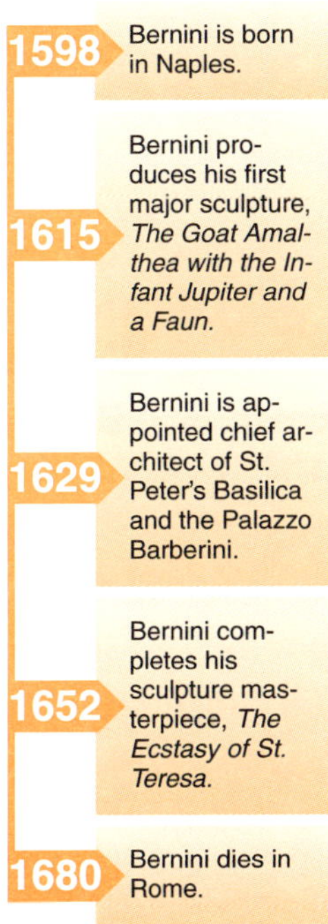

Bernini's early sculptures are steeped in the Hellenistic classicism in which he was trained. For instance, *The Goat Amalthea with the Infant Jupiter and a Faun*, completed when he was 17, was so accomplished a work that many observers assumed it to be a Greek original. Bernini's prodigious talent attracted the admiration and support of Cardinal Scipione Borghese, an influential figure in the papal court. Under his patronage Bernini produced his first major works. By the 1620s he was diverging from the **mannerist** custom of presenting a group scene from several views, rendering his group sculptures from a unified, principal view that endowed his work with greater coherency and enhanced emotional impact; his *Apollo and Daphne* (1623), for example, achieves an almost feverish intensity. In these years Bernini also sculpted a number of remarkably penetrating busts that achieve in marble a subtlety of form and expression, a sinuously palpable rendering of the details of skin and hair, previously associated with more tractable materials such as bronze.

mannerist: an artist in the mannerism genre who composed pieces that made an effort to reflect the enormous amount of tension on the European continent between 1520 and 1600; mannerists specialized in reflecting emotion and distortion.

The unstinting patronage of Pope Urban VIII, who reigned from 1623 to 1644, established Bernini as the preeminent Italian artist of the day. His first important architectural projects were the façade for the church of Santa Bibiana (1624–1626) in Rome and the huge gilt-bronze badalchin (altar canopy) over the tomb of St. Peter, perhaps the first monument conceived in a fully realized baroque style. Shortly thereafter he oversaw the sculptural adornment of St. Peter's four supporting piers, although only *St. Longinus* is Bernini's own design.

In 1629 Bernini was appointed chief architect of St. Peter's Basilica and the Palazzo Barberini. Bernini's commissions were by now so copious and diverse that he was at times engaged on 100 different projects at once and often employed nearly all of the leading Roman sculptors in his studio. Many of his largest works were actually executed from his drawings by closely supervised assistants, yet the rapidly growing body of his work retained the distinctive impress of his devout Roman Catholic faith. Other major projects under the patronage of Urban VIII included the tomb of Urban VIII; a series of tomb memorials; and, most notably, his graceful fountains such as the Barcaccia in the Piazza di Spagna (1627–29) and the Triton Fountain in the Piazza Barberini (1642–43).

While serving under six more pontiffs after the death of Urban VIII in 1643, Bernini surpassed himself in public architecture of unrivalled scale and splendor.

While serving under six more pontiffs after the death of Urban VIII in 1643, Bernini surpassed himself in public architecture of unrivalled scale and splendor. Notable from this period is the wondrous Fountain of Four Rivers in Rome's Piazza Navona (1648–51), in which four marble sculptures, each symbolizing one of the world's great rivers, support a replica of an ancient Egyptian obelisk. Bernini's greatest achievement of those years—perhaps of his career—is the sculpture that forms the centerpiece of the Cornaro Chapel in Santa Maria della Vittoria in Rome. Called *The Ecstasy of St. Teresa* (1645–52), it depicts Theresa in a swoon of mystical rapture as she is about to be pierced through the heart by an angel's golden arrow. Framed between dark columns, the polished white marble figures of the main group—awash in sunlight that beams ethereally from a hidden source—seem like paintings sprung passionately to life. As one noted scholar has written, "If we compare the face of his swooning saint with any work done in previous centuries, we find that he achieved an intensity of facial expression which until then was never attempted in art."

Bernini also produced a number of outstanding busts, both allegorical, as in *Damned Soul and Blessed Soul* (1619), and realistic, as in his portrait of Cardinal Scipione Borghese (1632). His bust of Francesco d'Este (1650–51) is widely regarded as his most fully realized union of psychological insight with the dramatic flamboyance of the baroque ideal of the hero.

In 1665 Bernini's long-time admirer from afar, King Louis XIV, then the most powerful sovereign in the world, summoned him to France to formulate plans for a new royal residence. His arrival in Paris occasioned great waves of adulation, but his insistence on the superiority of Italian art alienated many members of the royal court, and his designs for the Louvre were spurned. The only fruit of this otherwise disastrous five-month detour is his bust of Louis XIV, a magnificent conjuring of the pomp and arrogance of absolute royal power.

Striving to incorporate his sculpture into aesthetically complementary surroundings, Bernini turned increasingly to architecture in his mature years. His greatest church design is that for Sant'Andrea al Quirinale in Rome, featuring an oval dome, an interior lavishly inlaid with colored marbles, and a soaring altar above which St. Andrew ascends dramatically to heaven. Bernini's architectural peak is St. Peter's Square in Rome, with its huge oval framed by freestanding, curved colonnades. The plaza forms a majestic entrance to St. Peter's Basilica, accommodating crowds of up to 500,000 for special benedictions by the pope. Bernini envisioned the oval colonnade as the comforting arms of the church reaching out to embrace the massed worshippers.

"[Bernini's] total control over his medium allowed him to introduce into sculpture a hitherto unknown level of physical naturalism. . . ."
Roderick Conway Morris, *International Herald Tribune*

Bernini's prolific output continued well into his old age, although he came to rely increasingly on assistants as his eyesight and stamina faded. Honored in his own lifetime as one of the great men of his era, he set an exalted standard that dominated European architecture and sculpture for several generations after his death in 1680. ◆

Blake, William

November 28, 1757–August 12, 1827 ● Artist and Writer

Blake's work was largely unknown to his contemporaries and only achieved full public recognition and acclaim in the early 20th century. Throughout his life Blake remained something of a lonely individualist with a reputation for eccentricity; indeed, one journalist called him "an unfortunate lunatic whose personal inoffensiveness secures him from confinement."

The struggle for personal and political freedom that infuses Blake's work was something he shared with the wave of revolutionary radicalism sweeping across late 17th-century Europe. Blake's modest upbringing as the son of a London haberdasher provided him with the opportunity to observe the suffering of the lower classes in England's newly industrialized capital. Throughout his life Blake was violently opposed to injustice and he is the first poet to describe the nightmare urban legacy of the industrial revolution, notably in poems such as "Jerusalem" and "London."

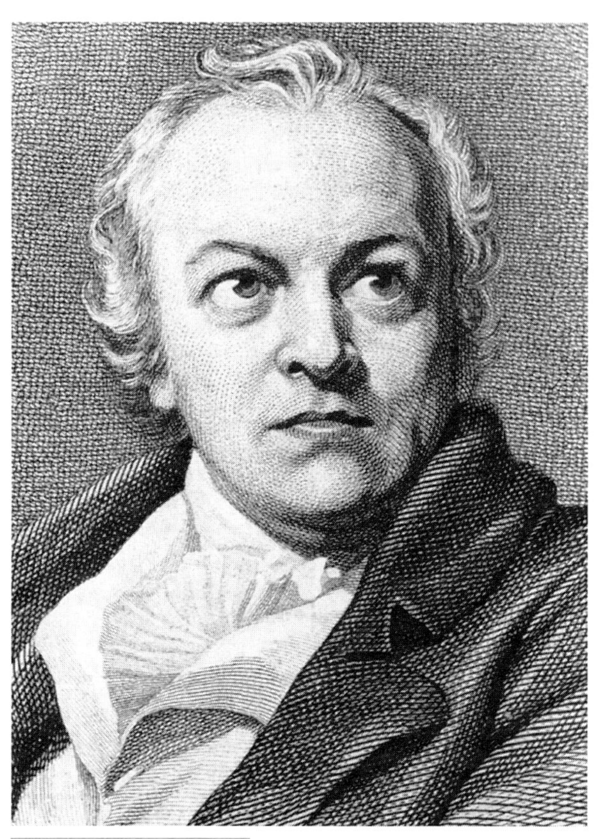

William Blake

He had no formal education until, at age ten, he went to an art school and was apprenticed to engravers; when he was 22, he went to study at the Royal Academy. Blake was as much a champion of spiritual freedom as he was of intellectual freedom and sharply criticized the Rationalist philosophy of John Locke and his followers who dominated contemporary English thought. Largely self-taught, Blake was nevertheless widely, if somewhat eclectically, read. His claim to "know nothing except the Bible" was quite untrue, although biblical metaphors and language permeate both his art and his poetry. Blake was also profoundly influenced by the work of Emmanuel Swedenborg, the Swedish mystic who subscribed to the view that the appearance of ordinary objects was a veil concealing their true essence and that it was necessary to break through this veil to a higher form of reality. This was contrary to the Rationalist opinion that reality is derived from a rational interpretation of our sensory perceptions. Blake's work represents a persistent attempt through verse and art to break through the barriers of ordinary daily life to a higher world of the imagination, a world to which from childhood he believed he had access in visions.

Blake believed that as children, men and women are intuitively closer to the world of the imagination, and his theme of childhood innocence giving way to the perils of adult experience is expressed in the lyrics of his second book of poems. In *Songs of Innocence* (1789) and its sequel, *Songs of Experience* (1794), he shows a strikingly modern perception of childhood. He portrays a world where children are often subject to strong negative and sexual feelings; for the Lockean Rationalist the child's mind was a blank page dependent on external influences to develop its identity. According to Blake, however, man enters the world fully formed mentally as well as physically and only the vicissitudes of adult experience cause him to lose his way. The role of the parent is not to indoctrinate the child with harsh moral codes, for he already has an intuitive morality of his own; instead, all that is required from the adult is security and gentle guidance.

Blake himself had no children. In 1782 he married Catherine Boucher, the illiterate daughter of a market gardener (she signed her name on her marriage document with a cross), whom Blake taught to read and write and even produce engravings in the manner of his own work. Despite severe financial problems in later life and Blake's unpredictable temper, Catherine Blake remained in devoted awe of her husband; a visitor to their home, remarking on the absence of soap, was met with the angry retort from Catherine, "Mr. Blake don't dirty."

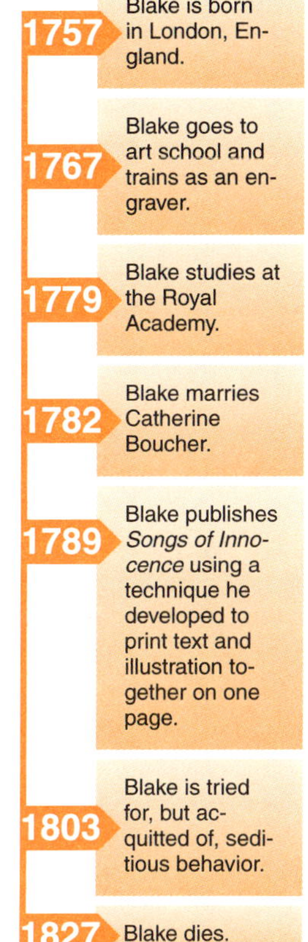

It was as an artist, never as a poet, that Blake was able to make a livelihood. Trained as an engraver from the age of ten, he developed a technique which enabled him to print both text and illustration together on one page, which he later colored by hand. It was unfortunately a laborious and time-consuming process which limited the number of copies Blake could produce, a contributing factor in his failure to reach a wider reading public. This technique, which was used for all except his first book of verse, *Poetical Sketches* (1783), emphasizes the integral nature of Blake's illustrations to any interpretation of his poetry. Initially Blake lived comfortably from the sale of his engravings, but in later life his favorite method of engraving became unfashionable and demand for his work slackened. Blake was forced to rely increasingly on the help of patrons such as the arts enthusiast William Hayley and the sculptor John Flaxman.

The death of Blake's favorite younger brother in 1797 and his trial and acquittal for seditious behavior (alleged criticism of the king, the army, and the country) in 1803 were traumatic events which, coupled with increasing poverty and frustration at home, increased Blake's disillusionment with existing social and religious systems and led him to retreat into a world of private mythology, most clearly expressed in later philosophical works such as *Jerusalem* and *Milton* (1804). In contrast to the approachable lyric poetry of his early books, these last two works are dense with obscure references to ominous and destructive forces, leading the reader into the strange phantasmagoric world of Blake's private symbolism.

Despite the failure of a one-man exhibition of his art in London in 1804. Blake did eventually manage to achieve limited fame as an artist. Toward the end of his life he gave up poetry to concentrate on illustrating the work of other writers such as Geoffrey Chaucer, John Milton, Dante Alighieri, and also the Book of Job. Illustration for Blake was never merely decorative—it served him as a form of visual comment, even textual criticism. Whether expressed in poetry or illustration, Blake's philosophy, while increasing in complexity, remains consistent. The modern dilemma of psychic disintegration, resulting from alienation with oneself and one's environment, is a repeated motif. The only solution envisaged by Blake is reintegration through art or nature, a theme to be reiterated by all the great romantic poets. As Napoleon's rise to power in France signaled the failure of the French Revolution and the government in England showed little sign of becoming more liberal, art became Blake's last hope of freedom: he died disappointed in the efficacy of political revolution but convinced of the redemptive power of artistic creation. ◆

"Forced to live a life of commercial subservience and drudgery, [Blake] nonetheless left us a legacy of provocative poetry and art that still shines with dreamlike brilliance …"
Morton N. Cohen on William Blake in *Insight on the News*, June 3, 1996

Boccioni, Umberto

OCTOBER 19, 1882–AUGUST 17, 1916 ● PAINTER

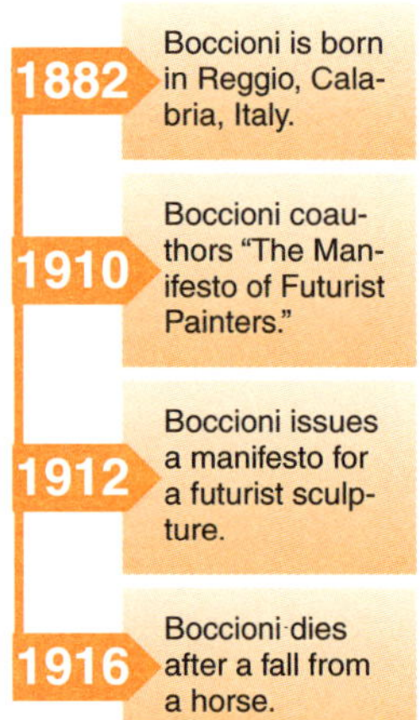

The Italian artist Umberto Boccioni was one of the leading exponents of futurism, one of the most important movements in early 20th-century modernism. The first futurist sculptor and its most important painter, Boccioni strove to create a modern art that would be both reflection and a prophecy of the explosive power and soaring dynamism of industrial technology.

Boccioni was born on October 19, 1882, in Reggio, Calabria. His initial intellectual passion was literature, but after moving to Rome in 1900, his interests shifted to painting. He attended the Scuola Libera del Nudo and came under the influence of Giacomo Balla, who schooled Boccioni in the theory and practice of divisionism, which included interpenetrating brushstrokes, corollary colors, photographic perspective, and exacting attention to the details of the natural world.

After several years of painting and sketching under Balla's tutelage, Boccioni yearned for a more cosmopolitan ambience and traveled to Paris in 1906. There he was intoxicated by the pulse of modern life, which he set about trying to render on

Futurism

The father of futurism was Filippo Tommaso Marinetti, an Italian writer and poet who penned the "Futurist Manifesto" (1909). In 1910 the "Technical Manifesto of Futurist Painting," by Italian artists Giacomo Balla, Umberto Boccioni, Carlo Carrà, Luigi Russolo, and Gino Severini, who were influenced by Marinetti, appeared. These works announced a rejection of conventional art, indeed a call for its destruction, and a criticism of government corruption and a plea for social justice and reason. The futurists looked for art not only in the studios of trained artists, but also in the works of children and blue-collar workers, believing as many romantics did that all people had an intuitive sense of art within them and that too much training could destroy this intuition.

Unlike romantics, however, futurists accepted and celebrated progress, technology, city buildings, noise, speed, and machines. In painting, they reveled in distortion, in an attempt to break free of established styles. They also showed interest in taking ordinary objects and elevating them into something unexpected and beautiful. Some practitioners regarded "motion" as the key to futurism—they endeavored to use static media such as paintings to depict objects in motion, to convey their dynamic nature. One trademark technique, as with Balla's *Hand of the Violin* (1912), was to represent in a single work of art several successive positions of a subject, as though the subject were moving and being photographed at intervals. In terms of color, the futurists shared the impressionist view that art should depict the color of things as perceived by the human eye in various settings, not just the objective color.

The futurist movement was brash, with a strong sense of mission. The first major futurist exhibition, held in Milan in 1911, gave greater public exposure to these works and greater opportunity for the artists to meet and discuss their ideas. Marinetti, Balla, and Boccioni (*The City Rises*), among others, were present. Although futurism would be practiced for many more years, already by 1918 many prominent exponents were exploring other styles. It stylistic and political influence could later be seen in cubism, constructivism, and expressionism, especially German expressionism.

canvas. Late in the summer of 1906, he accompanied a Russian family to their homeland, although little is known about his cultural contacts there. Returning to Italy in December of that year, he sojourned in Padua but soon grew restive there. He spent most of the following year in Venice and then Milan, feverishly striving to strip his art of the remnants of tradition and free himself to express a clear vision of the accelerating rhythms of the modern world. As he wrote in his diary that year, "I don't know if I ought to transform a literary or philosophic vision into a pictorial one. . . ."

Floundering in his quest to find his own way amid the shifting currents of **neo-impressionism** and expressionism, Boccioni

neo-Impressionism: a painting movement composed of artists, led by Georges-Pierre, Seurat reacting to the impressionist school; Seurat perfected the pointillism technique, in which the artist brings together dots of pure color made by the paintbrush.

"Let us open the figure like a window and include in it the milieu in which it lives."
Umberto Boccioni on his creative process

undertook a variety of stylistic experiments from 1907 to 1909. In 1909 he finally found a firm direction, thanks to his meeting with the poet Filippo Tommaso Marinetti, the leading literary futurist of the day. Along with other important artists (Balla, Gino Severini, Luigi Russolo, and Carlo Carrà), they issued two important manifestoes in quick succession: the *Manifesto dei pittori futuristi* ("The Manifesto of Futurist Painters") on February 11, 1910, and *La pittura futuristica—Manifesto tecnico*. Viewing the aesthetic heritage of Italian painting as a debilitating burden, the group limned the requirements of an art as innovative and unbridled as the restless juggernaut of modern science and technology.

temerity: foolish or unwise casualness in the face of opposition or danger.

In contrast to its theoretical **temerity,** the movement's practice evolved only tentatively and gradually. The first exhibition devoted exclusively to Boccioni's work, held in 1910 at the Ca' Pesaro in Venice, was awash in figurative styles clearly rooted in the recent past. The futurists' first major group show in 1911 elicited critical scorn over the chasm between the group's intrepid verbal visions and its modest painterly achievements.

After absorbing elements of cubism during a visit to Paris in late 1911, Boccioni achieved a fresh fusion of color and space in *City Rises* (1910).

After absorbing elements of cubism during a visit to Paris in late 1911, Boccioni achieved a fresh fusion of color and space in *City Rises* (1910). In *States of Mind* (1911), he seeks to use line and color to infuse matter with the life of the mind, what he called a synthesis "of the internal and the external, of space and movement in all directions." *Forces of a Street* (1911) compellingly realizes Boccioni's concept of *linee forze*, "lines of force," a buzzing confluence of forms and colors—even "painted sounds"—that summons the primal fusion of human and natural energy in a modern urban intersection.

As futurism gathered momentum through a series of exhibitions in major European cities in 1912, Boccioni turned his attention to sculpture. In a manifesto published in April of that year, he called for a free combination of diverse materials to convey the seamless, invisible energies that animate and define all objects: "We proclaim that the environment must become part of the plastic block like a world unto itself, with its own laws; that the pavement can rise up on to your table and that your head can cross the street, while between one house and the other your lamp spins its web of plaster rays."

Deploying a wide array of materials, including wood, glass, and horsehair, he produced his first major sculptures, *Head and House and Light* (1912) and *Fusion of a Head and a Window*

(1912), which sought to vivify the relativist continuum of mass and energy. *Development of a Bottle in Space* (1912) and *Unique Forms of Continuity in Space* (1913) extend his effort to capture in a solid mass the temporal unfolding of elemental life energies. In 1914 Boccioni began to devote more time to theoretical reflections. His book *Pittura e scultura futuriste* (1914) remains the definitive statement of the futurist aesthetic.

Caught up in the patriotic fervor preceding World War I, Boccioni enlisted in the army and was wounded in action. While recuperating, he suffered a fatal fall from a horse in 1916. With the loss of its most brilliant theoretician and practitioner, the futurist movement gradually lost its vitality and was a spent force by the end of the 1920s. ◆

Bonnard, Pierre

October 3, 1867–January 27, 1947 ● Painter

The French painter Pierre Bonnard was associated with two variants of the impressionist movement: the Nabis and the Intimists. Throughout his career he was preoccupied with the creation of rich, sensual, intimate ambiences through shadings and combinations of color. Although his critical standing had ebbed by the time of his death in 1947, Bonnard has since regained the heights of scholarly regard and public interest, as manifested in the popular 1998 retrospective of his work at the Tate Gallery in London and the Museum of Modern Art in New York. According to the critic Stanley Meisler, Bonnard "is now widely regarded as one of our century's most complex and masterful painters."

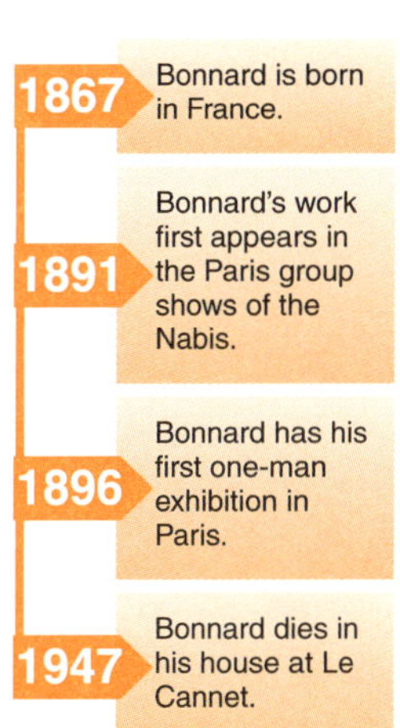

As a child Bonnard spent a good deal of time in the spacious, idyllic surroundings of Grand-Lemps in the Isère, where he grew to love nature during his wanderings through a nearby park and farm. He began drawing at an early age. In school he excelled in the classics, taking his baccalaureate at the age of 18 and then enrolling in law school at his father's insistence. Soon after his graduation from the law faculty at age 21, he took his oath as a barrister and took a job with the government.

His worldly vocational obligations never deterred Bonnard from his higher calling as an artist, however. While still in law school he was also attending the École des Beaux-Arts. After failing to win that school's scholarship competition for study at the French Academy in Paris, he enrolled at the less structured and competitive Académie Julian, where he met a number of innovative, influential young artists—Maurice Denis, Paul Ranson, Ker-Xaniver Roussel, Paul Sérusier, Edourard Vuillard, and Félix Vallotton. The young men were bound by a shared passion for the work of Gauguin, which they discovered at an exhibition at the Café Volpini in Paris in 1889.

By 1890 this informal coterie had formed an artistic society to promote their vision of impressionism. Calling themselves the Nabis (from the Hebrew word for "prophets," *neblim*), they gathered frequently at Rason's studio to exchange ideas and nurture their aesthetic of intimacy, chromatic density, and curvilinear composition. Denis summarized their outlook in these words: "Remember that a painting, before being a battle horse, a nude, or some anecdote, is essentially a flat surface covered with colors which have been arranged in a given order."

In these early years Bonnard was fascinated by Japanese art, with its fluid simplicity of form and its flat, saturated blocks of color.

In these early years Bonnard was fascinated by Japanese art, with its fluid simplicity of form and its flat, saturated blocks of color. Despite his liberal borrowings from this style—so pervasive in those years that his friends dubbed him "the Japanesque Nabi"—in early paintings such as *Croquet Party* (1892) and *Woman with Rabbit* (1891) there is a playful irreverence that delights in bending and occasionally breaching the conceptual strictures of formal aesthetic doctrine.

Bonnard's work first appeared in 1891 in group shows of the Nabis at the chateau of Saint-Germain-en-Laye, the Salon des Indépendants, and the galleries of Le Barc de Boutteville, an early champion of the group's work. But it was a single advertising poster, more than any gallery show, that secured Bonnard's reputation in the art world. Entitled *France-Champagne* (1889–90, named for the sponsoring beverage), the poster became a familiar and striking presence around Paris with its hand-drawn letters, its erotic evocation of a woman's arm, and its distinctive three-color scheme against a largely black background. It was this poster that inspired Toulouse-Lautrec to try his hand at commercial posters, a field soon ceded to him by Bonnard.

Flush with the 100 francs he earned from the poster, Bonnard was emboldened to turn away from the law and devote himself full time to his art. Sharing a Montmartre studio with Denis, Sérusier, and Vuillard, he not only worked on his own canvases but also collaborated with his Nabis associates in designing sets for several Paris theater companies.

During the 1890s, Bonnard's paintings increasingly reflected his fascination with the quotidian details of urban life: the interiors of homes, domestic vignettes such as a woman primping before a mirror, the view from a bedroom window, and so on. Such glimpses in to the private domain of everyday life, typical of the work of Bonnard and Vuillard, soon became known as *Intimisme*. Much of his finest work in this vein can be found in his lithographic illustrations for the book *Quelques aspects de la vie de Paris* (*Some aspects of Parisian life*; written by Claude Terrasse, his brother-in-law) and *Petites scènes familières* (*Small familiar scenes*).

"There is a formula that perfectly fits painting: lots of little lies for the sake of one big truth."
Pierre Bonnard in his interpretation of painting

On the strength of Bonnard's first one-man exhibition, held in 1896 in Paris at Durand-Ruel, the publisher Vollard hired Bonnard to do the illustrations for Verlaine's collection of symbolist poems, *Parallèlement* (1900), and for *Daphnis and Chloe* (1902). Notwisthstanding his success, Bonnard never yielded to complacency. He set out with Vuillard to explore the landscapes and museums of England, Belgium, Holland, Spain, and Italy, and he journeyed through new artistic territories as well, incorporating elements of cubism and especially the brash colorings of **fauvism** in pressing his art beyond the limits of impressionism.

fauvism: a French style of painting during the early twentieth century; the word Fauves means "wild beast" in French, and was used to describe the artists of this style who reflected an uncontrolled and violent use of intense colors in their paintings.

By 1908 his expressly Intimist impulse had run its course as he turned increasingly to the landscapes of northern France for inspiration. Enraptured by the splendors of southern France on his first visit there in 1910, he began to make regular trips there, eventually buying a house at Le Cannet and settling there in 1925 with his new bride and longtime companion, Maria Boursin. Thereafter, the light and classical heritage of the Mediterranean figured prominently in his work, which laid increasing emphasis on form without sacrificing the gentle sensuality that had always graced his paintings. *Summer in Normandy* (1912), *Country Dining Room* (1913), *Breakfast Room* (1931–32), and *Studio with Mimosa* (1939–40) are among the major works of his later years.

Pierre Bonnard died in his house at Le Cannet on January 27, 1947. ◆

Bosch, Hieronymus

c. 1450–August 9, 1516 ● Painter

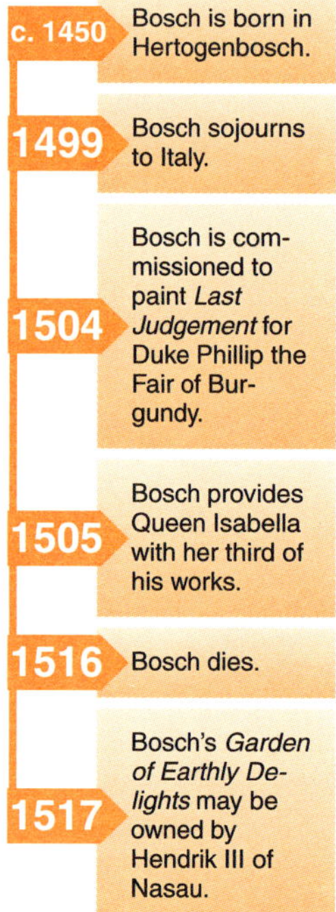

Born in Hertogenbosch, Hieronymus Bosch was a member of the van Aken (or van Aeken) family of painters, probably from Aachen, that worked in Hertogenbosch from the early 15th century.

First mentioned in 1474, Bosch presumably trained with his father, Antonius, but little is known about earlier painting in Hertogenbosch, and Bosch's artistic origins are obscure. His earliest works show affinities with the art of the northern Netherlands, although no evidence exists that he traveled outside Hertogenbosch. An assumed sojourn in Italy circa 1499–1504 is based on a triptych in Venice, often identified as the martyrdom of St. Julia, who was venerated chiefly in northern Italy, but the subject of this triptych is uncertain. Bosch's presumed portrait in the *Recueil d'Arras* is of doubtful authenticity.

Sometime before 1481 Bosch married Aleyt Goyaerts van den Meervenne, who was from a wealthy family. No children are recorded. Tax records place Bosch among the wealthiest citizens in his town. After 1486 Bosch and Aleyt were members of the Brotherhood of Our Lady, whose records indicate that he executed a number of commissions for them, including two altar wings (depicting David and Abigail) for a sculptured altarpiece completed in 1476–1477 by Adriaen van Wesel. Later sources record an *Epiphany* for Saint John, scenes from the stories of Judith and Esther, and *Creation of the World* on two shutters for a carved altarpiece.

Bosch's patrons included leading members of the church and aristocracy. Duke Philip the Fair of Burgundy commissioned a *Last Judgment* in 1504, which is often identified with the Vienna *Last Judgment* or Munich *Last Judgment* fragment. Queen Isabella of Spain owned three of his works by 1505. Bosch's paintings were also owned by Margaret of Austria; Anthony of Burgundy, bishop of Utrecht (a *Stone of Folly* and an unspecified cosmic subject); and Cardinal Domenico Grimani at Venice (probably Venice *Heaven* and *Hell* panels). Hendrik III of Nasau may have owned the *Garden of Earthly Delights* by 1517.

No surviving work by Bosch is dated or securely documented, nor does his name on a painting or drawing guarantee its authenticity. Attributions and chronology are based on stylistic analysis, complicated by the many existing copies of his paintings. Earlier scholars attributed 30 to 50 paintings and 19 to 24 drawings to Bosch; other scholars, based on scientific examination, have reduced these estimations to about 25 paintings and 14 drawings, plus putative copies of lost works and a few paintings perhaps from Bosch's immediate workshop.

Bosch painted traditional christological scenes (such as the Brussels *Crucifixion*), images of saints, and highly original moral allegories. Although not without humor, Bosch presents a pessimistic view of sinful humanity. The *Haywain* and probably *Garden of Earthly Delights* (although this is disputed) show the origins of human sin, its progress in the world, and its punishment in hell. Conversely, the lives of Christ and the saints are posited as models for salvation. Often drawing his subjects from traditional Christian writings and imagery, he treated them with remarkable virtuosity, especially the hell scenes.

Bosch's stylistic development is controversial, but it is generally divided into three periods (c. 1470–1490, 1490–1500, and 1500–1516). His early works are fairly homogenous in style, reflecting the art of his Dutch predecessors: *Epiphany* (Philadelphia), *Christ Carrying the Cross* (Vienna), *Ecce Homo* (Frankfurt), and *Tabletop of the Seven Deadly Sins and Four Last Things* (Madrid). Three panels that are probably fragments of a single work, *Death of the Miser* (Washington, D.C.), *Ship of Fools* (Paris), and *Gluttony and Lust* (New Haven), lead to a middle period that shows the earliest manifestations of Bosch's genius, including *Last Judgment* (Vienna) and *Haywain* triptychs (Madrid), the latter an expansive allegory of avarice. The great triptychs of the third phase, *Garden of Earthly Delights* (Madrid), *Temptation of St. Anthony* (Lisbon), and *Epiphany* (Madrid), show brilliant formal innovations and a new compositional clarity. *St. John in the Wilderness* (Madrid) and *Christ Carrying the Cross* (Ghent) are also probably late works.

The chronology and function of Bosch's drawings are unclear. He nourished his visual imagination on a wide range of sources, including prints, late Gothic decoration, and possibly hermetic symbolism. Dutch manuscript illumination perhaps contributed to his "archaizing" tendencies, especially the bright colors and flatly modeled forms. But he was equally an heir to early Netherlandish realism. In this vein, Bosch also created some of the finest landscapes of the period, including *Vagabond* (Rotterdam) and *St. John on Patmos* (Berlin). Underdrawings are fairly elaborate in Bosch's early paintings, but can be summary in his mature pictures, often restricted to the basic compositional elements. Bosch frequently deviated from his later underdrawings, introducing major changes as he painted; this suggests to some scholars that he improvised his imagery as he worked, rather than following a predetermined program, as is frequently assumed.

Bosch had assistants, and some works, such as the *Job* triptych, may be workshop productions, but no pupils can be identified. Engravings reflecting his inventions were made in Bosch's lifetime by local designer-architect Alaert du Hameel. After Bosch's death, copies of his paintings and new compositions in his style were produced by many followers, chiefly at Antwerp. Best known are Pieter Huys, Jan Mandyn, and above all Pieter Bruegel the Elder. These followers contributed to Bosch's reputation as a "maker of devils," whose creations were merely "dreams." Bosch's moral seriousness was recognized, however, by Spanish writers Felipe de Guevara (c. 1550) and José de Siguënza (1605); many of his paintings were acquired by Philip II of Spain. No less controversial today, Bosch's art is interpreted along three basic lines: as an expression of his mental state, amenable to psychoanalysis; as inspired by various medieval heresies, witchcraft, or alchemy and astrology; or as reflecting the religious and social concerns of his time. ◆

Botticelli, Sandro

c. 1444–May 17, 1510 ● Painter

Filipepi, nicknamed Botticelli, was the son of a tanner. He perhaps briefly trained as a goldsmith before being apprenticed to the painter Fra Filippo Lippi, whose influence can be discerned in Botticelli's early work. *The Adoration of the Magi* is considered by several critics to be Botticelli's earliest surviving painting. However, it owes so much to Fra Filippo Lippi that some writers believe it was begun by him. Some critics also emphasize the importance of Andrea del Verrocchio's and even Antonio Pollaiuolo's work on Botticelli's developing style.

Botticelli almost certainly became an independent master before 1470, when he was recorded as one among a number of

Florentine masters with a workshop. In that year he painted the vigorous, plastically conceived *Fortitude* (Florence, Uffizi), his earliest dated picture. It completes the series *Seven Virtues* commissioned from Piero Pollaiuolo for the hall of the Mercanzia (where the tribunal of six judges governing the Florentine guilds met) on Piazza della Signoria, Florence. The wealthy Medici supporter Tommaso Soderini recommended Botticelli for this task, perhaps at the behest of Lorenzo de' Medici, the Magnificent. In 1472 Botticelli joined the Compagnia di San Luca (the confraternity of Florentine painters), where his late teacher's son, Filippino Lippi, was listed as his pupil. Filippino eventually became the most gifted artist to come out of Botticelli's excellent and prolific workshop.

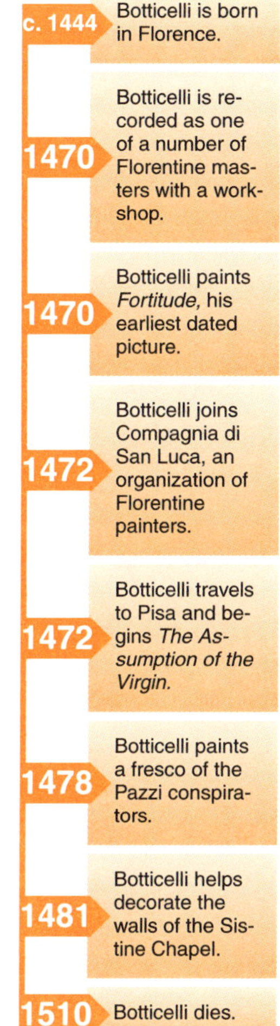

In January 1474 Botticelli traveled to Pisa to paint frescoes in the Camposanto (monumental graveyard) but instead began a fresco, *The Assumption of the Virgin,* in the cathedral, which was left unfinished and is now lost. In Florence, Botticelli painted decorations (all lost), including Giuliano de' Medici's standard with an allegorical image of Minerva, for the joust won by Giuliano in January 1475 and celebrated in Angelo Poliziano's *Stanze* (Stanzas), which was begun the following year and left unfinished. Five prominent male members of the Medici family and presumably the artist can be recognized among the Magi and their followers in the altarpiece *The Adoration of the Magi* (1475–1476), commissioned by Gaspare del Lama for his family chapel in Santa Maria Novella, Florence. The fresco *Adoration of the Magi* (now lost) was painted in 1475 at the Palazzo della Signoria, and in 1478 Botticelli painted a fresco (now lost) of the Pazzi conspirators—who were hanged that year for the murder of Giuliano—on the exterior of the same palace.

In 1480 Botticelli and Domenico Ghirlandaio painted their frescoes *St. Augustine's Vision of the Death of St. Jerome* and *St. Jerome,* respectively, in the choir of Ognissanti, Florence (now transferred to the nave). Botticelli's fresco *The Annunciation* (Florence, Uffizi) was completed in May 1481 for the Hospital of San Martino alla Scala. Several weeks later Pope Sixtus IV ordered Botticelli, Ghirlandaio, and Cosimo Rosselli to join Perugino (Pietro Vannucci) in decorating the walls of the recently erected Cappella Magna (the Sistine Chapel) in Rome. In the chapel's second register Botticelli frescoed the *Temptations of Christ* on the right wall reserved for scenes from *The Life of Christ* and *Moses and the Daughters of Jethro* and the *Punish-*

ment of Korah on the opposite wall showing *The Life of Moses*, which prefigures Jesus's life. In the third register Botticelli and his workshop painted a number of early popes standing inside illusionistic niches, thereby reinforcing the intricate program exalting papal primacy.

Following his return to Florence in 1482 Botticelli was invited on October 5th to join Perugino, Piero Pollaiuolo, and Ghirlandaio in decorating the new Sala Magna (a state anteroom now known as the Sala dei Gigli) of the Palazzo della Signoria; however, only Ghirlandaio seems to have delivered work. In 1485 Botticelli completed his altarpiece *Madonna with SS. John the Baptist and John the Evangelist* for the Bardi Chapel in Santo Spirito, Florence. In 1489 he received the commission for an *Annunciation* for the Guardi Chapel in Cestello (later named Santa Maria Maddalena dei Pazzi), Florence, and in the late 1480s he painted *The Coronation of the Virgin with Four Saints* for the goldsmith's chapel dedicated to St. Eligius in San Marco, Florence.

The works Botticelli executed from roughly the time of *Primavera* (c. 1478) to the *Coronation*—a period of considerable activity that includes *The Birth of Venus* (c. 1484) and the circular *Madonna of the Magnificat* and *Madonna of the Pomegranate* tondi—combine a late-Gothic sinuosity of line and opulence of color with the range of emotions and *contrapposto* (in antithesis) poses derived in large measure from the study of antiquity. This remarkable synthesis was achieved in the milieu around Lorenzo de' Medici, which included many of Botticelli's most prominent patrons as well as the poet Poliziano and the philosopher Marsilio Ficino, both of whom supplied the subjects, explanations, and underlying values of a number of Botticelli's secular paintings.

The frescoes *Youth Presented to the Liberal Arts* and *Young Lady with Venus and the Graces*, from a cycle in the Villa Tornabuoni (now Villa Lemmi) near Florence, were presumably painted on the occasion of Lorenzo Tornabuoni's second marriage, in 1491. Lorenzo de' Medici's death in April 1492 undoubtedly affected Botticelli, as did Girolamo Savonarola's preaching and the expulsion of the Medici from Florence in November 1494.

In this period Botticelli's precious, courtly style was gradually replaced by a simpler, more direct, and more nervous mode of expression, communicating even greater moral and religious fervor. *The Calumny of Apelles* and the *spaliera* panels (installed at shoulder-height above a bench) depicting *The Story of Virginia* and *The Story of Lucretia* belong to these years. Among the religious paintings one should mention the four panels of *The Life and Miracles of Saint Zenobius*, *Mystic Crucifixion*, and *Mystic Nativity*, Botticelli's last dated picture, completed in early 1501. On November 15, 1499, Botticelli matriculated as a painter in the Guild of Doctors and Pharmacists, which had absorbed the painter's guild in the previous century.

Botticelli spent his later years in a state of melancholy, poverty, and religious despair, commenting on Dante and illustrating *The Divine Comedy*, an ambitious project that remained unfinished.

Botticelli spent his later years in a state of melancholy, poverty, and religious despair, commenting on Dante and illustrating *The Divine Comedy*, an ambitious project that remained unfinished. The late 15th and early 16th century was characterized by a shortage of major commissions in Florence, for reasons that have yet to be clarified. When the high Renaissance style became firmly rooted following the return of Leonardo and Michelangelo in 1501, and the arrival of Raphael in 1504, Botticelli's pictorial language presumably struck most potential patrons as a distant echo of the Laurentian Golden Age.

Botticelli was praised during his lifetime by the humanist poet Ugolino Verino, the mathematician Luca Pacioli, and agents to Duke Ludovico Sforza of Milan and Marchioness Isabella d'Este of Mantua. His wit, intelligence, sophistication, and early success were noted by the writer and court artist Giorgio Vasari in 1550, and three of his jokes were recorded in Poliziano's *Detti piacevoli* (Pleasant sayings; 1477–1482). However, he was almost completely forgotten from the time of his death until the reevaluation of his unparalleled achievements in the late 19th century.

Botticelli's mythological pictures are of fundamental importance to our understanding of the Florentine Renaissance. His paintings of ancient myth offer a pictorial equivalent of the humanist study and imitation of ancient poetry and the development of a highly refined vernacular poetry of love, all of which were successfully promoted and practiced by Lorenzo the Magnificent himself.

The humanist Leon Battista Alberti played a significant part in Lorenzo's thinking about the arts. In his treatise on painting of 1435, *De pictura*, he had recommended poetic invention in painting. Such *inventio* eventually helped raise the painter's status from that of mere craftsman to that of a thinking and highly creative individual whose imagination rivals the divine inspiration or genius of the poet. Botticelli's pictures exemplify in both form and content Horace's dictum *Ut pictura poesis:* "As is painting, so is poetry."

Primavera and *Pallas and the Centaur* were painted for Lorenzo di Pier-francesco de' Medici (a second cousin of il Magnifico), for they were recorded in 1499 in his Florentine palace, in the room next to his bedroom. Botticelli's mythologies are among the few surviving large secular pictures from 15th-century Florence.

The subject of the lush and exquisitely detailed *Primavera* is love. The picture depicts spring in the garden of the Hesperides, with Venus, standing in her dress and cloak, in the center and middle ground of the composition. Above the goddess of love blind Cupid shoots a flaming arrow toward the three Graces dancing in the foreground on the left. Farther left, Mercury disperses ominous clouds with his wand. On the right the wind god Zephyr embraces the nymph Chloris, who, as his bride, is transformed into Flora, scattering flowers on the fertile ground. The allusions to the birth of love and the transformation of a nymph, through wedlock, into the goddess of flowers may characterize this work as a wedding picture.

The rich iconographic program, conceived by Poliziano and so brilliantly interpreted by Botticelli, does not illustrate an episode from ancient myth. Instead, it borrows motifs from the classical poets Lucretius, Ovid, and Horace, as well as the philosopher Seneca and the writer on agriculture Columella, combining their ideas into a highly original, visual poem. The identity of the images and sources influencing this type of Albertian *inventio* remains the subject of scholarly debate, as does the way in which the linked themes should be interpreted and the amount of emphasis that should be placed on the various motifs (ranging from personification to the potential symbolism of fruits and flowers). A number of scholars see a reflection of Ficino's Neoplatonic philosophy of love in this painting. *Primavera*, with its references to classical and Renaissance poetry and ideas, expresses the values of Florence's cultural elite.

The Birth of Venus, painted about half a decade later, is more archaizing. It shows the goddess freshly risen from the sea, standing on a scallop shell in the center of the composition. She is shown in the nude, perhaps for the first time since antiquity, modestly covering herself with her hair and hands in the guise of a classical *Venus pudica*. Zephyr and Chloris, on the left, blow the goddess toward a shore on the opposite side, where Flora rushes forward to wrap Venus in a cloak. The theme is derived from Poliziano's *Stanze*, and the painting's celebration of the birth of love may make it yet another wedding picture.

Mars and Venus (c. 1485), with its languorously reclining deities and mischievous little satyrs, is also probably a wedding picture. *Pallas and the Centaur* (c. 1482–1483)—another allegorical invention—alludes to the Renaissance fascination with the theme of nature overcome by rationality and order through its depiction of luxury (symbolized by the centaur) conquered by chastity.

In *The Adoration of the Magi* (1475–1476), the Virgin is seated at the apex of a wide triangle formed by the gracefully converging men almost occupying the entire width of the altarpiece. This picture was praised by Vasari for the varying poses of the many heads and for the differentiation of the retinues of the three kings. In *The Madonna of the Magnificat* (c. 1480–1481) Botticelli shows his skill in accommodating large figures to the difficult format of a round panel. The Virgin, crowned before a landscape by angels as queen of heaven, dips her pen in an inkwell as she prepares to write once more in the codex in which she has recorded the Magnificat (the canticle praising the Lord in Luke 1:46–55). The magnificent curve of her back and thighs echoes the contour of the panel and is repeated in the pose of her son, seated on her lap and looking up lovingly toward his mother and bride.

Botticelli's skill as a draftsman is evident in the quality of his compositions and the linear grace of his paintings. Unfortunately, most of his sheets are lost. Several were used by engravers, including Baccio Baldini, and it is probable that Botticelli provided designs for other artists and artisans as well. However, 93 exceptional drawings, executed over a period of years for Dante's *Divine Comedy*, survive. Most of these crisply executed line drawings are unfinished, and only four are almost completely colored. They are additional testimony to Botticelli's passion for literature and to his unmatched skill in translating words into poignant imagery. ◆

Boucher, Francois

SEPTEMBER 29, 1703–MAY 30, 1770 ● PAINTER

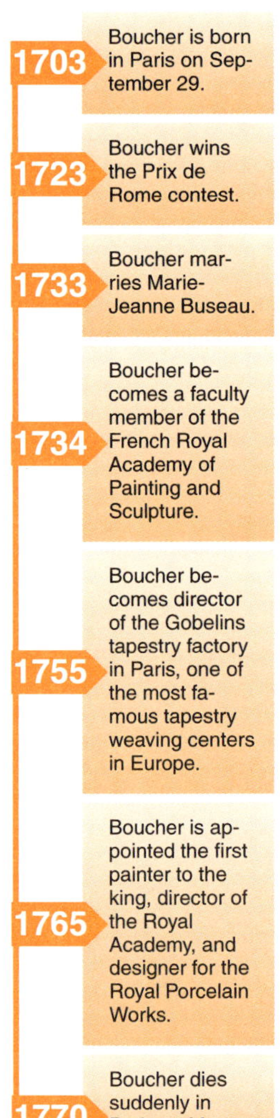

In pre-Revolutionary France of the 1770s, the fashion in art reflected a lifestyle that valued elegance, manners, and charm. The painters of this period, which came to be called "rococo," indulged in this focus on refinement, pleasure, frivolity, and sentimentality. Francois Boucher became a leading painter in France during this time, a master of the ornate and sometimes erotic art of the period. His paintings contain pretty, idealized pastoral and mythological scenes with a glowing softness and gaiety that represented the lightness and sensuousness of the rococo style. His lush and erotic nudes seemed later to symbolize the decadence of the political environment in France that was soon to cause the French poor to rebel against their extremely wealthy leaders.

Boucher was highly productive in many different media. Not only did he produce many paintings, he designed opera and ballet settings as well as tapestries and porcelain. He also made etchings, book illustrations, and numerous drawings. Boucher oversaw hundreds of students who spread his style far and wide, making Boucher one of the most imitated and influential artists of his day.

Francois Boucher was born into a humble family in Paris on September 29, 1703. His father, Nicolas, a lace designer and painter, was probably Boucher's earliest teacher. At age 17, Francois attracted attention for an exceptional painting, *Judgement of Susanna,* from the painter François Le Moyne, who helped Boucher compete for the Prix de Rome. Boucher won the contest in 1723, but the money was diverted to political favorites, forcing Boucher to begin working before completing his education.

From 1723 to 1728, Boucher worked for an engraver and publisher. He also created etchings during this time, imitating the delicate style of his contemporary Jean-Antoine Watteau. Etching is a process of creating a design on a metal plate with the use of acid and making prints from the design.

This work finally earned Boucher enough money to go to Rome. In Italy from 1727 to 1731, Boucher studied the great masters of the baroque, an art era that produced large-scale works filled with dramatic details. During Boucher's career, baroque art developed into the more intimate style of rococo. The word rococo came from the French word, "rocaille," which means "rock" or "pebbles." The term referred especially to the fancy shell and rockwork used to decorate the fountains and interiors of grottoes. The rococo style had a feminine look to it, and the age was dominated by the taste and the social initiative of women. These women, such as Madame de Pompadour—the powerful mistress of King Louis XV of France—held some of the highest positions in Europe.

After returning to France, Boucher continued making prints, but he tried to gain a reputation as an artist. He painted a series that featured three main subjects: mythological figures, religious scenes, and compositions containing cupids and cherubs.

In 1733, Boucher married Marie-Jeanne Buseau, who became a model for many of his paintings. A famous portrait of her, *Madame Boucher* (1743), now hanging in the Frick Collection in New York City, shows a girlish woman reclining in a domestic setting. The couple had a son in 1736, Juste-Francois Boucher, who became a furniture designer.

Boucher's work achieved the recognition he sought, and in 1734 he became a faculty member of the French Royal Academy of Painting and Sculpture. In 1735, he received his first royal commission, which was to paint four large cherubs representing Plato's four virtues of wisdom, courage, temperance, and justice in the palace of Versailles. He followed this with several other paintings for the palace.

Boucher actively sought the business of private painting for collectors, which proved profitable for him. He also created designs for the Beauvais tapestry works, and in 1755 he became director of the Gobelins tapestry factory in Paris, one of the most famous tapestry weaving centers in Europe. From 1749 onward, Boucher used some of the themes of his paintings to create a series of drawings for porcelain pieces. In addition, he created stage designs for the royal opera and other theatrical productions.

Boucher's painting career reached its height in the 1740s. His delicate, lighthearted visions of classical figures and lushly dressed French peasants and noblewomen made him the most fashionable painter of his day. His work, filled with dimpled cupids, billowing clouds, cooing doves, and flowers, seems overly sentimental to modern tastes, but it showed exceptional talent. His skill in rendering detail and producing luminous color is remarkable for any era.

Rococo: a style of painting emerging in the eighteenth century that emphasized the lesiurely lives of aristocrats as opposed to religious martyrs or heroes; the focus was on love and romance and was characterized by freeflowing movement, use of line, and color.

Rococo artists made the ancient Roman goddess Venus their virtual queen, and Boucher rendered her in various paintings. The lovely *Triumph of Venus* (1740) illustrates the story of Venus being born of the sea. She hovers on a canopy of mother-of-pearl, upholstered with pink and pearl-gray silk and held up by the winds and cupids. She is attended by a court of white nymphs and bronzed demigods. In a swirl of blue and turquoise are dolphins, fabrics, gods, water, and clouds. In *Venus Consoling Love*, a delicate, alabaster-skinned nude Venus lounges among chubby cupids and doves in a dreamy wooded setting.

Boucher's work for royalty continued, especially under the influence of Madame de Pompadour, who doted on Boucher as her favorite painter. She generated several commissions that resulted in some of Boucher's major works, including some in the palace of Versailles where she lived. Boucher also painted several portraits of the Marquise, which she became, bedecked in lavish ruffles and bows.

Although the Marquise de Pompadour died in 1764, Boucher's status remained high. In 1765 he was appointed the first painter to the king, director of the Royal Academy, and designer for the Royal Porcelain Works. The appointments gave Boucher virtual control of all the official French art of the day.

Boucher's style was copied endlessly in his era. Among well-known artists, his influence is seen in the work of his star pupil, the rococo painter Jean Honoré Fragonard. Perhaps because Boucher's style became so widely imitated, it soon fell from favor. The style that followed rococo was called **neoclassicism,** which developed in France in reaction to rococo. Neoclassical artists returned to more formal elements, and many criticized the work of Boucher and others as frivolous.

neoclassicism: an artistic style in nineteenth century France that responded to the Baroque school of artistic expression, and is characterized by the revival of ancient Roman and Greek ideals of classic form to express love of country, courage, and sacrifice.

However, during his lifetime, Boucher enjoyed success not only with collectors and patrons but also with critics. In the late 1800s, American collectors amassed the largest collection of Boucher's works in public and private collections. They and modern viewers appreciate Boucher's work as an expression of the spirit of his time.

Boucher died suddenly in Paris on May 30, 1770. ◆

Brancusi, Constantin

FEBRUARY 19, 1876–MARCH 16, 1957 ● SCULPTOR

Constantin Brancusi became one of the most influential 20th-century sculptors, producing pieces that embodied pure form and breaking radically from the tradition of pictorial sculpture of previous centuries. Brancusi's abstract sculptures profoundly influenced modern concepts of form in sculpture, painting, and even industrial design.

Constantin Brancusi was born in Pestisani, in the Gorj district near Tirgu Jiu, Romania, on February 19, 1876. He was the fifth of seven children in a large peasant family. At about the age of 18, he became a student at the School of Arts and Crafts in Craiova, the capital of Oltenia province. He then went on to the new Academy of Fine Arts in Bucharest, Romania's largest city and chief cultural center. Although Brancusi did not receive a traditional academic instruction in sculpture at either school, he produced a number of unique sculptures.

Constantin Brancusi with one of his sculptures.

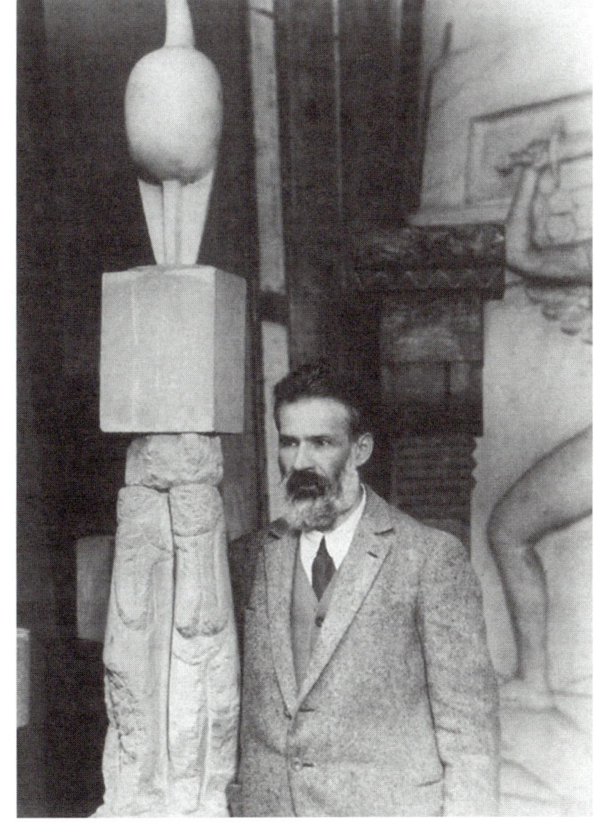

According to Brancusi, he left Romania in 1903 and traveled on foot to Paris, arriving in the summer of 1904. He settled in Paris and lived there the remainder of his life. He began supporting himself by washing dishes in a restaurant. From April 1905 to 1907, Brancusi studied at the Academie des Beaux-Arts, and several sculptures of this period show his early attempts to learn various styles.

One of the most interesting of Brancusi's works resulted when a rich Romanian widow commissioned him to create a monument to her dead husband. The woman wanted a figure of a weeping woman and a portrait bust based on a photo of her husband. Brancusi boldly

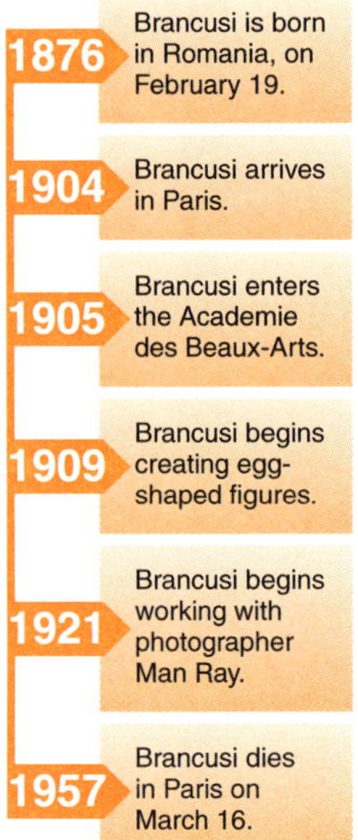

scrapped the original plan and created a nude figure kneeling in prayer. The work includes the figure *The Prayer*, and the portrait of *Petre Stanescu*, still located in a Romanian cemetery.

Brancusi entered the bracing atmosphere of greatness when he worked briefly for French sculptor Auguste Rodin, often considered the greatest sculptor of the 19th century. Rodin created many sculptures of the human figure that fairly came alive with emotional intensity and human passion. Rodin employed many assistants, and Brancusi's early works reflect his time with Rodin.

After 1908, Brancusi's personal style rapidly evolved, and by 1910 a very distinct style had gelled. One of his first unique sculptures became a subject he would return to several times. *The Kiss* (1908) is a limestone carving in a simplified, block-like form. On the block, lines create an image of two figures merged in a kiss and embrace. The sculpture is somewhat humorous as well as charming. The complete melding of the couple in one block of stone speaks volumes about romantic love.

Along with many other artists of his era, such as Gauguin and Picasso, Brancusi turned to primitive sources such as African masks for artistic inspiration. His own Romanian heritage offered a rich source of material, and it seems Brancusi imitated masks of ancient Romanian celebrations. Using his folk roots for inspiration placed Brancusi in the avant-garde.

In 1909, Brancusi began creating the figures that were perhaps his most characteristic. These figures were *ovoid*, egg-shaped, and the first of them were smooth, rounded shapes with recognizable human features. *Sleeping Muse* (1910) is simply a stylized ovoid head. His most extreme ovoid sculptures became so smooth that the human features are barely recognizable. Brancusi was influenced by his friendship with Amedeo Modigliani, an important Italian painter who preferred oval and cylindrical forms. Modigliani painted subjects with elongated bodies, long necks, and oval heads. The two friends—Brancusi and Modigliani—influenced each other's work.

Brancusi continued to simplify his sculptures to basic abstract forms, eliminating all unnecessary details. He concentrated on a few subjects, such as the egg, the bird in flight, and the human head and torso. He highly polished his bronze and marble sculptures to allow reflected light to play off the surfaces. *Bird in Space* (1919), at the Museum of Modern Art, New York City, is a long, graceful cylinder of polished metal, with lines like the curve of a bird's wing. Brancusi made 27 sculptures of birds over more than three decades. In *Golden Bird* (1919) at the Art Institute of Chicago, details such as feet, tail, and a crowing beak are barely suggested in an elegant, slim silhouette of bronze. The high polish of the metal mirrors the surrounding space.

Brancusi moved into woodworking, and many of his woodcarvings were inspired by Romanian folk carvings. He created wooden bases for his sculptures, some of which became unique sculptures of their own. One geometric pedestal of rough-hewn wood—with a bird perched on it—soon evolved into an independent, tree-sized sculpture that Brancusi called *Endless Column*.

Brancusi moved into woodworking, and many of his woodcarvings were inspired by Romanian folk carvings.

In 1921, Brancusi met the well-known photographer Man Ray, an experimental and unconventional artist who worked in many media simultaneously, including filmmaking and photography. Dissatisfied with the photos taken by others of his sculpture, Brancusi set up a darkroom in his studio and asked his friend Ray to help him improve his own photographing technique. The result was photos of Brancusi's works and his studio that highlighted his sculptures in an appealing light. A large archive of Brancusi's photographic work survives in France's National Museum of Modern Art in Paris. The collection holds about 1,250 photographic prints and 560 negatives, mainly glass.

One of the Romanian artist's greatest works and his only monumental piece, became a complex consisting of various types of his sculpture. Inaugurated in 1938, the Tirgu-Jiu Complex in Romania consists of a sculpture called the *Endless Column*, which is of iron and steel and commemorates the soldiers of World War I. The nearby *Table of Silence* is a circular table with 12 surrounding hour-glass chairs. The *Gate of the Kiss* completes the piece with stone benches.

When Brancusi died in Paris on March 16, 1957, he left a somewhat small body of work, in view of how influential he was. About 215 sculptures survive, and about 50 are thought to have been lost or destroyed. ◆

Braque, Georges

MAY 13, 1882–AUGUST 31, 1963 ● PAINTER

An artist experiences the world visually, and for many centuries the artist copied the visual world as closely as possible. That suddenly changed when artists began distorting visual reality, twisting it, blurring it, softening it, hardening it, and coloring it in new ways. Painters explored new realities on canvas instead of simply repeating what they saw. These explorations reached a very intellectual and intriguing point with the cubists, who splintered reality into geometrical forms, slicing and dicing the world into colors and shapes, fragments and planes. The leaders of this movement were the French painter Georges Braque and his great friend and fellow artist Pablo Picasso.

Braque was born May 13, 1882, in Argenteuil-sur-Seine, a small community near Paris that had been one of the centers of the impressionist movement in the 1870s. His father and grandfather owned a successful house painting and decorating business. They were also amateur artists, and Braque accompanied his father on painting expeditions. In 1890 the family moved to the port city of Le Havre, also an early center of impressionism. Braque attended local schools and became active in sports, giving him an athletic build.

Georges Braque in his studio.

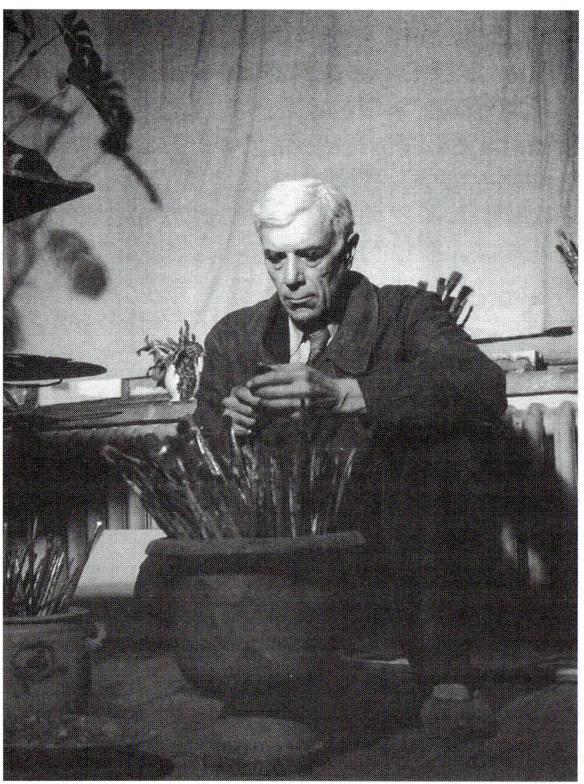

At age 15, Braque enrolled in the municipal art school. He left school at 17 to apprentice as a house painter and interior decorator, during which time he learned the professional skill with materials and the knowledge of artisan's tricks that later appeared in his paintings.

After a year of military service, Braque decided—with the help of an allowance from his family—to become an artist. Between 1902 and 1904 he studied in a Paris private academy and, very briefly, at the official École des Beaux-Arts. In his free hours he frequented the Louvre museum.

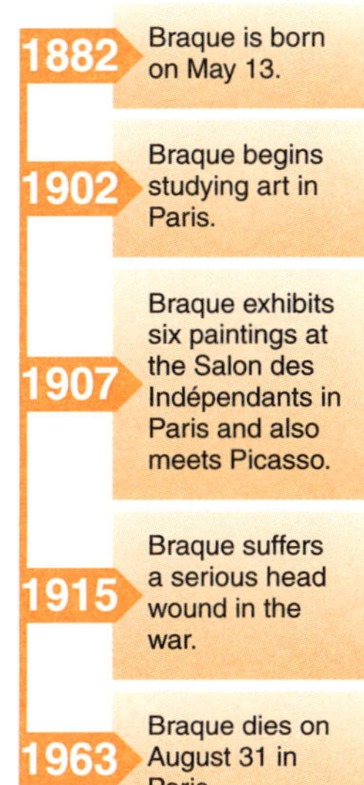

It is clear from Braque's works of 1905 to 1907 that he admired the style called fauvism, from a group nicknamed the Fauves (wild beasts). The Fauves painted with brilliant colors, a loose structure, and dark, thick lines to create intense emotional responses. In the spring of 1907, Braque exhibited six paintings at the Salon des Indépendants in Paris and sold them all.

That year continued to be hugely significant in Braque's life. He signed a contract with a famous dealer, Daniel-Henry Kahnweiler, whose small Paris gallery came to influence the history of modern art. Kahnweiler introduced Braque to Picasso that year at Picasso's Montmartre studio.

The two artists became close friends, and soon the Braque and Picasso duo became one of art history's most creative collaborations. They bounced ideas off each other on a daily basis, and their works of this period are so alike that even trained eyes often cannot distinguish them from each other. Together they gave birth to the style that came to be called cubism. Although Picasso set off the trend with his shocking *Les Demoiselles d'Avignon* (1907), a fragmented image of five nude women, Braque pushed their work toward the geometric forms that the cubist style became most known for.

In his works of 1908 to 1913, Braque conducted an intense study of the effects of light and perspective, challenging artistic conventions. He reduced architectural structures to mere cubes or rectangular prisms, calling attention to the nature of visual illusion and artistic representation.

By 1911, Braque was teamed inseparably with Picasso. Both men experimented with collage, a technique of constructing images from such everyday materials as newspapers, fabric, or glass. In 1912, Braque created the first recognized papier collé (pasted-paper picture) by attaching three pieces of wallpaper to the drawing *Fruit Dish and Glass*. In other collages, Braque glued bits of cloth and other materials to paintings to enrich the design. He also painted surfaces that imitated the textures of marble and the grain of wood, a technique he learned as a house painter.

In 1912, Braque married Marcelle Lapré and rented a house at Sorgues, a small town in the Rhône valley near Avignon.

His fertile collaboration with Picasso was interrupted when Braque enlisted in the French army at the outbreak of World War I. He served with distinction, being decorated twice in 1914 for bravery. In 1915, he suffered a serious head wound, followed by several months in the hospital and a long period of convalescence at home at Sorgues.

Braque resumed his artistic career without his former companion, Picasso, in 1917. The cubist movement was by then in its synthetic phase, referring to a tendency to use more color and to represent objects with large planes. In 1917 to 1918, Braque worked with his friend Juan Gris, a Spanish-born synthetic cubist master. Braque soon moved toward softer forms, and his style evolved to a more personal variation of the style of his day.

Braque became a prosperous modern master, receiving great acclaim among art lovers and buyers.

Braque became a prosperous modern master, receiving great acclaim among art lovers and buyers. In 1930, he acquired a country residence at Varengeville, a group of hamlets on the Normandy coast near Dieppe. There he created several series of paintings. From 1922 to about 1926, he painted a series of canephores, pagan-looking women carrying fruit. Overlapping with this group in time is the series of cheminées, fireplace mantelpieces laden with fruit and perhaps a guitar. By 1928 he was doing a series of gueridons, pedestal tables that held decorative items.

In 1931, Braque undertook a new medium of expression: incised white drawings, reminiscent of ancient Greek pottery designs, executed on plaster plaques painted black. During World War II he produced a collection of small decorative sculptures in a style calling to mind ancient Greece and mythological themes. After the 1940s, Braque continued working in a variety of media. He painted series of single subjects, first a series of billiard tables, then one of studio interiors, and then one of birds.

Braque continued to work throughout his life, producing art that remains richly inspiring and thought provoking to viewers. During the last years of his life, Braque was honored with important retrospective exhibitions throughout the world, and in December of 1961 he became the first living artist to have his works exhibited in the Louvre. After suffering from a chronic illness that began in 1959, he died August 31, 1963, in Paris. ◆

Bruegel the Elder, Pieter

c. 1525–1569 ● Painter

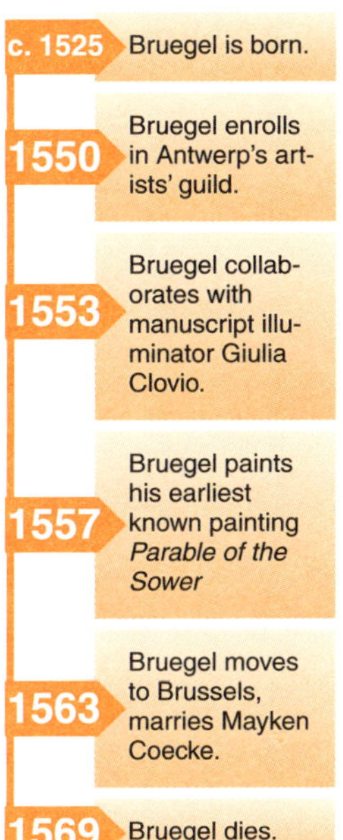

The Bruegels were a dynasty of Flemish landscape, genre, and still life painters active from the mid-16th to the early 18th century chiefly at Antwerp. The founder and the most famous member was Pieter Bruegel the Elder, but his sons, especially Jan, achieved considerable reputation in their own right. The name is spelled in various ways. Pieter the Elder favored "Bruegel," but his sons used "Brueghel" or "Breughel."

Pieter Bruegel was a pupil of Pieter Coecke van Aelst, the leading Flemish artist of his day, after which he worked (1550–1551) with Pieter Baltens for Claude Dorizi, an artist and art dealer in Malines. Bruegel enrolled in the Antwerp artists' guild in 1550–1551, before departing on an extended trip to southern France (including Lyon), Italy, and the Alps. In Rome about 1553 he collaborated with the manuscript illuminator Giulio Clovio. Bruegel was in Antwerp from about 1555 to 1563, when he moved to Brussels and married Mayken Coecke (called Bessemers), daughter of Pieter Coecke; they had two children, Pieter the Younger and Jan. His association with the print publisher Hieronymus Cock probably introduced him to the mapmaker Abraham Ortelius, the printer Christophe Plantin, and other Flemish humanists.

Remarkably versatile in style and subject matter, Bruegel produced landscapes, religious and allegorical subjects, scenes of peasant festivities, depictions of Flemish proverbs, and compositions in the manner of Hieronymus Bosch. Bruegel's career falls into two major phases. In Antwerp he produced many designs for Cock's printmakers, among them the so-called *Large Landscapes*, *Vice* and *Virtue* series, satirical subjects (*Elck*, *The Alchemist*), and two scenes of a peasant kermis, or church festival (*Hoboken Kermis*, *St. Joris Kermis*). Bruegel made only one print himself: *Landscape with Rabbit Hunters*, etched in 1560. His earliest known paintings were done in Antwerp. *Parable of the Sower* (1557), *Fall of Icarus* (known in two versions), his first multifigured paintings, *Netherlandish Proverbs*, and two panels in Vienna, *Children's Games* (1560) and *Carnival and Lent* (1559). All were inspired by Flemish speech and folk life, but with allegorical content, and possibly all three paintings were done in the manner of Bosch.

Once in Brussels, Bruegel continued producing designs for Cock but concentrated on painting. His patrons included Cardinal Antoine Perrenot de Granvelle and two wealthy government officials in Antwerp, Niclaes Jonghelinck and Jean Noirot (the latter's collection was unknown to scholars until 1995). For Jonghelinck, Bruegel painted the *Labors of the Months* (1565), a series of either six or 12 landscapes (the number is disputed), of which five survive, three in Vienna (*Hunters in the Snow, Gloomy Day, Return of the Herd*), and one each in Prague (*Haymaking*) and New York (*Harvesters*). Granvelle owned Bruegel's *Flight to Egypt* (1563) and other pictures, and Noirot possessed five paintings, four of them depicting peasant kermises or weddings (none can be identified with extant works). Bruegel's most important commission according to Van Mander came from the Brussels magistrates shortly before his death. Never executed, it was for a series of paintings, presumably landscapes, commemorating a recently completed canal linking Brussels with Antwerp.

Bruegel's art represents the culmination of the Flemish realistic tradition, often-reviving styles and compositions of earlier generations. In his *Procession to Calvary* (1564), his largest surviving painting and perhaps owned by Jonghelinck. Bruegel drew upon a traditional composition, possibly invented by Jan van Eyck, and adapted the holy figures from Rogier van der Weyden. His *Death of the Virgin* (1565) reworks deathbed scenes in earlier books of hours. Bruegel's interest in Bosch appears in some of his earliest print designs (*Big Fish Eat the Little Fish*) and in three paintings, *Fall of the Rebel Angels* (1562), *Dulle Griet* and especially *Triumph of Death* which is closest to Bosch in its apocalyptic view of human destiny.

vistas: distant views along or through an opening or avenue.

His landscapes range from depictions of the Flemish countryside, best seen in *Peasant and Bird Nester* and *Misantrhope* to great **vistas** that infused the traditional Flemish world landscape style of Joachim Patinir and Herri de Bles with a new grandeur inspired by Bruegel's Alpine experience, especially in the *Large Landscapes* prints, *Months*, and *Conversion of Paul* (1567). The same vast space and heroic scale distinguish his two paintings of the *Tower of Babel*, one dated 1563 the other probably done later. Bruegel's allegorical subjects, often satires of human folly presented with biting wit, share themes and attitudes with the literature and pageantry of the Flemish rhetoricians of his day, suggesting his participation in the *Violieren* chamber of rhetoric (which produced allegorical plays, farces, and poetry for various occasions), which was closely associated with the Antwerp artists' guild. A robust good humor pervades Bruegel's peasant scenes; the *Wedding Dance* (1566) and two late pictures in Vienna, *Peasant Dance* and *Peasant Wedding*, also contain acute observations of human forms and psychology.

A robust good humor pervades Bruegel's peasant scenes; the *Wedding Dance* (1566) and two late pictures in Vienna, *Peasant Dance* and *Peasant Wedding*, also contain acute observations of human forms and psychology.

Despite his stay in Italy, Bruegel showed little interest in Italian art until his Brussels period. Many of his works from 1565 on, especially *Christ and the Woman Taken in Adultery*, *Land of Cockaigne* (1567), the Vienna peasant scenes and two drawings. *Calumny of Apelles* and *Summer* (1568) show more concentrated compositions, larger-scaled, often monumental figures possibly influenced by a study of Raphael's Vatican cartoons. Some of Bruegel's late paintings, *Massacre of the Innocents* and *Census at Bethlehem* (1566) as well as three emblematic pictures of 1568, *Parable of the Blind*, *Peasant and Bird Nester*, and *Misanthrope*, may comment on the troubled times inaugurating the Eighty Years' War (the war of Netherlands independence from Spain, 1568–1648). According to Van Mander, before his death Bruegel destroyed a number of his satirical drawings to save his wife from persecution, and he left her the *Magpie on the Gallows* (1568), an enigmatic picture evoking an earlier Flemish landscape style. Several lost paintings are perhaps recorded in copies, including a *Crucifixion*, *Unfaithful Shepherd* (copy attributed to Marten van Cleef in Philadelphia, and *Peasants Fighting over a Card Game*.

Many of Bruegel's paintings were later acquired by Rudolph II, Holy Roman emperor (1576–1612), as well as by two Habsburg governors of the Spanish Netherlands, Archduke Ernst (1594–1595) and Leopold Wilhelm (1645–1656); many of their paintings are part of the great Bruegel collection now in Vienna. Bruegel's paintings and prints were endlessly copied and imitated; his peasant subjects and landscapes influenced later Netherlandish artists, among them Adriaen Brouwer and Peter Paul Rubens (who owned several Bruegel pictures). Drawings in Bruegel's style, some apparently done as forgeries by Roelant and Jacob Savery, circulated under his name until the 1980s and 1990s. In his lifetime Bruegel was famed as a second Bosch, but Ortelius, who owned his *Death of the Virgin* and had it reproduced in a print for distribution to his friends,

epitaph: a short statement or expression honoring and summing up a dead person or past event or ceremony.

erudite: possessing a knowledge gleaned nearly exclusively from books and bookreading.

hermetic: invulnerable to outside influences or beliefs; keeping to oneself.

warmly praised Bruegel in a 1574 epitaph as a consummate imitator of nature who was the most perfect painter of his century.

For Van Mander, Bruegel was chiefly a humorist of peasant origins, an image that persisted until the publication of Ortelius's **epitaph** in 1931. Pointing to his highly placed patrons and association with Ortelius and his circle, many scholars have seen Bruegel as a painter-philosopher whose art, even his peasant scenes, expresses profound philosophical or moral concepts, often expressed in disguised symbolism. In reaction to this view of an **erudite** and "**hermetic**" Bruegel, some critics emphasize both Bruegel's humor and the sources of his subject matter in traditional popular culture, especially its more festive aspects. Since 1970 the number of drawings thought to be by Bruegel has shrunk considerably through reattribution of a number of Alpine scenes and other landscapes, as well a series of peasant figures supposedly done after life, to artists working a generation later, possibly the Savery brothers.

The elder son and major successor of Pieter the Elder, Pieter the Younger (1564–1638) was a pupil of Pieter Goetkindt and possibly Gillis van Coninxloo. He remained all his life in Antwerp, where he entered the artists' guild in 1585. He painted religious subjects and scenes of hell and conflagrations but specialized in copies or reworked versions of his father's pictures, including the *Massacre of the Innocents*, *Netherlandish Proverbs*, *Triumph of Death*, and many pictures of peasant weddings and kermises. In his finest pictures, Pieter the Younger approaches his father in quality, but many inferior pictures attributed to him suggest an active workshop or were done by his son, Pieter III (1589-after 1634), who continued his father's style.

The younger son of Pieter the Elder, Jan lived after his father's death with his grandmother, Marie Bessemers, a miniaturist who, according to Van Mander, taught him watercolor; he was also a pupil of Pieter Goetkindt and perhaps the landscape painter Gillis van Coninxloo. After traveling in Germany, Brueghel was in Italy by about 1589. He worked for Cardinal Federigo Borromeo in Rome and Milan, and continued to paint pictures for him after returning to Antwerp in 1596. Jan entered the Antwerp painters' guild in 1597, becoming its dean in 1602. He was a friend of Pieter Paul Rubens, who painted a portrait of Jan and his family. Jan was the court painter to the governors of the Spanish Netherlands. Archduke Albert and the Infanta Isabella, for whom he painted a number of pictures. Among his pupils were his son Jan the Younger and Daniel Seghers.

A versatile artist like his father, Jan specialized in landscapes, flower pieces and other still-life subjects, and animals. Often painted on copper, his detailed, delicately executed pictures with their glowing, jewel-like colors earned him the epithet of "Velvet." He often collaborated with other artists, including Hans Rottenhammer (while in Rome), Rubens, and Hendrik van Balen, adding the flora and fauna; a joint effort with Rubens is their *Adam and Eve in Paradise* (1620). Jan also painted floral borders around images of the Madonna and Child by other artists.

Jan the Elder was a prolific artist and his paintings can be found in many museums. His earliest landscapes, such as *Harbor* (1599) and *Battle of Arbela* (1602), reflect the world landscapes of his father, but he developed his own repertoire of forest and mountain views, as well as rural scenes showing country people at work and play, as in *Landscape with River* (1612) and *Landscape with Windmills*. Some of his early landscape drawings were engraved by Aegidius Sadeler. Jan's detailed realism and love of nature also characterize his **allegorical** paintings, among them *Five Senses* and *Four Elements* in collaboration with Rubens and Van Balen respectively. His pictures were very popular and were copied and imitated into the 18th century. Two of his sons were also painters; Jan the Younger (1601–1678), who imitated his father's pictures, and Ambrosius (1617–1675). Both artists in turn had sons who followed their fathers' profession. ◆

allegorical: posessing veiled spiritual meaning transcending the literal interpretation of a sacred work.

Burne-Jones, Sir Edward Coley

AUGUST 28, 1833–JUNE 17, 1898 ● PAINTER AND DECORATIVE DESIGNER

A group of young British painters joined forces in 1848 to react against what they thought to be the unimaginative and artificial painting of their day. Inspired by Italian art of the 14th and 15th centuries, they called themselves the Pre-Raphaelite Brotherhood, in admiration of what they saw as the simple and natural images typical of Italian painting before the time of the painter Raphael. The Brotherhood's ac-

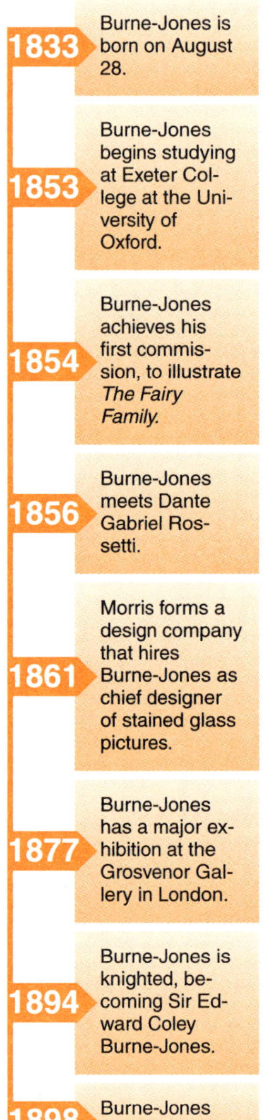

tive life lasted less than 10 years, but their influence reached into other arts and influenced future movements.

Sir Edward Coley Burne-Jones became one of the most successful of these Pre-Raphaelites, with a style characterized by dreamy, sensuous medievalism. His work is also characterized by the use of vivid color and the presence of architectural backgrounds. The women who appear in his works, usually draped in intricate classical gowns, fit the Pre-Raphaelite model of soft, luminous, ethereal faces with high, regal cheekbones and abundant, flowing hair. Burne-Jones became strongly influenced by the artistic styles of the Italian Renaissance, and he blended those styles with elements of Greek myths and the legends of King Arthur.

Born on August 28, 1833, in Birmingham, England, and christened Edward Coley Burne Jones, he went by the name Edward Jones until his late twenties then began using the name Burne-Jones. His father, Edward Richard Jones, ran a carving and gilding business. His mother, Elizabeth Coley, was the daughter of a prosperous jeweler. Young Edward loved to draw, though he did not intend to go into art. He attended the local grammar school and then attended classes at a school of design, with an engineering career in mind.

Burne-Jones developed a strong interest in religion and began studying at Exeter College, at the University of Oxford, in 1853. There he met fellow divinity student William Morris, who became Burne-Jones's lifelong friend and working partner. The two young men became steeped in fascination for Romantic literature, mysticism, and for all things medieval, themes that would fill their later artwork. They became interested in art through the writings of the influential art critic, John Ruskin. Burne-Jones's drawings led to his first commission in 1854, to illustrate *The Fairy Family*, a collection of fairy tales.

Through Ruskin, the two young friends learned of the Pre-Raphaelite Brotherhood and went to see their exhibits. After a vacation spent touring French cathedrals, the two young men decided to study art instead of becoming ministers. In 1856, Burne-Jones met one of the leading Pre-Raphaelites, Dante Gabriel Rossetti, who became one of the most famous English poets and painters of the 19th century. The Brotherhood had at first exhibited together anonymously, signing all their paintings with the monogram PRB. They had ceased exhibiting together by 1854, though, and had gone their individual ways by the time Burne-Jones and Morris met Rossetti.

Burne-Jones left Oxford without graduating, settled in London with Morris, and began training under Rossetti. The three men—Burne-Jones, Morris, and Rossetti—formed a bohemian group of friends who romanticized the Middle Ages. Rossetti and several of the other Pre-Raphaelites were students of England's highly prestigious Royal Academy. The group aimed at "truth to nature," which was to be achieved by attending to detail and painting from nature outdoors.

Burne-Jones became successful quickly, showing his work in several exhibitions and receiving commissions to design stained glass windows for architects.

Burne-Jones became successful quickly, showing his work in several exhibitions and receiving commissions to design stained glass windows for architects. In 1861, Morris and several partners formed a design company that revived the medieval applied arts of stained glass windows, mosaics, and tapestries. Burne-Jones became the company's chief designer of stained glass pictures, and he also created mosaics and other designs for Morris's firm. Today, Burne-Jones's influence is seen less in painting than in these areas of decorative design. His mosaics and stained glass windows can be seen in many English churches, including Christ Church, Oxford, and Birmingham Cathedral. He even created designs for tapestries, including the *Adoration of the Magi* (Exeter College Chapel, Oxford). Burne-Jones also illustrated books printed by Morris's prestigious Kelmscott Press. He made 87 designs for *Chaucer* (1896), considered to be among the world's finest printed books.

In June of 1860, Burne-Jones married Georgiana Macdonald (1840–1920) and one of the couple's children, Philip, later became a painter. After meeting his hero, Ruskin, Burne-Jones became inspired to tour Italy several times, finding inspiration for his style in the Italian Renaissance.

Around 1870, Burne-Jones experienced several personal and professional crises. He had an affair with a beautiful Greek woman and also had to resign from a prestigious painting group, the Old Water-Colour Society, when they objected to a male nude he painted in *Phyllis and Demophoon* (1870). He also had a disagreement with Ruskin, and his friendship with Rossetti declined after Rossetti had a breakdown. In 1875, Morris's firm dissolved, and the two friends drifted apart somewhat.

In spite of those setbacks, in 1877 Burne-Jones reached a successful height with a major exhibition at the Grosvenor Gallery in London. His works included oils such as *Days of*

Creation (1871–76), *The Beguiling of Merlin* (1873–77), and *The Mirror of Venus* (1867–77). This and further exhibitions at the Grosvenor raised Burne-Jones to the status of one of the great painters of England.

His highly sentimental, dreamlike, and romanticized works had reached maturity. In his stunning painting *The Golden Stairs* (1880), a circular stairway that seems to go nowhere in particular holds 15 or more lovely, angelic, glowing women in flowing gowns, walking in dreamy fantasy. His famous paintings of medieval chivalry include *King Cophetua and the Beggar Maid* (1884), in which the handsome, darkly clad king gazes up at the delicate young woman clad in a transparent gown, while an innocent pair of angelic scribes works in the background.

Burne-Jones was knighted in 1894, becoming Sir Edward Coley Burne-Jones. He died June 17, 1898, in London. ◆

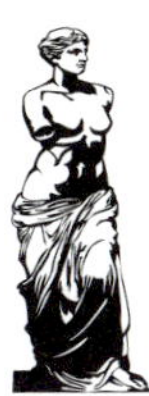

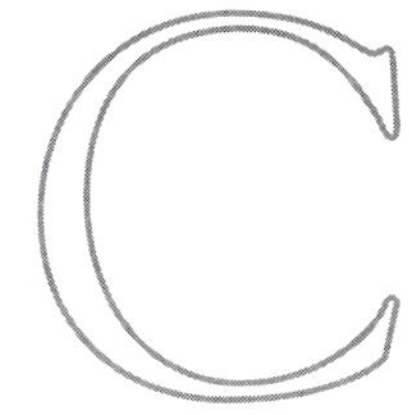

Campin, Robert

c. 1375–April 26, 1444 ● Painter

During the heart of the Renaissance, around 1400, an area of northern Europe called Flanders generated a rich and unique art genre. Flanders lay in parts of what are now France, Belgium, and the Netherlands. People from Flanders were called Flemish, and the Flemish painters created original uses of light and color. Robert Campin was one of the earliest and greatest Flemish masters. He has also been identified by scholars as possibly the same artist known as the Master of Flémalle, one of the founders and great masters of the Flemish school of painting.

Little more is known of Campin's life than what can be found in public records. He was born between 1375 and 1379 and lived in Tournai, Flanders, until his death in 1444. Documents show that he was established as a master painter in Tournai in 1406, and public records show payment for such works as altarpieces, religious panels, and portraits.

Campin's art is notable for its departure from the idealized, artificial International Gothic style and his pursuit of realism. The three main elements that set Campin's art apart from the Gothic are his solid, three-dimensional human figures, his grasp of perspective, and his interest in details of everyday life. These qualities can be seen in the famous triptych of the Annunciation, the *Mérode Altarpiece* (c. 1425), one of Campin's masterpieces. The Virgin is portrayed in a realistic setting, where

c. 1375	Campin is born in Tournai, Flanders.
1406	Records show Campin established as a master painter in Tournai.
1438	Campin produces his masterwork, the *Werl Altarpiece.*
1440	Altarpiece depicting the *Virgin and Child* and *St. Veronica* is created by Campin.
1444	Campin dies in Tournai, Flanders.

interior furnishings are rendered with an attention to detail that became characteristic of Flemish art. Also in his late masterwork, the *Werl Altarpiece* (1438) in the Prado, Madrid, Campin included realistic Flemish interiors of his day, skillful perspective, and figures dressed in realistic, well-contoured folds of material.

Campin drew from the style of manuscript illumination common in his day. His paintings also contain disguised symbolism, meaning that everyday objects in a scene convey symbolic meaning. For example, in his ***Annunciation,*** a burned-out candle may refer to Jesus extinguished on the cross. A basin and towel may refer to the purity of the Virgin Mary.

Annunciation: a painting depicting Robert Campin's interpretation of the church festival celebrating the announcement of the Incarnation to the Virgin Mary.
altarpiece: the work of art and ornamentation that decorates the space behind and above an altar in a church.

Another important work attributed to either Campin or the Master of Flémalle and now in Frankfurt, Germany, consists of two wings of an **altarpiece** dating about 1440. They depict the *Virgin and Child* and *St. Veronica.* Among other works generally ascribed to Campin are the *Virgin and Child before a Firescreen* and a *Nativity* at Dijon (c. 1430).

Although the identity of the Master of Flémalle cannot be confirmed, by the late 20th century, many scholars agreed that the works of the Master of Flémalle are those of Robert Campin. They base this on the stylistic similarities of paintings attributed to the two names. The name, "Master of Flémalle," came from four paintings attributed to him that were mistakenly thought to have hung in an abbey in Flémalle, Belgium, near Liege. It is known that the Master of Flémalle lived around 1430. Two artists—Rogier van der Weyden and Jacques Daret—are known to have been pupils of Campin's. An altarpiece executed for the Abbey of St. Vaast by Jacques Daret looks much like works by Rogier van der Weyden and also like works by the Master of Flémalle. Since the Tournai records give the name of Campin as master of both Daret and Rogier, it has been assumed that the Master of Flémalle may be identified with Campin. Some scholars, however, have considered the works of the Master of Flémalle as early works by Rogier van der Weyden himself.

Campin's work influenced two later masters of Flemish art, his pupil Rogier van der Weyden, who became a famous painter of portraits and religious subjects, and Jan van Eyck, one of the greatest Flemish painters of altarpieces and portraits in the 15th century. ◆

Canova, Antonio

NOVEMBER 1, 1757–OCTOBER 13, 1822 ● SCULPTOR

As a master carver of pure white Italian marble, Antonio Canova drew his inspiration from the classical art of ancient Greece and Rome. Classical artists pursued images of physical perfection, seeking to portray the essence of pure beauty. Canova, though, was a leading sculptor of Europe's Napoleonic period, the late 1700s and early 1800s. His intentional imitation of antique forms is known as neoclassicism, and Canova's subjects look as if they could have graced ancient temples, endowed as they are with godlike heroism and grace. Indeed, he was commissioned to render sculptures of popes as well as the Emperor Napoleon.

Canova was born November 1, 1757, in Possagno, Republic of Venice, in northern Italy. Canova's father, a stone mason, died in 1761, leaving Canova to be raised and trained by his stone mason grandfather, Pasin Canova. Under the patronage of a Venetian senator, Canova went at the age of 11 to work with a sculptor called Torretti. When Torretti moved his studio that same year to Venice, Canova went along. In a traditional student-master relationship, Canova helped Torretti, studied classical art, and drew sketches of nude models. He also created a few modest works for hire.

Antonio Canova

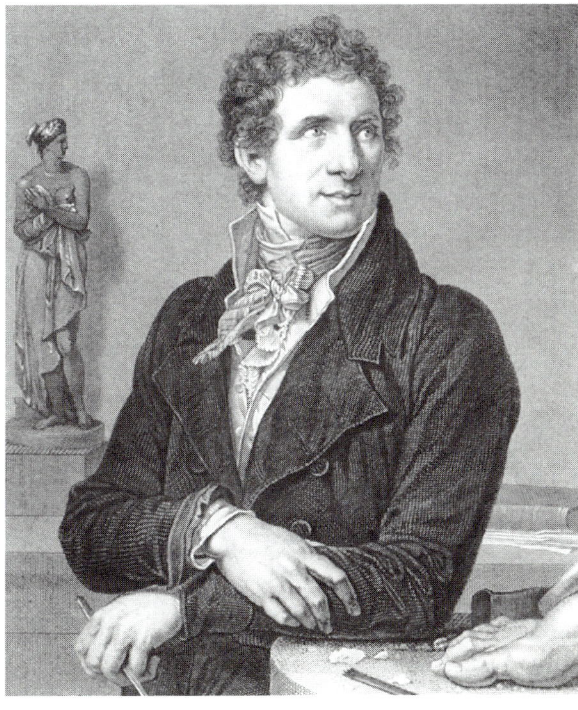

In 1775, Canova set up his own studio in Venice. In 1779, he sculpted his first important work, the marble statue *Daedalus and Icarus*, which had been commissioned by a Venetian politician. The wrinkles of the old man and the sweet-faced youth make the figures look so realistic that people accused Canova of making plaster casts from live models.

1757 Canova is born in Possagno on November 1.

1779 Canova sculpts his first important work, the marble statue *Daedalus and Icarus.*

1781 Canova settles in Rome.

1792 Canova's *Monument to Clement XIII* becomes the first neoclassical sculpture to be placed in St. Peter's.

1802 Canova accepts Napoleon's invitation to go to Paris, where he becomes the court sculptor and a major influence on French art.

1810 Canova becomes president of the Accademia di San Luca in Rome.

1815 Canova is sent to Paris to retrieve the art treasures Napoleon had taken from Italy.

1822 Canova dies on October 13 in Venice.

On visits to Rome, Canova met leading artists of the period, including the Scottish painter-dealer Gavin Hamilton, who directed Canova's studies toward a more profound understanding of the antique. Canova visited Naples and the ancient archaeological sites of Herculaneum, Pompeii, and Paestum.

After settling in Rome in 1781, Canova spent most of the rest of his life there, becoming an influential figure in the artistic life of the city. Several portraits show a stylish, attractive man with warm eyes and dark curly hair. He reached heights of fame throughout Europe, and he often helped young artists by finding them patrons.

In the 1780s Canova presented the art world with a bounty of work that gave life to the nude body. In a series of nearly life-size sculptures, he explored the graceful human form as well as mythological figures. In the exquisitely delicate and balanced composition, *Cupid Awakening Psyche* (1783–93), the winged Cupid leans tenderly over the naked Psyche in an embrace that is erotic but also spiritually transcendent. This depiction of Cupid reviving Psyche, who was put to sleep forever by inhaling a magic perfume, is as much a tribute to the immortal soul as it is a hymn to love. Canova sculpted many other mythological figures through his career, such as Orpheus, Eurydice, Adam and Eve, and Venus.

Canova's love of the classical and his presence in Rome led to several important commissions from the Roman Catholic Church. In 1783, the church commissioned him to carve the *Mausoleum of Pope Clement XIV* in the Santi Apostoli church in Rome. In 1787 crowds flocked to see the first display of the tomb, with its carved figure of the pope at the top, and the front draped with two female figures guarding the tomb entrance. That same year, Canova received a commission to sculpt another papal tomb, this time in the great St. Peter's Basilica in the Vatican. The interior of the basilica, the world's largest church, contains numerous sculptures by some of the world's greatest sculptors, including magnificent tombs. Canova's massive and ornate *Monument to Clement XIII* (1792) became the first neoclassical sculpture to be placed in St. Peter's. Huge carved lions and an adult male angel provide a powerful guard at the tomb's entrance.

Canova's moving *Statue of Pius VI in Prayer* (1822) took a place in the area under the altar of St. Peter's known as the Sacred Grottoes, home to numerous artifacts and memorial artwork. The image is of a kneeling pope, a man who died impoverished in exile, asking only to be buried near St. Peter, whose ancient tomb also lies in these underground chambers.

As his status grew, Canova received commissions from Napoleon Bonaparte, emperor of France, as well as the Bonaparte family. He sculpted a handsome marble bust of Napoleon and two massive statues of Napoleon, one a naked bronze of the emperor standing with a royal toga draped over one arm and a scepter in the other, looking like a great Caesar. In 1802, at the Pope's nudging, Canova accepted Napoleon's invitation to Paris, where he became the court sculptor and a major influence on French art.

About 1807, Canova finished one of his most famous works, a sculpture of Napoleon's sister, Pauline Borghese, the wife of Prince Camillo Borghese, reclining on a couch as *Venus Triumphant*. Today the famous sculpture resides as a centerpiece in the lavish museum galleries of the elegant Villa Borghese in Rome, once the family estate. Pauline lies on her side in a gracious pose, naked from the waist up with a cloth entwined sensually around her legs. Each fold of the velvety mattress and plump pillows are sculpted in marble, and the marble couch features gold decorative carvings.

In 1805, Canova received the prestigious appointment of inspector general of fine arts and antiquities for the Vatican.

In 1805, Canova received the prestigious appointment of inspector general of fine arts and antiquities for the Vatican. In 1810, he became president of the Accademia di San Luca in Rome, a position he held for life. After Napoleon's defeat in 1815, Canova was sent to Paris to retrieve the art treasures the emperor had taken from Italy. As a reward for a successful mission, the pope made Canova the marquis of Ischia, a small island near Capri, across the Bay of Naples.

Canova worked on commissions in England and Austria and even on a monument of George Washington in 1820 that was destroyed by fire in 1830. Canova was also a painter, but his few paintings are not considered high in quality. They include a few portraits and re-creations of antique paintings discovered at Herculaneum.

Canova died October 13, 1822, in Venice and was buried at Possagno in a temple he designed to look like the Pantheon in Rome. Canova's supremacy among European sculptors at the turn of the 18th century and the beginning of the 19th was seen in countless memoirs, poems, and newspaper stories. However, his reputation declined during the following century, perhaps because his subject matter was classical and much copied. Now his work is recognized for the great skill it shows and is viewed by millions every year. Most of Canova's statues remain in European collections, though the Metropolitan Museum of Art in New York City owns important works, including *Perseus with the Head of Medusa* (1804–06) and *Cupid and Psyche* (1793). ◆

Caravaggio

SEPTEMBER, 1571–JULY 18, 1610 ● PAINTER

Michelangelo Merisi was probably born in Milan but lived in nearby Caravaggio, where his father was steward to Marchese Francesco I Sforza. Apprenticed in the late 1580s to the conservative Milanese painter Simone Peterzano, he is intermittently recorded in Caravaggio until 1592, when he arrived in Rome. Certain aspects of Caravaggio's north Italian heritage were clearly influential throughout his career. Beyond figural and compositional borrowings from local artists such as Giovanni Girolamo Savoldo and Peterzano, he more importantly absorbed the north Italian traditions of naturalism and dramatic **chiaroscuro** (contrasts of light and dark), using the latter, like Leonardo da Vinci and his Milanese followers, to enhance the sculptural relief of figures. This lyrical, naturalistic tradition emphasized still life painting, portraiture, and genre scenes; meanwhile, the towering figures of Counter-Reformation Milan, archbishops Carlo and Federico Borromeo, who later owned Caravaggio's *Basket of Fruit*, encouraged naturalism and simplicity in Milanese religious art.

chiaroscuro: the method painters use to depict light and shade by making them constrast drastically; the word chiaroscuro is taken from the Italian word for dark.

Caravaggio's early Roman production (c. 1593–1595) is notable both for its reliance on the Lombard naturalist tradition and, conversely, for its failure to imitate respected artistic models from antiquity and the high Renaissance. These earliest canvases, not done on commission, are technical demonstration pieces intended to highlight Caravaggio's insistent, sharp naturalism taken directly from life study. Yet the contrived system of lighting and affected pose of models betray a refined atmosphere and sophisticated design process. The *Sick Little*

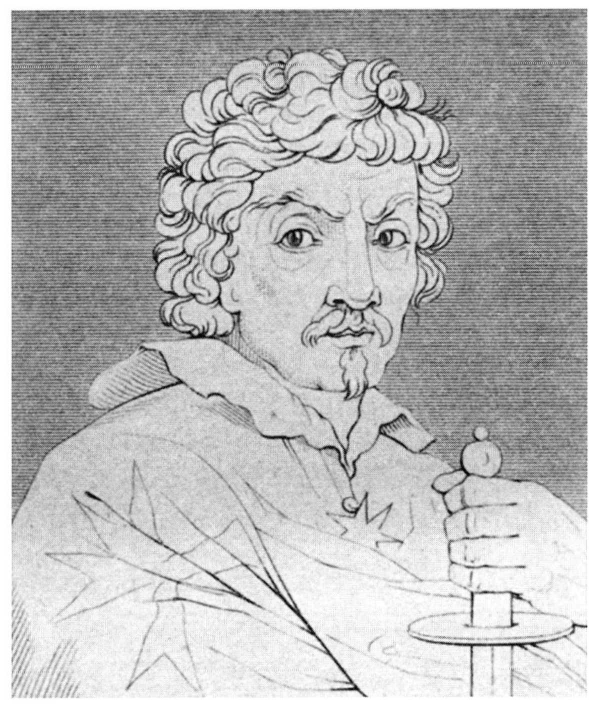
Caravaggio

Bacchus, *Boy with a Basket of Fruit*, *Boy Peeling a Fruit*, and the *Boy Bitten by a Lizard* are characterized by the depiction of a single half-length figure, an androgynous youth clad in classicizing garments, who addresses the viewer. Eschewing a defined background setting and any sense of atmosphere or depth, Caravaggio focuses on still life objects with an exaggerated, tactile literalness. Objects tend to be placed against, and sometimes beyond, the picture plane, allowing for virtuoso displays of foreshortening.

In these early works Caravaggio attempts to capture momentary gesture, expression, and emotion, qualities best seen in the *Boy Bitten by a Lizard*. In the *Magdalene*, a full-length figure placed away from the plane, the mood is quiet and introspective, a feeling enhanced by the dark background shadow, two features important to his later religious images. In a horizontal format, the *Cardsharps* and *Fortune-teller* are Caravaggio's first essays in multifigure narrative composition. Duplicity is the theme of these genre scenes, which represent foolish youths in contemporary clothing, yet the blank, bright backgrounds reveal Caravaggio's staged, studio realism.

From 1595 to 1601, Caravaggio joined the household of the Florentine Cardinal Francesco del Monte, a well-known patron of music and art, who influenced Caravaggio's imagery by commissioning canvases of musical subjects. Although Caravaggio depended on north Italian precedents for composition, the instruments and various scores belonged to his patrons and were studied with consummate skill. It has recently been hypothesized that the seemingly erotic, androgynous model in the musical images is a Spanish castrato singer in del Monte's retinue.

Caravaggio's contemporary religious works, such as the *Rest on the Flight into Egypt* and *St. Francis in Ecstasy*, signal a change in style and mood from his secular scenes. Both canvases include landscapes, which contribute to the quiet, intimate at-

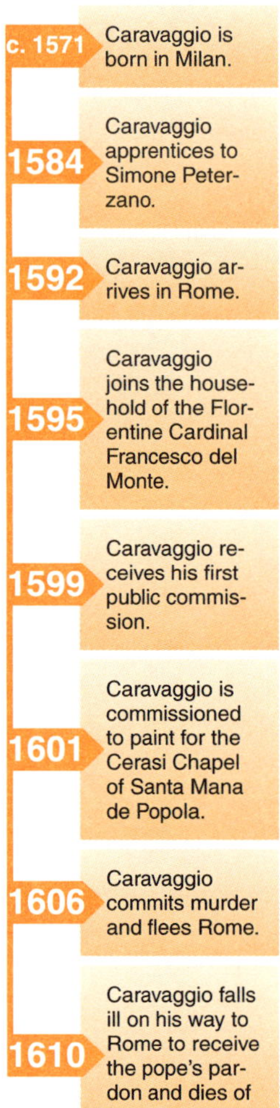

mosphere, and androgynous angels, adopted from the secular pictures. Caravaggio begins to concentrate on spiritual meaning and initiates his famous exploitation of the effects of strong chiaroscuro, especially in the nocturnal *St. Francis*, where light is employed as the sole indicator of divinity. The introspective feeling of the tender *St. Francis* is a precocious intimation of Caravaggio's extraordinary ability to communicate images of spiritual profundity. *St. Catherine* demonstrates Caravaggio's development by depicting a monumental, full-length figure comfortably situated in space by the dramatic contrast of light and dark. Likewise, the *Judith and Holofernes* and *Conversion of the Magdalene* elaborate the narrative format of the *Cardsharps* and *Fortune-teller*, although here chiaroscuro enhances drama and the sharp, sculptural relief of figures.

In 1599 Caravaggio received his first public commission, to paint the lateral canvases depicting the *Calling of St. Matthew* and the *Martyrdom of St. Matthew* in the Contarelli Chapel of San Luigi dei Francesi, Rome. This project secured Caravaggio a lasting reputation and much notoriety. Completed by 1600, the Contarelli canvases successfully synthesized diverse elements from both his early secular and sacred images. Apparently, two systems of lighting are employed: directed sunlight entering at an angle from a window and diffuse, overhead light from an artificial source such as a lamp. Light conveys sculptural form to figures while simultaneously serving as a metaphor for the divine. Dramatic gesture and movement also gain significance. Furthermore, sacred figures are depicted as unidealized, realistic human beings while secular actors are identified by a closer attention to costume, appearing as contemporary dandies. After the original version of the altarpiece was rejected, Caravaggio executed a more dignified, corrected replacement with a stately Matthew and distant angel.

Caravaggio was next commissioned, in 1601, to paint the two lateral canvases in the Cerasi Chapel of Santa Maria del Popolo, in direct competition with Annibale Caracci, who executed the altarpiece. Caravaggio's original versions of the *Conversion of Paul* and *Crucifixion of St. Peter* were rejected (only the *Paul* survives), but he quickly completed two astounding replacements. Hereafter, Caravaggio's religious works tend to convey deep concentration and utter seriousness enhanced by dark, contemplative shadow; yet, through the foregrounding of figures, they still appeal directly to the viewer. The deeply moving *Death of the Virgin* was also refused because, although touching and emotional, the scene was devoid of heavenly apparitions and resembled too much a common, realistic ceremony of mourning. Yet Caravaggio never lacked for private patrons.

In 1606, after committing a murder, Caravaggio fled Rome under the protection of the Colonna family, painting a *Supper at Emmaus* and a *Magdalene in Ecstasy* while in exile. He is next recorded in Spanish Naples, safe from papal jurisdiction and a capital sentence.

Between 1606 and his death in 1610, Caravaggio rapidly moved from Naples to Malta, where he spent a year, was knighted and later imprisoned, only to escape to Sicily and return again to Naples. In July 1610, on his way to Rome to receive the pope's pardon, Caravaggio stopped at Port Ercole, where he became ill and died of fever. Throughout this period Caravaggio, although a fugitive, continued to receive **patronage** at the highest levels of society. His brushwork becomes more rapid and broader, causing greater visibility of the red-brown middle ground, which now acts almost as a middle tone contributing to greater pictorial unity and evocative atmosphere. Precise naturalism yields to softer, more expressive forms, as the mood of these predominantly religious images is one of melancholy, sobriety, and humility. Figures are reduced in scale, placed in a middle ground, and arranged in geometrical groups and clear compositions. A dark, open space or void, which occupies the top portion of the canvas, contributes to the contemplative, tragic atmosphere. Gestures are subdued and posture restrained as Caravaggio concentrates on simple, intense inner emotion. The *Beheading of St. John*, *Burial of St. Lucy*, and *Raising of Lazarus* demonstrate well the geometrical organization of space and figural grouping. Massive architecture also gains significance in these canvases, for it contributes monumentality and solemnity while lending intimacy to the humble figures.

patronage: the financial, emotional, and professional support supplied to an artist by a patron.

Caravaggio and Annibale Carracci were the two major opponents of **mannerism** and exponents of a return to **naturalism** at Rome from the decade of the 1590s. Both wished to clarify the subject matter and intensify the message of religious art through the realistic depiction of figures and legible composi-

mannerism: the style of art reflected in the works of European artists between 1520 and 1600 and characterized by emotion and distortion symbolizing the enormous tension in Europe during that time period.

naturalism: an artistic style that attempts to portray an object in nature in its most realistic state on a canvass or paper.

Caravaggio, however, while frequently availing himself of artistic precedent, always remained far more devoted to direct, observable naturalism.

tion, initiating the baroque by emphasizing the appeal to sensory perception and directly engaging the viewer. Yet Annibale's idealized naturalism was tempered through the study of artistic tradition, of antiquity and the high Renaissance, and laborious preparatory drawing. His highly selective realism utilized and combined only what was most beautiful in nature.

Caravaggio, however, while frequently availing himself of artistic precedent, always remained far more devoted to direct, observable naturalism. In his singular experimentation with the dramatic effects of light and chiaroscuro, he employed light to increase the solidity of form, add pictorial or expressive interest, and represent the presence of the divine, sometimes all simultaneously in a single image. Yet Caravaggio consistently subordinated realist practices to a comprehensive sense of design; his famed naturalism was clearly regulated and studio-based. He achieved such stunning immediacy and presence from his figures by skipping the intermediary drawing process and instead painting from posed studio models directly onto the canvas. But perhaps Caravaggio's greatest achievement was his unparalleled communication of profound spiritual meaning and a searching exploration of human nature. His uncompromising realism dictated that sacred figures be depicted as unidealized and common human types, so that frequently, the witnesses to supernatural, divine events are clearly destitute members of the lower classes. Some patrons rejected these humble examples of faith, devotion, and piety; for other groups and audiences, they seemed to embody Counter-Reformation ideals.

Ironically, Caravaggio's spirituality was also the least understood and imitated feature of his output. Giovanni Battista Caracciolo, the Neapolitan painter, was possibly the only follower of Caravaggio to comprehend the style and mood of his mature spiritual sentiment. The majority of the Caravaggisti, as his imitators are called, in the first two decades of the 17th century focused on genre scenes, figural naturalism, and chiaroscuro, with little grasp of underlying content. As a group they lacked his sense of composition and subtle, sophisticated atmosphere. His most important Italian emulators were Orazio Gentileschi, Orazio Borgianni, and Carlo Saraceni; French followers include Valentin de Boulogne and Georges de la Tour; Dirck van Baburen, Gerrit van Honthorst, and Hendrick ter Brugghen reinterpreted his style in the north. ◆

Cellini, Benvenuto

NOVEMBER 3, 1500–FEBRUARY 13, 1571 ● ARTIST

Benvenuto Cellini was a Florentine goldsmith, sculptor, medallist, and writer who is generally considered to be one of Italy's greatest mannerist artists. He led an itinerant life in his early years and worked for various illustrious patrons, including Popes Clement VII and Paul III in Rome, Cosimo I de' Medici in his native Florence, and Francis I in France. Cellini chronicled many of the events from his brilliant career in his highly engaging autobiography, the *Vita di Benvenuto Cellini*, begun in 1558 but not published until the 18th century. His own account of his life gives invaluable insights into his volatile personality, his turbulent relations with his patrons, his views on art and fellow artists, and the working processes linked to his craft.

A statue of Benvenuto Cellini in Florence, Italy.

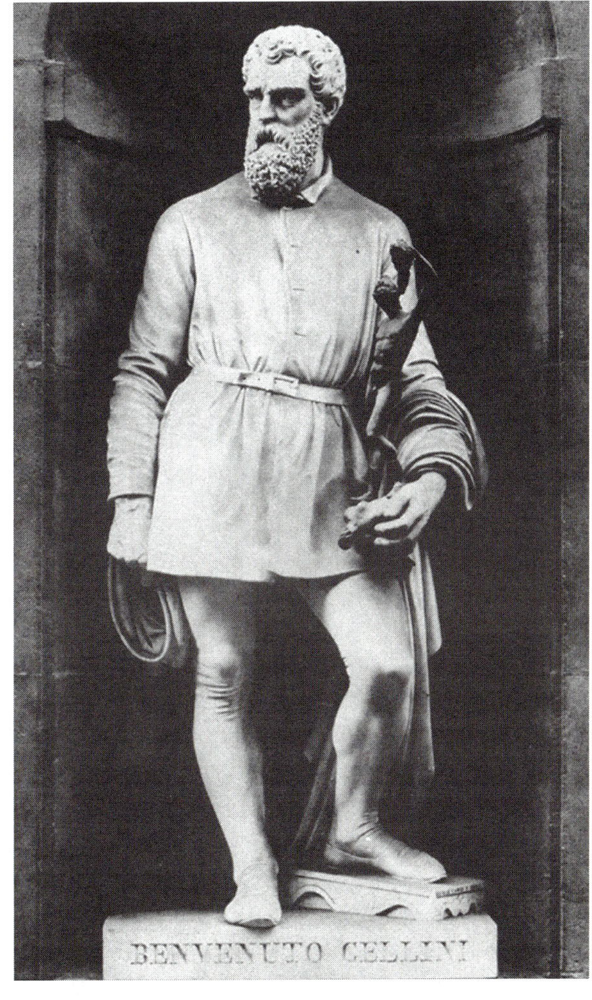

Cellini was born into a family of prosperous, well-respected craftsmen: his grandfather was a mason and his father, Giovanni Cellini, was a master carpenter who constructed scaffolding for one of Leonardo da Vinci's Florentine artistic projects. In 1513 Cellini began to train in the art of the goldsmith with Michelangelo de' Brandini in Florence and two years later moved to the workshop of Andrea di Sandó Marcone, but in 1516 he was forced to leave the city following a brawl and moved to Siena. Subsequently he traveled to and worked in Bologna, Pisa, and Rome while periodically visiting his native city. In the early 1520s, he returned to Florence, where he worked or was associated with the artists Francesco

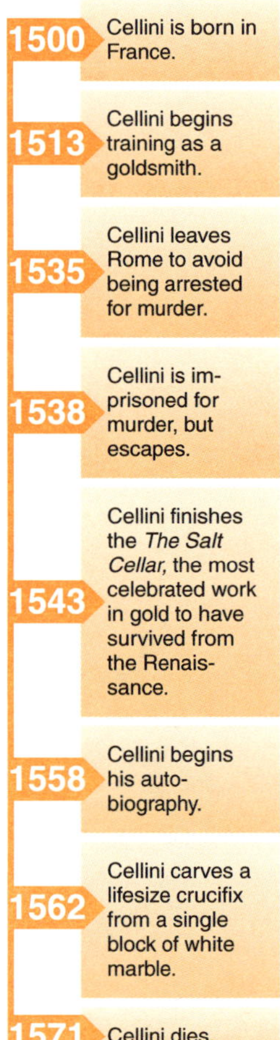

Salimbeni and Giovanbattista Sogliani. But in 1523 Cellini was prosecuted for sodomy, and he fled Florence after he had a violent confrontation with fellow goldsmiths. The following year in Rome he worked for several goldsmiths, then opened his own shop at the end of the same year. In this period he worked in precious metals for important members of the church and the nobility; none of the items for these patrons is thought to have survived. This successful and productive phase of his career came to an abrupt end in May 1527 with the Sack of Rome by imperial troops.

Cellini left Rome in 1527 and returned to Florence and then, after a short stay, made his way to Mantua, where he worked for the Gonzaga family. In 1529 he was again in Rome, where he entered the service of Pope Clement VII and was employed in the papal mint. Among his works of this moment are two silver gilt medals (1533–1534 and 1534; Florence, Bargello) with the bust of the pope on the obverse, or front. Although small in scale, Cellini's designs are extremely effective as portraits and are characterized by psychological suggestiveness and an attention to minute detail. The reverse of the earlier of the two medals depicts an allegory of Peace: the other shows Moses striking water from the rock. Both testify to Cellini's skill in organizing a complex composition within a restricted area. For the pope he also worked on a splendid jewel-encrusted morse or clasp, which is now lost but was fortunately recorded in 1729 in Francesco Santi Bartoli's watercolors (London, British Museum).

Following the death of Clement VII, Cellini was charged with the murder of a fellow goldsmith, but was pardoned by the newly elected Pope Paul III, who also commissioned him to work on a die for a gold coin depicting Saint Paul. Despite papal intervention, Cellini left Rome in 1535 to avoid arrest, and he traveled first to Florence and then to Venice. Back in Florence later in the same year, he was employed by Alessandro de' Medici to work on coin dies. The artist returned to Rome in 1536, but left the city the following year and headed for Padua, where he worked on a portrait medal of Pietro Bembo (Florence, Bargello). He then went to Paris, where he may have designed a bronze portrait medal of King Francis I (Florence, Bargello). After a brief stay in France he returned to Rome at the close of 1537 via Ferrara. In Rome, however, his earlier misdeeds caught up with him, and in October 1538 he was imprisoned in the Castel Sant' Angelo, from which he managed to escape. By 1540 Cellini had decided to return to France, but before leaving Italy he stopped in Ferrara, where he worked for members of the Este family.

Throughout his second stay in France Cellini carried out a variety of projects for Francis I. Among the earlier commissions (1542) was the decoration for the Porte Dorée at the château of Fontainebleau, which consisted of two bronze Satyrs (never cast), and a bronze lunette of the Nymph of Fontainebleau, (1543), his first surviving monumental sculpture. The iconography of the relief is partly connected to a now-destroyed fresco by Rosso on the Fontainebleau legend (a hunting dog discovered a spring and its goddess). The style of Cellini's reclining nymph, in the pose of an ancient river-god, resembles that of the mannerist sculptures designed in the 1530s by Primaticcio and Rosso Fiorentino for Fontainebleau. Accordingly, the **nymph**'s anatomy is defined by elongated limbs that create the effect of perfect poise and studied elegance. But her **languid** sophistication contrasts with the vibrant naturalism of the stag (an emblem of the French king), dogs, and boars, which have all been designed with the goldsmith's eye for detail and finish. The relief, however, was never placed on the Porte Dorée; it was instead set up in the entrance to the château of Anet by Philibert de L'Orme.

nymph: in classical mythology, the minor divinities represented as beautiful maidens who lived in nature.

languid: sluggish or lacking in forcefulness.

While in the service of Francis I, Cellini occupied the post of goldsmith to the king and executed the *Salt Cellar* (1540–1543), the most celebrated work in gold to have survived from the Renaissance. With Earth and Neptune, the two principal figures of the piece, Cellini successfully communicated a sense of the monumentality of sculpture, although he was working in the more delicate scale of the goldsmith's art. With their abstracted anatomical forms and composed manners, both figures are characterized by a mannerist refinement typical of the Fontainebleau school. Decorating the base are personifications of Morning, Day, Evening, and Night, which reflect Cellini's interest in Michelangelo's sculptures in the new sacristy of San Lorenzo, Florence. Cellini, however, transformed Michelangelo's expressive force into sheer delicacy and grace. Alongside the four times of day are the four winds or seasons and, beneath the principal figures, allusions to Francis I, such as the salamander and the elephant. Furthermore, colored enameling enriches the already gleaming, finely detailed surfaces of the work and is to be found on the miniature Ionic temple (for the peppercorns) and the boat (for the salt).

Despite the privilege of being granted French citizenship, Cellini was forced to leave Paris in July 1545 after he was accused of embezzling a quantity of silver given to him by the king to make a set of candlesticks.

Cellini returned to Florence in the summer of 1545 and entered the service of duke Cosimo I, received the commission for a bronze statue of Perseus with the head of Medusa (1545–1553) in August. Positioned close to Donatello's *Judith* (c. 1446–1460), the *Perseus* was conceived as an emblem of Florentine civic pride, and it may also have been intended to symbolize the strength of Cosimo's leadership. The commission also gave Cellini the opportunity to establish his reputation in monumental sculpture in his home city. He is thought to have used an **Etruscan** statuette as the basis for the pose of his triumphant figure. But the poise, graceful forms, and eight intended points of view of Cellini's statue are typical of mannerist works of art. Although large, the *Perseus* displays all the intricately wrought surfaces found in the artist's small-scale works in precious metals. The hand of the goldsmith is especially evident in the base, which is encrusted with a wide range of decorative motifs and is adorned with four bronze statuettes of Mercury, Danaë, Jupiter, and Minerva, and a bronze relief of Perseus and Andromeda.

Etruscan: of or relating to citizens of the ancient nation of Etruria.

In 1545 Cellini also set to work on a bronze portrait bust of Cosimo I. He intended the design to compete with a marble bust by Bandinelli, Cellini's great rival in Florence. Cellini's engaging and vibrantly characterized portrait evokes a sense of nervous energy that is, in part, also created by the turn of the head, deeply drilled eyes (once silvered or enamelled), and windswept locks of hair. The bust clearly displays the artist's skill in differentiating surface textures, especially in the precious and elegant effects of Cosimo's cuirass, or upperbody armor, which is embellished with carefully chiseled emblems of the duke. In 1557 Cellini's work was sent to Portoferraio on the island of Elba and replaced by a portrait by Bandinelli, who had closely modeled his design on an antique bust and, as a result, presented a less revealing and more conventional public image of Cosimo.

While working on the Cosimo I bust, Cellini executed the bronze bust of the Florentine banker resident in Rome, Bindo Altoviti (c. 1550). A successful design in the field of portraiture, the work was apparently praised by Michelangelo. The degree of psychological introspection and careful rendering of detail (see, for example, the furrowed brow, wrinkles around the eyes, and thick eyebrows) suggest that Cellini may have modeled the portrait from life. Like the Cosimo I work, the Altoviti bust displays the sitter caught in a moment of action. In the case of the latter, the head is gently inclined to the left, and the chest and shoulders appear to move beneath the tunic and cloak.

On his return to Florence, Cellini was also involved in restoring works of antiquity in marble and bronze from Cosimo's collections.

On his return to Florence, Cellini was also involved in restoring works of antiquity in marble and bronze from Cosimo's collections. Some time after 1548 the artist designed a marble *Ganymede* which incorporated an antique torso given to the duke by Stefano Colonna (Cellini carved the remaining sections). Inspired by the pose of Jacopo Sansovino's *Bacchus* (1511–1518), the *Ganymede* exhibits subtly carved surfaces that define delicate areas of flesh and the gentle feathers of the eagle. Aiming to establish a reputation as a marble sculptor, and in direct competition with Bandinelli, Cellini designed two other statues on mythological subjects: the *Apollo and Hyacinth* and the *Narcissus* (c. 1548–1557). He carved the former work from an imperfect block of marble presented by Bandinelli, and, despite its unfinished state and weathered surfaces (it was placed in the Boboli Gardens in the 18th century with the *Narcissus* and only rediscovered in 1940), it displays a careful arrangement of lithe, gracefully moving forms. With the languorous *Narcissus*, Cellini manifests his concerns with elegant outline, the poised body, and more than one intended viewpoint.

With the completion of the *Perseus* in 1553, Cellini reached the high point of his career. In the subsequent years his relations with the Medici administration became strained, and he experienced personal problems that eventually led to his imprisonment. During this difficult period Cellini carved a life-size *Crucifix* (1562) from a single block of white marble, and this is considered to be the masterpiece of his last years. Originally intended for his own tomb, the *Crucifix* was presented to Cosimo I, but in 1576 Francesco I de' Medici gave it to Philip II of Spain, who installed it in the Escorial. Characterized by a masterful handling of the marble, the *Crucifix* displays the crisply delineated facial features and anatomical forms of a deeply moving Christ.

In 1565 Cellini started writing his treatises on sculpture and the art of the goldsmith, which were printed in 1568. He died on February 3, 1571 and was interred in the Chapel of the

Accademia del Disegno in the Florentine church of the SS. Annunziata. ◆

Cézanne, Paul

JANUARY 19, 1839–OCTOBER 22, 1906 ● ARTIST

A founder of impressionism, Cézanne was born and grew up in Aix-en-Provence. His parents married when Paul was 10 years old. During this time the elder Cézanne had become the owner of a successful bank and the family prospered financially. Still, because of the illegitimacy of Paul and his younger sister Marie, and the couple's humble origins, they were always ostracized by what was considered respectable society in this provincial town.

As a result, the young Cézanne was something of an outsider who found it difficult to form social relationships, a trait that continued throughout his life. Perhaps the most influential person in Cézanne's life was his closest friend from childhood, the writer Émile Zola. Of their early friendship Zola wrote, "Opposites by nature, we became united forever, attracted to each other by secret affinities, the as yet vague torment of a common ambition, the awakening of a superior intelligence in the midst of the brutal mob."

Paul Cézanne, self-portrait, c. 1879

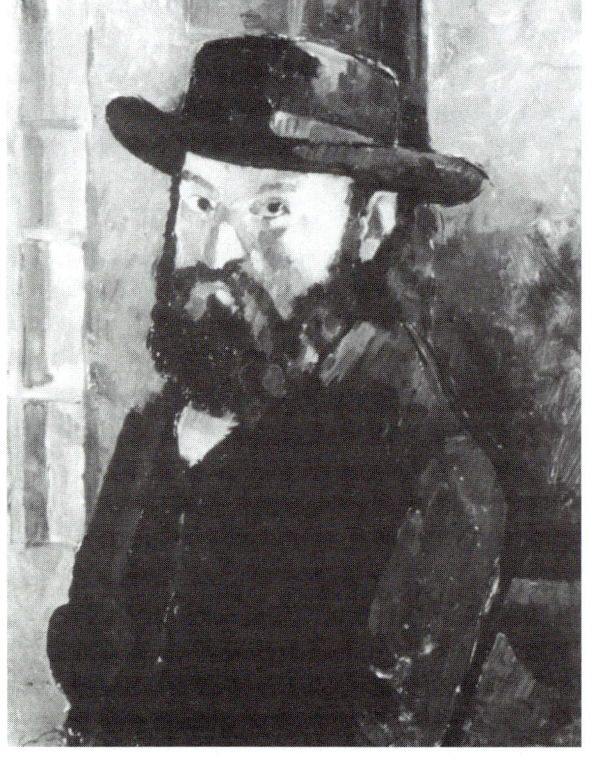

After school Zola went to live in Paris and Cézanne stayed in Aix to study law in accordance with his father's wishes. He gave up his studies as soon as his father agreed and moved to Paris to be reunited with Zola and begin painting seriously. He produced very little during this period and drifted away from Zola. Always prone to melancholy and fits of temper, he began to have periods of depression and withdrawal that lasted on and off for the rest of his life.

Cézanne returned to Aix determined to please his father; he planned to give up painting and take up the family business. Soon both father and son realized that Paul would never become a banker and he returned to Paris. There he failed to gain acceptance at the École des Beaux Arts. His work, along with that of Camille Pissarro, Pierre Renoir, Claude Monet, and others, was rejected by the art establishment. Cézanne returned to the countryside, where he remained, except for brief intervals, for the rest of his life.

It was in one of these intervals that he fell in love with a 19-year-old model named Hortense Fiquet. He lived with her first in Paris, then in the country, hiding her from his father. His relationship with his father was strained; although the older Cézanne was still supporting his son financially, the allowance was barely enough to live on. Cézanne lived off this allowance, and later his inheritance, for his entire working life.

Hortense and Cézanne had a son in 1872 also named Paul, and they married a few years later. Although he was a tender and attentive father, his relationship with his wife was far from ideal. He took sides with his mother, with whom he was very close, and who neither liked nor approved of Hortense. The couple lived apart for most of their married life.

Both official and popular rejection continued to plague Cézanne. He submitted paintings to the salon each year and each year his work was summarily rejected, but eventually his work found a sponsor, a customs official with independent tastes named Victor Chocquet.

Cézanne's technique and style of painting changed gradually throughout his life. His early work was characterized by dark colors. Later, greatly influenced by the impressionist Pissarro, he began using lighter shades and chiseling and softening his style. He finally broke with the impressionists, feeling they too often sacrificed form for color.

Ultimately overwhelmed by criticism, though, Cézanne retired to the countryside, nearly a misanthrope and hermit but still confident of his work. During his last 20 years he concentrated on the landscapes around Aix. He had few visitors as he more or less cut himself off from all his former contacts, including Zola who, after supporting his work for many years, offended Cézanne with his unflattering, thinly veiled portrayal of the artist in his novel *L'Oeuvre*. Locally, he was regarded as an eccentric failure, and the head of the museum in Aix swore

Postimpressionism

Postimpressionism is not a single well-defined movement, and many of its principal figures painted in isolation. Art critic Roger Fry coined the term in 1910 to describe a predominantly French movement (about 1880–1910) in which painters began to move beyond impressionism, without necessarily attempting to repudiate it. Impressionism had been an attempt to portray subjects (especially nature) with great emphasis on light and bright color. As a rule, postimpressionists strove to preserve the exciting use of color, while paying more attention to form. One central artist was Paul Cézanne, who beginning in the late 1870s sought to focus greater attention on the three-dimensionality of subjects such as still lifes and landscapes; his novel use of space would later influence cubism. Another key postimpressionist figure is Paul Gauguin, who largely painted in Tahiti and sought inspiration from primitive art, including the art of the South Pacific. His attempt to be more pictorial, using exotic, flat colors, while giving his work more emotional intimacy than the works of his impressionist predecessors, would influence fauvism. Vincent Van Gogh, painting in Arles, used curved lines of vivid colors as a means for highly personal and emotional expression. Georges Seurat is sometimes also included with these figures.

What unites the practitioners of postimpressionism is not their subject matter or style, but the fact that they had learned, and largely respected, the goals of impressionism, while distrusting its naturalism and being more interested in expression and (for most painters) surface pattern. In addition to the influences already noted, Odilon Redon, who exhibited with the postimpressionists, was a link between this style and symbolism; the movement also influenced expressionism and abstract art.

that none of Cézanne's paintings would hang on its walls as long as he was director.

His subjects, in the early years, were literary and historical. As his work matured he moved toward more naturalistic subjects: portraits, still lifes, landscapes. His portraits, one of the most famous being *The Portrait of Madame Cézanne*, are a remarkable combination of deadpan, almost inhuman, facial expressions that somehow through color and spacial distortion convey startling humanity.

In his last years the landscape was his only regular companion. Cézanne often chose to paint the same scene from different angles and at different times. These works of Cézanne's differ from similar series by true impressionists because of the presence of a sharp underlying form; however, the roots of his art lie in impressionism. He studied its love of light and shade, but he found impressionism insubstantial, whereas he sought to create something lasting. In his last period he often returned to the theme of people in nature, especially bathers, whom he painted not from life but from other art. To the end, he sought after the universal harmony between nature and mankind.

By the time of his death he had become recognized by his peers but it was not until later that he was acknowledged by the public at large as one of the great painters of the 19th century, of whom Pablo Picasso said, "He was the father of us all." In his last years Cézzane wrote, "The world does not understand me and I do not understand the world. That's why I have chosen to withdraw from it." ◆

Chagall, Marc

JULY 7, 1887–MARCH 28, 1985 ● PAINTER

Marc Chagall was born in Vitebsk, Russia. Scenes of his native town and of the village of Lyozno where he used to visit his grandfather and scenes of his childhood—the family and their friends, the homes, the life of the Jewish community and its spire and officials, the landscapes and the skyscapes—were to crowd his paintings, seemingly out of time and space in a dreamlike world of fairy-tale imagination.

Although in a spiritual sense he never left Vitebsk, he needed broader horizons and moved to Saint Petersburg to study at the School for the Imperial Society for the Encouragement of the Arts. He lived in poverty and, as a Jew, was forced to dwell outside the city. For a time he studied with the famous Leon Bakst, the designer for the Diaghilev Ballet.

Thanks to assistance from a patron, he was able to move to Paris in 1910, and soon found his place in what was then the artistic capital of the world. Many of his paintings at this time continued to be based on his life in Russia. His colors were exuberant. (Bakst, who visited him, said, "Now, your colors sing.") Many of his works show the influence of cubism and fauvism although he could never be pigeonholed as belonging to a particular school.

In 1914 Der Sturm gallery in Berlin held a one-man exhibition of his works. Chagall visited Berlin, where there were over 200 of his pictures that he was destined never to retrieve. He went on to Vitebsk, where he was caught by the outbreak of World War I. There he married Bella Rosenfeld, and began a

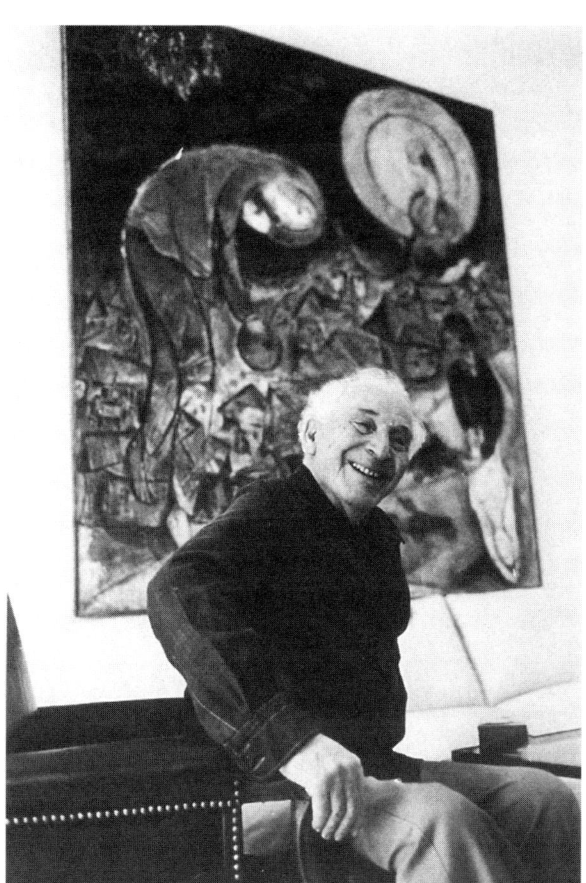

Marc Chagall with one of his paintings.

joyous series of pictures featuring Bella, as well as further paintings of Vitebsk scenes. Often two lovers, representing himself and Bella, wafted aloft above the roofs of the houses. For a time he was drafted into military service and stationed in Saint Petersburg.

After the Revolution of 1917 he was appointed commissar of fine arts in Vitebsk and director of the Vitebsk Art Academy. He also started a museum. In the first official exhibition of the new government, two rooms were reserved for Chagall's work and the state purchased 12 of his paintings. However, he was soon disillusioned with the official attitude to art and one day, returning from Moscow, found that he had been displaced as director and his Free Academy had been turned into a Supremacist school. He and his family moved to Moscow and never returned to Vitebsk.

He was invited to design the sets and costumes for the new State Jewish Theater. On the theater's long wall, he painted a mural. *Introduction to the Jewish Theater*, his largest work, showing Jewish actors, dancers, and musicians. In his designs, he had a particular affinity for the works of Sholem Aleichem. He also taught in a settlement for war orphans. It was at this period that he began to write his autobiography, published as *My Life*.

In 1922 he left Russia for Berlin, where he studied etching with Hermann Struck, but was unable to settle down because of the difficult economic situation. Paris beckoned and he returned there. The paintings he had left were gone, but he set about reconstructing his old works as well as painting new ones. He worked on etchings for Gogol's *Dead Souls*, La Fontaine's *Fables*, circus scenes, and pictures influenced by the light and colors of southern France.

In 1931 he visited Palestine with his family for the opening of the new Tel Aviv Museum and toured Egypt and Syria. The results of this journey were 105 biblical etchings, which have been called some of the finest masterpieces of the art of etching. He was profoundly affected by the anti-Semitic developments of the 1930s. In 1937 the Nazis exhibited some of his paintings as "degenerate art." A famous picture of this period is *White Crucifixion*, in which the Christ figure obviously symbolizes the tragedy of the Jewish people.

After the fall of France in 1940, it was not safe for Chagall to remain there, and the following year he arrived in New York. Americans were charmed with Chagall's work. His distortions and defiance of the laws of gravity—in both senses of the word—his unique blend of sophisticated techniques, his lively colors, and his evocation of folk art were irresistible. When asked why he painted a calf in a cow's head and why a milkmaid's head floated above her body in his *Country Life in Russia*, Chagall answered: "In the first instance, I had to fill an empty place. In the second, I had to create one." However, the terrible events in Europe during those years were reflected in a new gloominess in his canvases. This was heightened when his wife died in 1944. For nine months he was unable to work until he illustrated *Burning Lights*, a book she had written, and worked on the sets, scenery, and costumes for Igor Stravinsky's *Firebird* for the Ballet Theater.

In 1947, he again returned to France, and represented France in the Venice Biennale, receiving a prize for the graphic arts. He lived first in Paris, then at Saint-Jean-Cap-Ferrat, eventually establishing his home at Vence, near Nice. He was honored with several important exhibitions including a retrospective at the New York Museum of Modern Art and the opening show of the National Museum of Modern Art in Paris.

Chagall began at this stage to turn to new media and to experiment. He did major work in stained glass, designing the Twelve Tribes of Israel for Hadassah Hospital, Jerusalem, the Peace Window for the U.N. Secretariat, New York, and windows for the Vatican and for the cathedral of Metz. Although the designs were rendered by skilled craftsmen, Chagall worked closely with them and always did the grisaille. He designed three Gobelin tapestries for the Israeli Knesset (parliament) and a mosaic floor for its state reception hall. He also worked in sculpture and ceramics. He painted the ceiling of the Paris Opera and two large murals for New York's Lincoln Center. The National Museum of the Biblical Message of Marc Chagall opened in Nice in 1973, with many of his works—paintings, stained-glass windows, and a mosaic—on biblical themes. For

1887 Chagall is born in Vitebsk, Russia.

1910 Chagall moves to Paris and finds a patron to assist his artistic endeavors.

1914 Chagall's works are showcased in a one-man exhibition at Der Sturm gallery in Berlin.

1917 Chagall is appointed commisar of fine arts in Vitebsk and director of the fine arts academy.

1931 Chagall visits Palestine for the opening of the Tel Aviv Museum.

1944 Chagall's wife dies. He is unable to work for nine months.

1985 Chagall dies.

his 90th birthday in 1977, he was given an exhibition at the Louvre, the first ever for a living artist, and received the grand cross of the Legion of Honor. In 1981, after 60 years' absence, he was able to visit Moscow for an exhibition of his work at the Tretiakov Gallery. After his death, the Pushkin Museum held an exhibition of 250 of his works.

Although critics have criticized his art for its facility, it has retained its almost magical popularity. In a period when art was becoming increasingly obscure, the public appreciated the art of Chagall, which did not challenge them, and were happy to participate in the world he created. He is renowned as a particularly Jewish artist but his appeal was universal. ◆

Chardin, Jean-Siméon

NOVEMBER 2, 1699–DECEMBER 6, 1779 ● PAINTER

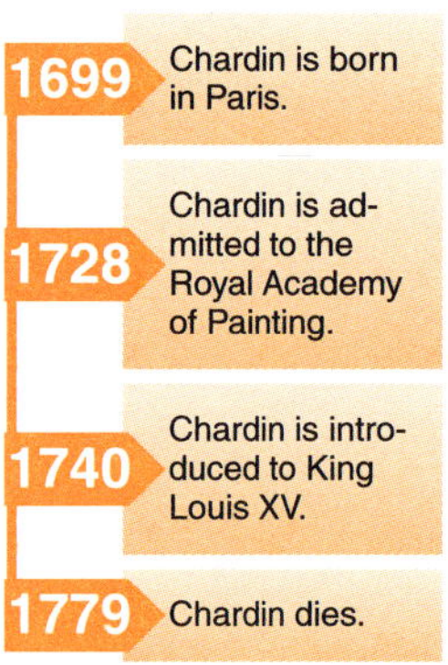

Jean-Siméon Chardin was one of the most highly esteemed painters of the 18th century. The sober candor of his still lifes and quiet scenes of petit-bourgeois domesticity elicited plaudits from quarters as diverse as the encyclopedist Diderot and King Louis XV. Although his reputation declined in the later years of the 18th century, his work was rediscovered in the mid-19th century and has remained among the most admired and coveted in the world since then.

Chardin's native genius carried him to the heights of French painting despite his humble background and paucity of formal training. The son of a prosperous cabinetmaker, he was born on November 2, 1699, in the Parisian quarter of Saint-Germain-des-Prés, from which he seldom strayed throughout his life. Little is known about his early training and evolution as an artist, apart from his work with the history painter Pierre-Jacques Cazes around 1718 and another history painter, Nol-Nicolas Coypel, in about 1720–21. There is very little in the artwork of either of Chardin's teachers that would account for the unique qualities that eventually emerged in the paintings of their student.

Chardin's lifelong friend and biographer, the engraver Charles-Nicolas Cochin, recounts one of Chardin's early efforts to work directly from nature, a still life of game in the early

1720s. It was in struggling with this project that Chardin first came to terms with the futility of precise replication and turned instead to a freer, more subjective approach to capturing the essence of his subject.

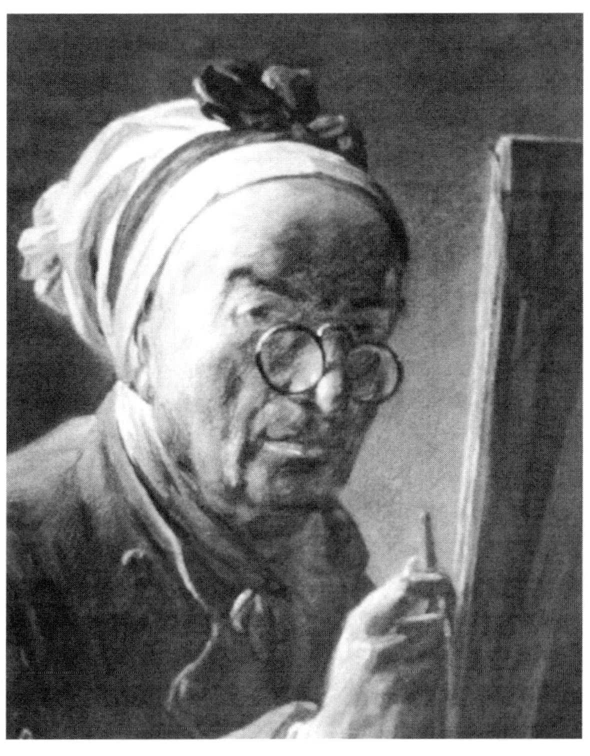

Jean-Siméon Chardin, self-portrait, 1771

In 1724 Chardin gained entrance to the Academy of Saint Luc, which one historian called "a kind of painters superlative guild." Throughout the 1720s Chardin began to evidence a preference for still life studies of everyday household tools, fruits, and vegetables, perhaps because their simplicity provided a firm and manageable focus for his inchoate artistic yearning to penetrate to the visual life of things rather than simply mirroring their exterior contours. With little taste or talent for the history painting in which he had been trained, he cast his fate with the simple objects that surrounded him, determined to render them more truly than anyone ever had before. As he told a friend, "I must forget all I have seen, including even the manner in which these objects were handled by others." Examples of Chardin's work in this period are *Still Life with Bottle and Cucumbers*, in which he uses vigorous brushstrokes to render objects arrayed randomly on stone shelves; *Hare and Copper Cauldron* (1726–28); and *Rabbits, Partridge and Game Bag* (1731). These works provide early evidence of his mastery in depicting fur on mammals and feathers on birds.

Sponsored by the portrait painter Nicolas de Largillière, Chardin was admitted to the Royal Academy of Painting in 1728. His appointment was based on the strength of two works, both of which now hang in the Louvre: *The Buffet*, a still life of wine and assorted fruits and foodstuffs arrayed on a sideboard, and *The Rayfish*, a realistic portrayal of the gutted rayfish on a counter amid various kitchen implements, oysters, fish, and an arched cat. The stark evocation of the homeliest details of everyday life—at once captivating and oddly unsettling—drew admiring comparisons to the 17th-century Flemish masters. Sadly, his subject matter relegated his membership status in the academy to that of "a painter of animals and fruit," a category wanting in prestige but aptly descriptive of Chardin's peculiar virtuosity.

impetus: a driving force or stimuli resulting in an increase of activity.

Chardin's reputation gathered **impetus** throughout the 1730s. Perhaps his marriage in 1731 to Marguerite Saintard enhanced his sensitivity to the quiet rhythms of domestic life. In the ensuing decade his painterly attention turned increasingly from objects to humans, whom he captured with unavailing frankness in their **myriad** everyday, **pedestrian** attitudes, postures, and gestures—what he called *la vie silencieuse* ("the silent life") of the Parisian middle class, the modest, unpretentious milieu of his youth. The major canvases of this period include *The Grace*, *Young Man Drawing*, *Child with Top*, and *Scouring Maid*. One critic wrote of his 1733 painting, *Lady Sealing a Letter*: "The painter's mastery in rendering the woman seated at a table, bending as she raises a stick of sealing wax between two finders, points to years of practice." In 1737 he produced *La Fillette au volant*, considered by many to be his finest achievement.

myriad: a wide array of activities or contents.
pedestrian: description of mundane, common, and unexciting day-to-day activities or actions.

"No French artist of the period came anywhere near Chardin's manner: supremely sophisticated, restrained, full of reminiscences of the towering figures of Dutch and Spanish art."
Souren Melikan, art critic, on Jean-Simon Chardin

The estate documents assembled after his wife's death in 1735 reveal that by then Chardin was a man of some means, well established in his profession. His reputation flourished not only among connoisseurs and collectors but also among a broader public audience, as engravings of his paintings made his work more widely accessible. His renown crested in 1740, when he was introduced to Louis XV, to whom he presented *Working Mother* and *The Grace*; the king subsequently purchased another of his works, *The Bird-Organ*. Chardin's rising stature in the academy led to his appointments, in 1755 and again in 1761, as supervisor of the hanging of paintings for the Salon, the academy's biannual exhibition. In 1757 the king bestowed upon Chardin an apartment in the Louvre.

Chardin's final years were beset with personal and professional reverses, beginning with the suicide in 1767 of his only son, a promising painter. Around this time Chardin's eyesight began to fail, obliging him to switch to **pastels,** works that are now highly regarded but met with indifference then. As public taste shifted from realism to neoclassicism, Chardin's work fell out of popular and critical favor. The newly installed director of the academy, eager to reestablish historical painting as France's preeminent genre, relieved Chardin of most of his official duties and reduced the pension he had been granted by Louis XV. He died in obscurity on December 6, 1779.

pastels: pigments mixed with gum that are pressed into a stick form and used as crayons; the works of art done with such a substance are called pastels.

In the mid-1800s, Chardin's work was rediscovered by a new generation of realist critics and connoisseurs, among them Jules Champfleury and Théophile Thoré in the 1840s and Edmond and Jules de Goncourt in the 1860s. Since then, few have disputed Chardin's greatness, which is perhaps best summarized in his reply to a young painter who once questioned him about the proper selection of colors. "But who told you that one paints with colors?" Chardin said. "One uses colors, but one paints with feeling." ◆

De Chirico, Giorgio

JULY 10, 1888–NOVEMBER 20, 1978 ● PAINTER

Known as the "father of surrealism," Giorgio de Chirico was born in Vólos, Greece, on July 10, 1888. He was the second of three children born to Evaristo de Chirico and Gemma Cervetto, both of Italian descent. Evaristo, an engineer and architect, encouraged Giorgio's early artistic tendencies. He gave Giorgio his first drawing lessons and then hired private art tutors for his son. When Giorgio was 12 he began attending, at his own request, the Polytechnic Institute in Athens. He studied there for four years, learning the technical aspects of art.

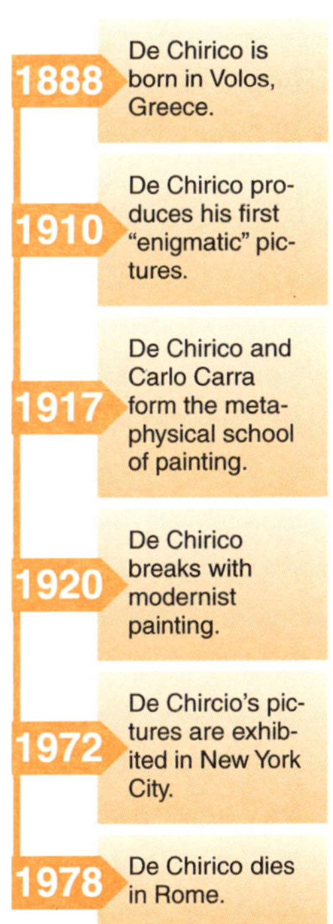

After his father died in 1905, de Chirico, his mother, and his brother moved to Munich. There he studied at the School of Fine Arts for two years. He was influenced by the work of symbolist Max Klinger and Swiss artist Arnold Böcklin, who juxtaposed the familiar and the fantastic. De Chirico moved to Italy in 1909 and divided his time between Florence, Milan, and Turin.

In Florence during 1910 he produced *The Enigma of an Autumn Afternoon*, the first of the "enigmatic" pictures that would characterize his painting for the next decade. These paintings, many of them depicting Italian piazzas, had a haunting, desolate, lonely, and foreboding quality achieved through the use of unrealistic perspective, the sharp clash of light and shadow, unexpected juxtapositions of objects, and the use of tailors' mannequins and statues instead of people. Later examples of this work included *The Enigma of the Hour* (1912), *The Joys and Enigmas of a Strange Hour* (1913), *Nostalgia of the Infinite*

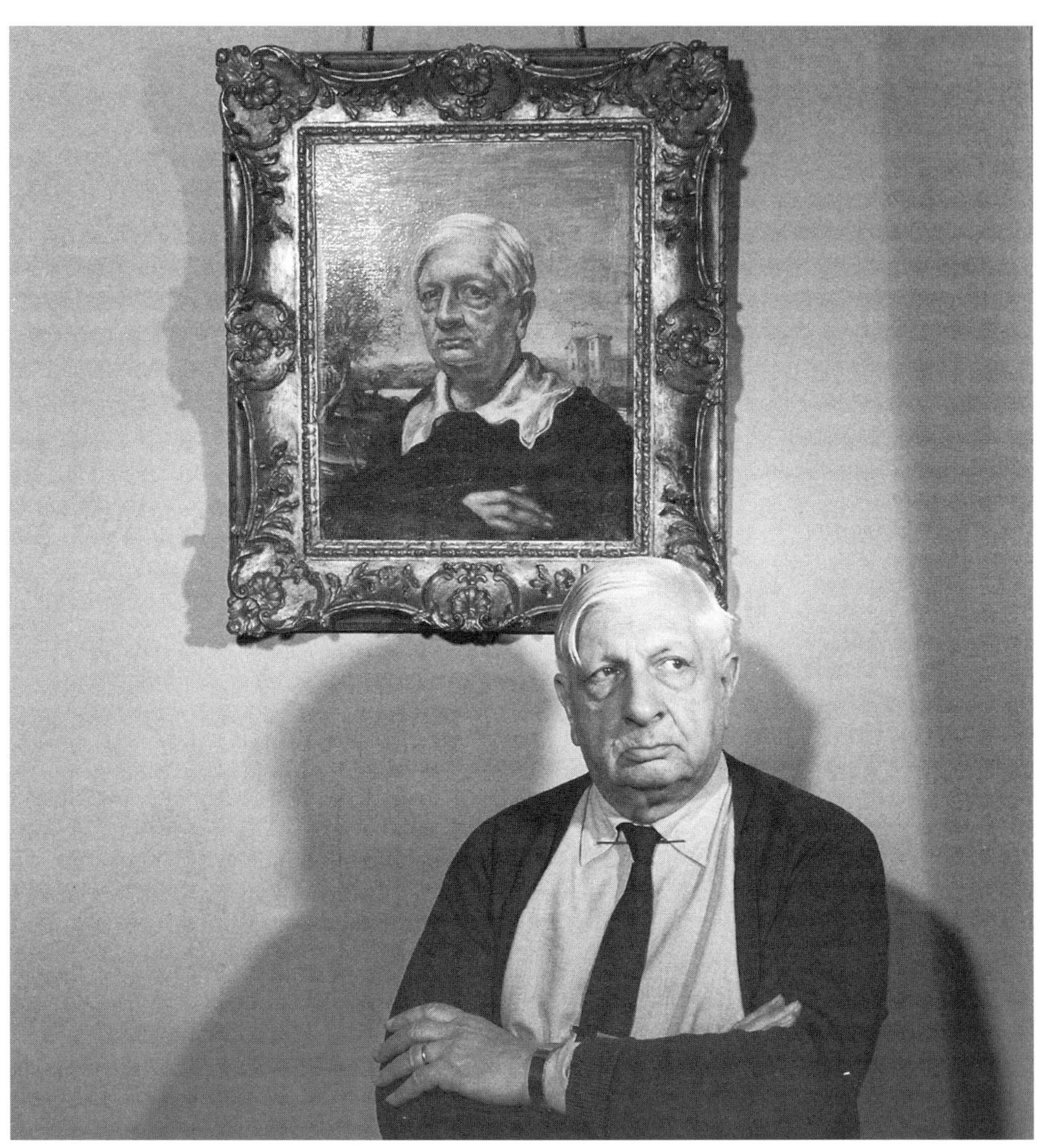

Giorgio de Cherico stands in front of his self-portrait.

(1913–14), *The Mystery and Melancholy of a Street* (1914), *The Soothsayer* (1915), and *The Sacred Fish* (1919). He described these paintings as "metaphysical" and developed a theory of "metaphysical insight" by which paintings see beneath the surface of things by stripping objects of their usual associations and placing them in new and strange relationships.

From 1911 to 1915, de Chirico lived in Paris, where he became friendly with many avant-garde artists, including Guillaume Apollinaire and Pablo Picasso. His association with them brought a greater maturity to his work. In 1915 he returned to Italy for military service in World War I. He was stationed at Ferrara, where he had a nervous breakdown in 1917. While in a military hospital, de Chirico met the futurist painter Carlo Carrà. De Chirico converted Carrà to his views, and the two formed the *scuola metafisica,* or **metaphysical school.** In 1918 the two exhibited their metaphysical paintings at the Galleria dell'Epoca in Rome.

metaphysical school: a movement in Italian art during the early twentieth century that strove to present an alternative reality by utilizing ordinary subject material and expressing it in a stark fashion.

As a movement, however, the metaphysical school did not last long; de Chirco and Carrà quarreled and went their separate ways in 1919. But de Chirico's influence endured through his influence on surrealism. Poet André Breton, founder of the surrealist movement of the 1920s, along with surrealist painters Paul Klee, Jean Arp, Pablo Picasso, and Joan Miró all acknowledged their debt to de Chirico. When the influence of the surrealists peaked in the late 1920s, de Chirico gained an international reputation.

In the meantime, however, de Chirico had made a sharp break with modernism around 1920. In his memoirs he claimed that while looking at a painting by Titian, the 16th-century Italian Renaissance painter, he had a "revelation of what a great painting should be." During the 1920s his pictures were more traditional, as he dedicated himself to what has been described as "recovering the techniques of the Old Masters, the craft of the tradition of the great Renaissance painters to which he felt he belonged." Classical references, including gladiators, Greek temples, broken classical columns, and horses moving through ancient ruins, often appeared in paintings such as *Furniture in the Valley* (1927) and *Horse and Gladiators* (1930).

"His celebrated paintings of deserted Italian piazzas, featureless manikins and fantastic still lifes, in which the logical was made to seem credible, were of major importance for the development of surrealism in the 1920s."

Alden Whitman on Giorgio de Chirico in *The New York Times,* November 21, 1978.

Influenced by the praise of the surrealists, in the late 1920s de Chirico sometimes executed imitations of his metaphysical paintings of the previous decade. By 1930, however, he had broken completely with surrealism and denounced modernism. From then on he devoted himself to painting in the style of the great painters of preceding centuries. De Chirico said that he was trying "to create a renaissance in painting that will restore art to its true masterfulness and beauty." But his post-1920 work was not highly regarded and has been described as repetitive and obsessed with technical issues.

During the 1920s and 1930s, de Chirico lived much of the time in Paris. From 1936 to 1938 he lived in the United States. His metaphysical paintings were exhibited at the Museum of

Modern Art in New York City in 1941 and 1945. De Chirico lived in Rome from 1944 onwards. He was largely forgotten until 1972, when the New York Cultural Center mounted a retrospective of his work over the preceding 50-odd years. In his later years there was a strong demand for his paintings from the 1910–1920 period. De Chirico acknowledged that as a result, "I now paint so-called metaphysical works or 'Italian piazza' pictures for anyone who wants to order and pay for them." He even backdated some of these pictures, which resulted in scandals and lawsuits.

In addition to his painting, de Chirico wrote art criticism; a dreamlike autobiographical novel, *Hebdomoros* (1929); and two volumes of memoirs, published in 1945 and 1960. He also designed costumes and scenery for the ballets *Bacchus et Ariane* in 1930 and *Protée* in 1938, and for the operas *Das Leben des Orest* in 1930 and *I Puritani* in 1933. He died in Rome on November 20, 1978. ◆

Constable, John

June 11, 1776–March 31, 1837 ● Painter

The English painter John Constable was one of the most accomplished European landscape artists of the 19th century, a naturalist and romantic who defined painting as both "a science ... an enquiry into the law of nature" and as "another word for feeling." He profoundly influenced later artists, especially the French painters of the Barbizon school and, more immediately, the early impressionists, who admired his freedom from academic convention and his novel methods of capturing natural light.

Constable's early aesthetic evolution—indeed, his very sense of calling as an artist—can be traced to the lush, verdant countryside of the Stour valley in Suffolk that surrounded him as a child and infused him with a deep love of nature. As he later wrote to a friend, "Those scenes made me a painter." His father was a wealthy owner of local corn and wheat mills, so young John grew up in close intimacy with the cycles and rhythms of the natural world. An intellectually gifted child, he abandoned his early religious studies to learn the family business, all the while harboring a yearning to paint. His artistic ambitions were encouraged first by John Dunthorne, a local plumber and artist, and later by Sir George Beaumont, a local amateur painter and art collector. Beaumont called Constable's attention to the watercolors of Thomas Girtin and the paintings of Claude Lorrain; the latter's work made an especially strong impression on the aspiring young artist.

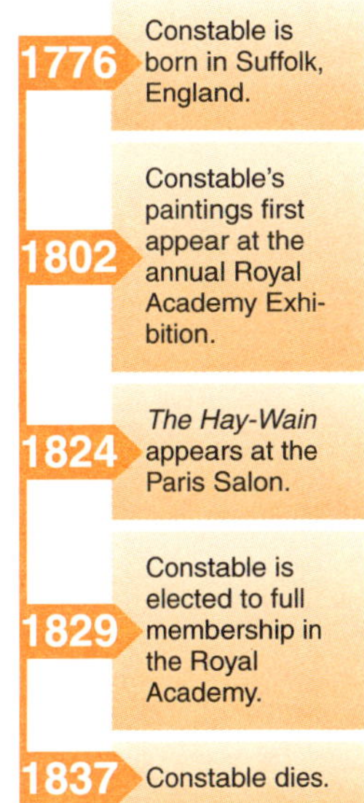

During a stay in London in 1796, Constable became acquainted with J. T. Smith, an engraver. Under Smith's guidance, Constable undertook systematic sketch studies of local cottages. By 1799 his technique had developed sufficiently to gain him admission into the Royal Academy, where he was intensively schooled in the basics of anatomy. His early work there was methodical but undistinguished, but he had begun to nurture a unique vision of painterly expression that would soon distinguish him from the academic conventions in which he languished. Resolving to become a "natural painter," he set out on a sketching tour of the Peak District in Derbyshire.

In 1802 Constable's paintings made their first of many annual appearances in the Royal Academy exhibition. Yet for him this was only a beginning. His quest to perfect his technique took him on still further drawing expeditions. His 1803 journey to Deal, where he sketched sailing vessels under what he described as "a natural history of the skies," ignited a painterly preoccupation with the firmament that endured throughout his career. Constable made a two-month tour of the Lake District in 1806, a journey that helped him to narrow his scope from sweeping natural spectacle to the telling details of village life that permeated his boyhood: country roads, riverboats, farm chores, and such. That trip also resulted in three paintings that he showed at the Royal Academy exhibition in 1807.

Throughout the next decade Constable was obliged to spend prolonged periods in London, the center of the art trade, all the while yearning to spend more time in the fields and meadows of Suffolk, where he managed to make yearly visits, still sedulously sketching his surroundings. The sketchbooks from 1813 and 1814 have survived, and their roughly 200 drawings give eloquent testimony to Constable's exacting and unremitting commitment to capturing the essence of nature.

His driven labors in these years produced modest successes but no breakthrough into a compellingly distinctive style. Some highlights of this period include *Dedham Vale: Morning* (1811), *Boatbuilding near Flatford Mill* (1815), and *The Stour*

"The sound of water escaping from mill-dams, etc., willows, old rotten planks, slimy posts and brickwork, I love such things."
John Constable, on the sources of inspiration for his art

Secure and settled in his personal life, Constable was finally able to focus his energies on realizing his potential as an artist.

Valley and Dedham Village (1808). His many painted sketches from this period, regarded as mere studies by Constable, are now more highly regarded than some of those finished pieces. He made his first sale only in 1814, when a bookseller paid him a mere pittance—20 guineas—and gave him some books in exchange for Constable's entire output for the previous year.

The pressures of his travels and work in these years were compounded by personal travails, principally his frustrating courtship of Maria Bicknell, whom he had hoped to marry in 1809. She was unable to accept his proposal due to the unyielding objections of her grandfather, the influential rector of East Bergholt. Then came the loss of his parents in successive years—his mother in 1815 and his father in 1816. His father's bequest did, however, provide the financial security that finally allowed the determined lovers to join in marriage on October 2, 1816.

Secure and settled in his personal life, Constable was finally able to focus his energies on realizing his potential as an artist. He turned out a series of nature paintings in which his vision fully emerges, bringing him the wider recognition and influence that had previously eluded him. The most notable achievements of this period are *The White Horse*, *Stratford Mill*, *The Hay-Wain*, *View on the Stour near Dedham*, *The Lock*, and *The Leaping Horse*. By 1819, his work was, in the words of one writer, "too large to remain unnoticed." A major breakthrough for Constable was the exhibition of three of his works, including *The Hay-Wain*, at the Paris Salon in 1824. They won a gold medal and drew adulation from the likes of Eugène Delacroix, who was so humbled by Constable's work that he was spurred to redo one of his own nearly finished paintings.

Throughout the 1820s and 1830s, Constable's canvases gradually ventured beyond Suffolk pastorals. He spent much of 1821 and 1822 on a series of precisely observed studies of the sky and clouds, and he gradually forsook his typical summer settings for the more turbulent vistas of churning seas and menacing winds, as in *Chain Pier, Brighton; Hadliegh Castle;* and *Salisbury Cathedral, from the Meadows*. But satisfaction at his growing professional recognition was offset by the death of Maria of tuberculosis in 1828; afterwards he wrote, "The face of the world is totally changed to me." Even his artistic renown was clouded with disappointment. Finally elected to full membership in the Royal Academy in 1829, at age 52, Constable was reminded by the president that his selection was "peculiarly fortunate" in view of the competition from historical painters.

In his final years Constable sought to buoy his reputation by collaborating with David Lucas on a series of mezzotints modeled on his major works. The project, however, was not a success, prompting Constable to comment, "Every gleam of sunshine is blighted to me in the art at least. Can it therefore be wondered at that I paint continual storms?"

Although Constable's work was well regarded in his own day, his genius received its full measure of recognition only in posterity. He died on March 31, 1837. ◆

Corot, Jean-Baptiste Camille

JULY 16, 1796–FEBRUARY 22, 1875 ● PAINTER

One of the greatest artists of the 19th century, Jean-Baptiste Camille Corot, painted in a style often called "romantic realism." Within that genre, Corot's work resembled that of a group of French painters who came to be known as the Barbizon school. They were painters who settled in the village of Barbizon, about 35 miles south of Paris, during the 1830s and 1840s. Although Corot did not live in Barbizon, he was a friend of many in the group, including Theodore Rousseau and Jean Francois Millet. The Barbizon painters admired the Dutch landscape painters of the 1600s and attempted to convey the simple beauty of nature. Corot painted gentle, picturesque landscapes that often featured French peasants at work or play.

Jean-Baptiste Camille Corot was born in Paris on July 16, 1796, toward the end of the French Revolution. When Camille, as he was called, was about eight years old, Napoleon I crowned himself emperor of France. Corot's father, Louis-Jacques Corot, was a successful merchant of cloth and related items, and his mother, Françoise Oberson, came from a wealthy family of Swiss wine merchants. She operated a prosperous millinery shop in Paris that attracted wealthy customers. Camille's sister, Victoire-Anne, died in young adulthood. The Corots spent the first 30 years of Camille's life in an attractive area of Paris, where the Seine River, the Tuileries gardens, and the

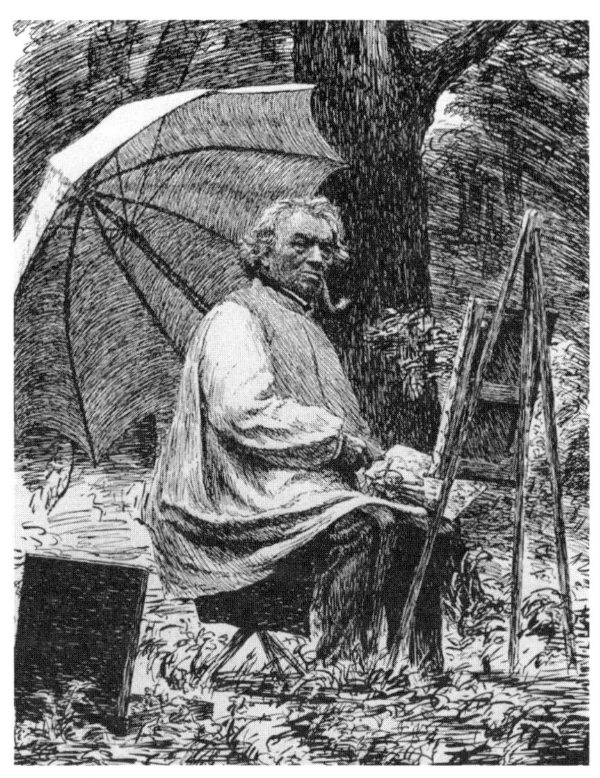

Jean-Baptiste Camille Corot

Louvre museum influenced Corot's artistic sensibilities. After his early years at a local school, the Corots could afford to send Camille to the College of Rouen from 1807 to 1812, where he formed lifelong friendships and developed the love of nature that would become a key element in his work. He then studied humanities at a boarding school in Poissy, on the outskirts of Paris.

As a young adult, Corot apprenticed to cloth merchants, attending drawing classes in the evenings. The family had purchased an elegant house at Ville-d'Avray, a country area outside Paris that became a rich source of artistic inspiration for Camille throughout his life. When he showed much greater interest in drawing than cloth, his father reluctantly agreed to let Camille become an artist. The Corots began giving Camille a generous annual allowance that freed him from earning a living for the rest of his life.

Corot set up a studio in Paris in 1823, exploring and sketching the wharves, forests, seashore, and countryside of surrounding areas. He learned classical principles of composition from academic landscape painter Jean-Victor Bertin. He also was influenced by the neoclassical school of landscape, in the tradition of artists Claude Lorraine and Nicolas Poussin. This style focused seriously on line and form more so than on the delight of color.

Following the academic route of many painters, Corot traveled to Italy to study art more intensively. Before he left, his parents had him paint a self-portrait to remember him by, which now hangs in the Louvre. From 1825 to 1828, Corot lived in Rome, where he frequented the cafes and earned a reputation among fellow artists who nicknamed him "our master." Corot traveled about Italy, painting ancient ruins, city scenes, and nature. He toyed with light and color, painting in solid masses in order to produce light and dark patterns of color. His early works show the influence of various French and

Dutch landscape painters. Two of Corot's paintings from that period in Italy, the *Forum* (1826) and the *Bridge of Narni* (1827), now reside in the Louvre.

After returning to France in 1828, Corot lived there for the rest of his life, traveling throughout Europe during the warm months of the year. His lifelong practice was to paint outdoors in the spring and summer and spend the winter in his studio. During winter months in his studio, Corot produced large salon pieces with biblical or historical subjects. In 1834, he spent the summer in the picturesque Tuscany region of Italy, producing such beautiful pieces as *Lake Como* (1834).

The lovely Alexina Ledoux, a seamstress in his mother's shop, became a subject of a Corot portrait about 1830. Alexina may have been the most serious love of Corot's life, but he chose his art career over marriage.

Corot came under the influence of the group of nature painters in the village of Barbizon. Corot was called "the lyric poet" of this group. He changed his style and began painting everything as if seen through a delicate gray veil, accented by a few details of bright color. His landscapes became imaginary creations bathed in a filmy romantic atmosphere. Examples of this style, for which he became famous, are versions of *Vile d'Avray* and *Memory of Mortefontaine* (1864). Corot's artistic style underwent a final change in 1871. He again painted in the style of his youth, but his works were now drenched in impressionist light and color. Although he tended to repeat his success in this vein to meet popular demand, he also painted such outstanding works as *The Belfry at Douai* (1871) in his earlier classical style.

During his lifetime, Corot showed his work in many group exhibitions in Paris and other French cities. Beginning in 1827, he often showed works he considered his best at the annual Salon Carre of the Louvre. In 1833, the Corot family rejoiced when Camille, age 37, earned his first official award when the Salon gave him a second class medal for *Ford in the Forest of Fontainebleau*.

Corot did not receive general recognition until his fifties, when he finally began to sell his work and gained wealth from sales and commissions. As he already had enough money, Corot became very generous with friends, pupils, and others in need.

Corot painted portraits for his own pleasure throughout his career, and they became some of his most cherished works. His

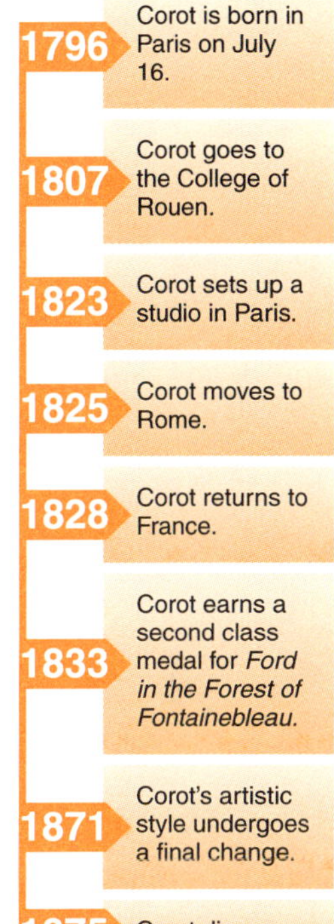

subjects included children, family members, peasants, and friends. He also painted religious pictures. Corot earned the nickname "Little Papa Corot" among his many beloved friends and was known for his cotton cap, tobacco pipe, and twinkling smile. He was said to be kind and gay but with a trace of melancholy from the many years of solitary work. His maid, Adele, attended to him. As he aged, Corot suffered from gout, a chronic disease that produces swelling of the joints. He developed stomach cancer but continued working until he died in 1875.

Corot paved the way for impressionist painters such as Claude Monet and Pierre Auguste Renoir, who credited Corot for his influence. Today, museums around the world exhibit highly valued Corots. ◆

Correggio

c. 1489–March, 1534 ● Painter

illusionism: style of art that distorts imagry to create an optical illusion to the viewer.

Correggio was one of the most influential artists of his generation, despite a relatively short career. Pervasive visual **illusionism** and psychological directness characterize his mature work, dating from 1518–1519 until his death in 1534. Correggio's figures are often powerful in physique, boldly foreshortened, and posed in dynamic *contrapposto* (counterposition, or "weight shift"), yet their eloquent gestures and sweetness of expression, rendered by a subtle use of value and sensual application of color, result in images of immense emotional appeal. Correggio is best known for frescoes that visually transcend their architectural settings as well as paintings that revivified the traditional formula of Renaissance altarpieces in Italy.

Apart from Giorgio Vasari's profile in his *Lives of the Artists* (1550; 2d ed. 1568), documentary evidence about the artist is scant, and precise information about Correggio's biography, artistic training, early work, and commissions is subject to debate. The artist died in his native town of Correggio on March 5, 1534; his birthdate has been variously calculated between 1489 and 1494. Modern scholarship favors the earlier birthdate and postulates that Correggio received his initial artistic training from his uncle, Lorenzo Allegri (d. 1527), believed to have been a local painter. Other aspects of his formal training remain unknown, although artists as diverse as Andrea Mantegna, the Modenese painter Francesco Bianchi de' Ferrari, and Francesco Raibolini of Bologna, better known as Francia, have been forwarded as possible teachers.

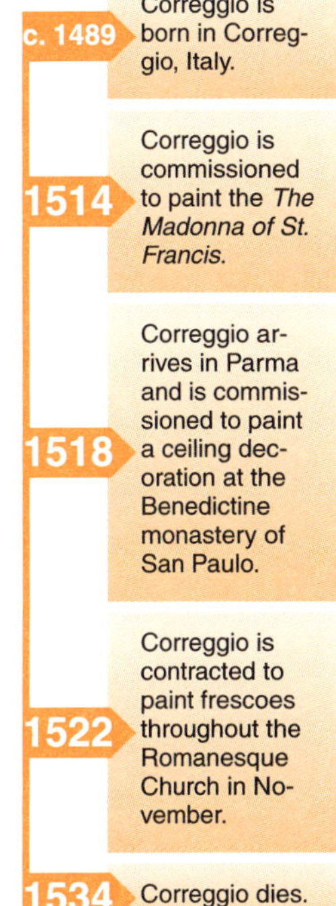

Whatever the specifics of his workshop experience and early career, it is clear that Correggio's style developed on a matrix of artistic principles nascent in 15th-century Lombard illusionism, particularly as practiced by Andrea Mantegna in Mantua, linked with a concern for compositional unity based on light and color found in Leonardo da Vinci's Milanese works. The influence of Raphael and Michelangelo is also evident in Correggio's artistic evolution and has led scholars since the 18th century to suggest that Correggio may have visited Rome, notwithstanding the absence of written documentation for such a trip and Vasari's assertion to the contrary. The presence of works by Raphael and Michelangelo in northern Italy as well as the increased availability and dissemination of drawings and engravings during this period may account for the influence of these Renaissance masters on Correggio's artistic thinking.

Correggio's career is generally divided into two parts. Paintings created prior to the artist's arrival in Parma, c. 1518–1519, are considered early works, although few are signed or well documented. Two late 20th-century discoveries—the appearance of Correggio's name in notarial records from 1512 concerning Andrea Mantegna's son, Francesco, and the attribution of two panels representing *David Before the Ark of the Covenant*, commissioned by the abbey of San Benedetto Po in 1514—confirm a long-standing tradition placing Correggio in Mantua within the circle of Mantegna and attest to Correggio's involvement with both Gonzaga and Benedictine patronage at an early point in his career. Correggio's name has also been connected with the decoration of Mantegna's funerary chapel in the Benedictine church of Sant' Andrea in Mantua, as well as two, much damaged, roundel frescoes, originally located in the atrium of the same church.

Only two securely documented works survive from this early period. Both are altarpieces painted for the artist's native town: the *Madonna of St. Francis* commissioned for the high altar of S. Francesco in August 1514, and the *Four Saints Altar-*

piece (c. 1514–1517), associated with the church of Santa Maria Verberator. Passages of subtle modeling in color and the delicacy of facial expression in these paintings anticipate qualities that characterize Correggio's later work. As manifestations of the artist's thinking, both altarpieces demonstrate Correggio's rapid assimilation and synthesis of significant pictorial trends in early 16th-century Italy.

Correggio's arrival in Parma is perceived as coincident with the advent of his mature style, initiating a prolific decade during which he worked on a number of commissions simultaneously. A ceiling decoration painted circa 1518–1519, for Abbess Giovanna da Piacenza at the Benedictine monastery of San Paolo, is acknowledged as Correggio's first significant fresco commission in Parma. Within the private apartment of the abbess, Correggio's frescoes transform a small chamber into a fictive **pergola,** a **verdant** gazebo open to the sky, where the goddess Diana presides over a collection of classically inspired statues, accompanied by rambunctious putti, nude infants inspired by ancient Roman art, who playfully threaten to spill into the interior from the roof. The illusionistic structuring of space in this small chamber known as the "camera di San Paolo" became a hallmark of the artist's subsequent fresco work in Parma.

pergola: a column-lined walkway supporting a roof of trelliswork on which ivy and other plants grow.
verdant: green in tint or color; green growing plants.

Documents dating from July 1520 through January 1524 detail Correggio's activity at the neighboring Benedictine monastery of San Giovanni Evangelista. This extensive commission included frescoes in the nave, cupola, choir, and apse, as well as a charming lunette depicting St. John above the door connecting church and cloister. Although the sequence of their execution is debated, Correggio's frescoes brought visual unity to the vast church interior, punctuating the visitor's experience of the building. Moreover, Correggio's iconographic and stylistic treatment of standard Christian narrative was inventive. Approaching the celebrated **cupola** frescoes, spectators are summoned by Christ, who descends earthward in a golden aura of light; only after shifting position does the viewer become privy to the *Vision of Saint John on Patmos*, as described in the Book of Revelation.

cupola: a small structure constructed on top of a roof or ceiling.

Beyond the cupola, Correggio's apse frescoes presented the *Coronation of the Virgin* as a timeless event, witnessed in the presence of several carefully selected saints: John the Baptist is paired with St. Benedict adjacent to Christ on the right while

John the Evangelist appears on the left with St. John, first abbot of the church. Correggio's original work was destroyed in 1587 when the choir was extended but was soon replaced with a full-scale copy by Cesare Aretusi. A central fragment representing Christ and Mary and its sinopia underdrawing are preserved in Parma; three smaller fragments exist in London. Correggio's innovative decorative scheme for the Del Bono chapel, with its paired lateral paintings of the unusual *Martyrdom of Four Saints* and dramatic *Lamentation*, was widely adapted by the end of the century.

Instantaneous recognition of Correggio's achievement at San Giovanni Evangelista resulted in a prestigious commission to decorate the cathedral of Parma, dedicated to Santa Maria Assunta in honor of Parma's special veneration of the Virgin. As part of a comprehensive 16th-century renovation, Correggio was contracted to paint frescoes throughout the Romanesque church in November 1522. His cupola portrayal of the *Assumption of the Virgin* was a radical departure from prior representations of the scene. Yet despite its innovation and later influence, the extravagant foreshortening of Correggio's figures and the dizzying *di sotto in su*, the spectator's experience of looking up from underneath the images, in which Correggio presented the Virgin's ascent were not considered an unqualified success and may have prompted the artist's return to his native Correggio (c. 1530).

Correggio's unique ability to represent the nuanced iconography of the miraculous as a concrete reality is apparent in other religious work from this period with three remarkable altarpieces, all in the Gemäldegalerie, Dresden, portraying the Virgin and Child as the tranquil focus of emotions so powerful as to elicit a **palpable** physical response. The maidservant who recoils from the numinous brilliance of the infant Christ in the *Adoration of the Shepherds*, known since the 17th century as "La Notte," is contrasted by the donkey pressing eagerly toward the Child, despite St. Joseph's robust restraint. Similarly, altarpieces such as the *Madonna with St. Sebastian* (c. 1524) and the *Madonna with St. George* (before 1530) both painted for **confraternities** in Modena, render the spiritual joy felt in the presence of the Christ child and his mother as a profound corporeal experience.

palpable: easily noticeable and tangible.

confraternities: religious or charitable societies or unions.

Physical pleasure in experiencing the divine also distinguishes Correggio's late masterpieces, the "Loves of Jupiter" series, painted for Federico II Gonzaga, duke of Mantua, after 1529. These four mythological canvases are the most erotic of Correggio's entire oeuvre and are more explicitly carnal than his earlier *Venus with Mercury and Cupid,* or "School of Love," and *Venus and Cupid with Satyr,* both painted circa 1523–1525 and known to have been in the collection of Nicola Maffei in Mantua before 1589. Undoubtedly aware of the tastes of his patron, the artist has consistently represented the literal and figurative climax of each narrative; *Io* enraptured by the Jupiter cloud; *Ganymede* submissively transported upward by means of an improbably levitating eagle; and *Danaë* in stunned acquiescence to Jupiter's golden shower from anatomically suggestive clouds. *Leda* differs from the others in that it was the only myth presented in episodic fashion and not based on Ovid's *Metamorphoses*.

Whether promising ecstatic union with God or the more terrestial pleasures afforded by visions of ancient goddesses or nude nymphs, Correggio's mature work appeals directly to the senses. Emotional directness anchors formal complexity: physical, psychological, and **spatial** relationships are intricate without appearing strained. Correggio's use of color, wedded to a structuring of pictorial space as a visual metaphor of spiritual transcendence, was essential to the development of baroque illusionism and a formative influence on subsequent principles and theory. ◆

spatial: occupying, related to, or having the character of space.

Courbet, Gustave

JUNE 10, 1819–DECEMBER 31, 1877 ● PAINTER

The artist as social visionary and activist: this was the distinctively modern vocation of the French realist painter Gustave Courbet, who wielded the paintbrush as a rapier of social critique, slashing away layers of romantic embellishment to reveal the hypocrisies and injustices at the core of mid-19th-century French society. No one has surpassed his own summation of his calling as a radical artist: "To be able to represent the customs, the ideas, the appearance of my own era according to my own evaluation; to be not only a painter but a man as well; in short, to create living art."

Jean Désiré Gustave Courbet was born in 1819 to a wealthy farming family in Ornans, France, near Bescançon. His radical political proclivities were already in evidence at the age of 18, when, chafing under the strictures of his traditional classical courses at the Collège Royal at Bescançon, he led a student rebellion against the school's curriculum. His interest in art was spurred by the classes he took with Charles Faljoulot, the director of the École des Beaux-Arts; his first work of note came in 1839, when he contributed four lithographic illustrations to Max Buchon's *Essais poétiques* (*Poetic essays*).

Sent to Paris to study law in 1841, Courbet soon forsook his law classes for the Louvre museum, where he spent hours refining his painting technique by making copies of masterpieces. When Courbet's father learned of his son's artistic ambitions, he offered his full support—moral and financial—enabling Courbet to devote all his time to his technical exercises at the museum, which he pursued with unremitting zeal and self-discipline.

Undeterred by the initial spurning of his work for exhibition at the Royal Academy's annual Salon, in 1844 Courbet won a place at the show with his *Self-Portrait with Black Dog* (1842). Of the five works he submitted the following year, only *Le Guitarrero* (*The guitar player*) was accepted, and he was shut out from the exhibition in 1847.

Courbet's realistic style was swept from the periphery to the center of the art world in the wake of the radicalizing wave of the Revolution of 1848. Among the 10 Courbet entries that were accepted at that year's exhibition, his *Walpurgis Night* aroused the enthusiasm of the influential critic Champfleury, who thenceforth became an important champion of Courbet's work.

After repairing to Ornans to visit his family and refresh his spirits in 1849, Courbet produced *After Dinner at Ornans*. This work, shown at the 1849 Salon, represents an important step forward in Courbet's project of portraying the lives of the poor and disenfranchised with unsparing honesty. This goal was fully realized in two subsequent masterpieces, *The Stonebreakers* and *A Burial at Ornans*, both of which appeared at the 1850 Salon.

The Stonebreakers realistically depicts the soul-flattening monotony of repetitive manual labor. In the words of the French socialist theorist Pierre Proudhon, "Here indeed is the mechanical or mechanized man in the state of ruin to which our splendid civilization and our incomparable industry have

1819 Courbet is born in Ornans, France.

1844 Courbet's painting *Self-Portrait with Black Dog* wins him an appearance the Royal Academy's annual Salon.

1850 Courbet's masterpieces *The Stonebreakers* and *A Burial at Ornans* appear at the Salon.

1871 Courbet is elected as a delegate to the Paris Commune.

1872 Courbet flees to Switzerland to escape a crippling fine for his activities in the Commune.

1877 Courbet dies in La Tour-de-Peliz, Switzerland.

Realism

The term realism has appeared in many different eras in philosophy and science. In art and literature, however, the term refers to a mid to late nineteenth-century movement to portray human beings, actions, and other subjects in literal, natural, representational ways. In literature, this movement includes writers such as Gustave Flaubert, George Eliot, and Henry James, who sought to imbue their stories with the details of human life—the minor gestures, descriptions of objects, and so forth—without imposing a preconceived form or ideal. In painting, this impulse represents a reaction against Romanticism, which was seen as focusing too often on subjective emotions and grand themes, such as classical myths and Bible stories. The subject matter of realism, especially in France, was often humble, as in some forms of Romanticism, but where that movement showed nostalgia for the rural life, the realists were willing to portray the misery and tedium of the poor. In fact, the depiction of wage laborers and the poor can challenge the viewer's sense of social justice, as in the social realism of Honoré Daumier (*Third–class Carriage,* 1862) and Gustave Courbet (*The Stonebreakers,* 1849); Courbet led the French realists in the mid-century. Nature settings can also form the subject for realist paintings, whenever the artist's emphasis is on detail and accuracy of representation rather than on preconceived ideals, as in the landscape works of American William Sidney Mount.

As a general artistic outlook, realism has never died. Many of the later movements that shared part of its name, like surrealism and magic realism, do not attempt to depict the world in literal ways, however, and are "realist" mainly their shared rejection of abstraction and their depiction of distinct situations and objects.

reduced him." A *Burial at Ornans*, which Courbet described as the "debut of my principles," is a wide canvas crowded with 40 figures, local peasants and clergy, rendered with a combination of large scale and unsentimental intimacy. The work shocked a conservative Parisian bourgeoisie more accustomed to—and far more comfortable with—patronizing romantic fantasies of cheerfully resigned country folk inhabiting prettified pastorals. One typically discomfited conservative critic sneered, "He paints pictures as you black your boots." But in the post-revolutionary glow of 1850, such sour notes were the exception. The most succinct and apt summary of the painting's importance is Courbet's own: "The basis of realism is the negation of the ideal .... *Burial at Ornans* was in reality the burial of romanticism ...."

With the advent of the Second Empire in 1851, Courbet once again found himself swimming against a conservative political tide. He was an implacable foe of Emperor Napoleon II, who contemptuously dismissed as "obscene" *The Bathers*, one of three Courbet works shown at the 1853 Salon. The work was bought by Alfred Bruyas, a hotel proprieter from Montpellier, who became one of Courbet's key supporters and patrons. On a visit to Bruyas in 1854, Courbet was moved to paint seascapes for the first time, the most notable of which is *Seashore at Palavas*, which shows Courbet saluting the vast ocean with his hat, as if to underscore his representational mastery over the natural environment.

"I am not only a socialist but also a democrat and a republican; in brief, I support the entire revolution, and above all else I am altogether a Realist ... because to be a realist means to be the sincere friend of actual truth."
Gustave Courbet, on his beliefs and how they affected his art

Further travels that year took Courbet briefly to Switzerland and then back to Ornans, where he set to work on one his most important paintings, *The Artist's Studio* (or *Real Allegory, Representing a Phase of Seven Years of My Life as a Painter*). This work depicts Courbet painting a landscape under the close scrutiny of a child, a nude woman, and—more distantly—a crowd that Courbet described as "all the people who serve my cause, sustain me in my idea, and support my activity ... the whole world coming to me to be painted." The painting's self-conscious symbolism was a radical departure that disconcerted many of his supporters, including Champfleury, who found the combination of allegory and realism unworkable.

When *The Artist's Studio*, along with three of his other works, was rejected by the politically conservative jury at the 1855 Salon, Courbet mounted his own realist exhibit near the official one. However admirable in intent, the show failed to attract a sizable audience. As his reputation waned in France, however, it waxed abroad, especially in Germany, where he was received with enthusiasm on visits in 1856 and in 1858, and in Belgium, where his 1861 lecture on realism was a great success.

When *The Artist's Studio*, along with three of his other works, was rejected by the politically conservative jury at the 1855 Salon, Courbet mounted his own realist exhibit near the official one.

His political impulse muted by France's conservative political climate in the 1860s, Courbet produced more landscapes and sensual nudes of women, some of them steeped in classical mythology, including *Venus and Psyche* (1864), *Sleeping Women*, and *Woman with a Parrot* (1866).

But his dormant radicalism was rekindled by the collapse of the Second Empire at the onset of the Franco-German war in 1870. Courbet rallied to the support of the Paris Commune, established in March 19, 1871, and he was elected an official delegate to its governing body several weeks later.

Disgusted by the Commune's increasingly destructive bent, however, Courbet resigned his post on May 2. On May 16 the Commune destroyed the column of the Place Vendome that honored the memory of Bonaparte. After the conservative forces seized power, Courbet was arrested on June 7 and falsely charged with complicity in the column caper. After serving six months in prison, Courbet returned to Ornans. The case against him was reopened in 1872, and he fled to Switzerland to escape an impending crippling fine levied against him to reimburse the government's costs in rebuilding the column. At length he settled in the Swiss town of La Tour-de-Peliz, where he bought an inn to sustain a modest livelihood. Impoverished and demoralized, he died there in 1877, at the age of 58. ◆

Cranach, Lucas

OCTOBER, 1472–OCTOBER 16, 1553 ● ARTIST

Known as "the Elder," German painter, printmaker, and book illustrator Lucas Cranach was born in Kronach, near Bamberg. Cranach was trained by his father, Hans Maler. Almost nothing is known of his Kronach period, save that he absorbed the revolutionary style of Albrecht Dürer, either through trips to Nürnberg or through seeing Dürer's woodcuts. Taking the name of his birthplace as his own, he arrived in Vienna in 1502. There he entered a humanist circle centered on the university and led by the poet laureate Conrad Celtis (1459–1508). In Vienna Cranach made religious paintings of novel expressive power. Applying contrasting colors loosely, he gave figures a turbulence of arrangement and gesture that fit their pathos, and he set these in an agitated landscape that seems to respond sympathetically. These works, especially their rendering of nature, influenced other artists along the Danube, including Albrecht Altdorfer.

Lucas Cranach

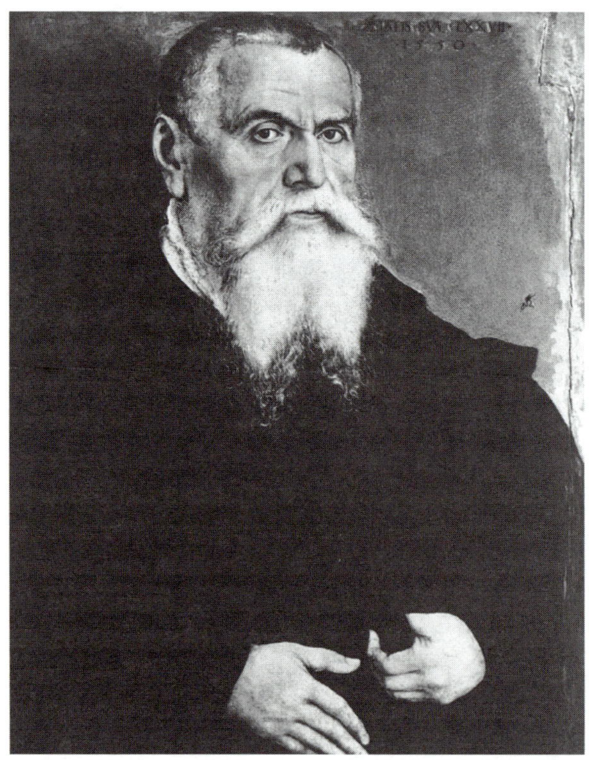

By 1505, Cranach moved to Wittenberg, where he became court painter of the Saxon elector, Frederick the Wise. Over the next half-century, he dominated the art of northern and eastern Germany through his output for the Saxon princes (he served three successive electors), and through work for the Protestant cause. His shop employed his sons Hans (c. 1513–c. 1530) and Lucas, called the Younger (1515–1586), plus some ten apprentices and more assistants. Cranach adapted his Vienna style to collaboration by formalizing spontaneity; emphasizing linear outline and detail, he made a virtue of the quickness required by huge commissions.

Today Cranach's most prized later works are his secular allegories. In these gently erotic paintings, the outline of nudes plays against a dark, flat ground. Other works, such as his hunting scenes, resemble patterned tapestry, reflecting their use as palace decoration. Cranach was Renaissance Germany's most prolific portraitist. Along with iconic likenesses of Saxon nobles, he portrayed Protestant reformers in paintings and prints that projected their cause well beyond Wittenberg.

Cranach's links to Martin Luther were both personal and professional. Godfather to each other's children, they collaborated on key projects, such as antipapal pamphlets, diagrams of reformed doctrine, and illustrations to Luther's Bible translations. In response to iconoclasm, Luther fostered through Cranach a legible style appropriate to a word-based faith. Cranach continued to work for Catholic patrons, notably Luther's foe, Albrecht of Brandenburg.

In 1550, after the 1547 defeat by Catholics of Prince Johann Frederick, Cranach accompanied his patron to Augsburg and then in 1552 to Weimar, where Cranach died in 1553. His shop still thrived under Lucas the Younger. Various and collaborative, Cranach's art coined a recognizable style that helped define visual culture for Lutheran Germany. ◆

1472 Cranach is born in Kronach and subsequently trained by his father.

1502 Cranach arrives in Vienna where he begins to make religious paintings.

1505 Cranach moves to Wittenberg for the next 45 years, where he becomes court painter.

1550 Cranach accompanies his patron to Augsburg.

1553 Cranach dies.

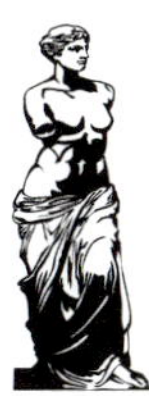

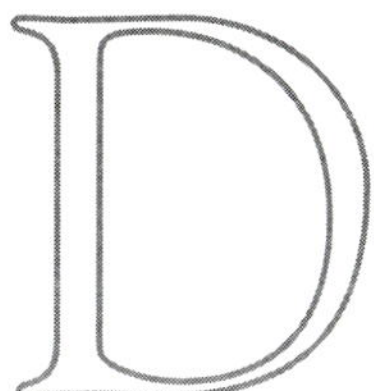

da Vinci, Leonardo

April 15, 1452–May 2, 1519 ● Painter, Sculptor, and Inventor

Leonardo da Vinci is the embodiment of universal genius, known as a Renaissance man. The illegitimate child of a notary and a peasant girl, he was brought up on his father's estate in Vinci, a Tuscan village between Florence and Pisa. As a boy he was talented in writing and music, but painting was his greatest interest, and he was placed in the studio of Andrea del Verrocchio, the Florentine sculptor, whose intellectual curiosity and pursuit of knowledge were inspiring to his young assistant. He worked with Verrocchio until 1478. At 20, da Vinci became a member of the guild of artists. While he was working with Verrocchio he was arraigned on a charge of sodomy and imprisoned for two months, but the case was dismissed because of lack of evidence.

In 1481 he started work on the *Adoration of the Magi* and a *Saint Jerome*, but left for Milan before they were completed. In Milan he applied to Duke Ludovico Sforza for a commission to sculpt an equestrian statue of the duke's father, saying that he was also competent as a military engineer. He received the commission and worked on the statue for 16 years. Although he had interested himself in the process of casting in bronze, he had never learned the requirements of the process for sculpting. "The Horse" was therefore never cast and the clay model was eventually destroyed by French soldiers.

In addition to designs of canals and artillery pieces for the duke, da Vinci designed pageants and masquerades for the

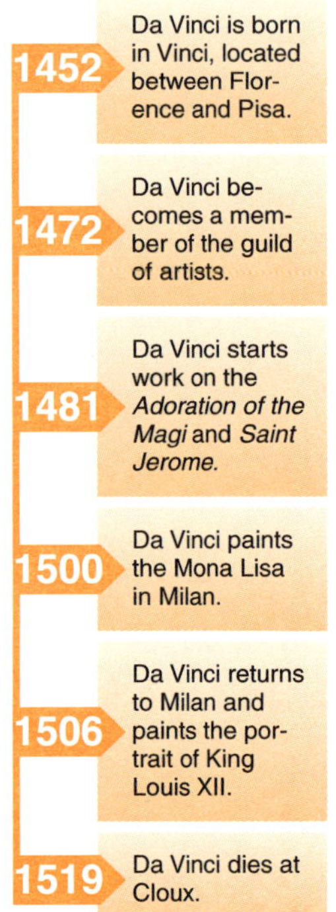

duchess's entertainments. He painted the duke and duchess and many of their courtiers and was rewarded with expensive gifts and a good salary. He also painted the beautiful *Madonna of the Rocks* for the Confraternity of the Immaculate Conception, but sued for the return of the painting when they paid him a meager sum. The suit dragged on for years.

Duke Ludovico ordered the artist to paint the *Last Supper* on the refectory wall of the convent of Santa Maria della Grazie. The artist worked very slowly, making many studies for the heads of Jesus and the disciples, and spending much time just looking at what he had done before he took up his brushes again. Unfortunately, da Vinci's compulsion to experiment resulted in the use of a medium that was not compatible with the ground. He completed the painting but 20 years later the paint had begun to flake off.

In 1497 the duchess died, and with her death da Vinci's salary stopped. The duke was forced to leave Milan, which shortly afterward was captured by the French; by that time da Vinci had already left.

In the spring of 1500 the painter was in Florence, where he was inspired by the atmosphere. He did more work in his six years in Florence than in all the years he had worked in Milan. It was there that he painted the *Mona Lisa,* one of the world's most famous portraits. He worked on it for four years; it is said that he used a compass to construct the famous "enigmatic" smile. The model was Lisa Gherardini, wife of a wealthy merchant. The critic Giorgio Vasari reported that da Vinci engaged musicians, singers, and jesters to keep her merry "and remove that melancholy which painting usually gives to . . . portraits." King Francis I of France bought the painting, and it found its home in the Louvre.

He was commissioned to paint an altarpiece for the church of Santissima Annunziata. His first cartoon, on the subject of the Virgin and Child and Saint Anne, was rejected because it was "only beautiful," not instructive. The second, however, showed Saint Anne with the Virgin in her lap, both rising to support the Child, who is reaching for a lamb (the symbol of sacrifice). This version was accepted and the painting was highly acclaimed.

Da Vinci left Florence to work on military projects for Caesar Borgia, who was campaigning in the Romagna, but when Borgia ordered the assassination of da Vinci's good friend Vitellozzo Vitello, who was one of Caesar's own officers, da Vinci returned to Florence. There he received a commission to make a fresco mural for the Sala di Gran Consiglio in the Palazzo della Signoria. Michelangelo received the commission to do a mural for the opposite wall. The rivalry of these two giants divided the city into two camps. The two cartoons were made and exhibited—much visited and copied. However, neither da Vinci nor Michelangelo finished his fresco. da Vinci, as usual, experimented. The new plaster which he used did not set; he started the work but soon gave up.

In May 1506 he went to Milan for nine months to work for the French king Louis XII and painted the king's portrait. Although he was the official architect and engineer for the French government in Milan, da Vinci spent much time designing pageants and studying various branches of life sciences and geology. In 1509 he wrote his *Divina Proportione* (*Divine Proportion*), for which he made 60 geometric designs.

Da Vinci met a handsome young artist, Francesco Melzi, and visited him at his family's home in Vaprio for two months. When Giovanni de' Medici became Pope Leo X, da Vinci, with Melzi, went to Rome. The pope's brother, Giuliano de' Medici, da Vinci's patron, arranged for da Vinci to occupy an apartment in the Vatican.

Da Vinci was now over 60 years of age and not too pleased with his new situation. His neighbors complained to the pope about him because he studied anatomy by dissecting cadavers. He lived quietly and modestly, tending to be withdrawn and antisocial; his neighbors intruded on his privacy and got on his nerves. Nevertheless, he continued with his studies and writings and completed several paintings.

After Giuliano de' Medici died, Francis I, who had ascended the throne of France the previous year (1515), invited da Vinci to come to live in France, appointing him First Royal Painter, Architect, and Engineer. Francis sincerely admired da Vinci for his artistic genius and his intellect and gave him a liberal pension, as well as the castle of Cloux near the royal residence at Amboise. He appointed Melzi to the position of Gentleman of the Chamber, and often visited da Vinci.

To the great grief of King Francis, da Vinci died at Cloux. He left his manuscripts, his drawings, and his books to Francesco Melzi. None of his writings—several thousand pages, all written in his left-handed "mirror-writing"—had been published. These included his many notebooks, and treatises on the art of painting, on harmony, optics, and aeronautics (he designed a flying machine). There was nothing that did not interest him. If there were phenomena that puzzled him he devised experiments to help him understand—experiments which often resulted in important contributions to the field he was exploring. He also left thousands of pen and ink and chalk sketches on a wide range of subjects.

Da Vinci's powerful mind and the diversity of his accomplishments have remained an object of wonder and admiration. He is appreciated as much for his contributions to knowledge and thought as for his artistic genius. ◆

Dalí, Salvador

May 11, 1904–January 25, 1989 ● Painter and Writer

Long before performance art became an officially recognized genre, the Spanish painter, printmaker, and writer Salvador Dalí was its master. A flamboyant self-dramatist and canny self-promoter, Dalí was also a prodigally gifted craftsman whose name became synonymous first with surrealism and then with the rampant vulgarization and mass merchandising of 20th-century art. By turns brilliant innovator and shameless huckster, Dalí was a pioneer in the now-fashionable blurring of boundaries between highbrow and mass culture.

Salvador Dalí was born on May 11, 1904, in the Catalan town of Figueras, near Barcelona, Spain. His family's image of stable bourgeois prosperity fronted profound inner contradictions: his father, a highly regarded notary, was a militant atheist and political radical, while his mother was a temperamentally conservative, pious Catholic. He later said that his having been named Salvador, after his deceased brother, early on instilled in him a sense of the malleability and fragility of personal identity. This theme would later inform his surrealist voyages to the frontier between consciousness and the unconscious.

Dalí's father was so determined to shield him from religious ideas that he sent him to public school, where Dalí's sartorial finery made him an object of ridicule and bullying from his tattered, often barefoot classmates. His father and sister encour-

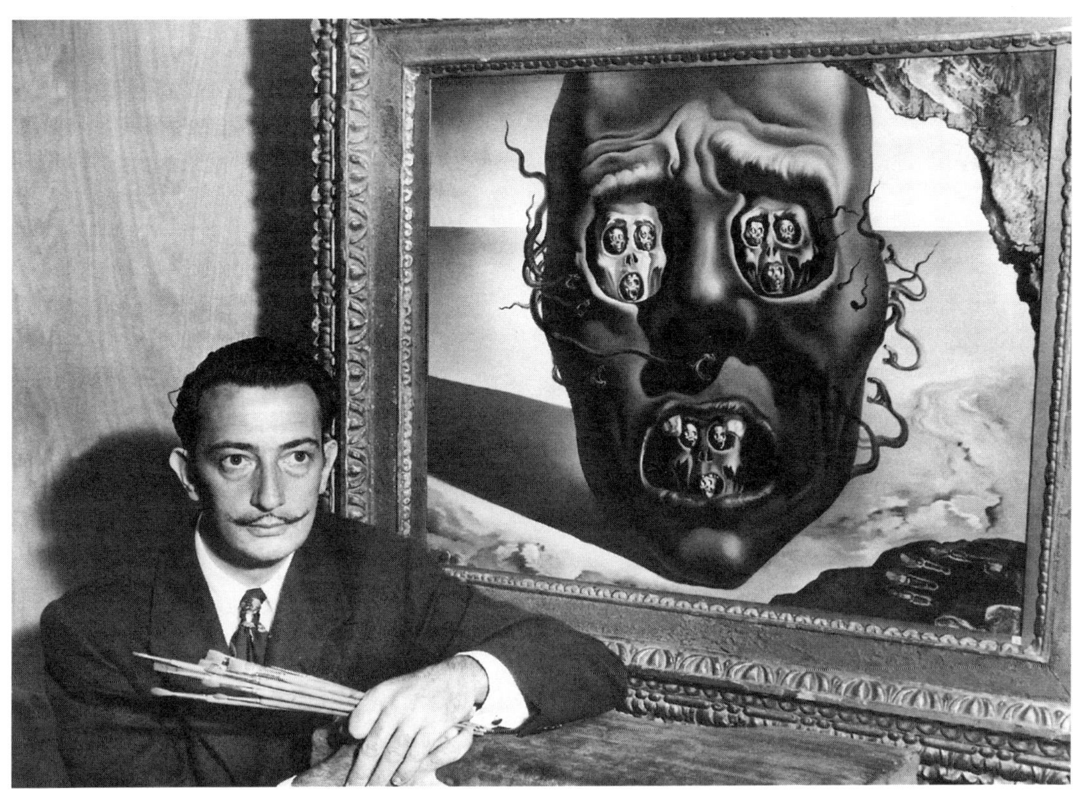

Salvador Dalí in 1941 with his painting *The Face of War.*

aged his youthful interest and talent in art, setting aside a room in the family home as his studio. In 1921 he entered the San Fernando Royal Academy of Fine Arts in Madrid. There his innovative impulses vied with his open admiration for classic masters such as Velazquez, Goya, El Greco, Dürer, Leonardo, and Michelangelo, thus prefiguring the admixture of exacting realist figuration and surrealist imagery that marked his mature style.

At the academy Dalí became part of a group of rebellious avant-garde students that included Federico García Lorca (the future playwright and poet) and Luis Bunuel (later to become a world-famous film director). At length he was expelled for fostering student unrest and refusing to take a required examination on the grounds that the professor was unfit to judge his work. His academic failure was overshadowed by growing recognition as an artist, certified by his first one-man show in Barcelona in 1925. With all the breathless impressionism of youth, his work at this time dashed exuberantly through the main currents of modernist style—cubism, futurism, purism—

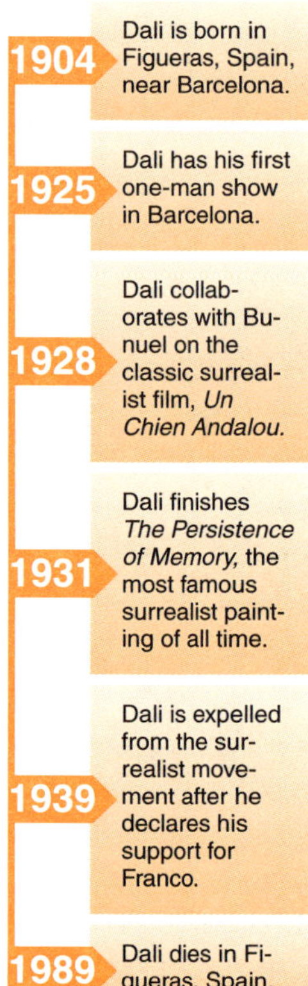

while retaining impressive neoclassical gestures. He also began contributing to intellectual journals and designed the sets for Lorca's first play, *Mariana Pineda* (1927).

The influence of the metaphysical painting of Giorgio de Chirico propelled Dalí toward surrealism, as evidenced in the randomly associated images in paintings such as *Senicitas* (1926–27). In 1928 Dalí collaborated with Bunuel on the screenplay of the surrealist movie classic *Un Chien Andalou* (released in 1929), whose startling, dreamlike flow of arresting, sometimes grotesque images sparked international controversy and acclaim. The film brought Dalí to the notice of André Breton, the French writer and leading surrealist.

Throughout 1929 Dalí's distinctive surrealist painting style began to crystallize: oneiric panoramas of oddly juxtaposed everyday objects and suggestive erotic symbols, each component rendered with exquisitely detailed realism unsettlingly at odds with the hallucinatory whole. Some of the more notable of these "hand-painted dream photographs," as Dalí called them, are *Dismal Sport* (1929), *The Lugubrious Game* (1929), *Great Masturbator* (1929), and *Persistence of Memory* (1931). The last of these, perhaps the most widely reproduced surrealist painting, depicts flaccid, melting wristwatches floating in an airless atmosphere of menacing calm.

The Dismal Sport was Dalí's passport into the inner circle of surrealism. His formal public initiation took the form of Breton's declaration in the preface to the catalogue for Dalí's one-man show at the Galerie Camille Goemans in November of 1929: "It is perhaps with Dalí that for the first time the windows of the mind are opened fully wide." Dalí called his aesthetic philosophical approach to painting "paranoiac-critical," which he defined as a "spontaneous method of irrational knowledge based on the critical and systematic objectivation of delirious associations and interpretations." For Dalí an understanding of inner and outer reality was a game of guile and double guile, a house of mirrors in which nothing was really as it appeared on the surface of perception. Taking the unconscious as revelatory palimpsest, he probed ever deeper for symbols within symbols, seeking the final gateway to the mind's secret store of truth, it's elusive and tantalizing promise of truth and deliverance.

Dalí's muse in this spiritual-aesthetic odyssey was his future wife, Gala Eluard, who became his confidant and lover after their meeting in 1929. Leaving her husband, she helped guide

Surrealism

Surrealism is an early 20th-century artistic movement, centered in Europe, that directly emerged from dadaism, from which some of its earliest advocates came. Like dada, surrealism rejected intellectualized ideas about the role of art and recognized the arbitrary and unpredictable element of artistic production; unlike dada, the movement was highly organized, and its various views were fully articulated. Surrealists shared a fascination with psychology, the use of the subconscious or unconscious, not intellect, to discover the deeper working of the mind, and the use of art to reproduce dreamlike images. In such works there was no interest in giving art a literal "meaning."

The term surrealism (sur–real, or exceeding the real) was coined by poet Guillaume Apollinaire in 1917. A prominent movement in literature as well as art, its central artistic ideas can be seen in poet André Breton's "Surrealist Manifesto" (Paris, 1924). A 1925 exhibition brought greater public attention to surrealist art.

Many surrealists believed in the possibility of automatic painting, in which the artist could paint as spontaneously directed by the subconscious rather than the intellect, as with the drawings of André Masson (*Furious Sons,* 1925). Max Ernst, prominent in dada, introduced frottage (French: "rubbing"), a technique for wrapping a simple object like a twig in a piece of paper and rubbing pencil over the object so that the paper would record a pattern. Hans (Jean) Arp produced highly abstract sculptures designed to represent and evoke subconscious images rather than represent identifiable objects. Other notable figures were Man Ray and René Magritte.

In addition to surrealism's avowed members, the movement welcomed the occasional association of other artists such as Marcel Duchamp, Marc Chagall, Joan Miró, and Pablo Picasso. By far the most famous figure popularly associated with the movement, Salvador Dalí, was in fact widely considered an outsider, because of his originality, his right-wing political views, and his perceived commercialism. Dalí often represented the images of dreams and nightmares not as purely abstract but as distorted transformations of objects recognizable from everyday life.

Surrealism flourished for over two decades, first in Paris, then in New York City, where Breton and many of the prominent figures went to live. Many of its works continue to enjoy great popularity, and its influence can be seen in the magic realist movement in the United States, and early abstract expressionism.

Dalí through his inner torments to achieve enough personal peace to unleash his visions on canvas. Other surrealists view her as a malign influence who steered Dalí toward his later commercialization and self-parody.

Dalí's pictorial penetrations of the recesses of the unconscious drew inspiration from his readings in Sigmund Freud, who distanced himself from surrealism as a whole but found in Dalí's work an interesting, if inverted, expression of his own in-

> **"The only difference between me and a madman is that I am not mad."**
> Salvador Dalí

sights. Freud told Dalí in 1938: "It is not the unconscious that I seek in your pictures but the conscious."

Throughout the 1930s Dalí remained a vigorous champion and promoter of the surrealist movement, helping to formulate manifestoes and contributing to shows such as the 1938 International Surrealist Exhibitions in London, as well as a major exhibit at the Galerie Beaux-Arts in Paris in 1938. But by the late 1930s political and aesthetic fissures appeared in the surrealist movement. Breton frowned upon Dalí's growing preference for academic formalism in his canvases but was even more alarmed by his flirtation with fascism. On shaky ground with Breton after he painted a laudatory portrait of Hitler in 1937 (*The Enigma of Hitler*), Dalí was expelled from the surrealist movement after he declared his support for the fascist Spanish general Francisco Franco in 1939.

Dalí lived in the United States from 1939 to 1948, where he was much in demand in high society as a party guest and cultural icon. He played his role to the hilt, masterfully parlaying his carefully cultivated image as a flamboyant aesthete-genius into unprecedented commercial success and eliciting Breton's derogatory anagram of his name: "Avida Dollars." Throughout the 1950s, while living in Spain, Dalí's prodigious and increasingly eclectic output covered a wide swath of themes from history, religion, and art. Among the highlights of this period are *Madonna of Port Lligat* (1949), *Sacrament of the Last Supper* (1955), *Exploding Raphaelesque Head* (1951), and *Christ of St. John of the Cross* (1951). Commercial success and international celebrity coincided with growing critical disfavor, as many scholars accused him of degenerating into self-parody by cannibalizing his early work rather than creatively renewing it.

By the 1970s Dalí was in serious financial straits because of mismanagement and theft by his longtime business manager, Peter Moore, who sold all of Dalí's copyrights. In 1980 a Cleveland businessman organized a foundation, Friends to Save Dalí, to assure the painter's material security. In the wake of a major retrospective of his work at the Centre Georges Pompidou in Paris in 1979, Dalí's reputation began to reacquire some of its lost luster. Another major retrospective was held at the Museum of Contemporary Art in Madrid.

Dalí spent his last years in a wheelchair after suffering injuries in a fire in 1984. He died on January 25, 1989, in a hospital in Figueras, Spain. ◆

Daumier, Honoré

FEBRUARY 26, 1808–FEBRUARY 10, 1879 ● SCULPTOR, PAINTER, AND LITHOGRAPHER

Honoré Daumier, French lithographer, sculptor, and painter, was born in Marseilles, France, on February 26, 1808, the son of a glazier and frame maker. He moved with his father to Paris in 1816. Because of the family's financial position, Honoré had to quit school and earn an income. He worked first as a messenger in a court of law and then as a bookseller's assistant.

Meanwhile, Daumier developed strong interests in drawing and politics. Impressed by his work, his parents hired Alexandre Lenoir as his teacher. (Later, Daumier would mock what he considered to be the grandiose, pompous style of conventional artists like Lenoir.) Subsequently, he worked as an assistant to a lithographer.

Daumier published his first lithograph in the satirical weekly *La Silhouette* in 1829. In the revolution of July 1830, Louis-Phillipe became France's constitutional monarch, and the nation's middle-class businessmen became the dominant class under his rule. Daumier was a republican and a sympathizer of the French Revolution, so a few months later he began publishing anti-government satire in a new anti-monarchist weekly, *La Caricature* (*The caricature*). Some of his lithographs featured caricatures of members of Louis-Philippe's parliament, as in *The Legislative Belly*. Another was called *Freedom of the Press*, a right that Daumier held dear. He had the impressive ability to capture and exaggerate his subjects' prominent physical features in such a way as to draw out their distinctive mental landscape as well.

The December 15, 1831, issue of *La Caricature* ran a lithograph in which Daumier represented Louis-Phillipe as "Gargantua, swallowing bags of gold extorted from the people." For his pains he was jailed for six months, from August of 1832 to February of 1833. He also worked for the daily *Le Charivari*, founded in December of 1832. But when the government banned political satire in 1835, *Le Charivari*—and Daumier—turned to social satire. Daumier's lithographs now used scenes of everyday life to satirize the many types of scoundrels and

1808	Daumier is born in Marseilles, France.
1830	Daumier begins publishing satiric lithographs in the weekly *La Caricature.*
1835	Daumier shifts from political to social satire after censorship is imposed.
1851	Daumier attacks the enemies of the Second Republic in his sculpture, *Ratapoil.*
1870	Daumier does illustrations for Victor Hugo's book *Chatiments.*
1879	Daumier dies in Valmondois, France.

clownish individuals to be found in society. His favorite target was what he considered the banality of the bourgeoisie.

The range of Daumier's lithographic subject matter is illustrated by the titles of his various series of drawings, including *Bathers* (1839–42), *Professors and Pupils* (1845–46), *Divorcées* (1848), *Bohemians of Paris* (1841–42), *Men of Justice* (lawyers and judges, 1845–49), and *The Good Bourgeois* (1847–49). After the revolution of 1848 had established France's Second Republic, Daumier returned to political **satire.** Among his targets were Bonapartist politicians seeking to overthrow the new republic. In 1870 he made drawings for Victor Hugo's book, *Châtiments*.

satire: a form of writing or speaking that utilizes wit, irony, and sarcasm to express commentary on human follies and foibles.

Daumier's lithographs were characterized by strong but controlled satire. They were robust and vivacious. Crisp, direct, uncluttered, and free of mawkishness, Daumier's work placed him in the realist school. Over his career, he produced over 4,000 lithographs, which amounted to an average of eight a month. Daumier claimed that this volume of work left him exhausted, yet his lithographs suffered no loss of energy over time. Contemporary critics placed him at the same level as the artists Goya—although he did not share the Spanish painter's pessimism—and William Hogarth. He has also been compared to novelists Charles Dickens and Honoré de Balzac. Like Dickens's characters, for example, Daumier's subjects are often defeated by their gullibility and vanity.

Daumier's sculpture and painting embraced the same qualities as his lithographs. He was an early experimenter with sculpture as a device for caricature. Perhaps his most famous sculptures were a series of busts, executed from about 1831 to 1833, depicting in grotesque fashion various members of the French legislature. Less than eight inches high, they captured the individuality of each of the subjects. They were modeled in terra cotta and cast in bronze after his death. Of the 45 originals, some 36 still exist.

The Emigrants, executed from approximately 1848 to 1850, is a **bas-relief** of desolate figures, undistinguished from each other, marching in a grim procession. The work, however, still conveys dignity and compassion. The sculpture was modeled in clay, transferred to plaster, and later bronzed. Executed in the same sequence of materials was another important sculpture, *Ratapoil* (1851). It presented the kind of bullying, corrupt thug who, as Daumier saw it, supported Louis Napoléon, who

bas-relief: a sculptural relief in which the projecting image from its surrounding surface is slight, and no part of the model is undercut.

shortly after became a dictator through a December 1851 *coup d'état*.

In the late 1840s, Daumier began to paint on a regular basis. Altogether, he generated over 300 oils and a large number of watercolors. Daumier painted more for his own pleasure than to earn income. His work was selected for display at the annual state-run exhibitions, or Salons, in 1849, 1851, 1861, and 1869. Otherwise, though, his paintings were rarely exhibited and were little known during his lifetime. Like his lithographs, Daumier's paintings consisted almost exclusively of figures. The subjects of many his of paintings came from daily life, as with his lithographs. In both mediums he employed the same vigorous, energetic drawing techniques and satiric exaggerations. His coloring was muted. The size of his paintings was usually very small.

[Daumier] had the impressive ability to capture and exaggerate his subjects' prominent physical features in such a way as to draw out their distinctive mental landscape as well.

During the Second Republic, Daumier received several commissions from the state to do religious paintings, one of them being *We Want Barrabas!* (circa 1850). Late in his career he painted *Don Quixote and Sancho Panza* in various versions. He used this theme to portray the universal human condition, bringing together the ridiculous and the exalted. These paintings exhibit Daumier's artistic abilities at their most accomplished. During his lifetime he was best known for his lithographs, but since his death his paintings have come to be regarded as the most impressive part of his work.

Among Daumier's contemporary French admirers were artists Paul Cézanne; Vincent van Gogh; Eugène Delacroix; Jean-Baptiste-Camille Corot; and Edgar Degas, who collected his work. Others holding him in high esteem were poet Charles Baudelaire, historian Jules Michelet, and novelist Honoré de Balzac. A modest, unassuming man, Daumier was also admired as a person. After his death, French painter and illustrator Jean-Louis Forain said of him, "Oh, he was different from all of us . . . he was generous."

Daumier went nearly blind during the 1870s and lived in obscure poverty at Valmondois, north of Paris. To raise money for him, his friend Corot organized an exhibition of his paintings. However, it failed even to pay for costs. Daumier died at Valmondois on February 10, 1879.

In the United States and Germany, Daumier's reputation is higher than in France, where it is still debated. Reflecting that status, an exhibition of his work on the 100th anniversary of his death was held not in Paris but in Marseilles. ◆

David, Jacques-Louis

AUGUST 30, 1748–DECEMBER 29, 1825 ● PAINTER

Jacques-Louis David, French neoclassical artist, was born on August 30, 1748 in Paris, France. He was from a middle-class family; his father was a successful dealer in textiles, albeit on a small scale. After his father died in 1757, Jacques-Louis was raised by his uncles. He studied under the famous rococo painter François Boucher, but left Boucher to become the pupil of Jacques-Marie Vien, who supported the revival of interest in Greek and Roman art.

In 1771 David began submitting paintings in an attempt to win the Prix de Rome. After failing three times in a row, he attempted suicide by starvation in 1773. The following year, however, David finally won the competition with *Antiochus and Stratonice*, which although it had a classical theme, showed some rococo influence. Using the proceeds of the prize, David went to Rome in 1776 with Vien, who had been appointed director of the French Academy at Rome. Awed by the vast quantities of ancient sculpture and architecture in Rome, David stopped painting for several years in order to study and sketch what he saw. The monumentalism of ancient Roman art strongly influenced his painting.

Jacques-Louis David

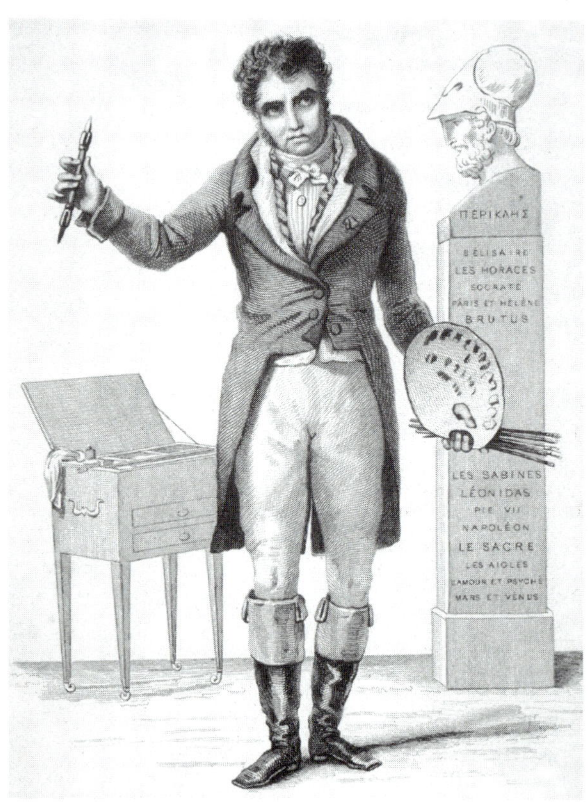

Soon after David returned to Paris in 1780, he became leader of the neoclassical revolt against the rococo style in France. The conflict was not solely about art; it also had moral and political implications. For David and the other neoclassicists, rococo and its excesses represented frivolity, while neoclassicism meant a revival of the moral and heroic virtues of the ancient world. For example, his *Oath of the Horatii* (1785), painted after he had returned from another visit to Rome in 1784, depicts the readiness of a father to sacrifice his son for the good of the Roman Republic. The painting created a political as well as an artistic sensation; although David's primary purpose had been to make an artistic statement, some saw the work as a call to end aristocratic corruption and reestablish the virtue of the ancient republics. Such sentiments underpinned the French Revolution, which began four years later. David's *Death of Socrates* (1787) and the *Lictors Bringing Back the Bodies of the Sons of Brutus* (1789) were two more artistically outstanding tributes to virtuous self-sacrifice that had a similar political impact. For his work during the 1780s, David was virtually idolized by much of the French public.

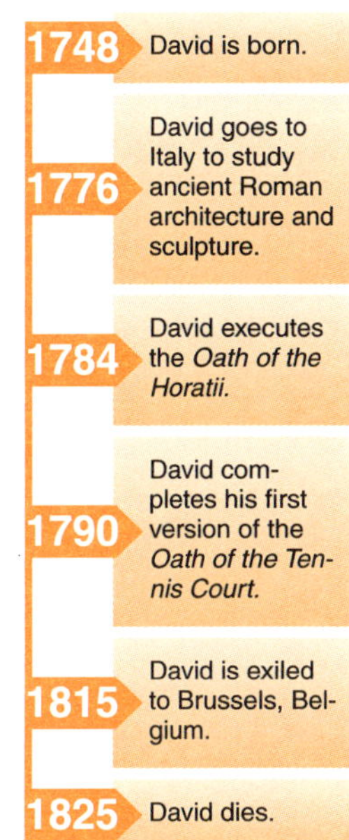

David was an ardent supporter of the French Revolution, which began in 1789. That year he was commissioned to paint *Oath of the Tennis Court*. The initial version was completed in 1790. The work depicts a famous oath taken on June 20, 1789 by the French Estates-General, in which its members swore not to dissolve until they had drawn up a constitution. In subsequent versions, David deleted figures who had fallen out of political favor—a practice that some have seen as foreshadowing the historical distortions of 20th-century Stalinist art.

A Jacobin and an associate of Robespierre, David became a member of the National Convention in 1792 and voted for the execution of King Louis XVI. When the Jacobins came to power, David became the virtual dictator of artistic taste and a spokesman for the Revolution. His *Death of Marat* (1793) and *Death of Bara* (1784) were tributes to revolutionary martyrs. During the Revolution he turned away from classicism and toward realism, although remaining enthralled with antiquity. David was not only the painter of the Revolution but its pageant master, developing stage and costume designs for public spectacles.

"Of all the major artists whose creative lives coincided with the revolutionary era, not just in France but throughout Europe, David was most directly involved in the conflicts and struggles of the age."

Warren Roberts in *Jacques-Louis David*, 1989

After the fall of Robespierre in 1794, David was sent to jail. He was released in 1795 upon the plea of his wife, Marguerite Pécoul, whom he had married in 1782 and who had later divorced him because of her royalist views; they remarried in 1796. David's *Intervention of the Sabine Women* (1794–99), which he began in prison, was one of his few post-revolutionary paintings with a classical theme. It is believed to be a tribute to his wife. But since it showed the women attempting to stop a battle between Roman and Sabine men, the work was also regarded as a call for the suspension of political animosities and the healing of the nation after the divisive revolutionary years.

Napoleon correctly believed that his self-exaltation could be effectively advanced with the help of David's artistic skills.

The painting brought David back into the good graces of France's establishment at the end of the 1790s. It also impressed Napoleon Bonaparte, who became the ruler of France in the same year as the Sabine painting was completed. Napoleon correctly believed that his self-exaltation could be effectively advanced with the help of David's artistic skills. In the years of Bonaparte's consulate (1799–1804), David was his official painter, beginning a series of works that glorified the new ruler. After Napoleon became emperor in 1804, David executed a huge work, *The Coronation of Napoleon* (1805–07). This was followed by *Napoleon Distributing the Eagles* (1810) and *Napoleon in His Study* (1812), a probing portrait underneath its propagandistic surface. Beginning in the late 1790s, David began displaying a Greek classical style as opposed to his Roman classical style of the 1780s. This was visible in *Intervention of the Sabine Women* and *Leonidas at Thermopylae* (1814).

Napoleon was sent into exile in 1815. David refused to support the restored Bourbon monarchy and was exiled that same year to Brussels, where he lived for the remaining 10 years of his life. Critics have had a low opinion of David's paintings from the last period of his life, but recently their sensuous aspect has won them some applause. The better ones are said to include *Cupid and Psyche* (1817), *Telemachus and Eucharis* (1822), and *Mars Disarmed by Venus* (1824).

As a teacher of art, David believed that he should help his pupils find their own way. Still, he had a great influence on French painting through his many students, who included François-Pascal-Simon Gérard, Jean-Auguste-Dominique Ingres, and Antoine-Jean Gros. David died in Brussels on December 29, 1825. ◆

Degas, Edgar

JULY 19, 1834–SEPTEMBER 27, 1917 ● PAINTER

Hilaire-Germain-Edgar Degas, a French painter, was born in Paris on July 19, 1834. He was the eldest son of Pierre-Auguste de Gas, a wealthy banker. Edgar attended the Lycée Louis-le-Grand. In 1854 he began studying under Louis Lamothe, who had in turn studied under Degas's hero, French painter Jean-Auguste-Dominique Ingres. During the following year Degas was a pupil in the painting and sculpture section of the École des Beaux-Arts in Paris. From 1854 to 1859 he spent periods of time in Italy, where some of his relatives lived, and studied art in Rome, Florence, and Naples.

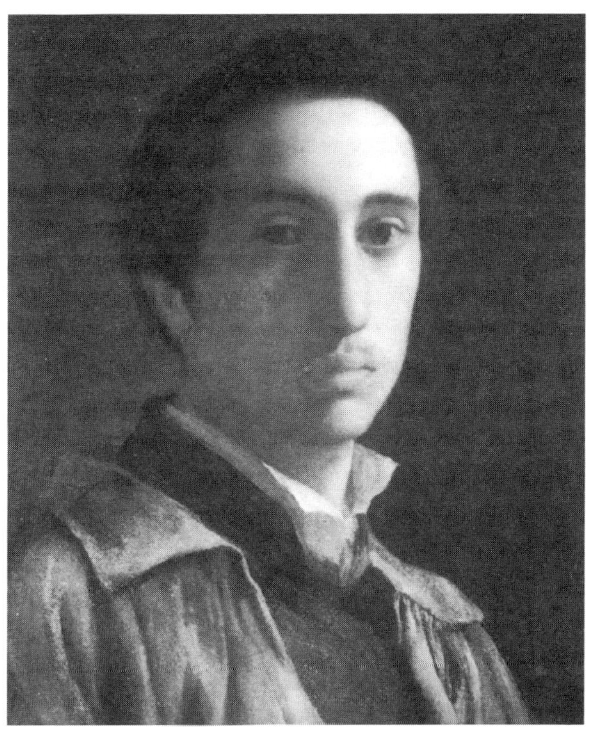

Edgar Degas, self-portrait, 1857

In 1859 Degas set up his own studio in Paris. In his early years as a painter he did portraits of relatives and friends and, under the influence of Ingres, depicted historical themes from the ancient world in such works as *Young Spartan Girls Challenging Spartan Boys* (1860) and *Semiramis Founding Babylon* (1861). Around the mid-1860s he stopped depicting historical themes. The paintings of this early phase of Degas's career have a somewhat stiff and formal quality.

In the early 1860s Degas began going to the Parisian cafés—particularly the Café Guerbois—attended by artists and intellectuals, and he became an integral part of their social scene. He had a difficult personality; Degas was haughty and often caustic in his criticism of others. Yet he made many friends among his colleagues and came to be greatly respected by them for his skill and dedication. Not known to have ever had a romantic involvement, Degas spent the great majority of his time on his work.

By 1865 Degas, influenced by Édouard Manet and Jean Désiré Gustave Courbet, had abandoned historical themes and was depicting scenes from everyday contemporary life. He was particularly interested in portraying places where people went for relaxation and entertainment, such as racetracks, seashores, concert halls, and cafés, and in depicting entertainers such as singers, acrobats, musicians, and ballerinas. Early examples are *Racehorses before the Stands* (1866–68) and *The Orchestra at the Opéra* (circa 1870), considered one of his best works. He is particularly well known for his ballet paintings, one of the earliest of which was *Mlle. Fiocre in the Ballet "La Source"* (1867–68). Female nudes, often shown drying off after bathing, as in *After the Bath* (about 1883–84), also became an important segment

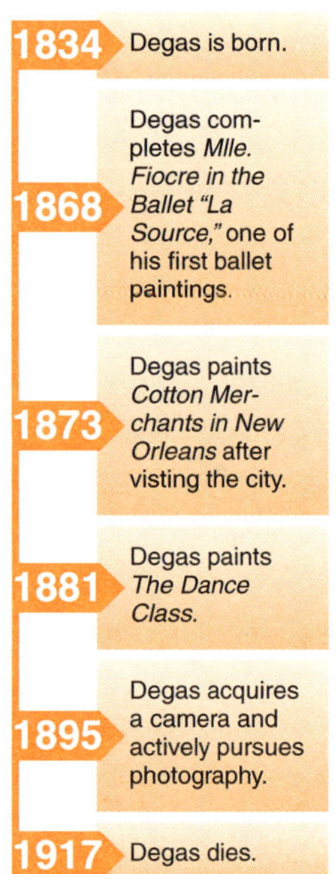

of his work. At the same time as he changed themes, his subjects became more relaxed; individuals now looked as if they had been caught unawares.

Degas was considered an impressionist. Following his military service in the Franco-Prussian War in 1870 and 1871, he was represented at seven of the eight impressionist exhibitions during the 1870s and 1880s, the decades of his best work. Unlike most impressionists, however, he had little interest in landscapes—only about 100 of his approximately 1,500 paintings were pure landscapes—nor was he interested in the play of natural light. Degas resembled the impressionists, on the other hand, in his effort to convey spontaneity (a difficult job, as he once noted in the observation that "no art was ever less spontaneous than mine"). Also like the impressionists, he used broken color and avoided historical and literary themes in favor of contemporary scenes.

Motion and the strain of work are at the heart of Degas's art, whether he is depicting performers or ordinary workers. His ballerinas are often caught with arms and legs akimbo, as in *The Rehearsal* (1874) and *The Dance Class* (1881), with the latter displaying the unusual composition in some of his later work. The faces of his singers show the effort required by their labors. Women workers, such as milliners and laundresses, are depicted in stress. In *Women Ironing* (circa 1884–86), for example, there are two figures: the strain of hard work is shown in the face of one; the physical stress on the arms of the other is evident as she presses down hard on a garment. Even his *Cotton Merchants in New Orleans* (1873), executed after a visit to that city, depicts the motion of those in a relatively sedentary profession.

At his prime Degas was also known for his great skill in the use of colors, which were lighter than in his earlier work. The unusual croppings, spatial tilting and distortion, and heightened decorative quality of his mature work have been attributed to the influence of Japanese prints and photography. During the mid-1880s his favorite medium became pastels, which he used either in crayon form or as a powder, applied with a brush. Degas used a special, secret formula for making his pastels. His pastel drawings were characterized by a luminous suffusion of light and a bold use of colors. Also in the 1880s, he executed small sculptures of women dancers and bathers as well as other subjects. These were meant not for exhibition but for Degas's own study of motion.

"One day at the Cirque Fernando ... [Degas] said to a landscape painter, 'For you, natural life is necessary; for me, artificial life."

Degas: His Life, Times, and Work, 1985, Roy McMullen

As a result of an injury that he sustained during the Franco-Prussian War, Degas became increasingly blind during the 1880s. Eventually he was totally blind in one eye and almost blind in the other. Yet Degas continued to work during the last two decades of his life. He became adept in photography; a friend noting that around 1895 Degas "acquired a camera and used it with the same energy he put into everything." He became increasingly reclusive, however—Degas disliked having his work interrupted by visitors and screened out those he considered unworthy of his attention.

Around 1870 Degas had some connection with socialist clubs, but he later shifted to the right politically. By the 1890s he had become a reactionary **anti-Semite** who refused to associate with defenders of Albert Dreyfus, a Jewish officer in the French army who was convicted of treason in 1894.

anti-Semite: an individual or state of thought hostile towards Jews and the Jewish faith.

Degas died in Paris on September 27, 1917. He left a large collection of paintings by his contemporaries and a collection of his poems, most of them in sonnet form. The famous French impressionist painter Camille Pissarro described him as "certainly the greatest artist of our epoch," and Degas had a strong impact on 20th-century art. ◆

Delacroix, Eugène

April 26, 1798–August 13, 1863 ● Painter

The preeminent French romanticist of the 19th century, Eugène Delacroix captured the imagination of the European art world with his provocative use of color and his mastery of a wide array of subjects, ranging from mythology and literature to politics and history. His work unleashed the anti-classical impulses that eventually flowered into impressionism and postimpressionism. The poet Charles Baudelaire called him "the last of the great artists of the Renaissance and the first modern."

The fourth child of a high-ranking public official, Ferdinand Victor Eugène Delacroix was born on April 26, 1798, in Charenton-Saint-Maurice, France. The product of a privileged household steeped in high culture, he concentrated on the mastery of Greek and Latin literature at the Lycée Impériale, the standard curriculum of that era. At the age of 17 he began

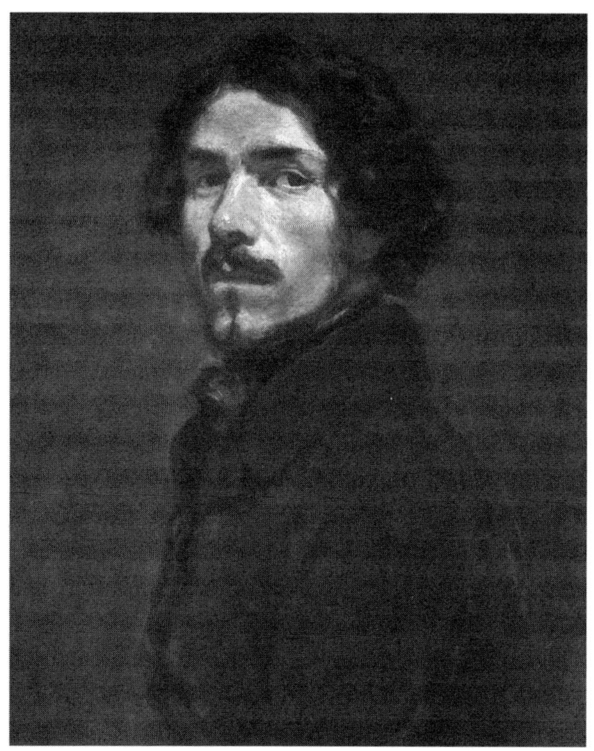

Eugène Delacroix, self-portrait, mid-1800s

studying at the studio of Pierre Narcisse Guérin, a prominent painter of the day. During his stay there, Delacroix encountered several important artists who helped to shape his sensibility: Antoine-Jean Gros, Baron François Gérard, and Théodore Géricault, with whom Delacroix shared a close personal and professional bond until Géricault's death in 1824. Delacroix's early career also benefited from the patronage of Louis Thiers, an influential politician and historian who later became the president of France.

The arrival of an important new talent was evident with the showing of Delacroix's *Dante and Virgil in Hell* at the Salon of 1822. Its use of a vivid and arresting palette to convey the emotional complexity of a daunting subject evoked the grandeur of masters such as Michelangelo and Rubens. The painting's emotional tempests were a foretaste of Delacroix's infatuation with romanticism, especially in its early English manifestations. A longtime Anglophile and student of Shakespeare, he was inspired by the works of Byron and Scott as well as the canvases of Bonnington and Constable. These influences were evident in his 1824 contribution to the Salon, *Massacre at Chios*, a huge work depicting a blood-drenched episode in the modern Greek struggle for independence. Both celebrated and reviled—Baron Gros called it "the massacre of painting"—the work reinforced Delacroix's stature as a major new force in French art.

Not content to absorb English influences from afar, Delacroix traveled to London in 1825 to make a more thorough study of the works of Turner, Constable, and Lawrence. The salutary effects of the journey are evident in the fertile output of the ensuing five years. *Death of Sardanapulus*, one of 12 works on display at the 1827 Salon, is a vibrantly colored, heady swirl of decadence and lust. Another important allegorical canvas from this period is *Combat between the Giaour and the Pasha* (1827). Delacroix's literary ventures extended into li-

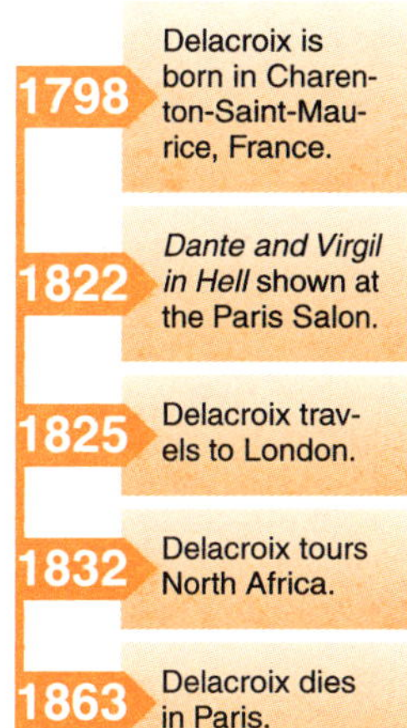

thography with his 17 illustrations for an 1827 edition of Goethe's *Faust*.

Delacroix also explored historical subjects during these years, most notably in *The Execution of the Doge Marino Faliero* (1826), *The Battle of Nancy* (1831), and *The Battle of Poitiers* (1830). *Liberty Leading the People* (1830), a tribute to the Revolution of 1830, is perhaps Delacroix's most famous painting, a singular and successful melding of symbolism and contemporary history. In his masterly traversals of literature, myth, and history, Delacroix was unique among his contemporaries. As one critic has written, "Delacroix admired in Rubens a quality that he himself possessed in abundance: the ability to unite allegory and history, and mould into a tumultuous whole figures mythological, historical, literary, and real. He, too, could convey the turbulent movement of brightly colored forms without disturbing the harmony of their arrangement and their overall composition in light and space."

Having weathered controversy to emerge as a major figure in the French art world, Delacroix fended off complacency by seeking new sources of inspiration on a six-month voyage to North Africa made in 1832 in the company of the Count de Mornay, a French diplomatic envoy. He first toured Algeria and Spain but spent most of his time in Morocco, which provided a cornucopia of exotic visual and emotional impressions that informed all of his remaining work. Delacroix's first rendering of his Moroccan journey was *Women of Algiers in Their Apartment* (1834), notable for its enhanced freedom of line, luxuriant density of color, and poetic intensity of effect. Other significant impressions of his North African journey include *Fanatics of Tangier* (1838) and *Jewish Wedding* (1839).

Although North African themes pervaded his work until the end, Delacroix also revisited classical themes during the 1830s, as in *Medea* (1838). Delacroix fully acknowledged the competing impulses at work in his canvases during this period. He declared: "I am a pure classic," but also proclaimed that "if by romanticism they mean the free manifestation of my personal impressions … then I am a romantic and have been one since I was 15."

Delacroix's growing renown brought him a number of significant architectural projects for French government buildings, including murals and ceiling decorations. Classical themes predominated in these works, but his work on several churches spurred an interest in Christian iconography later in

"[Delacroix was] the last of the great artists of the Renaissance and the first modern."
The poet, Charles Baudelaire, on Eugène Delacroix

his career, especially during the 1850s. In 1854 he wrote in his journal, "I was much impressed by the Requiem Mass. I thought of all that religion has to offer the imagination, and at the same time of its appeal to man's deepest feelings." A major example of this tendency in his later work is *Christ on the Lake of Gensareth* (1854), rendered with the freedom of line and grittiness of texture that became more prominent in his later work.

tepid: lukewarm in enthusiasm.

Controversy hounded Delacroix to the end. His offering to the 1859 Salon occasioned as much derogation as praise, ending his involvement with that institution. Discouraged by the **tepid** response to his major mural group for St.-Suplice *(Jacob Wrestling with the Angel)*, Delacroix gradually reduced his output as failing health sapped his energy and determination. He died in Paris on August 13, 1863, leaving behind an unsold inventory of some 6,000 works of various kinds—canvases, watercolors, pastels, engravings, and lithographs. All told he produced more than 9,000 works in his lifetime, a monument to what one scholar has called "the highest manifestation of French genius in art." ◆

Donatello

C. 1386–DECEMBER 13, 1466 ● SCULPTOR

paradigms: typical examples and patterns of behavior.

Considered one of the founders of the Italian Renaissance style. Donatello extended the visual **paradigms** of every genre of sculpture, from freestanding figures, portraiture, and sacred narrative in relief to commemorative tomb monuments and chapel decoration, working across an impressive range of media, including marble, wood, bronze, terra-cotta, glass, brick, and stucco.

The earliest biography of Donatello is found in Giorgio Vasari's *Lives of the Artists* (1550). Yet Donatello is among the best-documented artists of the 15th century, with more than 400 documentary references detailing his activities from 1401 until 1461 and frequent mentions in a variety of contemporary sources. Incidents recorded in contemporary biographies mentioning Donatello attest to his forceful personality and support the wealth of anecdote encountered in Vasari. Donatello was among the artists to whom Leon Battista Alberti dedicated his

Della pictura (1436); he was praised for his talent and skill by Bartolomeo Fazio in *De viris illustribus* (Lives of illustrious men; 1456) and was celebrated posthumously in Cristoforo Landino's *Apologia* (1481). Significantly, these humanists note Donatello's artistic achievement in specific reference to antiquity. Donatello's acute interest and participation in the revival of classical culture were reflected in a number of activities, from restoring antiquities to advising collectors as distinguished as the humanist Poggio Bracciolini.

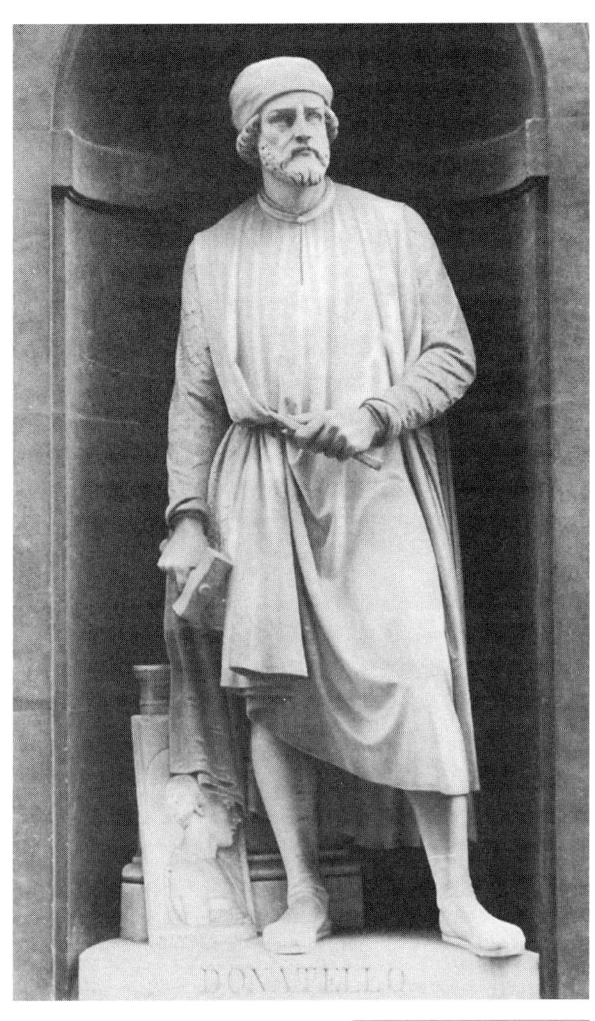

Statue of Donatello in Florence, Italy.

Donatello is first documented as an assistant in Lorenzo Ghiberti's Florence workshop (1403–1407), while Ghiberti was at work on models for the first set of bronze Baptistery doors. Although Donatello was described as a goldsmith and stonemason in the guild registry of St. Luke in 1412, earlier payment records from the cathedral workshops of Santa Maria del Fiore suggest that he was already autonomous; beginning in 1408 and continuing into the early 1420s, Donatello received a number of public and corporate commissions, mostly single figures in marble and terra-cotta. The earliest independent commissions that brought him to prominence were for Florence Cathedral and include the life-size marble *David* (1408–1409), and a seated *St. John the Evangelist* (1408–1415), commissioned to flank the west doors of the cathedral facade. Too small for its intended location on a northern tribune buttress of the cathedral, the *David* was acquired by the Florentine city council for display in the Palazzo della Signoria in 1416. *David*'s decorative sway and original ornamentation—painted, gilded, and installed on an elaborate base inlaid with colored glass and mosaic—reflect contemporary taste for the International Gothic style. By contrast, the marble *St. John*, with its concentrated realism and optical cor-

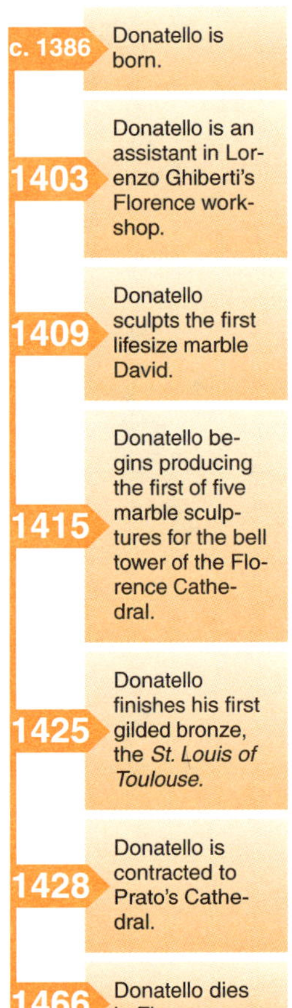

rections, carved to compensate for a viewer's angle of vision below, is often mentioned as a forerunner to Michelangelo's *Moses* (1513–1516).

During the second decade of the 15th century, Donatello received two commissions for Orsanmichele, a multipurpose structure that functioned as a center for the Florentine guilds: a marble *St. Mark* (1411–1414), commissioned by the Linen Drapers' Guild (noted for Donatello's realistic rendering of the Evangelist's robe and cushion), and a marble *St. George* (1414–1417), patron saint of the Armorers' Guild, whose alert and tense expression was much admired for its realism. The exterior of the niche below marks the pioneering debut of Donatello's "rilievo schiacciato," or flattened relief technique, to illustrate the saint's rescue of the princess of Cappadoccia. Departing from earlier conventions. Donatello treated the surface of marble like wax, drawing with the cornor of his chisel to create atmospheric effects and employing perspective to enhance the illusion of spatial depth.

At the same time, 1415–1418, he produced five marble sculptures for the bell tower of Florence Cathedral: the earliest were a *Bearded Prophet, Prophet with Scroll,* and *Abraham and Isaac.* Execution of *Habakkuk* and *Jeremiah* lasted into the 1430s; an early tradition claiming these as portraits testifies to their realism. The sandstone lion, the *Marzocco* (Bargello), was commissioned in 1418 and completed in 1420 for the entrance to the papal chambers at Santa Maria Novella, on the occasion of Pope Martin V's visit.

Donatello's growing engagement with bronze as well as an increase in private commissions can be observed throughout the 1420s. He produced his first gilded bronze, the *St. Louis of Toulouse* (1421–1425), for the Guelph party at Orsanmichele in collaboration with Michelozzo, an experienced metallurgist in Ghiberti's workshop, resulting in an official workshop partnership from 1425 into the early 1430s. The vivid realism of the gilded bronze reliquary bust of *St. Rossore* has suggested to scholars that it was the earliest revival of classical portrait bust in the Renaissance.

The polychrome marble and bronze Tomb of Baldassare Coscia. Antipope John XXIII, in the Florentine Baptistery, was one of the most prestigious commissions of the 1420s. Its innovative composition features a vivid effigy in gilded bronze, lying "in state" under a marble baldachin. Three other tomb commissions date from this period: the Aragazzi Tomb in Montepulciano, the bronze Pecci Tomb relief with its unusual illusionism in the Siena cathedral, and the Brancacci Tomb ordered for Sant' Angelo a Nilo in Naples, where it was shipped from Pisa in 1428. In many respects a typical Neapolitan tomb updated with classicizing elements. Donatello's central marble relief of the *Assumption of the Virgin* reflects his increasing interest in narrative and his rapidly developing technique. Similar concerns were brilliantly explored in the gilded bronze panel of *Feast of Herod,* 1423–1427, for the Siena Baptistery font, assigned to Donatello after Jacopo della Quercia failed to fulfill the commission. Using multiple vanishing points, Donatello manipulated perspective as an expressive device linking pictorial space to narrative time; viewers watch the head of the Baptist move inexorably closer, from background to foreground, toward Herod, the banqueters, and us. In a series of small marble reliefs, which date from this period and include a number of Madonnas as well as the *Delivery of the Keys/Ascension of Christ,* Donatello's disregard for traditional finish and obvious chisel marks add to the works' expressiveness.

Donatello's central marble relief of the *Assumption of the Virgin* reflects his increasing interest in narrative and his rapidly developing technique.

Donatello's exceptional experimentation with materials, techniques, and modes of expression continued in the 1430s, while his interest in ancient art intensified. Although tradition maintains that Donatello explored the ruins of Rome with Filippo Brunelleschi circa 1403, the artist's only documented trip occurred circa 1432, evidenced by the Crivelli Tomb in Santa Maria in Aracoeli and *Tabernacle with Burial of Christ,* now in the Beneficiati Sacristy of St. Peter's.

Upon his return to Florence, Donatello embarked on his first large-scale Medici commission, the decoration of a sacristy constructed by Brunelleschi to house the tomb of Giovanni de Medici at the church of San Lorenzo. In addition to two sets of bronze doors, whose paired and actively gesticulating figures raised issues of decorum and finish, Donatello revived an ancient technique by modeling eight polychrome stucco roundels on site.

Difficulties in executing an exterior pulpit on the southwestern corner of Prato's cathedral, initially contracted to both Donatello and Michelozzo in July 1428, form a backdrop for Donatello's activities during this decade. In 1434, Donatello alone signed a second contract for the Prato Pulpit, required for the semiannual outdoor display of a highly venerated relic, the girdle of the Virgin lowered to Thomas as a sign of her Assumption. Finally completed in 1438, individual marble panels on

Prato's circular gallery present a continuum of joyously dancing angels.

Donatello's *Cantoria,* a choir gallery commissioned for the cathedral of Florence in 1433 and completed in 1440, is related conceptually to the Prato pulpit but richer in ornamentation and expression. Its uninterrupted **frieze** of wildly cavorting angels is viewed through a screen of columns supporting a massive cornice. Other significant work from this period includes a stained-glass window of the coronation of the Virgin for the cathedral's dome; the deeply carved and tenderly expressive *Cavalcanti Annunciation Tabernacle* sandstone relief, Santa Croce; the **polychrome** and gilded wood *John the Baptist*, made in Florence for the Florentine merchants' chapel in Santa Maria Gloriosa dei Frari, Venice, 1438; and two iconographically mysterious bronzes now in the Bargello, the *Attis/Amor* and the controversial *David,* first recorded in the courtyard of the Medici palace in 1469.

frieze: any ornamentally sculptured band on furniture, a gallery, or a wall.

polychrome: multicolored.

Why Donatello left Florence for Padua around 1443 is uncertain; however, he was soon occupied with distinguished projects near and within the church of Sant'Antonio. Donatello's bronze equestrian portrait of the mercenary captain Erasmo da Narni (Gattamelata) was erected on its base outside Sant'Antonio in 1453. Inside the church, Donatello undertook an ambitious enterprise for a high altar complex entailing seven freestanding bronze figures and a series of reliefs in both marble and bronze that included four complex narratives recounting St. Anthony's miracles. The anatomically powerful bronze *Crucifix* (1444) was the earliest figure contracted for Sant'Antonio but probably not part of the original altar. The altar itself was left unfinished when Donatello left Padua in 1454, was dismantled in 1579, and reinstalled in 1895. Its intended appearance is subject to speculation.

Documents indicate that Donatello resided in Florence from 1454 to 1457, when he moved to Siena to design a set of bronze doors for the Siena cathedral. He returned to Florence in 1459, where he remained until his death. Donatello's last works reveal a wide range of emotional tension, narrative invention, and drama. The penitent *Mary Magdalen* (c. 1455) in polychrome wood, and the bronze *John the Baptist* (c. 1457) both appear as introspective aged ascetics empowered by their faith. The heroic and allegorical bronze *Judith Slaying Holofernes* (c. 1453–1457) was probably commissioned as a fountain sculpture for the Medici palace. Donatello's final commission for the Medici, the so-called Resurrection and Passion Pulpits in San Lorenzo, remained unfinished at the time of his death and were not installed until 1515, yet their intricate perspectives and almost claustrophobic crowding of figures impart a new sense of urgency to their narratives. Donatello died in Florence on December 13, 1466 and was buried with obsequies in the crypt of San Lorenzo. Donatello's last works demonstrate the same profound intellect, restless imagination, expressive power, and confident handling of materials that marked the artist's work throughout his entire career. ◆

Dubuffet, Jean

JULY 31, 1901–MAY 12, 1985 ● PAINTER

For Jean Dubuffet, one of the key figures of high modernist painting, iconoclasm was not an option but an imperative. "For me, insanity is super sanity," he said. "The normal is psychotic. Normal means lack of imagination, lack of creativity." He conquered the international art world from without, zealously upending hallowed aesthetic conventions yet ironically rising to the peak of the very institutional culture he so fiercely assaulted. He sought the power of subversion in the primal **reveries** of the innocent and insane, using simple, ordinary materials and subject matter to fashion rough-hewn, seemingly primitive canvases that sounded a refreshingly barbaric yawp through the decorously abstract corridors of postwar modernism.

reveries: daydreams.

The son of a prosperous wine merchant, Jean Philippe Arthur Dubuffet was born in Le Havre, France, on July 31, 1901. Rebellious by temperament, he sought escape from bourgeois convention by immersing himself in art, beginning with local classes at the age of 15 and moving to Paris two years later to study painting at the Académie Julian. Chafing under the constraints of formal study, Dubuffet dropped out art school six months later to paint on his own; after several years of floundering, he grew disillusioned with the entire realm of culture and art and set out to see the world.

After two years of travel in Italy and Brazil, the prodigal son reappeared in Le Havre and immersed himself in the conventional bourgeois life he had spurned, enrolling in a business

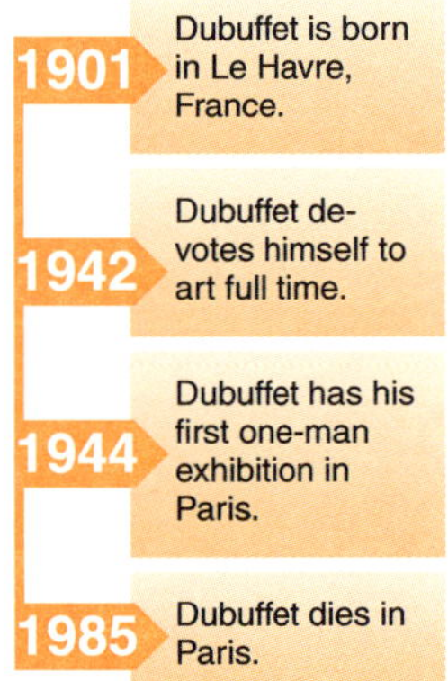

class in 1925 and marrying in 1927. (The marriage lasted only a few years and was followed shortly thereafter by another.) Dubuffet returned to Paris in 1930 to establish himself as a wine merchant but within a few years heard the call of the painting muse and turned his business over to a manager. The business faltered in hired hands, however, and in 1937 Dubuffet was obliged to resume wine selling. By 1942, however, he had resolved to devote himself full time to painting and hired another manager to run the business until he was able to sell it on favorable terms after the war.

A partisan of the French *art brut* (raw art) movement of the 1940s, Dubuffet made his public debut in 1944 in Paris with paintings of everyday subjects rendered in a provocatively childish manner. In fact, Dubuffet had been making extensive studies of the art produced by young children and mental patients in order to replicate their elemental energies. The paintings at his 1946 show in Paris featured the found objects and materials of everyday life—old newspapers, broken glass, chunks of plaster—to distill its essence in art. The show elicited a chorus of derision from conventional critics and admiration from the chroniclers of the avant-garde. Both factions recognized—with glee or dread—the arrival of an irrepressible original.

Dubuffet's reputation as an artistic provocateur climaxed with a 1947 show at the Galerie Rene Drouin in Paris devoted mainly to acidulous caricatures of prominent French writers and artists of the day. A typical entry was his portrait of the surrealist writer Georges Limbour, titled *Limbour Fashioned from Chicken Droppings*. Dubuffet characterized his aesthetic in typically blunt terms: "The persons I find beautiful are not those who are usually found beautiful.... Funny noses, big mouths, teeth all crooked, hair in the ears; I'm not at all against such things. Older people don't necessarily appear worse to me than younger ones." As one critic wrote, "Dubuffet's interest in the rudimentary and the inchoate meant that conventional subjects were dissected into their most ignoble components. His excremental landscapes and turnip-men, set down in meandering lines and harrowed clods of pigment, were not ordinary—they were frighteningly banal."

Fascinated by the power of the primitive, Dubuffet made several visits to North Africa and the Sahara during 1947 and 1949. The trips infused his canvases with a renewed vigor and a growing appreciation for landscape. His taste for the grotesque was on vigorous, unembarrassed display in a series of female nudes he executed in the early 1950s, *Corps de Dames*, "rosy-brown, squashed-flat, gross and scarily funny," in the words of the critic Robert Hughes.

"[Dubuffet's] excremental landscapes and turnip-men, set down in meandering lines and harrowed clods of pigment, were not ordinary—they were frighteningly banal."

Art critic Robert Hughes, commenting on Jean Dubuffet's often harsh style

Dubuffet moved to Venice in the south of France in 1955, seeking a milder climate for his ailing wife. While there he reimmersed himself in landscapes, many of which incorporated the material of nature in portraying its form: some featured scattered sand, others patterns of butterfly wings. The 1950s series *Texturologies*, an evocation of the soil itself, borders on abstraction but remains rooted in Dubuffet's project of radically reimagining the natural world rather than transcending it altogether.

After moving back to Paris in 1961, Dubuffet resumed his studies of people and the byproducts of daily urban life, the most notable example of which was *L'Hourloupe* (a word made up by Dubuffet). Much of his work in the 1970s and 1980s was a cross between painting and sculpture, mostly formed of painted polyester resin and marked by a characteristically macabre humor.

Jean Dubuffet died in Paris in 1985. ◆

Duchamp, Marcel

JULY 28, 1887–OCTOBER 2, 1968 ● PAINTER, SCULPTOR, AND CONCEPTUAL ARTIST

Reveling in his reputation as the Clown Prince of modern art, Marcel Duchamp was equal parts artist, anti-artist, prankster, and provocateur. A founder of **conceptualism,** the movement through which art became pretty much anything the artist verbally declared it to be, Duchamp gleefully dynamited the very foundations of traditional aesthetic theory and practice by proclaiming the artistic worth of found objects such as urinals or by painting a mustache on a reproduction of the *Mona Lisa*. Yet Duchamp cultivated a serene indifference to the subject of his ridicule, calmly turning away from art for years at a time to indulge his passion for chess. Theorists of art have taken him more seriously than he took himself; at times this breezy nihilist seemed merely to play at art in order to strip it of its high solemnity, but without

conceptualism: a twentieth century artistic movement characterized by the artist's own verbal interpretation of his or her work.

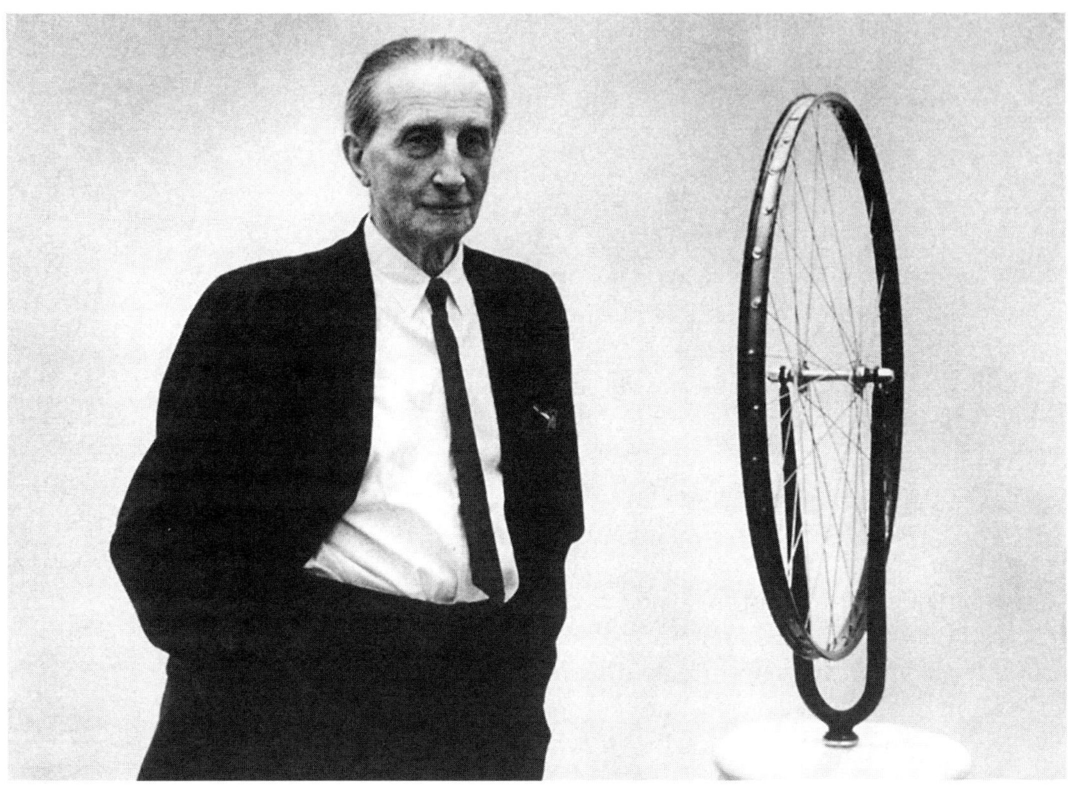

Marcel Duchamp, with his work *Bicycle Wheel* (1913).

proselytizing for any alternative vision. He once declared that, "as a religion, [art is] not even as good as God."

Duchamp grew up in a family that prized art—three of his five siblings became artists as well. His grandfather was a shipping agent by vocation and an engraver by avocation; his father, a prosperous provincial notary, eagerly supported his children's artistic ambitions for the contact it brought him with the bohemian life he himself could not attain. After some preliminary training in his hometown of Blaineville, Marcel moved to Paris, where his two older brothers—Jacques Villon and Raymond Duchamp-Villon—were already established in the art world. They helped to guide his mostly self-taught steps toward artistic maturity. The initial influence of postimpressionism and fauvism (the latter especially evident in his early work *Portrait of the Artist's Father*) had, by 1911, yielded to cubism, deployed by Duchamp in a series of introspective experimental canvases.

Quickly exhausting cubism's expressive possibilities, the restless Duchamp hungered for an even freer modality, especially after his discussions with the painter Francis Picabia. Together they began to formulate a radically nonobjective aesthetic that seemed to partake of elements of then-germinating movements such as **abstractionism** and **futurism** but went beyond them in questioning the very primacy of the visual. As Duchamp later wrote, "I am interested in ideas—not merely the visual products. I want to put painting once again to the service of the mind."

abstractionism: an artistic movement characterized by the artist's use of imagery that departs from traditional and representational accuracy, and the simplification or exaggeration of forms.

futurism: an early twentieth century artistic movement with roots in Italy that emphasized an effort to give an expression to mechanical functions and processes.

Duchamp's first major step in this direction was *Portrait*, a 1911 painting that superimposes five successive stages of the movement of a silhouette. Duchamp expanded this kinetic concept in what proved to be his most famous painting, *Nude Descending a Staircase, No. 2*, which deploys a superficially cubist style to transcend cubism. The work depicts the staggered downward progress of a machinelike entity, thus emphasizing the irony of the title and issuing a bold challenge to cubism's essentially static framework. Spurned by the committee in charge of the Salon des Indépendants in Paris in February of 1912, the work went on display at New York's famous Armory Show in 1913, where it became the center of attention, arousing as much indignation as admiration.

Rather than basking in his instant notoriety, Duchamp retreated to a hermetic, anonymous existence in Munich, where he began work on what proved to be a ten-year undertaking, *The Large Glass, or The Bride Stripped Bare by Her Bachelors, Even*. Constructed on glass, it depicts a bride surrounded by a group of panting, unrequited suitors. The work, described by one critic as a "mechanistic coitus-interruptus," is considered by many to be Duchamp's masterpiece, even though he grew discouraged and pronounced it definitively unfinished in 1923, declaring that a shipping accident that had splintered its glass surfaces had improved it.

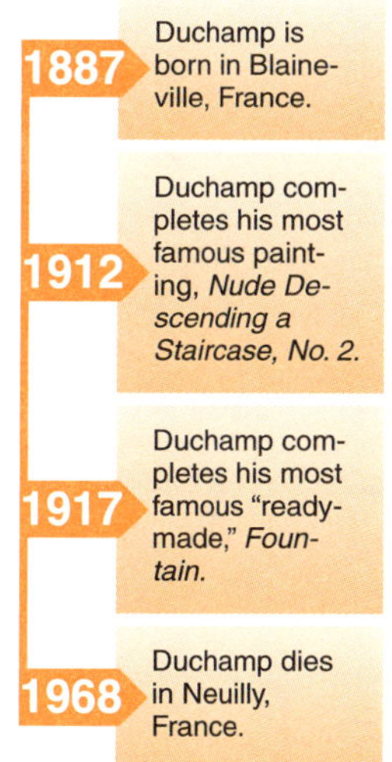

In 1913 Duchamp pronounced himself bored with painting, chafing under the constraints of what he called a purely "retinal" art. His restless quest to transcend the boundaries of the visual led him to what he later called "the most important single idea to come out of my work"—the "ready-made," manufactured objects whose mere insertion into a display case with philosophical intent endowed them with the power of art—or,

"[Marcel Duchamp] is certainly the most intelligent and, for many, the most troublesome *genant* man of this first half of the 20th century."
André Breton, on Marcel Duchamp's role as the Clown Prince of modern art

in Duchamp's terms, the subversive power of anti-art. His first work in this vein was *Bicycle Wheel*, which was just that—a found bicycle wheel. The following year saw the debut of *Pharmacy*, a commercially reproduced winter landscape before which Duchamp placed two medicine bottles.

At the outbreak of World War I, Duchamp traveled to the United States, where, thanks to the sensation stirred by *Nude* at the Armory Show, he was showered with adulation from the press and art community. The wealthy art patron Walter Arensberg created a studio for Duchamp in which he returned to work on *The Large Glass* but rebuffed offers from various art galleries, no longer wishing to devote himself full time to art. Instead he earned money by giving private French lessons.

Duchamp's next major exercise in calculated affront to art was the ready-made entitled *Fountain*, which was rejected for exhibition at the first show sponsored by the Society of Independent Artists because Duchamp had signed it "R. Mutt." With the proceeds of his sale of the still-unfinished *Large Glass* to Arensberg in 1918, Duchamp traveled to Buenos Aires for nine months before sailing to Paris in 1919. While there, consorting with his kindred spirits and disciples among the Dadaists, he kicked aside another sacred column of the temple of Western art when he issued a reproduction of the *Mona Lisa* with a superimposed mustache and goatee.

Throughout the 1920s and 1930s, Duchamp's chief preoccupation was chess, but he did devote sporadic intervals to explorations in cinema and mechanically reproduced sound. His involvement with the surrealist movement engaged the attention of André Breton, who published a major **treatise** on his work in a Paris journal in 1935 and enlisted Duchamp's collaboration in mounting the surrealist exhibitions from 1938 to 1959. During World War II Duchamp decamped to New York along with numerous other luminaries of the European avant-garde and made the United States his home thereafter.

treatise: a systematic written demonstration that includes examples of fact and principle, and a summation and presentation of a final conclusion.

After marrying in 1954, Duchamp retreated from the creative **maelstrom** of the art world and receded into anonymity until the 1960s. Then the young radicals of American art rediscovered his startling inversions of tradition and raised him to an unprecedented eminence, redeeming his reputation from the academic critics who had dismissed him as a crank.

maelstrom: a powerful and violent whirlpool that envelops objects within a particular radius.

Marcel Duchamp died on October 2, 1968, in Neuilly, France. ◆

Dürer, Albrecht

MAY 21, 1471–APRIL 6, 1528 ● ARTIST

A talented painter, printmaker, draftsman, designer, and theoretician, Albrecht Dürer spent most of his career in his native city of Nürnberg. He was the third of 18 children of Albrecht the Elder (d. 1502), a noted goldsmith, and Barbara Holper (d. 1514). By the time of his death, Dürer was arguably Europe's best-known artist because of the broad dissemination of his prints. His works reveal a remarkable breadth of interests. Although many generations of scholars have overemphasized Dürer's significance, his influence was felt throughout Germany and beyond. For later audiences, he was the quintessential German artist.

Dürer initially trained to become a goldsmith with his father. He learned to work with a burin (a cutting tool) and to appreciate the characteristics of different metals. His fledgling talents as a draftsman were already evident in 1484 when he drew a delicate and slightly awkward silverpoint *Self-Portrait at Age Thirteen*. Produced at a time when artists rarely represented themselves, this proved to be the first of many self-portraits by Dürer. From November 1486 until 1489 Dürer apprenticed with Michael Wolgemut, a neighbor and Nürnberg's leading painter. Although Dürer later remarked on how difficult these years were, especially the inevitable torments that be suffered at the hands of the older apprentices in the studio, he learned the arts of drawing, painting, and printmaking.

Upon completing his training in 1489, Dürer began his extended *Wanderjahr*. Although the precise itinerary of his travels as a journey-

Albrecht Dürer, self-portrait, 1498

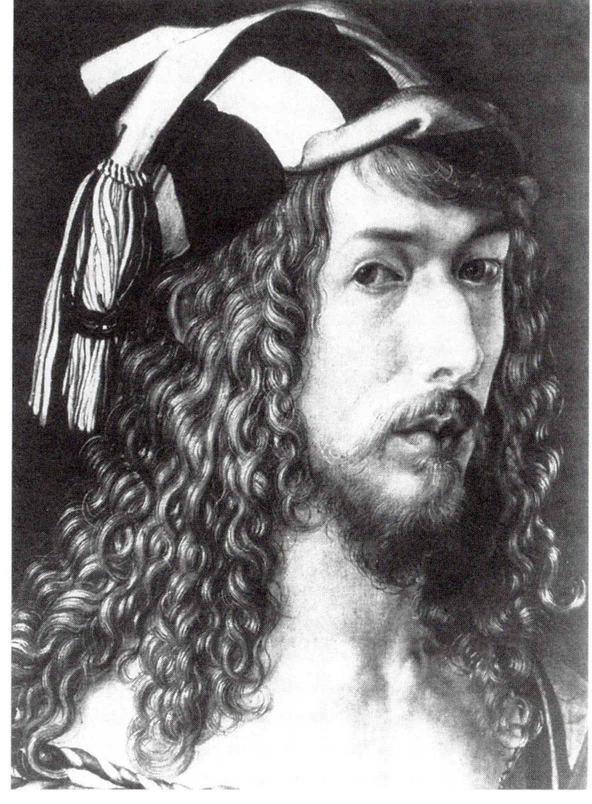

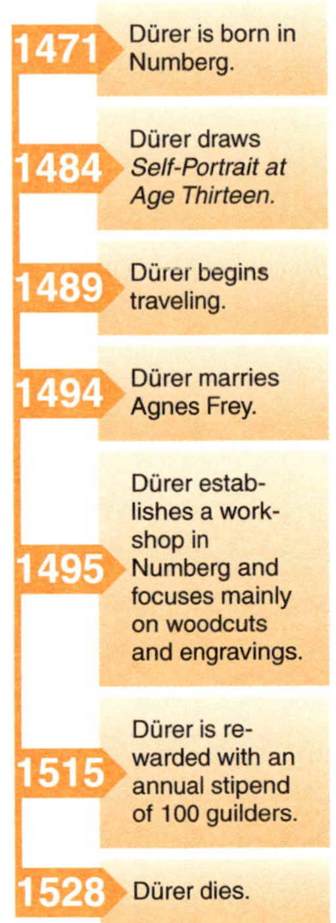

man is unknown, the documentary and artistic records indicate that he arrived in Colmar only to discover that Martin Schongauer, the famed engraver and painter, had died. Dürer worked in Basel and Strasbourg, both active publishing centers, where he made designs for book illustrations, including Terence's *Comedies* (unpublished) and, less certainly, Sebastian Brant's *Das Narrenschiff* (*Ship of Fools;* 1494).

The artist returned to Nürnberg in 1494, apparently at his father's bidding, where he married Agnes Frey, the daughter of Hans Frey, a talented coppersmith. Much has been written about their relationship and their lack of children. Even though Agnes did not always get along with Willibald Pirckheimer, the noted humanist and Dürer's best friend, she seems to have been a highly supportive spouse who helped manage the large workshop and often traveled to fairs to sell his prints. In the fall Dürer first journeyed across the Alps to Venice and other towns. Several exquisite watercolors record his route. While in northern Italy he first discovered the art of Andrea Mantegna, with its powerful evocation of classical antiquity, concern for the human body, and explorations of perspective, and that of Giovanni Bellini, Venice's leading painter, who taught Dürer new approaches to the use of color.

Back in Nürnberg in 1495 Dürer established a workshop and entered one of the most productive periods of his career, in which he focused primarily on **woodcuts** and engravings. In his *Men's Bath* woodcut of 1496–1497 he explored complex spatial constructions, varied material surfaces, including the stunning use of the whiteness of the paper to suggest both solids and open passages, and complex poses. Here and especially in the woodcuts for his famed *Apocalypse* series of 1496–1498, published as a book in collaboration with Anton Koberger, his godfather. Dürer experimented with the expressive and descriptive potentials of line to communicate form, surface, texture, and light. Never had the terror of the *Four Horsemen* seemed so palpable as in Dürer's woodcut. Likewise, Dürer convincingly evoked the immateriality of an angel dissolving into a band of clouds in *St. John Eating the Book.* Through prints like these and the first edition of the *Large Passion* (1497–1499), Dürer's artistic ideas and fame reached a growing audience well beyond the walls of Nürnberg.

woodcuts: a print fashioned by a cut design in the grain of a side of a block of wood; ink is transferred from the raised surfaces to the paper.

Dürer's early facility with a burin and his youthful admiration for the art of Martin Schongauer attracted him to engraving as early as 1494. The *Sea Monster* (c. 1498) offered the artist the opportunity to represent a **voluptuous** nude woman set against an exquisitely detailed landscape, one reminiscent of the watercolors from his first Italian trip. In several instances Dürer used his engravings as a means for communicating his growing fascination with antiquity and human proportions. *Nemesis* (1501–1503) is ostensibly an allegory of fortune and retribution, reward and punishment, based upon a humanistic text by Angelo Poliziano. His personification, a winged nude woman hovering above the Alpine town of Klausen, is actually an experiment in correct human proportions based upon the writings of the ancient Roman architect Vitruvius. Her head measures 1/8 the length of the body, the face is 1/10, and her right foot is 1/7. Although in later years he would abandon Vitruvius's scheme for one that better accommodated the variety of human bodies, the artist already was seeking a theoretical basis for his art. This quest is best observed in *Adam and Eve* (1504). The first couple is based loosely upon canonical examples of classical sculpture, the *Apollo Belvedere* and the *Medici Venus*, which he knew only indirectly. These are among the most complex and compelling nudes in German art. They inspired dozens of subsequent copies by other artists in a variety of media. His interest in the human body and the classical tradition are, however, couched in a northern artistic language, one stressing surfaces, varied lighting, and vivid contrasts between the figures and the dense forest behind.

voluptuous: complete delight to the senses, especially as related to sensual gratification.

Throughout this period Dürer also painted and created designs for stained glass, table fountains, and a host of other objects. In 1496 the artist executed a portrait of Frederick III the Wise, elector of Saxony (now in Berlin). This commission was the start of a long **patronage** by Frederick that resulted in such works as *Seven Sorrows of the Virgin* and the *Mater Dolorosa* (1496), *Mary Altarpiece* (1496), possibly the *Jabach Altarpiece* (1503–1504), *Adoration of the Magi* (1504), and *Martyrdom of Ten Thousand* (1508).

patronage: financial, emotional, and spiritual backing of an artist or group of artist by a wealthy individual or group interested in promoting the arts.

Dürer's theoretical ambitions are evident when comparing his self-portraits of 1498 in Madrid and 1500 in Munich. Adopting a compositional formula developed earlier in Netherlandish and Italian art, the 26-year-old artist rests his arm on a ledge parallel to the picture plane. Behind, an Alpine vista appears through the open window. Dürer stresses his attractive appearance, notably his long flowing hair, and attentive gaze. This painting depicts a successful, if mildly narcissistic, sitter. By contrast, the 1500 portrait confronts the viewer. Dürer positions himself frontally. He gazes intensely outward, an effect heightened by the reflection of an unseen window off the surface of each eye. Intentionally iconic, indeed consciously Christlike, the likeness stresses the artist's creative capacities, especially his mathematical prowess in the generation of the picture's proportions and his phenomenal skill in rendering material textures. The accompanying Latin inscription reads "Albrecht Dürer of Nürnberg has [depicted] myself in everlasting color at age 28," an allusion that the artist's likeness and his fame would be everlasting, too.

When Dürer returned to Venice in the late summer of 1505 he was a far more renowned artist. As 10 of his surviving letters written to Pirckheimer in Nürnberg attest, his fame prompted a certain jealousy in some of the Italian artists. Dürer reported that he was awarded a much-coveted commission to paint the *Feast of the Rose Garlands Altarpiece* (1506) for the German merchants' Chapel of Saint Bartholomew. Stung by criticism of his painting talents, the artist labored on this picture. His colors and technique reflect the influence of the aged Giovanni Bellini, with whom he maintained friendly contacts. Dürer also had to contend with Marcantonio Raimondi's direct copying of his prints. In Venice and in his travels to Bologna, Rome, and likely Florence, Dürer continued his studies of perspective and the human body. He copied several of Leonardo's anatomical sketches and, indirectly, caricatures, as seen in his *Christ among the Doctors*, executed in Rome in 1506.

pendants: an object hanging from another object, such as an ornament hanging from a necklace.

Back home by January 1507 Dürer soon entered another highly productive period. As if to demonstrate the lessons of Italy, he painted life-size **pendants** of *Adam and Eve* (1507). In contrast with the rigidity and rather academic quality of his 1504 engraved couple, the pair are far softer, more fluid, and more graceful. Perhaps his Venetian experience encouraged the artist to paint two large pictures: the *Heller Altarpiece* (1508), which exists only in drawings and in a copy (c. 1614) made by Jobst Harrich: and the *All Saints' Altarpiece* (1508–1511), done for the Landauer Chapel in Twelve Brothers' House in Nürnberg. Both pictures show heavenly visions that occur just above deep, panoramic landscapes. Each includes a prominent portrait of Dürer holding an inscription tablet. The financial success of these and other projects permitted the artist to purchase a large stone and half-timber house near the Tiergärtner gate just beneath the castle.

Dürer's graphic activity also increased dramatically. In 1511 he published his *Mass of St. Gregory* and *Trinity* woodcuts, which with their elaborate shading systems are two of the most technically accomplished of his career; his *Life of the Virgin* series (c. 1504–1511); *Large Passion* series (1497–1499 and 1510–1511); and *Apocalypse* series, each now reissued with a new title page. *His Engraved Passion* series of 1508–1512 is perhaps Dürer's most complex narrative and emotional exposition. Next follow the three "master" engravings: *Knight, Death, and the Devil* (1513), *St. Jerome in His Study* (1514), and *Melencolia* I (1514). The precise perspectival design and the careful mimicry of textures in his *St. Jerome in His Study*, however brilliant, are secondary to the print's remarkable lighting effects. Warm sunlight bathes the saint's study. This symphony of light and shadow sets a tranquil mood conducive to Jerome's scholarly enterprise. Jerome's radiant halo conveys a convincing aura of sanctity. Dürer created the *Agony in the Garden* (1515) and the *Angel Holding the Sudarium* (1516), two of his most expressive etchings, a technique he used only rarely. The rough and energetic lines heighten the emotion of Christ's lonely burden and the angel's anguish.

***His Engraved Passion* series of 1508–1512 is perhaps Dürer's most complex narrative and emotional exposition.**

Around 1512, if not a year or two earlier, Dürer started working for the emperor Maximilian I. The artist made now-lost drawings (c. 1512) for the bronze statues of King Arthur, King Theodoric, and Charlemagne for the emperor's tomb that later in the century was erected in the Hofkirche in Innsbruck. Soon after meeting Maximilian, who visited Nürnberg in 1512, Dürer and his workshop, following designs by imperial court artist Jörg Kölderer, began production of the 192 woodcuts for the *Triumphal Arch of Maximilian*, which was finished by 1515 but not published until 1517–1518. When assembled, the arch measures 134 inches by 115 inches, making it the largest graphic project ever. Together with Albrecht Altdorfer, Hans Burgkmair, Lucas Cranach, and Hans Baldung, Dürer contributed pen drawings to the margins of the emperor's *Book of Hours* (1515). In 1515 Maximilian rewarded the artist with an annual stipend of 100 guilders drawn from Nürnberg's imperial taxes. Three years later Dürer traveled with a city delegation to the imperial diet in Augsburg, where he sketched Maximilian's portrait, now in Vienna. The emperor died the following January before the artist had completed either the two painted portraits, today in Nürnberg and Vienna, or the large commemorative woodcut portrait (1519). He also was in the midst of designing the *Large Triumphal Chariot;* the drawing in Vienna was finished in 1518 but the subsequent woodcut was published only four years later. This composition was one of the models that Dürer provided for the redecoration of the great hall and exterior of Nürnberg's city hall that was painted by others in 1521–1522.

stipend: a fixed amount of money disbursed periodically for services or work.

Dürer's fourth great journey occurred in 1520–1521 when, together with Agnes and a servant, he traveled to the Low Countries. Although prompted by his desire to have Charles V, the new emperor, reaffirm his annual **stipend,** the Nürnberg master used this occasion leisurely to explore the Netherlands from his primary base in Antwerp. As recounted in his remarkable diary—or, more accurately, annotated account book—Dürer was treated as a celebrity. He was feted by artists in most of the towns he visited. He befriended Joachim de Patinir, the noted landscapist, and exchanged works with Lucas van Leyden, Bernard van Orley, Jan Provost, and others. He supported his trip through the sale of prints, which apparently he brought in considerable quantities, through the execution of numerous portrait drawings and the occasional painting, and through the completion of a few other projects, such as *St. Jerome* (1521). The diary records Dürer's visits to view Jan van Eyck's *Ghent Altarpiece*, among other works of art, and his quest to view a beached whale. From the latter trip he developed a fever, perhaps **malaria,** that permanently damaged his health.

malaria: tropical disease caused by parasites in red blood cells and transmitted by mosquitoes; characterized by attacks of chills and fevers.

During the last years of his life, Dürer concentrated on portraiture and writing. He experimented with printed portraits that range from the huge woodcut of *Ulrich Varnbüler* of 1522 to the refined engraved likenesses of *Cardinal Albrecht von Brandenburg* (1519 and 1524), *Frederick III the Wise* (1524), and, from 1526, *Erasmus*, *Philipp Melanchthon*, and *Willibald Pirckheimer*. Most are arranged with a laudatory inscription tablet beneath the portrait. Melanchthon's reads, "Dürer was able to picture the features of the living Philipp, but his skilled hand was unable to picture his mind." Equally impressive are the three painted portraits of *Jacob Muffel*, *Hieronymus Holzschuher*, and *Johann Kleberger*, all dating to 1526.

In 1512 or 1513 Dürer began drafting a manual entitled *Speis der Malerknaben* (*Food for Young Painters*), in which he argued that art is a combination of craft and knowledge. Although this project was never completed, he eventually wrote *Vnderweysung der Messung* (*Art of Measurement;* 1525), *Etliche*

Vnderricht, zu Befestigung der Stett, Schlosz vnd Flecken (*On Fortification;* 1527), and *Hierinn sind begriffen vier Bücher von menschlicher Proportion* (*Four Books on Human Proportions;* 1528). The last was published posthumously through the efforts of Agnes and Pirckheimer. In a land without a strong theoretical tradition and virtually no history of writing about art, Dürer's texts were pioneering. Indeed, he often had to invent his own artistic terms. While these texts were popular with later theoreticians, the practical impact on contemporary artists was limited.

Like others of his age, Dürer was keenly interested in the emerging religious debate. He belonged to the Sodalitas Staupitziana, a group of humanists and patricians who met in the local Augustinian church to discuss theological issues. Although Dürer avidly collected the writings of Martin Luther and in his 1520–1521 diary fretted over the rumor of the reformer's death, it is not clear whether he ever abandoned Catholicism; he probably assumed, like others at the time, that the different groups would ultimately reconcile. In 1526, the year after Nürnberg formally adopted Lutheranism, Dürer presented his *Four Apostles,* two life-sized panels (now in Munich), to the city council. The images of Saints John the Evangelist, Peter, Paul, and Mark, together with the accompanying inscription, stress the artist's faith in the word of God and the need to be steadfast in safeguarding it.

The course of German art would have been quite different without Dürer. Unlike most artists, Dürer's posthumous reputation continued to grow. Collectors avidly hunted for his drawings, prints, and paintings. The taste for his work or new works in his style between about 1570 and 1620 has been dubbed the Dürer Renaissance. By 1828 elaborate ceremonies honoring Germany's "greatest artist," the Teutonic counterpart to Italy's Raphael, were held in Nürnberg, Berlin, and other locales. For much of the 19th and early 20th century, Dürer's fame tended to overshadow the very real contributions of his peers. Subsequently, a more nuanced understanding of both Dürer's art and the complexities of the Renaissance in Germany has emerged. ◆

Unlike most artists, Dürer's posthumous reputation continued to grow.

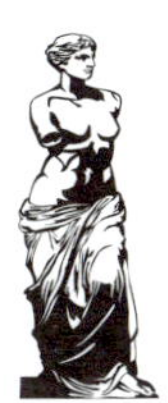

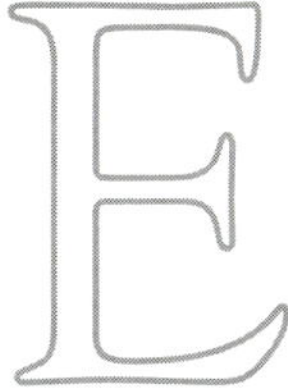

Ensor, James Sydney

APRIL 13, 1860–NOVEMBER 19, 1949 ● PAINTER

The Belgian painter, printmaker, and draftsman James Ensor languished in obscurity for most of his career in Ostend, a small seaside summer resort. From that unlikely location he turned out decades of uncompromisingly original art, by turns whimsical, bleak, and **macabre** in its blend of symbolism and realism. Mostly reviled and ridiculed in his own lifetime, his work is now celebrated as a forerunner of important 20th-century movements such as expressionism, surrealism, and dada. Ensor's own summary of his career's trajectory is apt: "I overthrow all the pictorial conformities. A hailstorm of criticism crashes down on me. People abuse me, people insult me, I am crazy, I am stupid, I am wicked, bad, incompetent, ignorant ... my calm interiors, my 'bourgeois salons,' are sources of revolution."

macabre: dwelling on death or ghastly thoughts and occurances.

"I was born," Ensor wrote, "at Ostend, on April 13, 1860, on a Friday, the day of Venus. At my birth, Venus came towards me, smiling, and we looked into each other's eyes. She smelt pleasantly of salt water." Venus must also have sensed the outsized family dysfunctionality that seemed to preordain Ensor's calling as scorned **aesthetic** visionary. His father, James Sr., was an English engineer who had studied at leading German universities. Stopping by Ostend on holiday, he was beguiled by Catharina Maria Haegheman, heir to a local curio and novelty shop. After James Jr.'s birth, James Sr. set out for the United States to sell his engineering designs but was compelled to re-

aesthetic: responding to or being enthusiastic over the appreciation of artistic endeavors.

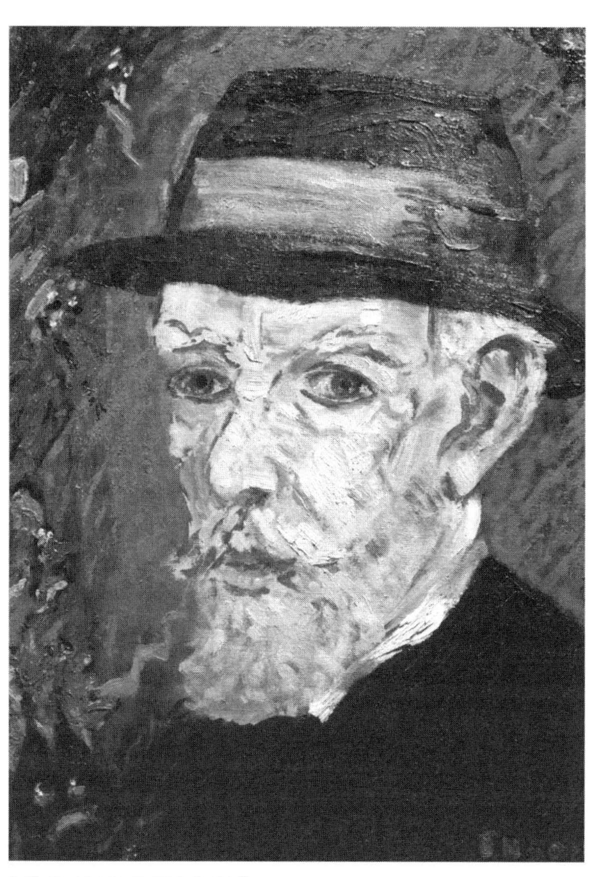

James Ensor, self-portrait, 1933

turn early, no deal in hand, because of the American Civil War. Upon his return he became the director of the family store, which he mismanaged into bankruptcy by 1875. Thenceforth he became an idle drunk, leaving his wife and her sister to revive the foundering business.

It was against this turbulent emotional background that young James's fascination with art began to blossom. He took his first private art lessons at the age of 13 and enrolled in art classes at the Ostend Academy at 16. By the time he entered the Académie Royale des Beaux Arts in Brussels at 17, Ensor was already producing landscapes of stunning maturity, as evinced in his early canvases *Dunes* and *Beach Hut* (1877). Loathing the formal constraints of academic training, Ensor returned to Ostend in 1880, where he remained, aside from a few minor side trips, for the rest of his life.

Ensor set up a studio in the attic of the family house. Although basically realistic, his work from the early 1880s verged on symbolism in uncannily bearing undercurrents of menace and oppression not suggested by the literal details of the paintings. Notable achievements of this period include *The Cabbage* (1880), *Afternoon in Ostend* (1881), *Middle-class Drawing Room* (1881), and *Woman in Distress* (1882). First shown in the early 1880s at two exhibitions in Brussels—one at the Chrysalide gallery and the other at the Cercle Artistique—Ensor's paintings were criticized for their "turpitude." Undaunted, Ensor ventured even further into experimentation with works that flirted with abstraction: *Man Seen from Behind* and *Two Figures in the Rain* merely suggest human figures amid rough patches of color. In the Turneresque *After the Storm (Rainbow)*, the wispiest hint of clouds and sails are the only recognizable objects in an otherwise nonfigurative haze of form and color.

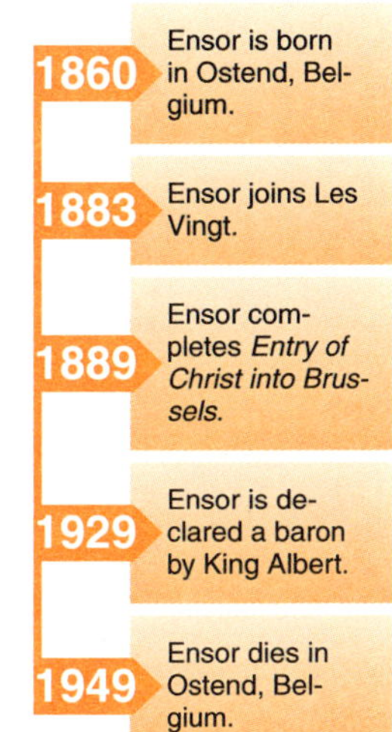

Spurned by the Brussels Salon in 1883, Ensor made common cause with the artistic rebels of Les Vingt (The Twenty). By the mid-1880s Ensor had reverted to figuration, but with a distinctly angular, foreboding aspect, using a scuffed brushstroke and garish color to realize a freedom of conception that set him apart from his contemporaries. Inspired by the Chinese theater masks sold in his sister's store, he evoked the hidden terrors of the human face in *Scandalized Masks* (1883), inaugurating a prolonged preoccupation with masks through which he conveyed what one critic called a "vision of humanity as sinister, jolly, and hollow."

Hampered by an ulcer, Ensor cut back on his output in the mid-1880s. He sought fresh inspiration in 1887 by traveling to London, where he is thought to have made a close study of Turner's work. The English influence was already apparent in *Brussels Town Hall* (1885), a notable example of Ensor's attunement to light, not merely in its aesthetic dimension but as a form of mystical revelation. "I have no children," he declared, "but light is my daughter, light one and indivisible, light, light, shed light on us! Breathe light into us, show us ways of attaining joy and happiness!"

Ensor's desperate investment in the revelatory powers of light was, perhaps, a counterforce to the morbidity of his life's enveloping emotional darkness, which inspired painted human figures and masks as grotesque as his landscapes were transcendent. According to a friend, "His mother, who was continually complaining about her husband, tried to set the son against the father." James Sr., long since lost to alcohol, died on a Brussels street in 1887. Devastated, Ensor called his father "truly a superior man, finally preferring to be drunk than to be like the rest of us."

His tenuous emotional foothold now further weakened, Ensor took refuge in paintings of an increasingly funereal tone, haunted by whispers of death. *Skeleton Studying Chinoiseries* portrays the withered form of an art connoisseur, while a self-portrait depicts skeletons squabbling over the remains of a hanged man. In *The Fall of the Rebellious Angels* (1889), Ensor evokes the advent of the human race as a ghoulish catastrophe. In the words of one critic, "Ensor succeeds in imbuing his entire painting with a veritable stench of carnality. It is simultaneously a condemnation and a celebration of the event that made human life, to him, a sometimes intoxicating but mostly

"Ensor's masks conceal nothing: they are the visible signs of corrupted flesh and decaying moral values."
Richard Dorment, writer for *The Daily Telegraph*, on Ensor's work

vicious hell." Such unavailing bleakness aroused extremes of invective and adulation; the Belgian symbolist poet Fernand Séverin wrote that "the visions of the illiterate Ensor are more ridiculous than terrifying," while Alfred H. Barr, Jr., wrote, "indeed, at this moment of his career, Ensor was possibly the boldest living painter."

The work that prompted Barr's comment was *The Tribulations of St. Anthony* (1887), the first in a series of religious paintings that reflect Ensor's deepening spiritual concerns as well as his personal identification with the torment and vilification of Christ. The painting shows a man being attacked by a pack of devils. In *Sad and Broken, Satan and the Legions of Hell Tormenting Christ on the Cross* (1886), Christ's face is clearly Ensor's self-portrait. He repeats this device in his famous *Entry of Christ into Brussels* (1889), depicting a beleaguered Christ (the face, again, is clearly Ensor's own) ushered along past a mocking array of taunting, vile masks and the figure of Death in a correct bourgeois top hat. This painting outraged even the radicals of Les Vingt, who sought to expel him from their group but were thwarted by a single vote—Ensor's own.

Ensor's prolific but disturbing canvases enticed scant interest from the staid bourgeois collectors and dealers of the day. In desperation, Ensor offered to sell his entire output for the equivalent of $210 in 1893. Even at that humiliating price, he found no takers. Over the next decade, with the rise of modernism, the critical tide turned, and Ensor's genius was finally acknowledged in the art world. Unfortunately, by the early 1900s his vital creative energies had waned and, until his death in Ostend in 1949, he never produced anything to rival the masterworks of the 1880s. He was declared a baron by King Albert in 1929.

Ensor's tormented path to greatness is best traced through the shifting images of his face.

Ensor's tormented path to greatness is best traced through the shifting images of his face. Once portrayed by the artist himself as the haunted, haggard visage of a broken and reviled Christ figure, it has since been appropriated as the centerpiece of Belgium's 100-franc bill, the symbol of the bourgeois stability and convention against which Ensor fervently pitched his creative life. The works that were unsalable at $200 a century ago were the subject of a spectacular retrospective at the Beaux-Arts Museum in Brussels in 1999. Ensor doubtless would have found in such bitter ironies a fitting epitaph. ◆

Ernst, Max

APRIL 2, 1891–APRIL 1, 1976 ● SCULPTOR AND PAINTER

The German printmaker, sculptor, and painter Max Ernst was a leading figure in dadaism and surrealism, two radical cultural movements of the 20th century that redefined the very notion of art. An early specialist in collage who then moved on to frottage and sculpture, Ernst tapped the power of unconscious association to create startling images that "continue to detonate in the mind like unexploded land mines left on the old battlefield of modernism," in the words of the critic Robert Hughes.

Max Ernst was born on April 2, 1891, to a devout Catholic family in Brühl, Germany, near Cologne. Ernst remembered his

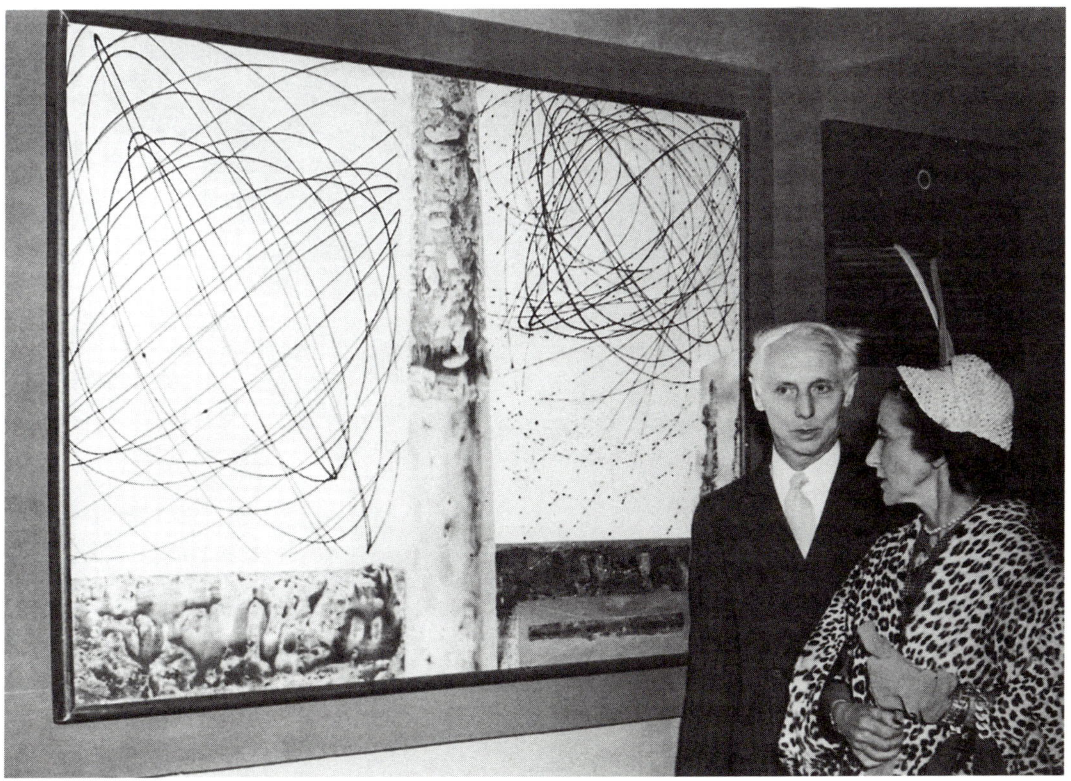

Max Ernst showing his work.

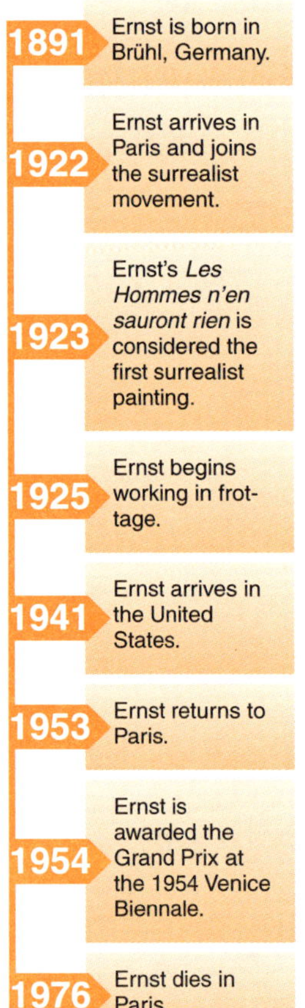

childhood as "marked by some dramatic incidents but was not particularly unhappy." Max's childhood interest in art was inspired in part by his father's amateur painting efforts, but he grew to despise the authoritarian piety of his father, a teacher of deaf schoolchildren. Ernst later located the source of his implacable radicalism in his fierce Oedipal enmity toward his father.

At his parents' behest Ernst entered the University of Bonn in 1909. He immersed himself in philosophy, art history, and psychology, drawing special inspiration from the works of Freud and Nietzsche. While there he encountered August Macke, with whose encouragement he began to turn out some early paintings. One of them, *Crucifixion*, was included in the Erster Deutscher Herbstsalon in 1913. Ernst left the university in 1912 to devote himself full time to painting, absorbing influences as a diverse as van Gogh and futurism. Not even his four-year stint in the German army derailed Ernst from his artistic ambitions; in 1916, while on leave, he managed to mount a show in Berlin along with Georg Muche.

Like other artists and intellectuals of his generation, Ernst was permanently radicalized by the mass carnage he witnessed during the war. In 1918 he married Louise Strauss, an art historian, and then dedicated himself to helping to launch the dadaist movement in Germany, especially in Cologne, where he settled from 1919 to 1922. By now an active collaborator with the movement's leading figures, such as Paul Eluard, Tristan Tzara, Jean Arp, and André Breton, Ernst began to develop the collage form that dominated the early period of his work. Eluard arranged for Ernst's collages to appear at a group show in Paris in 1921, and the two became so close that Ernst left his wife and child in Cologne in 1922 and moved in with the Eluards in Paris. While there, Ernst created numerous canvases suffused with dream imagery, many of which he drew from distant childhood memories. Highlights of this period include *Les Hommes n'en sauront rien* (*The men will never know*; 1923), considered by some critics to be the first true surrealist painting; *Elephant Celebes* (1921); *Pietà* or *Revolution by Night* (1923); and *Two Children Are Threatened by a Nightingale* (1924).

By 1925 the surrealists, seeking new methods for plumbing the depths of the unconscious, were experimenting with automatism, committing the word to the page or the image to paper or canvas without premeditation or conscious direction. It was this impulse that led to Ernst's development of frottage, placing a paper over an object. Ernst used floorboards, tiles, bricks, and so on, rubbing the paper with graphite to create various shapes and random images. His first collection of frottage drawings was *Histoire naturelle* (*Natural history*), shown in 1926, and he applied the technique in subsequent works such as the *Forest* series of paintings.

From 1929 to the late 1930s, Ernst reverted to the collage form. He began with the symbol-laden anti-narratives *La Femme 100 têtes* (*Woman [with] 100 heads;* a pun in French) a series of 124 captioned pictures—many of them culled from 19th-century magazines—and continued with *Rêve d'une petite fille qui voulut entrer au Carmel* (*Dream of a little girl who wanted to be a Carmelite;* 1930) and *Une Semaine de bonté* (*One week of goodness;* 1934). From the mid-1930s onward, as surrealism's radical impulses placed it at **loggerheads** with the reactionary fascist regimes in Germany and Italy, Ernst's collages grew more turbulent and abrasive, as in *Angel of Hearth and Home* (1937).

loggerheads: a condition or state of disagreement or debate between individuals and/or groups.

With the onset of World War II, Ernst was among the Germans detained by the French government, but he managed to escape to the United States in 1941. In New York he met the wealthy art patron Peggy Guggenheim, whom he eventually married, if rather briefly. Although he was an instant celebrity in New York's avant-garde circles, Ernst was not content to rest on his reputation and pressed forward in his experimentation with new expressive techniques. The most notable of these was dripping paint onto the canvas from a can swung above the canvas, a method later used to powerful effect by Jackson Pollock, a pioneer of abstract expressionism.

"What's the matter with everyone wanting to make a museum piece out of Dada? Dada was a bomb ... can you imagine anyone, around half a century after a bomb explodes, wanting to collect the pieces, sticking it together and displaying it?"

Max Ernst, and the influence that Dada had on his work

In 1953 Ernst returned to France with his new wife, the American painter Dorothea Tanning. Despite his declining output, Ernst's fame grew during the postwar years, culminating in the Grand Prix at the 1954 Venice Biennale. There were also major exhibitions of his work in the 1960s in New York, Cologne, and Stockholm; a major retrospective that traveled from New York to Paris in 1975; and another extensive retrospective exhibition was mounted in 1991.

Max Ernst died in Paris on April 1, 1976, one day short of his 85th birthday. ◆

Eyck, Jan van

c. 1380–July 9, 1441 ● Artist

According to 16th-century Ghent sources, Jan van Eyck trained under his brother Hubert, also an artist, and may have begun as a book illuminator. Jan is first documented in August 1422 in The Hague, already a mature artist serving John III, Count of Holland (John of Bavaria, ruled 1419–1425). In 1423 Jan became official court painter, with two assistants. No actual works from this period survive, although scholars speculate as to echoes of lost paintings in other pictures and drawings. The death of John III terminated Jan's employment. He is next recorded in Bruges, where on May 19, 1425, Philip the Good (ruled 1419–1467) engaged him as court painter and *varlet de chambre*, a post (also held by Jan at The Hague) denoting personal service to the ruler, but not predicated on the profession of an artist. This title designated its bearer as a member of the ruler's *familia*, extended to him valuable benefits including room, board, and medical services, and made him subject to the laws of the court rather than those of the city.

Jan van Eyck

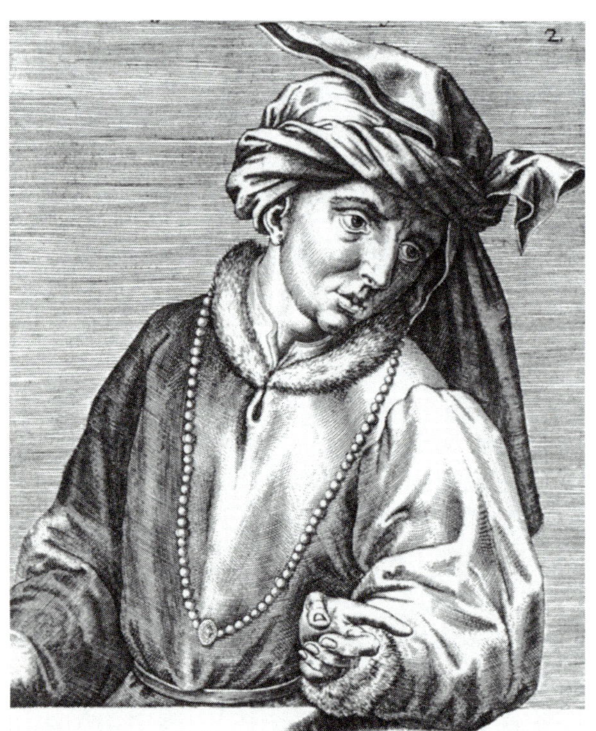

Jan's reputation was clearly established by this time, for Philip already knew of "his aptness in the art of painting" and counted on his loyalty and honesty. Throughout their association the duke greatly valued Jan and remunerated him generously. Indeed, when in 1435 the ducal exchequer sought to reduce Jan's salary and pension in accordance with a general program of austerity, Philip dispatched a stern letter ordering prompt and full payment, for he "would never find a man equally to his liking nor so outstanding in his art and science." Reciprocally, the prestige of his employer enhanced Jan's renown domestically and internationally.

Jan's service under Philip entailed frequent travels, both between numerous ducal residences and abroad on diplomatic missions. He worked in Lille on the newly built ducal palace from 1425 until at least 1428; in Bruges from 1431 until his death; at Hesdin in 1432; and in Brussels in 1433. His only unequivocally documented foreign journey, from October 1428 to December 1429, took him to the Iberian Peninsula as part of an embassy negotiating marriage between Philip the Good and Isabella of Portugal. Jan was required to paint a portrait of Isabella for Philip's approval (a standard practice for dynastic marriages). While waiting for the **ducal** reply, the ambassadors made a pilgrimage to Santiago de Compostela and paid visits to several rulers on the Iberian Peninsula. As a *varlet de chambre*. Jan was not merely a craftsman, but also a **courtier,** and traveled as such. Ducal accounts record several "secret missions to distant lands" undertaken by Jan on Philip's behalf. As a courtier, moreover, Jan could travel on assignments unrelated to art: on August 26, 1426, he was paid for performing a certain pilgrimage in Philip's name. However, Jan's travels to Italy and the Holy Land, proposed by many scholars, are conjectural.

ducal: of or relating to a duke or dukedom.

courtier: an individual in the attendance of a royal court.

Jan executed a variety of projects for the duke, as well as for private patrons in court circles. He decorated Philip's residences, and probably participated in staging lavish festivities on such occasions as the wedding of Philip and Isabella, and the tournament between Philip and the duke of Bedford held in Lille in June 1427. He also served as an agent in procuring works of art and services of other masters: in 1439 he hired Jean Creve of Bruges to pain gold initials in a book for Philip, and in 1441 he bought the duke some paintings. In 1435, moreover, Jan gilded and painted six statues and tabernacles for the facade of the town hall of Bruges. His paintings ranged from portraits of his employers, to religious pictures, to scenes of women bathing, and merchants going over their accounts (the latter two lost, but recorded in Italian collections), as well as *Mappamundi* (that is, a map of the world), which he probably produced in collaboration with a cartographer at Philip's court. Most of these works do not survive, but those that do often bear Jan's signature. He was almost unique among his contemporaries in signing his paintings, usually in Latin, and frequently including his motto *Als Ich Can*, apparently punning on his name (and possibly playing on a common medieval scribal phrase, "As I was able, but not as I wished"), which seems simultaneously to signal humility and pride.

Jan's works for members of Philip's entourage are those best known today, for they alone are preserved. The *Virgin and Child with Chancellor Rolin* (c. 1435) was commissioned by the ducal chancellor for his family chapel at Autun; the *Portrait of Baudouin de Lannoy* (early 1430s) depicts the governor of Lille and one of the leaders of the embassy to Portugal; the *Arnolfini Betrothal* (1434) was painted for a member of the Italian colony in Bruges, traditionally identified as Giovanni Arnolfini, a Lucchese merchant who supplied most of Philip's silks and velvets—the identity of the sitters, however, was reconsidered in the late 20th century. (Not only are the double-portrait format and the narrative subject uncommon, but the painting also bears a florid, legalistic signature declaring "Jan van Eyck was here" on the back wall of the room—above the convex mirror, which reflects the interior backwards and reveals two witnesses in the doorway).

Anselm Adornes, a Genoese aristocrat in Bruges who was prominent in the civic and court affairs, purchased from Jan two pictures of *The Stigmatization of St. Francis* which he willed to his daughters in 1470. Georg van der Paele (d. 1443), canon of St. Donatian's in Bruges, commemorated his founding of a chaplaincy by commissioning a large painting of *Virgin and Child with SS. Donatian and George*, which included his portrait (1436). Jan also painted a *Portrait of His Wife, Margaretha* (1439).

Jan's fame resounded well outside the Burgundian territories.

Jan's fame resounded well outside the Burgundian territories. Indeed, the earliest eulogies of his art come from Italy, where his work was admired and sought after: Italian humanists, including Bartolomeo Fazio and Cyriac of Ancona, as well as 15th century inventories reveal that King Alfonso I of Naples, the Medici of Florence, the Este of Ferrara, Ottaviano della Carda at Urbino, and other Italian worthies eagerly collected Jan's paintings. In the 16th century Georgio Vasari ascribed to Jan the invention of oil painting. Actually, this technique had been employed since the Middle Ages, but Jan clearly took it to new levels of proficiency and refinement. By systematically layering multiple coats of tinted oil glazes, he created enamel-like surfaces that possessed both depth and translucency. The use of fine glazes also enabled him to blend brushstrokes to the point of imperceptibility, and to build up painted images gradually and in minute detail. In addition to oil painting Jan probably also used other media, including tempera and watercolors. He is, moreover, believed to have produced book illuminations.

Jan's work is distinguished by a meticulous depiction of the physical world: one can discern in his pictures individual hairs and highlights on jewels in the foreground, and entire cityscapes, landscapes, and a wealth of human activity rendered on an almost microscopic scale in the background. He paid particular attention to sumptuous display, presenting with striking tangibility the shimmer of costly textiles and metalwork, and rich architectural interiors furnished with marble columns, carved relief, pictorial tiles, and oriental carpets. His emphasis on the material opulence likely reflected the values and desires of his courtly clientele. The complexity of the visual world within Jan's paintings, and the combination of everyday details with religious allegories have given birth to the notion of "disguised symbolism," according to which every narrative element within these pictures—light effects, flora, architectural elements, gestures of characters—bears theological significance, which can be decoded with the help of contemporary texts. Numerous scholars have sought to uncover such "hidden" meanings in Jan's paintings.

Jan's work influenced artists both in the Netherlands and abroad in Germany, Italy, and Spain. Karel van Mander, the first historian of Netherlandish art, extolled Jan as the founder of northern **Renaissance** artistic tradition. He occupies this position in scholarly literature to this day. ◆

Renaissance: a period of time in Europe in which a cultural and intellectual rebirth took place during the fourteenth and fifteenth centuries, concentrated in Italy, Germany, and other European nations; the period was marked by a renewed interest in Greek and Roman art, design, and philosophy.

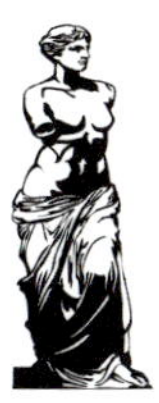

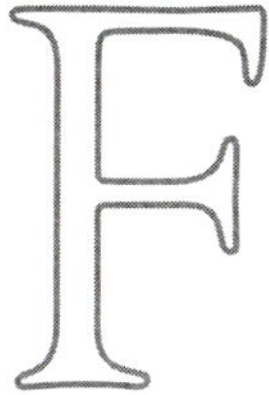

Fragonard, Jean-Honoré

APRIL 4, 1732–AUGUST 22, 1806 ● PAINTER

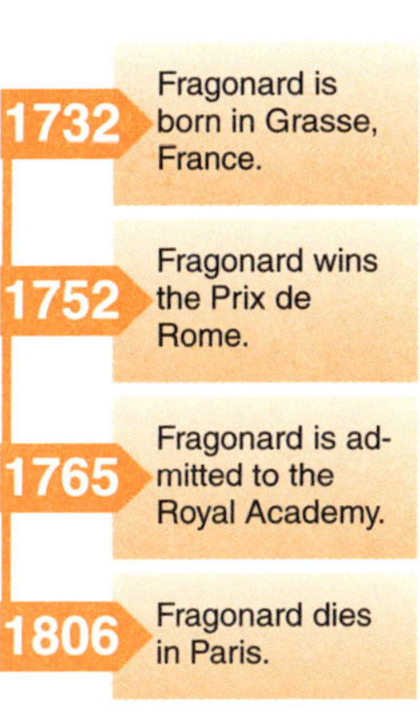

The 18th-century painter Jean-Honoré Fragonard was one of the leading exponents of the rococo style, an aesthetic whose buoyant hedonism and elaborate ornamentation dominated French painting and architecture during the reign of King Louis XV (1715–1774).

The son of an assistant glove maker, Fragonard was born in Grasse, France, on April 4, 1732, but spent most of his youth in Paris, where his family had moved when he was six years old. Fragonard's avid childhood sketching prompted his father to seek out an art apprenticeship for the boy, and he succeeded in placing him in the studio of Jean-Baptiste Chardin in 1748. Later that year Fragonard became the pupil of François Boucher, with whom he studied until 1752, when Boucher helped him to obtain the prestigious Prix de Rome grant from the Royal Academy of Painting and Sculpture. For the next four years, Fragonard, along with the cream of France's young artistic talent, studied under Carle Van Loo, the king's court painter, at the École des Élèves Protégés (School for Protected Children), which prepared students for study in Rome.

Having distinguished himself in the four-year program at the École, Fragonard was sent to Rome in 1756 for advanced study at the French Academy. Fragonard's penchant for independence did not endear him to the Academy's conservative faculty, but he made the most of his three years there, assiduously copying baroque masterpieces and making frequent

"Fragonard was probably the most versatile of the great masters of 18th-century French art."
John Elson, in Time magazine, February 15, 1988

sketching tours of the rural environs of Rome. With the expiration of his grant in 1761, Fragonard secured the patronage of the Abbé de Saint-Non, who took him and Hubert Robert, a fellow student at the Academy, on extensive sketching expeditions throughout Italy.

Fragonard returned to France in 1761 with a bounty of landscape paintings. A major historical canvas, *Corseus Sacrifices Himself to Save Callirhoe*, was widely acclaimed at that year's Salon and was sold to the royal court. That success earned him an important court commission for another historical canvas, which earned him admission to the Royal Academy in 1765 and a coveted studio in the Louvre. Resisting pigeonholing as a historical painter, however, Fragonard turned instead to landscapes, many of them in the romantic mode of idealized **pastoral** scenes that he conjured from his Italian sketches. He also turned out portraits, some of elderly men and others of aristocrats in outlandish attire or suggestive poses. Other works exhibit exuberantly sensual party scenes, such as *The Swing*, which depicts a beautiful woman, skirts aflutter as she guides a swing while under furtive observation by a male admirer hidden in the bushes.

pastoral: relating to shepards, herdsmen, and countryside images in an idealized form.

It was precisely the carefree hedonism and ripe carnality of such scenes that defined the aristocratic spirit of the rococo, which flourished in the middle and late years of the reign of Louis XV. But by the 1760s the rococo began to recede before an advancing tide of antiaristocratic sentiment compounded of rationalism in philosophy, republicanism in politics, and neoclassicism in the arts. The eminent encyclopedist Denis Diderot denounced Fragonard's work as frivolous and lacking in self-respect. Nevertheless, Fragonard's work remained popular among aristocratic patrons and afforded him sufficient financial security to allow him to marry Marie-Anne Gérard in 1769.

The following year Fragonard was chosen by Louis XV's mistress, the Comtesse du Barry, to contribute four large paintings to her new chateau, the Pavilion de Louvecinnes. Collectively entitled *Loves of the Shepherds*, the individual panels bear titles that convey their romantic content: *Storming the Citadel*, *The Pursuit*, *The Declaration of Love*, and *The Lover Crowned*. Two years later he undertook another major decorative project for a renowned actress of the day, Madeleine Guimard. But these works met with a mixed reception among connoisseurs already attuned to the more Spartan sensibility of neoclassicism.

In 1772 Fragonard made an extended journey to the Low Countries, in part to make a close study of the portraiture of Hals and Rembrandt. The following year he returned to Italy, spending a year indulging his penchant for landscape sketching. Back in Paris in 1775, he painted some of his most highly regarded landscapes, most notably *Fête at Saint-Cloud*. In the late 1770s he completed a flurry of work on blissful domestic scenes (*The Happy Family*, *The Schoolmistress*). Many of these works centered on fetching young women, a fixation most likely inspired by his ripening passion for his wife's 14-year-old sister, who had moved in with the Fragonards in 1775.

Late in the 1770s and 1780s Fragonard did attempt to adapt to the growing taste for neoclassical themes and styles, but his efforts in this direction were halting and stilted, lacking the natural fluency and grace of his earlier work. After the French Revolution in 1789, Fragonard's intimate association with the ancien regime rendered him a **pariah** in Paris, and he retreated to the safety of Grasse in 1790.

pariah: an individual outcast from society for criminal or immoral actions as deemed by that society.

Under the protective aegis of the impeccably republican neoclassicist painter Jean-Louis David, Fragonard returned to Paris the following year and was appointed to a post with the commission of establishing a new national museum. But renewed political turmoil cost Fragonard this job in 1797.

Thereafter there was little demand for his work, and Fragonard all but ceased painting. He died in poverty in Paris on August 22, 1806. It was not until the late 19th century that Fragonard's work was recognized as one of the great achievements in the history of French art. ◆

della Francesca, Piero

c. 1412–October 12, 1492 ● Painter

Piero della Francesca was the second born but eldest surviving son of Benedetto di Piero dei Franceschi of Borgo San Sepolcro, a small town in Tuscany (now called Sansepolcro), and his wife, Romana. The date of della Francesca's birth is estimated from the fact that his parents' marriage contract is dated 1410. His date of death is known from the record of his burial in the Badia at Borgo (October 12, 1492). The family surname was properly dei Franceschi, but the form della

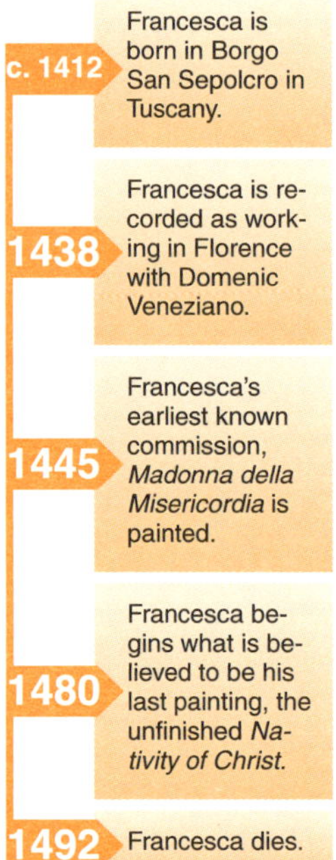

Francesca, by which (following Giorgio Vasari) Piero is generally known, was used by Piero's grandfather, also called Piero di Benedetto. The explanation of the feminine form given by Vasari—that the boy was brought up by his widowed mother—may apply to this della Francesca. The painter's mother died in 1459, about 14 years before his father. Throughout his life, della Francesca spent a considerable amount of time in Borgo San Sepolcro; he owned property both in the town and nearby. His fresco *The Resurrection of Christ* was painted for the town hall (now the Museo Civico of Sansepolcro).

We have no direct information about della Francesca's early education. Studies of educational practices during the appropriate period indicate that he might have attended an "abacus school," one of the schools set up to teach mathematics to boys who intended to pursue a career in, for example, commerce or banking. Della Francesca's father was a moderately prosperous merchant, and della Francesca seems to have maintained connections with the family firm throughout his life, so it is not surprising that the kind of mathematics in his treatises closely resembles what was taught in abacus schools. However, it is possible that della Francesca was taught by a private tutor. His autograph, marginal comments in Latin manuscripts of his perspective treatise, and his apparently active collaboration in making the Latin version from the vernacular original, suggest strongly that he was able to read some Latin. No specimen of della Francesca's handwriting is known from his early years, but his later style, a highly legible humanistic cursive with more than enough character for easy identification, suggests contact with the learned tradition of the day. Della Francesca was apprenticed to Antonio da Anghiari, a local painter about whose style nothing is known. In 1438, della Francesca is recorded as working in Florence with Domenico Veneziano. By then della Francesca was no longer an apprentice.

Vasari tells us della Francesca wrote "many" mathematical treatises. Three are now known: *Trattato d'abaco* (Abacus treatise), *Libellus de quinque corporibus regularibus* (Short book on the five regular solids), and *De prospective pingendi* (On perspective for painting). Their dates of composition are uncertain. The *Trattato,* in Tuscan and probably composed before 1460, is dedicated to a member of the Picchi family of Arezzo, a whose wish the dedicatory letter says the work was written. It is an ideal version of the textbooks used in abacus schools, dealing with elementary arithmetic, algebra, and geometry. Instruction proceeds by a series of worked examples, with almost no discursive text. The algebra includes very advanced examples, and there is far more geometry than was usual in textbooks, including three-dimensional examples. Both the algebra and the geometry of the *Trattato* are "state of the art." Some of the problems found in the *Trattato* appear in a neater or more developed form in the *Libellus,* which survives in a single Latin copy (probably translated from della Francesca's vernacular original), dedicated to Guidobaldo da Montefeltro (1472–1508). It thus seems that the *Libellus,* which is almost entirely concerned with geometry, was written after the *Trattato.* Between them, the *Trattato* and the *Libellus* describe six of the "Archimedean solids" (polyhedra with regular faces of more than one kind which meet in the same way at each corner of the solid). Della Francesca seems to have rediscovered six solids.

De prospectiva pingendi, the earliest known work on the mathematics of perspective, was written in the vernacular, but the Latin title is found in all manuscripts. The **treatise** is divided into three books. The first deals with basic **theorems** and then with plane problems, such as how to construct the perspective image of a regular hexagon. The second considers prisms, erected on the bases formed by the figures in the first book, so that we have, for example, a hexagonal wellhead. The method of construction employed in della Francesca's first two books is close to, but not identical with, that described by Leon Battista Alberti (1404–1472) in *De pictura* (*On painting;* 1435). The third book employs a different method to draw perspective images of more complicated shapes, such as the human head. This method effectively constructs the lines of individual "visual rays," using front and side views and sections of the solids. All della Francesca's examples are presented in full detail, as a series of drawing instructions. The text is tremendously repetitive. Comparing the examples proposed with known works by della Francesca, it seems that *De prospectiva pingendi* was probably completed in the late 1460s.

treastise: a thorough and complete exposition of in writing that includes a discussion of facts and principles in a methodical fashion.

theorems: statements, formulas, or propositions in mathematics or logical deduction.

We know only a rather small number of commissions for paintings. Della Francesca never ran a workshop. He probably did not rely exclusively upon his painting for his livelihood but drew income from the family business.

Della Francesca's earliest known commission, apart from a painting on a ceremonial candle, was for the **polyptych** *Madonna della Misericordia* (1445), but the panels seem in fact to

polyptych: a painting that is arranged in four or more panels which are folded or hinged together.

have been painted in the period 1460–1462, after he had started work on his major fresco cycle. *The Legend of the True Cross* (1455–1466). Part of the difficulty that scholars find in dating della Francesca's works may be due to his habit of working slowly. He is said to have used cloths to keep the plaster wet so that he could work on frescoes over a longer time. The Arezzo frescoes employed egg tempera and oils as well as standard fresco colors. Infrared reflectograms of both panel paintings and frescoes show extensive use of detailed underdrawings. These are strong evidence that the painstaking methods described in his perspective treatise were part of della Francesca's practice as a painter.

All della Francesca's works show a complete absorption of the new classicizing manner of his Florentine predecessors, in particular the powerful figure style of Donatello (1386–1466) and Masaccio (1401–c. 1428), and the concern with lighting of Domenico Veneziano and others. Della Francesca's work is also characterized by his skill in balancing composition in depth with composition in the picture plane, and by the extreme delicacy of his handling of detail. Lighting is often used to impose unity. The construction in depth is usually an art that hides art: there is very little explicit visible use of constructed perspective. The single exception is the small panel painting *The Flagellation of Christ* where it has proved possible to reconstruct a complete ground plan. In contrast, there are no construction clues in the portraits of Federigo da Montefeltro (1422–1482) and his wife, Battista Sforza (1446–1472), the parents of the dedicatee of della Francesca's *Libellus* or in his *Madonna di Sinigallia* (1469–1480). Della Francesca's last painting is believed to be the unfinished *Nativity of Christ* (1480s).

Vasari says that in his old age della Francesca lost his sight, but if this is true it must refer only to the painter's very last years, since we have an autograph draft of his will dated 1487.

There is evidence that the painter Luca Signorelli (c. 1450–1523) was della Francesca's pupil. On stylistic grounds, the same has been asserted of Melozzo da Forli (1438–1495) and others. Della Francesca never taught mathematics. Luca Pacioli (c. 1445–1517), who used della Francesca's *Trattato* extensively for his *Summa de arithmetica* (Treatise on arithmetic; Venice, 1494)—a work of great historical importance as the first printed algebra—probably came into possession of della Francesca's manuscripts after the painter's death. A vernacular text of della

Francesca's *Libellus* appeared, without his name, in Pacioli's *De divina proportione* (On divine proportion: 1509).

Della Francesca's reputation as a painter declined quickly, overtaken by changes of taste in the 16th century. Art historians rediscovered him in the early 20th century. The perceived formality of his work harmonized with current concern with abstract qualities in art. Unfortunately, this linkage has encouraged persistence in the anachronistic 1920s practice of drawing complicated mathematical figures over reproductions of della Francesca's pictures, implying that these figures "explain" the composition. Della Francesca's posthumous reputation as a mathematician mainly rested on his perspective treatise. Up to 1600, all perspective treatises show substantial traces of his work. Daniele Barbaro (1513–1570) incorporated large parts of it, sometimes verbatim, into his *La pratica della perspettiva* (The practice of perspective; Venice, 1568, 1569). Like Pacioli's *Summa*, this work was widely read and very influential. However, della Francesca's mathematical afterlife contained a large dash of anonymity. Only in the last 20 years or so has it become clear that he is in fact an important figure in the history of mathematics. ◆

Della Francesca's reputation as a painter declined quickly, overtaken by changes of taste in the 16th century.

Freud, Lucian

DECEMBER 8, 1922– ● PAINTER

The British painter and draughtsman Lucian Freud has been hailed as "the best realist painter alive" by the influential critic Robert Hughes. The scion of a great intellectual and cultural estate—his father was the architect Ernst Freud and his grandfather the founder of psychoanalysis, Sigmund Freud—Lucian Freud was an artist of modest repute until the 1980s. Since then, his unavailingly probing nude portraits of his friends and relatives—though still controversial—have elicited wider appreciation from critics and the public.

A scrupulously private man, Freud has seen his reputation flourish with minimal self-promotion. He was born on December 8, 1922, in Berlin, where his father was a prominent architect. After the Nazis took power in 1933, the Freud family took refuge in England. Lucian's early education was at Dart-

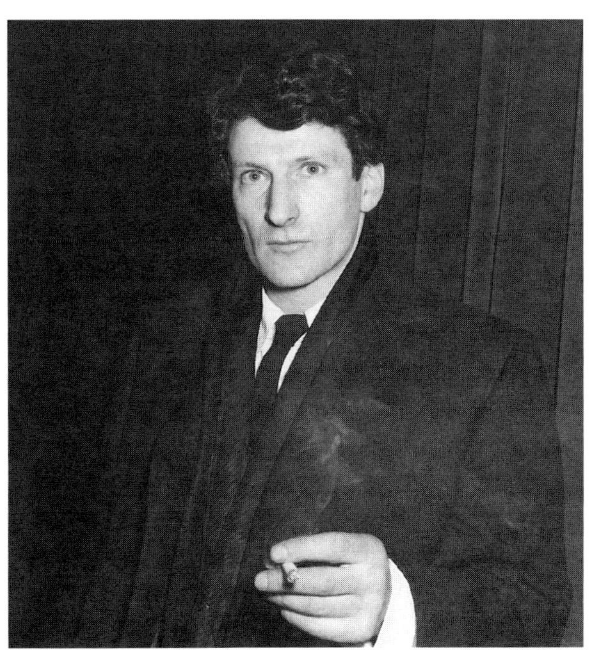

Lucian Freud

ington Hall, popular with avant-garde exiles from the continent, and Bryanston, a progressive school whose students came mostly from the artistically inclined haut bourgeoisie. Determined to become an artist from his early youth, Freud began attending art schools in the late 1930s, including the Central School of Arts and Crafts and Cedric Morris's East Anglian School of Painting and Drawing in Dedham, the rural area that inspired the landscapes of John Constable. Freud became an English citizen in 1939 while studying in Dedham.

Morris's tutelage seems to have consisted not so much in steering Freud toward a particular school but rather in helping him to find his own unique style. Freud attained early renown both for his obstreperousness and talent: he inadvertently set the school ablaze with a cigarette; and, in 1939, *Horizon*, an avant-garde journal of the arts, published his self-portrait. Despite such recognition—or perhaps because of it—Freud grew restive in the rural confines of Dedham and abruptly left the school in April of 1941 to sign up with the Merchant Navy. After a three-month stint, he sporadically resumed his studies at the East Anglian school at its new home in Hedleigh in Suffolk. In 1943 Freud rented an apartment/studio in the Delamere Terrace area of Paddington, where he remained for three decades, working its inner-city grit into his often brooding canvases, which led to his characterization by the critic Herbert Read as "the Ingres of **existentialism.**"

existentialism: a twentieth century philosophical movement centering on the study of the individual's existence in an endless universe and the acts of the individual who assumes responsibility for his acts without the knowledge of what is right and wrong.

After the war Freud made an art-study tour of the continent, spending the fall of 1946 in Paris and then moving on to a long sojourn in Greece. He then returned to London, where he married Kitty Garman (daughter of the controversial artist Jacob Epstein) in 1948. It was during this period that his mature style began to crystallize after an earlier flirtation with surrealism, evident in efforts such as *Painter's Room* (1943), with its odd juxtapositions of disparate objects and images. There are strains of neo-romanticism in his 1952 portrait of John Minton.

But it was in his portraits of his wife—most notably *Girl with Roses* (1947–48)—that he began to work out the distinctive figurative style that he gradually extended to paintings of his fellow artists, friends, relatives, and his children, most of whom he portrayed in the nude. *Interior in Paddington* (1951)—a vivid evocation of a prototypical angry young man of Britain's postwar generation—and *Girl with a White Dog* (1951) are additional landmarks in the emergence of Freud's probing visual meditations. His work from the early 1950s brought him his first official recognition in the form of the Arts Council purchase prize from the 1951 Festival of Britain. From 1949 to 1954 he lent his talents as a visiting tutor at the Slade.

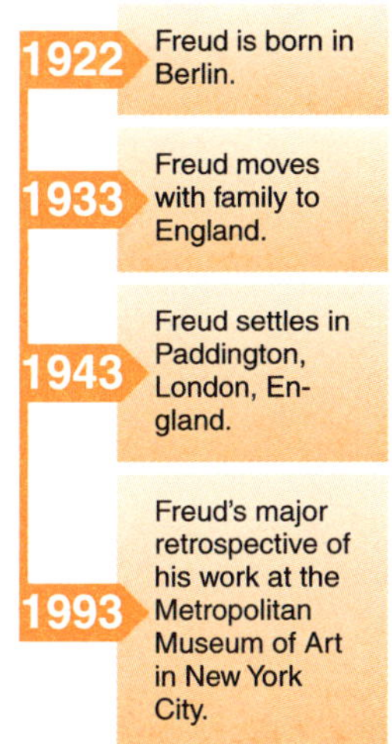

Freud's penchant for remorselessly honest portrayals of his intimates achieved an even more compelling mode of expression in the late 1950s, as he abandoned the smooth surface of his earlier work and achieved a ruder immediacy through the use of stiffer brushes and freer brushtstrokes. As Hughes has written, "This 'Freud effect' is not unlike the quick, coarse expressiveness of Frans Halls, but less benign." One notable early example of this later technique is *Pregnant Girl* (1960–61). In its later manifestations, the technique yields refinements of detail at once exquisite and discomfiting, as in *Paddington* (1970–72), *Two Plants* (1977–80), and *Reflections (Self-Portrait)* (1987).

In 1943 Freud rented an apartment/studio in the Delamere Terrace area of Paddington, where he remained for three decades, working its inner-city grit into his often brooding canvases, which led to his characterization by the critic Herbert Read as "the Ingres of existentialism."

The canvases of the 1980s are more imposing and ambitious in scale, many of them featuring his sisters, mother, and daughters. The anatomical starkness of his portraits have roused the indignation of feminist critics. Freud has replied succinctly to such criticisms: "I think the idea of misogyny is a stimulant to feminists, and it's rather like anti-Semites looking for Jewish noses everywhere." Another critic has commented: "The unclothed single figure, female or—increasingly, in the last few years—male, is not only Freud's specialty. It is also the best conduit for his formidable sense of worry about the vulnerability of flesh."

Freud's work was the subject of a major exhibition at the Metropolitan Museum of Art in New York City in 1993. ◆

Friedrich, Caspar David

SEPTEMBER 5, 1774–MAY 7, 1840 ● PAINTER

Solitary and brooding, tormented by personal tragedies, the German painter and printmaker Caspar David Friedrich personified the 19th-century romantic philosophy he helped to pioneer with his emotionally charged, spiritually fraught landscapes. Although a meticulous observer of nature, Friedrich viewed his paintings as more lamp than mirror: he portrayed the sky and earth as metaphors for the divine, the language in which God summons humans to their spiritual destiny. As one critic put it, "This is German Romanticism with all the stops pulled out; this is Beethoven and *The Sufferings of Young Werther* rolled into one."

The son of a wealthy manufacturer, Caspar David Friedrich was born in Greifswald, Pomerania, Germany, on September 5, 1774. His early years were marred by crushing personal losses that haunted him throughout life, accounting in part for the tormented mysticism that pervaded his paintings. When he was seven, his mother died. Six years later, while he and his brother were skating, his brother suffered a fatal accident for which Caspar always blamed himself.

A painting of Caspar David Friedrich at work.

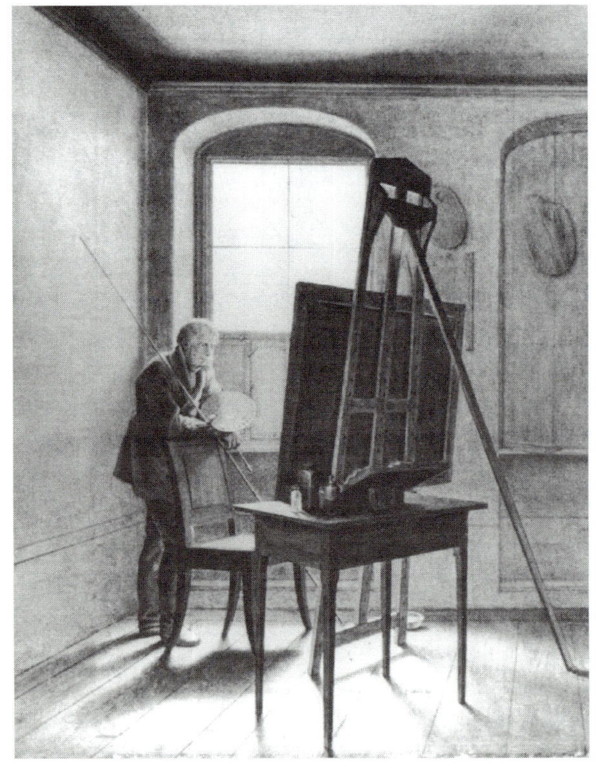

Privately educated for most of his childhood, Caspar began studying drawing in 1788 and at the age of 16 began a four-year course of study with Johann Gottfied Quistorp. When he was 20 years old, Friedrich enrolled at the Akademi for de Skønne Kunster in Copenhagen, Denmark, a school known for favoring the progressive philosophy of drawing from nature rather the traditional approach of emulating the work of the Old Masters. While there, Friedrich was strongly influenced by Jens Juel, a landscape specialist, and Nocolai Abraham Abilidgaard, whose devotion to Nordic mythology helped to ignite Friedrich's romantic leanings.

After completing his studies in Copenhagen in 1798, Friedrich stopped briefly in Berlin before moving to Dresden, which became his permanent home. Following a course of study in life drawing at the Hochsschule der Bildenden Künste, Friedrich showed his works publicly for the first time at the school's 1799 exhibition. His early paintings, sketches, and etchings are mostly landscapes; although derivative of his teachers' styles, they are already layered with the inchoate symbols that emerged more fully in his mature work.

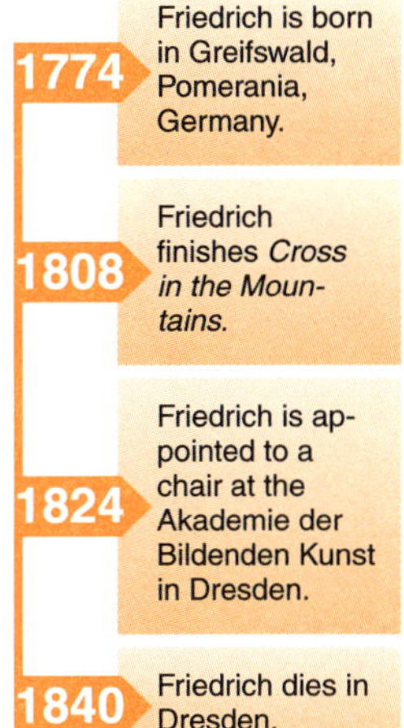

In 1801–02, during a year-long stay in Greifswald, Friedrich traveled to the island of Rügen, where he executed several monochromatic landscapes in the sepia style reminiscent of Adrian Zingg. These sketches caught the notice of the renowned German writer Goethe and earned him a prize at the 1805 Weimarer Kunstfruende exhibit. During this period Friedrich seems to have fallen under the influence of the prominent landscape painter Philipp Otto Runge, who lived in Dresden from 1803 to 1805 while painting his *Times of Day* series.

Working in oils after 1807, Friedrich began to develop his signature style, as evidenced in *Cross in the Mountains* (1807–08) whose imposing scale and sweeping pantheistic conception seemed a visual realization of the romantic. The painting's transcendental auguries did not sit well with the entrenched classicists of the critical establishment, however. F. W. B. von Ramdohr doubted that "it is a good idea to use landscape allegorically to represent a religious concept or even to arouse a sense of reverence," adding: "It is the greatest arrogance when landscape painting seeks to worm its way into the churches and crawl onto the altars."

But the romantic genie was out of the bottle. Spurred rather than dampened by the fierce critical controversy it sparked, Friedrich's work helped to spawn a movement that transformed modes of thought, perception, and feeling throughout Germany and Europe. His own devotion to romantic ideals was unshakable—he wrote, "The noble man (artist) recognizes good in everything.... Shut your corporeal eye so that you first see your picture with your spiritual eye. Then bring to light that which you saw in darkness so that it may reflect on others from the exterior to their spiritual interior." Friedrich's visionary gleam is evident in other notable canvases

"[Friedrich] is now considered the most important German painter of the nineteenth century."
John Zeaman, art critic, on Caspar David Friedrich

from this period, including *Mountain Landscape with a Rainbow* (1810) and *Morning in the Riesengebirge* (1810–11).

After the French occupiers were driven out of Dresden in 1814, Friedrich expressed his ardent patriotism in *On the Sailing Ship* (1813–14) and *Two Men Contemplating the Moon* (1819). Both paintings feature figures in traditional Germanic attire, a fashion popular with the young pro-republican students of the day. In fact, figures began to assume a more significant role in his landscapes as well, as in *Wanderer in a Sea of Fog* (1818) and *Woman at a Window* (1822). But the figures in Friedrich's paintings always seem archetypal rather than specific, tenuously embodied spirits rather than flesh-and-blood human beings. Some critics have made the same point about his rendering of nature. In John Zeaman's words, "Despite his Romanticism and his love of nature, the world of Friedrich's paintings is a curiously artificial one. The figures look like porcelain statues. Objects—even mountains—seem weightless and insubstantial. His execution is as dry and as tightly controlled as Andrew Wyeth's. Nothing of nature's randomness gets into this geometric compositions.... His approach to art was essentially literary. He never found a painterly equivalent for what he was trying to express."

Friedrich was appointed to a chair at the Akademie der Bildenden Kunst in Dresden in 1824 but suffered a profound disappointment when he was passed over as the academy's landscape teacher after Klengel's death that year. As Friedrich's style gradually fell out of critical favor through the 1820s and 1830s, his health and output began to decline, although he still managed to turn out works of great power, such as *Great Enclosure* (1832) and *Stages of Life* (1835). Temporarily disabled by a stroke in 1835, Friedrich returned to sepia painting for his remaining years.

anachronism: an individual or idea whose time has past and is considered severely and drastically outdated.

At his death on May 7, 1840, Friedrich was already an **anachronism,** mourned only by his closest friends and relatives. His work was rediscovered early in the 20th century by the Norwegian scholar Andreas Aubert, after which it won renewed admiration among a generation attuned to the emotional complexity of expressionism. Friedrich's work was also championed by the Nazi regime in Germany, which considered his landscapes a unique expression of what it saw as the exalted mission of the German *volk*. Despite the taint of Nazi approbation, Friedrich's achievement is held in high regard by contemporary critics and scholars. ◆

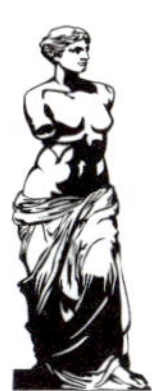

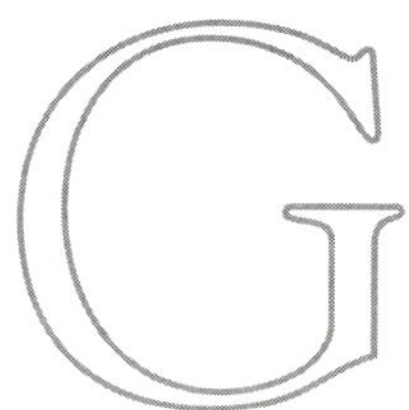

Gainsborough, Thomas

May 14, 1727–August 2, 1788 ● Painter

Although he became famous for his portraits, Thomas Gainsborough much preferred to paint the landscapes that first drew him to art as a young man. A founding member of the Royal Academy in 1768—the only provincial painter so honored—he came to rival Sir Joshua Reynolds as the preferred portraitist of British aristocracy of the late 18th century.

Baptized on May 14, 1727, in Sudbury, Suffolk, England, Thomas Gainsborough was the youngest of nine children of John Gainsborough, a prosperous cloth merchant. While a student at Sudbury Grammar School, Thomas showed extraordinary artistic gifts, especially at drawing landscapes. At the age of 13, Thomas convinced his father to send him to London to study with the influential French illustrator and engraver Hubert Gravelot, who schooled him in the rococo style just then coming into fashion. His other early London activities included assisting Francis Hayman in creating decorative paintings for Vauxhall Gardens, and copying and restoring landscapes of Dutch masters.

Gainsborough's early struggles to establish himself in the London art world were eased by his marriage, in 1746, to Margaret Burr, an **illegitimate** daughter of the Duke of Beaufort. The union afforded Gainsborough emotional security and an annual income of 200 pounds. The couple settled in Sudbury, where Gainsborough indulged his passion for landscape art. His

illegitimate: description of a child born out of wedlock.

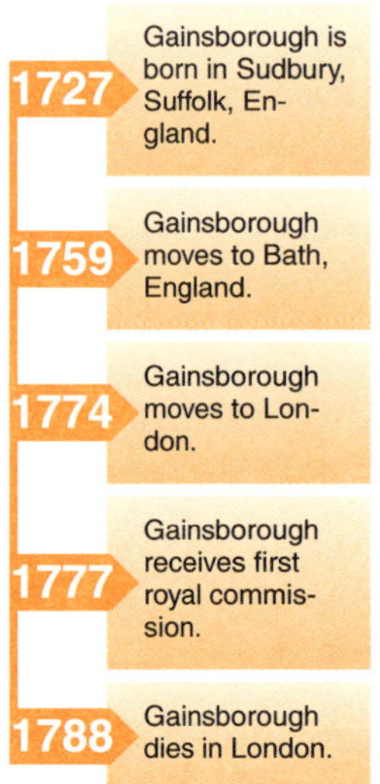

earliest influences were the Dutch landscape specialists Jan Wynants and Jacob van Ruisdael—the latter's influence is especially evident in *Cornard Wood* (1748). Many of his early landscapes are so fanciful and inventive that most scholars contend that he painted as much from his imagination as from direct observation.

By 1748 Gainsborough's growing reputation secured him a coveted invitation, along with England's other leading artists, to contribute a painting to London's Foundling Hospital. The resulting work, *The Charterhouse*, is typical of the imaginative rococo flair Gainsborough brought to his early work, other notable examples of which are *Mr. and Mrs. Robert Andrews* (1749) and *Henéage Lloyd and His Sister* (1750).

In 1752 Gainsborough, his wife, and two daughters (born in 1748 and 1752) moved to the seaside town of Ipswich. After seven years there Gainsborough had exhausted the possibilities for local patronage. Seeking a larger, more prosperous clientele, in 1759 he relocated to Bath, a spa resort frequented by the rich and well-born. He was soon surfeited with portrait commissions, but he persisted in his landscape work. While in Bath he acquainted himself with the work of Anthony van Dyck and Peter Paul Rubens, and their influence registered increasingly in his work.

Gainsborough's instant success at Bath emboldened him to make an assault on the London art world, then dominated by Sir Joshua Reynolds. Gainsborough sent his first painting to the London Society of Artists in 1761 and received his first review in a London newspaper a year later. After several well-received exhibitions of his work in London during the 1760s, in 1768 Gainsborough became the only provincial artist voted in as a founding member of the Royal Academy.

Spurred by his study of van Dyck and Rubens and by the expectations of his discerning patrons at Bath, Gainsborough began to turn out portraits that flattered and ennobled his subjects while retaining a playful vitality and inimitable spark of warmth. These distinctive qualities were enhanced, in part, by his insistence on executing his portraits in their entirety, without assistants—a rare practice in those days. Notable work from his late Bath period includes *Isabella Countess of Seton* (1769) and *The Blue Boy* (1770), one his most famous works, which appeared at the Royal Academy exhibition in 1770 under the title *A Young Gentleman*.

Rococo

The rococo style, which flourished during the reign of Louis XV of France (1715-1774), has no precise origin or founders. Rococo draws its name from the French *rocaille,* or "rock work," as in the stone decoration of garden grottoes and fountains. In architecture and decoration, the style is marked by elaborate curves and ornamentation, pastels, and asymmetrical design; in painting, by moving away from somber subjects and style (as in Louis XIV style) to light and playful styles. It is evident in the arabesque architectural designs of Pierre Le Pautre (as in the royal residence at Marly, 1699). One masterpiece of the style is the Hôtel de Soubise, Paris, decorated in part by René Alexis Delamaire and Gabriel Germain Boffrant. In painting, high notes include Jean Honoré Fragonard and François Boucher, whose robust, rose-pink nudes were very popular.

The popular rococo style later influenced art in other countries. In Germany and Austria, the marriage of rococo and baroque led to highly elaborate works of art, as in the Amalienburg Pavilion in Germany (1730s), a masterpiece of architect François de Cuvilliés, which explodes with beautiful ("feminine") plasterwork, mirrors, and filigree. In Britain, rococo had little influence on architecture. Britain's main rococo painters were Joshua Reynolds and Thomas Gainsborough; Gainsborough painted prolifically in portraits and landscapes.

Toward the end of the 18th century, rococo, which was associated with opulence, wealth, and privilege, gave way to the neoclassical style, perceived to be more democratic and "masculine"; the neoclassical style would become particularly strong in America and France after the revolutions there.

By 1774 Gainsborough was ready to make his move to London. That year he and his family moved to a section of Schomberg House in Pall Mall. Although Reynolds was already installed as the official court painter, Gainsborough's Tory sympathies helped him to find favor with George III, who in 1777 bestowed upon Gainsborough the first of many royal commissions, which eventually included a 1781 request to paint the king and queen. Although his reputation by now rested chiefly on his portrait work, Gainsborough returned frequently to his beloved landscapes, taking a sketching tour of the Lake District in 1783 to replenish his store of inspiration. He also began to experiment with printmaking techniques, principally soft-ground etching and aquatint. He even built a peep-show box for the candle-lit display of transparencies.

Gainsborough's growing wealth afforded him an added measure of artistic independence. After a dispute with the Royal Academy in 1784 over the mounting of his works, he

[Thomas Gainsborough] came to rival Sir Joshua Reynolds as the preferred portraitist of British aristocracy of the late eighteenth century.

forsook the academy's annual exhibitions and arranged his own. In Gainsborough's late landscape style a new-found freedom of conception and execution anticipate by a century the departures of impressionism and even border on abstraction, as in *Diana and Acateon* (1788), one of his few attempts to tackle a mythological theme.

The powers of empathy that animate Gainsborough's art were evident in his overall approach to life, which was, by most accounts, goodhearted and free of the petty snobbery that so often marked the social circles in which he traveled. In the words of the critic Michael Podger, "Gainsborough drew no distinction in terms of dignity between his agricultural labourers and his aristocratic patrons. It is in this instinctive morality that is perhaps the defining characteristic of his portraiture. In *The Morning Walk*, say, or *Mrs. Sheridan*, his subjects depicted in feathery strokes in a parkland setting, are distinguished not by their social rank but by their innate sensibility."

On his deathbed in 1788, Gainsborough sent a note to his arch-rival Reynolds asking for a last visit. He wrote: "I can from a sincere Heart say that I always admired and sincerely loved Sir Joshua Reynolds."

Thomas Gainsborough died in London on August 2, 1788. ◆

Gauguin, Paul

June 7, 1848–May 8, 1903 ● Painter

The French postimpressionist Paul Gauguin was "entitled, more than anyone else, to be called the creator of modern painting," according to his biographer David Sweetman. A bitter critic of Western industrial civilization, Gauguin journeyed to **rustic** outposts in France and to distant tropical islands to capture, in lushly colored flat images, the earthly delights and otherworldly inspirations of Edens that had eluded what for him were the spiritual toxins of modern materialism.

rustic: an individual who lives in a rural area or affects the behavior of an unsophisticated or coarse person.

The legend of Gauguin as modernist master—in no small measure self-perpetuated—arose not only from his groundbreaking paintings but also from his tumultuous life. Visionary artist, spiritual prophet, political revolutionary, restless traveler—these dramatic roles converge in art that one early critic called the "fantastic shadows in the forest of the enigma." He was the son of a radical republican journalist and a half-French, half-Peruvian mother. After the anti-republican Napoleon III assumed power in a coup d'etat, the Gauguins fled to Lima, Peru, in 1851. Paul's father died en route, and the family remained there for four years before returning to France to live in Orléans, where his mother supported Paul and his sister as a seamstress.

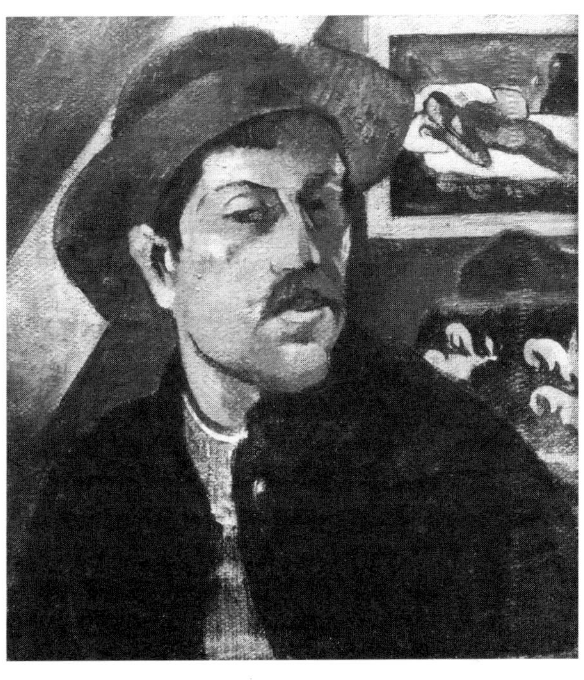

Paul Gauguin, *Self-Portrait With a Hat*, c. 1893

A rebellious and difficult student, Gauguin happily bid farewell to school at the age of 17 and spent the next six years sailing around the globe, first in the French merchant marine and then in the military. Back in Paris in 1871, Gauguin was taken under wing by his wealthy guardian, Gustave Arosa (Gauguin's mother had died four years earlier), whose large art collection sparked Gauguin's interest in painting. With the salary from his new job as a stockbroker and the proceeds from an inherited trust fund, Gauguin began not only to collect art but also to try his own hand at painting, taking sporadic instruction and working from a model at a studio.

Despite increasing family responsibilities—in 1873 he married a Danish woman, Mette Sophie Gad, who eventually bore him five children—Gauguin deepened his commitment to painting, taking lessons from professionals—including Pissarro during 1875–76—and devoting all his leisure hours to his canvases. His *Landscape under the Tree Canopy at Viroflay* was accepted for exhibition at the 1876 Paris Salon. Over the next five years he became fascinated with impressionism, studying and collecting works by its leading practitioners such as a Pissarro, Manet, Cézanne, and Monet. On Pissarro's recommendation, Gauguin became a member of the "Independents" (impressionists), and his work appeared at the annual impressionist exhibitions in 1880, 1881, and 1882 as he was refining his technique in continued studies with Pissarro and Cézanne.

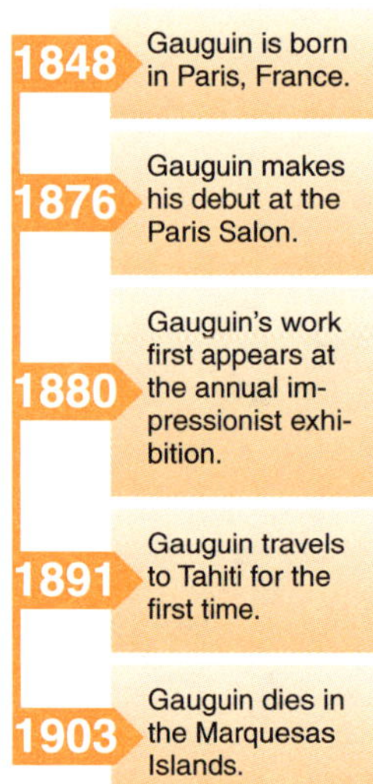

After the Paris stock market crashed in 1882, Gauguin lost his brokerage job. He moved with his wife and children to Rouen, where he supported his family as a sales representative, all the while pursuing his painting and making forays to the Spanish border to support the republican movement in Spain. His wife, dismayed by Gauguin's evident preference for art and politics over his domestic responsibilities, moved with her children to her hometown of Copenhagen. After a brief attempt to reconcile there in 1884, Gauguin and his wife separated, and he set out on the life of the restless artist/nomad, bouncing between odd jobs, living on the margins of an industrial commercial civilization he abhorred.

He careened from Panama to Martinique and, in 1888, back to France, settling for a time in Pont Aven, Brittany. There he worked with Emile Bernard, Paul Sérusier, Maurice Denis, and Charles Laval, a circle known as the School of Pont Aven (and later the Nabis), which admired the simple piety of the local peasants and their harmony with nature's rhythms. It was during his sojourn in Pont-Avon that Gauguin developed his aesthetic philosophy of synthetism, which stressed a flat, two-dimensional perspective and vibrant colors.

In October of 1888, Gauguin received a letter from Vincent van Gogh, whom he had met in Paris two years earlier, imploring Gauguin to work at a studio the two would share in Arles, in the south of France. Financially strapped, Gauguin was lured by a generous subsidy from Vincent's brother, Theo, and accepted the offer. At first the two thrived in collaboration, turning out more and better work than they ever had before. But within a few weeks, artistic exaltation yielded to personal turmoil as the volatile van Gogh hurtled toward the insanity that eventually resulted in his suicide. After van Gogh threatened him with a knife, Gauguin fled. Reflecting on those frenetic weeks in Arles, Gauguin later wrote, "But I owe something to Vincent, and that is, in the consciousness of having been useful to him, the confirmation of my own original ideas about painting. And also, at difficult moments, the remembrance that one finds others unhappier than oneself."

After his stormy interval with van Gogh, Gauguin was more intent than ever on realizing an art utterly shorn of artifice, a clear window on transcendent human perception and feeling. As he wrote in 1888: "Primitive art proceeds from the spirit and makes use of nature. The so-called refined art proceeds from sensuality and serves nature. Nature is the servant of the former and the mistress of the latter. She demeans man's spirit by allowing him to adore her. That is the way by which we have tumbled into the abominable error of naturalism." This was a self-conscious primitivism, dedicated to the expression of ideas and thus receptive to the symbolist doctrines that Gauguin absorbed from the poet Mallarmé and his followers. Gauguin's synthesis of the elemental and the symbolic is evident is such canvases as *The Vision after the Sermon*, *Bonjour Monsieur Gauguin*, and *The Yellow Christ* (1889).

"Civilization makes you suffer. Barbarism which is to me rejuvenation."

Paul Gauguin on where he found the inspiration to paint

By now hardened in his contempt for the regimentation and repression of "civilized" life, Gauguin left for Tahiti in 1891, heading up a government-sponsored study of life and customs there. Although captivated by the surroundings, he was also disillusioned by the rivalries among local groups and the meddling of French and local authorities. Nevertheless, he produced a stream of brilliant canvases recording the **primordial** rhythms of life there. He returned to France in 1893, and, after spending two more years there, returned to Tahiti to stay in 1895. Despite the increasing poverty, despair, and illness of his final years in Tahiti, Gauguin continued to turn out brilliant paintings such as *Nave Nave Mahana* (1896), and his masterwork, *Where Do We Come From? What Are We? Where Are We Going?* (1897–98).

primordial: the earliest formed growth of an individual, movment, or society.

Increasingly isolated and tormented by the ravages of syphilis, Gauguin attempted suicide in 1897. In 1901 he moved to the Marquesas Islands, where he remained until he died, alone, in 1903. ◆

Gentileschi, Artemisia

JULY 8, 1593–1653 ● PAINTER

Of the handful of women artists who achieved international stature in the Renaissance, Artemisia Gentileschi stands out for her progressive style, ambitious thematic range, and overtly feminist expression. Gentileschi was born in Rome and trained in printing by her father, Orazio Gentileschi. She adopted Caravaggio's dramatic realism and strong chiaroscuro lighting but departed from his and other models in her preference for themes featuring biblical and historical women and in her humanizing and heroizing of female

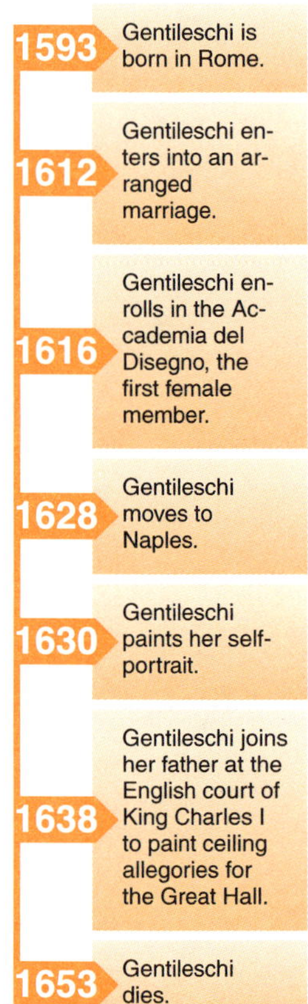

characters. In her first signed painting, *Susanna and the Elders* (1610), Gentileschi presented the heroine as a protesting victim of the lustful Elders. She constructed the first of four interpretations of the Judith theme (1612–1613) as the gory decapitation of a helpless Holofernes by two powerful and determined women.

Gentileschi's rare ability to dramatize credibly the acts and emotions of women was grounded in her experience of sexual intimidation. In March 1612 Orazio sued the painter Agostino Tassi, hired to teach Gentileschi perspective, for the rape of his daughter. The seven-month trial resulted in Tassi's conviction and light punishment and Gentileschi's arranged marriage to a Florentine artist in late 1612. In her eight-year stay in Florence, Gentileschi received commissions from Michelangelo Buonarroti the Younger, contributing *The Allegory of Inclination* (1615–1617) to a gallery glorifying his famous great-uncle, and from Grand Duke Cosimo II de Medici, for whom she painted a replica of her Naples *Judith* (c. 1620), a *Penitent Magdalen* (1617–1620), and other works.

Gentileschi's interest in female characters, fortified by her insider knowledge of female anatomy, was encouraged by her patrons, who typically regarded women artists and their paintings of women as twin specimens of female beauty. In 1616 Gentileschi matriculated in the Accademia del Disegno, becoming the first female member of the prestigious Florentine academy. She befriended Galileo Galilei, then court mathematician to the grand duke; subtle tributes to the famous astronomer have been found in two of her pictures.

Gentileschi returned to Rome around 1620 and is recorded in 1624 (presumably already separated from her husband) as head of a household that included a daughter and two servants. Lacking access to large church commissions, Gentileschi found important private patrons. Her paintings were purchased or commissioned by the Genoese nobleman Pietro Gentile (*Cleopatra*, *Lucretia*), the Roman collector Vincenzo Giustiniani (*David*, lost), and the sitter who ordered her only surviving portrait (*Gonfaloniere*, 1622). After returning to Rome, she abandoned the refined elegance that briefly marked her style at the still somewhat mannerist Florentine court and renewed her baroque realism and strong tenebrist lighting. The major work of this period is her third *Judith* (c. 1625), a large, grand painting that represents the suspenseful climax of the story, when the heroic tyrannicides pause, frozen by a sound that alerts them to danger. The picture's theatrical lighting and isolation of a dramatic moment can be connected with the popularity of the Judith theme in Roman Jesuit theater in this period. Perhaps also of the mid-1620s is the majestic *Esther and Ahasuerus*.

About 1628 Gentileschi moved to Naples. In 1630 she painted a self-portrait (one of several mentioned in the literature) for the Roman scholar-collector Cassiano dal Pozzo, probably identical with her *Self-Portrait as the Allegory of Painting*. This complex picture combines the traditionally female allegory with a prevalent Renaissance concern, the intellectual and social status of the artist, to convert a convention repressive for women into an image that celebrates both female capability and the intrinsic worth of artistic practice.

In Spanish-ruled Naples, Gentileschi gained commissions for religious pictures. In this period, her style modulated from Roman Caravaggism to a more decorous classicizing now favored in Italy, and she began to hire collaborators to paint architectural and landscape backgrounds in her pictures. Other patrons in the 1630s included Francesco I d'Este, duke of Modena; Cardinals Francesco and Antonio Barberini; and Ferdinando II de' Medici.

In 1638–1641 Gentileschi joined her aging father at the English court of King Charles I and Queen Henrietta Maria; together they painted ceiling allegories for the Great Hall of the Queen's House at Greenwich (1638–1639). King Charles's extensive Italian art purchases included six or more paintings by Gentileschi; none is known today. The artist spent her final decade in Naples, where she painted for Dotore Luigi Romeo a *Bathsheba* (early 1640s), *Susanna*, and *Lot and His Daughters* (1640s).

Some of Gentileschi's late paintings are overpainted or otherwise dubious; even the secure works tend toward a formal and expressive conservatism. An exception is *Corisca and the Satyr*, identified in the early 1990s, which, in a rarely depicted episode from Battista Guarini's *Il pastor fido*, presents a nymph gleefully outwitting a lustful satyr. In her last years, Gentileschi produced for Don Antonio Ruffo of Sicily a *Galatea* (1649), *Diana and Actaeon*, and (in progress in 1651) *Andromeda Freed by Perseus* and *Joseph and Potiphar's Wife*; none has survived.

Some of Gentileschi's late paintings are overpainted or otherwise dubious; even the secure works tend toward a formal and expressive conservatism.

Gentileschi's letters reveal both her acute consciousness of the presumed inferiority of women artists in a masculine art world and her own fierce determination to excel. Her success is partly seen in her demonstrable influence (in one or more instances) upon contemporary artists, including Bernardo Cavallino, Simon Vouet, Guercino, Rembrandt, and perhaps Velazquez. Resistance to Gentileschi's achievement is reflected in the paucity of biographical accounts and in her persistent characterization in sexual terms. Many of her paintings were reattributed to her father, Orazio, her artistic identity nearly subsumed into his, before 20th century art historians began to reclaim her. Gentileschi's singular achievement was her transformation of the image of females in art, from passive ciphers into autonomous agents. ◆

Géricault, Théodore

September 26, 1791–January 26, 1824 ● Painter

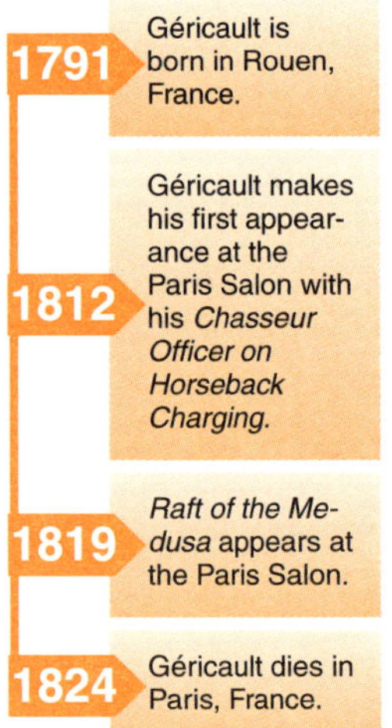

The French painter and printmaker Théodore Géricault made a powerful and lasting impression on the Western art world during his brief and eventful life. His passionate, mercurial personality was reflected in dramatic, controversial paintings and prints—most notably *The Raft of the Medusa*—that broke the decorous mold of neoclassicism and helped to unleash the stormy spirit of romanticism in the visual arts.

Jean-Louis André Théodore Géricault was born to a wealthy family in Rouen, France, on September 26, 1791. After graduating from the Lycée Impériale in 1808, Géricault was determined to become an artist despite the objections of his father, a prominent lawyer. Fascinated by horses, Géricault furtively sought out Carle Vernet, an artist renowned for his equestrian paintings, and became his student for the next two years, mastering the technique of capturing animal motion on the canvas. He then moved on to the studio of Pierre Narcisse Guérin, who sought to impart the fundamentals of neoclassical composition to his refractory and tempestuous pupil, whose passions drove beyond his master's taste for stately restraint. Guérin once admonished him, "As for your figures, they resemble nature the way a violin case resembles a violin."

Géricault's first major professional breakthrough was the acceptance by the 1812 Paris Salon of his painting *Chasseur Officer on Horseback Charging,* which the state declined to purchase even though the jury awarded it a gold medal. Evidently influenced by the Gros's taste for recent history and Rubens's somber way with color, the painting's operatic depiction of a battlefield officer atop a soaring horse anticipates the gusts of high emotion that animated Géricault's later works. Less successful was his 1814 Salon entry, *Wounded Cuirassier*, whose rough execution and turbid color scheme aroused critical controversy and the retrospective scorn of the artist himself.

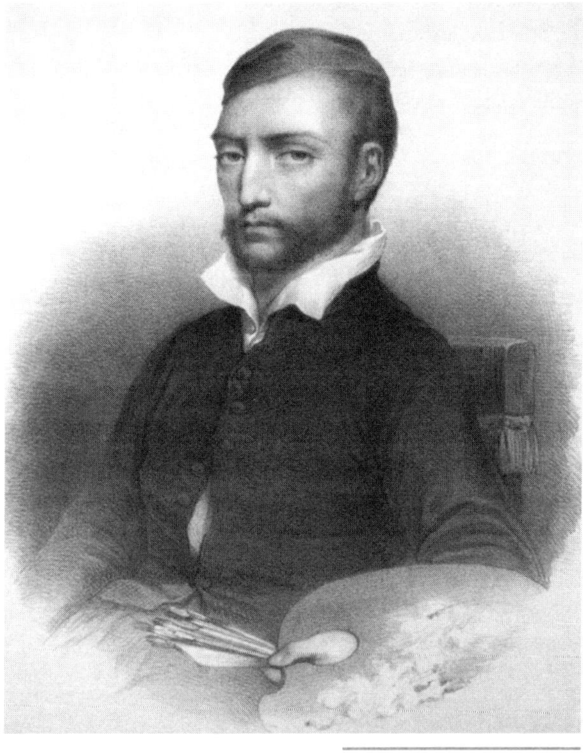

Théodore Géricault

Géricault's brief tour of duty with the royal musketeers, begun shortly after the Bourbon restoration in 1815, was notable chiefly for a passionate love affair that resulted in the birth of his son, Hyppolyte Georges. Upon his return to civilian life, Géricault resolved to further his artistic development by traveling to Italy to study the works of the Old Masters. In the fall of 1816, he set off for Rome, where he spent most of the next year, aside from a month in Florence and a two-month trip to Naples. While in Italy he immersed himself in the works of Raphael and Michelangelo. Later that year, while in Rome, he began a large-scale tableau, *Race of the Riderless Horse*, seeking to combine a sense of topical urgency with classical heroism, but he left the project unfinished.

Upon returning to Paris in the fall of 1817, Géricault applied himself to the art of **lithography.** His copious drawings of martial scenes introduced an unprecedented expressive fluency to that medium. With his success in a smaller format, Géricault was inspired to reconquer the larger territory of the canvas. He embarked on his most ambitious composition, based on a horrific real-life event: the desperate struggle of the survivors of the wrecked French frigate *Medusa*, who floated for 12 days on a raft and reportedly resorted to murder and cannibalism before their rescue.

lithography: the process of printing an image, which is to be printed in ink, from a plane surface.

The extraordinary emotional range of Géricault's *Raft of the Medusa*—a gripping blend of the desperation of the dying, the heroic determination of the living, and the morbid peace of the dead—stirred both acclaim and bitter denunciation. Some critics and government officials saw the work as an attack on

"It's as though Romanticism is born all of a piece in Géricault."
Art critic Robert Hughes on Theodore Géricault's work

the regime by the committed liberal Géricault. Just as neoclassicists were discomfited the work's emotional charge, so the champions of the nascent romantic movement hailed it as the dawn of a new era in the arts. In the words of the historian Jules Michelet, "It is our whole society that embarked on the raft of the *Medusa*." Gericault compensated for the painting's critical rebuff at the Salon of 1819 by taking it on a tour of England, where it generated high praise and substantial revenues for the artist. He remained in England until 1822, working in lithography, watercolors, and oil on mostly equestrian subjects.

motif: a reoccuring or dominant, salient theme in a work of art.

chasm: a wide breech between two points, individuals, nations, or other entities.

The depth of Gericault's achievement, according to the critic Robert Hughes, "lies not just in his release of tragic and horrific imagery but in the way this hot and black subject matter is formalized and disciplined by his study of both classicism and nature, the concrete **motif.** And in this process, classical stereotypes themselves are given new life—or rather, old life, since the murderous irrationality of fate and the pressure of human cruelty lie at the original core of Greek tragedy."

Fixated on the gruesome **chasms** that yawned beneath the serene surfaces of Western civilization, Gericault turned his painter's eye toward death and madness, composing canvases of autopsy remains, the severed heads of guillotine victims, and the faces of inmates of mental asylums, all undertaken in a spirit of unflinching exposé. An ardent opponent of slavery, he planned a series of political canvases, including *Slave Trade* and *Victims of the Inquisition*. But years of reckless living and the cumulative effects of falls from horses cut short his ambitions, and Géricault died in Paris on January 26, 1824, at the age of 32. As Hughes commented, "Live fast, die young, and have a good-looking corpse—except that, as one can see from his death mask, Gericault's beauty was destroyed by the long, painful battle with spinal damage and ulcers brought on by repeated falls from horseback; it is the face of a withered man of 70." ◆

Ghiberti, Lorenzo

1378–December 1, 1455 ● Sculptor

Lorenzo Ghiberti was an Italian Renaissance sculptor and bronze caster. Many of the renowned artistic personalities of the age, including Donatello, Paolo Uccello, and

Michelozzo di Bartolomeo, assisted him or trained in his busy, well-organized workshop. Ghiberti was supremely versatile and, throughout his life, worked in a variety of media: in this respect he should be considered one of the greatest universal artists of the early Renaissance.

In his youth Ghiberti trained as a goldsmith with his stepfather and in 1400 left Florence for Pesaro, where he collaborated with an unknown painter on decorating a room for the Malatesta family. Ghiberti rushed back to Florence in the winter of 1400–1401 so that he could participate in the competition, announced by the Arte di Calimala (guild of cloth dealers and refiners), to design bronze doors for the Baptistery. Seven artists reached the final stage, but only the trial pieces by Ghiberti and Filippo Brunelleschi of the *Sacrifice of Isaac* survive. The young Ghiberti was given the commission, perhaps on the strength of his superior technical abilities in bronze casting, and executed 28 partially gilded bronze reliefs on New Testament themes and saints by April 19, 1424. In the early panels, Ghiberti attempted to balance his compositions with the quatrefoil format (the framing device adopted by Andrea Pisano in the earlier Baptistery doors, the model for Ghiberti's work), and the elegant poses of the figures, spirited drapery forms, and graceful lines of these reliefs are in keeping with contemporary developments in Florentine painting, especially with the art of Gherardo Starnina and Lorenzo Monaco. Ghiberti's style evolved significantly in these years, and the later scenes display a more subtle use of the height of relief. The later figures, furthermore, emerge from the background almost in the round and are characterized by a heightened sense of movement. As time progressed, Ghiberti also took a greater interest in creating depth to the background of his panels, and the later designs appear more sophisticated in perspectival construction.

In 1413 Ghiberti worked on the bronze statue of *St. John the Baptist* for the Calimala. It was cast in one piece and testifies to Ghiberti's expertise with bronze. Enhanced by the finely chased details of its smooth surfaces, the figure is characterized by an air of rare elegance. Rich folds of fabric envelop the saint in a series of calligraphic curves, and these lyrical rhythms are a feature of what is sometimes called a late Gothic or International Gothic style. In 1419 the Arte del Cambio (guild of moneychangers) commissioned Ghiberti to execute the bronze statue *Saint Matthew*, completed in 1422 for the guild's niche on the facade of

1378 Ghiberti is born in Florence and trained as a goldsmith by his father.

1400 Ghiberti leaves Florence for Pesaro to decorate a room for the Malatesta family.

1406 Ghiberti participates in the planning of the Florence cathedral as an architect.

1413 Ghiberti works on the bronze statue *St. John the Baptist.*

1419 Ghiberti is commissioned by the Arte del Cambino to execute the bronze statue *Saint Matthew.*

1447 Ghiberti begins writing three books on art and his autobiography.

1455 Ghiberti dies.

Orsanmichele. Compared to the *Baptist* the Cambio sculpture exhibits a greater awareness of the structure and movement of the body (in line with developments in the oeuvre of Donatello and Nanni di Banco), and an obvious debt to antique art. The energized drapery forms of the earlier bronze statue are here replaced by calmer, more form-defining folds.

Ghiberti's third bronze statue for Orsanmichele, *Saint Stephen*, was commissioned by the Arte della Lana (wool guild) in 1425 and finished in 1429. The graceful pose, sweet expression, and fluid drapery forms of the statue contrast with the openly classicizing spirit of the earlier *Saint Matthew*.

Ghiberti executed fire-gilded bronze reliefs of *John the Baptist before Herod* and the *Baptism* for the font of the Baptistery in Siena by 1427. In these scenes he continued to develop his ideas on the placing of figures in space and on the organization of setting and background.

The pictorial relief of the *Baptism* is developed to the full in Ghiberti's second bronze door, commissioned by the Arte di Calimala for the Florence Baptistery in 1425. The rectangular format of the Siena reliefs is adopted for the scenes of the door, which comprises 10 gilded bronze panels on Old Testament subjects. These larger sections present a greater illusion of depth and space and exhibit a wider range of detail in the shallow relief of their backgrounds. The style of the doors, apparently named *Porta del Paradiso* (Gate of Paradise) by Michelangelo, is enriched with classical influences; Ghiberti was also aware of contemporary developments in architecture, especially Brunelleschi's, and linear perspective. The sculptor is also responsible for the lyrical designs of floral ornamentation on the jambs and interior borders.

In 1432, as work progressed on the doors, the wool guild commissioned from him the bronze shrine *Saint Zenobins* for Florence Cathedral. Completed in 1442, the work includes some reliefs that display certain affinities in style and composition with the doors.

Ghiberti was also active as an architect, and he participated in the planning of Florence Cathedral.

Ghiberti was also active as an architect, and he participated in the planning of Florence Cathedral. From 1406 to 1408 and 1418 to 1436 he advised on the construction of the dome, but his precise contribution to the final project is not known. He also provided designs for the building's stained-glass windows. Another of his architectural projects is thought to be the facade of Santa Trinità, Florence (1417–1424).

Around 1447 Ghiberti started writing the three books of *I commentarii* (Commentaries), which comprise a survey of the art of antiquity, a history of the art of "modern times," including his autobiography, and notes on the sciences necessary to a sculptor. His writing is characterized by a humanistic belief in the preeminence of the art of antiquity, and it draws on Vitruvius and Pliny the Elder. The second book is particularly valuable for its astute observations on painters' styles and its appreciation of Sienese art. Ghiberti's suave figures and elegant drapery forms, so different in character from Donatello's vigorous style, appealed to the artists of the later 15th century, from Benozzo Gozzoli to Andrea del Verrocchio and Sandro Botticelli. The influence of Ghiberti's lyrical art endured into the 16th century, as aspects of Benvenuto Cellini's work attest. ◆

Giacometti, Alberto

October 10, 1901–January 11, 1966 ● Painter and Sculptor

The son of successful postimpressionist Giovanni Giacometti, Alberto Giacometti was born in the town of Stampa, Switzerland. Through his father, Alberto was introduced to art while still very young and executed his first drawings before reaching his teens. As a schoolboy he worked mostly with portraiture, but when he went to Geneva for a year to study at the École des Beaux-Arts he expanded his artistic scope, adding painting to his already well-developed drawing skills. He also began to study sculpture at this time, at the École des Arts et Métiers (School of Arts and Crafts).

After a year of academic study in Geneva, Alberto traveled in Italy from 1920 to 1921. There he worked on his own, exploring sculpture and painting intensively. In 1922 he moved on again, this time to Paris, where he began five years of **intermittent** study at the Académie de la Grande Chaumière, working under the sculptor Emile-Antoine Bourdelle. By 1925, sculpture was occupying all his efforts, and in 1927 he opened a studio with his brother, Diego Giacometti, in Montparnasse.

intermittent: the coming and going of a career or other happening; going in intervals.

Like many artists of his day, Alberto Giacometti was strongly influenced by a number of different sources. For one, he found inspiration in the work of the cubists, including

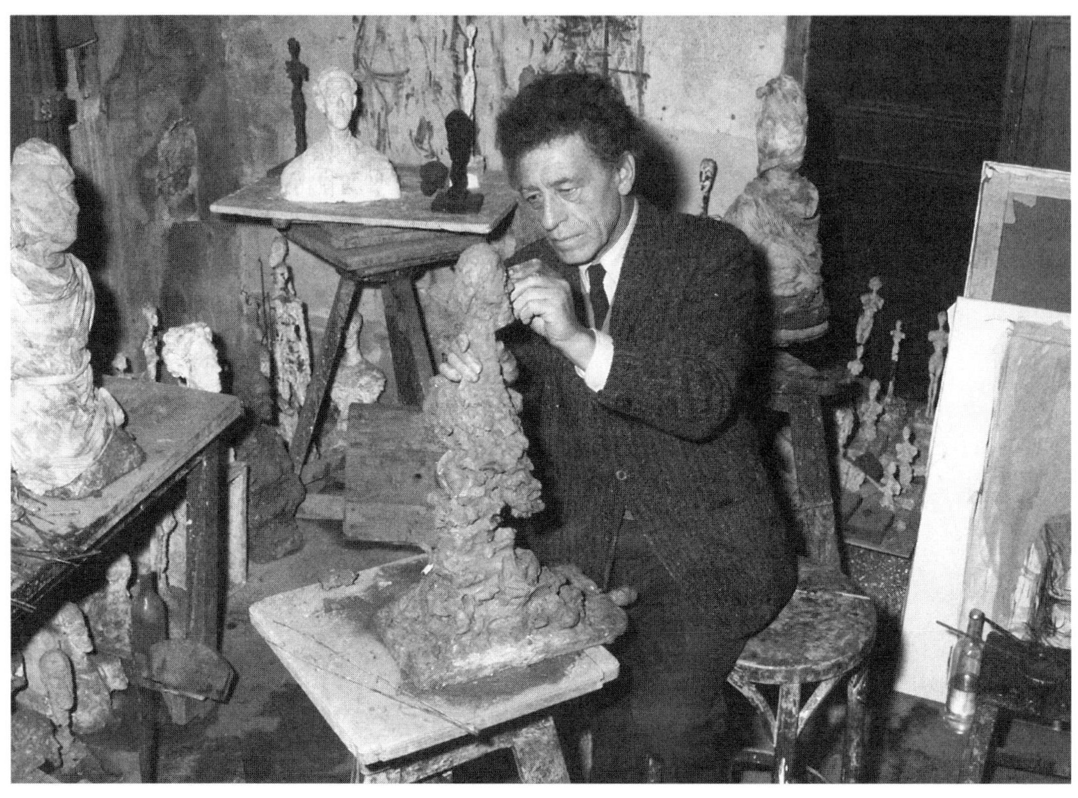

Alberto Giacometti in his studio, 1958.

Jacques Brancusi and Henri Laurens. For another, he was excited by the possibilities of incorporating elements from African art, which was enjoying a vogue in many European museums at the time. These and other influences found their way into many of Giacometti's early sculptures, including *Spoon Woman* (1926). However, it was the work of the surrealists that touched off his first real burst of creativity.

Along with the other surrealists, such as Max Ernst and Joan Miró, Giacometti was intrigued by the theories of Freud, particularly as they applied to ideas about sexuality, violence, and dreams. His sculptures began to take on dark and dramatic themes. Examples from this period include *Reclining Woman Who Dreams* (1929), *Study for a Surrealist Cage* (1930), and *Hands Holding the Void* (1934). Giacometti remained an active member of the surrealist circle in Paris until the mid-1930s, coming to be known as their premier sculptor, but he broke with them in 1935 when he decided to take his themes and images from the real world, rather than from theories, dreams, or literature.

In his post-surrealist period, Giacometti first returned to cubism, then became fascinated with rendering in sculpture the true human experience of perception, capturing the effects of distance, orientation, and other natural aspects of the process of seeing. This harmonized with his own philosophical development, as he had become increasingly convinced that isolation formed the cornerstone of the human condition. This was a period of great frustration for the artist, and very few significant pieces survive.

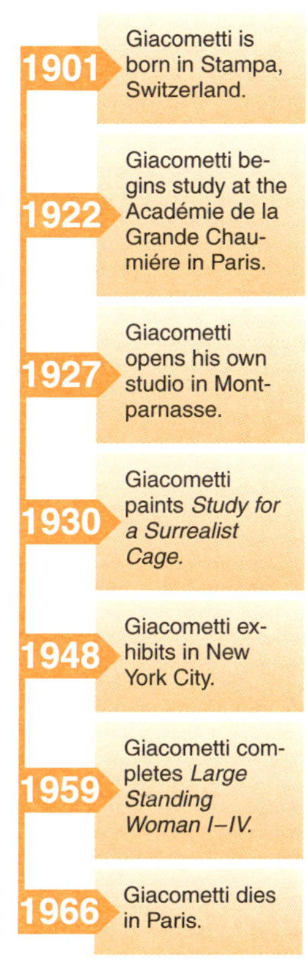

In 1940, with World War II looming on the horizon, Giacometti returned to Switzerland. There he would stay for the next five years, still struggling to find a way to express his artistic vision. After the war he returned to Paris, taking up residence in his Montparnasse studio once again, and finally all his years of struggle began to bear fruit. The post-war vitality that pervaded Parisian intellectual circles no doubt contributed to Giacometti's renewed creativity, as did his friendship with Jean-Paul Sartre and other existentialist thinkers. His work of the early post-war years ranks among his best, and demonstrates that he had conquered his earlier conceptual problems of expressing distance, movement, and perception. As he had been for the surrealists, Giacometti again became a sort of sculptural spokesman for an intellectual ideal, and his art came to be viewed as a visual representation of the existentialist movement.

As he had been for the surrealists, Giacometti again became a sort of sculptural spokesman for an intellectual ideal, and his art came to be viewed as a visual representation of the existentialist movement.

The post-war period also marked Giacometti's return to drawing and painting, which he had nearly abandoned for the previous 20 years. His paintings of human figures reflect the direction he had taken in his sculpture, portraying movement and power, but expressing isolation through the cavernous settings in which the figures are often presented. He also painted still lifes, using the same materials for most of his paintings, and restricting his palette to a very few muted tones: grays, browns, black, and white.

Giacometti's mature style received great acclaim from critics around the world. Three major exhibitions were mounted in New York City, in 1948, 1950, and 1958. His work was shown in Paris in 1951, 1954, and 1957. Museums in Berne and London both held major shows in 1954 as well, and Venice followed suit in 1956. For all this acclaim, however, Giacometti still struggled with the conviction that he had yet to capture his conceptual vision in his finished work. He became obsessive, constantly reworking his pieces until, often, he went too far and destroyed them. This terrible period of self-doubt would plague him for the next few years until, sometime around 1959, he seems to have overcome it.

From 1959 until his death, Giacometti crafted work that shows a steady increase in certainty, intensity, and power. A group of major pieces from this period typify his newfound sense of mastery in sculpture: *Large Standing Woman I-IV, Monumental Bust*, and *Walking Man I-II*. These were executed during the period 1959–60. His paintings, too, exhibited a new power. By the early 1960s, however, there were new obstacles to Giacometti's creativity. His fame had become so great that a stream of visitors began to invade his studio, providing near-constant interruptions. Then, in 1963, the artist fell ill and was diagnosed with stomach cancer. He continued to work, but at a reduced pace, until his death, in Paris, in 1966. ◆

Giorgione

c. 1477–October 24, 1510 ● Painter

Giorgione is among the most intriguing and enigmatic figures in Renaissance art. He was hailed by Baldassare Castiglione (1528) as one of the greatest painters of the age and claimed by Giorgio Vasari as the originator of "the modern style"(*maniera moderna*) of painting in Venice. But documentation of Giorgione's unusual, brilliant, and brief career is scanty. Mythification began soon after his death, and interpretation of his artistic personality is to some degree determined by subjective response to the hauntingly **evocative,** poetic works that have been associated with him. Consensus is lacking regarding which paintings should be considered autograph; the number of works assigned by individual scholars has varied widely. Dating of the majority of the most securely attributed pictures is problematic and further complicated by alternate views as to whether Giorgione's apparently earliest works were executed circa 1495 or circa 1500; the latter represents the traditional view.

evocative: serving to evoke a particular spirit or emotion.

Giorgione's origin in the Venetian subject city Castelfranco is unquestioned; the birth date assigned him by Vasari, who names Giovanni Bellini as his teacher, is generally accepted. No signed works are known. A female portrait now entitled

Laura bears on the reverse an early 16th-century inscription with the date 1506 and an attribution to him. A *Portrait of a Man* is similarly inscribed with attribution and a no longer legible date. Documents record that in 1507–1508 Giorgione painted a now-lost canvas for the Sala dell'Udienza (audience chamber) in the Doge's Palace. In 1508 Giorgione received payment for frescoes decorating the facade of the Fondaco de' Tedeschi (German merchants' warehouse) in Venice. These depicted monumental, classicizing female nudes in niches. Already faded and damaged in the 18th century, when copied in engravings by Zanetti, the frescoes are lost except for fragments detached in 1937. In October 1510, Isabella d'Este of Mantua requested that her agent in Venice acquire "a night" (*una nocte*, meaning "Nativity") by Giorgione; in November, the agent replied that the artist had died of plague.

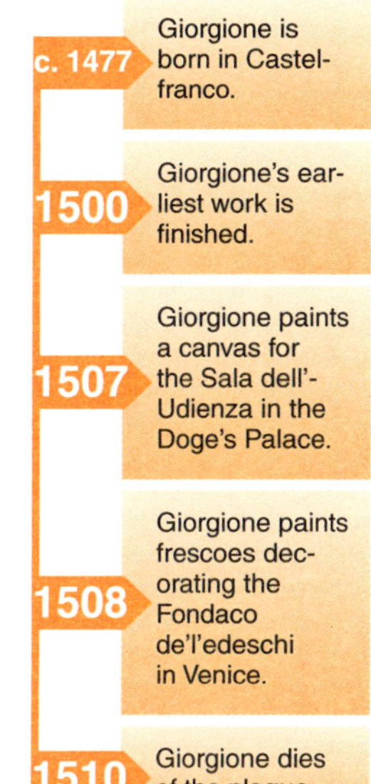

In notes compiled between 1521 and 1543, the Venetian patrician Marcantonio Michiel recorded several paintings—then in Venetian private collections—as by Giorgione. Three are now surely identifiable: *Boy with an Arrow; Three Philosophers in a Landscape* (both Vienna, Kunsthistorisches Museum); and *The Tempest*. Identification of a fourth, the *Sleeping Venus*, is usually accepted. The first three and the *Laura* share the feature of having uncommon subject matter, seemingly elusive of precise meaning. The latter three include landscapes of extraordinary beauty. The sleeping nude, the naked mother in the *Tempest*, the stately *Laura* exposing her breast, and the androgynous youth with the arrow are all subtly erotic. These pictures are stylistically cohesive. Although complicated by his statements that the Venetian painter Sebastiano del Piombo completed the *Three Philosophers* and that Titian completed the *Sleeping Venus*, Michiel's information is thus invaluable to establishing Giorgione's style and range of activity. Michiel (1530) locates *The Tempest* in the collection of Gabriele Vendramin; it appears in later Vendramin inventories (1567–1569; 1601), as does a picture of an old woman. This reference is now identified with *La Vecchia* (The old woman) a painting inscribed *col tempo* (with time) and accepted as autograph.

An inventory (1528) of the collection of Domenico Grimani lists a *Self-portrait of Giorgione as David with the Head of Goliath*. An engraving by Wenceslaus Hollar (1650) records this work; a painted fragment of the same composition is identified by some scholars as Giorgione's picture and thought by others to be a copy. In this picture, the San Diego portrait,

Boy with an Arrow, and *La Vecchia*, the subject is presented startlingly close up, emerging from a dark background and looking out as if to engage the viewer in a penetrating psychological exchange. A close-up image of *Christ Carrying the Cross*, dated by document to 1508–1509, has been attributed to Giorgione and alternatively to Titian. In 1648 the Venetian art historian Carlo Ridolfi cited a work that is now universally attributed to Giorgione and placed near the start of his career: an altarpiece in the Cathedral of Castelfranco. Surprisingly, and except for St. Francis, the figures here do not look out or at each other but rather appear to be rapt in inward contemplation, their reverie enhanced by the soft, dusky modeling, golden light, and long shadows.

Unrecorded works accepted by modern scholars and usually dated early in Giorgione's career include: *Judith*, which may reflect the classicism of the Venetian sculptor Tullio Lombardo; *Portrait of a Man in a Pink Quilted Jacket*; and *Adoration of the Magi*. A *Nativity with Shepherds* shares landscape and compositional features with the *Three Philosophers*. It is most often assigned to Giorgione, but has alternatively been attributed to Titian, as is also true of the later, large *Pastoral Concert*.

Many of the works associated with Giorgione indicate a taste for the sensual and the pastoral—equivalent to a contemporary revival of the classical genre by Venetian poets—among the humanistically educated patrons that must have constituted Giorgione's major clientele and may have encouraged his influential break with tradition in exploring landscape and mood as subject matter for "painted poems" (*poesie*). Most extraordinary is the *Tempest*. Despite numerous reasonable interpretations put forward for the subject as political **allegory** or mythological story, the eerie light and heavy air of the impending meteorological climax may be considered the essential subject.

allegory: an expression by utilizing symbolic fictional characters and actions of truths or generalizations about the human condition.

In justifiably citing Giorgione's technique as revolutionary, Vasari stated that the Venetian eschewed drawing, sketching with brush on his canvas. X-radiography of his paintings confirms that Giorgione often made significant compositional changes in the paint layer. Recent observation, through infrared reflectography, of contours that are only loosely indicated by underdrawing has also tended to support Vasari's assertion. Giorgione's swift progression away from the precisely delineated and smoothly layered application of pigment characteristic of Giovanni Bellini toward an irregularly layered (*im-*

pasto) application exploiting texture of canvas and brush, was quickly taken up by a generation of Venetian painters and established not only the direction but also the renown of Venetian 16th-century painting. Vasari's suggestion that Leonardo da Vinci's stay in Venice (1500) inspired Giorgione's innovations, although dismissed by the early Venetian writers on art, has recently been reconsidered for stylistic and thematic analogies (as in the newly cleaned *Concert* or *Three Ages of Man)*, as has the influence of the German painter Albrecht Dürer, who also visited Venice during the same decade. ◆

Giotto

c. 1267–1337 ● Painter

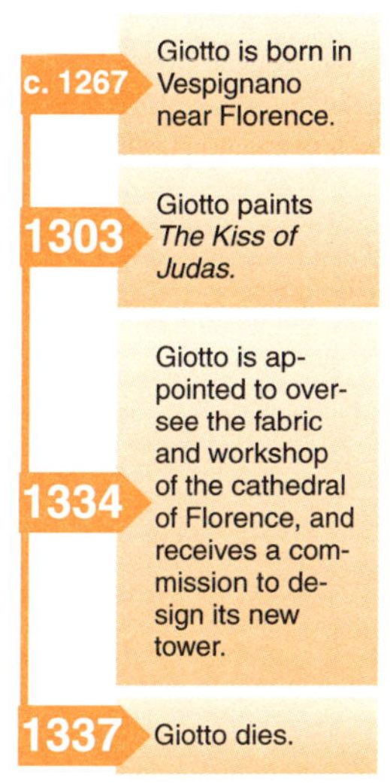

Little is certain regarding the details of Giotto's life, as sources are scarce and often unverifiable. According to a literary tradition, Giotto was born as Giotto di Bondone, a peasant in the village of Vespignano, near Florence. The tradition dates at least to around 1447, when it appears in a passage of the Tuscan sculptor Lorenzo Ghiberti's *Commentaries* concerning the beginning of painting's rise in central Italy.

Giotto is mentioned in writings of 14th-century poets such as Dante Alighieri, Giovanni Boccaccio, and Petrarch (Francesco Petrarca), as well as in the Florentine chronicles of Filippo Villani. His renown among these authors attests to his early fame in Tuscany. Yet the Giotto lauded by these figures is a man of maturity and artistic accomplishment. The beginnings of his life became important only in later centuries, when he figured in laudatory histories written about artists and their works, such as Ghiberti's work and the Tuscan painter Giorgio Vasari's *Lives of the Artists* (1550; revised 1568). Giotto is characterized as a boy of precocious intellect and artistic genius, qualities whose fruition is recounted in both texts. For both authors, Giotto's greatness as an artist was magnified by the story of his rise from rural poverty and obscurity to civic refinement and celebrity. The extent to which the narrative is factual cannot be ascertained.

Both Ghiberti and Vasari relate that the Tuscan painter Cimabue (Bencivieni di Pepo) discovered Giotto as a boy in the countryside, drawing a nearby sheep on a slab of stone. As the

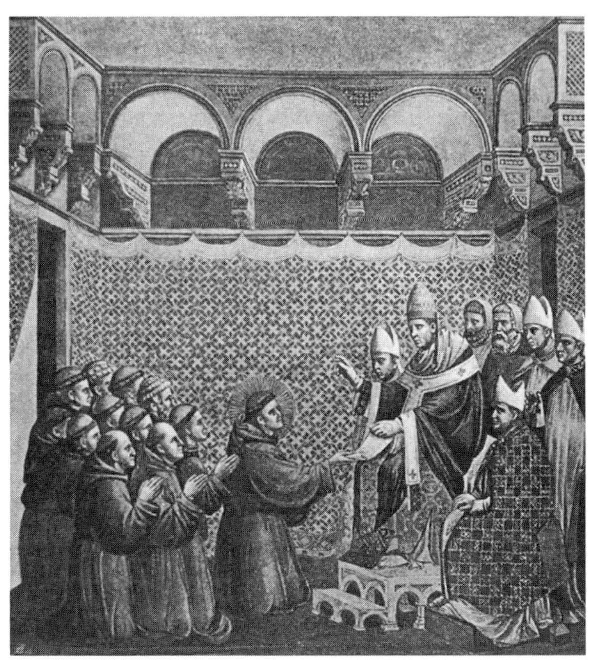

Giotto's *St. Francis of Assisi Presenting his Rule to Pope Innocent III*.

story goes, the painter was struck by the boy's artistic abilities and obtained his father's permission to take Giotto as a student. After an unspecified amount of time, Giotto matched and surpassed his master's art. What Giotto then achieved and widely propagated, according to both authors, was a revolution of artistic style. His accurate drawing from life replaced what Vasari considered a derivative tradition of crude quality practiced by the famous Cimabue.

Giotto and Cimabue are associated already in literature of the early 14th century, during Giotto's lifetime. In the 11th canto of his *Purgatory* (c. 1307–1321), Dante names both figures in an example of the transience of fame and the folly of vainglory. Giotto is here said to have replaced Cimabue in the field of painting. Toward the end of the century, Villani recapitulated Giotto's succession as an accomplished fact in his *Liber de origine Florentiae et eisdem famosis civibus* (On the origin of the Florentine state and its famous citizens; c. 1395). Yet Ghiberti was the first to use narrative to elaborate a process of artistic succession over time. The author's attention to Giotto's youth prepared readers to understand not only that Giotto was an artist worthy of highest praise, but also that the painter's achievement derived from a combination of innate talent and formal training by an artist who was exceptional in his own right. Vasari repeats and expands the details found in Ghiberti's image of Giotto, with some variation.

Vasari amplifies Giotto's historical role, which was related as early as around 1353 in Giovanni Boccaccio's *Decameron*. The Giotto of Boccaccio resurrects a lost art of rendering objects naturalistically to the point of deceiving viewers. In Vasari, Giotto is the catalyst in a vaster and more complex history. Here Giotto ushers in art's rebirth or second rise to perfection, following a previous cycle that began in remote antiquity, culminated in ancient Greece and Rome, and declined during the twilight of the Roman empire. In this position

Giotto is a hero who rescues and restores a lost art sought in vain by incompetent artist since the fall of Rome.

Behind Giotto's triumph, according to Vasari, is the divine source of the painter's talent, an aspect highlighted through the biographical treatment of his youth. The preface of Vasari's *Lives* portrays God as the first artist and ultimate teacher of human artists, enabling them to perfect imperfect materials through the application of the same principles by which God ordered nature. Giotto's talents are therefore understood not only as God-given, but also as instruments of God's will for the Tuscan people to reach divine perfection in the arts. The painter thus becomes both a Tuscan hero and a primary redeemer on a universal scale of absolute artistic value. In this capacity he is shown to have laid the foundation upon which subsequent artists discussed by Vasari built in persisting to use nature as a model to imitate and reproduce.

Vasari's scheme of progress in the arts culminated in the careers of the 16th-century artists Leonardo da Vinci, Raphael of Urbino, and Michelangelo Buonarroti. And while modern scholars have left behind the theological underpinnings of Vasari's history, Giotto's pivotal status in art history has remained; most of the thousands of Giotto studies written internationally in the 20th century note how the art of Giotto anticipates the work of later Renaissance painters. Where they were concerned to show Giotto's importance in the history of painting, scholars in the 20th century transformed the idea of Giotto as a historically pivotal figure in the history of art. Vasari's focus on Giotto's naturalistic style was retained as a primary indicator of the fundamental change he effected in the art of painting, although modern studies approach his images with different notions of what constitutes the painter's style.

Many aspects of the painter's career, aside from claims made by Vasari, mark Giotto as an exceptional figure in his time. The works of art commonly attributed to him and his workshop, while vexed with questions of authorship, suggest an astonishing breadth of mastery in the media of fresco, tempera, gold leaf, and mosaic, as well as a conceptual inventiveness in meeting the demands of a variety of important projects. Giotto's artistic endeavors include diverse types of panel painting, from complex altarpieces to monumental crucifixes. He was also hired to paint church and chapel murals with dramatic narrative programs comprising several scenes—if not dozens of them—representing the lives of popular religious figures. In 1334, toward the end of his life, Giotto was appointed to oversee the fabric and workshop of the cathedral of Florence, and also received a commission to design its new tower. Such versatility was unprecedented for a single artist up to Giotto's time.

The patronage of these projects equally reveals the singularity of Giotto's career. The Florentine commune's appointment of Giotto to the works of its cathedral crowned a lifetime of prominent positions. Among Giotto's other employers in Florence were the Bardi and Peruzzi families, some of Italy's wealthiest bankers. He was also engaged by great religious orders in Florence, including the Dominicans at the church of Santa Maria Novella, the Franciscans at the church of Santa Croce, and the Umiliati at the church of Ognissanti. His other important patrons resided well beyond Florence. In Padua he painted for the commune of Padua and also for the private citizen Enrico Scrovegni, the wealthy son of a prosperous moneylender. Giotto's patrons south of Florence included a cardinal of old St. Peter's in Rome and Robert I, King of Naples. At the headquarters of the Franciscan order in Assisi, an extensive fresco cycle of the *Life of St. Francis* in the Upper Church of the Basilica of San Francesco stands as Giotto's most disputed attribution. Aside from issues of other possible patrons and the difficulties of attribution and dating of particular works, the cultural breadth of these examples is sufficient to suggest that Giotto's professional itinerary encompassed the principal centers of wealth, power, and artistic sponsorship in early 14th-century Italy. By contrast his followers, who included Taddeo Gaddi and perhaps Maso di Banco, worked mainly in Florentine milieus, such as the church of Santa Croce.

The ways in which Giotto depicted space through his rendering of architecture and figures, color and light have been shown to set him in advance of previous artists, as he forged new relationships between pictorial representation and visible reality.

A prevalent current of American and British scholarship examines the painter's novel evocations of reality in the depiction of human drama. The ways in which Giotto depicted space through his rendering of architecture and figures, color and light have been shown to set him in advance of previous artists, as he forged new relationships between pictorial representation and visible reality. The painter's powers of observation emerge, for example, in the minute attention given to foliage and the distinctions made between birds in the fresco painting of *St. Francis Preaching to the Birds* in the Upper Church of San Francesco in Assisi [see the color plates in this volume], which scholars have dated variously from the 1290s to the 1320s. Moreover, the tonal contrasts and lines that define the friars' bodies contribute to an impression of spatial depth within the frame by giving the bodies volume. The disappearance of an elbow behind the left vertical frame suggests the extension of a unified space beyond the surface of the painted wall. *St. Francis's Sermon before Honorius III* in the same fresco cycle also conveys spatial depth through volumetric figures, but here spatial recession is defined by the architecture of a chamber rather than expanded laterally beyond the frame.

Where Giotto sets standards for painting illusionistic spaces, however, the character of spatial depth varies to amplify the particular subject represented. In the case of the Assisi frescoes, both the subjects and their spaces enhance the official image of the founder of a new and powerful religious order. *Preaching to the Birds* presents a rural space expressive of the wandering life of a radical figure that sought to reform the Church through dedication to material poverty and preaching beyond ecclesiastical walls. The *Sermon before Honorius III*, by contrast, takes place within a splendid interior. At the center, flanked by high clerics, sits Pope Honorius III, here depicted as a captive audience to Francis's preaching. Focus on the attentive pope affirms his supreme authority on church-related matters. This is the pontiff who formally approved Francis's Second Rule for his newly founded order of mendicant friars; his receptive posture in the Assisi fresco conveys a sense of inevitability to this crucial decision in the order's history. In sum, Giotto's art conveys both groundbreaking illusionism and spatial settings that recollect both the saint's commitments to itinerant preaching and his eventual attainment of papal recognition. Each of the remaining scenes in Assisi makes a similarly compelling point about Francis and his mission.

In addition to Giotto's attention to visible reality, modern observers of Giotto's work have been struck by a psychological realism in his human figures. A disturbing example is *The Kiss of Judas* from Enrico Scrovegni's chapel (Arena Chapel) in Padua, painted around 1303–1305. The scene, a highlight of Giotto's talent as a visual storyteller, follows upon a lengthy narrative cycle representing Jesus' birth, childhood, and ministry. Throughout the story plots build against Jesus, and now reach a **crescendo** as dense groups of armed soldiers and Jewish men converge to surround him. His captors bear down with a hatred that becomes accute in a foreground confrontation between Judas' glare and Jesus' **equanimity.** The enveloping ges-

crescendo: the peak of a gradual increase; usually associated with music.

equanimity: attribute characterized by a balanced mind and sense of fairness and equity.

ture dramatized by Judas' bright cape signals that Jesus has been overwhelmed. Yet Giotto's Christ shows by his calm expression that the capitulation is only physical, heightening the psychological tension between his figure and those of his adversaries.

The scene initiates a sequence of episodes representing the Passion, a popular subject of artistic and dramatic representation in this period. Here Giotto's introduction to the Passion with *The Kiss of Judas* is novel in the emotional charge that governs the attitudes of Jesus' persecutors, who appear at once as identifiable individuals and faceless hordes. With this image the painter magnifies anticipation of the expansive sequence of pictures that shows the human God suffering at the hands of malevolent figures in the short time before his execution on the cross. ◆

Goes, Hugo van der

c. 1440–1482 ● Painter

Hugo van der Goes was probably born in Ghent; it is not known where or under whom he trained. In May 1467 the painter Joos van Wassenhove sponsored his enrollment as master in the Ghent painters' guild, which van der Goes served as dean in 1474–1475. Van der Goes periodically furnished decorations for Ghent pageants between 1468 and 1474 and was among the artists summoned to Bruges in 1468 to provide adornments for the marriage celebrations of Charles the Bold and Margaret of York. About 1476–1477 he entered the monastery of the Rode Klooster in the Forêt de Soignes at Auderghem near Brussels as a lay brother. In his early 16th-century chronicle of the monastery, Gaspar Ofhuys states that van der Goes was allowed to continue painting at the Rode Klooster, where he also welcomed dignitaries, including Archduke Maximilian. Ofhuys also says that on his return trip from Cologne in 1481 van der Goes—who suffered from depression ("melancholia"), feared damnation, and was inundated with commissions—lapsed into madness, from which he briefly recovered before his death.

Van der Goes's few surviving works are not signed, dated, or documented as autograph paintings. However, the writers Giorgio Vasari, in 1550, and Lodovico Guicciardini, in 1567, mention a painting by "Ugo d'Anversa," or Hugo of Antwerp, at the hospital of Santa Maria Nuova in Florence. They are almost certainly referring to van der Goes and his painting the *Adoration of the Shepherds*, which was sent from Bruges by Tommaso Portinari and arrived at Santa Maria Nuova in 1483. The central panel of the huge triptych ordered by Portinari for the high altar of the hospital's church of Sant' Egidio shows the vividly characterized Virgin, Joseph, angels, and shepherds encircling the nude Christ child lying on the ground as they adore him. The wings depict the donor and his family kneeling in the foreground, with their huge patron saints standing behind them, before a continuous landscape, with the *Flight into Egypt* on the left and the *Procession of the Magi* on the right. The central panel includes the *Annunciation to the Shepherds* in the top right. The exterior of thc wings depicts the *Annunciation*, painted in grisaille, with simulacra of statues of Mary and Gabriel placed in separate niches. Van der Goes's remarkable powers of illusion are indebted to Jan van Eyck, while the monumentality and plasticity of his forms, their unexpected shifts in scale, the abrupt spatial transitions, and the nervousness of his compositions are his own highly expressive and original creations. The picture is dated about 1475, based on the birth dates of the donor's children.

The Adoration of the Magi, with its virtuoso foreshortenings, is generally dated several years before the Portinari Altarpiece, while the *Nativity* and *The Death of the Virgin* are usually dated after it, due to their greater spatial ambiguities, dramatic eloquence, and cooler coloring. In the unusually wide *Nativity* two half-length prophets in the immediate foreground draw curtains aside, offering a vision of shepherds bursting into the shed, where Mary, Joseph, and the angels adore the child lying in the manger. In *The Death of the Virgin* the apostles, beside themselves with grief, collapse around the Virgin's bed, as Christ appears above her—accompanied by angels in a halo of light—to receive her soul. Van der Goes's devotional paintings enjoyed tremendous appeal, and a number of lost works can be reconstructed through the many copies made after them. ◆

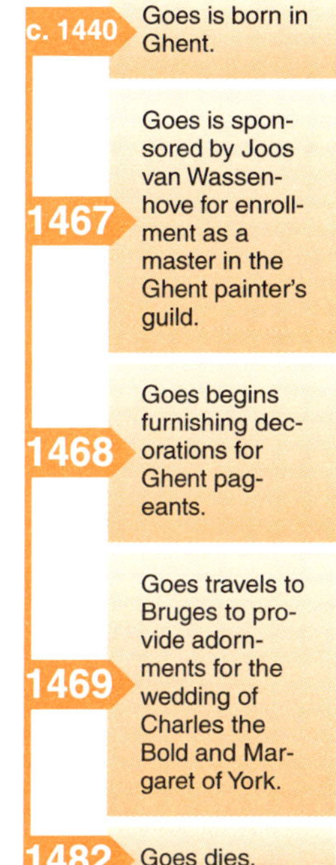

Gogh, Vincent van

MARCH 30, 1853–JULY 29, 1890 ● PAINTER

Vincent van Gogh was born in Groot-Zundert, Holland; his father was a pastor and his uncle a partner in the famous firm of art dealers Goupil. Both Vincent and his younger brother, Theo, worked for Goupil in the Hague and in Paris; in 1873 Vincent was sent to the London office, where he learned English. He collected more than 1,000 prints by English, French, American, and Japanese artists and for a time he taught languages and was a lay preacher in England. He became fanatically interested in religion and in 1878 went to work in the Borinage (Belgium), where he lived in utter poverty and tried to teach the miners his religious ideas. In December 1881 Van Gogh went to the Hague, where he studied painting with Anton Mauve and lived on the little money Theo was able to send him. Then for two years he lived with his parents in Nuenen, Holland, painting peasants and weavers in somber earth colors.

Vincent van Gogh, self-portrait, 1887

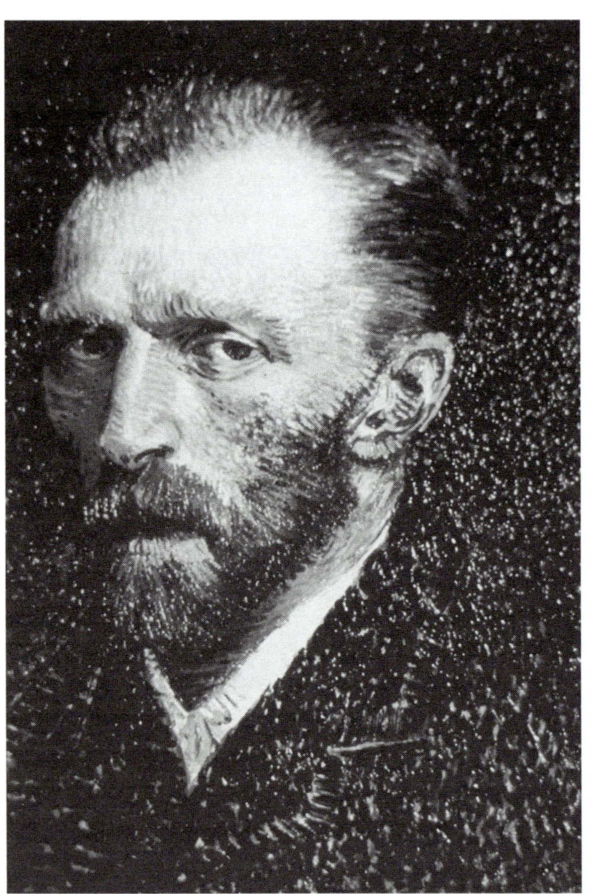

In 1886, van Gogh went to stay with Theo in Paris, where he met Camille Pissarro, Edgar Dégas, Georges Seurat, and Paul Gauguin and his palette brightened under the influence of the impressionists and Japanese prints. Although his work was included in a few exhibitions, no one bought it. In February 1888, he went to live at Arles in southern France. He wrote to Theo, "Everywhere— all over the vault of heaven is a marvelous blue, and the sun shade a radiance of pale sulphur, and it is as soft and lovely as the combination of heavenly blue and yellow in a Van der Meer of Delft… As long as the fall lasts, I shall not have hands, canvas, and colors enough to paint the beautiful things

I see." But he tried, completing painting after painting, forgetting to eat, subsisting almost entirely on coffee and alcohol.

He invited Gauguin to come and stay with him at Arles. For a long time Gauguin did not respond but van Gogh persisted, asking Theo to pay Gauguin's expenses and, at last, Gauguin came. The encounter proved disastrous. Gauguin provoked van Gogh into pointless arguments that lasted through the night, adding exhaustion to the ill health caused by his drinking and lack of food.

At Christmas, after one of these quarrels at a cafe, Gauguin took van Gogh home, drunk. Gauguin's story was that the following morning van Gogh cut off his ear and sent it to a prostitute as a gift. Van Gogh was found, bleeding and unconscious, by neighbors, who thought he was dead; the police went to arrest Gauguin for murder. When van Gogh regained consciousness in a hospital the next morning, he remembered nothing. He asked for Gauguin and, upon being told that he had left Arles, his first question was had he taken their money.

Theo hurried to Arles. Depressed, Vincent decided to go to an asylum in Saint Rémy, where the doctor wrote that due to difficulties with his sight and hearing, he had cut off his ear. The doctor diagnosed his problem as incipient epilepsy and advised him to stay for observation. Van Gogh was distressed by his epileptic episodes but his sharp, analytic intelligence remained untouched and he never faltered in his work.

In 1890 an article praising his work appeared in *Mercure de France*, and he sold a painting (the first ever) in Brussels, where he exhibited with The Twenty. In May he left the asylum and went to Paris for three days to visit Theo, his young wife, Johanna Bonger, and their three-month-old baby, Vincent. From there he went to Auvers, to stay with a homeopathic doctor, Paul-Ferdinand Gachet, who was also an artist and whose portrait he painted. On July 27 he took a gun, went out into the fields, stood against a tree, and shot himself. He died two days later, in his brother's arms. Theo, heartbroken, survived him by only six months, and the two brothers are buried at Auvers, side by side.

Johanna van Gogh-Bonger devoted the rest of her life to earning for Vincent's work the appreciation she felt it deserved. She published his correspondence with Theo in Holland and Germany, and translated over 650 of the letters into English.

Van Gogh painted for only 10 years, but in that short period he produced more than 800 oil paintings and 700 draw-

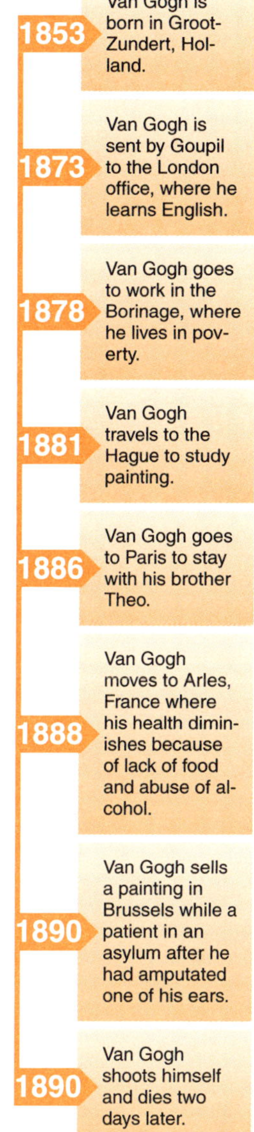

ings. In spite of his ill health, malnutrition, and dependency on alcohol, he was a highly disciplined painter. Although he often spent four or five days on one painting, at one period he painted 70 paintings in 70 days. He liked to paint people, but his forthright drawing, his fluid lines, solid forms, and brilliant colors were not flattering to his models, and many refused to sit for him because, they said, he did not know how to draw.

Van Gogh's work (and that of Gauguin) inspired the generation that followed—in particular the group called Les Fauves (the wild beasts), which included Henri Matisse, André Derain, Georges Braque, Georges Rouault, and Raoul Dufy, as well as Chaim Soutine and the German expressionists. Strength, vitality, vibrant colors with a strong touch of decorativeness were the new criteria. These are, to a great extent, still the criteria for contemporary art.

Today van Gogh is one of the best-known and best-loved of all artists and is regarded as the greatest Dutch painter after Rembrandt.

Today van Gogh is one of the best-known and best-loved of all artists and is regarded as the greatest Dutch painter after Rembrandt. Reproductions of his works can be found in millions of homes, and an entire museum is devoted to him in Amsterdam. He is the subject of books, films, and popular songs, and his paintings—of which only one sold in his impoverished lifetime—now command prices of over $20 million. ◆

Goya y Lucientes, Francisco Jose de

MARCH 30, 1746–APRIL 16, 1828 ● PAINTER

Francisco Goya was born in a small Spanish town, the son of an unsuccessful notary and gilder who was forced to take up farming to feed his family. Francisco Goya grew up among the peasantry and received very little formal education save the bare rudiments of reading and writing. As a craftsman himself, the elder Goya had little objection to his son's chosen profession, which was at the time little more than a skilled trade like any other. At the age of 18 Goya set out for Madrid, armed with a notebook from his mother listing rich Spanish families that was meant to be his order book when he gained prominence in his field. Both firmly believed he would achieve his stated goal, to become a "painter of the great."

Goya himself said he had three masters: "Velászquez, Rembrandt, and Nature."

Goya began his training under the tutorship of José de Lujan y Martinez, a devoted teacher whose official title was Reviser of Indecent Paintings, as his main source of income was adding clothing to figures deemed indecent by the Inquisition. Martinez gave Goya his first break by passing on a commission to paint a small church.

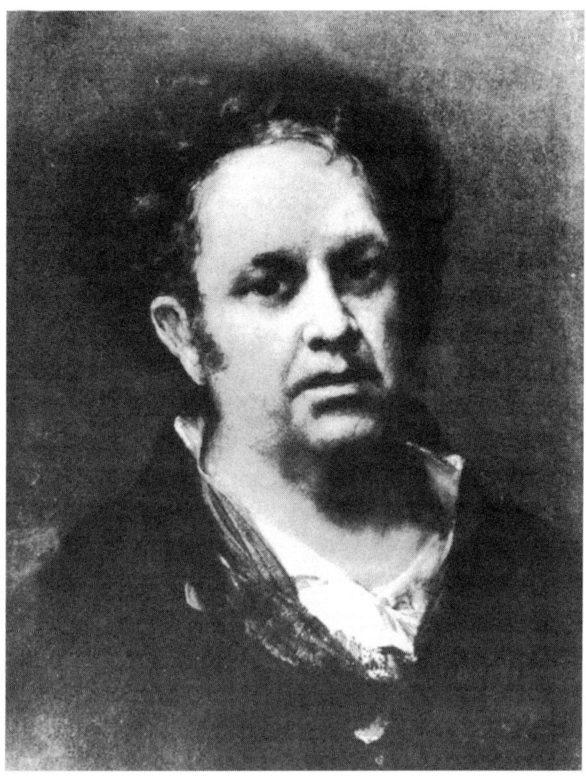

Francisco Goya, self-portrait, c. 1815

In 1766 Goya began a work that he planned to enter in the Royal Arts Academy competition in order to win a free trip to Italy; the painting received no mention and the artist scraped up the money to visit Italy himself. The journey, despite a variety of rumors about his scaling the dome of Saint Peter's and kidnapping nuns, was basically unproductive. His work was rejected in another competition and he returned to Spain determined to stifle the originality and creativity that made him unpalatable to the conservative establishment.

At the age of 30 he married Josefa Bayeu, sister of his former master Francisco Bayeu. Bayeu got him a job producing tapestries and assisting in other projects that helped him support himself and his family. It was not, however, until the age of 40 that Goya finally achieved success on his own merits. He was given a commission to decorate part of the church of San Francisco el Grande, which, it was rumored, was to be the Christian Parthenon. Though his portion looked much like the others in the church, it was critically well received and this, coupled with his recommendation from a prince who noted that the artist enjoyed hunting almost as much as royalty did, initiated his successful career as a court artist and portrait painter.

Strangely enough, his first period of artistic success also coincided with the onset of periods of artistic block, depression, and paranoia about other artists conspiring against him. The optimism symbolized by his mother's notebook was being real-

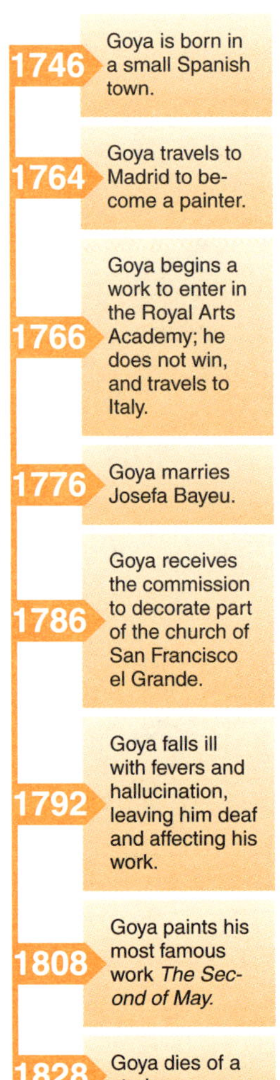

ized but his personal life consisted of a series of tragedies, including the death of all his children save one. At the age of 46 Goya was struck with an undiagnosed illness that brought on fevers and hallucinations and rendered him deaf, which led to his spiritual isolation. From this period, his work changed dramatically. He began to portray subjects that were purely imaginary, often nightmarish, as if he were transcribing hallucinations from his illness. One of the most famous of these is *Caprices*, a series of etchings on women, communication, and social satire that were narrated by the artist with such commentary as "The sleep of reason produces monsters." They were directed against superstition, dandies, ignorance, and hypocritical priests. The subject matter of these etchings and further paintings caused some critics to say they were works produced during periods of insanity, but there is little evidence that Goya was anything but lucid. They annoyed the Inquisition, who ordered their withdrawal, but Goya was protected because the king had accepted a set.

The artist remained married but was also famed for his studio seductions. It was said that whenever he seduced a woman in his studio he covered the statue of the Virgin Mary so as not to offend her. He began a passionate affair with Maria Teresa, the duchess of Alba and one of the outstanding women of her time, whom he depicted in many of his pictures. It was to her that he gave his famous works, the *Maja*, and the *Naked Maja*, whose very existence got him indicted by the Holy Office of the Inquisition, although the matter was hushed up for many years. The *Maja* was hung in front of the *Naked Maja*, for propriety.

In the years that followed, Goya was appointed first painter to the king and painted portraits of the royal family and the court. He was also, unofficially, the documentarian of the political turmoil Spain was enmeshed in, generated by both the Napoleonic wars and, later, internal strife. From this emerged perhaps his most famous painting. *The Second of May, 1808*, which chronicled the gore and carnage of the Napoleonic wars. His series of etchings, *The Disasters of War*, are among the most powerful visual indictments of war and its horrors. Many of the paintings of his later years are devoted to the dark, wild, and fantastic sides of life, haunted by spirits and demons.

His wife died in 1812 and Goya retired to the country at the age of 73, no longer taking orders and painting only what he wished. He became involved with a woman, Leocadia, who served as both his mistress and his housekeeper, and her young daughter Rosarito, whom he adored.

When the constitutional monarchy was overthrown, Goya, like many others who had supported it, fled to France, where he lived out his remaining days in Bordeaux until he collapsed of a stroke, paintbrush in hand. He was buried in France but was later exhumed; it was discovered that his skull had been stolen, possibly by a group he had befriended while working on *Caprices*, that believed in phrenology, the ability to read a person's character from the bumps on his skull. ◆

Greco, El

1541–April, 1614 ● Painter, Sculptor, and Architect

Born in Candia, Crete, El Greco's first training was probably with icon painters in Crete at the monastery of Saint Catherine at Candia. The early influence of this Byzantine tradition persisted in his mature painting despite his assimilation of the Italian tradition. He always remembered his Greek origin and signed his works with his Greek name written in Greek letters. It is unclear when he left Crete but he probably arrived in Venice about 1560 and remained in Italy, where he studied the Renaissance and mannerist masters, until about 1575. During the early years in Venice he painted hundreds of small panels of Gospel scenes in the style of the Byzantine madoneros, the icon painters who formed part of the large Greek colony there.

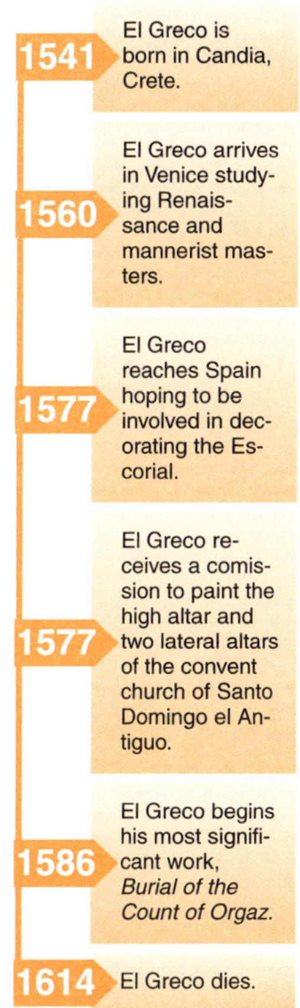

El Greco soon became a disciple of Titian although it is not clear whether he actually spent time in Titian's workshop as an apprentice or assistant. He also borrowed motifs and ideas from other Venetians including Parmigianino, Schiavone, and Tintoretto.

El Greco lived in Rome between 1570 and 1572 but was apparently unpopular with the jealous Roman painters. He acquired a reputation as haughty and arrogant after commenting to Pius X that if the Sistine Chapel frescoes were taken away he could paint better ones in their place. He is said to have remarked that "Michelangelo was a good man—a pity he did not know how to paint." Of course, while living in Rome he did

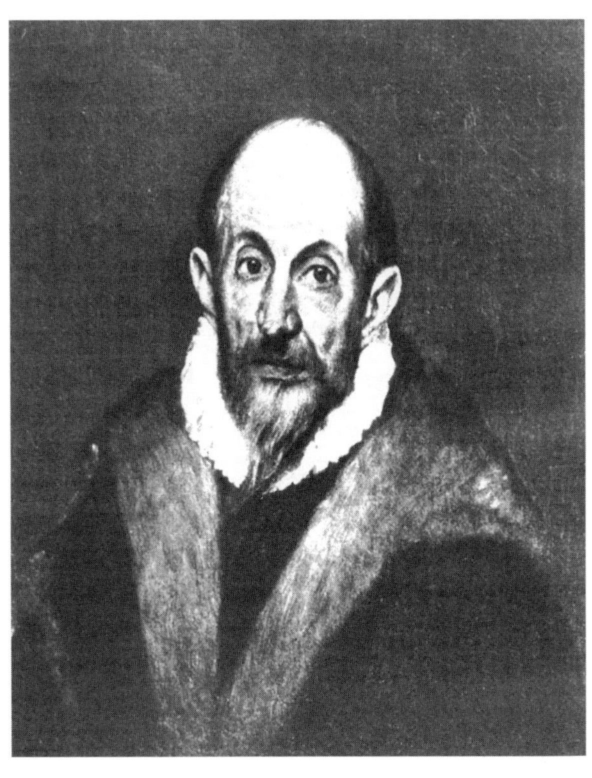

El Greco, self-portrait

study the frescoes of Michelangelo and Raphael in the Vatican and he was influenced by Michelangelo's grand vision of the human form. In the 1560s many Italian painters were involved in decorating the Escorial, which was being built in Spain, and the news from Spain probably influenced El Greco to seek his fortune there. He reached Spain in 1577 as a full-fledged Italian master and upon his arrival in Toledo immediately received an important commission to paint the high altar and two lateral altars of the convent church of Santo Domingo el Antiguo. He painted the two huge panels of the *Trinity* and the *Assumption of the Virgin*, and also devised the architecture for the altar, breaking with Spanish tradition by creating a Venetian Renaissance rather than a Gothic design.

By the late 1570s El Greco had gained the admiration of Toledo and, eager to become a court painter of the king, sought to woo King Philip II, presenting him with a gift of two sketches. The king commissioned El Greco to paint pictures of the *Adoration of the Name of Jesus*, and the *Martyrdom of Saint Maurice*. The *Martyrdom*, with its mystical mannerist mood and dramatic composition was, however, not appreciated by the king and El Greco never again received a royal commission. His wish to become a court painter was never realized but he was very successful as a portrait painter, being favored by church figures and the aristocracy. He received so many commissions that he was forced to collaborate with his disciples, especially in his later years. El Greco's portraiture style—bringing life to the sitter psychologically and physically—was greatly admired in 17th-century Spain.

As he grew older El Greco concentrated his efforts on capturing exalted religious feeling and depicting the spiritual realm, utilizing various symbolic motifs. His visionary concep-

Mannerism

The art of the Italian Renaissance in the early 16th century was largely characterized by harmony, balance, and naturalism. Later in that century, artists, particularly painters and sculptors, began experimenting with ways to preserve the classical styles while introducing greater emotion and tension in their works. The word that describes this powerful style, mannerism, comes from the Italian maniera ("style"). One common mannerist technique is to represent a human figure in an exaggerated way, as highly angular, or by elongating the neck or showing a body in a twisted pose, to highlight the anguish of the figure. Mannerist colors were often vivid and clashing. In their use of space, the mannerists often eliminated the middleground, so that the scene immediately jumps from foreground to background. Influenced by Michelangelo, they also used foreshortening, a technique that makes objects appear to emerge from the canvas or other two-dimensional surface. Key figures in mannerism include Jacopo da Pontormo, Rosso Fiorentino (*Descent from the Cross,* 1521), Michelangelo in his later works (such as the *Last Judgment,* 1541), Florentine Agnolo Bronzino, Francesco Mazzola (Parmigianino), and the architect Giulio Romano. El Greco used this style in some periods of his work and remains Spain's best-known mannerist.

Mannerism is very difficult to define because, as with many art movements, the "mannerists" did not see themselves as part of a single school, and even today there are different ideas about what mannerism was. In any case, mannerist art was not widely appreciated in its own day—the public often misunderstood its technique and sophistication, and church authorities found it irreverent—and by 1600 the style gave way to baroque. In the 20th century, however, especially under the influence of German art historian Max Dvorák, mannerism was appreciated by new generations for its willingness to play with space and proportion to convey intense drama and emotion.

tion of the real and spiritual world was expressed with supernatural light and flamelike, ethereal forms. His most significant work, *Burial of the Count of Orgaz* (1586–1588), combines mystical and earthly images, portraying the three stages of human existence: life on earth, the grave, and heaven. A modern author has ascribed his characteristic style—a vertical elongation on a slightly oblique axis—to astigmatism, but in fact this was a style familiar in other painters of the time.

El Greco was strongly influenced by Spanish mysticism, and his work is marked by an exalted spiritualism. He was also something of a philosopher and wrote philosophical treatises as well as treatises on art and architecture, but his writings are lost. A self-taught architect, he designed altarpieces for his paintings, developing an individual language of architecture to complement the figures in his paintings. Essentially a painter of religious works, El Greco also painted many fine "psychological" portraits and a number of landscapes. His reputation faded after his death and it is only in the 20th century that he has been acclaimed as a great visionary artist. ◆

Gris, Juan

MARCH 23, 1887–MAY 11, 1927 ● PAINTER

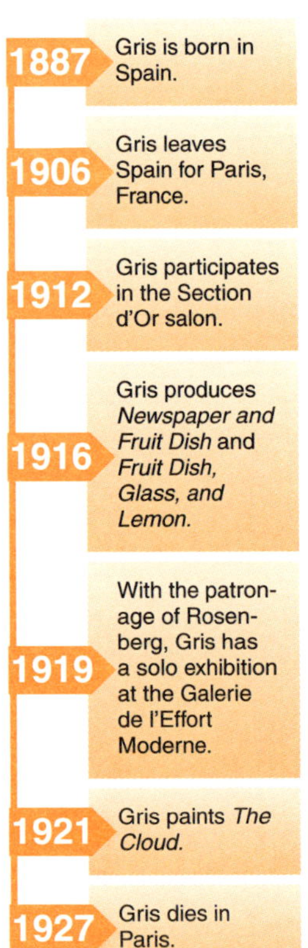

The artist known today as Juan Gris was born José Victoriano Gonzáles in Madrid. Little is known of his earliest childhood, but in 1902, he entered Madrid's Escuela de Artes y Manufacturas (School of Arts and Crafts), where he spent two years learning mathematics and technical drawing. He left the school before completing his degree in order to study painting under José Moreno Carbonero, and never returned to the more technical and scientific work of his school days. During his first year out of school, Gonzáles supported himself as an illustrator, and in 1904 or 1905 first used the pseudonym "Juan Gris." He contributed drawings to the periodical *Renacimiento latino* and also illustrated a book of poetry by José Santo Chocano, entitled *Alma América*. In 1906, motivated by a desire to participate in the great artistic ferment going on in Paris, and perhaps as well by a desire to avoid compulsory military service, he moved to France, never to return to his native Spain.

Arriving in Paris, Gris immediately fell in with the already formidable Pablo Picasso and a brilliant circle of artists and writers, including Guillaume Apollinaire and Georges Braque. With Picasso's help he founded a studio in 1908. He continued to earn his living as an illustrator, contributing work to Parisian and Spanish publications. There is no evidence, however, that any paintings he may have executed during his first four years in Paris have survived. In 1910, however, Gris committed himself to a career as a painter. For some time his association with Picasso had made him privy to the evolution of cubism, and in 1911 he was ready to make his own contribution to the development of that style. He was not, however, prepared to go to the extremes that marked the work of Picasso and Braque. While he employed the flattened planes that typify cubist art, he retained some fidelity to the depiction of recognizable objects through the use of light and shadow.

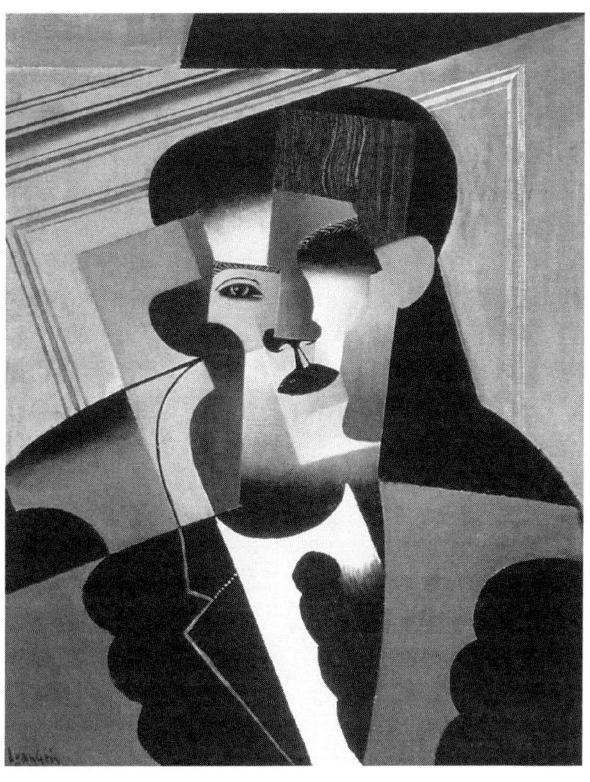

Portrait of the Artists (1916), by Juan Gris

Gris's close association with some of the major actors in the Parisian art scene quickly brought him to the attention of the renowned agent Daniel-Henry Kahnweiler, who also handled Picasso. Kahnweiler secured for Gris the opportunity to participate in a number of prestigious exhibitions. As his fame and acceptance grew after the salon of the Section d'Or in 1912, Gris became increasingly free to explore new areas of interest, and in 1913–1914 he began working intensively with collages, in which medium he became known as a particularly creative innovator. One of his most impressive works of this period is *The Coffee Packet* (1914), which combined colored drawing with an underlying base of paper cut-outs.

The year 1914 saw the beginning of World War I and with it the disruption of the Parisian art circles, as most of their members were called for military service. Gris, as a resident foreigner, was exempt from such obligations, however, and for him the wartime period was a time of great experimentation and productivity. By 1916 he was exploring pointillism, and produced such still-life collages as *Newspaper and Fruit Dish* and *Fruit Dish, Glass, and Lemon*. Within two years, however, he began turning away from the collage form and began experimenting with thickly textured layers of paint to achieve his effects.

The war did have a damaging effect on Gris's financial stability, however, when his formidable agent was exiled in 1914 for having German ancestry. During this period Gris's friendship with Gertrude Stein, among others, was important, for

Gris's approach, he felt, was a synthetic one, to be contrasted to the "analytic" approach that worked from real objects to their more abstract components.

these friends offered him financial support when commissions and sales of his art were lagging. It was not until 1916 that Gris was free to sign with a new agent, Léonce Rosenberg. With his fortunes once again secure, Gris became one of the leading lights of what was left of Paris's cubist movement, and he provided friendship and support for younger artists, such as Amédée Ozenfant.

By 1920, Gris was beginning to articulate his own theory of cubism, writing articles to Parisian journals that spoke of "working deductively" from flat shapes to recognizable objects. His approach, he felt, was a synthetic one, to be contrasted to the "analytic" approach that worked from real objects to their more abstract components. At about the same time, he was continuing his prolific artistic output. In 1919 he had an important solo exhibition at the Galerie de l'Effort Moderne (Gallery of Modern Endeavor), owned by Rosenberg, and in 1920 he was again included in an exhibition at the salon of the Section d'Or. Works during this period include *The Cloud* (1921) and others depicting still-lifes in the foreground, with an open window in the background revealing the landscape beyond.

After a bout of illness requiring hospitalization interrupted his work in 1920–1921, Gris enthusiastically returned to his painting. A series of prestigious commissions underscored his professional success in 1922, 1923, and 1924, some of them for work outside his customary medium. Significant among these was the commission, by Serge Diaghilév, for costume and set design for the Ballets Russe. However, some of his peers saw in his paintings of this period the early signs of compromise, believing that Gris was allowing himself to be influenced by the growing voices of critics of cubism. Gris himself denied any such compromise. He was, however, becoming increasingly intrigued by the work of the surrealists, having been introduced by his old agent, Kahnweiler, to proponents of surrealism such as Antonin Artaud.

Although illustrations for books no longer formed a major part of Gris's artistic production, he continued to take on such projects for his friends through the first half of the 1920s, including four drawings he supplied for a volume by his old friend and supporter, Gertrude Stein. While he continued to paint, he suffered a return to ill health, possibly tuberculosis, and his decline was rapid. He died in Paris. ◆

Grünewald, Matthias

C. 1475–AUGUST, 1528 ● PAINTER

The painter and writer Joachim von Sandrart mentions a painter named "Matthaeus Grünewald," also known as "Matthaeus von Aschaffenburg," in his *Teutsche Academie der Edlen Bau-, Bild- und Mahlerey-Künste* (1675). This person is almost certainly the painter "Mathis Gothart Nithart" referred to in early 16th-century documents.

Nothing is known regarding the training and early career of Grünewald, who was probably born in Würzburg. The *Mocking of Christ* (c. 1504–1506), is among his earliest surviving pictures.

Grünewald was recommended in 1510 as a hydraulic engineer. In 1511 he is recorded as a painter, stonecutter, superintendent of works, and architect at the court of Uriel von Gemmingen, archbishop of Mainz, at Aschaffenburg. Around that time, he painted four grisaille (gray-toned) *Saints* which became the fixed wings of Dürer's (lost) *Assumption and Coronation of the Virgin* (1508–1509), ordered by Jakob Heller in 1507 for the Dominican church of Frankfurt.

In 1512 the Antonite preceptor Guido Guersi commissioned three sets of painted wings from "Mathis Nithart" to complete the carved altarpiece on the high altar of the church of the monastery of Saint Anthony, near Isenheim in Alsace. The monumental polyptych dated 1515 shows in its closed state a *Crucifixion* rising above a *Lamentation* in the predella and flanked by fixed wings depicting *Saint Sebastian* and *Saint Anthony* as statues miraculously come alive. Once we open

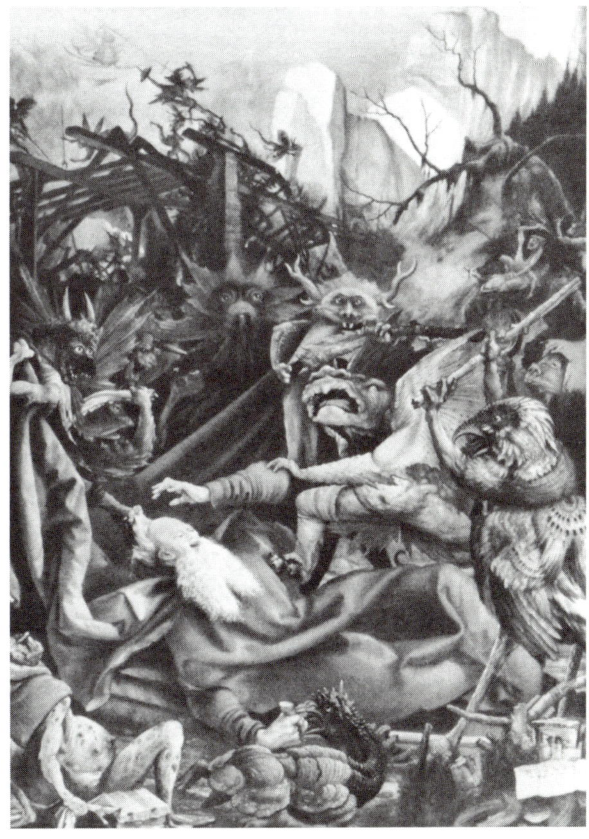

The Temptation of St. Anthony (1515), by Matthias Grünewald.

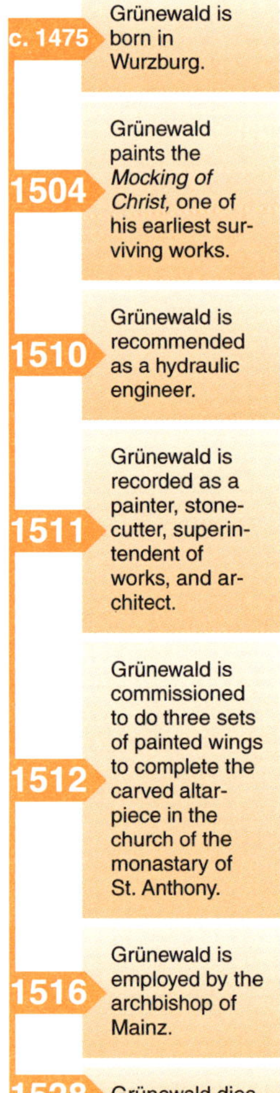

the first set of movable wings, we see: the *Annunciation* on the left, the so-called *Angels' Concert* and *Virgin and Child* in the center (above the *Lamentation*), and the *Resurrection* on the right. When the altarpiece is completely opened, we see Nikolaus Hagenower's polychrome wood sculpture group of circa 1505 depicting *Saint Anthony* enthroned between the standing *SS. Augustine* and *Jerome*. Bust-length depictions of *Christ and the Twelve Apostles* carved by Desiderius Beichel appear in the predella below. Hagenau's ensemble is flanked by the interior of Grünewald's third set of painted wings, depicting the *Meeting of SS. Anthony and Paul the Hermit* and the *Temptation of Saint Anthony*.

This altarpiece was presumably closed during most of the liturgical year; the first set of mobile wings was opened on Sundays and special feast days, and the second set was opened to uncover the sculpture within on the feasts of Anthony and other patron saints of the Antonine order. Grünewald's highly unusual imagery—comprising gruesome depictions of the dead Christ—has been interpreted in light of the fact that the monastery included a hospital. Christ's stiff, lacerated body harbors the promise of salvation (symbolized by the *Resurrection*) for those who suffer greatly—in "imitatio Christi"—and repent. In addition, SS. Sebastian and Anthony were venerated by people seeking to ward off or cure diseases. However, Grünewald's pictures—with their accent on the mystery of Christ's incarnation, sacrifice, and resurrection, and on the trials of Anthony's ascetic way of life—also perfectly suited the monks' contemplative needs. Their expressive vocabulary goes back to certain types of German Gothic devotional images, such as the so-called Plague Crucifixes, as well as to the *Revelations* of the mystic Bridget of Sweden.

Grünewald returned to the theme of Christ's sacrifice in his harrowing *Crucifixions* (c. 1510–1520 and c. 1525–1526). His altarpiece dedicated to *The Virgin of the Snow* for a chapel of the (former) collegiate church in Aschaffenburg is dismembered. Only the central panel depicting the *Madonna and Child in a Garden* and one side panel showing the *Miracle of the Snows* survive. This painting's frame bears the date 1519 and the artist's monogram MG (in ligature) beneath an N.

Grünewald was employed by the new archbishop of Mainz, Albrecht von Brandenburg, from circa 1516 to 1526, and completed *The Meeting of SS. Erasmus and Maurice* for him by 1525. Several scholars suggest the artist was dismissed by Albrecht in

1526, either because of his (supposed) participation in the Peasants' War of 1525 or as a result of his (documented) enthusiasm for Lutheranism. Grünewald moved to Frankfurt and later to Halle, where he worked in his final year as a hydraulic engineer.

In his *Elementorum rhetorices libri duo* of 1531, Philipp Melanchthon ranked "Mathias" just after Dürer and before "Lucas" (Cranach). Grünewald conveys the emotional intensity and spiritual dimension of his religious subjects through his singular powers of invention, symbol-laden transformation of natural phenomena, and subtlety as a colorist and painter of ethereal light. Unlike Dürer, he appears to have been largely untouched by antique visual and literary sources, and hardly inspired by the achievements of the Italian Renaissance. His **oeuvre** proves the continued importance of medieval images, ideas, and modes of expression in some of the major cultural centers of Germany at the beginning of the 16th century. ◆

oeuvre: a French word meaning or representing a substantial body of work by an artist, composer, or writer.

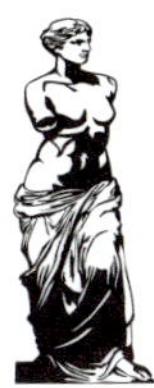

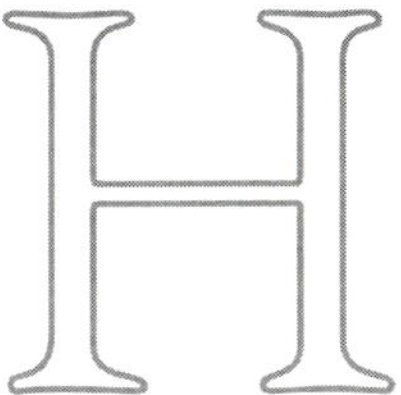

Hals, Frans

c. 1581–August 29, 1666 • Painter

Dutch portrait painter Frans Hals was not well known during his lifetime, but he strongly influenced the development of **portraiture** through his spontaneous, lively, and highly distinctive paintings of individuals and groups. Hals was born in Antwerp, the son of a clothmaker. In 1585 the family left Antwerp, which had fallen under Spanish control, and settled in Haarlem, which would remain the center of Hals's work until his death. As a young man Hals studied with Karel van Mander. In 1610, he joined the Haarlem Guild of St. Luke and married his first wife, who died just five years later.

portraiture: the art of creating portraits.

No known work survives from Hals's earlier years as a painter. His earliest surviving works suggest that he developed his portraiture style early. In a departure from his predecessors, Hals gave his subjects more individual characteristics, seeking in a sense to capture their uniqueness. One painting from 1611, *Jacobus Zaffius*, reveals several elements that would become important in Hals's work, especially lighting from the left, the brightly-lit head against a dark background, and the portrayal of a highly distinctive face, not an emotionless subject sitting passively while having his portrait taken.

In 1612, Hals joined the St. George Civic Guard, a group that had once served in war but had become largely ceremonial. It was common for members to commission portraits of themselves. Before Hals, painters had tended to show these

One painting from 1611, *Jacobus Zaffius*, reveals several elements that would become important in Hals's work, especially lighting from the left, the brightly-lit head against a dark background, and the portrayal of a highly distinctive face.

military groups in bland ways, with little to distinguish one man from another except his face. In *Banquet of the Officers of the St. George Civic Guard Company* (1616), Hals gave each man some attribute to make him stand out—a special facial expression or stance. Viewed as a whole, such a picture also conveyed a more lively and interesting group than earlier portraits following a more repetitious approach. This and other group pictures were quite successful, and Hals also began painting individual and smaller group portraits, such as his *Portrait of Isaac Abrahamsz Massa and Beatrix van der Laen* (1622), which show Hals's attention to close detail. Against the backdrop of a long open field, cut off by a grove of trees, the two figures playfully recline in a half-seated posture, both full of joy. While elements of the clothing are so loosely painted they almost resemble charcoal sketches, the lace on the collars and wrists is rendered with exquisite detail, as are the faces of the newlyweds. In particular, the face of Beatrix is so well lit, detailed, and shown with such a spontaneous smile of pleasure that it appears lifelike.

In the 1620s, Hals also painted several "genre" paintings, paintings that deal with certain established themes or scenes. Influenced by Utrecht Caravaggisti, these include playful children and carousing young men out drinking or playing music. Examples include *Jonker Ramp and his Sweetheart* (1623) and *The Merry Drinker* (1630).

Throughout the 1620s and 1630s, Hals's fame as a portraitist grew. People responded to the way he made faces leap off the canvas through lighting, realistic depiction, and interesting gestures and emotions. In the late 1630s and early 1640s, however, his portraits and scenes became somewhat less exuberant and joyful. He used more muted colors such as browns and grays, and his subjects had more serious facial expressions, while facing the viewer directly ("frontal poses"). This is probably because public tastes were changing, and people preferred to be represented in more somber ways. Still, Hals's talents matured throughout his lifetime, and his *Regents of the Haarlem Old Men's Alms House*, painted in 1664, just two years before his death, is a masterpiece of dignity and simplicity.

Besides subject matter and the composition of his work, Hals is remarkable for his technique. Unlike most artists, he rarely used preliminary studies to plan the works he was about to do. Later in life, he rarely used underpainting, a technique where an artist applies a layer of paint as a background to the surface paint. He used very broad strokes, applied in a loose manner. Taken together, these qualities gave his work a sense of liveliness and exciting light, and later painters such as Claude Monet appreciated and even attempted to copy Hals's style.

In his own day, however, Hals was not universally admired. While some painters, such as Hendrick Po and Pieter Claesz, cited his influence, and some critics admired the naturalness of his style, others thought his loose brushwork was a sign of carelessness and lack of skill. Hals also faced another challenge in his own lifetime—financial difficulties. While it is hard to be certain about the details of his life due to the existence of another F. Hals (a relative recorded in historical documents of his time), Hals appears to have faced financial troubles repeatedly. They may have made it difficult for him to travel more widely and meet many artists in other countries. His reputation did not spread widely in his lifetime, and only after his death were his skills fully recognized. Gustave Courbet emulated him, and Vincent van Gogh praised his ability to make his characters come to life. While the neglect he suffered in his own lifetime still undermines his fame—especially because many critics are not sure exactly which paintings are his own—he is now generally acknowledged as second only to Rembrandt in producing vivid, intimate portraits of his contemporaries. ◆

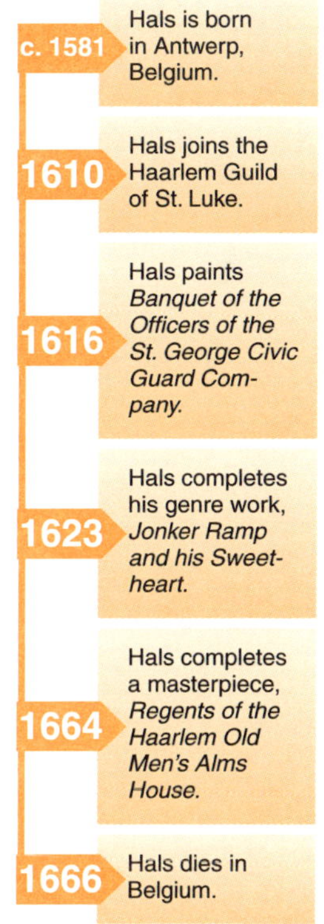

Hockney, David

JULY 9, 1937– ● PAINTER AND DESIGNER

British painter, graphic artist, and designer David Hockney is still considered to be a leading European artist and is one of the most well-known painters on the contemporary scene, but there is no question that his big move to California in 1963 changed his perspective and altered his artistic style. Hockney was born in Bradford, Yorkshire, England, in 1937. He was one of five children born to Kenneth Hockney, head of an accounting firm, and Laura Hockney. David's early precocity as an artist was nurtured in the household, for his father dabbled in art, and his brother John would later pursue a career in the arts as well. Young David received further encouragement when he entered the Bradford School of Art in 1953.

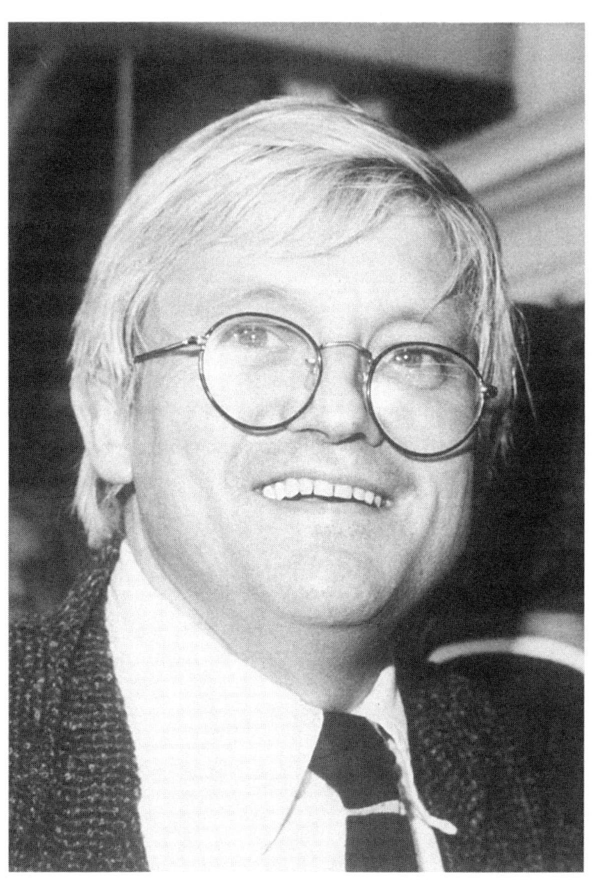

David Hockney

There he immediately excelled in his courses in draftsmanship. During his years at the Bradford School, Hockney refined his skills under the direction of Stanley Spencer. Upon leaving school he faced a mandatory two-year term of national service, claiming conscientious objector status and serving in hospitals.

Upon completing his national service requirement in 1959, Hockney returned to formal training, enrolling in a three-year postgraduate course offered by London's Royal College of Art, where he was introduced to the theory and techniques of modernism. There he met R. B. Kiraj, a fellow student, with whom he began exploring new, more personally satisfying ways to express himself on canvas. This led to experiments in integrating painting and poetry, and he began inserting bits of poetry or other textual messages into his work. Already in his early works, his "naive" style was emerging—forms that the viewer at first glance might regard as simple and childlike, though he used them in highly sophisticated ways.

In the early 1960s the idea of homosexual love became an important theme in Hockney's work, first turning up in his treatment of Walt Whitman's poem, "We Two Boys Together Clinging." Hockney's homosexuality would always play an important role in both his art and his reputation. Works such as the elegant etching *In the Dull Village* (1966) show men reclining in bed together, but there is no implication of shame or titillation; the work's title can in fact be interpreted to suggest the almost mundane quality of the relationship.

pop art: an artistic style originating in the 1950s in England and the United States in the 1960s; characterized by vivid colors and the use of familiar commercial images and products.

Hockney earned his earliest international recognition in the early 1960s as a painter of **pop art.** His works of this period were witty and well-designed, but the artist's interest in the pop art idiom was short-lived. He moved to California in 1963, hoping to find there a society in which his dream of unselfconscious love could flourish. The paintings he began producing after the move reflect that desire, as he left pop art behind and began working in a more realistic, representational style. He chose to represent a vision of a brightly-lit California, as in his 1967 painting, *A Bigger Splash,* which, while still somewhat modernist in tone, shows the beginning of his shift to naturalism. During this period Hockney also produced what has become one of the best-known paintings in modern British art: *Mr. and Mrs. Clark and Percy* (1970), which can be interpreted as a depiction of a couple's profound alienation and distance, set against a brightly-lit, cleanly painted interior. For this and many other paintings, Hockney worked from photographs rather than live models, and some critics complained that the resulting work is stilted. It is more likely, however, that this stiffness was an intended effect, since in his drawings and etchings Hockney clearly displays an elegant and graceful style.

While best known as a painter, Hockney is also highly regarded for his proficiency as a draftsman and printmaker. In the late 1960s he concentrated for a time on etching, and he produced the illustrations for a collection of poetry by C. P. Cavafy (1967) and for a volume of *Grimm's Fairy Tales* (1969). He also produced a series of 16 prints inspired by William Hogarth's *A Rake's Progress.* In 1975 he became interested in the theater as a new venue for his art. He designed sets for a wide range of productions, from Mozart's *The Magic Flute* to Wagner's *Tristan and Isolde.* His design work for opera was seen in venues as diverse as the Glyndenbourne Opera Festival in England and the Metropolitan Opera in New York City, the Lyric Opera in Chicago, and the Royal Opera House at Covent Garden.

Hockney's openness to experimentation led him to work in other media as well, from pulped paper constructions such as the *Paper Pools* (1978) to photography in the 1980s. Through these and other experiments the artist has explored theories of perspective and memory. In the early 1990s he began a series entitled *Very New Paintings,* in which he attempts to convey his personal experience of the Pacific coastline. In these works the abstract sensibility of his school days begins to re-emerge, although they remain well within the naturalist idiom. ◆

1937 Hockney is born in Yorkshire, England.

1959 London's Royal College of Art accepts Hockney for post-graduate study.

1966 Hockney completes *In the Dull Village.*

1969 Hockney's etchings for *Grimm's Fairy Tales* appear.

1970 Hockney paints the well-known *Mr. and Mrs. Clark and Percy.*

1978 Hockney finishes *Paper Pools.*

"In the mid-'60s, Hockney moved from London to Los Angeles, where he's lived on and off ever since and where he has created his most famous paintings—of his boyish lovers swimming in brilliant blue pools and of the city's crazy-colored streets."

Michael Joseph Gross, in the *Boston Phoenix,* 1998.

Hofmann, Hans

MARCH 21, 1880–FEBRUARY 17, 1966 ● PAINTER

Hans Hofmann was born in Weissenberg, Bavaria. From an early age he showed great skill in science and music (including violin and piano) as well as drawing. When only 16, however, he left school to take a position with the public works department in Bavaria. There he proved himself to be an inventor of great ingenuity, developing a refrigeration device and radar apparatus for naval use. Although his family pressured him into pursuing a technical career, and his talents in that direction were great, his love for art triumphed. By 1898 he was again studying art with Moritz Heymann, who ran an art school in Munich.

While at Heymann's school, Hofmann explored a wide variety of different painting styles, most notably the then strongly influential French impressionist school. Over time, Hofmann gradually established a reputation as an important artist in his own right. His work of this period is strongly influenced by impressionism, as in *Self-portrait* (1902). Willi Schwarz, Hofmann's teacher, was profoundly impressed by his talent and introduced the young artist to art patron Phillip Freudenberg. Freudenberg quickly took Hoffman under his wing, providing the artist and his companion, Maria Wolfegg, with sufficient funds to underwrite a ten-year sojourn in Paris, from 1904 to 1914.

By the time of his arrival in Paris, Hofmann was recognized for his mastery of impressionism. In the French capital, he enrolled in the Académie Colarossi and the Académie de la Grande Chaumière. He now found himself surrounded by an explosion of new ideas and styles. He studied the works of artists such as Robert Delaunay, Georges Braque, and Pablo Picasso and built a network of associations with influential art dealers and collectors in France, Germany, and the United States. He showed his work at summer exhibitions in Berlin in 1908 and 1909, and at last achieved his first solo exhibition at Berlin's prestigious Paul Cassirer Gallery in 1910.

It is impossible to say how vast a legacy of paintings Hofmann might have left behind if this life of contact with many of the greatest painters of his day had continued uninterrupted. Unfortunately, World War I intervened. War between France

1880	Hoffman is born in Weissenberg, Bavaria.
1910	Hofmann's first solo exhibition is held at Berlin's Paul Cassirer Gallery.
1915	The Hofmann School for Modern Art opens in Munich.
1933	Hofmann opens his School of Fine Arts in New York City.
1942	Hofmann paints *The Wind.*
1962	Hofmann paints *Magnum Opus.*
1966	Hoffman dies.

and Germany was declared while Hofmann was visiting his homeland, and the artist was barred from re-entering France. In addition, the bulk of his artistic output was destroyed during the war. However, out of this double tragedy came one of the most important developments in modern art—Hofmann's decision to devote himself to teaching. In Munich in 1915 he opened the Hofmann School for Modern Art (Schule für Moderne Kunst). Soon, promising students from all over the world—including Louise Nevelson and Wolfgang Paalen—were flocking to his courses. Although his influence upon the younger artists of the day was profound, his own artistic output almost completed ceased.

Today, Hofmann is primarily remembered as a brilliant teacher who introduced European modernist theories into the United States.

In 1929 Hofmann married his long-time companion, Maria Wolfegg, and during the next few years he took summer trips to the University of California at Berkeley, where he taught a series of courses. In 1932, the couple decided to move to the United States permanently, and Hofmann took a teaching position at the Art Students League in New York City. His direct and vast experience of the artistic creativity then sweeping Europe made him an influential mentor for students curious about the latest developments in modern art. In 1933 he began the Hans Hofmann School of Fine Arts, where he taught modernist theory. Through this school he exerted a powerful influence over the development of many of the most important young artists of his day, including Larry Rivers.

Although Hofmann devoted some time to his own painting during this period, he eventually closed his school in 1958 in order to resume painting full time. Prior to this decision he had explored a number of genres, including landscapes and portraits, and had experimented in a variety of techniques, including automatism, a favorite of the surrealist school.

Today Hofmann is primarily remembered as a brilliant teacher who introduced European modernist theories into the United States. The destruction of so many of his earlier works in World War I, and the fact that he painted little from the outbreak of World War I to the 1930s, has interfered with the widespread appreciation of his own artistic oeuvre. Hofmann's body of work is, however, quite substantial. Even during the period 1914–1935, he produced many drawings, and from the mid-1930s onward his painting became increasingly prolific. His work in the 1930s shows the powerful influence of Henri Matisse, best exemplified in paintings such as *Japanese Girl* (1935) and *Table with Fruit and Coffee Pot* (1936). Hofmann's later work shows his immense receptivity to new styles and techniques. His 1942 painting, *The Wind,* is a forerunner of the drip technique made famous by Jackson Pollock, and in the 1950s he produced some fine examples of action painting, a major branch of the school of **abstract expressionism.** Among these works are *Le Gilotin* (1953) and *Fantasia in Blue* (1954). At the same time he had an important influence on the development of abstract impressionism's other main branch, **color field painting,** particularly in the work of his student, Helen Frankenthaler. By the 1960s, he began experimenting with the manipulation of contrasting shapes so that various parts of his paintings seem to emerge, and then retreat, from the canvas. This is clearly apparent in his *Magnum Opus* (1962).

abstract expressionism: an artistic movement in painting characterized by the artist applying paint rapidly and with force onto giant canvases in an attempt to convey emotion and feeling.

color field painting: a form of painting in which a large canves is covered with solid areas of color.

Given Hofmann's experimentation in so many different styles, it is not surprising that some have criticized his work as lacking focus, as though he was more a mirror of contemporary trends than a leader in them. His paintings have a continuity, however, characterized most of all by his imaginative and bold use of color and his consistent focus on the composition of shapes. ◆

Hogarth, William

NOVEMBER 10, 1697–OCTOBER 25, 1764 ● PAINTER AND ENGRAVER

William Hogarth is remembered primarily for his innovative, populist engravings of morality tales. Through these works he virtually invented the satiric tradition in British art. His series of prints such as *A Harlot's Progress* and *A Rake's Progress* brought him not only wealth but also fame as a social observer.

Born in London, Hogarth was the son of a schoolmaster. His father also owned a coffeehouse in the city, but this business went broke in 1708, and the entire family was sent to debtor's prison for four years. The family's financial difficulties made it necessary for young William to find work, and in 1713 he became apprentice to a London silver engraver. He quickly mastered the engraver's trade, and by 1720 he had opened up a shop of his own.

Hogarth's early engraving work was commercial, but his artistic interests would not be denied for long. In the autumn of

1720 he signed up for courses in life drawing. One year later he completed his first artistic engraving, *South Sea Scheme*. He would soon make a name for himself for his satirical eye, and the financial scandals of the period provided him with ample subject matter, presented in such works as *The Lottery* (1724) and *Bad Taste of the Town* (1724).

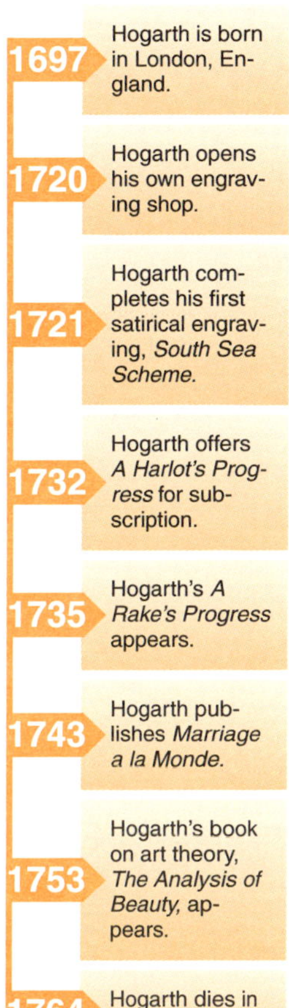

By this time, Hogarth's work had achieved such popularity that his prints were being pirated. Ever practical about financial matters since his childhood experiences in debtor's prison, Hogarth placed an advertisement in the London papers announcing that his work could only be sold through his own shop and a handful of other, authorized print-sellers.

By 1724 the young engraver moved on to study at a school run by James Thornhill. Ever on the lookout for ways to make his income more secure, Hogarth noted that Thornhill published his prints by subscription only. This meant that he would not begin work on a volume of engravings until a body of patrons had already paid for them. Hogarth recognized the financial advantage of this strategy and used it consistently once he began publishing his own work.

By the late 1720s, Hogarth had found a new reason to increase his income; in 1729 he married Jane Thornhill, his art teacher's daughter. He found portrait painting a congenial way of earning a living and soon built a reputation for group portraits. He also quickly built an audience for a new type of artwork—a series of pictures intended to tell a story and sold as a collection of prints. His first attempt at this new style was *A Harlot's Progress* (1732), the pictorial chronicle of a young woman's life from her arrival in the city, through her corruption, to her dismal death and funeral. The six-print series, sold by subscription, earned the artist an impressive sum of money. However, the success of Hogarth's work again inspired others to copy his theme, siphoning off potential subscribers. In retaliation, Hogarth appealed to Parliament for legislation that would grant engravers copyright over their works.

Meanwhile, Hogarth sought to duplicate the success of his *Harlot* series, and found it in a new chronicle of a young man's fall from wealth into debauchery, ending in madness and death. This eight-print work, *A Rake's Progress* (1735), is perhaps the best-known of Hogarth's pictorial morality tales, and his paintings upon which the prints are based are among the finest examples of rococo art in England.

The eight-print work, *A Rake's Progress* (1735), is perhaps the best-known of Hogarth's pictorial morality tales.

As concerned as he was with commercial success, Hogarth also hungered for social acceptance and began working to establish himself as a portraitist of the British elite. He was somewhat successful, securing commissions to paint a number of eminent society folk. He lost his commission to depict the royal family, however, because of a rival's interference. Still, Hogarth's greatest artistic legacy was never based upon his conventional portraiture. Even in his own day such works met with little enthusiasm, largely because he was unwilling to portray his subjects in conventionally bland and flattering poses. Fortunately, Hogarth's satires continued to be popular, as were his treatments of sensational subjects, such as *Sara Malcolm in Prison* (1732), one of several pieces depicting notorious criminals.

While continuing to seek acceptance as a high society painter, Hogarth kept up with his popular moralistic and satirical works. In 1743 he published *Marriage à la Monde*, which details the sorry fate of a young man who enters into an arranged marriage. In 1747 he published *Industry and Idleness*, addressing the vice of **sloth.**

sloth: inactivity or apathy of the spirit; insolent and lazy behavior; said to be one of the seven deadly sins.

Hogarth's quest for respectability periodically inspired him to paint religious and historical themes, including *Moses Brought before Pharaoh's Daughter* (1746) and *Paul before Felix.* As a result of these works and in recognition of his more populist pieces, Hogarth was appointed Sergeant-Painter to the King in 1757, an honor previously held by his father-in-law.

Hogarth had great success in the following years, particularly when he returned to popular themes, but his longtime paranoia that his fellow artists were conspiring to destroy him only grew worse. He lost an important commission in 1757, and the rejection appears to have made him ill for a year, during which time he could not work. Also severely troubling to him was the criticism he received for a piece he submitted for exhibition in 1760 and later withdrew. In 1762 Hogarth produced *The Times: Plate I*, supporting the end of the war with France and insultingly portraying a number of London's statesmen as corrupt. This touched off a new round of criticism by both fellow artists and public figures, and Hogarth responded with attacks of his own, in the engravings *John Wilkes* and *The Bruiser* (both published in 1763). He died of an aneurysm the following year and is buried in London.

Because of his efforts to secure copyrights for engravers, Hogarth has been credited with sparking tremendous growth in the English printmaker's art. His book *The Analysis of Beauty* (1753) is also the first English example of a sustained attempt at a theory of art. ◆

Holbein the Younger, Hans

1497–OCTOBER, 1543 ● PAINTER

Hans Holbein the Younger worked with his elder brother Ambrosius in their father's Augsburg workshop until he transferred to Hans Herbst's studio in Basel as a journeyman in 1516. One of his earliest commissions involved marginal illustrations to theologian Oswald Myconius's copy of Erasmus's *Praise of Folly*, dimly alluding to Erasmus's own sponsorship of the artist a number of years later. In 1516, Holbein completed a double portrait of the mayor of Basel, Jakob Meyer, and his wife. Several monumental commissions followed: in 1517, the illusionistic facade of Jacob von Hertenstein's house in Lucerne and, after his 1519 receipt into the Basel guild as master, works for the town council chamber and the facade of the Haus zum Tanz.

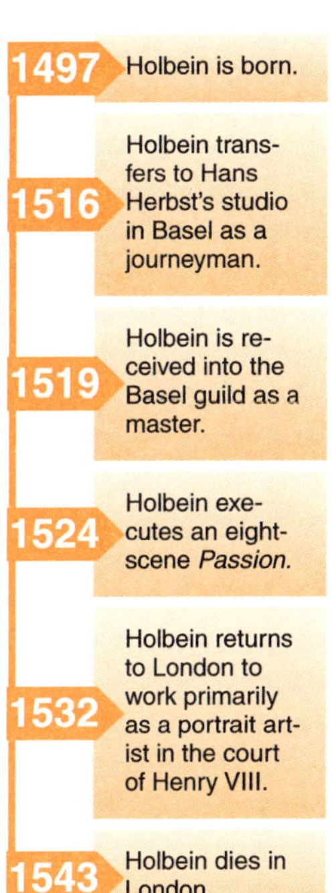

Holbein's 1521 *Body of the Dead Christ* testifies to his growing conviction that a new human form inhabits religious personages. This recumbent and decomposing Christ was probably suggested by the predella of Matthias Grünewald's *Isenbeim Altar* (1512–1515), which he might have seen in 1516. In 1524, Holbein executed an eight-scene *Passion*. In part inspired by his father's 1502 altar in Kaisheim, its innovation lies in its use of dramatic lighting dictated by the unusual and predominant choice of night scenes.

Holbein's services as a portraitist were recommended to the humanist Erasmus of Rotterdam by Johannes Froben, Erasmus's publisher, for whom Holbein had done some illustrative work. Erasmus actively commissioned portraits of himself as gifts for a network of colleagues, including the 1523 *Erasmus* for his protector, William Warham, the archbishop of Canterbury. A 1524 sojourn in France put Holbein in contact with French court styles and under the influence of Lombard painting prevalent there around the time of Francis I. Holbein's *Laïs Corinthiaca*, *Darmstadt Madonna*, and the *Last Supper* reflect such Leonardesque inspiration.

Holbein's first stay in England dates to 1526–1528. Recommendations from Erasmus won him commissions from Sir Thomas More and members of the royal court, whose images Holbein aggrandized in frontal portraits. By the time he returned to Basel in 1529, the city was beseiged by anti-Catholic iconoclasts. He soon found untenable the practice of creating Catholic religious imagery while simultaneously generating anti-Catholic woodcuts in the name of Protestant propaganda. By 1532, Holbein was back in London. *The Ambassadors* of 1533 is a double portrait of the French ambassador to England, Jean de Dinteville, and the bishop Georges de Selve. The table between them supports items of **Byzantine** iconography, topped by a foreground anamorphic image of a skull, which comes into focus only when the perspective system governing the rest of the picture drops away. Between 1532 and 1538, Holbein was retained by Henry VIII's court and executed numerous title-page and jewelry designs, miniatures, murals, and portraits. Henry's 1536 portrait by Holbein is perhaps that by which we know the king best. Holbein made some additional trips to the Continent to capture the likenesses of Henry's potential wives. He died in London in 1543. Holbein remained a great influence on the next generation of English portraitists and miniaturists, particularly Nicholas Hilliard, as well as Flemish painters Peter Paul Rubens and Anthony van Dyck. The Dutch painter and writer Karel van Mander gave the first real biographical account (1604) of Holbein as a northern foil to the idea of Italian genius propagated by Giorgio Vasari. ◆

Byzantine: relating to the Byzantine Empire and its architectual styles, particularly the fifth and sixth century domes carried on pendentives over a square, and marble veneers incrusted with mosaics on gold grounds.

Houdon, Jean-Antoine

MARCH 25, 1741–JULY 15, 1828 ● SCULPTOR

The noted French sculptor Jean-Antoine Houdon was literally born into the world of art. His father worked for the Comte de Lamotte, owner of the building where Royal Academy prize-winners in French sculpture and painting trained. This gave young Jean-Antoine the opportunity to meet many of the greatest artists of that day, even before he was old enough to begin his own formal training. When the time came, Houdon's early mentors included Jean-Baptiste Pigalle and René-Michel Slodtz, and under their tutelage he took third prize for sculpture by the age of 15. Already by 1761 he had won the ultimate prize, the Prix de Rome. This prize carried with it a stipend and studio space in Rome, but before taking advantage of this opportunity, Houdon chose to spend three years studying at the École des Elèves Protégés (School for Protected Children). He moved to Rome in 1764.

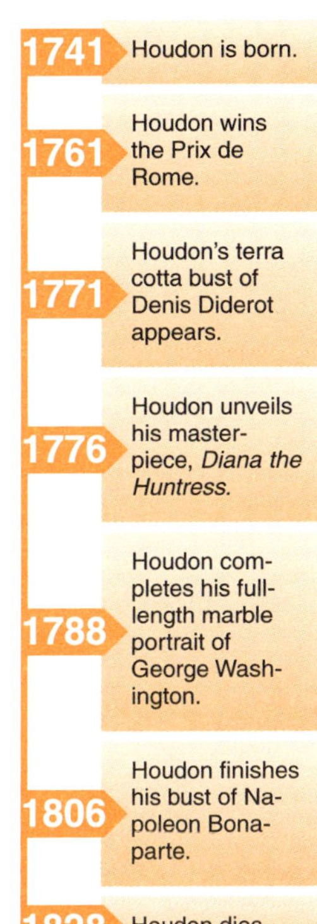

In Rome, Houdon studied at the Academy of France, where he also taught classes in drawing and modeling, while quickly making a name for himself as a sculptor. One of his early commissions called for two statues, of Saint John the Baptist and Saint Bruno, for the Church of S. Maria degli Angeli. Houdon's tranquil, meditative rendering of the latter subject displayed what would become his hallmark—his ability to portray the humanity of his subjects without recourse to the more overwrought emotionalism that typified the work of his mentors, most notably Slodtz. The statue of Saint John the Baptist was never completed, but it became the basis for Houdon's later work *Ecorché au bras tendu* (*Flayed man with outstretched arm*). Houdon's four-year stay in Rome was a time of great creativity. In addition to producing the requisite pieces demanded of all Academy students, he contributed works to a number of important exhibitions, working in plaster, terra cotta, and marble. His studies at the Academy gave him the time and the opportunity to hone his skills in the form of sculpture for which he would be remembered—powerfully expressive, classically inspired portrait busts.

At the end of his time in Rome, in 1768, Houdon returned to Paris and was accepted into the Académie Royale as a result of the success of his *Morpheus*, which he sculpted as a reclining figure. This return to France marked the true beginning of his career as a portrait sculptor. He began a series of sculptures of famous contemporaries, among them his famous terra cotta bust of the philosopher Denis Diderot (1771). To convey a lifelike awareness to his subject, Houdon inserted small pieces of marble into the terra cotta sculpture to represent the pupil of the eyes. It is believed that Houdon was inspired in this technique by the work of Giovanni Lorenzo Bernini, whose influence on his work would remain powerful throughout Houdon's life.

Houdon's fame as a portrait sculptor spread, and collectors began vying for his work. He exhibited portraits at the Paris Salons of 1771 and 1773, the latter exhibition marking the first public showing of his bust of Ernest Ludwig II. Also presented at this exhibition was his bust of Catherine the Great, no doubt created in part as homage to the woman who, like a number of others in Russia, had become an admirer and collector of his work. Through the Russian queen's patronage, Houdon soon received many prestigious commissions from the Russian elite families, including the Russian ambassador to France, Prince Dmitry Alekseyevitch Galitzin.

The middle of the 1770s, however, saw a true explosion of creativity. Houdon's list of patrons and collectors grew, and he contributed a number of important pieces to the salons of 1775 and 1777. Houdon's works of this period demonstrate both his great technical skill and his ability to give his subjects emotion and individuality. This is particularly true of his famous *Diana the Huntress* (1776). The piece, done in plaster, is still greatly admired, both for its anatomical realism and its dynamic quality. The Goddess Diana is posed in such a way that the sculptor seems to have captured her in mid-step. This piece would later be reproduced in both marble and terra cotta, and it was also cast in bronze.

Houdon's works of this period demonstrate both his great technical skill and his ability to give his subjects emotion and individuality.

Houdon produced a vast number of sculptures of living men and women, and he would often render the same person in several different pieces of art. His fame soon spread beyond Europe, and in 1778 he sculpted a bust of his friend Benjamin Franklin. In 1781 he produced the bust of Voltaire (now displayed at the Comédie Française). Four years later, in 1785, Thomas Jefferson—then the American ambassador to France—invited him to the United States to sculpt a massive bronze depicting George Washington mounted on a horse; this was to be placed at the Capitol in Richmond, Virginia. In the same spirit that led him to refuse the title of king when he assumed leadership of the new American republic, however, Washington declined to be represented in such a grandiose and heroic way, and the commission was changed to a full-length portrait in marble. The plow that stands behind the figure expressed Houdon's respect for this American leader, for it alludes to the life of the great farmer-statesman of classical times, Cincinnatus.

Throughout his career as a portraitist of the historical, literary, and intellectual giants of his day, Houdon also accepted and executed commissions for religious works from various churches and cathedrals in France. Of these, few remain, for most were destroyed during the tumult of the French Revolution. The upheaval of those years, however, did not stop the artist from his work, and he produced several new busts. With Napoleon's rise to power, Houdon was commissioned to create a bust of the new emperor, which he completed in 1806.

Today, Houdon is considered to be foremost among his contemporary sculptors, and many regard him as the finest sculptor who ever lived. His work in marble displays a mastery of the medium, and he was able to elicit from the stone a remarkable humanity and vitality—particularly in his busts, but also in his full-length figures, as in his *Saint Bruno* and *Diana*. Whether working from life or from death masks, as he did for his bust of Rousseau, he never failed to capture the essence of his subjects. His works remain as powerfully moving today as they did at their first unveiling. ◆

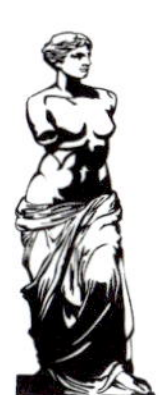

I

Ingres, Jean-Auguste-Dominique

AUGUST 29, 1780–JANUARY 14, 1867 ● PAINTER AND DRAFTSMAN

Born in Montauban, France, Jean-Auguste-Dominique Ingres received his earliest training from his father, Jean-Marie-Joseph Ingres, who was himself a respected painter and sculptor. Ingres developed his sensibility, skills, and technique by copying the masters of the day—including Raphael, Titian, and Rubens. These exercises were later supplemented by formal academic training in Toulouse, where he studied painting with Guillaume-Joseph Roques and sculpting with Jean-Pierre Vigan, later adding training in watercolors under the mentorship of Jean Briant.

When he was 17, Ingres joined the Paris studio of J.-L. David in 1797. Here he met a lively circle of artists, including his fellow students Etienne-Jean Delécluze and Jean-Pierre Granger. He studied the work of Giotto and Fra Angelico, but the painter whose works had the deepest influence on his developing aesthetic was Raphael, whom Ingres felt **epitomized** the classical ideal in artistic expression.

epitomized: described or characterized perfectly a situation or individual.

Little remains from his days at David's studio. In 1801 Ingres won the prestigious Prix de Rome for his *Envoys of Agamemnon*, a powerfully beautiful example of history painting in the style of the French modern school. The Prix de Rome brought Ingres his first portrait commissions, which enabled him to support himself while he continued to refine his tech-

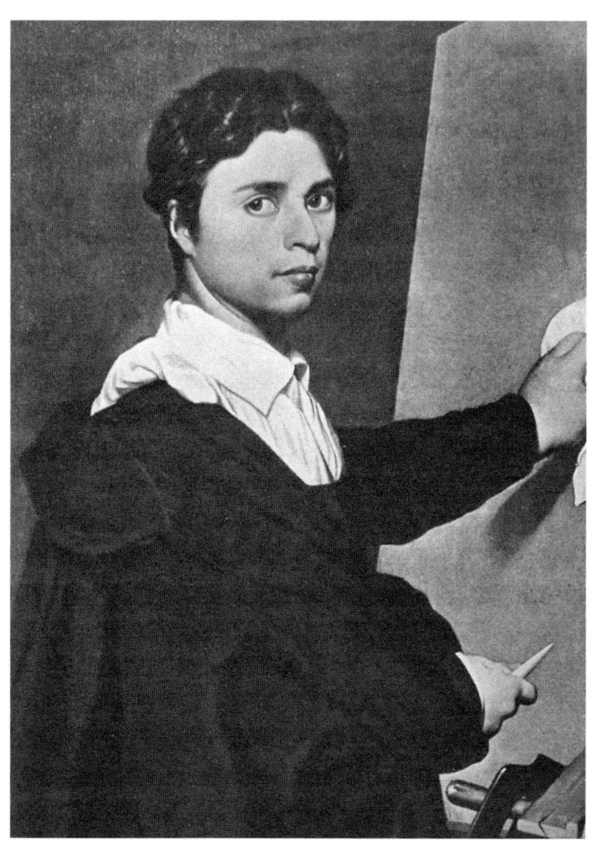

Jean-Auguste-Dominique Ingres, self-portrait

nique and his skills. His *Bonaparte as First Consul* (1804), painted at the government's request, is one such commission. Unfortunately, critical reception of this and some of his other works of the period was largely negative.

Additional benefits of winning the Prix de Rome were a small stipend and access to studio space at the Villa Medici in Rome, but Ingres was unable to take advantage of these opportunities until 1806. Disheartened by the critical reaction to his work in Paris, Ingres was determined to use his stay in Italy to earn the respect of his peers back in France. He threw himself into his work, at first concentrating on paintings and drawings of the Roman landscape, but soon taking on historical themes. During this time he began work on *Venus Anadyomette* and *Antiochus and Stratonice*, both of which would remain unfinished for more than 30 years (1848 and 1840, respectively).

Ingres actively solicited the patronage of important figures in French government during this time, and had great hopes of gaining the support of Lucien Bonaparte, but these hopes were dashed. Ingres now turned his talents to a study of the nude, producing, among other works, the *Bather* and *Reclining Woman* (both 1808). These paintings, however, like his earlier work, received a cool reception from the critics, for they were perceived as too sensual, violating the standards of propriety that prevailed at the time.

Though unsuccessful in gaining an important patron, Ingres had greater luck in making connections with other artists in France and Italy. Among these was Jacques-Edouard Gatteaux, who gave Ingres both his friendship and access to lucrative government portrait commissions. With his income secured, Ingres was able to remain in Rome after his Prix funding and studio access ended in 1811. In that year he completed one of his master works in the history genre, *Jupiter and Thetis*.

However, this painting also met severe criticism, for the artist's penchant for combining intimate themes and massive scale—a quality that characterizes Ingres's historical works—was deemed unacceptable by French critics.

Nonetheless, Ingres continued to work on the monumental scale, producing *Romulus Victorious over Acron* in 1812 and *Virgil Reading from the 'Aeneid' before Augustus and Livia* in that same year. With these and other works of this period, Ingres had firmly established his reputation in Rome but still hungered for acceptance in his native France. He therefore prepared to participate in the Salon of 1814, to which he intended to send several important pieces. Distractions in Rome, including his marriage to Madeleine Chapelle in 1813, curtailed his originally ambitious plans. His submissions to the Salon, ultimately, numbered only three: *Interior of the Sistine Chapel, Don Pedro of Toledo Kissing the Sword of Henry IV,* and *Raphael and La Fornarina*.

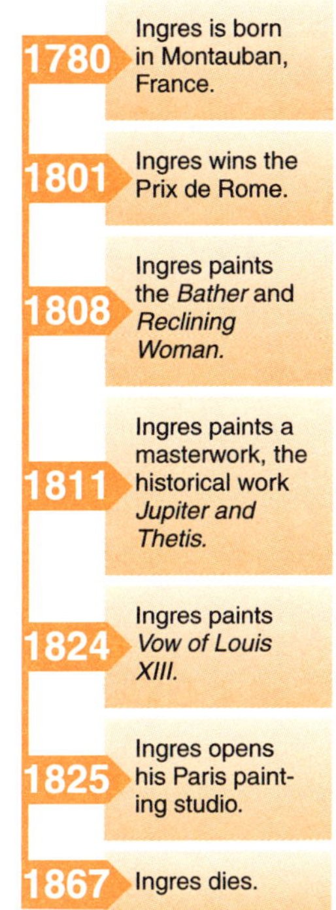

The newly married Ingres remained happily ensconced in Rome, though he was forced to rely heavily on portraits for the tourist trade after the Napoleonic forces—and their lucrative government commissions—were withdrawn from Italy. He did receive some assignments from members of the Italian aristocracy, however, and he enlisted the support of Charles Thévenin, who became director of the Académie de France. Through this new patron he received several important commissions from the French community in Rome. Nonetheless, his work continued to shock the French art critics.

Drawn to the beauty and history of Florence, Ingres moved his family there in 1820 for a four-year sojourn. During his first year in Florence, Ingres received a commission through Thévenin for a religious painting to be installed in the Montauban Cathedral. As was his lifelong habit, Ingres conceived of a work so ambitious that the actual installation of the finished painting, *Vow of Louis XIII* (1824), was delayed several years.

The monumental *Vow* for once silenced Ingres's French critics. Ingres therefore finally returned home in 1825, opening a studio in Paris. Once again he assiduously cultivated favor among Paris's notables. He also sought to make the French art circles better aquainted with the work he had done in Rome and Florence, and to that end sold contracts for the engraving rights to printmakers, realizing a substantial income that freed him from the need to scramble for more commissions. Unfortunately, all his efforts failed to permanently win the critics

Neoclassicism

In the mid-18th-century rococo style of French painting and architecture, artists emphasized exaggerated refinery and lightheartedness. Toward the end of the century, around the time of the American and French Revolutions, artistic interest shifted to a more serious style, one with moral purpose. The neoclassical style that emerged there largely drew its inspiration from recent archaeological discoveries making it possible to closely study the varieties of architecture and art from classical Rome. Neoclassical art, which flourished in the last two decades of the 18th century and continued into the 1850s, was named for its attempt to duplicate Roman and Greek styles in painting, architecture, and sculpture, in order to instill in its viewers the virtues of truth, beauty, heroism, and nobility associated with the classical period.

A central figure in French neoclassical painting was Jacques-Louis David, an ardent supporter of the Revolution. He took as his subject matter classical and historical themes, as in the *Oath of the Horatii* (1784) and *Lictors Bringing Brutus the Bodies of His Sons* (1789). Here the loveliness, lushness, and humor of rococo are replaced by logical and austerely represented dramatic tensions. Similar styles are found in the work of Jean-François-Pierre Peyron and others, where color and light become less important than stark design. In such works, the clothing and decoration of the Roman period are depicted with great accuracy, and the themes are drawn from classical mythology and history. Also central to the movement was Jean Auguste Ingres, the last major painter of the movement, who continued to refine the style for decades. Neoclassicism also influenced furniture, vaseware, tapestry design, and sculpture, where the use of colored marble and emotionally charged faces gave way to more tranquil poses depicted in white marble. Neoclassicism influenced American art through figures such as Benjamin West (as in *Agrippina Landing at Brundisium with the Ashes of Germanicus,* 1760). The style's influence on architecture can be seen in many of the American republic's earliest buildings, such as Benjamin Henry Latrobe's House of Representatives (1807) and Charles Bulfinch's Massachusetts State House (1798).

While neoclassical painting's austerity gave way to richer forms of art in the romantic period, romanticism carried on the neoclassical interest in Greek and Roman themes.

over to his style, and the painting he entered in the Salon of 1834, *Martyrdom of St. Symphorian*, was roundly condemned.

Devastated, Ingres closed his studio and returned to Rome in 1835. He stayed there until 1841, spending much of his time reworking or completing paintings he had begun years earlier. Among these works was *Antiochus and Stratonice*, which was now wanted by the Duc d'Orléans, an important Parisian art collector. This painting was highly acclaimed, and an encouraged Ingres returned once again to Paris.

The Revolution in 1848 disrupted French society and the steady flow of commissions Ingres had again begun to enjoy, but he continued to work. In 1849, the death of his wife precipitated a health crisis for the artist, and although he continued to draw during his illness, his painting ceased. In 1851 he returned once again to his easel. Only one work after this date was an attempt to return to the monumental scale of his earlier years, and from this time until his death in 1867 he concentrated almost exclusively on private commissions. Ironically, though during Ingres's life critics had often attacked his work as too radical, by the time of his death his work was widely considered conventional—perhaps a tribute to his tireless work to promote his own work and his vision for the possibilities of historical painting. ◆

By 1812, Ingres had firmly established his reputation in Rome but still hungered for acceptance in his native France.

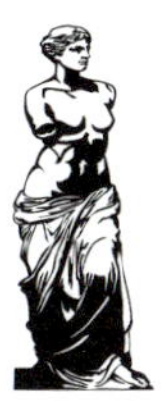

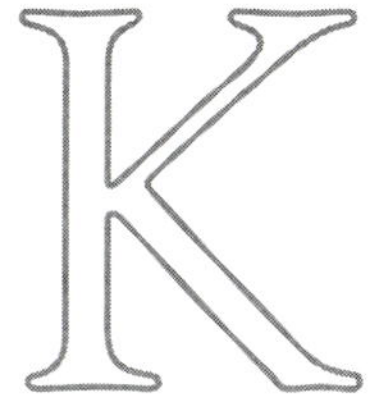

Kandinsky, Wassily

DECEMBER 4, 1866–DECEMBER 13, 1944 ● PAINTER

Wassily Kandinsky was the son of a Moscow merchant whose business called for him to travel in Europe often, and to settle temporarily in cities like Rome and Florence. The elder Kandinsky took his family with him on these trips, and young Wassily thus received an early exposure to some of the finest art of the day. Nonetheless, when he was old enough to attend Moscow University, it was enthnology and the law that claimed his attention, and he earned advanced degrees in both fields.

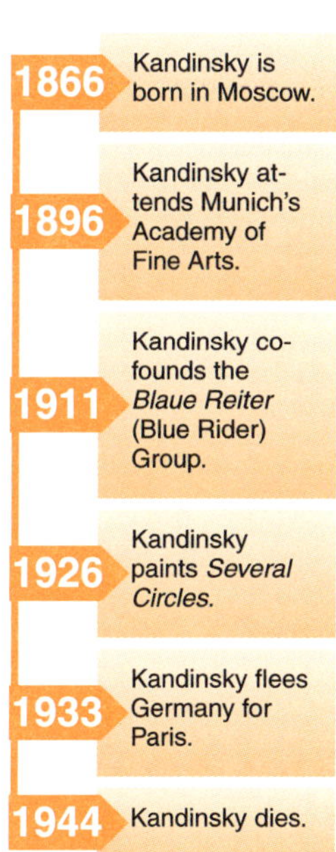

In 1889, however, while conducting a field study in peasant law in the Volga region, Kandinsky became acquainted with the local folk arts. The experience so profoundly moved him that within a year he had left his professional studies behind. In 1890 he visited Paris to learn more about current art theory and practice, and by 1896 he had devoted himself fully to becoming a painter. That year he traveled to Munich to study at the Academy of Fine Arts, where he remained a student until 1900.

It was not long before Kandinsky came to the notice of the European art world. In 1901 he founded the Phalanx, a group of **avant-garde** artists working in Munich, and in 1902 he began teaching painting to other aspiring artists. His work during this early period was naturalistic, and his subject matter was

avant-garde: French term for vanguard; symbolizes artists at the forefront of creative and original ideas that often oppose established tradition and methods.

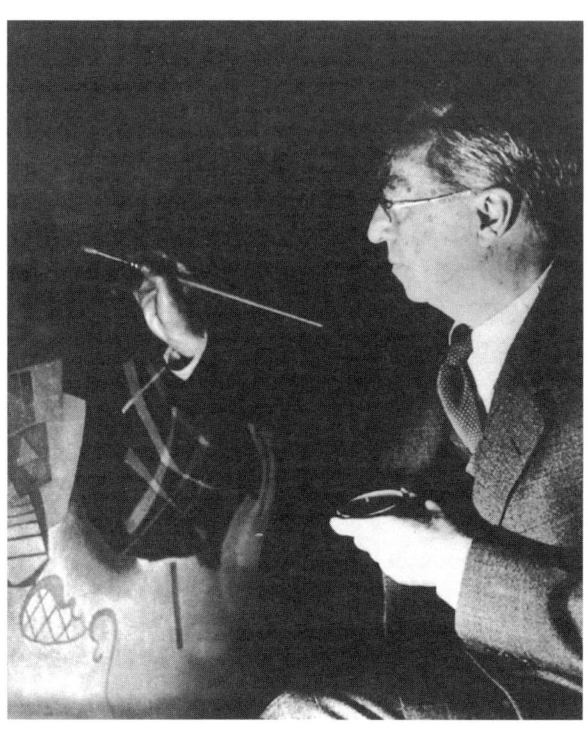

Wassily Kandinsky

primarily portraits, landscapes, and fairytale subjects. He worked in both watercolor and oil, turning his hand to woodcut and printmaking as well. During this first decade of the new century, Kandinsky also did a great deal of traveling, visiting several European countries and drawing on his experiences as subject matter for his paintings. During his stay in Paris he viewed the work of some of the most prominent fauves, including Paul Gauguin and Henri Matisse. These artists rekindled Kandinsky's early attraction to the vitality and exuberance of Russian folk art, and his paintings from this period onward show a great freedom in color and expression.

By 1908, Kandinsky's style had already become highly distinctive as he moved more and more toward the abstract. For him, the interplay among color, line, and form was far more interesting than simple representations of objects and scenes could ever be. The paintings could still be called landscapes, but the connection between the subject matter and its presentation on the canvas was becoming increasingly remote.

Kandinsky was torn between his impulse toward abstraction and his belief that art was, essentially, a communicative act. It was this contradiction that delayed him from fully abandoning the effort of producing representational images. By 1911 he had resolved his philosophical difficulties, however, and his paintings were no longer concerned with representation.

Kandinsky's move toward greater abstraction was more daring than the critics in his circle were prepared to handle, and he broke with his peers by the end of 1911. Along with a few like-minded colleagues, he founded Die Blaue Reiter Group (The Blue Rider). In an effort to communicate his new philosophy of life and art, he turned to writing, and a collection of his essays was included in an anthology entitled *Der Blaue*

Abstract Art

In abstract art, artists explore form and color without representing identifiable objects like people or landscapes. In this way, it is the opposite of realism, which attempts to portray objects as naturally as possible. As a movement, abstract art began in the early years of the twentieth century, with the work of Vassely Kandinsky. In writings such as his influential "On the Spiritual in Art" (begun in 1910), he drew from writer and philosopher Johann Wolfgang von Goethe to discuss the value of the visual arts, like the value of music, to evoke the inner life of the artist without trying to mirror the everyday world. Kandinsky even chose the titles of his works, such as "Improvisations" (from 1911) and "Compositions," to point to the parallel between visual art and music. Kandinsky's earliest abstract works still showed some traces of representation, but these traces were largely absent in later works. Kandinsky was deeply influenced by cubism and symbolism, as was Paul Klee in Switzerland, in his watercolors. Czech Frantisek Kupka ("Hot Chromatics") embraced the abstract style as well, as well as working out a detailed theory of how abstract color and form could signify universal ideas.

Because the principles underlying abstract art are so basic—a break from natural representation—it is easier to say when abstract art as a movement began than when it ended. The Russian constructivists clearly embraced nonrealism, as did De Stijl artists such as Theo van Doesburg and Piet Mondrian. In fact, not 20 years after Kandinsky burst upon the scene, abstract art was influencing many first-rate artists in several countries. Despite waning somewhat around the time of World War II, the movement in its various forms has continued, from Francis Picabia, Morgan Russell, Karel Appel, Kurt Schwitters, and Joachim Torres-Garcia to Henri-Georges Adam, Wilem de Kooning, Isamu Noguchi, Jackson Pollock, and Mark Rothko.

Reiter Almanach (1912). He was also making new connections among his fellow artists, particularly Paul Klee and Hans Arp, both of whom were exploring surrealism at the time. Over the next few years he showed his work extensively, at exhibitions in places as diverse as Moscow, Zurich, Cologne, and New York.

Kandinsky's base up to 1914 had been in Munich, but the onset of World War I forced him to leave Germany and, ultimately, to return to Russia. He abandoned working in oils entirely for long stretches at a time, executing a number of watercolors and drawings, some of which seemed to presage the artist's return to representationalism. However, other pieces of this period remain fully abstract, and abstraction would remain his principle stylistic choice.

For Kandinsky, the interplay among color, line, and form was far more interesting than simple representations of objects and scenes could ever be.

In Moscow, Kandinsky quickly became an important figure in the city's artistic circles. He was invited to participate in the Department of Visual Arts, which had been founded by the People's Commissariat for Enlightenment, a cultural department in the government. He was also selected as a teacher in the newly formed Svomas, a fine arts studio collective. His work brought him into active participation in other areas of creative expression, most notably the theater, which he felt was an ideal medium for the integration of the arts. Kandinsky's administrative, writing, and teaching duties took up much of his time, but he managed to continue to paint. He began experimenting with shapes, particularly with oval and circular forms. Examples of his work during this period include *Multicoloured Circle* (1921) and *Several Circles* (1926). This fascination with geometric forms can be dated to when Walter Gropius invited Kandinsky to visit the Bauhaus in Berlin. Kandinsky accepted a professorship there, where he taught painting and theory on a faculty that also included Paul Klee and others. Kandinsky also began exhibiting his own works once again and had several important shows in 1922 and 1923. Kandinsky's tenure at the Bauhaus was an extremely productive time, during which he completed over 300 oil paintings and an even greater number of watercolors. His fascination with geometric forms continued, and he added a variety of new shapes to his original repertoire of circles and ovals.

Kandinsky also continued to explore alternative means of artistic expression, including the theater. He did scenery and costume design for a production mounted at the Friedrich Theater in Dessau, Germany, and even designed the props. However, the Nazi party's rise to power soon spelled the end for the Bauhaus, because the party considered the art produced there to be "**degenerate.**" In 1933 Kandinsky left Germany to settle in a small town near Paris, where he would stay for the next 11 years. His work of this period shows the influence of surrealism, and he began exploring new subject matter—including biology and **embryology**—in search of inspiration.

Kandinsky was denied the opportunity to return to Germany in 1939, so he obtained French citizenship just a month before World War II was declared. His painting and his writing continued throughout the war years, but shortages of art supplies reduced him to painting on boards. He died in Neuilly-sur-Seine in 1944. ◆

degenerate: description of a person or thing that has sunk below what would be considered the normal standards of decency and taste; term was applied by the Nazi Party in Germany to describe artists with whom the party disagreed.

embryology: the branch of biology that examines the development of embryos.

Kauffmann, Angelica

OCTOBER 30, 1741–NOVEMBER 5, 1807 ● PAINTER

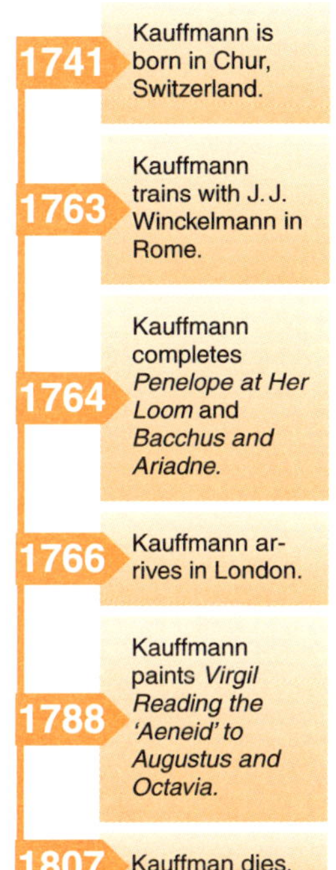

Although Angelica Kauffmann's passion was for history painting, today she is best known as a portrait painter and decorative artist. The sentimentalism of her historical paintings, appropriate to her era, soon fell out of fashion. Nonetheless, her entire body of work constitutes an important legacy, and she was a pioneer in breaking down the gender barriers within the highest echelons of the art world of her time.

Kauffmann was born in Chur, a commune in Switzerland. She came by her art naturally, as the daughter of Joseph Johann Kauffmann, a minor painter in his own right. Her father rewarded her early curiosity about painting by training her in technique and the use of color, and she acted as his assistant. Together they traveled throughout Austria, Italy, and Switzerland, and her precocious talents in both painting and music soon became widely known.

Before turning 13, Angelica received an independent commission to paint the portrait of Bishop Nevroni of Como, Italy. This added to her growing reputation as an artist, but she continued to assist her father for several more years. Traveling with him to Florence in 1762, Angelica became acquainted with an international group of artists who were then exploring the neoclassical style, among them the American Benjamin West. In the following year the Kauffmanns arrived in Rome, and Angelica began studying with Johann Joachim Winckelmann. She quickly secured commissions to paint the portraits of Abbe Peter Grant (1763) and Winckelmann himself (1764).

Up to this point, Angelica's art was largely confined to portraiture, but she had begun to explore other modes of expression and even studied sculpture for a time. Historical subjects in particular caught her imagination. This was a daring choice for a woman because history painting, as this field was called, required training in anatomy—a subject that well-bred women of her era were not permitted to study. While Kauffmann could not be permitted to work with live male models, she overcame this difficulty by using statues and augmented her training with classes in perspective. By the end of 1764 she had completed

"Poverty does not terrify me, but the loneliness kills me."

Angelica Kauffman after the death of her husband in 1795

two significant works inspired by classical literature, *Penelope at Her Loom* and *Bacchus and Ariadne*.

During the following year, Kauffmann further extended her studies, adding etching to her artistic accomplishments. By this time she had formed close associations with many of the principal artists working on the continent, and respect for her talents had spread widely. While visiting Venice with her father, she received an invitation to come to England and, traveling on her own for the first time, she arrived in London in 1766. There she quickly joined company with Benjamin West and Nathaniel Dance. Although still strongly drawn to history painting, she soon realized that portraiture was a better way to earn a living. She quickly received a number of prestigious commissions, and she produced portraits of such notables as the Duchess of Richmond and Joshua Reynolds, a leading exponent of neoclassicism and the moving force behind the establishment of the Royal Academy of Art in 1768.

To participate in the Academy's first annual exhibition, Kauffmann returned to her love of history painting, earning particular notice for *Hector and Andromache* and *Venus Showing Aeneas and Achates the Way to Carthage*. Her personal life during this period was less satisfying. In 1767 she met a man who presented himself to society as a Swedish count and, thoroughly infatuated, she married him. Only a year later, her "noble" husband was exposed as a fortune hunter and fraud, and upon learning of his masquerade she left him. As a devout Catholic, however, she was not able to divorce him, and she would not be free to remarry until his death 12 years later. Domestic tragedy notwithstanding, Kauffmann produced a significant body of work during the next several years. Drawing from literary and historical sources, she continued to produce history paintings, and even her portraits often incorporated classical themes. For example, her portrait entitled *The Marchioness Townshend and Her Son* depicts her contemporary subjects as Venus and Cupid. Also during this period, Kauffmann became involved in decorative art, paintings incorporated in the walls and ceilings of fashionable homes and public buildings.

In 1781 Kauffmann was free to remarry, and she wed the Venetian painter Antonio Zucchi. Her new husband, less passionate about his own art than his wife's, quickly assumed control of her finances, a task he managed well. Together with Kauffmann's now elderly father, the newlyweds determined to return to Italy. Stopping first in Venice for a time, Kauffmann painted *Leonardo da Vinci Dying in the Arms of Francis I*. Here, Kauffmann captured the attention of Grand Duke Paul of Russia, an avid supporter of the arts, who extended his patronage to her. But this Venice sojourn was not an entirely happy time, for during their stay her father died, in 1782.

Upon the death of her father, Kauffmann and her husband once again moved on, first to Naples, then to establish permanent residency in Rome. There she opened her studio to the notable artists, writers, and thinkers of the day. Johann Wolfgang von Goethe was a visitor, as were Johann Gottfried Herder and the Grand Duchess Anna Amalia of Saxe-Weimar. During his travels in Italy, the Emperor Joseph II commissioned work from Kauffmann, including *The Return of Arminius Victorious over the Legions of Varus* and *Aeneas Celebrating the Funeral Rites of Pallas*. Additionally, her *Virgil Reading the 'Aeneid' to Augustus and Octavia* (1788) is considered one of her most striking and vivid works.

With the death of her husband in 1795 and the loss of his deft financial management, Kauffmann's finances soon fell into disarray, and the **Napoleonic Wars** interfered with her ability to secure commissions. Still, she reigned as the acknowledged leader of the Roman school of painting and received numerous honors. She took her reduced circumstances with good grace, confiding to a close friend that "poverty does not terrify me, but the loneliness kills me." She died 12 years after the death of her beloved husband. ◆

Napolenonic Wars: wars commenced by Napoleon I of France in his ambition to rule Europe.

Kiefer, Anselm

March 8, 1945– ● Painter

Born in Donaueschingen, Germany, painter Anselm Kiefer began his schooling intending to pursue a career in law, which he studied at the Albert-Ludwigs-Universität in Freiberg for a year (1965–66). He soon changed his focus, however, and in 1966 began studying painting with Peter Dreher, who was on the faculty of that university. In 1969 he continued his art studies at the Staatliche Akademie der Bildenden Künste, working under Horst Antes. That same year he also began experimenting in book design, using a combina-

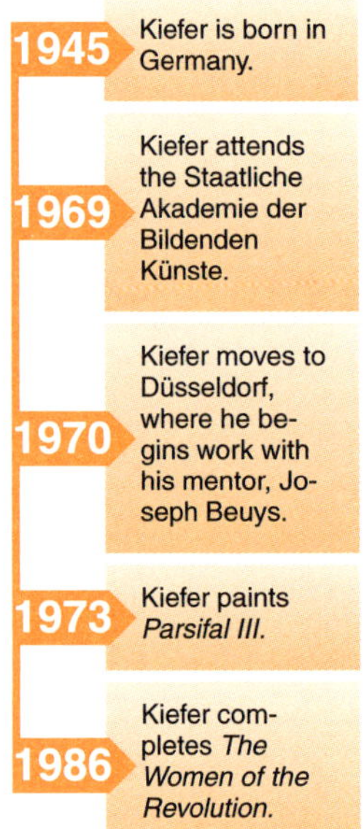

tion of unorthodox materials intended to convey symbolic meaning. A year later he moved to Düsseldorf to continue his studies at the Staatliche Kunstakademie. There he trained under Joseph Beuys, who became his mentor.

Beuys is renowned for his strong conviction that art serves a mystical function, and his belief that the role of the artist is to be something of a magician-priest. Kiefer has adopted these ideas and incorporated them into his own work, which has a strong mythological component entwined with a profound concern for history, particularly Germany's mid-20th-century experiences under Nazism. Kiefer's early efforts at rendering these themes and ideas in his art resulted in dark, brooding landscapes of barren or scorched earth, portrayed in a neo-expressionist style. In a very real sense, we can see his work as his personal quest to come to terms with the violent legacy of World War II, which had just ended when he was born.

In 1971, Kiefer moved to Hornbach, where he began working on a larger scale than he had in his earlier pieces. He began a series of landscapes, including *Heath of the Brandenburg March* (1974). He used a combination of oils and blood on paper that was then applied to the canvas, as in his *Parsifal III* (1973). This exploration of his country's Nazi history is also apparent in his architectural paintings, some of which featured buildings that had been designed by Nazi architect Albert Speer. His insistence on employing symbols from the Nazi era, an important part of his mythical and historical explorations through his art, has resulted in profound disagreements among art critics—some find his techniques powerful and evocative, others find them manipulative or even insulting.

Kiefer's preoccupation with the recent history of Germany required, he believed, an investigation of the country's older myths and legends. This belief inspired him, in 1975, to explore the Nibelung tales, the great epic cycle that decades earlier had inspired the composer Richard Wagner—and, through Wagner's music, Hitler himself. Kiefer later expanded his mythological base and drew his subject matter from a variety of other sources, including the Hebrew scriptures and the stories of Alexander the Great's military conquests. In his work he rejects the use of abstraction, embracing instead a subjective, narrative style.

Although Kiefer's earliest work was principally done in oils, during the 1970s he began incorporating a variety of other materials, from sand and wood to photographs and cloth. For example, his 1986 piece, *The Women of the Revolution,* is done in acrylic on lead and incorporates wood, glass, and flowers. The 1970s also saw Kiefer exploring sculpture, a natural outgrowth of his investigations of new media in his painting. During this time he produced a series of aircraft sculptures. He also began what became a characteristic practice of inserting into his painting long text passages, meant as titles. Eventually these textual additions to his paintings went beyond titling to directly communicate the artist's intended meaning, or at least to provide broad hints about the meaning of his symbols.

Kiefer's insistence on employing symbols from the Nazi era . . . has resulted in profound disagreements among art critics.

Kiefer attained greater international fame in the 1980s, with a number of important exhibitions in the United States, including at the Metropolitan Museum in New York. While much of his work is serious, even somber, critics have remarked upon his "goofy" sense of humor, particularly in his manipulation of what have long been considered taboo symbols of Nazi Germany. For example, in his *Germany's Heroes* (1973), he painted a tiny figure of himself dressed as Hitler. This humor, intended to convey the artist's own ambivalence about his country's history, has earned Kiefer the outrage of many critics, particularly in Germany. At the same time, many American art critics applaud his courage in using powerful, evocative symbols to explore the difficulties of coming to terms with Germany's past. ◆

Kirchner, Ernst

MAY 6, 1880–JUNE 15, 1938 ● PAINTER AND SCULPTOR

Born in Aschaffenburg, Germany, to a middle class family, Ernst Kirchner received art lessons while still a schoolboy. Although willing to educate their son in these skills, the Kirchner family was less enthusiastic about young Ernst's decision to pursue an art career. Instead they sent him to study architecture at Dresden's Königliche Technische Hochschule. Kirchner went along with this arrangement, but concentrated on courses in art nonetheless. He interrupted his coursework in 1903 to travel to Munich and study drawing and painting with Wilhelm von Debschitz and Hermann Obrist for several months, then returned to Dresden to complete his degree. He graduated in 1905.

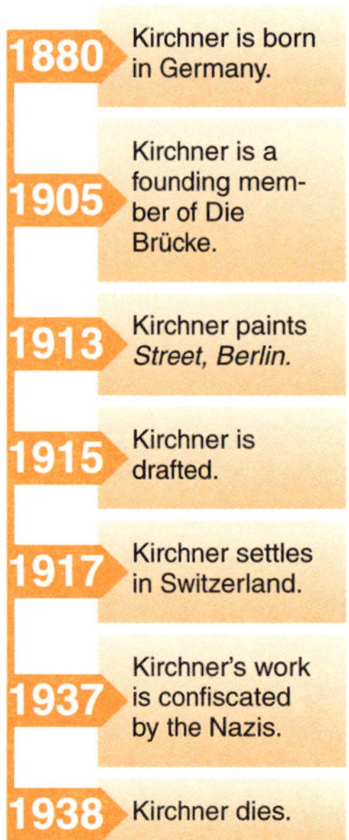

Having fulfilled his parents' wishes academically, Kirchner was now determined to devote himself to his art. With three of his fellow graduates, Fritz Bleyl, Erich Heckel, and Karl Schmidt, Kirchner formed Die Brücke (The Bridge, 1905), a closely knit group of artists who would contribute greatly to the emerging expressionist movement. Kirchner was already working in a neo-impressionist style, influenced by Henri Matisse, among others. Like the fauves, he was fascinated by non-Western art, such as Dresden Art Museum's collection of African and South Pacific art, a collection that would influence many important contemporary painters.

The group initially came together, often in Kirchner's studio, to share ideas and techniques with one another. The founding members were joined in 1906 by Emil Nolde, Max Pechstein, Cuno Amiet, and Axel Gallén-Kallela. They experimented in new, bold uses of color and form, and they explored various artistic media as well, including sculpture, woodcuts, printmaking, and lithography. Over time, the group developed a signature style, in part characterized by their use of color and form, and particularly in their treatment of the human figure as represented on paper or canvas. Kirchner himself declared that the nude was "the foundation of all visual art," and the members of Die Brücke spent much of their time attempting to capture the grace and movement of the body in a variety of media. Representative works of this period include *Interior with Bather* (1909) and *Standing Nude with Hat* (1910). Throughout this period, the expressionist side of Kirchner's work is seen is his desire to transcend the external form to reveal the emotions and desires beneath the surface.

Many of his writings disparaged his former associates in Die Brücke [The Bridge], and he energetically denied any influences on his own artistic development, presenting himself as *sui generis*.

These early years were a time of great artistic ferment for the group, as they explored the trends of the international modern art movement. They had also begun exhibiting their work and had gained the attention of several important collectors. In 1911 it was time for a change, however, and the group moved to Berlin, where Kirchner and Pechstein founded an art school, the MUIM-Institut (Moderner Unterricht in Malerei-Institut). Although all the other members of Die Brücke were also in Berlin at this time, the unity of their Dresden days was lost as they began moving in their own separate directions, and by 1913 the group was formally dissolved.

Working on his own now, Kirchner sought new sources for inspiration, and he found them in the urban landscape surrounding him. From 1913 to 1917 he devoted much of his time to a series of 14 figure paintings depicting the variety and interconnectedness of people in city life, including the well-known *Street, Berlin* (1913). The tone and style of these paintings differed from his earlier street scenes, displaying an edgier quality, sharper angles, and more muted colors. During this time Kirchner produced a number of other important pieces, including a series of nudes painted on the island of Fehmarn in the Baltic Sea.

The onset of World War I interrupted this period of artistic productivity, as Kirchner was called for army service in 1915 and assigned to the mounted artillery. Within months of this devastating experience he suffered a breakdown, spending several months in a hospital. Out of this experience came *Self-portrait as a Soldier* (1915). Two years later, Kirchner remained deeply troubled, and in 1917 concerned friends arranged for him to **emigrate** to Switzerland, hoping that the move would speed his recovery.

emigrate: to leave one's place of origin to live elsewhere.

Settling in Frauenkirch, the artist lived in a rustic log cabin and became fascinated with the life of the peasants who lived and worked nearby. The subject matter of his work during this period underwent a profound shift, featuring studies of the local people and the rugged landscape of the region. Important works from this time include *Alpine Cabin* (1919) and *Winter Landscape by Moonlight* (1919).

Kirchner's return to health in 1920 was marked by a simultaneous shift in his artistic style and focus. He began working with a local weaver, providing designs later reproduced as tapestries. These designs also found their way into his paintings. Over the next several years he worked on ever larger canvases, and he also began retouching or overpainting many of his earlier works, in some cases radically altering them in tone, color, and style.

The 1920s were also a time of personal reflection for Kirchner, and he began writing essays exploring his own theories of art and artistic expression. Many of his writings disparaged his former associates in Die Brücke, and he energetically denied any influences on his own artistic development, presenting himself as ***sui generis.*** In the latter half of the decade he made several trips back to Germany to solidify his reputation as an important artistic talent. By the start of the 1930s he had succeeded in these efforts, and the most important museums in Germany displayed his pieces. This period marked a new emphasis in Kirchner's art, as he developed an abstract form of painting.

sui generis: making up a class or category that stands alone in uniqueness.

War, or the threat of war, once again signaled a shift in Kirchner's artistic development. In 1933 the National Socialist Party attained power in Germany. By 1937, the Nazis had confiscated all of Kirchner's works that were held in Germany and had stripped him of his membership in the Prussian Academy of Berlin. Dispirited by the lingering effects of his illnesses and by the rejection of his work by his homeland, he committed suicide. ◆

Klee, Paul

DECEMBER 18, 1879–JUNE 29, 1940 ● PAINTER AND WRITER

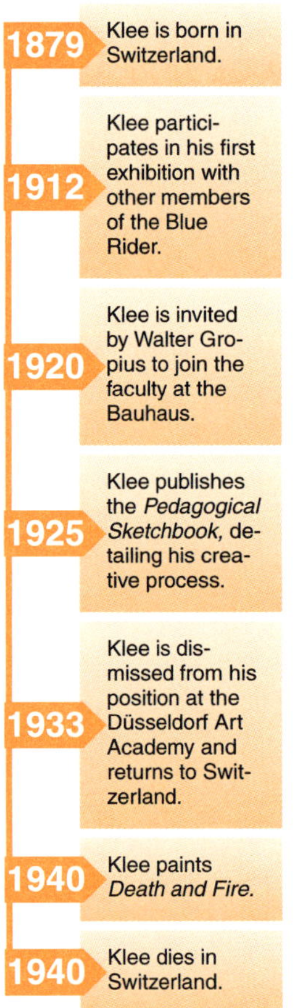

Once disparaged by the Nazis as "degenerate," Swiss painter Paul Klee's work is now given a position of first rank, acknowledged as influential in its inventive use of color, symbol, and form, and representative of the greatest work of 20th-century art. Klee was born in the town of Münchenbuchsee into a family of musicians. As a young adult, he wavered between a career in music or art. Klee spent his childhood in Switzerland, moving to Munich in 1900 to study art with the symbolist Franz von Stuck. After striking out on his own, Klee initially suffered several years of disappointment and lack of critical success. He relied on his wife's earnings as a piano teacher to supplement his own meager income. Still, this period was crucial for his artistic development, as it allowed him to absorb influences—including Francisco de la Goya and James Ensor—and to experiment with different media, especially etchings and pen and ink drawings.

Klee got his first major opportunity in 1911, after being introduced to the Russian artist Wassily Kandinsky and other avant-garde artists in Kandinsky's collective, known as The Blue Rider. These influential modernists welcomed Klee into their group and invited him to display his work in their second major exhibition in 1912. It was during this period that Klee began to develop an elaborate creative theory that he continued to refine throughout his life. Like many modern artists in the early 20th century, Klee sought to reject purely representational art. A representational artist might see a fish and try to paint it as realistically as possible, detailing the gills, the head, and so forth, in natural colors. Modern artists such as Klee would see the same fish and try to capture what they perceived as its internal, essential qualities—the underlying planes and curves, its internal organs, distortions of the features, and so forth. The transformation could be so striking that the outward form of the fish would be barely recognizable in the painting. Klee also flattened fish against abstract backgrounds or surrounded them with strange, dynamic symbols, as in *Around the Fish* (1926).

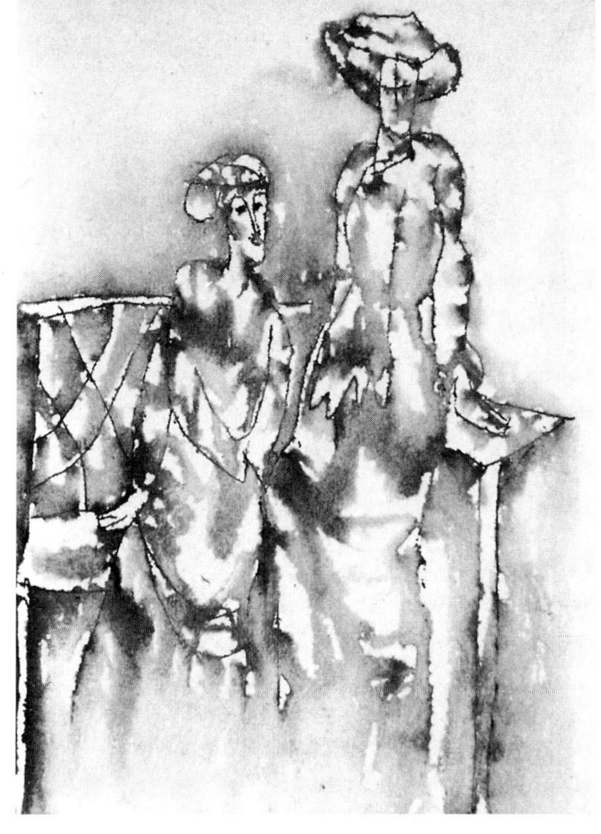

Two Ladies (1911), by Paul Klee

From 1914 to 1920, Klee continued to experiment with color, shape, and form to further distance himself from literal interpretation. He originated his own language of symbols—including arrows, hearts, eyes, exclamation points, and abstract shapes—to expand his vocabulary of styles. His use of color increased dramatically after a trip to Tunisia in 1914. "It has me in its grip; color and I are but one," he commented. Works illustrating his bold new use of color include his painting *Red and White Domes*. Klee also drew inspiration from nature and spent much of his career trying to capture in his art what he regarded as its internal structure. He employed different media in pursuit of new forms, even creating, as a present for his young son Felix, fanciful puppets out of bits of cloth borrowed from his wife's sewing basket.

After 1920, Klee increasingly devoted himself to writing and teaching, while still continuing to produce major works of art. Walter Gropius invited Klee to teach at the new Bauhaus School in 1920. Klee joined the faculty there, one that included some of that era's most famous names in architecture, industrial design, painting, and sculpture. The Bauhaus was committed to an artistic vision emphasizing function and encouraging artistic collaboration and experimentation. Klee flourished in this environment, engaging in successful collaborations with Lyonel Feininger and Kandinsky, while writing and teaching extensively. Klee harnessed his tremendous facil-

"Art does not reproduce the visible, it makes the visible."
Paul Klee, on how he viewed art

ity with language in his writing and teaching, as in his *Pedagogical Sketchbook* (1925), discussing his intentions and internal creative process to an unusual extent and passing on to his students his most intimate reflections on his years of experimentation with color and form. Many of his writings and lectures focused on moments of tension, ambiguity, and spontaneous creation. His work during this period includes the imaginative ink and watercolor *Twittering Machines* (1922), in which birds are strung on a wire controlled by a machine. This work can be interpreted as a commentary on the role of nature in a technological age.

Klee's years at the Bauhaus were the pinnacle of his career. After the horror of World War I, the viewing public was prepared as never before for Klee's artwork, which drew on the internal workings of the subconscious for many of its themes. His work attracted international acclaim with extensive exhibitions in Berlin and at New York City's Museum of Modern Art (1929, 1930). In the 1930s, however, Klee's career plummeted due to forces beyond his control—politics and physical illness. Adolf Hitler's National Socialist Party seized control of the mechanisms of power in Germany in 1933. Hitler's all-encompassing vision of a pure racial community left no room for non-representational modern art, which he considered "degenerate." Klee, a key figure in modern art, represented a convenient target for propagandists like Hitler and his assistants. Shortly after Hitler's rise to power, Klee was forced to resign a post he had accepted two years earlier at the Düsseldorf Art Academy. By Christmas of 1933, Klee had fled to his native Switzerland.

So great was the Nazis' hatred of Klee, in fact, that their attacks on his artwork continued long after his departure. At the 1937 Nazi exhibition of "degenerate art," 17 works by Klee were held up as examples of art that was "the monstrous offspring of insanity, **impudence,** ineptitude, and sheer degeneracy."

impudence: the state of being impudent, which is to lack modesty or to display brash and brazen boldness in attitude towards others.

Compounding the misery of Nazi attacks on his reputation, in 1935 Klee developed the degenerative skin disease scleroderma. This made it difficult for Klee to work. His output declined until 1937 when, seized by the need to create again before his health could decline even further, Klee increased his activity. His canvases in these last few years of his life are characterized by somber subjects such as war, and drawn with heavy black lines to heighten the mood of foreboding. Shortly before his own death, Klee painted *Death and Fire*, representing his own metaphysical musings about death.

Klee died in 1940 in the peaceful Swiss resort of Muralto-Locarno. At the time of Klee's death much of Europe, including France, had succumbed to the military might of Hitler and his allies. Though Klee did not survive to see it, his reputation was restored in the post-war era and his place in modern art assured. ◆

Klimt, Gustav

JULY 14, 1862–FEBRUARY 6, 1918 ● PAINTER AND DECORATOR

Born in Baumgarten, near Vienna, Austria, Gustave Klimt was the son of a respected local engraver. At the age of 14 he began his studies in Vienna at the School of Decorative Arts, from which he graduated in 1883. While at school, Klimt joined forces with his brother, Ernst, and another fellow student, Franz von Matsch, who would later go on to a career as a society painter. The three pursued a successful commercial career, securing commissions to decorate public buildings in Vienna and beyond. Their joint work includes the Bucharest National Theater (1885) and Vienna's Kunsthistorisches Museum (1891). Their work brought them important recognition, and Klimt was awarded the Gold Cross for Merit by the Austrian government in 1888.

"Whoever wants to know something about me ... ought to look carefully at my pictures and try and see in them what I am and what I want to do."

Gustav Klimt, quoted at the online Gustav Klimt Gallery

In addition to participating in these public projects, Klimt was also perfecting his painting technique. Here, as in his more commercial endeavors, he quickly achieved success. In 1890, for example, Emperor Franz Joseph awarded him a cash prize in recognition of his watercolor painting *View of the Interior of the Old Burgtheater*, which the artist had painted two years earlier.

At the outset of his career, Klimt had yet to find his own artistic voice. While the complaint of some critics that he was content merely to make faithful **renditions** of subjects according to the academic conventions of the day is too harsh, it is true that he had not yet brought forth a wholly individual style. His skill at following conventions was great enough to win him widespread approval, but little in his early paintings suggests that he would come to be known as his era's premiere dec-

renditions: performances or interpretations.

orative painter. In any case, his conformity to the accepted standard was soon to end.

By 1894, Klimt had been exposed to a wide range of work coming out of Europe's disparate avant-garde circles, from Aubrey Beardsley and Fernand Khnopff to Jan Toorop. Not surprisingly, then, when he received a commission to produce three paintings, depicting philosophy, medicine, and the law, for the Vienna University, many of these influences came to the fore. This is particularly apparent in the painting *Philosophy* (1894) which incorporates elements of symbolism, impressionism, and **art nouveau.**

art nouveau: French term for "new art"; a nineteenth and early twentieth century style characterized by depicting flowers and leaves in undulating lines and flowing vines.

Klimt's departure from the accepted academic style was not, however, immediately greeted with praise. In fact, his submission to the university touched off loud public criticism. Klimt responded by putting his commission work on hold for a time to concentrate on a piece he was preparing for exhibition in 1902. This work, the *Beethoven Frieze,* was intended as a visual representation of the great composer's Ninth Symphony. At the exhibition, Klimt also showed the trio of paintings originally destined for the Vienna University, the earlier-reviled *Philosophy, Medicine,* and the unfinished *Jurisprudence.* By this time it was clear that the university was never going to accept these paintings, and the artist bought them back. Unfortunately, these works, like so much great art of the early 20th century, were destroyed in World War II.

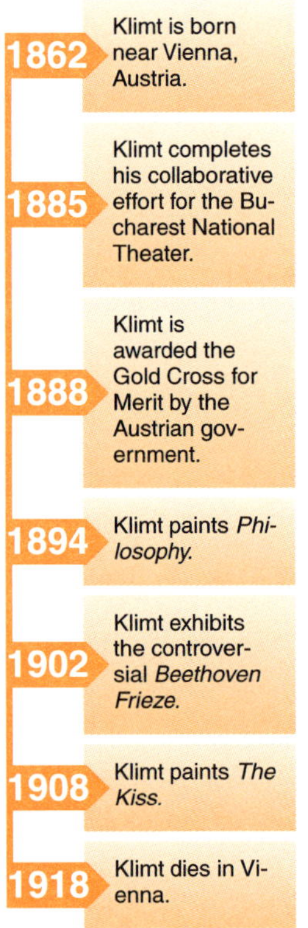

From 1898 onward, a signature characteristic of Klimt's later work was coming to the fore—his treatment of the female form and, more particularly, female sexuality. As early as 1898 Viennese censors rejected a poster of his as pornographic. Similarly, his inclusion of a naked female figure in *Medicine* was publicly denounced. In the latter years of the 19th century, Viennese sensibilities could accept male nudes but demanded that females be rendered in proper attire.

Klimt's ability to outrage his Viennese critics was not limited to his depiction of nude females. Public outrage was further inflamed by the strong eroticism pervading these images. Although he frequently obscured this sexuality in his paintings, it was nonetheless apparent to his thoroughly disapproving critics, and in his drawings there is no attempt at all to hide the explicit eroticism of his subjects under a veil of ornamentation.

By 1905, Klimt recognized that his work would never receive the acceptance of his peers in Vienna, so he broke with the art establishment there, withdrawing to work on his own and supporting himself through a successful career as a portraitist. During this period he also produced what has remained his best-known work, *The Kiss* (1908). This work depicts a couple embracing, but little of their bodies appear—they are covered with bright shapes, suggesting their immersion in erotic pleasure.

Unlike most successful artists of his time, Klimt never founded a school of his own, although he was a steadfast mentor and supporter of young artists whose work he found worthwhile and promising. He died in Vienna in 1918. ◆

Kokoschka, Oskar

MARCH 1, 1886–FEBRUARY 2, 1980 ● PAINTER

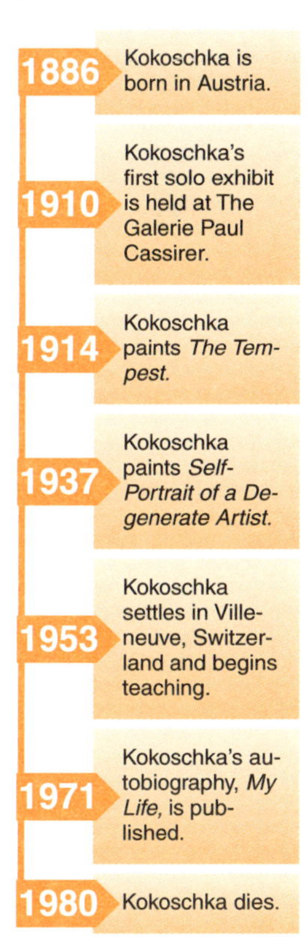

Oskar Kokoschka is best remembered for his early portraits, which go far beyond the external appearance of the subjects to reveal their interior lives, as well as for his landscapes, which show many of the cities of Europe as vibrant and beautiful locations, bathed in color and light. Kokoschka was born in Pöchlarn, on the Danube in Austria, to an Austrian mother and Czech father whose family were goldsmiths. He trained at the Vienna School of Arts and Crafts (Kunstgewerbeschule, 1905–1909), where he was influenced by Gustav Klimt and art nouveau symbolism. In a 1908 show in Vienna, he exhibited tapestry designs and a self-portrait plaster bust that caught the attention of Adolf Loos. Using Loos's connections, he was able to put his great skills toward painting portraits of many of that city's prominent citizens. Works of this period include *Hans Tietze and Erica Tietze-Conrat* (1909) and *August Forel* (1910).

Already at this early stage of his career, Kokoschka was fascinated by expressionism, and his portraits (especially his self-portraits), often dominated by grays and browns, convey not just the surface features of the subjects' faces but also their intense emotional tension, sadness, or loneliness. In 1909 his writings, including his *Murderer, Hope of Women*, stirred controversy in Vienna, in part because of sexual themes. Seeking a more receptive climate for his work, he left that city for Switzerland and then Germany, where he joined Herwarth Walden's *Der Sturm* circle of Berlin artists (1910). There his

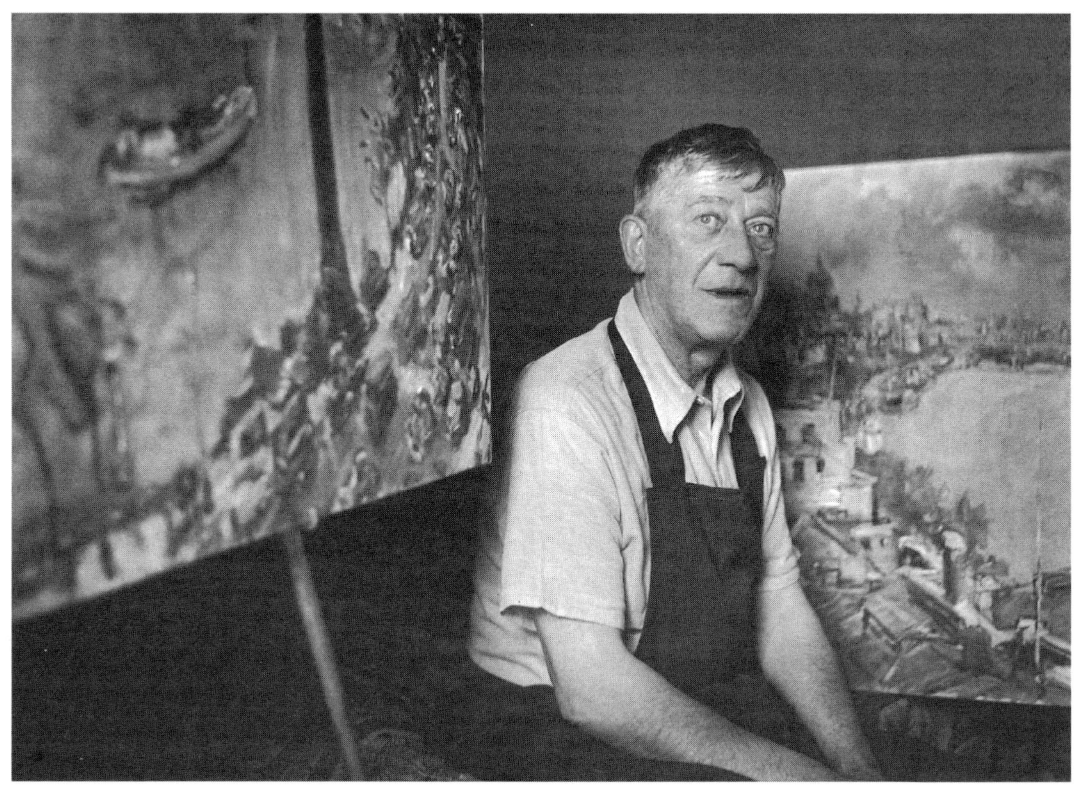

Oskar Kokoschka with two of his paintings.

fortunes changed, as he was surrounded by a vibrant community of German expressionists. His pen drawings for *Der Sturm* were well-received, and his first solo exhibition was held in Berlin that same year at the Galerie Paul Cassirer. In 1914, he painted one of his best-known works, *The Tempest,* featuring the entangled bodies of himself and a woman with whom he was in love, Alma (Schindler) Mahler, widow of the famous composer Gustav Mahler.

Kokoschka's work was interrupted by World War I, when he volunteered for cavalry duty. He was shot and stabbed by Russians on the Ukrainian front in 1915 but was rescued by his comrades. He recounts the details of this gruesome but deeply spiritual experience in his autobiography, *Mein Leben* (My Life, 1971). After the war he moved to Dresden (1916) and took a teaching post at Dresden's art academy (1919–1923) while continuing to paint. Works during this time include *The Power of Music* (1919) and the brightly-colored *Girl with Doll* (1921). After the end of his teaching in 1923, he began producing a large number of landscapes as he traveled widely throughout

North Africa, the Middle East, and Europe; works of this period include *Harbor of Marseilles* (1925), *Tower Bridge* (1926), and *Jerusalem* (1930). His landscapes and outdoor scenes reflect his expressionist taste for bright color and emotion, with his own contribution of an elevated perspective and sense of each city as a dynamic and living whole.

With the rise to power of the Nazis, Kokoschka was in danger, because they had labeled him a dangerous and subversive artist. His oil painting *Self-portrait of a "Degenerate Artist"* (1937) is a powerful reply to this form of tyranny. Though the work uses bold color and background, the face emerging from the painting appears thoughtful, alert, intelligent, possessing a spirit that only a corrupt regime could view as a threat. In 1934 he left Vienna for Prague, where he met Olda Palkovská, whom he would later marry. To flee from the **encroaching** Nazi armies in Czechoslovakia, the couple moved from Prague to England in 1938, and later Oskar became a British citizen. He continued to use his art to protest the war in works such as *Help the Basque Children* (1937) and *What We Are Fighting For* (1943).

With the cessation of hostilities in 1945, Kokoschka resumed his travels, including travel to the United States. He continued his work with visual media as well as writing short stories *(A Sea Ringed with Visions*, 1956), plays, and poetry. He settled in Villeneuve, Switzerland, in 1953. For 10 years (1953–1963) he organized a painting school in Salzburg, featuring what became an internationally **renowned** and influential course, while doing increasing work in set design and lithographs on classical themes. A large retrospective of his work at London's Tate Gallery in 1962 was one of many exhibits featuring his work. He died in Montreux, Switzerland. ◆

"I consider myself responsible, not to society, which dictates fashion and taste suited to its environment and its period, but to youth, to the coming generations, which are left stranded in a blitzed world, unaware of the soul trembling in awe before the mystery of life."

Oskar Kokoschka, 1948, quoted on *The Meaning of Art* website

encroaching: movement of an individual or group in a gradual or unwelcome fashion into an area where they are unwelcome.

renowned: well-known and recognized for a body of work in the arts or other area of life.

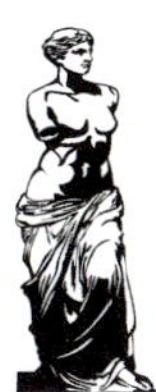

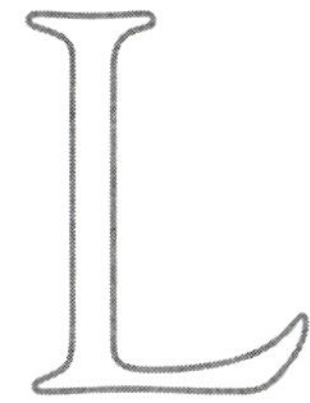

La Tour, Georges de

MARCH 14, 1593–JANUARY 15, 1653 ● PAINTER

Georges La Tour, a French painter, was baptized on March 14, 1593 at Vic-sur-Seille in Lorraine, an independent duchy until 1633 and subsequently a province of France. His father was a baker. Little is known about his life, especially his youth. It is believed by some that he studied painting with Jacques Bellange, court painter to the duke of Lorraine at Nancy, Lorraine's capital. He may have traveled to northern Europe or Italy, but that is just a guess based on the painters who apparently influenced his work, including Caravaggio, Hendrik Terbrugghen, and Gerrit van Honthorst.

The first concrete evidence of La Tour's existence after his baptism is a document dated October 20, 1616, which records that he became a godfather in Vic-sur-Seille. On July 2, 1617, he married Diane Le Nerf. In 1620 he moved to Lunéville, in Lorraine, his wife's native town. There he hired an apprentice and opened a studio. The reason for the move may have been that the duke of Lorraine was erecting a residence there, which meant that by living in Lunéville, La Tour would have a greater chance of receiving commissions for paintings from the duke. In fact, La Tour is known to have received only two such commissions.

However, early in his career La Tour began to purchase property, which suggests that he was financially successful. In 1639 he became a "Painter to the King," Louis XIII of France. In his later years, purchasers paid high prices for his paintings.

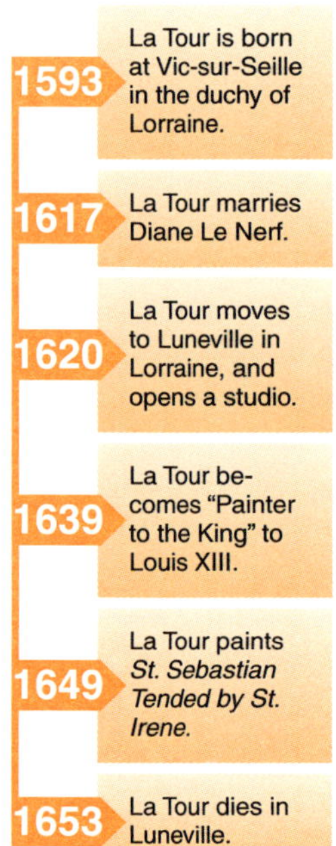

In modern times, there has been considerable controversy about the order of his paintings, since most of them are undated; there is even uncertainty in identifying which works are his.

La Tour was a Catholic. Lorraine itself was a Catholic stronghold located near the Protestant states of western Germany. Therefore, it was a battleground during the Thirty Years War (1618–48), a fact that surely influenced his painting. His two areas of specialization were religious subjects—which increasingly dominated his work—and genre paintings, or paintings that depict scenes of ordinary life. Often it is hard to distinguish between the two. Much of his genre work, which seems at first glance to be purely secular, has religious overtones; his *Dice Players* and *Payment of Dues* have been cited as examples. In his religious paintings, on the other hand, holy themes are presented in a subtle fashion, as in *Repentance* and *Job and His Wife*. La Tour usually did not use obvious holy symbols, like haloes above the heads of saints; instead, he tended to employ everyday objects that had acquired a religious significance. Still, religious themes dominated his work, especially in his middle and later years.

With time, La Tour's composition became ever more spare. His figures were executed in a realistic style, painted in ordinary postures. His paintings were uncrowded: he never included more than seven figures. La Tour used little scenery; it is not possible to identify the locations of his paintings. It has been said that this austerity helps to concentrate the viewer's attention on the figures—and hence on the Catholic implications of their attitudes. His paintings from 1645 on, such as *Nativity* and *St. Sebastian Tended by St. Irene* (1649) have a simple, smooth, geometric appearance that makes them highly appealing in the modern era.

One of the outstanding qualities of La Tour's work is what has been described as its "solemn quietude" or "steady stillness." His *Musicians' Quarrel* depicts an apparently violent dispute, but La Tour captures a moment of balance when one of the quarrelers is using his hand to hold back the other's sword. Also, in his two versions of *St. Jerome*, a man is whipping himself in religious penance but is depicted at an instant of rest between strokes. La Tour also uses color to advance a quiet, thoughtful depiction of human feelings. He often uses muted colors and avoids sharp contrasts between them.

Among La Tour's early paintings, daytime scenes prevail. Increasingly, however, he painted nocturnal scenes lit by candlelight, nightlight, or torch. His use of light in the latter paintings has been one of the most admired aspects of his work. Sometimes the source of light is visible, sometimes it is hidden with great skill. It is in these paintings that the muted, solemn, contemplative qualities of his work are most artfully apparent, qualities that have been described as "contrary to the pervasive exuberance of the baroque age" in which he lived.

After La Tour's death at Lunéville on January 15, 1653, his work was ignored for more than 300 years, and many of his unsigned paintings were attributed to other artists. Only in the early years of the 20th century was his reputation revived. Since then his works have been shown at the Les Peintres de la réalité au XVIIe siècle France (Realist Painters in Seventeenth-Century France) exhibition at the Musée de l'Orangerie in Paris in 1934, The Age of Louis XIV exhibition in London in 1958, and at a solo exhibition at the Musée de l'Orangerie in 1972. His paintings are owned by museums around the world, including the Metropolitan Museum of Art and the Frick Collection in New York City, the Louvre in Paris, and museums in Stockholm, Berlin, Cleveland, and Detroit, and elsewhere. ◆

"It was against this backdrop of burgeoning secularism that La Tour and his fellow Lorrainese struggled. Their efforts were perhaps less a renewal of Christian devotion than a last beleaguered effort to stem an unstemmable tide."

From the essay "Lorraine in the Time of La Tour," by Patricia Behre Miskimin in *Georges de la Tour and His World,* 1996

Léger, Fernand

FEBRUARY 4, 1881–AUGUST 17, 1955 ● PAINTER

The son of a cattle merchant, Fernand Léger was born in Argentan, in Normandy, France. He served an apprenticeship at an architect's office, and he continued in that line of work when he moved to Paris in 1900. He served briefly in the military as a member of the corps of engineers from 1902 to 1903. On leaving the military he returned to employment with an architectural firm, but also enrolled in the Ecole des Arts Décoratifs, while studying under Jean-Léon Gérôme and Gabriel Ferrier.

During his first years in Paris, Léger shared an apartment with another painter from his hometown, André Mare, and together the two young men began to explore the avant-garde of

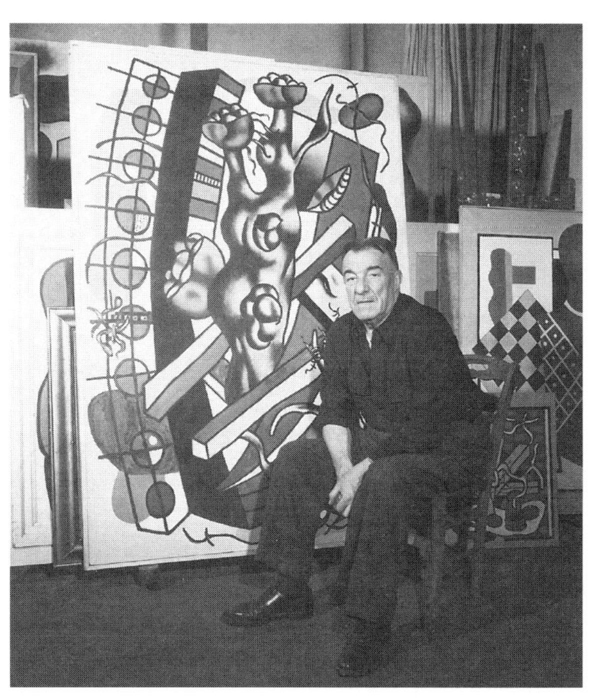

Fernand Léger, 1948

the Parisian literary and artistic scenes. By 1908 Léger had established himself in a studio in Montparnasse and had made the acquaintance of such notables as Guillaume Apollinaire, Blaise Cendrars, Marc Chagall, Robert Delaunay, and Jacques Lipchitz. His work during this early period showed strong impressionist influences, but soon he began experimenting with different styles, particularly after viewing an exhibition of Cézanne's paintings at the Salon d'Automne in 1907.

Very little of this early work survives, for Léger destroyed nearly all of it. Of the few examples that remain, it is clear that impressionism dominated his early years, and that later on he explored fauvism. However, by 1910 cubism became the dominant force in his painting style. Early on he was greatly interested in exploring contrast, such as the contrast between the ephemeral quality of rising smoke against the sharp detail and static shape of buildings. His early works were far from abstract, and even in his cubist works, such as *Nudes in a Forest* (1911) the figures are not as fragmented as they would be in the works of many other cubist painters of the time. His greatest preoccupation remained the study of contrast.

By 1912, Léger had already achieved respect and acceptance among his fellow artists and among collectors and critics. He participated in a cubist exhibition at the Salon d'Automne in that year and signed on with Daniel-Henry Kahnweiler, an important dealer who also handled the work of Picasso and Braque. By the following year Léger had embarked on his important series, *Contrasts of Forms*, and was a lecturer at the Académie Wassilieff.

Léger's career was interrupted by the outbreak of World War I, when he was called for military duty. He was gassed during a battle at Verdun (1916) and hospitalized until 1917. Before the end of the war he also met Jeanne Lohy, the woman that he would marry in 1919. Out of his experiences in battle came a series of powerful paintings and drawings, among them

Soldiers in a Dugout (1915) and *The Card Game* (1917). His wartime service also awakened in him a commitment to making his art accessible and relevant not only to a few collectors and critics, but to the general public, whom he now regarded as his true audience.

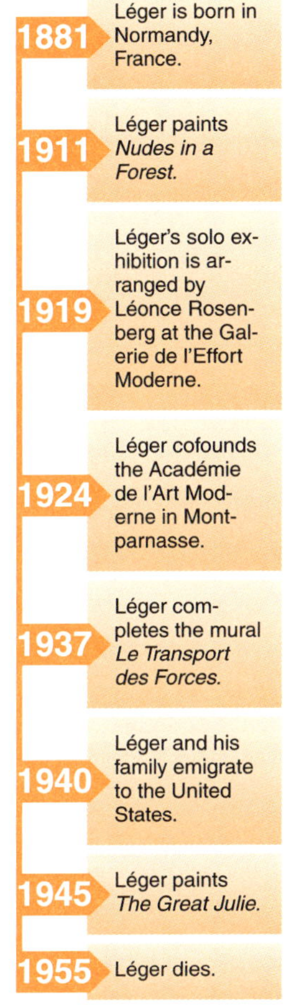

In the aftermath of the war, Léger began exploring an entirely new direction in subject matter. The machine gun, a relatively new invention, had impressed the artist as a symbol of power, and machines became his primary motif. During this period he produced several series of paintings, each exploring the beauty and power of some mechanical device or component. Among these series are *The Discs* and *The Propellers*. In these works he turned away from delicate colors, which he associated with effete sensibilities, and employed the stronger, more vivid colors that he associated with the reality recognized by ordinary people.

The end of the war saw a further change in Léger's career. His new agent, Léonce Rosenberg—an influential figure in artistic circles—quickly secured for Léger a one-man exhibition at the Galerie de l'Effort Moderne (1919). By 1920, Léger began integrating his mechanical theme with figures, resulting in such paintings as *The Mechanic*, in which the human form is composed of machine-like parts. However, the artist was also exploring other avenues of expression, briefly indulging a passion for printmaking. He also continued to do book illustrations and began to explore film as a result of his profound admiration for Charlie Chaplin's work in cinema. Léger's early film work included set design and promotional posters, but in 1924 he made the film *Ballet mécanique*, which used rapidly shifting **montages** juxtaposing mechanical images with human figures.

montages: a single composition comprised of juxtaposed or superimposed images or designs.

Working in film inspired Léger to explore further collaborations between visual arts with other types of expression. He collaborated with choreographers, writers, directors, and architects, and tried his hand at costume design. Throughout this period, he also continued his solo work on paintings that were now monumental in scale and more abstract than his earlier works. He had several important exhibitions during the 1920s, began contributing articles on art theory to art journals and, in 1924, co-founded the Académie de l'Art Moderne in his studio in Montparnasse.

In the 1930s Léger returned to less abstract, more accessible representations in his paintings. This shift in style reflected

Léger was greatly interested in exploring contrast, such as the contrast between the ephemeral quality of rising smoke against the sharp detail and static shape of buildings.

Léger's political idealism, which was strongly influenced by socialist and communist theory, and shows his belief that art should be for the common people, directly recognizable and relevant to their lives. During this decade Léger corresponded with the Russian filmmaker Sergei Eisenstein and made several trips to the United States to learn more about American filmmaking techniques. In 1937 he completed his massive mural, *Le Transport des Forces*, his vision of a mechanistic utopia and its break from nature.

World War II and the coming Nazi occupation in Paris drove Léger and his family from their beloved Montparnasse, and he ultimately moved to the United States in 1940. He settled in New York but took teaching engagements at Yale University and, later, at Mills College. During this period he produced a number of paintings, including *The Great Julie* (1945), and he believed that his American sojourn yielded the best paintings of his career.

Léger and his family returned to France in 1946 and plunged into political action, driven by his powerful identification with the common people and the cause of world peace. He also revived his academy and attracted students from throughout Europe and the United States. During the 1950s he again began to explore new media, from stained glass and ceramics to **mosaics** and **tapestries.** As with his painting, he concentrated on public installations, remaining true to his conviction that art was an essentially public form of expression. His artistic output and collaborations remained prolific up to the time of his death. ◆

mosaics: pictures or designs made up of small pieces of glass, colored stone, tile, or paper attached to a surface; typically seen on walls, floors and ceilings.
tapestries: heavy handwoven textiles with pictoral designs that are utilized as curtains, hangings, and upholstery.

The Limbourg Brothers—Paul, Herman, and Jean

c. 1370–1416 ● Manuscript Illuminators

The Limbourg brothers, Paul, Herman, and Jean, were born in Nijmegen, the Netherlands, to an artistic family. Their uncle, Jean Malouel, had been a successful artist for well-placed clients such as the Duc de Bourgogne; their father, Arnold Limbourg, was a sculptor. Documents suggest that in the late 1390s the younger brothers, Herman and

Jean, worked for a Parisian goldsmith. Paul, the eldest, was later the leader of their illumination workshop. Because so few historical records about the brothers exist, much information on their early lives remains obscure. The brothers were not obscure to their contemporaries, however, and by 1402 their artist skills were respected enough to earn them a contract to prepare an illuminated Bible for the Duke of Burgundy, known as Philip the Bold. The duke died just two years later, however, before the project, the *Bible moralisée* (*Moralized Bible*), could be completed, and the duke's brother, Jean, Duc de Berry, inherited their labors. The Limbourg brothers could not have asked for a more suitable patron—the duke was one of the most wealthy and devoted art patrons of his era, commissioning castles, jewels, tapestries, and paintings of all varieties. The brothers became members of the duke's entourage, and he was fond of showering them with gifts as tokens of his appreciation for their talents.

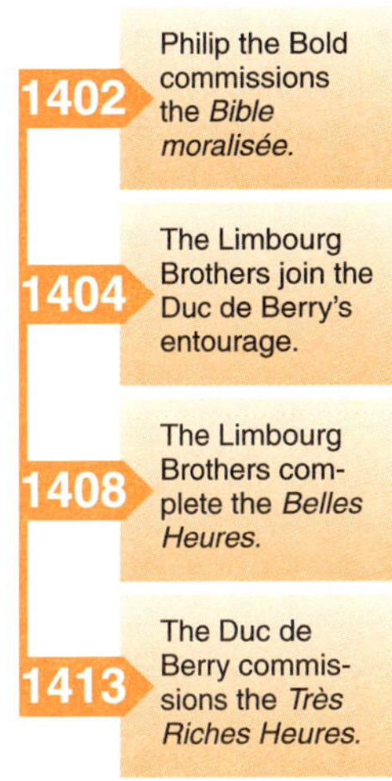

While the duke commanded a fortune, his position in French society (he was brother to King Charles V) implicated him in a number of political intrigues. During one attack by a hostile mob, his Bicetre Castle was burned to the ground, destroying many of the illuminated manuscripts the brothers had prepared for him. Moreover, the Limbourg brothers would all die young, apparently succumbing to the plague, before completing their last work, commissioned by the duke in 1413. Luckily, the works they had already achieved were so remarkable that even today they are regarded as the greatest masterpieces of manuscript illumination.

The Brothers show an attention to detail unrivaled in manuscript illumination, portraying traditional stories such as the passion of Jesus Christ in new and imaginative ways.

One of the works they finished for Philip the Bold was a *Bible moralisée*. It features miniature illustrations, with Latin and French texts. While it was in many ways similar to previous such books, and may show the influence of illuminator Jacquemart de Hesdin, it features a wider range of color, and its human figures are endowed with dramatic gestures and movements. It is possible that the Brother's experience in gold working helped train them for the painstaking tasks of illumination, which required tiny brushes for detail.

The first major work the brothers produced for the Duc de Berry was the illustrated manuscript *Belles Heures* (*Beautiful hours;* 1408 or 1409). In this work, the Limbourg brothers were quite innovative both in subject matter and style. Earlier works had featured "cycles," series of pictures clustered around a single person or theme. In this work, however, the brothers gave special attention to new subjects in their cycles. The great medieval mystic Catherine, a favorite of the Duc de Berry's wife, is featured with attention to lesser-known incidents in her life. Twelve scenes are devoted to the Christian patristic leader Jerome, others to Antony—probably because of the duke's own spiritual interests. These scenes are rendered with great imagination and a sensitive use of color.

The Limbourgs' greatest work for the duke was their last. The *Très Riches Heures* (*The Very Rich Hours*), like the *Belles Heures*, is a book of hours, an extremely popular genre in the late medieval period. The book of hours was a religious book used by lay people as an aid to their prayer lives. Though the exact content of books of hours could vary, a typical book contained the text of prayers, arranged according to the appropriate season, month, week, day, and canonical hour (such as morning or "matins" prayers and **vespers**). Other elements could include psalms and special holy day masses. In the hands of the Limbourg brothers, this popular genre took on exciting new life in the late Gothic style. The brothers reorganized the conventional arrangement of **zodiac** signs to include detailed information such as lunar phases. The Greek god of the sun, Apollo, is powerfully portrayed in the center of the zodiac with his chariot. In the pictures devoted to each of the 12 months, the brothers showed scenes from peasant life and from the courtly life they had been lucky enough to join. In January, their patron is seen hosting a banquet; three other months are devoted to courtly scenes. Even the peasant scenes of activities such as sheep shearing are often set against the backdrop of the Duc de Berry's castles or those of his relatives.

vespers: relating to the evening; the sixth of the canonical hours said or sung in the late afternoon.

zodiac: the imaginary belt in the heavens that is said to encompass the paths of each of the principal planets with the exception of Pluto, and is divided into 12 signs or constellations for astrological purposes.

In such depictions, the brothers show an attention to detail unrivalled in manuscript illumination, portraying traditional stories such as the passion of Jesus Christ in new and imaginative ways. Clearly, many of the scenes were influenced by earlier works, especially art in Florence, but the Limbourg brothers were the first to introduce certain styles to illumination, with greater attention to perspective and space than their predecessors. Their vivid rendering of color was certainly aided by the patronage of the wealthy duke, who made it possible for them to use colors such as the exotic *azur d'outreme* ("ultramarine") derived from lapis lazuli, a semi-precious stone.

At the time of the brothers' untimely deaths in 1416, painting of the *Très Riches Heures* remained largely unfinished. Decades later, Charles I de Savoie would commission Jean Colombe to continue the illumination, which he finished in the years 1485–1489.

The brothers' influence on later manuscript illumination is immense. The original *Très Riches Heures* volume is housed at the Condé Museum, Chantilly, France. ◆

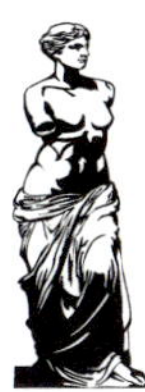

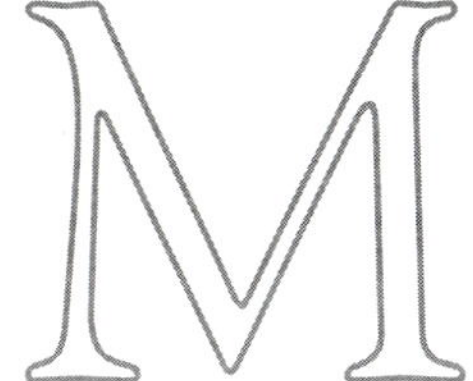

Magritte, René

NOVEMBER 21, 1898–AUGUST 15, 1967 ● PAINTER

So many images from René Magritte's paintings—like the bowler hat perched atop a green apple—have been so widely reproduced in ads and posters that they are better known than the artist himself. Often acclaimed as the greatest Belgian artist of the 20th century, Magritte worked and reworked his signature pictorial counterpoint: precisely realistic figures arrayed in jarringly surrealistic **juxtapositions**—"snapshots of the impossible," in the words of one critic.

juxtapositions: instances in which two or more objects or ideas are placed together.

René François Chislain Magritte was born on November 21, 1898, in Lessine, Belgium. He was inspired to become an artist during childhood after happening upon an outdoor painter at work; he was taking classes at a local art school by the age of 12. His chronically suicidal mother finally succeeded in ending her life in 1903, after which the family moved to Charleroi. Two years later, at a local fair, Magritte met Georgette-Marie-Florence Berger, whom he did not see again until 1922; they married that year and remained together until his death.

From 1916 to 1918, Magritte studied at the Académie des Beaux-Arts in Brussels, where he was trained in the prevailing impressionist aesthetic that pervades his earliest canvases. In 1919 he worked with Gisbert Combaz, a Belgian painter, to create a series of posters, his first publicly exhibited works. That same year, as he gravitated toward the innovative precepts of futurism and cubism, he participated in the publication of an

"[Magritte] was a storyteller of hallucinatory ordinariness."
Andrew Lambith on the contradictory aspects of René Magritte's paintings

avant-garde review entitled *Au Volant!* and had his first painting accepted for public exhibition: the Cubist-influenced *Three Women*.

A brief detour into military service in 1921 was followed, a year later, by his marriage to Georgette, after which he earned money by designing wallpaper and posters. Magritte had experimented with abstraction in the early 1920s, but he reverted to figurative painting after an inspiring encounter with a reproduction of Giorgio de Chirico's painting *The Song of Love* (1914), whose odd, dreamlike juxtapositions came as a revelation to Magritte, setting him on his trajectory toward surrealism. An important transitional work was *Blue Cinema* (1925), a semiabstract depiction of a toplike object portrayed with a severe, skewed geometry rendered in a skewed, oddly menacing perspective.

Magritte's flirtation with surrealism had ripened into a full embrace by 1926, when he cofounded the Belgian surrealist group, helping to formulate its theoretical precepts, which harked back to the writings of the 19th-century French poet Lautréamont, especially his dictum that nothing is "as beautiful as … the chance encounter of a sewing machine and an umbrella on a dissecting table." (Years later, Magritte contributed 77 drawings to a definitive edition of Lautréamont's works [1948]).

Magritte's career prospects advanced apace with his aesthetic development as he signed a contract in 1926 with the influential Brussels gallery owner Paul Gustave van Hecke, who mounted Magritte's first solo exhibition the following year. The show featured his first explicitly surrealist canvases such as *Lost Jockey* (1926) and *The Threatened Assassin* (1926); the latter work, with its aura of frozen menace, reflects Magritte's longstanding fascination with French and American detective fiction and the cinema.

In the wake of the show's chilly critical reception, Magritte and his wife moved to France, where they settled in a Paris suburb. There Magritte joined forces with the French surrealist movement, then at is peak of influence, and grew especially close to its leaders, André Breton and Paul Eluard. By 1930, however, Magritte had wearied of the movement's **internecine** quarrels, and he returned to Brussels, where he lived for the rest of his life.

internecine: a confrontation characaterized by bitter and conflict and mutual destruction.

Struggling for a livelihood in the depths of the Depression, Magritte and his brother Paul founded Studio Dongo, a graphic arts firm that produced posters, illustrations, advertisements, and so on. Although van Hecke's gallery closed in 1930, his huge inventory of Magritte's paintings—some 200 in all—was acquired by E.L.T. Mesens, who became the director of the London Gallery in 1938 and helped to promote Magritte's work in England.

During the 1930s Magritte's reputation continued to thrive in Belgium, where his work was the subject of two major museum exhibitions: a one-man show in 1933 and, in 1937, a group show along with Man Ray and Yves Tanguy. Throughout that decade Magritte refined his distinctive pictorial idiom—painstakingly realistic figures placed in wildly **anomalous** contexts or absurd juxtapositions that sought to subvert the frozen perceptions of repressed human consciousness. For example, *Elective Affinities* depicts a huge egg inside a birdcage; *Eternity* (1935), in which the three pedestals of a museum are the head of Christ, a stick of butter, and the head of Dante; and *Red Model* (1935), in which human toes protrude from the tips of a pair of boots. As Magritte summarized his art, "Our secret desire is for a change in the order of things, and it is appeased by the vision of a new order.... The fate of an object in which we had no interest suddenly begins to disturb us."

anomalous: inconsistent with the normal or usual; irregular.

Aside from a brief foray into an impressionist visual style in the 1940s, Magritte stuck to his well-established visual formula for the rest of his career. After World War II his renown spread to the United States, thanks in large measure to his 1948 contract with the influential New York art dealer Alexandre Iolas. During the 1950s and 1960s Magritte **supplemented** his characteristic surrealist canvases with experimental projects in film and wax sculpture. Since his death in Brussels in 1967, his work has retained its critical and popular cachet, helping to inspire the pop and conceptual movements. ◆

supplemented: added or completed.

Malevich, Kasimir

FEBRUARY 26, 1878–MAY 15, 1935 ● PAINTER AND PRINTMAKER

The Russian painter and printmaker Kasimir Malevich was one of the seminal figures of modern art. His formally austere, geometrically precise painting, to which he applied the label "suprematism," was a watershed in the de-

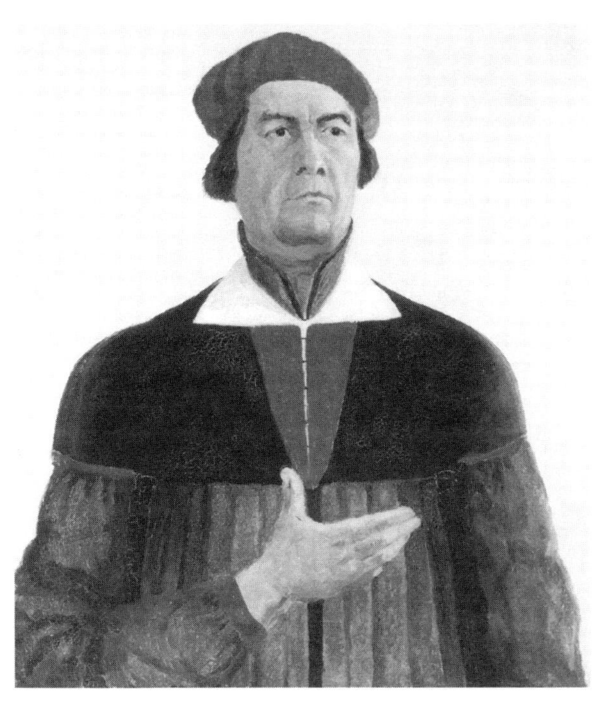

Kasimir Malevich, self-portrait, 1933

velopment of abstract art and its later ramifications, such as constructivism and minimalism.

Kasimir Serenovich Malevich was born near Kiev, Russia, on February 26, 1878. His father, who labored in the sugar factories around Belopolye, moved the family to Kursk in 1896, where both father and son took jobs with the local railroad. Despite an erratic early education, Kasimir was a precocious young artist and studied at the Kiev School of Art from 1895 to 1896. It took him eight more years to amass the funds needed to travel to Moscow to spend a year at the Stroganov School, after which he studied privately with the painter Ivan Renberg. He then enrolled at the Moscow School of Painting, Sculpture, and Architecture, where he was schooled in impressionist techniques. A committed radical, he also took part in the 1905 uprising but was spared government reprisals.

Malevich's training in impressionism was evident in his early canvases, which also bore traces of influence from the fauves and the nabis. His growing stature led to an invitation to contribute a painting to a 1907 group exhibit mounted by the Association of Moscow Artists. One of the Association's members, Mikhail Larionov, recruited Malevich to a newly formed modernist group, Jack of Diamonds, in 1910; two years later the two formed the nucleus of a splinter movement named Donkey's Tail (shortly thereafter renamed Target). By now Malevich had shed the last vestiges of **post-impressionism** and was incorporating elements of cubism in canvases like *Morning in the Country after the Rain* (1911), a semiabstract landscape.

post-impressionism: an art movement originating in France that immediately followed the Impressionist and neo-Impressionist school; the artists of post-Impressionism emphasized structure, form, and expression more so than ever and rejected the emphasis of nature and the depiction of light.

The Target group was a magnet for the leading avant-garde currents in Russian art, including cubism, futurism, and neoprimitivism, out of which Larionov proclaimed a nonobjective movement he dubbed Rayism. But personal acrimony led to the dissolution of the Target group, and Larionov and Malevich went their separate ways. Malevich increasingly identified with the burgeoning futurist movement, whose doctrinal influence was evident in Malevich's work from 1912–13, which had all but dispensed with representation and concentrated on the interplay of light and form.

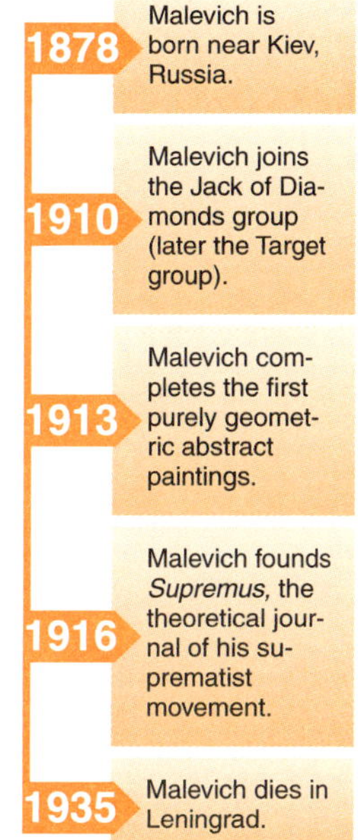

By the end of 1913, Malevich had begun turning out the geometric abstractions that marked a major departure in his work—and in the course of modern painting. His first such effort, a black rectangle on a white background, launched the movement Malevich called suprematism, which he described as "the supremacy of pure feeling in creative art," freed from the extraneous demands of representation. Malevich showed such works, some of them retaining elements of collage, in 1914 at the Jack of Diamonds exhibition in Russia and at the Salon des Indépendants in Paris. The 1915 Russian show entitled *Tramway V* featured a large sampling of Malevich's abstract canvases, in which he displayed a growing preference for rectilinear shapes. Subsequent highlights in Malevich's embrace of geometric austerity were *Black Square* (1915), *Black Circle*, and *Black Cross*. After turning out a flurry of polychromatic paintings in 1916, Malevich reverted to sparer monochromatic designs, including *White on White* (1917–18) and *White Square on White* (1918).

In 1916 Malevich attempted to establish a formal apparatus for the suprematist movement, to be centered on a journal called *Supremus*. But his plans were interrupted by the February 1917 revolution, which led to the call-up of Malevich's army regiment. After the decisive October revolution that brought the Bolsheviks to power, Malevich, initially a partisan of the anarchists, became a supporter of the new regime. In April of 1918 he joined the Fine Arts division of the People's Commissariat for Enlightenment, which was charged with the administration of museums and exhibits. He later taught at the Free Art Studios in Moscow and in 1919 wrote a book on his aesthetic theories, *On New Systems in Art*.

During a stint as a teacher at Marc Chagall's art school in Vitesk, Malevich founded a new movement called Unovis. Dispirited by the dismissal of Chagall in 1920, Malevich temporarily forsook painting for writing, concentrating on philosophical and theoretical issues. He came to Petrograd in 1922, when Unovis was merged into the just-founded Museum of Artistic Culture. Two years later the museum was reorganized as the Institute of Artistic Culture, with Malevich as its director. As his teaching began to supersede his painting, in 1926 Malevich or-

By the end of 1913, Malevich had begun turning out the geometric abstractions that marked a major departure in his work—and in the course of modern painting.

ganized an exhibition of the abstract works of his pupils. But the Soviet government, which by then had spurned modernism in favor of Socialist realism, bitterly criticized the show and closed the institute. Malevich and his students were transferred to the more pliant State Institute of Art History. Despite its hostility to his aesthetic, the government allowed Malevich to travel to Germany in 1927 to display his work and lecture at the like-minded Bauhaus, which published one of his books, *The Nonobjective World.*

Despite Stalin's increasingly repressive cultural policies, a major retrospective of Malevich's work was mounted at the Tetryakov Gallery in Moscow in 1929. The party-line critics were at pains to criticize the "reactionary" nature of his abstractions while acknowledging their historical importance. After he lost his position at the institute that year, Malevich came under great financial pressure, and his painting output markedly declined. He did, however, attempt to salvage his career by adapting to state-approved figuration in works such as *Three Peasants* (1930), *Running Man* (1933–34), and *Man with Horse* (1933). The last major exhibition of his work in Russia during his lifetime, held in 1932 in conjunction with the 15th anniversary celebration of the revolution, held up his paintings as a model of counterrevolutionary art, **inimical** to the goals and ideals of the Soviet state.

inimical: being purposely belligerent due to hositlity or malevolence.

In 1934 Malevich developed cancer, and he succumbed to the disease in Leningrad in 1935. ◆

Manet, Edouard

JANUARY 23, 1832–APRIL 30, 1883 ● PAINTER

Edouard Manet's work profoundly influenced the direction of modern painting. Manet was born in Paris, where his father was a high official in the ministry of justice. Expected to become a lawyer, at 16 he announced that he had decided to be an artist. His family encouraged him in an abortive attempt at a naval career, but he was soon back in Paris studying art with Thomas Couture (and piano with a young Dutch woman, Suzanne Leenhoff, with whom he lived and eventually married). In 1853 he traveled to Italy, where he visited Venice and Florence and painted copies of the Renaissance masters, and Spain, where he copied Velasquez.

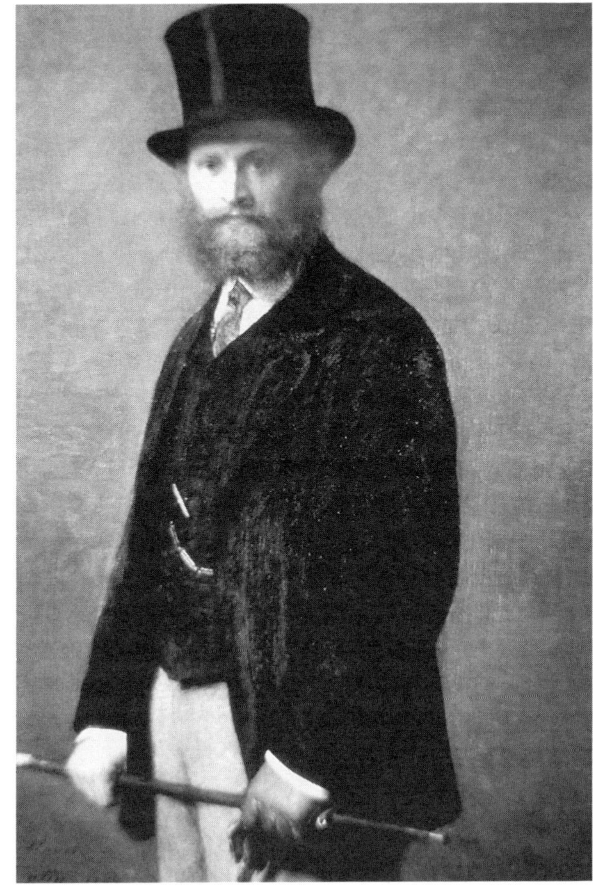

Portrait of Edouard Manet (1867) by Henri Fantin-Latour.

Manet's early original compositions, such as *The Absinthe Drinker*, won praise from fellow artists, including Eugène Delacroix, but were too radical for the conservative artistic sensibilities of the Salon of the French Academy. In 1863 his work *Déjeuner sur l'herbe* ("Luncheon on the Grass") was hung in the Salon des Réfusés, a gallery sponsored by Napoleon III to accommodate pictures rejected by the academy. Crowds flocked to the Salon to laugh at the "outrageous subjects and inept techniques" of the exhibits; they considered Manet's contribution scandalously shameless. In it, a lightly draped woman kneels over a little brook: two men are seated on the ground, conversing. In front of them, stark against the black of their clothes, is a nude woman, painted as only Manet painted, with not so much as a shadow or a nuance to soften the brilliance of her flesh.

Manet's painting *Olympia* (1863), showing a reclining nude staring boldly at the viewer, aroused such vehement public outrage that the painting was rehung in a spot in the salon where it was hoped that no one would see it. Manet's exhibition of his own work at the 1867 Paris World Fair promised its viewers "not flawless, but sincere" works, true to his dictum "instantly paint what you see."

Between 1862 and 1868 Manet made over 100 prints experimenting with different techniques. Many of these prints were based on works of old masters as well as his own paintings. He also used photographs as studies for portraits.

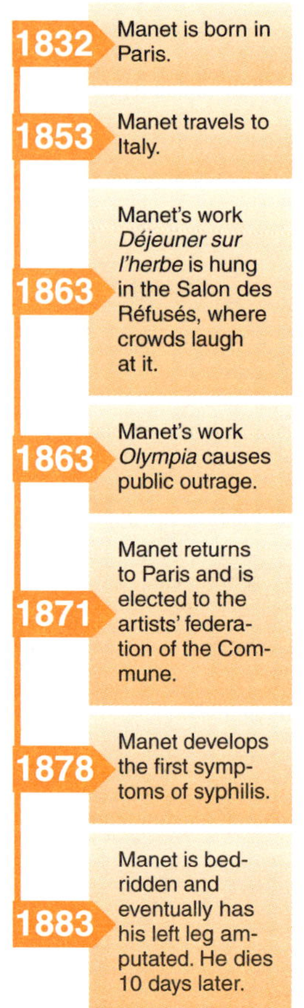

Returning to Paris in 1871, after military service in the Franco-Prussian War, Manet found his studio vandalized; luckily, he had stored his canvases safely. The city was controlled by the Communards, and Manet was elected to the artists' federation of the Commune. He made many sketches of the Paris of the Commune.

In 1875 refused by the salon once again, Manet decided to exhibit his paintings in his studio for two weeks. Thousands came and the occasion was so noisy and elicited so many complaints from the neighbors that he was evicted from his studio when the lease expired.

In 1878 a pain developed in Manet's left foot, the first sign of syphilis manifesting itself in a relentlessly progressive locomotion-ataxia. By 1883 he was bed ridden. His gangrenous left leg was amputated, but after 10 days of high fever, delirium, and great pain, he died.

Manet has been called "the first modern painter." His friend Emile Zola said that every time he placed his canvas on the easel, he departed for the unknown. His reality had nothing to do with "realism," his truth was not of flesh and blood or lace and velvet, but of paint and painting. One must paint the truth regardless of adverse critism, he believed. He had a revolutionary impact, even though his own goal had always been to achieve official recognition. ◆

Mantegna, Andrea

c. 1430–September 13, 1506 ● Painter

Born to a humble carpenter in a village near Padua, Andrea Mantegna was apprenticed at age 11 to the Paduan painter Francesco Squarcione, who became his adoptive father and with whom he later had a falling out.

Squarcione was no great painter, but in his studio apprentices were exposed to Renaissance artistic ideals and practices, such as copying after classical sculpture. Mantegna was therefore trained in the atmosphere of academic antiquarianism that was particular to mid-15th-century Padua, and with which he was temperamentally entirely in sympathy. This shows clearly in his first major works, his contributions to the fresco decoration (largely destroyed in 1944) of the Ovetari Chapel in the Church of the Eremitani. In *St. James before Herod Agrippa* (1450–1451) Mantegna incorporated classical motifs and details gleaned from Roman triumphal arches and tombs known to him in north Italy, placing these within a perspectival setting that indicates his knowledge of Leon Battista Alberti's treatise *Della pittura* (1436).

His Paduan works also show his strong response to the sculpture of the Florentine Donatello, who worked in Padua from 1443 to 1453. The combined influences of classical statuary and Donatello's Paduan bronzes led Mantegna to develop an exceptionally sculptural treatment of the human figure. This provided the foundation for the severe, statuesque figure style to be seen in mature paintings like the *St. Sebastian*, probably painted in the early 1480s.

In 1459 Mantegna completed the high altarpiece for San Zeno in Verona, one of the most influential north Italian altarpieces of the 15th century and still in situ. He left Padua in January 1460 to enter the service of Lodovico Gonzaga, marques of Mantua from 1444 to 1478, as his court painter. Mantegna's early works in Mantua were all small paintings on panel, some of which were made during the 1460s for the decoration of the chapel in the Mantuan castle. Although he never adopted a Netherlandish oil-painting technique, Mantegna was indebted to northern painting, as the intricate surfaces of these paintings demonstrate. The *Circumcision* perhaps best shows his brilliant, miniaturist painting of fine details. Using crystal-clear lighting and an evolved sense of the colors and surface textures (especially of minerals), Mantegna here showed a subtle feeling for the variety of expression required in narrative presentation.

The principal surviving work done for Lodovico Gonzaga is the fresco decoration of the Camera Picta (also known as the Camera degli Sposi), started in 1465 and completed in 1474. Using fictive classicizing architecture and elaborate illusionistic devices, Mantegna depicted the Gonzaga family within their court environment. On the west wall, set against an extensive landscape dotted with the ruins of classical buildings, Lodovico greets his second son Francesco, perhaps on his return from Rome after his investiture as a cardinal in December 1461. In contrast to the flat, tonally high-key treatment of these figures, Mantegna portrayed the assembled Gonzaga family on the north wall with rounded forms and a rich tonality, as though to suggest their physical presence within the space of the room.

Especially ingenious and witty is the painted oculus at the crown of the vault through which, silhouetted against the open sky, a group of women and sharply foreshortened putti peer down at the family group.

After Lodovico Gonzaga's death in 1478, Mantegna's next major patron was Lodovico's grandson Francesco, marquise of Mantua from 1484 to 1519, for whom probably Mantegna painted the nine canvases of the *Triumphs of Caesar.* Already under way in 1486, work on these huge canvases was interrupted by Mantegna's stay in Rome between 1488 and 1490, where for Pope Innocent VIII he decorated a chapel (destroyed in 1780) in the Villa Belvedere. The *Triumphs* are an inventive reconstruction of a triumphal procession of Julius Caesar, who is shown in the last canvas enthroned on his chariot. The procession includes sacrificial animals and enemy captives, the weaponry of classical warfare, and miscellaneous booty won in conflict, all represented with unprecedented archaeological accuracy.

The last phase of Mantegna's career was dominated by painting for Francesco Gonzaga's wife, Isabella d'Este.

The last phase of Mantegna's career was dominated by painting for Francesco Gonzaga's wife, Isabella d'Este. Soon after her marriage in 1490 she constructed a *studiolo* (a small room embellished with paintings and other objects of art) in her new apartments in the castle of Mantua. For this room Mantegna supplied the first two (and started a third) of a series of elaborate allegorizing paintings, in which Isabella sought to make visually evident her moral and intellectual qualities. Mantegna's own intellectual skills and profound knowledge of the antique world allowed him to match the complex allegorical programs of the *Parnassus* (installed in 1497) and the *Pallas Expelling the Vices from the Garden of Virtue* (completed 1502) with great pictorial inventiveness and brilliant surface treatment. The decoration of Isabella d'Este's *studiolo* also included two works painted to imitate bronze. These and other late paintings that imitate sculptural reliefs offer further indications of Mantegna's interest both in depicting minerals and in establishing visually the representational superiority of painting over sculpture. The final tribute both to Mantegna's intellectual learning and to his renown as a creative artist was the establishment of his funerary chapel in Alberti's great church of S. Andrea in Mantua. Mantegna's *all'antica* (in a classical style) bronze self-portrait bust, probably cast some 20 years before his death, was later installed at the entrance to his chapel.

In 1453 Mantegna married Nicolosia, daughter of the Venetian painter Jacopo Bellini and sister to Gentile and Giovanni Bellini. The latter in particular was powerfully affected in his early work by his brother-in-law's style and pictorial skills. In the later 15th century Mantegna's influence was felt, in part through his activities as a printmaker, throughout north Italy and beyond—by, for example, the German painter Albrecht Dürer (1471–1528). But the severity of Mantegna's style did not chime in well with new artistic directions at the start of the 16th century, and after his death his influence rapidly diminished. ◆

Marc, Franz

FEBRUARY 8, 1880–MARCH 4, 1916 ● PAINTER

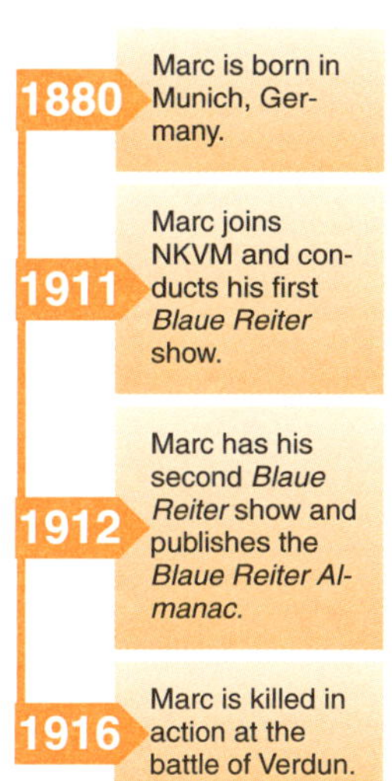

The German painter and printmaker Franz Marc was a leading figure in the avant-garde ferment that transformed art early in the 20th century. As a founder and coleader of the Blaue Reiter (Blue Rider) group, Marc developed a semiabstract style that sought to portray the spirituality he discerned at the core of the natural world.

A painter's son, Franz (Moriz Wilhelm) Marc was born in Munich, Germany, on February 8, 1880. Initially drawn to philosophy and theology, Marc shifted his sights to painting when he was 20 years old, when he enrolled at the Akademie der Bildenen Künste in Munich. While there he studied traditional academic landscape painting under Wilhelm von Dietz and Gabriel von Hackl. His early work, such as *Portrait of the Artist's Mother* (1902), displays a formidable talent for conventional representation.

But Marc's restlessly creative temperament strained against the confines of his academic training, and in 1902 he strayed from the academy in a quest for a less derivative style, initially by taking a sketching tour of the Bavarian Alps and later, in May 1903, by setting out for Paris, then the center of the burgeoning impressionist movement. Roused by the radical modernist ferment of the Parisian art world, Marc dropped out of the academy after returning to Munich and set up a studio,

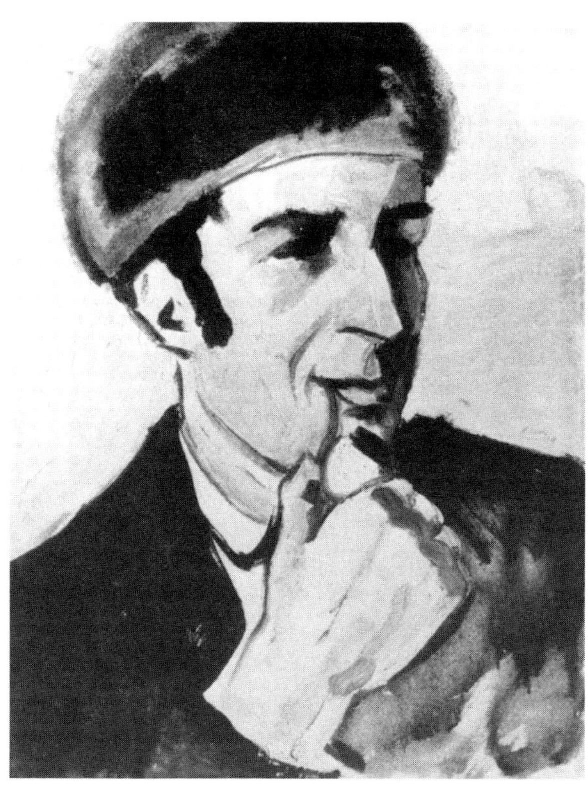

Franz Marc, painting by August Macke, 1910

where he spent most of his time on drawings that were to accompany the work of several modern German poets, including Richard Dehmel, Hans Bethge, and Carmen Sylva. He also experimented with various painterly means of conveying his mystical spiritual convictions on canvas.

Marc spent much of the year 1906 in Greece with his brother Paul, studying classical sculpture and architecture and making landscape studies. The following year saw him back in Paris, where he made an extensive study of the works of Gauguin and van Gogh. The next summer he returned to Bavaria, where his work, most notably *Larch Sapling* (1908), betrays the deep impression made upon him by van Gogh. Marc's extensive nature studies in Bavaria that summer for the first time evince a preoccupation with animals, for Marc the embodiment of a spiritual essence more pristine than that of humans. Marc remained in Bavaria through 1909, striving to refine his technique and sharpen his perception, still working in a figurative mode but increasingly blurring the boundaries between natural and spiritual vision.

Throughout 1910 Marc became close with Auguste Macke, another avant-garde painter, and Bernhard Koehler, Macke's uncle and a wealthy patron of the arts. Thanks to a subsidy from Koehler, Marc was able to resettle in Upper Bavaria to pursue his nature studies. In September of that year he attended the second annual show of the Neue Künstlervereinigung München (NKVM) and got to know many of its members, including Wassily Kandinsky, the group's leader. The show's impact is evident in the aesthetic distance between Marc's *Grazing Horses I* (1910) and the far more abstract and daring *Grazing Horses IV* (The Red Horses) (1911).

Sharing Kandinsky's vision of art as a vehicle of spiritual Marc joined the NKVM in February 1911, and his work was shown in May of that year at the Galerie Thannhauser in Munich. But not all of the members of the NKVM shared Marc's and Kandinsky's mystical inclinations, and fault lines between radicals and conservatives began to appear in the movement throughout 1911. In August of that year, Marc wrote to Macke, "I can foresee clearly, with Kandinsky, that the next jury (in the late autumn) will bring about a dreadful altercation, and then, or the next time, a split, or the resignation of one or other party; and the question will be, who *stays*...."

The final rupture came in December 1911, when the conservatives of the NKVM rejected Kandinsky's painting Composition Five for the society's third annual exhibition. Kandinsky and Marc resigned forthwith and proceeded to organize their own exhibitions—one in December 1911 that featured their own work and that of likeminded painters like Macke and Campendonck, and another in the spring of 1912 that featured major figures such as Picasso, Braque, and Delauny as well. Both shows bore the title Blaue Reiter; Kandinsky later explained their choice of the name: "We both loved blue: Marc—horses, myself—riders. So the name invented itself."

The pair used the same for an almanac of contemporary art they published in May 1912 that is now regarded as one of the key documents of 20th-century art. The volume contained important articles on aesthetics, including contributions by Kandinsky, Marc, Macke; several pieces on music; and more than 140 illustrations, including children's drawings, a liberal sampling of primitive and folk art from around the globe, and paintings by artists ranging from El Greco to Cézanne to Kandinsky and Marc.

Marc's 1912 meeting with the cubist painter Robert Delaunay proved to be another major spur to Marc's artistic development, reaffirming his commitment to art as a means of seeing through the **ephemeral,** shifting surfaces of matter to its spiritual essence. Significant works to emerge from this period include *In the Rain* (1912), *Deer in the Convent Garden* (1912), and *The Tiger* (1912), one of Marc's most famous paintings, in which the animal's primal ferocity seems both concentrated and dispersed by its **refraction** through its physical components. The following summer Marc executed a series of larger, more ambitious canvases, including *Tower of the Blue Horses* (1913) and *Animal Destinies* (1913). Marc's increasing distance from figuration is reflected even in the titles of works he completed during 1914: *Serene*, *Playful*, and *Struggling*.

ephemeral: lasting for a short period of time.

refraction: the distorting of an image by looking at it through a medium.

Marc enlisted in the army with the onset of World War I. While in military service he wrote copiously descriptive letters and carried a sketchbook; his letters and drawings were later collected in a posthumously published volume, *Franz Marc, Briefe, Aufzeichnungen, und Aphorismen* (1920).

Franz Marc was killed in the battle of Verdun on March 4, 1916, at the age of 36. ◆

Masaccio

DECEBER 21, 1401–C. 1428 ● PAINTER

Masaccio is considered the founder of 15th century Italian painting. Masaccio's style is characterized by volumetric and muscular figures placed in compositions organized according to the system of linear perspective. The directional light illuminating his scenes imparts to them further depth and three-dimensionality and makes the figures appear to inhabit measurable spaces.

Masaccio was born in San Giovanni Valdarno. His brief professional life was centered in Florence. He is first documented as a painter there on October 14, 1418; on January 7, 1422 he enrolled in the Florentine painters' guild; in 1424 he joined the Compagnia di San Luca, the professional organization of painters.

Masaccio's earliest extant work may be the *San Giovenale Triptych*, depicting the Virgin and Child flanked by angels and saints (dated April 23, 1422). It is attributed to the painter on stylistic grounds, and thus subject to debate.

The altarpiece of the *Virgin and Child with St. Anne* (c. 1424–1425) was attributed to Masaccio by Giorgio Vasari (1511–1574), although cleaning and close examination revealed involvement of additional artists, including Masolino (Maso di Cristofano Fini; 1383–c. 1440) with whom Masaccio collaborated on numerous commissions.

Vasari also ascribed to Masaccio a now dismantled and scattered triptych originally in the Carnesecchi Chapel of Santa Maria Maggiore in Florence (c. 1423); it depicted the Virgin and Child framed by SS. Catherine and Julian, and scenes from the lives of these saints in the predella below. Today the authorship of the panels is again in question, and Masolino's participation in this work is suggested as well.

Better documented is Masaccio's *Pisa Altarpiece*, commissioned in 1426 by the Pisan notary Ser Giuliano di Colino degli Scarsi da San Giusto for his chapel in the Carmine in Pisa. Following the remodeling of the church in the late 16th century, the altarpiece was dispersed; its original form is reconstructed from Vasari's description. It focused on the enthroned Virgin and Child entertained by musical angels and flanked by SS. Peter, John the Baptist, Julian, and Nicholas. The predella narrated episodes from the lives of these saints, while the upper story of the polyptych contained a crucifixion and additional saints. Today parts of the altarpiece belong to multiple museums: the *Virgin and Child* is in London, in the National Gallery; the predella scenes and four small saints are in Berlin, in the Gemäldegalerie; and other pieces are further dispersed.

Still in its original location is Masaccio's *Trinity* fresco (1425–c. 1427), thought to have been ordered by a member of the Lenzi family because the tombstone of Domenico Lenzi (d. 1427) and his family, dated 1426, was once in front of the fresco, and Domenico's relative Benedetto served as a prior of Santa Maria Novella in 1426–1428 and could thus have supervised the memorial. Masaccio's fresco depicts Christ on the cross upheld by God the Father and flanked by the Virgin and St. John. This group is set in an illusionistic classicizing chapel crowned by a coffered barrel vault. Kneeling in front and outside the chapel are presumably its donors. Below them is painted a skeleton reposing on a catafalque that bears an inscription: "I was once that which you are and that which I am you will also be."

Masaccio's most celebrated work is a series of frescoes in the Brancacci Chapel in the Church of Santa Maria del Carmine, Florence (the commission and its execution are not documented but dated c. 1425–1427). The chapel was founded by Pietro Brancacci (d. 1367). His son Antonio left a further bequest for it in his will (dated August 16, 1383). Pietro's nephew Felice owned the chapel from 1422 to 1434. In 1434, when Felice was exiled from Florence to Siena, the frescoing had not been finished; it was finally completed by Filippino Lippi in the early 1480s. The initial painting campaign was car-

1401 Masaccio is born in San Giovanni Valdarno.

1418 Masaccio is documented as a painter in Florence.

1422 Masaccio enrolls in the Florentine painters' guild.

1422 Masaccio paints *San Giovenale Triptych*, probably one of his earliest works.

1423 Masaccio joins the Compagnia di San Luca, the professional organization of painters.

1428 Masaccio dies.

ried out by Masaccio jointly with Masolino (the chronology of the work is uncertain). The cycle is devoted to the life and ministry of St. Peter. The entrance piers also feature the *Temptation of Adam and Eve* by Masolino, and the *Expulsion from Paradise* by Masaccio. The *Expulsion* vividly conveys the profound remorse and anguish of the first sinners through their body language and the facial expression. Similar psychological complexity characterizes other scenes of the cycle painted by Masaccio. The most famous episode, the *Tribute Money*, gathers the apostles in an intimate circle around Christ, who commands Peter to fetch the tribute money out of a fish's mouth and deliver it to a Roman official. The expressive interlocking arrangement and communication of the characters creates a **tangible** drama in front of the beholder. But here, too, as in other works associated with Masaccio, Masolino's hand has been discerned.

tangible: capability of an object or an idea to be clearly perceived by others.

In 1423–1425 or 1428 Masaccio and Masolino seem to have collaborated on the double-sided *Altarpiece of Santa Maria Maggiore* in Rome, likely commissioned by Pope Martin V (reigned 1417–1431). The front of the altarpiece depicted the *Assumption of the Virgin*, flanked by four saints; the rear, the *Foundation of Santa Maria Maggiore*, with saints in the wings. Today the altarpiece, like so many others, is scattered among European and American museums.

Masaccio's career ended tragically early, and many works attributed to him by Vasari and other authors do not survive. He was, however, admired and emulated by Florentines shortly after his death. Leon Battista Alberti in *Della pittura* (1436) lauded Masaccio, along with Brunelleschi, Donatello, Ghiberti, and Luca della Robbia, as in no way inferior to the ancient masters. Cristoforo Landino, in the *Commentary on the Divine Comedy* (1481), praised Masaccio for his ability to convey the true appearance of objects in nature, his volumetric construction of figures and spaces with the aid of perspective, and his technical mastery. Leonardo da Vinci, in one of his notebooks, praised Masaccio for taking lessons from nature and thus attaining perfection. Vasari eulogized Masaccio in his *Lives of the Artists* (1568) as the founder of the second period of Italian painting and reported that 25 Florentine artists (including Michelangelo and Raphael) studied and copied the Brancacci Chapel paintings. ◆

Matisse, Henri

DECEMBER 31, 1869–NOVEMBER 3, 1954 ● PAINTER

The French painter, sculptor, and lithographer Henri Matisse is widely regarded as one of the greatest artists of the 20th century, rivaled in importance only by Pablo Picasso. Initially influenced by impressionism and postimpressionism, he became one of the pioneers of fauvism, a movement that challenged the cerebral formalism of cubism by emphasizing the sensual warmth of color, line, and movement.

Henri Matisse was born in northern France, in Le Cateau-Cambrésis, on December 31, 1869, and grew up in Bohain-en-Vermandois, where his father sold grain. His mother's avocational painting seems to have sparked no early interest in art in her son Henri, who followed the conventional sequence toward a law career: five years at a secondary school in Saint Quentin (1882–87), a year of law studies in Paris, and then a law clerkship in Saint Quentin. His first approach to art was offhanded, as a diversion from the tedium of the law, when began arising early to attend drawing classes at a local art school. This mild flirtation quickened into a feverish embrace in 1890, the year he was stricken with appendicitis and his mother gave him an oil painting set to pass the time during his lengthy recuperation. Progressing rapidly from copies of color prints to original canvases, he found himself so deeply immersed in painting that he soon forgot about the law. "Henceforth," he wrote, "I did not lead my life. It led me."

Henri Matisse at work in his studio.

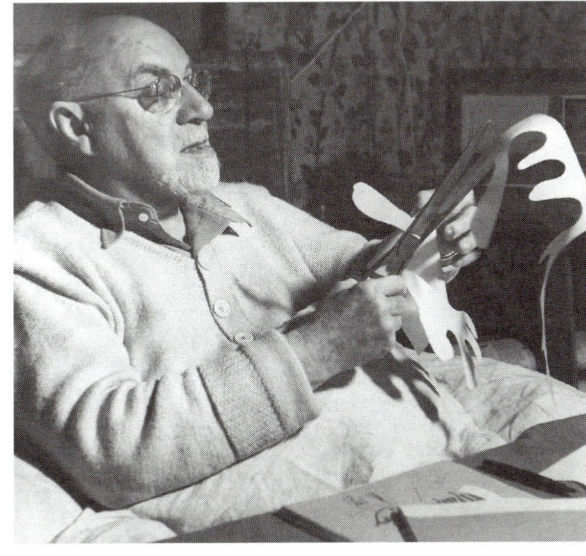

Matisse quit his law practice in 1891 and went to Paris to enroll as a full-time art student at the Académie Julian, where he studied with Adolphe-William Bouguereau, an academic traditionalist. Once he became aware of the modern impressionist currents streaming through the Parisian art world, he

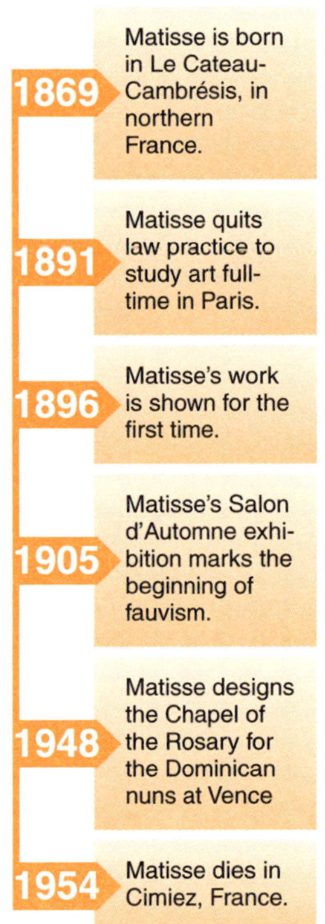

found Bouguereau's approach stifling, and in 1892 he transferred to the École des Arts Décoratifs (School of Decorative Arts), where he took evening classes while simultaneously studying at the École des Beaux-Arts (School of Fine Arts) with the symbolist painter Gustave Moreau, who encouraged his students to find their own styles. Thriving under Moreau's tutelage, he remained at his studio until Moreau's death in 1899.

Matisse's first public recognition came at the 1896 Salon, which exhibited four of his paintings, one of which, *Woman Reading,* was purchased by the French government. Emboldened by this success, Matisse grew more daring in his stylistic experiments, assimilating impressions and insights gleaned from sketching trips to Brittany, personal encounters with the impressionist Camille Pissarro, and his studies of the major works of impressionism. Now freer in his use of color, he enjoyed a *succés de scandale* at the 1897 Salon with his *La Desserte* (*The Sideboard*).

After marrying Amélie Parayre in 1898, he traveled to London, where he made an intensive study of the works of J. M. W. Turner, and then to Corsica to observe and sketch the scenic riches of the Mediterranean. Upon returning to Paris in 1899, Matisse read Paul Signac's famous essay, "*D'Eugéne Delacroix au Néo-Impressionisme*" ("From Eugéne Delacroix to Neo-Impressionism"), and was powerfully influenced by its advocacy of achieving chromatic effects through combinations of color dots, a style known as **pointillism.** So intensive was his study of color that he bought two important impressionist paintings—one by Cézanne and one by Gauguin—so that he could scrutinize them at liberty. He bought a bust by Rodin and in 1899 began taking a sculpture class.

pointillism: artistic technique in which the artist brings together dots of pure color made by the paintbrush.

In spite of the modest critical esteem accorded Matisse's unorthodox paintings, they did not sell well; financial pressure forced him to accept work as a decorator for the Grand Palais, and his wife opened a dress shop. Further derailed by a long convalescence from a bronchitis attack in 1901, the nearly penniless Matisse was obliged to move back to Bohain with his wife and three children the following year. Having abandoned the conservative Salon, in 1902 he showed his work at the modernist Salon des Indépendants and in a small group show at Berthe Weill's gallery. In 1903 his work was shown at the newly founded Salon d'Automne; the next year, when Matisse was 34 years old, he had his first solo exhibition, at Ambrose Vollard's Paris gallery, but it generated few sales and little critical notice.

Fauvism

The name fauvism derives from the French *les fauves* (wild beasts), a phrase art critic Louis Vauxelles used to describe the wild, seemingly undisciplined paintings of a small group of painters whose works were on display in France in the first decade of the twentieth century. Fauvism was influenced by neoimpressionism and drew inspiration from Paul Gauguin, for his non-literal use of color, Paul Cézanne, for his willingness to explore and innovate stylistically, and Vincent Van Gogh, who emphasizes intense color.

Fauvism burst onto on the scene with an October 1905 Paris exhibition at the Salon d'Automne, which included works by André Derain and Henri Matisse, the leader of the fauves. Derain's work (as in *Collioure,* 1905) was notable for its color (vivid yellows and reds) and its raw appearance—depending upon one's point of view, it was spontaneous and free or clumsy and unfinished. Such use of color was in contrast to the softer colors of the earlier impressionists. Matisse's work included *Green Strip,* which showed an otherwise typical representation of his wife, except that the long line of her nose was green. This use of non-naturalist colors was the hallmark of the fauvism.

Another prominent fauve was Maurice de Vlaminck (*House at Chatou,* 1906), who had collaborated and shared a studio in Chatou with Derain. Vlaminck was the boldest and most dramatic in his use of color and form, using thick brush strokes. Other fauves included Albert Marquet (*Fourteenth of July at Le Havre,* 1906), who like Matisse had studied with Gustave Moreau; Georges Braque, Raoul Dufy, and Othon Friesz would later come to the fauvism.

In a sense, fauvism was less a movement than a moment, both because of its short life and because many of its central figures worked in other styles before and after its flourishing. The fauves never were nor tried to be a single school of art, and by 1908 many of its members were already moving on to other styles. Despite its short life and the initial hostility of many critics, however, many critics now acknowledge fauvism's important influence on cubism and expressionism.

Gradually weaning himself from the strictures of pointillism, Matisse adopted a freer brush technique and a bolder, more imaginative palette, advances that yielded important works such as *Open Window* and *Woman with the Hat*, both of which were shown at the 1905 Salon d'Automne, where the artists' overall preference for violent effusions of color scandalized many observers, including the prominent critic Louis Vauxcelles, who called the young artists *les fauves*, "wild beasts"; the pejorative label stuck as a proud badge of the fauvist movement, of which Matisse became the de facto leader.

Thanks to the notoriety sparked by the Salon d'Automne, Matisse's work became fashionable among connoisseurs of the avant-garde, who began snapping up his paintings and thus re-

penury: an extreme and crippling lack of financial resources or extreme frugality.

manifestoes: statements of a philosophical belief on the part of an individual or organization.

> **"I go toward my sentiment, toward ecstasy. And then, there I find calm."**
> Henri Matisse, on how he created his paintings

lieving the **penury** that had hobbled him for so long. Especially important was the patronage of the influential writer Gertrude Stein and her family, who not only bought a number of Matisse's works but also helped him to found an art school in Paris where he taught intermittently through 1911.

The heyday of fauvism was relatively brief; by 1908 its major exponents had evolved toward other, more enduring expressions of modernism such as expressionism and Cubism. Matisse persisted in his unique stylistic quest, defying easy classification—too sensual for the analytical Cubists and too lyrical for the anguished expressionists, Matisse obeyed the promptings of his inner muse rather than the external dictates of **manifestoes.** From 1908 to 1913 he traveled to Spain, Germany, Russia, and Africa, accumulating a rich store of impressions that inspired a prolific output of paintings that are now deemed among the masterpieces of 20th-century art, including *Joy of Life* (1906); *The Dessert, a Harmony in Red* (1908); *The Red Studio* (1915); *Goldfish* (1916); and *Piano Lesson* (1918).

Matisse's renown began to spread throughout Europe and beyond, especially after 13 of his paintings appeared at the landmark Armory Show in New York in 1913. Highlights of his prodigious output in the ensuing decades include the *Odalisque* series he executed in the early 1920s; the famous mural *The Dance* (1932–33), created as a commission for the Barnes Foundation in Merion, Pennsylvania; the work that Matisse deemed his greatest achievement, his design for the Chapel of the Rosary for the Dominican nuns at Vence (1948–1951), who had cared for him during a serious illness in 1941; and, in the late 1940s and early 1950s, a series of vibrantly colorful abstract paper cut-outs, such as *Negro Boxer, Tristesse du roi* (*The king's sadness*), and *Jazz*.

Henri Matisse died in Cimiez, near Nice, on November 3, 1954. ◆

Michelangelo

MARCH 6, 1475–FEBRUARY 18, 1564 ● SCULPTOR, PAINTER, AND ARCHITECT

Born in Caprese in Tuscany, Michelangelo Buonarroti was sent to school in Florence and at age 13 was apprenticed to Domeni Ghirlandaio, who introduced him to the

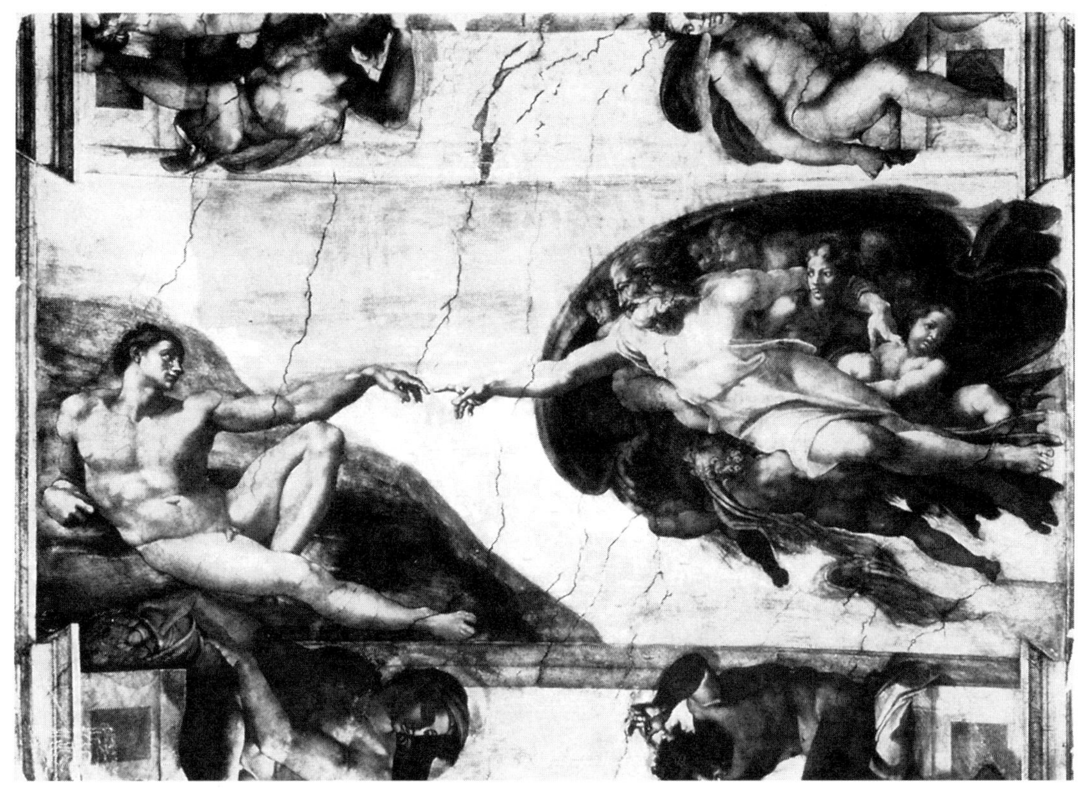

Michelangelo's *The Creation of Adam*, a fresco on the ceiling of the Sistine Chapel.

works of the Italian and Flemish masters. He lived in the home of Lorenzo de Medici who supported him. With Lorenzo, Michelangelo went to hear Girolamo Savanorola preaching against the corruption of Florence, a campaign that ended in the expulsion of the Medici from Florence in 1494, Michelangelo fled to Bologna but returned to Florence the following year. In 1498 his great sculpture *Pietà* was commissioned for Saint Peter's; it took two years to complete.

In 1501 he signed a contract with Cardinal Piccolomini—the first of several commissions he was unable to fulfill and which therefore made his life miserable. His great creative imagination was inspired by the proposed projects but he often failed to execute the monuments before a new and more enticing proposal came along. Because his patrons were cardinals, popes, and dukes, the commissions were as difficult to refuse as to complete. Cardinal Piccolomini (the future Pope Pius III) ordered 15 statues of apostles for Siena Cathedral; Michelangelo finished two and had three others made according to his design, but 60 years later the contract had still not been

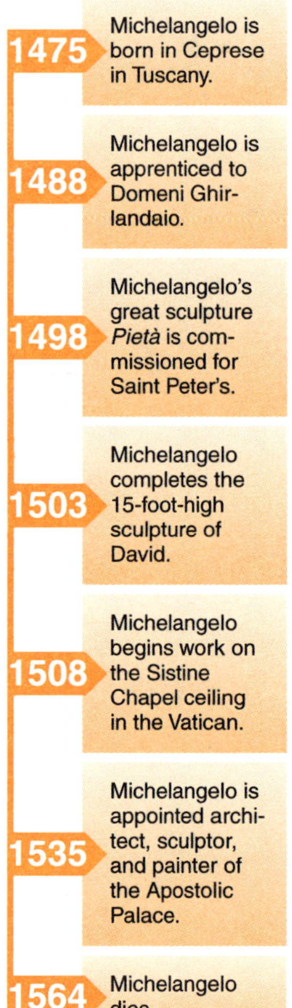

fulfilled. Similarly, in 1503 he agreed to produce 12 statues for the Cathedral of Florence; only one was ever blocked out, and this was never finished. In 1501, however, Michelangelo received a block of marble that had been given to another artist years before for a statute of a prophet; by 1503 he had completed the 15-foot-high *David*, an early example of his heroic, young male nudes.

Pope Julius II summoned Michelangelo to Rome to design a monument—40 statues and bas-reliefs surrounding the sarcophagus—for his tomb in Saint Peter's. Michelangelo purchased the marble but the pope decided instead to rebuild Saint Peter's, postponing the project, and refusing to reimburse the sculptor for the money he had laid out. Furious, Michelangelo left Rome for Florence but the pope sent five messengers with threats and entreaties; Michelangelo returned to Rome, where the pope now commanded him to make a gigantic statue of himself. The statue was eventually erected in Bologna but a few years later, when the fortunes of war had turned against the martial pope, it was removed and melted down to make a cannon.

Meanwhile, however, the pope had given Michelangelo his greatest commission—the Sistine Chapel ceiling in the Vatican. Work began in 1508 and was completed five years later, shortly before the pope's death. Perched on a scaffolding high above the floor, Michelangelo labored to create his depiction of the Creation and other biblical scenes and figures that have become one of the world's best-known masterpieces. Time dimmed the magnificence of the colors but restoration work has brought back the splendid brightness of the original.

Before Julius died he arranged for work to begin on his tomb, although on a somewhat smaller scale than the original plan, and Michelangelo worked on it for the following three years. Among the statues he completed for it was his famous *Moses*.

However, Julius's successor, Leo X, had other plans: he forbade the sculptor to continue work on the tomb and ordered him to begin creating the facade for the Church of San Lorenzo in Florence. The contract, which included 20 figures, was to be completed in nine years. Michelangelo, working under tremendous deadline pressures, secretly tried to continue his work on Julius's tomb at night. The tomb was eventually finished in 1545 and placed in the Church of Saint Peter in Vinculi.

In 1529 Michelangelo enthusiastically supported the republic which had been established in Florence and, during its short life, was in charge of the city's fortifications. When the republic was overthrown the following year the pope pardoned the sculptor on condition that he work on the new Sacristy of San Lorenzo. Michelangelo agreed without enthusiasm and finished three tombs there over the next two years.

In 1532 he met Tommasso dei Cavalieri, to whom he wrote passionate love poems; the handsome young Roman gentleman remained Michelangelo's close friend for the rest of his life. He also had a deep friendship based on religious feelings with Vittoria Colonna and wrote many beautiful sonnets for her.

Paul III became pope in 1534 and the following year appointed Michelangelo architect, sculptor, and painter of the Apostolic Palace, giving him the task of painting the *Last Judgment* on the altar wall of the Sistine Chapel. When the top part was completed the pope brought his master of ceremonies, Biagio de Casena, to see it. Biagio was shocked by the nude figures and said the painting belonged in a tavern or brothel. Michelangelo promptly painted Biagio in the lower region as a legendary judge in Hades. Later popes had the nude figures clothed.

Following the completion of this project Pope Paul III had Michelangelo paint frescoes in his Pauline Chapel. He completed two but suffered severe illnesses when working on them and never painted another fresco. He then began another major task, the rebuilding of Saint Peter's, working on a model and designing a great dome that was the most important element viewed both from within and outside. Michelangelo refused all remuneration, saying that it was God's will that he build Saint Peter's and that he was doing it for the love of God. His plan was almost completed when he died at age 89. His successors lengthened the nave (compromising its harmony with the dome) and added a colonnade.

In his will Michelangelo consigned "his soul to God, his body to the earth, his substance to his nearest relatives." His body was taken to Florence and buried in the **sepulcher** of the Medici family.

sepulcher: a tomb; a place of burial.

Michelangelo had burst upon the art world like a comet and his impact was historic. No preconceived idea was sacred to him; he shattered accepted criteria and pointed the way to be followed by future generations. The laws of perspective so diligently worked out by his predecessor, were swept aside as he discovered his own. His perspectives did not create a three-dimensional "illusion"—they were three-dimensional, and his use of architectural details in his paintings enhanced this feeling. Innovative in his use of materials, he brought new ideas even to the building of bridges. Michelangelo left behind a completely fulfilled body of work. ◆

Millais, John Everett

JUNE 8, 1829–AUGUST 13, 1896 ● PAINTER

John Everett Millais, an English painter, was born on June 8, 1829 in Southampton, England. His father, a man of means, came from a wealthy family based on the island of Jersey; his mother came from a family of affluent saddlers in Southampton. As a child, John lived in Southampton, Jersey, and Brittany before settling in London in 1838. A boy of remarkable artistic talent, he attended a private art school for a short time, and in 1840 became the youngest pupil ever admitted to the Royal Academy schools.

John Everett Millais, self-portrait, 1880.

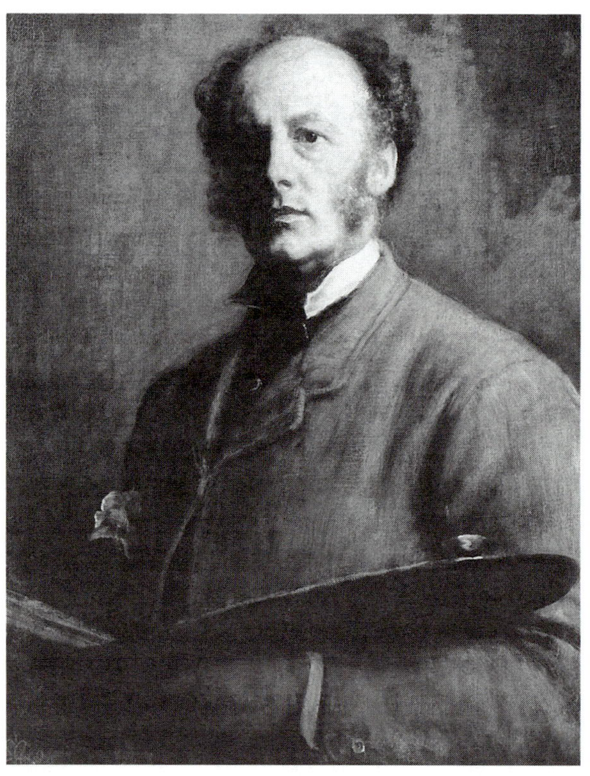

In 1843 Millais won a silver prize at the Royal Academy for one of his paintings, but his first painting to be shown was *Pizarro Seizing the Inca of Peru* (1846), a standard historical painting. The following year he won a gold prize from the Royal Academy for his *Tribe of Benjamin Seizing the Daughters of Shiloh* (1847).

In 1848 Millais, William Holman Hunt, Dante Gabriel Rossetti and other artists met at Millais's London home to form what they called the Pre-Raphaelite Brotherhood. Their movement represented a revolt against the dominant school of painting, which was inspired by the writings of Sir Joshua Reynolds, a late-18th-century portrait painter and the first president of the Royal Academy. Reynolds, who idolized Raphael, the late Renaissance Italian painter, advocated improvement on—and the glorification of—nature. The

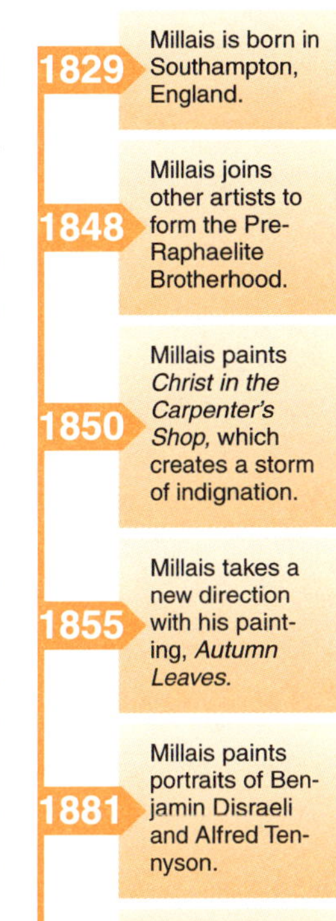

Pre-Raphaelites, influenced by medieval and Renaissance painters up to Raphael, believed that people and things should be presented just as they were, in careful detail. Their emphasis on detail was also linked to their call for a revitalization of craftsmanship in an era of increasing mechanization.

The first Pre-Raphaelite work by Millais was *Isabella* (1849), inspired by John Keats's poem of the same name. In this work his opposition to idealization of the subject is indicated by the stiffness of pose, which is a reference back to medieval art. This work won some approval, but Pre-Raphaelite paintings completed by Millais just afterward generated great controversy. That was particularly the case with *Christ in the Carpenter's Shop* (1850), which depicts an unprepossessing Christ, a gaunt Virgin, and an imperfectly groomed Joseph. This work was widely deemed blasphemous, and other Millais works at the time, including *Ferdinand and Ariel* (1849), were also denounced for violating Victorian notions of propriety.

The Pre-Raphaelites gained public acceptance beginning in 1852. In large measure this was due to the efforts of English art critic John Ruskin, who explained and defended their work. Millais won great admiration for his freshness of observation and his craftsmanlike attention to detail, as in *Huguenot* (1852). Ruskin and Millais became friends, but their amity evaporated when Ruskin's wife, Effie Gray, had their marriage annulled and then married Millais in 1855.

With *Autumn Leaves* (1855) Millais charted a new course. Previously his paintings were also stories that included hints to the viewer about what had happened before the depicted moment, and what would happen subsequently. However, *Autumn Leaves*, which shows young girls burning dead leaves, expresses a universal theme—the mortality of all life—instead of telling a story. Also, this painting, set at twilight, is less carefully detailed than earlier works and is somewhat blurred. The same is true of *A Dream of the Past: Sir Isumbras at the Ford* (1856–57) and *Vale of Rest* (1858–59). This in part reflected Millais's growing impatience with the arduous work involved in creating his earlier, more purely Pre-Raphaelite paintings.

From 1857 to 1864 Millais was a leading illustrator of books and magazines. Among his efforts were illustrations for poems of Alfred Tennyson and a series of novels by Anthony Trollope. During the 1860s Millais began painting attractive and innocent children, sometimes using his own offspring, and later his grandchildren, as models. His daughter Effie posed for *My First*

"The uncompromising composition [of *Isabella*], the precise detail of fabrics and the wall-hanging behind the table, the clarity of the palette, the portrait likenesses of the figures and their starkly meaningful expressions, ensured that it was noticed."

Claire Donovan and Joanne Bushnell in *John Everett Millais 1829-1896: Centenary Exhibition*, 1996.

Sermon (1863), and his grandson Willie James is the subject of *Bubbles* (1886).

By the late 1860s Millais had become an admirer of the Old Masters against whom he had rebelled in his youth. Subsequently, the major influences on his work included Spanish painter Diego Velázquez and Dutch painter Frans Hals, both of the 17th century, and 18th-century English portraitists—especially, and ironically, Joshua Reynolds. His depictions of young women in fashionable 18th-century clothing, as in *Stella* (1868) and *Vanessa* (1868), began an 18th-century revival in various arts.

In the 1870s and 1880s Millais painted portraits of some of the most famous people of his era. They included *Thomas Carlyle* (1877), *William Ewart Gladstone* (1879), *Benjamin Disraeli* (1881), *Lillie Langtry* (1878), and *Alfred Tennyson* (1881). He was also commissioned to paint many wealthy people and their children, commanding handsome sums for his efforts.

At around the same time, Millais began spending his holidays in Scotland. There he painted scenes around the River Tay. He particularly enjoyed painting gloomy, unattractive Scottish landscapes. Examples are *Chill October* (1870), *Murthly Moss* (1887), and *Dew-drenched Furze* (1890).

Millais became a baron in 1885. He was elected president of the Royal Academy in 1896. Later that year, on August 13, Millais died in London. ◆

Millet, Jean-François

OCTOBER 4, 1814–JANUARY 20, 1875 ● PAINTER

Jean-François Millet, French painter, was born in the Norman village of Gruchy, France, near Cherbourg. He came from a modestly prosperous family of peasants who owned their own land. His parents made sure that he received a solid basic education, and by the age of 18, Jean-François had a good command of Latin and an appreciation of literature.

Having demonstrated remarkable drawing skills as a boy, Millet went to Cherbourg in 1833 to study with Bon Du Mochel, a local portrait painter. Remaining in Cherbourg, in 1835 he began studying with Lucien-Théophile Langlois. In 1837 Millet received a scholarship to the École des Beaux Arts in

Paris. Two years afterward he returned to Cherbourg to set himself up as a painter. From then until 1849 Millet traveled between Cherbourg, Paris, and Le Havre, painting conventional mythological subjects, genre scenes, and portraits. He lived in severe poverty all the while; his refusal to abandon painting demonstrated his commitment to art.

By 1847 Millet had met artists of the **Barbizon School,** a group of painters living in and around the town of Barbizon, at the edge of the Fontainbleau forest in northern France. While the dominant French painters of the time drew historical scenes in an idealized style, the Barbizon painters chose a wider range of subject matter, leaned more toward realism, favored informality, and insisted on naturalness. Millet became associated with the Barbizon artists, especially his friend Théodore Rousseau. *The Winnower* (1848), the first of his many depictions of rural labor, was influenced by them. It laid the foundation for the many other works in which Millet portrayed humble scenes of rustic life, the subject that would dominate his work. In contrast to the other Barbizon artists, he did not paint wilderness scenes in the forest of Fontainbleau; he was only interested in man-made rural settings.

Barbizon: a philosophy of artistic work displayed by artists such as Bannister, Millet and Corot; Barbizon school emphasizes themes from nature and the natural world.

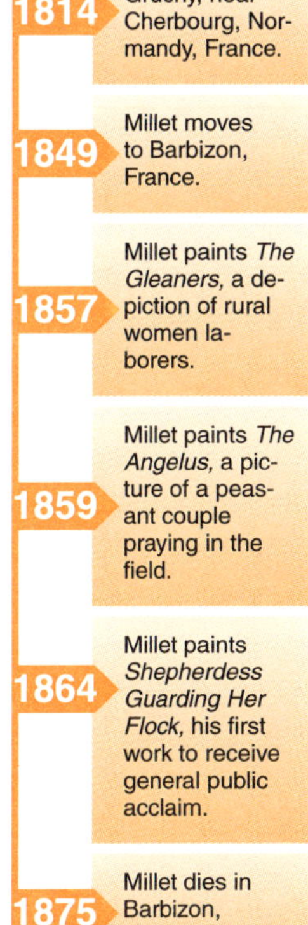

During a cholera epidemic in Paris in 1849, Millet moved to a cottage in Barbizon, near the home of Rousseau. A government commission to paint *The Haymakers Resting* (1853) made the move financially possible. He lived in this cottage for the rest of his life. Millet rarely traveled, making only a handful of trips to Cherbourg and Vichy. Travel, however, was not necessary for him, since he never painted out of doors and relied to a great extent upon memories of his childhood in Normandy.

Millet's *Sower,* first exhibited at the state-sponsored Salon of 1850–51, drew both praise and ridicule for endowing farm labor with dignity. *The Gleaners* (1857), perhaps his best-known work, drew similar responses. In the foreground, three women gleaners are in a bent-down, faceless pose, collecting the leavings of the harvest. Through color, Millet blends the women with the earth, implying that humble peasants are closer to the soil than the wealthy landowners who do not work the fields. The gleaners are also bathed in a golden light that elevates them above the mundane work they are performing.

Another famous painting of Millet's is *The Angelus* (1859). In the foreground, two typical peasants, a man and a woman, stand in the fields with their heads bowed in prayer; most likely they are responding to the ringing of the bells of the distant

Although Millet painted common scenes of peasant life, he cannot be—as he often has been—considered in the current of artistic realism.

church. The painting suggests that church attendance is not essential for the truly pious, and that the peasants are closer to God than their social superiors, who are relegated to the distant background, as in *The Gleaners*. In another similarity to *The Gleaners*, Millet's use of color blends the peasants with the soil.

Millet did not intend his paintings of humble rural workers to be political messages, but the political right in France denounced him for real or imagined socialist leanings, while the left praised him for his social enlightenment. The same reaction awaited *Man with a Hoe* (circa 1862). In this connection, it should be noted that in 1870 and 1871 Millet refused to associate himself with the radical Paris Commune and its Federation of Artists.

Although Millet painted common scenes of peasant life, he cannot be—as he often has been—considered in the current of artistic realism. Millet idealized and emotionalized what he saw, and so in these aspects of his work he is neither modern nor visually objective. His modernity and originality lie not in his subjects or the feeling that he brought to them, but in what have been called "his formal qualities, the power of his drawing and the boldness of his pictorial invention."

"They may call me a painter of ugliness.... I stand firm.... I am determined to say what I feel and paint things as I see them. The beautiful is that which is fitting or suitable."

Millet quoted in Leslie Thomson, *Jean François Millet, 1814-1875*, 1927

Millet's success as a painter did not begin until he won a first-class Salon medal for his *Shepherdess Guarding Her Flock* (1864). The public preferred his charming depiction of an attractive woman to his melancholy scenes of hard labor. Having become more widely accepted, Millet was awarded the cross of the Legion of Honor in 1865. Two years later nine of his paintings, including *The Gleaners* and *The Angelus*, were represented at the Paris Universal Exposition.

Millet was not interested in painting wilderness scenes during the early part of his career. Nevertheless, in his later painting, landscape became the dominant feature of his art. Examples are a landscape cycle of the four seasons begun in 1868 and *The Church of Gréville* (1871–74). In some of his later paintings the landscape is disturbed by an emotional tension reminiscent of the late work of Vincent van Gogh, who was a great admirer of Millet. One of his last works was *The Bird Nesters* (1874), a nighttime scene of torch-lit violence that diverges sharply from the stillness that usually characterizes his paintings.

After becoming seriously ill, Millet married his common-law wife in a church ceremony at the beginning of 1875. Millet died at Barbizon on January 20, 1875 and was buried at Barbizon next to Rousseau. ◆

Miró, Joan

APRIL 20, 1893–DECEMBER 25, 1983 ● PAINTER AND SCULPTOR

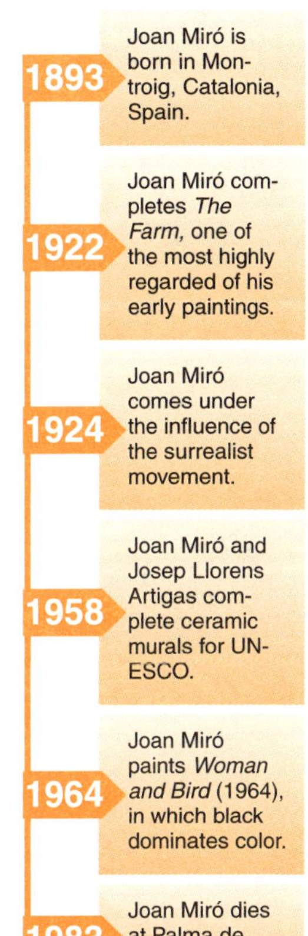

Joan Miró, Spanish painter and sculptor, was born on April 20, 1893 in Montroig, Catalonia, Spain, near Barcelona. His father, Miquel Miró, was a watchmaker and goldsmith; his mother, Dolors Ferrá, was the daughter of a carpenter. Joan grew up in his parents' country house in Montroig, to which he often returned in adulthood. The images of nature and rural life impressed upon him there had an important influence on his artistic work.

Following his parents' wish that he enter the business world, Miró studied at the Escuela de Comercio in Barcelona from 1907 to 1910. But following an emotional crisis in 1911, he abandoned his business studies and the following year entered the Barcelona art school, run by Francesc Galí. Miró showed strength in the use of color but not in defining shapes; Galí helped by encouraging him to feel objects before drawing or sculpting them. Miró took drawing classes at the Circulo Artístico de Sant Luc. During those years he was influenced by fauvism, and his paintings were marked by the use of brilliant colors. At the same time, Miró's *Portrait of E.C. Ricart* (1917) showed the influence of Vincent van Gogh, while his *Nude with Mirror* (1919) is witness to the impact of cubism. Even his earliest paintings contained the humor for which he later became well known.

Miró visited Paris in 1919. The following year he established a residence there and subsequently lived alternatively in France and Spain. In the French capital he met Pablo Picasso, who introduced him to the work of Henri Rousseau; the primitivism of Rousseau constituted another influence upon Miró. From 1918 to 1922, influenced by Paul Cézanne and cubism, he drew in precise detail the underlying construction of his works. Examples are *Vegetable Garden with Donkey* (1918) and *Montroig, the Church and the Village* (1919). The most famous of his early paintings is *The Farm* (1921–22), which exhibits a careful calculation of composition that belies the seeming simplicity and innocence of its organic and inorganic objects. He later sold this painting to his friend, Ernest Hemingway.

Following a nervous breakdown, Miró became in 1924 a significant part of André Breton's surrealist movement, al-

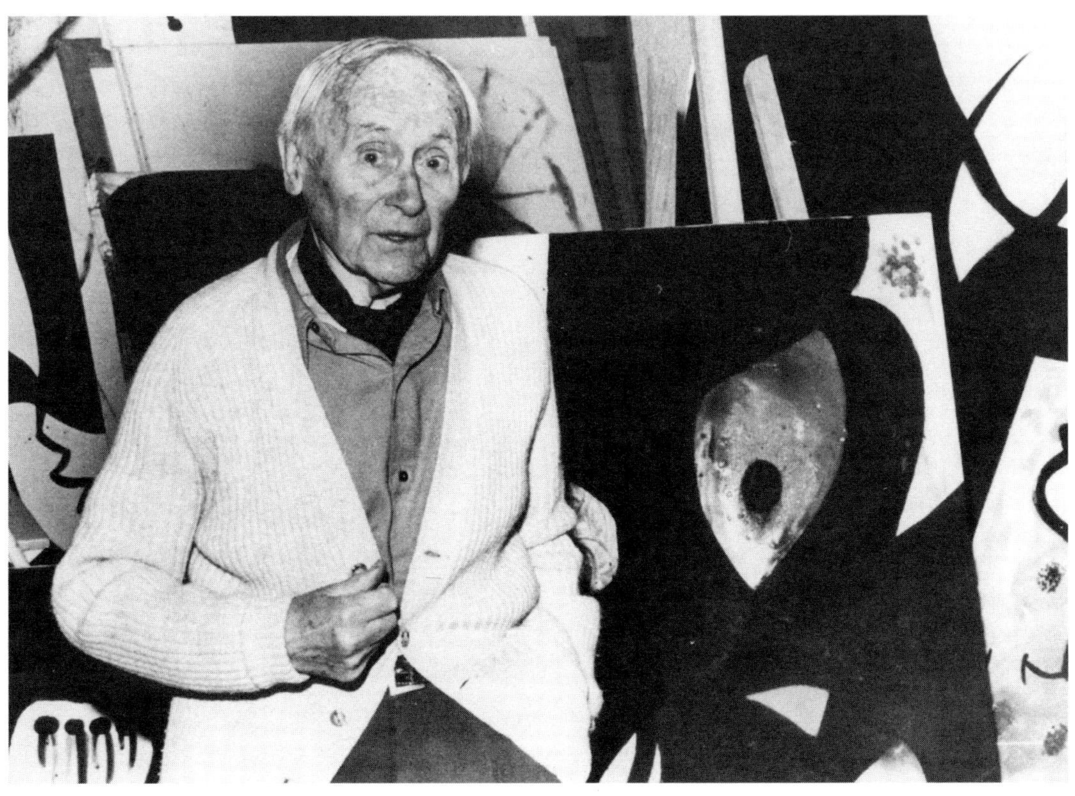

Joan Miró, with his paintings.

though he was not within the "official" circle of surrealist painters. Dadaism also had a major impact on him at this time. His pieces beginning in 1924 are characterized by fantastic-looking shapes that seem to be living organisms, shapes that became fixtures in his work.

This represents the outer limits of his abstractions, at least until his post-1960 years; they rarely became total abstractions divorced from the external world. Among Miró's works from this period are *Harlequin's Carnival* (1924–25) and *Head of a Smoker* (1925). In 1925 he collaborated with Max Ernst on sets and costumes for a ballet, *Roméo et Juliette*. Influenced by a visit to the Netherlands in 1928, Miró executed a series of paintings called *Dutch Interiors*. In these he transformed the literalism of Dutch masters such as Jan Vermeer and Jan Steen into surrealistic fantasy. His *Imaginary Portraits* series at about the same time incorporated collage into his painting.

From 1929 to 1931 Miró turned from painting and toward collages and sculptural assemblages such as *Sculpture-object* (1931). Returning to painting in the mid-1930s, he produced a series of works called *Wild Paintings* that expressed an aggressiveness and violence previously absent from his work. Normally nonpolitical, Miró took the republican, anti-Franco side during the Spanish Civil War (1936–39). His outlook was reflected in his *The Reaper* (1937), a painting made for the Spanish pavilion at an international exhibition in Paris, and in a poster, *Help Spain* (1937).

When the republican side lost the war, Miró moved from Spain to Paris, but when the Nazis occupied that city in 1940, he returned to Spain. His *Constellations* paintings, a series of small **gouaches** made during World War II, consist of asterisks, gracefully curving lines, and happily whirling dots, which demonstrate the influence of music and rhythm on his art.

gouaches: heavy opaque watercolor paints that produce a strongly colored and less watered looking picture than regular watercolor.

In 1945 an exhibition of the *Constellation* series was mounted at the Pierre Matisse Gallery in New York City. Its success helped Miró win a commission to create a mural for the gourmet restaurant at the Terrace Hilton Hotel in Cincinnati, which he completed in 1947. He also obtained a commission to paint a mural for Harvard University's Graduate Center, finished in 1950. The Matisse Gallery exhibit also influenced Jackson Pollock and other abstract expressionists. Miró in turn was influenced by American painters Mark Rothko, Robert Motherwell, and other abstract expressionists.

During the 1940s and 1950s Miró sought new forms of expression. He engaged in printmaking and lithography in the 1940s. In 1944 he finished a group of 50 black-and-white lithographs named *Barcelona*. That year Miró produced his first ceramics, working with Josep Llorens Artigas. Their best-known collaborative work was two ceramic murals—*The Sun* and *The Moon*—for the UNESCO headquarters in Paris, which won the Great International Prize of the Guggenheim Foundation in 1958. Beginning in 1948 he expanded his range of media to include color lithographs and etchings, **drypoints,** and woodcuts.

drypoints: a printing process in which burrs are left on a plate by a pointed needle that inscribes lines.

Beginning in 1960 Miró's work took a new turn. In 1961 and 1962 he created paintings on a monumental scale in which a single line is drawn over a monochrome background. Color became far less prominent, giving way to black as in *Woman and Bird* (1964). He began using black both to outline figures and to fill them in. His use of calligraphy in his art increased after he visited Japan in 1966. Following that visit, Miró gave some of his pictures haiku-sounding titles like *The Smile of the Star to the Twin Tree of the Plain* (1968) and *Hair Pursued by Two Planets* (1969).

"Pitting poet against craftsman, Miró s varied strategies aim, more often than not, at surprising existing aesthetic orders by discovering possibilities latent in them."
Carolyn Lanchner, in *Joan Miró,* 1993)

Miró did another ceramic mural for Harvard in 1960 and others for the Guggenheim Museum in New York City in 1966 and the Barcelona Airport in 1970. Massive sculptures of the mid-1960s, such as *Moon Bird* and *Sun Bird,* recapitulated old themes in his work, such as the battle between the sexes and the striving of humankind to rise above the animal level. Beginning in 1966 he worked on small sculptures that often were made of found objects.

Miró did book illustrations into the mid-1970s. Also, in the 1970s he did a number of political posters protesting political oppression in the waning years of the Franco regime. Three years after Franco's death in 1975, the first inclusive exhibition of Miró's painting and graphic work was held in Madrid. Retrospective exhibitions of his work during the 1970s in New York City, London, and Paris were indicators of the great fame and influence that his work had achieved. On December 25, 1983, Miró died at Palma de Mallorca on the Spanish island of Majorca, where he had made his home. ◆

Modigliani, Amedeo

July 12, 1884–January 25, 1920 ● Painter and Sculptor

Amedeo Modigliani was born in Leghorn (Livorno), Italy, to a family of small merchants. Ill health forced him to give up his general education and he concentrated on art. Leghorn had a lively artistic community and Modigliani's teacher, Gugliemo Michele, himself a student of an Italian impressionist, gave him a thorough training in the fundamentals of art and art history. Modigliani's uncle paid for his art classes, but after his death in 1905, Modigliani moved to Paris, where his mother sent him as much money as she could. He lived in cheap hotels, moving when he had no rent money, often leaving his paintings behind.

In 1906, the year Modigliani arrived in Paris, the retrial of Captain Alfred Dreyfus was held and anti-Semitism was rampant. Most of Modigliani's friends in Paris were Jewish artists. When he made sketches of customers in cafés to earn a few francs, Modigliani signed them, "Modigliani—Jew." Because of his poverty, he often painted on both sides of his canvases. He was greatly influenced by the work of Cezanne and he had close contacts with Picasso.

Between 1909 and 1914, Modigliani's work was mainly in sculpture, at first in wood. His wooden sculptures were made from railroad ties from the construction sites of the Paris subway. After he moved to La Cité Falguière, where Chaim Soutine and Constantin Brancusi were his neighbors, he began to work in limestone, which he found at building construction sites. Often the workers gave him stones, but if not, he went at night to take some home. On Brancusi's advice, he made a study of African sculpture.

Both wood and stone sculpture were carved—dusty work that affected his lungs. During these five years, he produced hundreds of drawings for sculptures and life drawings. He worked on drawings for a series of caryatids, but completed only two.

World War I halted Modigliani's work as a sculptor, for there was no more construction and he could never afford to buy stone. Even his small stipend stopped coming, and he sold nothing. Deprived of the means to work at sculpture, Modigliani resumed painting. He continued his sketching at cafés and would go to La Rotonde for food and drinks, often paying with his paintings. His deteriorating health, together with drink and drugs, made him irascible and often violent. He would attack his friends, including the English poet Beatrice Hastings, who lived with him. She said that he was an "enfant, sometimes terrible, but always forgiven."

He painted everybody—Beatrice Hastings more than a dozen times—and was able to get commissions, though prices were low. When he painted Jacques Lipshitz and his wife, he asked to be paid 10 francs and brandy for each sitting.

In 1916 the Polish poet, Leopold Zborowski, became his dealer. That year and the next, Modigliani painted a series of reclining nudes, which are among his outstanding works. Zborowski arranged an exhibition at the Berthe Weill Gallery. It was Modigliani's only one-man show, and it ended before it started. The police came, removed the nudes from the gallery window, and then from the walls. Over 50 years later, the United States Postal Service forced the Guggenheim Museum to withdraw a postcard reproduction of one of these nudes from its shop. Pubic hair was still illegal.

In 1917 Modigliani met and fell in love with Jeanne Hébuterne, a 19-year-old art student. The following year their daughter, Jeanne, was born. She was brought up by Modigliani's

1884 Modigliani is born in Leghorn, Italy.

1905 Modigliani moves to Paris and pays his way with his paintings.

1917 Modigliani meets and falls in love with Jeanne Heburterne.

1918 Modigliani receives the highest price of the show for one of his exhibition pieces.

1920 Modigliani dies.

sister and was to write an outstanding biography of her father. Zborowski found him a studio and models (he painted Jeanne 25 times) and gave him a stipend. He also sent Modigliani for two months to Nice, where he painted servants, peasants, children, and two landscapes.

In an exhibition of work by French artists in the Mansard Gallery in London arranged by Zborowski in 1919, the English author Arnold Bennett bought a painting by Modigliani—it brought the highest price in the show, substantially more that the 60 **francs** he sometimes received for a commission. In 1989, Sotheby's auctioned off a Modigliani portrait for over eight million dollars.

francs: French currency.

In November 1919, Modigliani began spitting blood. Legend has it that at a friend's house, he sang the Kaddish (mourners' prayer) for himself. In two months he was dead. The next day, Jeanne committed suicide by jumping out of a window on the fifth floor of her parents' house.

Modigliani's portraits are among the very best of the 20th century. He never painted a portrait without the sitter directly in front of him. Much has been written about the ovoid heads, long necks, and supposed blankness of the almond-shaped eyes. They show a natural kinship with the geometric forms of his sculpture. His work is unmistakably Modigliani, yet he caught the essence of the character of the model in every portrait.

His carvings, a series of heads—pure geometric forms—have been described, in spite of his affinity for African art, as Gothic. Here are no portraits of individuals, but universal icons of a contemplative **benign** humanity. ◆

benign: description of a gentle, unthreatening disposition.

Mondrian, Piet

March 7, 1872–February 1, 1944 ● Painter

Piet Mondrian, a Dutch painter and theorist originally named Pieter Cornelis Mondriaan, was born March 7, 1872 in Amersfoort, the Netherlands. He was the second child of Pieter Cornelis Mondriaan, Sr., a Calvinist headmaster. Piet received his first drawing lessons from his uncle, Frits Mondriaan, a member of The Hague school of landscape

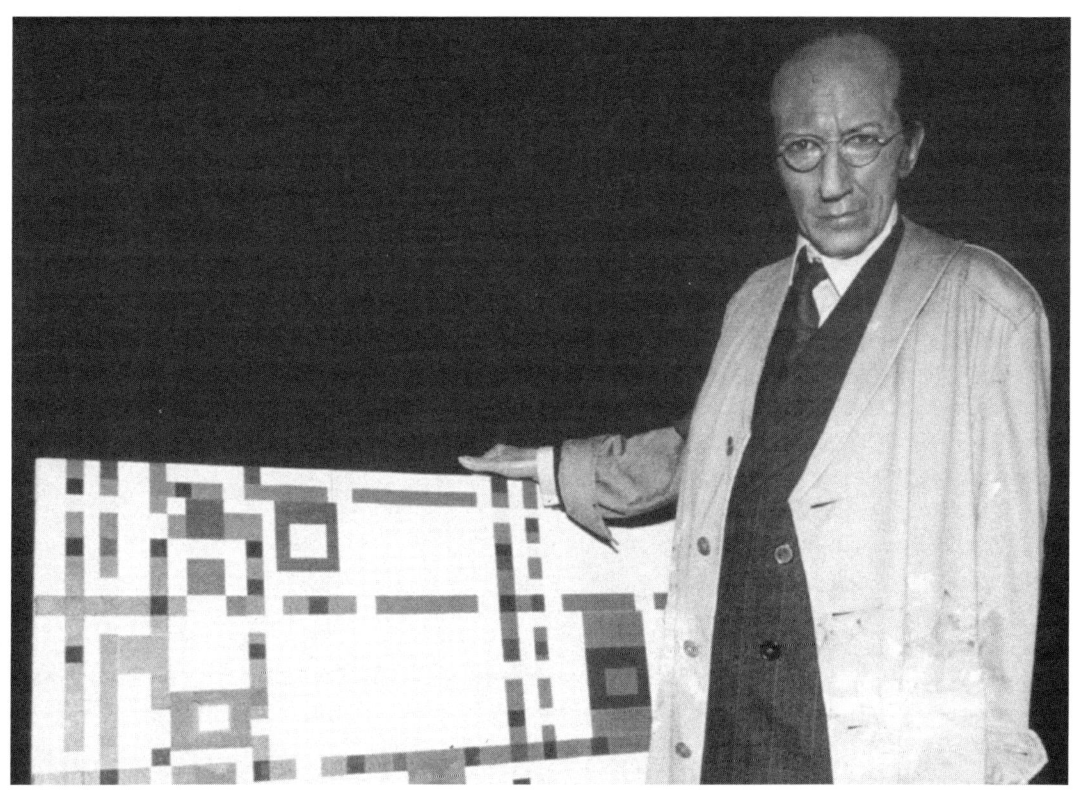

Piet Mondrian with one of his paintings.

painters. Piet qualified to teach drawing at the lower-school level in 1889 and in the middle schools in 1892. He studied at the Amsterdam Academy of Fine Arts from 1892 to 1894.

During the 1890s Mondrian painted landscapes of the countryside outside of Amsterdam; he also painted boats on Amsterdam's canals. His work was in a naturalistic style, with grays and dark greens serving as the major colors. However, Mondrian's paintings at Winterswijk, known as the Winterswijk group (1898), suggest his later movement away from naturalism. In 1904 and 1905 he visited the Brabant region in northern Belgium. Afterwards, windmills became a major theme of his until 1912. After his trip to Belgium, Mondrian also placed greater stress on composition and less on the play of light and shade.

In 1906 Mondrian joined the Theosophical Society, which claimed that all spirit and matter come from one source. This philosophy, which stressed commonality rather than distinctions, encouraged Mondrian's shift from naturalism, with its depiction of particulars, toward abstract forms that escape from

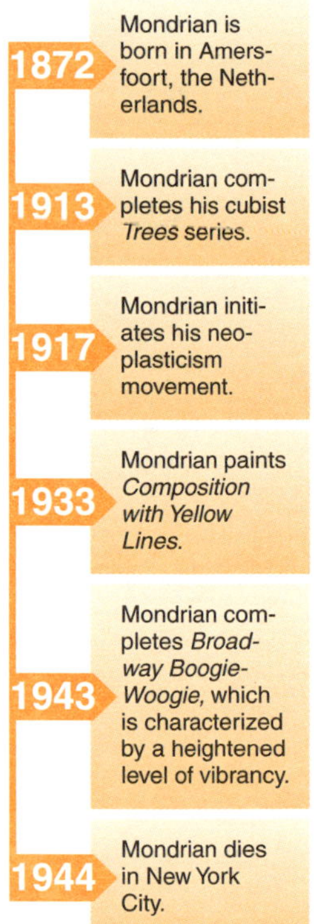

the specific. *The Red Cloud* (1907), with its bright colors, indicated the influence of postimpressionism, while his *Woods Near Ole* (1908) reflects expressionist values. In 1908 Mondrian met painter Johann Toorop, leader of the luminist movement, and for a time was influenced by Toroop's divisionism, a new approach to presenting light. Mondrian's luminist works were exhibited in Amsterdam in 1909; from then onward he was recognized as a member of the Dutch avant-garde.

At the urging of friends, Mondrian went to Paris in December of 1911. There he immediately came under the sway of cubism, which remained at the heart of his work until 1917. During that period his paintings became increasingly abstract as the rhythm of landscape forms was reduced to geometric patterns, a shift from the particular to the general. Like the other cubists, Mondrian focused the viewer's attention on the center of the work and left the corners untouched. Also in accord with cubism, he used subdued colors that would not draw the viewer's attention from his geometric structures. Early examples of Mondrian's cubist work are the *Trees* series (1912–13) and *Compositions* (1913–14). By mid-1914 he had moved further toward simplification by avoiding curved or diagonal strokes, limiting himself to vertical and horizontal lines. His *Composition No. 10* (1915) is an example of this development. The 1917 version of his *Ocean and Pier* series marks the furthest progress of his cubism.

Cubists sought to reduce forms from their visual appearance to their underlying elements; still, their work was not truly abstract, since their drawings remained connected with external, everyday forms. But beginning in 1917 Mondrian moved toward genuine abstraction by completely disconnecting his art from everyday reality. He now attempted to base his work not on forms but on a vision of a harmonic universe. Instead of attending to transitory perceptions of the specific, he argued, art should concern itself with the basic, eternal relationships of the cosmic order. To disseminate his ideas, Mondrian, with the help of Theo van Doesburg, established the publication *De Stijl* (The Style). He also wrote many articles explaining his views. Mondrian used the term "neoplasticism" to describe his new stage of development, but it was often known as the Style after the name of his publication.

In appearance, his new work was characterized by a rhythmic organization of straight lines (usually black) and colors—but only the primary colors, red, yellow, and blue, plus the

De Stijl

Architect and painter Piet Mondrian met Bart Van Der Leck and Theo Van Doesburg in the Netherlands in 1914, and out of their shared artistic and philosophical investigations came a new movement in building, home, and furniture design. De Stijl artists believed that art and style could be linked to all aspects of human life and could unite and harmonize humans and nature—hence the movement's name De Stijl (duh-STAY-uhl: "The Style"). In terms of color, they greatly emphasized the three primary colors—yellow, red, and blue—each of which was thought to have special significance in the forces of nature. In terms of form, they sought simplicity in a new imagery ("nieuwe beelding"), favoring solid geometric shapes, especially squares and triangles. Their preference for straight lines and right angles matched their belief that art should be logical, ordered, and intentional rather than chaotic and arbitrary.

The movement's origin is usually dated from 1916 or 1917, Amsterdam; in 1917 Van Doesburg's journal *De Stijl* appeared. The paintings, sculptures, and architectural models of this movement proved greatly popular, reaching their peak in the early 1920s. Over a period of several years Van Doesburg successfully collaborated with architect Eliezar Lissitzky, and the two held joint exhibits, such as Léonce Rosenberg's Galeria de l'Effort Modern in Paris. Other prominent figures included architects Gerrit Rietveld and J. J. P. Oud and sculptor and painter George Vantongerloo. Toward the end of the 1920s, however, personal disagreements and differences in artistic temperament led the principal figures to part company, while their own styles had evolved past the original vision of the movement; Mondrian's later work remained largely consistent with his earliest ideas, however. Later movements such as Bauhaus and the International Style owe much to the De Stijl movement, which also had a vast influence on architecture, sculpture, and popular fashion.

noncolors white, black, and (less often) gray. As a consequence, the paintings consisted of colored rectangles (or sometimes triangles) divided by lines in a grid pattern, as in *Composition* (1921).

For Mondrian's fiftieth birthday in 1922, his friends organized a retrospective of his work in Amsterdam. The exhibit showed his development from naturalism to cubism to the abstract painting of neoplasticism. But Mondrian's eventful artistic journey was not over. Throughout the 1920s and 1930s he worked to purify and clarify his abstract work. In the early 1930s Mondrian determined his composition from the center of his paintings in the horizontal as well as a vertical direction, as in *Composition with Yellow Lines* (1933). At the same time he began limiting color to only one certain area. Also, a series of parallel lines—horizontal and vertical, sometimes close together and sometimes not—mark off areas, thus making those

"What Mondrian makes in paintings is movement in stillness, an energy which the viewer can witness an action. They are both sensual and intellectual, personal and impersonal."
John Milner, *Mondrian,* 1992

areas more prominent; this increased the complexity of the relationships in the paintings.

By the 1930s Mondrian had gained wide recognition and appreciation as the most modern of modern artists. He continued to propagate his views during that decade; particularly notable is his article, "Plastic Art and Pure Plastic Art" (his first in English), in the international publication *Circle: International Survey of Constructive Art*. Mondrian's work was well known and heartily disliked by the Nazis, who had come to power in Germany in 1933. After the Munich Agreement of 1938, he felt endangered and moved from Paris to England.

When German bombs fell near his studio in a London suburb during 1940, Mondrian left for the United States. Establishing himself on East 56th Street in New York City, he spent about a year finishing works already begun. In completing them, he placed a more pointed emphasis on the rhythmic relationship between colored areas. Although remaining within the **neoplastic** principle of the horizontal-vertical, other important changes occurred in the next three years. Mondrian began using many more small rectangles than previously, alternating with larger ones. In *New York City* (1942), black lines give way to colored ones. Eventually, he replaced his continuous lines with series of small colored rectangles running horizontally and vertically in rhythmic flows. This development appears in *Broadway Boogie-Woogie* (1942–43). His unfinished *Victory Boogie-Woogie* (1943–44) also has the vibrant joyousness of his last paintings. Many have attributed these changes to the vitality of New York City and to the influence of American music. Mondrian died of pneumonia on February 1, 1944 in New York City. ◆

neoplastic: an art movement advocating simplicity and and abstraction reduced to the rectangle and colors to the primary colors and black and white.

Monet, Claude

NOVEMBER 14, 1840–DECEMBER 6, 1926 ● PAINTER

Oscar-Claude Monet, French painter, was born on November 14, 1840 in Paris, the eldest son of Adolphe Monet, a wholesale grocer. When Claude was five years old the family moved to Sainte-Adresse, near the Norman port of Le Havre, on the English Channel. The sea, the coast, and the quickly changing weather of the region would influence his painting. By the age of 15 Monet was known for his caricatures. In the late 1850s Eugène Boudin, a local landscape artist, encouraged Monet to become a *plein-air,* or outdoor, painter, advice that Monet followed throughout his career.

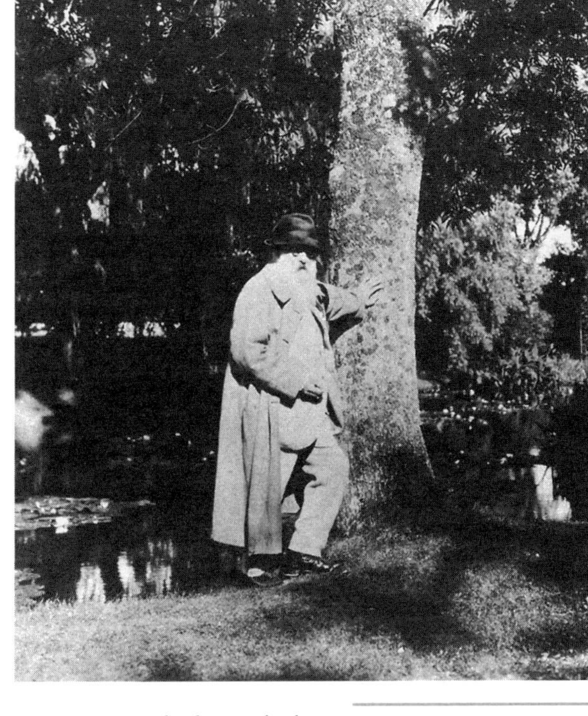

Claude Monet

Making his first trip to Paris in 1859 and 1860, Monet met Camille Pissarro. In Paris he was impressed by the painters of the Barbizon school, who challenged the traditional emphasis on religious and historical paintings and worked out of doors. In 1860 and 1861 he served out his military obligation in Algeria. After his discharge Monet returned to Le Havre where he painted with Boudin and Johan Jongkind. All three were interested in capturing shifts in light and weather.

In the fall of 1862 Monet returned to Paris to study under Charles Gleyre, and met Pierre-Auguste Renoir, Frédéric Bazille, and Alfred Sisley. During 1863 Monet painted landscapes in the Fontainbleau forest and along the English Channel coast. Like Édouard Manet, he painted actual, informal scenes of modern life, a novel and controversial choice of subject matter in the 1860s. In 1865 he began *The Picnic*, based on a Manet painting. It was an attempt to paint out-of-doors on a large canvas, with life-sized picnickers, but he never finished the work. He sold very few paintings in the mid-1860s and was in a terrible financial state. Monet attempted suicide at about this time.

Monet painted Parisian cityscapes in 1866, some from the roof of the Louvre. During the late 1860s he advanced toward his mature style, as in *The Beach at Sainte-Adresse* (1867) and *The River* (1868). He was not trying to copy the scene in front of him but capture the energy and motion of a moment.

After the Franco-Prussian War broke out in 1870, Monet moved to London to avoid the draft. There he painted *Westminster Bridge* (1871). The next year, back in France, he exe-

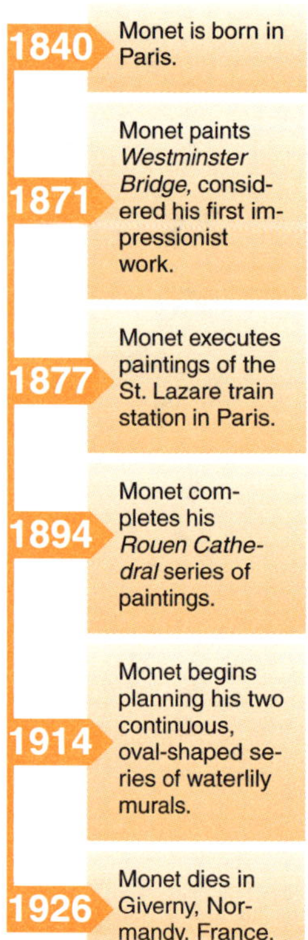

cuted *Impression, Sunrise* (1872). These came to be regarded as his first two impressionist paintings. (The term, originally meant to be derogatory, was coined by a critic from the title of the latter painting.) They were attempts to fix the momentary sensation of light and atmosphere before thought intervened. This was accomplished by the use of strong, short, broken strokes of color. (Monet preferred rainbow colors, and avoided earth tones.) The only value of these paintings was visual; touch, texture, and volume were ignored. Line and formal composition were abandoned for pattern. Figures and objects were painted in rapid brushstrokes that rendered them by resonant chromatic contrasts. Forms thus lost their solidity and became incorporeal.

Monet lived in Argenteuil on the Seine, west of Paris, from 1872 to 1876. There he worked on a houseboat-studio. He was joined in Argenteuil by Renoir, Manet, Sisley, and Pissarro and became the central figure of the impressionist movement. His paintings came the closest to the impressionist ideal of capturing the direct optical experience and of establishing the autonomy of the visual. Monet played a leading role in bringing the impressionists together in an organization, which in 1874 held the first of five impressionist exhibitions in Paris. It caused a scandal and was a financial disaster. In 1877 he again returned to Paris, this time to paint views of the St. Lazare train station.

By the 1880s impressionism was well in vogue and Monet's financial standing had improved. In 1883 he rented a house at Giverny in Normandy. During the 1880s he made a number of trips to the Normandy coast where he again addressed the sea, the rugged terrain, and the highly changeable weather. Visits to the Mediterranean coast enabled him to work with clear light and radiant color. In this decade his stress on atmosphere over solidity became so pronounced that his forms seemed almost to disintegrate.

Beginning in 1890 Monet executed a number of "series paintings" in which he painted specific scenes in different light, times of day, and types of weather. These series included *Haystacks* (1890–1891), *Poplars* (1891–1892), and *Rouen Cathedral* (1892–1894). In 1895 he did a series in Norway. Visits to London from 1899 to 1891 enabled him to do his *Views of the Thames* series, which included *Charing Cross Bridge and Westminster* (1902), *Waterloo Bridge, London* (1903), and *Houses of Parliament, Stormy Sky* (1904). Another set of series paintings was based on a trip to Venice in 1908.

"The art critic of *Le Charivari,* poking fun at a canvas by Monet called *Impression Sunrise,* coined the word 'Impressionism' as a gibe at the group. Monet adopted the name at once and launched it on its glorious career."

Denis Rouart in the book *Claude Monet,* 1958

Impressionism

Impressionism, a term coined by author Louis Leroy after a painting by Claude Monet (*Impression Sunrise,* 1873), was primarily a movement in French painting, from about 1864 to 1890. Its principal members shared a distaste for many earlier styles, which took as their subject matter themes from history or classical and Biblical mythology, depicting them in conventional ways. The impressionists sought to portray subjects with greater fidelity to the way the human eye actually perceives form and color. By painting ordinary scenes—such as outdoor nature settings or streets—that did not directly involve human drama, the impressionists also focused more attention on the color and technique of their work.

Édouard Manet, painting in the 1860s, was a major early influence. In his work, the subject itself is not the center of attention. By flattening the perspective from three dimensions to two, Manet invites the viewer to focus on surface color and texture. Influenced by Manet, Monet, Pierre Auguste Renoir, and Camille Pissarro preferred natural settings such as landscapes and rivers as their subjects. They too used a two-dimensional style. Regarding form, they rarely used solid lines dividing one object from another, preferring to use dots of color to suggest the boundaries among objects, pointing to the way the eye sometimes cannot distinguish precise borders. Regarding color, they used whatever hues accurately reflected the colors their eyes perceived. This led them to be more attentive than their predecessors to the differences between the effects of direct sunlight, reflected light, and shadow, and to use a broader range of brighter colors to represent their subjects—nature scenes as well as man-made scenes such as railroad stations and houses. In general, they preferred brighter colors to the somber colors of the French Academy that preceded them.

Other prominent impressionists include Berthe Morisot and Alfred Sisley (*Bridge at Argenteuil,* 1872). From 1874 to 1886, the central figures worked closely, conferring, drawing inspiration from one another's investigations, and exhibiting their works together. Eventually, they grew apart as their individual styles evolved in separate directions. With its movement away from a natural style, impressionism was one of the most influential movements in the history of art, beginning with its influence on postimpressionism and pointillism and, later, countless 20th-century movements, including cubism and expressionism.

Meanwhile, Monet purchased his residence at Giverny in 1890. In the 1890s he created a wildflower garden in front of his house. In 1893 he bought an additional parcel of land that included a pond and stream. Monet built a Japanese-style arched bridge across the pond and introduced waterlilies. During the first decade of the new century he enlarged the pond. From the 1899 to 1910 he executed a series of waterlily paintings, including *Japanese Bridge and the Waterlily Pool—Giverny* (1899). He exhibited nearly 50 of these paintings in 1909.

Beginning in 1914 Monet planned a waterlily project on a grand scale: two continuous, oval-shaped series of murals that would surround the viewer. Persisting despite failing eyesight, he executed the murals mostly between 1916 and 1921. They are regarded by many as the ultimate achievement of impressionism. In 1918 Monet, who since 1900 had been quite wealthy, declared that the murals would be donated to the state. Three years later the government announced that the murals would be installed in 80-foot oval rooms in a building call the Orangerie, at the opposite end of the Tuileries Gardens from the Louvre. The rooms have been described as the "Sistine Chapel of impressionism." They were opened to public viewing in May 1927, some five months after Monet's death at Giverny on December 6, 1926. ◆

Moore, Henry

JULY 30, 1898–AUGUST 31, 1986 ● SCULPTOR

"Basically, Moore was not interested in the idea of avant-garde innovation as an end in itself; rather, formal devices were, for him, simply a way of bringing about such transformations and metamorphoses of natural form as might enable him to intensify the emotive content of his work."

Peter Fuller in *Henry Moore*, 1993

Henry Spencer Moore, English sculptor, was born in Castleford, Yorkshire, England, on July 30, 1898, the seventh of eight children. Henry's father, Raymond Moore, was a miner. To assure that Henry would be able to earn a living, Raymond Moore insisted that his son acquire the credentials to be a schoolteacher before pursuing his interest in the arts. Henry worked as a student teacher in 1915 and 1916, but the following year was drafted into Britain's World War I army. In France he was gassed at the Battle of Cambrai.

Returning to England in 1919, Moore applied for and received a scholarship to the Leeds Art School. The school had no instructor in sculpture, which was Moore's major interest; at his insistence the school hired one. In 1921 Moore won a scholarship to study sculpture at the Royal College of Art in London. While attending that institution he began studying non-Western sculpture, which with its three-dimensional realization of form and direct carving made a decisive impression upon him. Four years later he became an instructor there, a post he would hold until 1932. He then became a teacher at the Chelsea School of Art. He retired from teaching in 1939 and from then on lived for the most part in the Hampstead section of London or in the countryside near the British capital.

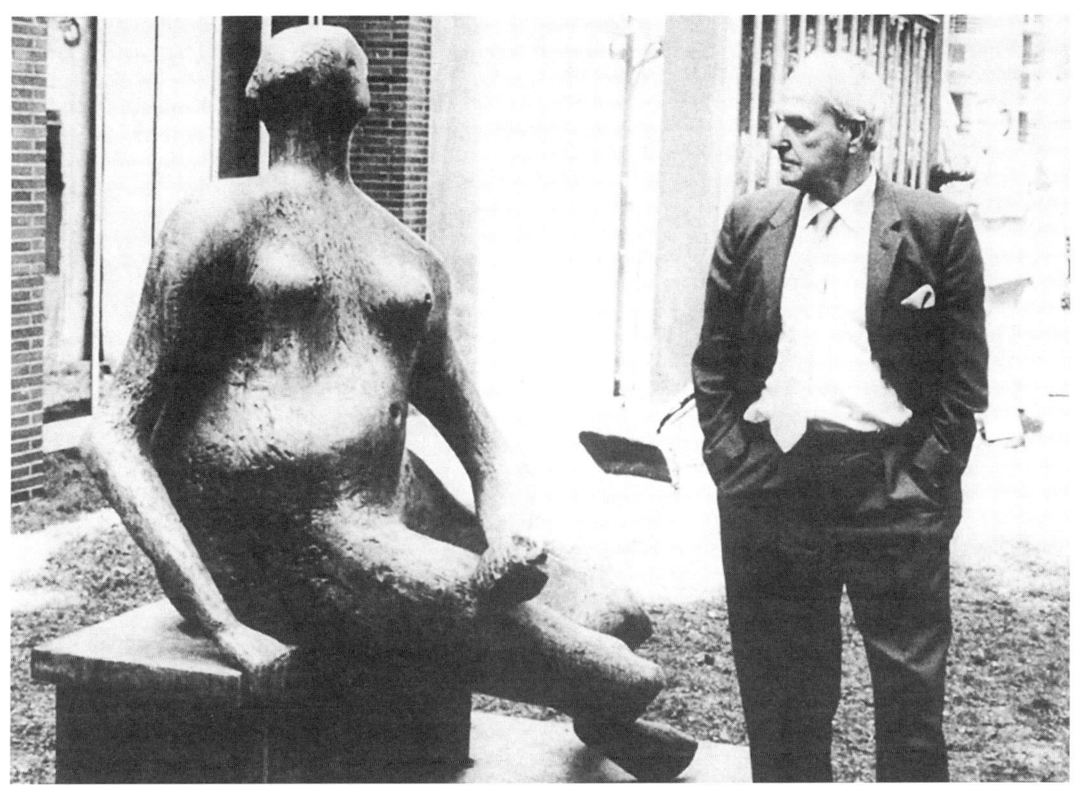

Henry Moore with one of his sculptures.

In the meantime, Moore had begun a sculpting career that would make him perhaps the leading British sculptor of the 20th century. From the beginning, Moore practiced direct carving and respected the inherent nature of his materials, which until the 1950s were usually stone and wood. His work of the 1920s exhibits the influence of Egyptian art, African masks, and in particular pre-Colombian Mexican sculpture. His *Snake* (1924), a small marble work, followed closely the rattlesnake carvings of the Aztecs. Moore's *Mother and Child* (1924–1925), made in stone, was the first of many major works with a maternal theme.

In 1928 Moore had his first exhibition. The same year he received his initial commission; it was for a sculpture relief called *West Wind,* which was installed at the new headquarters of London Transport. In 1929 he completed *Reclining Figure*, a stone sculpture inspired by a Toltec-Maya reclining figure of the warrior-priest Chacmool, found on the Yucatan Peninsula. Moore subsequently stated that this figure had the greatest impact on his early work; he admired what he later called "its

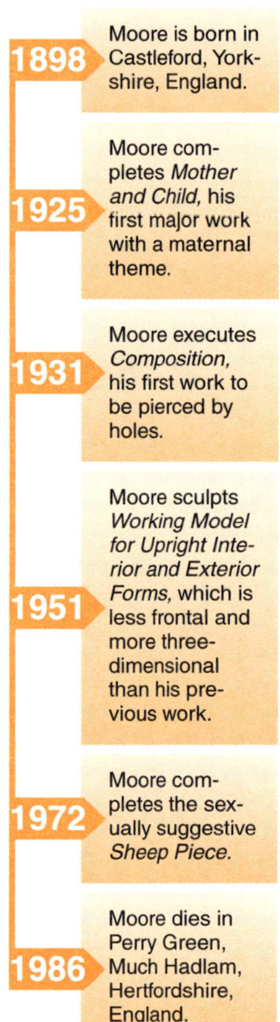

stillness and alertness, a sense of readiness." The Yucatan influence remained to the end of his career. Examples are the *Reclining Figure* (1957–58) at UNESCO headquarters in Paris, and *Reclining Figure, Lincoln Center Sculpture* (1963–65), at the Lincoln Center for the Performing Arts in New York City.

During the 1930s Moore's sculpture became more abstract under the influence of modern artists such as painter and sculptor Pablo Picasso; artist Hans Arp; and sculptors Alberto Giacometti, Constantin Brancusi, and Alexander Archipenko. The surrealist and constructivist movements impacted his work. Cubism had exerted an influence on his early work, but by the early 1930s he had ceased using the block forms of cubism. Instead, he began producing the undulating and swelling forms that became characteristic of his sculpture and that reflected Moore's belief in the close relationship of humanity and nature. Even from 1932 to 1936, when Moore's sculpture was at its most abstract, it retained what has been called "the human, psychological element."

During the 1930s Moore began to puncture his wood and stone sculptures with holes, starting with *Composition* (1931), which was apparently inspired by Picasso's sculpture *Metamorphosis* (1928). Sometimes the holes were threaded with wire. In 1934 Moore began executing small two-, three-, and four-piece figures influenced by the work of Arp and Giacometti. *Four-Piece Composition: Reclining Figure* (1934) is one of these; although it is an abstract work, separated body parts (head, legs, and navel) are readily discernable. Moore was not a political activist, but in 1936 he signed a petition of artists that called upon Britain to aid the republican side in the Spanish Civil War.

With the coming of World War II, Moore was appointed an Official War Artist, and in 1940 he began executing a series of drawings that depicted people in the stations of the London Underground railway, seeking refuge from German air attacks. These drawings, which conveyed an intense sense of common danger, caught the popular imagination and marked the beginning of the general public's appreciation of Moore. His *Madonna and Child* (1943–1944) illustrated the continuation of the maternal theme in his work. It also marked a return to a more naturalistic style that characterized most of his post-1930s work.

Beginning in the 1950s Moore worked mostly in bronze. His bronze *Reclining Figure* (1951) marked a major departure for him. Earlier the holes in his sculptures were small compared to the solid forms around them, but now space and form were, as Moore later remarked, "completely dependent on and inseparable from each other." Also during the 1950s Moore's sculptures became less frontal and more three-dimensional. An example is his bronze *Working Model for Upright Interior and Exterior Forms* (1951). In this semi-abstract work, his mother and child theme appears again: the outer shell of the sculpture enfolds the embryonic form within it. Influenced by carvings from New Ireland in the western Pacific, near New Guinea, this is one of few post-World War II Moore sculptures inspired directly by non-Western art.

Because of his improved financial standing in the 1960s and 1970s, Moore was able to produce larger sculptures, such as his *Reclining Figure* for New York's Lincoln Center. At the same time, he began more and more to execute drawings for their own sake rather than as preparatory sketches for his sculptures. While Moore had engaged in printmaking since the early 1930s, it became a large part of his work starting in the late 1960s. Although continuing to examine the mother and child theme, Moore in his late works also explored other human interactions. Strong sexual suggestiveness characterizes his *Large Two Forms* (1966 and 1969) and *Sheep Piece* (1971–72).

While Moore had engaged in printmaking since the early 1930s, it became a large part of his work starting in the late 1960s.

Moore received frequent recognition for his work. He won the International Sculpture Prize at the 24th Venice Biennale in 1948 and again at the 2nd São Paulo Bienal in 1953. In Britain, he was appointed as a Companion of Honour in 1955 and to the Order of Merit in 1963. From the 1970s on, Moore's work was widely shown, as at the Belvedere Fort in Florence in 1972, at a major Spanish exhibition in 1981, at the Metropolitan Museum of Art in New York City in 1983, and in Hong Kong and Japan in 1986. Moore died in Perry Green, Much Hadlam, Hertfordshire, England. ◆

Moreau, Gustave

April 6, 1826–April 18, 1898 ● Painter

Gustave Moreau, French painter, was born in Paris on April 6, 1826. From infancy, Gustave was weaned on the culture of antiquity. At the age of 10 his father gave him a two-volume work of neoclassical engravings illustrating

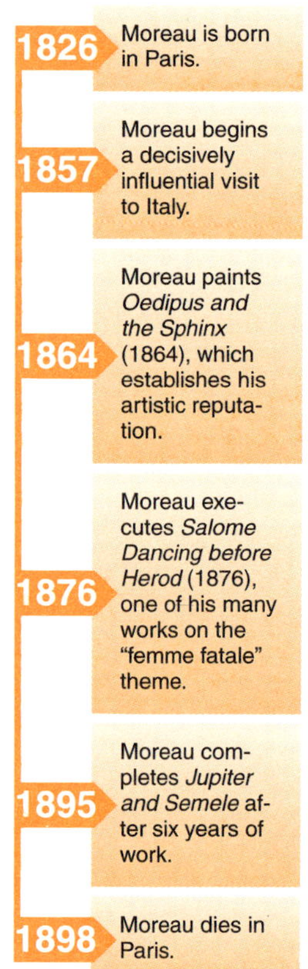

Homer, Hesiod, Dante, and the playwrights of ancient Greek tragedy.

Entering the École des Beaux-Arts in Paris at the age of 20, Moreau studied under François-Edouard Picot, a painter of history and allegory. A much greater influence on Moreau, however, was the romantic painter Théodore Chassériau, whom he met in 1848. The cryptic images of Moreau's work derived from the mysterious goddess figures of Chassériau. Eugène Delacroix was another influence on Moreau's early paintings.

From the beginning, Moreau's work was based on figures from the Bible and from Greek, Roman, Egyptian, and Asian mythology. The first of his paintings to be exhibited at one of the state-sponsored annual Salons was *Pietà* (1851). Two years later came the *Song of Songs* and *Darius*. Moreau received praise for his work, but he was dissatisfied with his efforts to combine the dramatic quality of romanticism with the ideals of order and balance derived from Renaissance classicism, as in *Young Athenians in the Labyrinth* (1855).

A trip to Italy from 1857 to 1859 had a decisive influence on Moreau. There, he studied Renaissance artists and ancient art in Rome, Florence, Venice, Milan, Siena, and Pisa. He was particularly impressed with the Venetian colorists. An inspired Moreau returned to Paris convinced of art's spiritual worth.

Integrating his Italian experience into a unique style of his own, Moreau devoted the early 1860s to working on the highly esteemed *Oedipus and the Sphinx* (1864), which won a medal at the Salon in 1864 and made his artistic reputation. It depicts a battle between Oedipus and the sphinx, but the violence is contradicted by the frozen composition and the passive expressions on the faces; the overall effect is a mysterious stillness. Here as in many of his other paintings—including *Jason and Medea* (1865), *Diomedes Devoured by His Horses* (1865), and *Salome Dancing before Herod* (1876)—Moreau is concerned with strife: between good and evil, male and female, physicality and spirituality.

From 1881 to 1885 Moreau produced excellent illustrations for the fables of Jean de La Fontaine.

A reclusive man who has been described as living in a world of dreams and fantasies, Moreau allowed his imagination to roam freely. He sought to capture what he called "the inner flashes of intuition which have something divine in their apparent insignificance and reveal magic, even divine horizons, when they are transposed into the marvelous effects of pure plastic art." His elaborate compositions and glowing colors give a dreamlike quality to his art. Moreau's works, especially his large ones, are amazingly rich in detail, both in their depiction of architecture and of crowded (and violent) street scenes.

Coming under criticism in the 1860s as his work became less novel, Moreau reconsidered his art in the early 1870s. His new style, visible in *Salome Dancing before Herod* and *Hercules and the Hydra of Lerna* (1876), was influenced by baroque art, particularly that of Rembrandt. Moreau's watercolor *Apparition* (1876), another of his many works based on the Salome legend of the *femme fatale*, earned great acclaim and represented the peak of his success. Beginning in the 1870s, Moreau exhibited watercolors.

From 1881 to 1885 Moreau produced excellent illustrations for the fables of Jean de La Fontaine. During the 1880s he began reworking some of his earlier art, going back as far as the 1850s. Such efforts were based on his belief that intuition should be tempered by intellect. That attempt at integration proved too difficult, however; none of his revisions were completed. From 1879 to 1886 Moreau worked on a large, multi-paneled work called *Life of Humanity*, in which each separately titled panel dealt with an historical theme. In 1883 he was made an officer of the Légion d'honneur and in 1888 was elected to the Académie des Beaux Arts of the Institut de France. Moreau never completed most of his large paintings, but *Jupiter and Semele* (1889–95) was one of the few exceptions. Its theme is the striving of humans to join with the divine, and it is characterized by a symbolist aesthetic. Moreau wrote two lengthy commentaries discussing *Jupiter and Semele*.

In 1892 Moreau became a professor at the École des Beaux-Arts, where he taught Georges Rouault, Henri Matisse, and Albert Marquet. Matisse lauded his pedagogical approach: "He didn't set his pupils on the right road. He set them off it. He made them uneasy.... He didn't show us how to paint; he roused our imagination."

Moreau was a perfectionist who educated himself by collecting thousands of prints, photographs, and periodicals. Over his lifetime he produced thousands of paintings, drawings, watercolors, and sketches. To house his collections and much of his prolific work, he transformed his Renaissance-style Parisian mansion into a museum—the Musée Gustave Moreau—in 1895 and 1896. Some four years after Moreau's death in Paris on April 18, 1898, it became an official state museum, with Georges Rouault as its director. Early in the 20th century, Moreau was much admired by the surrealist painters. ◆

"He consciously wanted to provoke a kind of awakening from 'the sleepwalking of life' to a contemplation of higher, more spiritual realities through the creation of visual situations that are more evocative than descriptive, imbued with 'an indecisive and mysterious character.'" Douglas W. Druick in the essay "Moreau's Symbolist Ideal,"
in *Gustave Moreau: Between Epic and Dream*, 1999

Munch, Edvard

DECEMBER 12, 1863–JANUARY 23, 1944 • PAINTER

Edvard Munch, Norwegian painter and printmaker, was born in Løteb, Hedmark, Norway, on December 12, 1863. He was the second of the five children of Christian Munch, a military doctor, and Laura Cathrine Bjølstad. Although of aristocratic descent, the family was poor.

Disease was rife in the working-class neighborhood in Oslo where the family lived; Edvard's mother died of tuberculosis in 1868, and his older sister Sophie succumbed nine years later. These deaths in turn led to the emotional deterioration of Edvard's father, who believed that he and his remaining children were doomed to hell. Edvard himself was sickly, suffering from episodes of bronchitis and tuberculosis. The horrors of his youth formed the underpinning of Munch's psyche; the artistic dramatization of his state of mind is central to his work.

Edvard Munch, self-portrait, c. 1882.

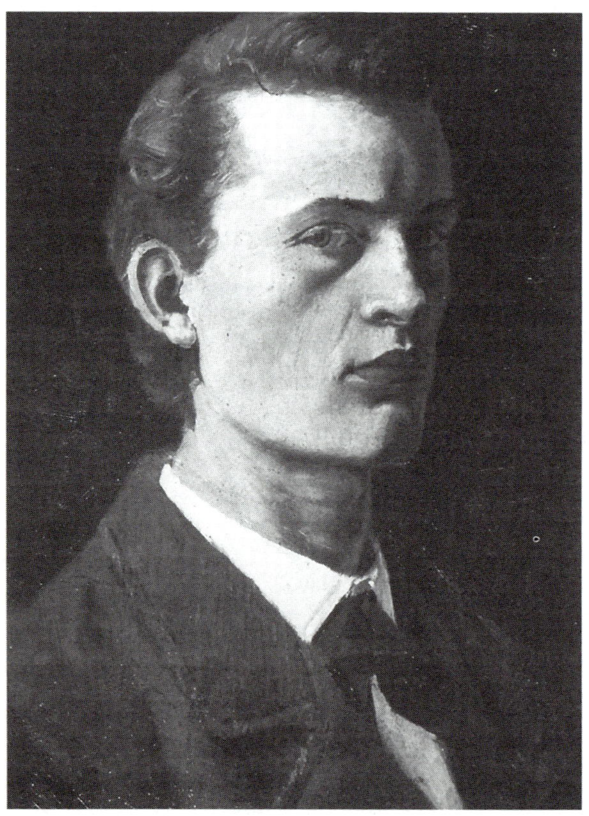

After studying engineering for a short while, Munch decided in 1880 to take up painting. In Oslo he studied under Christian Krogh. In the early 1880s his painting reflected impressionist influences drawn from Parisian artists, as in *Young Servant Girl Kindling a Stove* (1883) and *Morning* (1884). This new style of Munch and other Norwegian painters was linked to the political movement for Norwegian independence from Sweden.

After a trip to Paris in 1885, Munch began associating with a group of artists and writers known as Christiania Bohemia that was led by anarchist Hans Jaeger. Munch and the others lived bohemian lives and, partly because of political repression, produced subjective and inner-directed art. Munch's paintings at this time, such as *The Sick Child* (1885–86), were later considered forerunners of expressionism. Exhibited in 1886, *The Sick Child* was almost universally denounced. Upset by the reaction, Munch returned to a more naturalistic style. He had his first one-man show in Oslo in 1889. The exhibition featured *Spring* (1889), in which light streams into the room of a sick girl as a beacon of hope, and a huge portrait, *Hans Jaeger* (1889); these helped to restore his reputation.

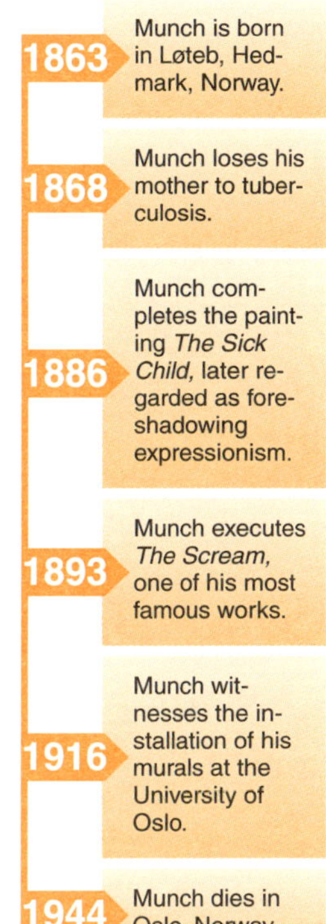

Living primarily in Paris from 1889 to 1892, Munch was influenced by symbolism, impressionism, and postimpressionism, all of which he used to strengthen the psychological content of his work. *Night* (1890), *Spring Day on Karl Johan Street* (1890), and *Rue Lafayette* (1891) are major examples of his subjectivism. His exhibit of such paintings in Berlin in 1892 was soon shut down because of the highly personal content of the paintings, a scandal that made him famous.

Munch lived mostly in Germany from 1892 to 1908 and had his greatest impact there. He continued to execute highly psychological work, one of the most famous examples of which is *The Scream* (1893) (sometimes translated as *The Cry*). It presents a genderless figure, hands to its head, emitting a cry that shakes the heavens in waves of intense red, orange, and violet. Another is *Jealousy* (1897), where green is used to convey emotion. These paintings were characterized by his typical flattened patches of color and swirling lines. In 1902 he exhibited in Berlin a frieze of 22 paintings—executed mostly during the preceding decade—that was then called *Love* and later known as *The Frieze of Life*. It has been remarked that this cycle "demonstrates above all how Munch extended the obsessive personal nature of his subjects into universal symbols of emotional states." Desire, anxiety, jealousy, loneliness, and death were the subjects of the paintings.

The last decade of the 19th century was a very busy one for Munch. He exhibited extensively. He designed sets for a production of Henrik Ibsen's *Peer Gynt*. He began to produce lithographs and woodcuts. Munch also became interested in photography, using it to document his work and to create prototypes for portraits, including self-portraits. In 1898 Munch began an intense love affair with Tulla Larsen, a Norwegian woman, from which he sought emotional and physical recuperation in a sanatorium during 1899 and 1900.

The end of his affair with Larsen in 1902 left Munch emotionally frazzled once again, but he accepted and completed many commissions for paintings and stage sets. In the first de-

Expressionism

In the Fauve movement in France, artists had embraced a bold style, influenced in part by "primitive" art, as with Vlaminck's interest in African styles. In Dresden, Germany, artists such as Erich Heckel, Ernst Ludwig Kirchner, Emil Nolde, and Karl Schmidt-Rottluff turned to primitive art as well. These artists, called *Die Brücke* (German: "the bridge"; 1905), combined the fauve taste for boldness and non-natural color with the depiction of human misery and anguish. They were called expressionists because they tended to viewed art as a way to record the feelings of the artists' emotions more than the impressions of the artists' sight (as with impressionism). This group also drew inspiration from artists like James Ensor, Vincent van Gogh, and Edvard Munch. In Munch's work, natural settings or people can be seen in the painting (they are not abstract), but the emphasis is on the intense emotion and tension of the subject, not realistic depiction. Another group in Munich, *Der Blaue Reiter* (*The Blue Rider;* 1911), drew from similar sources, but with greater abstraction, in part under the influence of Vassely Kandinsky; Kandinsky and Franz Marc were central members, with Alexei Jawlensky and Paul Klee. This group shared Die Brücke's emphasis on interiority; in their view, however, the interior world could also be a source of mystical harmony and pantheistic unity, not only repressed emotion, desire, and fear.

Expressionism also extended to printmaking and etching (as with Nolde's evocative *Prophet,* 1912), and sculpture (as in Ernst's Barlach's *The Avenger,* 1914). Expressionism moved beyond Germany to Belgium, Austria, and France. It would influence abstract expressionism, as with Jackson Pollock, and neo-expressionism, as with Julian Schnabel.

cade of the new century he also executed a new cycle on love relationships, known as *The Green Room*. In this series the accent shifts from individual to group relationships; that is also true in the triptych *Bathing Men* (1907–08), consisting of *Youth*, *Maturity*, and *Old Age*.

Suffering from a particularly extreme bout of anxiety and depression in 1908, Munch entered a sanatorium in Copenhagen, Denmark. Although institutionalized, he was still able to paint, make plans for a retrospective exhibition, and sell his paintings. After several months Munch left the clinic and settled in Kragerø, on the southern coast of Norway, where he lived for the remainder of his life.

Beginning in 1909 Munch's work became somewhat calmer. He concentrated less on inner torment and morbid scenes and more on exterior and active ones. Furthermore, his palette became lighter, and sunlight is often featured. In 1912 he exhibited 32 paintings in Cologne, Germany, at an exhibit on expressionism, of which he was by then considered a forerunner. During the same year he won a commission to paint murals for the newly opened University of Oslo. Installed in 1916, the most important of them were *History*, *Alma Mater*, and *The Sun*.

World War I temporarily severed Munch's contact with his German patrons, but he found new patrons in Norway among men who became rich thanks to Norway's neutral stance during the conflict. In the 1920s he reworked many of his paintings from the late 19th and early 20th centuries, but he also continued to experiment. He exhibited in Germany and Switzerland.

After the Nazis came to power in Germany in 1933, Munch was denounced as a "degenerate" artist and his work was taken down from the walls of German museums. In Norway, political disorder in the 1930s reduced Munch's opportunities for selling and exhibiting art. In addition, he suffered from temporary blindness caused by cysts in his eyes. Nevertheless, in his last years Munch experienced a spirit of **reconciliation** and humor that is apparent in a self-portrait of 1940.

After Germany conquered Norway during that year, Norwegian museums, too, removed Munch's paintings and prints. He rejected various attempts by Nazi sympathizers in Norway to "rehabilitate" his work as consistent with Nazi doctrine, along with efforts to enlist him as a Nazi sympathizer.

Munch died in Oslo on January 23, 1944. He willed most of his work to the municipal government of Oslo, which began displaying it in the Munch Museum in Oslo in 1963. ◆

"He was familiar with death . . . and did quail before it. . . . 'Without mortal danger and sickness I should have been a ship without a helm,' he said."

Edvard Munch quoted in Otto Benesch's, *Edvard Munch*, 1960

reconcilliation: a settlement or resolution of a conflict between two or more parties.

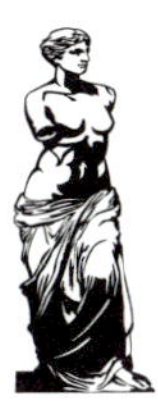

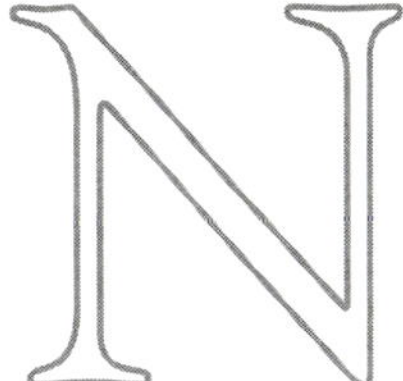

Nolde, Emil

AUGUST 7, 1867–APRIL 13, 1956 ● PAINTER

Emil Nolde, originally Emil Hansen, German painter and printmaker, was born in Nolde, Schleswig-Holstein, Prussia, in 1867. He received training as a decorative wood carver at Flensberg under Heinrich Sauerman. Subsequently, Nolde worked at furniture factories there and at Munich, Karlsruhe, and Berlin. He also was a student at the Arts and Crafts School in Karlsruhe. From 1892 to 1898 Nolde taught industrial design at the Saint-Gall crafts museum.

While teaching, Nolde made a considerable sum from postcards he designed, enough to devote all of his time to art. In 1898 he studied art under Friedrich Fehr at Munich, and the following year under Adolf Hölzel at Dachau. Influenced by Wilhelm Leibl and Arnold Böcklin, Nolde tried to bring together symbolism and realism at this point in his career.

While in Paris for a few months in 1900, Nolde studied at the Académie Julian, where he came under the influence of the impressionist painters. He painted mostly landscapes and flower arrangements with strong but generally dark colors. Throughout Nolde's career, the stark, primitive terrain of his native northern Germany strongly influenced his landscape painting. In 1900 he visited the Exposition Universelle, which reinforced an earlier interest in cultures far removed from his own, including so-called primitive cultures. Soon after his marriage to Ada Vilstrup in 1902, Nolde established a pattern of

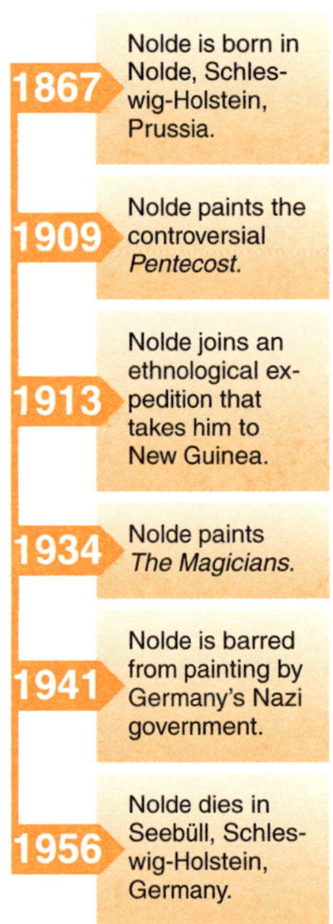

spending the winter in Berlin and the summer on the island of Alsen off the north German coast.

Nolde exhibited at the Galerie Ernst Arnold in Dresden in 1905. Impressed by his use of vivid, rich colors in such paintings as *Springtime in the Room* (1904), a group of young expressionists called Die Brücke urged Nolde to join them in 1906. Although close to the group for a few years, he never was fully in agreement with the other members. Over the next few years Nolde alternated scenes of urban bars and theaters with somber seascapes and landscapes.

Nolde started producing religious compositions in 1906. Some of his outstanding ones include *Last Supper* (1909) and the multi-paneled *Life of Christ* (1912). He also celebrated paganism in *Dance around the Golden Calf* (1910) and *Candle Dancers* (1912). Nolde stirred up a great deal of controversy with his *Pentecost* (1909); its primitivist approach to Christ and his and Apostles depicted them with mask-like heads. The painting was executed in radiant colors and with the daring, emotional brushwork of expressionism.

Passionately charged, visionary landscape and religious pictures would constitute Nolde's most valued work. His religious art was said to "express a violent, almost demonic feeling in brilliant, strongly opposed colors."

Nolde's interest in primitive art was again strengthened when he met Belgian artist James Ensor in 1911. In 1913 he joined an ethnological expedition that went to Russia, Japan, China, the South Seas, and New Guinea; in New Guinea he painted luminous watercolors such as *Tropical Forest* (1914) for several months before returning to Germany in 1915. Nolde admired what he regarded as the innocent, childlike qualities of "primitive" peoples. Again his penchant for the primitive was reinforced; severe simplifications and distortions of forms became more prominent in his painting.

His watercolors were less brutal and were characterized by a more delicate use of color.

After his voyage to New Guinea, Nolde no longer had any interest in executing scenes of modern life. He deployed primitive figures in scenes from the Bible, from fables, and from his imagination. *Christ and the Adulteress* (1926) and *The Magicians* (1934) are characteristic of this work. He also began to move along what would become a dangerous political path, opposing colonialism on the grounds that it defiled the "racial integrity" of primitive peoples. After returning from New Guinea, Nolde moved to the mainland of north Germany at Utenwarf, and in 1927 to Seebüll. In 1921 a biography of him by Max Sauerlandt was published. In 1927 Nolde's first volume of letters appeared, followed in 1931 by the first of his four autobiographical volumes. For his sixtieth birthday in 1927, a large retrospective exhibition was mounted in Dresden.

In 1933 Nolde joined the Nazi Party. He supported its belief in racial purity, not understanding the full import of the party's ideology. The Nazis did not approve of his work, which they considered part of "degenerate" modern art. In 1937 more than 1,000 of his paintings were seized. In 1940 additional paintings were taken from his studio, and the following year he was barred from painting.

Despite the ban, Nolde secretly executed over 1,000 small watercolors, called "unpainted paintings." After the war Nolde turned the watercolors into oils, as with *Jesus and the Scribes* (1951). For his eightieth birthday, exhibitions were held in several German cities. Nolde created a large number of engraved works, for which he won an award at the Venice Biennale in 1950. After the war he taught at the Berlin Academy. Nolde died at Seebüll, Schleswig-Holstein, Germany in 1956. The largest collection of his work is at the Ada and Emil Nolde Foundation in Seebüll. ◆

"In his memoirs, Nolde spoke of having certain clairvoyant qualities ... which, in the midst of peace ... caused him to paint apocalyptic scenes of destruction."

Robert Pois, *Emile Nolde*, 1982

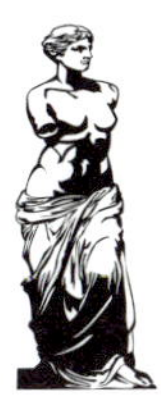

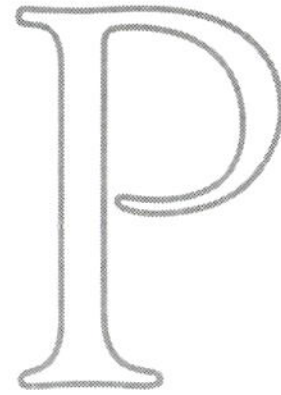

Phidias

c. 490 B.C.–430 B.C. • SCULPTOR

Phidias learned painting and sculpture from the master artist Hegias. Later, as the foremost sculptor of ancient Greece, Phidias perfected the idealized style of representing the human form that came to characterize **Hellenic** art. Although all that remains of Phidias's original works is a few statuettes and coins minted after his design, there are Roman copies and the accounts of ancient writers that provide a fuller knowledge of his accomplishments.

Hellenic: relating to the ancient Greeks and their language.

His greatest achievements were the three carvings of the goddess Athena created for the Parthenon and his monumental sculpture of the seated Zeus for Olympia. These works were commissioned by the Athenian ruler Pericles in 440 B.C. with Phidias also overseeing the building of Athens's national shrines. Pericles' projects were extensive and included a series of temples erected on the **Acropolis** and at Olympia aimed at proclaiming the greatness of Athens and its gods during this period of Athenian ascendancy.

Acropolis: the fortified hill of ancient Athens.

Working in bronze, marble, gold, and ivory, Phidias created forms that revealed lifelike contours of the body while achieving a magnificent grandeur absent in the later periods of Greek sculpture. Two all-bronze statues, the Apollo Parnopios and the Athena Promachos, stood on the Acropolis. The Athena Promachos was Phidias's first statue, completed around 456 B.C., and stood 10 meters high. The Amazon at Ephesus, done in marble, was probably the basis for the Amazon Mattei in the

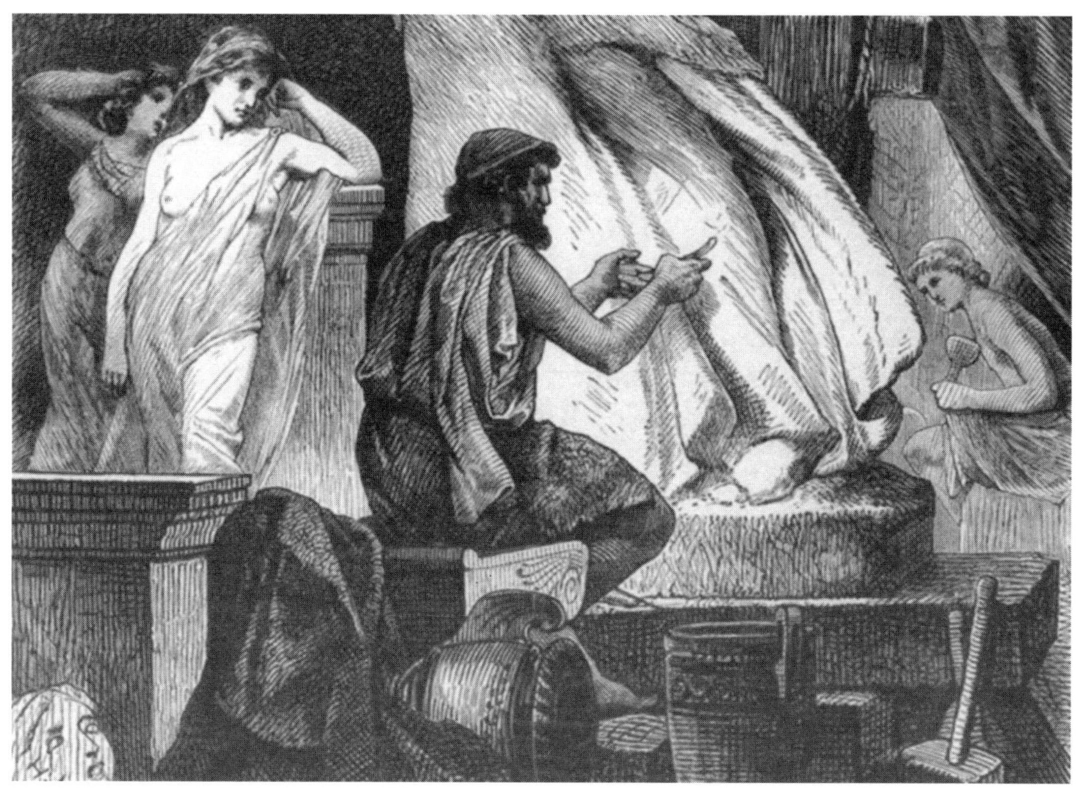

Phidias at work.

Vatican. The Athena Lemnia on the Acropolis was done completely in bronze, a thanks-offering commissioned by the Athenian colonists sent to Lemnos around 450 B.C. There are Roman copies of this statue in marble in collections in Bologna and Dresden.

Phidias also created works from gilded wood and set with ivory—the Athena at Pellene and the Aphrodite Ourania at Elis. These smaller chryselephantine works were dwarfed by two others done by him in the same style. The Athene Parthenos was completed in 438 B.C. and placed in the Parthenon, where it stood some 12 meters high; Roman and Greek copies of it are extant in Berlin and Athens. Phidias's Zeus was in this same style. This statue of the god sitting on his throne was made for the shrine at Olympia and reached to a height of 14 meters. Zeus's skin is ivory, his tunic gold and the god is shown holding Nike (the Greek goddess of victory) in one hand and a staff in the other. Ancient sources speak of it as Phidias's greatest work. His inspiration for the Zeus was Homer's descriptions, and the statue became one of the Seven Wonders of the world.

Phidias's statues on the Acropolis reached to such a height that they could be seen, reflecting the sun, by boats passing out at sea. Phidias's status in the ancient world is suggested by the saying that only he knew the true rendering of the gods; the forms he gave them were universally adapted.

Little is known about Phidias's last years. The enemies of Pericles accused Phidias of stealing the gold provided for his work, a charge he successfully denied. It appears, however, that he was subsequently jailed for the impious act of copying his own image and that of Pericles onto the shield of the Athene Parthenos. He went into exile at Elis where molds have been found in a studio thought to have been used for his creation of the Zeus at Olympia. ◆

Picasso, Pablo

OCTOBER 25, 1881–APRIL 8, 1973 ● PAINTER AND SCULPTOR

Picasso was born in Malaga where his father, José Ruiz Blasco, was a drawing master. His mother was Maria Picasso from Andalusia and from the age of 20, he was, following a Spanish custom, known by his mother's name. At first his father readily encouraged his son's artistry but became resentful of his obvious ability. At 15 Picasso was admitted to La Lonja, Barcelona's school of fine arts. A year later he entered the Real Academia de Bellas Artes de San Fernando in Madrid, but left soon after, unable to tolerate methodical training. In 1900 Picasso chose to visit Paris, unlike many of his contemporaries who followed the *Jugendstil* (decorative style) and went to Munich.

Already strongly influenced by the Spanish painters Isidro Nonell y Monturid and El Greco, in Paris Picasso became fascinated by the works of Vincent van Gogh and especially of Henri de Toulouse-Lautrec. Living in poverty, Picasso was strongly attracted by Montmartre's **bohemian** street life. His paintings, then done in an ethereal blue, were dominated by wretched scenes of beggars and prostitutes, evoking moods of melancholy and despair (*Celestine*, 1903; *The Old Guitarist*, 1903). During this Blue Period, he traveled between Paris and Barcelona.

bohemian: usually associated with artists characterized by living in an unconventional circumstance, such as in a colony with like-minded individuals.

Picasso finally settled in Paris in 1904 and took lodgings in the so-called Bateau Lavoir, a building in Montmartre. It be-

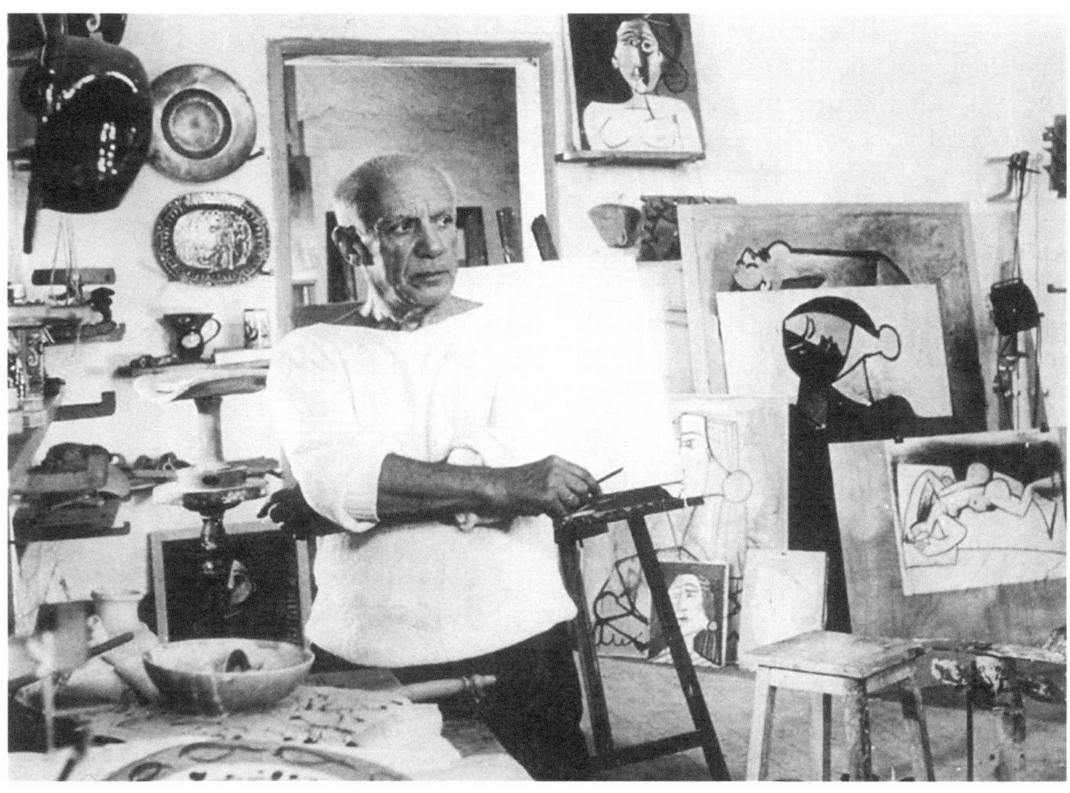

Pablo Picasso in his studio.

came the center of an avante garde circle that included the poets Max Jacob and Guillaume Apollinaire and the painter Marie Laurencin. Picasso also knew Henri Matisse, with whom he maintained a friendly rivalry, and Gertrude Stein, who had a great liking for his works. Fernande Olivier, Picasso's mistress, related that his jealousy, with its tragic Spanish overtone, led him to confine her to his studio with no shoes. Their relationship brought a new tenderness to his paintings, and although he liked attending bullfights and being considered a local tough, his works took on subtle rose tones. Sculpturelike figures, family groups, and circus scenes, especially those depicting harlequins, were often portrayed during the Rose Period (1904–1907). Picasso began sculpting for the first time and became interested in African sculpture and Paul Cézanne's work. He simplified form in this African Period (1907–1909), as in his revolutionary painting *Les Demoiselles d'Avignon* (1906–1907, now in the Museum of Modern Art, New York). As the fauve painters rebelled against the impressionist use of color, so this work made a statement against the impressionist use of form. *Les Demoiselles* was not exhibited until 1937, at which point art critics considered it the most significant turning point in contemporary painting and the forerunner to cubism.

Between 1910 and 1916 Picasso worked in close association with Georges Braque, then with Juan Gris, in developing analytical and synthetic cubism. They introduced the use of collage, *papier collé*, and real elements, as in Picasso's first constructed metal sculpture, *Guitar* (1912).

In 1917 Picasso began designing scenery and costumes for Sergey Diaghilev's Ballets Russes. The first ballet he worked on, *Parade*, was an adaption from a book by his friend Jean Cocteau and brought together the music of Erik Satie and cubism. From 1918 to 1925 Picasso was married to Olga Koklova, a dancer with the Ballets Russes. A social climber used to luxurious living, she introduced Picasso to the fashionable resorts of Biarritz and Juan-les-Pins.

Picasso continued painting in the cubist manner while also producing large classical nudes, notably *Two Seated Women* (1920), as well as *Three Musicians* (1921). Although Picasso stated he was not a surrealist, André Breton, the author of surrealist manifestos, considered him the initiator of surrealism. Picasso exhibited *The Three Dancers* (1928) at the surrealist exhibition at the Galerie Pierre Loeb in Paris and illustrated the cover of the movement's first journal, *Minotaure*. It was then that he started producing studies of the minotaur, a mythological image, and of the *Dying Horse* and *Weeping Woman*. In 1930 he began concentrating more on sculpture which was different from his cubist "constructions." In 1936 he returned to Madrid as director of the Prado Museum but his anger at Francisco Franco's fascism led him shortly after to a self-imposed exile for the rest of his life.

After the outbreak of the Spanish Civil War in 1936 and the bombing of the Basque capital, Guernica, Picasso produced his great political masterpiece entitled *Guernica*. This large composition was commissioned for the Spanish Republic pavilion at the Paris World Exhibition of 1937. For many years it was exhibited in New York as Picasso, while feeling his natural home was in Spain, refused to have it shown there under Franco's dictatorship. Only after the redemocratization of Spain was it finally displayed there.

During World War II Picasso remained in Paris, though he was forbidden to exhibit by the German occupying forces. He often hid members of the Resistance in his flat, and during the

1881 Picasso is born in Malaga, Spain.

1896 Picasso is admitted to La Lonja, Barcelona's school of fine arts.

1900 Picasso travels to Paris and becomes fascinated by the works of van Gogh and Toulouse-Lautrec.

1904 Picasso sculpts for the first time.

1917 Picasso begins designing scenery and costumes for the ballet.

1936 Picasso returns to Madrid as the director of the Prado Museum.

1949 Picasso designs the sign of a dove for the Paris Peace Congress.

1973 Picasso dies.

Cubism

The cubist movement began in Paris in the first decade of the 20th century and signals an early step in art history toward abstract art. The movement had no single unifying style or idea, but some recurring themes stand out. Taking its cue from South Pacific, Egyptian, and African indigenous art, cubism sought to turn impressionism on its head. Where impressionism had downplayed form and emphasized bright color and light, in cubism form would be inescapable, and, at least in earlier works, cubist artists would emphasize black and muted greens, grays, and browns.

In terms of form, cubism is often divided into two types. In the first, as in Pablo Picasso's *Ambrose Vollard* (1910), the subject is painted according to its underlying planes or geometrical solids—especially cubes and cones—that make up the subject. This way of viewing and representing a subject is "analytic," just as an analytic philosopher breaks a difficult subject down into the underlying ideas that compose it. "Synthetic" cubism, arising around 1912, represents a single object as it would appear at the same time but from different perspectives, while using more vivid shapes than its predecessor. This results in overlapping transparent images of the same object. Both styles result in a fragmented image that is far removed from natural depictions of the subject, though the styles are not yet abstract, because their subjects are often identifiable objects such as human bodies and musical instruments. Many examples of cubist art, however, do not quite fit these two types, such as Picasso's works exaggerating and distorting perspectives of room interiors.

The creation of new cubist works peaked in the 1910s, though its influence would continue for decades. Picasso (*Les Demoiselles d'Avignon,* 1907) and Georges Braque, working in Paris, were the leading cubist painters, and Braque's 1908 exhibition of paintings in Paris is sometimes considered the true beginning of the cubist movement. Other notable cubist figures include Marcel Duchamp, Albert Gleizes, Juan Gris, and Fernand Léger (*The Wedding,* 1911). Cubist painting would influence sculpture as well, as in the works of Aleksandr Archipenko and Raymond Duchamp-Villon.

liberation of Paris he sang aloud as he painted to drown out the sound of gunfire. Emerging from the war a declared communist, Picasso designed the sign of a dove for the Paris Peace Congress of 1949.

In 1946 Picasso met the painter Françoise Gilot and settled in Antibes and in 1947 the couple moved to Vallauris, where he took up pottery, often producing anthropomorphic designs. An intense and obsessional man, when he began his relationship with Gilot, Picasso made 10 portraits of her in one day, no two of which were alike. However, after a bitter breakup with her in 1953, Picasso, then 72, did 180 drawings in four months featuring the ravisher minotaur. Considered autobiographical, they portrayed the themes of age and love. That year he met

Jacqueline Roque and in 1955 they went to live in La Californie, a villa he purchased in Cannes. In 1958 they married and settled in the Chateau de Vauvenargues near Aix. There, Picasso continued investigating new techniques and materials for painting, sculpture, pottery, and, especially, lithography.

Picasso outlived most of his friends, including Matisse, which made him constantly aware of his own mortality. He was a prolific artist whose inventiveness influenced many of his contemporaries, including Jean Metzinger and Fernand Léger and the sculptors Aleksandr Archipenko and Jacques Lipschitz. Many important retrospective exhibitions were held in his later years, most notably that at the Louvre in 1971 commemorating his 90th birthday. ◆

Pisano, Nicola

c. 1220–c. 1284 ● Sculptor and Architect

Nicola Pisano, Italian sculptor and architect, was born around 1220, possibly in Apulia, a province in the southeastern region of the Italian peninsula. He studied at Apulia in the workshops of Holy Roman Emperor Frederick II, who ruled Apulia. In those workshops, Frederick encouraged a revival of the classical style so that the art of the empire would link him with the majesty of ancient Rome.

Around 1245 Pisano moved north to Tuscany, probably to Pisa, where he worked on imperial projects with artisans and craftsmen from both the Mediterranean and Europe north of the Alps. His work bridged the two regions, combining Byzantine and Islamic traditions with Romanesque and Gothic—especially the French Gothic associated with the Cistercian monastic order—along with the influence of ancient Rome. It also linked Christian and **pagan** traditions. His art did not, however, merely throw different traditions together helter skelter, but merged them into a brilliant new synthesis that re-energized Tuscan art at the approach of the Renaissance.

pagan: an individual who adheres to little or no religion and who revels in sensual pleasures and material wealth.

Of Pisano's early work at Apulia, only two grifffins' heads can be said with reasonable certainty to be his; their undulating, or wavelike, surface creates an effect of light and shade called chiaroscuro that is similar to the sculpture of late Rome.

> **"The middle of the 13th century marks the beginning of a new epoch in Italian sculpture which culminated in Michelangelo.... Nicola Pisano [was] the author of this revival."**
> G. H. Crichton and E. R. Crichton, in *Nicola Pisano and the Revival of Sculpture in Italy*, 1938

His earliest work in Tuscany was probably the lions on the portal of Prado Castle.

In 1259 or 1260 Pisano designed and helped carve the marble pulpit in the baptistery at Pisa. It is considered the best example of the integration of French Gothic and classical components. The work incorporated concepts that appeared in a sermon by Federico Visconti, the archbishop of Pisa, who was the pulpit's patron. The central column is surrounded by six columns, three on a plain base and three held up by lions. The leaf-shaped capitals of these columns, which are lavishly carved, support arches that have *Prophets* and *Evangelists* between the curves of the arches and the enclosing right angles, and the *Virtues*, *St. John the Baptist*, and *St. Michael* at the corners. The parapet above the columns is made up of five scenes from the life of Christ, with red marble separating them. The shafts of the columns are made of red and green marble, while the rest of the sculptures are of white marble.

The pulpit is hexagonal-shaped. Of the five panels—which relate a complex narrative—the first two are inspired primarily by ancient Roman art. This is apparent from the solemn, regal faces, and dignified movements of the figures, as well as the lifelike spatial arrangements. The first relief presents the *Nativity*, the *Annunciation*, and the *Annunciation of the Sheperds*, displaying multiple scenes in one composition. The second relief is the *Adoration of the Magi*. In both reliefs varying surface treatments, which highlight depth and projection, go beyond a simple mimicking of ancient prototypes. The energy of the figures is indicated by the small size of the heads in comparison to the bodies, a Romanesque rather than a classical feature. The faces are highly expressive, depicting the character of the individuals.

The third relief on the Pisan pulpit, the *Presentation*, is characterized by more refined carving. A sense of endurance and grandeur is conveyed by arranging the figures in groups that are related to the size of the structures in back of them. In the *Crucifixion*, the fourth panel, the elements are all centered around the figure of Christ. The fifth panel, *Last Judgment*, presents an overhead view of the saved and the damned in an amphitheater, facing Christ, their judge.

From about 1264 to 1267 Pisano worked on the Arca, or shrine, of St. Dominic in the city of Bologna. Six scenes from the life on St. Dominic are on the sides, two on the long sides and one on the short ones. Pisano's assistants carried out most of the project's carvings. The portions carved by Pisano stand out for the quality of their composition and for the sense of dynamic motion that they convey.

From 1265 to 1268 Pisano devoted most of his attention to constructing the octagonal pulpit of the Siena Cathedral. His assistants included his son, Giovanni, who would go on to become a distinguished sculptor himself. A central column is on a pedestal surrounded by seated figures of *Philosophy* and the *Seven Liberal Arts*. Around the central column are eight others—as with the Pisa **pulpit,** some are on plain bases and others on lions. The overall structure of the pulpit is similar to the one at Pisa but more complex. The narrative panels that tell the story of Christ from the *Visitation* of the Virgin Mary to the *Last Judgment* are more crowded than in the earlier pulpit. The French Gothic influence is stronger at Siena, and later on Giovanni Pisano would take it further than his father. The human figures at Siena are as emotionally expressive as the ones in Pisa. The carvings are cut more deeply than at Pisa, perhaps for the sake of visibility in the darker Sienese building.

pulpit: place on a church altar from which a minister delivers a sermon, usually an elevated platform.

Pisano's Great Fountain at the main square of Perugia was erected in 1277 and 1278. Three basins are superimposed one above the other. The lower one has 25 sides; each side has two reliefs, including scenes from classical mythology and the Old Testament. The middle basin is smaller and has 12 sides, each with two Old Testament figures. The top basin is made of bronze and is capped by three water-bearing women in the classical style. The overall design is Pisano's, and some of carving can be identified as his, but most of the sculpting was done by Giovanni. In contrast to the reliefs on the Pisan and Sienese pulpits, those at the Great Fountain do not form a narrative.

Nicola Pisano died somewhere between 1278 and 1284, possibly at Pisa. ◆

Pissarro, Camille

JULY 10, 1830–NOVEMBER 12, 1903 ● PAINTER

Camille Pissarro was born on Saint Thomas in the Virgin Islands, where his father, Frederic, had come as executor of his uncle's estate. A year later, Frederic and his uncle's widow went to arrange for their marriage in the syna-

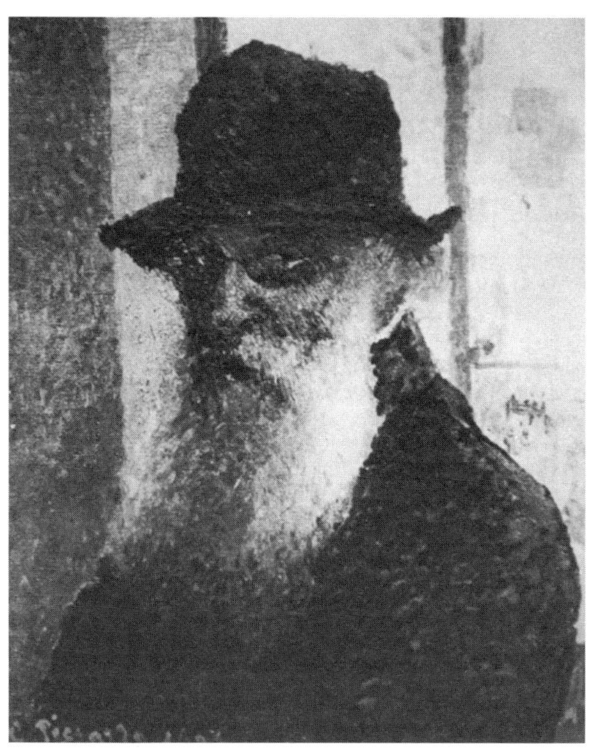

Camille Pissarro, self-portrait, 1903

gogue, but as aunt and nephew, were refused permission. However, their marriage in a private home was recognized by the Danish authorities, and eventually—after they had registered the birth of four sons at the synagogue—by the congregation.

Camille Pissarro studied art in Paris from 1841 to 1847. He returned to Saint Thomas to work in the family's general store, but after a few years left to paint in Venezuela. In 1855, he moved to Paris, never to return to the West Indies. One of his paintings was accepted for the Salon of 1859, a success that elicited financial aid from his family. Anton Melbye introduced him to J.B.C. Corot, who encouraged him and advised him, and later gave him permission to list himself in the salon catalogue as "pupil of Corot."

Before he left Saint Thomas, Pissarro had fallen in love with Julie Vellay, a servant in his parents' home. He asked his parents' consent to marry her—to protect property and inheritance rights—but his parents denied them permission.

The couple was constantly burdened with financial difficulties. In Pontoise, where they lived for over 10 years, Julie had a vegetable garden and raised rabbits and chickens to sustain the family. They received some financial aid from Pissarros' mother and from Julie's family. In 1868, Pissarro took a job painting landscapes on window shades. Painting out of doors in Pontoise, he explored the effect of the light on colors and contours.

In 1870, during the Franco-Prussian War, the couple went to England with money lent them by Pissarro's mother. There they married. When the Pissarros returned to France from England in 1871, they found that their house in Pontoise had been devastated by Prussian troops who had slaughtered the animals in the garden, spread paintings on the ground, and used others as aprons to protect their uniforms. The government gave Pissarro an indemnity to cover his losses during the war, but 15 years' work had been destroyed, as well as many paintings of Claude Monet, left with Pissarro for safekeeping. Paul Cézanne and his family came to live nearby and Pissarro urged him to paint out of doors, and to paint what he observed. They often went out together searching for a "motif."

Pissarro, Monet, and Alfred Sisley organized a group to bypass the Salon and arranged an exhibition in 1874, in which 30 artists participated, including Edgar Degas and Cézanne. A critic, reacting negatively to Monet's painting *An Impression: The Rising Sun* gave the group the name "Impressionists." The exhibition ran for a month and admission was one franc. Costs outweighed profits, and in the end, each artist had to pay 184.50 francs. The second exhibition was somewhat more successful—each artist made a profit of three francs.

Pissarro spent days going around Paris trying to sell paintings. Pierre Auguste Renoir as badly off, went on much the same rounds, with little luck, because, he said, everybody who could buy had already bought from "poor Pissarro with all those children." To make matters worse, a collector of impressionist paintings was forced to auction his collection. After that, it was impossible for Pissarro to find a buyer. He earned a little money by painting ceramic tiles and fans.

At last, in 1878, he found a dealer who began to sell his paintings. Paul Gauguin, who was working in finance, also sold a few for him. Pissarro encouraged Gauguin in his artistic endeavors, and Gauguin exhibited a piece of sculpture in the fourth impressionist exhibition. In the 1880s, impressionist paintings began to be in demand. The critic J.K. Huysmans said that Pissarro was one of France's most remarkable and audacious painters and called him the most original landscape painter of the period.

The eighth and last impressionist exhibition was held in 1886. Pissarro and his son and pupil, Lucien—who was also a leading impressionist painter—were among those whose work was exhibited in a special "Neo-Impressionist" room.

In 1890 the dealer Durand-Ruel took 300 paintings to the United States for a show in Madison Square Garden in New York, in which he included work by Pissarro, Paul Signac, and Georges Seurat. Pissarro's work found so many buyers that Durand-Ruel, in 1892, bought all the canvases that had not been sold when the exhibition ended. The seminal nature of his work was recognized: "Pissarro's work," wrote Georges Lecomte, "seems to preface the work of tomorrow."

1830 Pissarro is born on St. Thomas in the Virgin Islands.

1841 Pissarro travels to Paris to study art.

1868 Pissarro takes a job painting landscapes on window shades to make ends meet.

1870 Pissarro journeys to England and marries before returning home.

1874 Pissarro organizes a group of artists later known as The Impressionists.

1878 Pissarro finds a dealer and finally starts selling paintings.

1903 Pissarro dies.

Pissarro developed a recurring eye problem, and was obliged to wear a bandage over his eye for long periods. He started working indoors, staying in hotels in Paris, Rouen, and Le Havre, and painting the view from the windows. These are beautiful cityscapes, full of movement and crowds, masterful in composition.

The Alfred Dreyfus affair had a profound effect on Pissarro. He was overwhelmed by the injustice of the sentence and by the frenetic anti-Semitism that raged through France. His friendships with Cézanne, Armand Guillaumin, and Renoir, all anti-Dreyfusárds, were strained. Degas, contaminated by anti-Semitism, never spoke to him again.

In spite of his eye problem, in the last three years of his life Pissarro produced about 160 paintings and sold two paintings to the Louvre.

In spite of his eye problem, in the last three years of his life Pissarro produced about 160 paintings and sold two paintings to the Louvre. He became ill, needing an operation, which was delayed due to a dispute between his two doctors. Blood poisoning ensued and Pissarro died on November 13, 1903.

Pissarro was an outstanding painter and etcher always open to new ideas. His search for basic principles led him to experiment with light and color. When Henri Matisse asked him what an impressionist was, Pissarro replied that an impressionist is someone who never makes the same painting twice. He was a natural teacher, and always encouraged younger artists and willingly passed on to them what he had discovered. ◆

Polykleitos

c. 450 B.C.–c. 415 B.C. ● SCULPTOR

This celebrated Greek sculptor is often referred to as Polykleitos the Elder in order to distinguish him from Polykleitos the Younger. The latter was a sculptor and architect who flourished in the 4th century B.C. and who may be a descendent of the 5th-century master.

The historical record on Polykleitos the Elder, the preeminent sculptor of the High Classical period in Greece, is understandably sketchy. None of his original works survive. Today they can only be seen represented in copies made by admiring Roman and Greek sculptors in later centuries. Nonetheless, Polykleitos holds an honored place in the history of sculpture for many reasons. He is credited with perfecting the art of bronze casting, and he wrote a book about his theory on rendering proportion; his theory became the standard for depicting male beauty in sculpted form. This book, which may well be the first formal treatise ever written on the theory of art, is known today as the *Canon*.

Polykleitos is also credited with having been the first sculptor to break away from the earlier standard pose for full-length, standing statuary, which presented a figure facing forward and resting its weight equally on both feet. Instead, Polykleitos used a pose known as *contrapposto*. In this more casual pose, the figure stands with the weight apparently supported on one leg, the other leg being bent at the knee, giving the impression that the figure may be just on the verge of taking a step. This pose gives the sculpture a sense of dynamism and action previously unknown in sculpted art.

The most famous of Polykleitos's sculptures today is *Doryphoros*, a *contrapposto* male nude known from several Roman copies, the best of which is on display in the National Archaeological Museum in Naples. The title of the piece means "spear-bearer." It depicts an athletic young man who appears to be walking casually, his spear held at rest over his shoulder. The copies that survive today are done in marble, but originally this statue was possibly cast in bronze. Polykleitos, after all, was a member of the Argive School of sculptors, who produced bronze statues of athletes.

Other statues by Polykleitos for which we have copies include two that depict gods and demigods of the Greek pantheon—*Herakles* (Hercules) and *Hermes*. He also sculpted a statue of the goddess Hera from gold and ivory, and it was installed in her temple in the city of Argos sometime after 423 B.C. No copies exist of this piece, but it is described by such ancient authors as Strabo, who admired it for its beauty and workmanship. Another sculpture attributed to Polykleitos is the depiction of an unnamed youth whose arms are raised to tie his hair back (copies exist at the British Museum in London and the National Museum in Athens).

The Greek encyclopedist, Pliny the Elder, writing in the first century A.D., recounts the tale of a great competition among the four greatest sculptors of the Greek classical period: Polykleitos, Phidias, Cresilas, and Phradmon. All were challenged to produce a statue of a wounded Amazon; the winning piece would be honored by being installed in the temple of Artemis in the Greek city of Ephesus. In due course, Polykleitos submitted his statue, and his competitors began talking among themselves, evaluating their work. Each named his own statue as the finest, of course, but all named Polykleitos as second best. The judges discounted the self-serving claims of each artist on behalf of their own work but noted that all were unanimous in their appreciation of Polykleitos's statue. Accordingly, Polykleitos was judged the winner.

While the story may sound too good to be true, there may be some historical accuracy in it after all. The Capitoline Museum in Rome displays a copy of a work by Polykleitos that appears to be an Amazon, in which the figure is represented as bearing her breast to expose her wounds and leaning on her spear. But even if the details of this tale, like so many told by Pliny the Elder, are fictitious, they clearly show how greatly people in antiquity honored the name of Polykleitos, a name that continues to be honored 2,500 years later. ◆

Poussin, Nicolas

JUNE 1594–NOVEMBER 19, 1665 ● PAINTER

Nicolas Poussin was born in Les Andelys, Normandy, to a well-established family. While details about his earliest years are sketchy, he appears to have trained with Quentin Varin. His move to Paris around 1612 signaled the beginning of the most important early phase of his career. There, he studied with Ferdinand Elle and Georges Lallemand, while being exposed to a wide variety of styles and artists. Raphael's influence was everywhere, but so were the mannerist works of Caravaggio and Giulio Romano, with their emphasis on heightened dramatic scenes.

Some of Poussin's earliest surviving works are mythological drawings to accompany the classical poet Ovid's *Metamorphosis*. These drawings show young Poussin's highly developed technical skill and give hints of creativity in his choice and treatment of subject matter. He remained in Paris almost constantly for 11 years, until 1623.

By 1624 Poussin, like many of his day, had made the artistic pilgrimage to Rome. There he continued working in a manner-

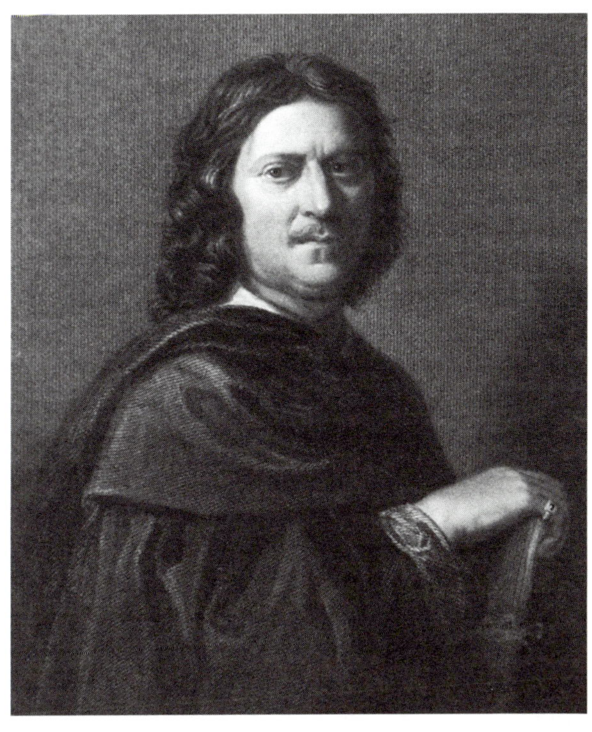

Nicolas Poussin, engraving of self-portrait

ist style, as with his *Battle of Gideon against the Midianites* and *Battle Scenes* (1625), both of which include such typical mannerist touches as twisted poses. While in Rome, he aligned himself with Cassiano dal Pozzo, a man of great learning and experience, with access to some of the artistic and intellectual elite of that day. Cassiano gave Poussin access to many great art collections as well, and as a result of Poussin's investigations came a series of landscape drawings and a number of paintings with themes drawn from classical Roman literature. These include *Venus and Adonis with a View of Grottaferrata* and *Arcadian Shepherds*, where he was able to convey intense mood not through the use of exaggerated perspective or comic depictions, but by applying his careful observations of landscape and light. In 1628 he also completed a larger work, *Death of Germanicus*, marking a great leap forward in his art. The view, though clearly arranged according to certain rules of composition, is highly realistic, and though the figures overlap and interact, they are not crowded one on top of another—the effect is not one of chaos or disorder but somber reverence for the departed leader.

Poussin began treating human subjects as individuals in their own right, with their own emotions, motivations, gestures, and particularities.

Poussin's talent did not go unnoticed, and ever more commissions came his way, including for religious works and altarpieces, such as the *Virgin Appearing to St. James the Greater* (1629–30). These decorative works were never Poussin's preference, however. Perhaps because he was an "artist's artist" and other artists valued his skills so highly, he took greater satisfaction from producing private works. Perhaps his serious illness in 1629–30 gave him a more pressing sense of the need to pursue his highest artistic vision without distraction. In any case, throughout this period his skills evolved, as he increasingly began treating human subjects as individuals in their own right, with their own emotions, motivations, gestures, and particularities; the scene or story in which they found themselves was not the only focus of dramatic interest.

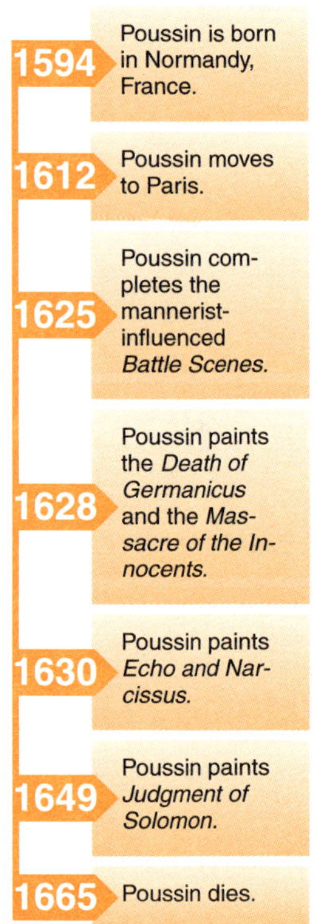

Examples of this evolution include *Echo and Narcissus* (1630) and *Massacre of the Innocents* (1628). In the latter work, Poussin deals with mass suffering by giving it a distinctly individual human face. Poussin focuses on the fate of one parent and child—the mother's terrified expression reflects her certain knowledge that her child will be slaughtered; the child's face reflects its happy ignorance of the carnage occurring all around it. Another such work is *Rape of the Sabine Women* (1635), where each figure is given its own precisely planned emotion and pose. In these serious and elevated treatments of classical themes, Poussin was bucking a baroque trend of representing classical themes in gentler, more romantic ways.

Poussin's art to this point was hardly lighthearted, but after he traveled to Paris and developed a keen interest in stoic thought, he imbued his works with even more precision and rigor. The figures in his works continued to show expression, but in a highly planned, formal way. One great example is Poussin's *Judgment of Solomon* (1649). The work is not without emotion—in fact, the scene is charged with feeling. But the poses of the principal figures are highly stylized and exaggerated, not at all natural. Poussin displays his Stoic influence not by removing all traces of feeling but by using every element in the painting in the most efficient, unambiguous way possible—the viewer cannot miss the shock of the audience or the two women claiming to be the mothers of the child.

Around 1650 Poussin returned to landscapes, this time with extreme rigor in his use of detail, though by the late 1650s geometry and human architecture, which reflected his excellence as a draftsman, become less important in his landscapes, as untamed nature begins to move to the fore.

Among all artists, Poussin is one of the hardest to reduce to one or two simple stories, as he changed styles and emphases throughout his career. Perhaps the one constant theme of his work is that he gave attention to rigor in composition and, throughout his life, explored newer ways to call attention to the role of individuals in his paintings, even when several individuals appeared in the same setting. He is also remembered as one who experimented with the use of light and color to their greatest effect. His influence never completely waned, but he was most influential in the later neoclassical movement and, later, in the art of Edgar Degas and Pablo Picasso. ◆

Praxiteles

375 B.C.–330 B.C. ● SCULPTOR

Praxiteles, the son of an Athenian sculptor, was one of the greatest sculptors in the ancient world. His style greatly influenced the work of future generations of artists. Although Praxiteles worked in bronze, he preferred to work in marble. As was the style at the time, his marble statues were painted after they were sculpted. Praxiteles paid great attention to the finish on his works, preferring to employ the painter Nicias over other painters. Praxiteles specialized in religious statues, especially those that portrayed gods and goddesses, such as Apollo and Dionysus, at a younger age than was usual for other artists.

Among the features of his work that influenced later sculptors was Praxiteles' use of the female nude. His ideal of the female body—wide hips, small breasts, oval face, and hair parted in the middle—characterized his masterpiece, the *Aphrodite at Cnidus*. While Aphrodite, the Greek goddess of love, had long been a popular subject for Greek sculptors, earlier statues showed her fully or partially clothed. Praxiteles was the first sculptor to show her completely nude.

Praxiteles was believed to have completed more than 75 sculptures during his career, although few, if any, of his original works still exist. The *Aphrodite of Cnidus* is known only from Roman copies. Many other statues that were once considered to be his originals have been shown to be copies as well. Although the famous statue of the god Hermes holding the infant Dionysus is considered by some experts to be the original work as described by the Greek writer Pausanias, others doubt its authenticity. ◆

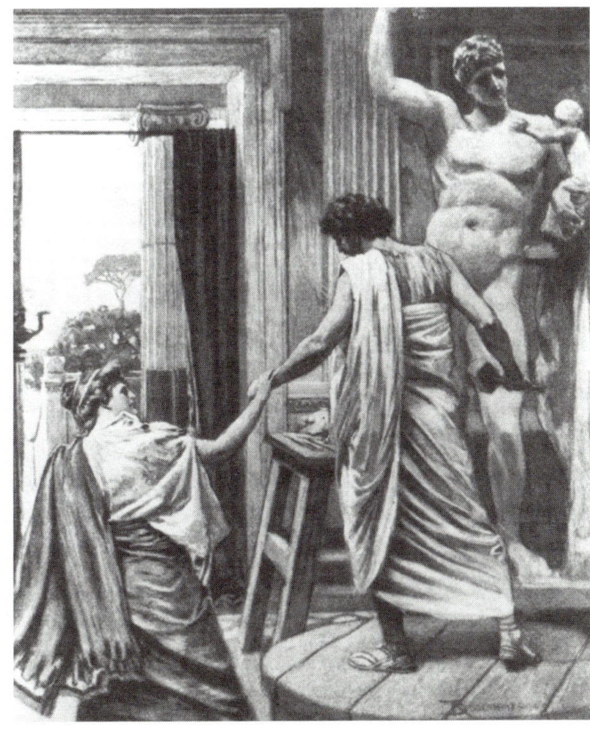

Praxiteles at work.

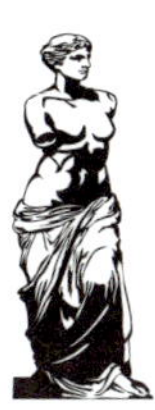

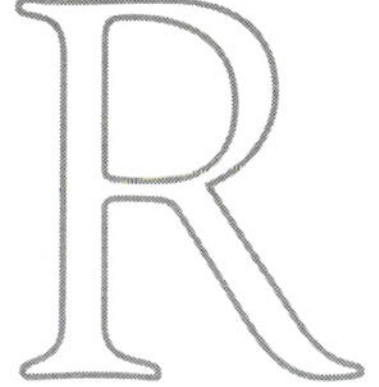

Raphael

APRIL 6, 1483–APRIL 6, 1520 ● PAINTER

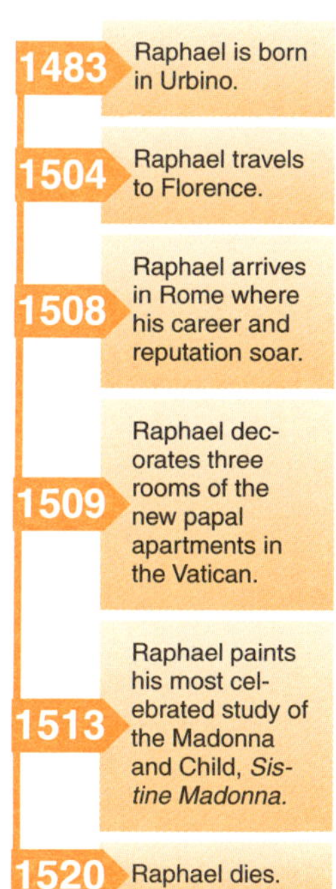

Raphael's work exemplifies the Renaissance interpretation of the classical ideal of perfect beauty. He was an inspired borrower who absorbed the best of the art of his time and renewed and perfected the forms, compositional devices, and motifs of antiquity. His style is characterized by an idealized representation of nature and a sweet and graceful manner by which he sought to capture the high ideals of humanism combined with a representation of the Divine. The renowned historian Giorgio Vasari held him in great esteem and his interpretation of Raphael's work formed the basis of much later study.

Raphael was born in Urbino, son of a poet painter, and trained in the style of Perugino. In 1504 he went to Florence, then the center of the Italian Renaissance. The fevered tone of the Florentine style exemplified by Botticelli and Pollaiuolo contrasted sharply with the calm, disciplined style Raphael had developed. He was, however, always eager to emulate other artists' work in order to enhance his own style. He mastered the Florentines' drawing style and adapted their robust sculptural forms so well that his paintings eventually became the yardstick for fine draftsmanship. He worked on commissions all over central Italy, developing techniques of naturalism, perspective, color, and composition. Fra Bartolomeo, whose sweet, simple style was closely influenced by Leonardo da Vinci, was a formative influence on Raphael, as was Leonardo himself,

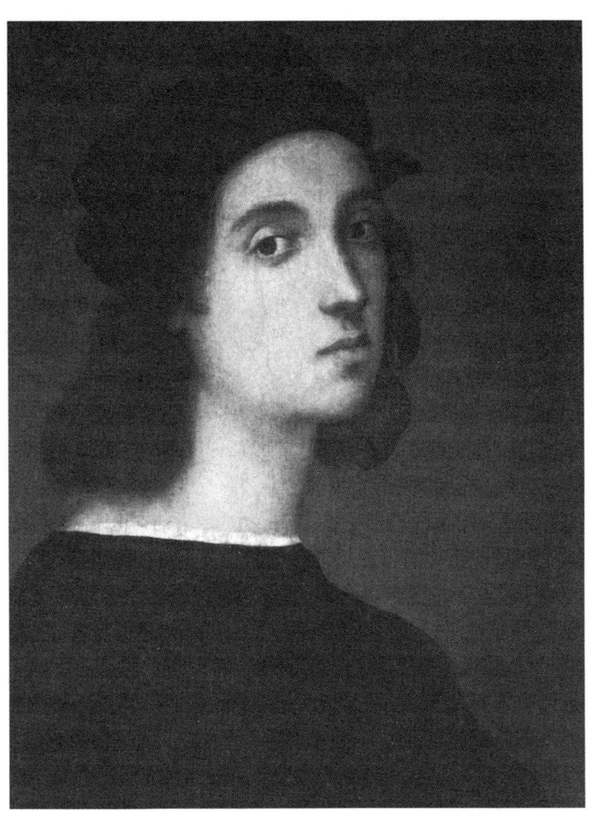

Raphael, self-portrait

whose Battle Cartoons prompted him to enliven his technique.

Donato Bramante, the leading architect of the Renaissance, was a townsman of Raphael's, and it is likely that it was he who suggested to him to leave for Rome, which had become the new center of Renaissance art. Raphael arrived there in 1508 and studied the numerous remains of antiquity and the works of masters such as Michelangelo. He was criticized for emulating Michelangelo's style too closely; the latter even commented that "all he knows he learnt from me."

In Rome, Raphael's career and reputation soared. He received numerous commissions for portraits easel pictures, religious and secular decorations, and tapestry cartoons. He was also commissioned to list and conserve the antique remains of Rome and was chosen by Pope Leo XI to succeed Bramante as architect of Saint Peter's.

A humane and charming person who exhibited the manners of a gentleman, Raphael was famous for his enthusiastic appreciation of women (Vasari ironically attributed his early death to this passion). His major commission (from Pope Julius II) and the culmination of his work came in 1509, when he decorated three rooms of the new papal apartments in the Vatican—the Stanze. The frescoes of the middle room, Stanza della Segnatura (1509–1511), explore the theme of divinely inspired intellect as represented by theology, philosophy, poetry, and law. In the second room, Stanza dell'Eliodoro (1511), Raphael's depiction of scenes from the New Testament was strongly influenced by Michelangelo's Sistine Chapel ceiling, the first part of which was completed in 1510.

After the Stanze, Raphael worked on architectural designs as well as painting. He received commissions for palaces in Rome and designed a villa for Cardinal Giulio de Medici. Throughout his career Raphael experimented with the theme of the Madonna and Child. While working on the Stanze he painted his most celebrated study of this theme, the *Sistine Madonna* (1513).

Raphael's last work, a study of the heads of apostles for the Transfiguration, was exhibited unfinished over the bier at his funeral; he was buried in the Pantheon. Despite the brevity of his career, his ability was universally admired and his work became the model for beauty and idyllic charm. ◆

Redon, Odilon

April 20, 1840–July 6, 1916 ● Painter

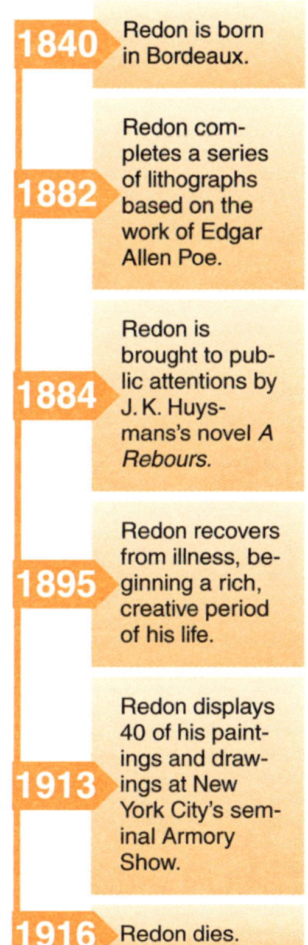

Odilon Redon was born to a Bordeaux merchant and his American wife in 1840. Since young Odilon was frequently sick, he spent his earliest years apart from his immediate family, being sent to live with an uncle on the family's wine-growing estate in the Medoc countryside. Left alone much of the time, Redon became an avid student of nature. After a "miracle cure," performed at a local church, the 11-year-old boy moved back with his family in Bordeaux and started school, including art instruction. He trained with various local masters, but his greatest influence was the lithographer Rodolphe Bresdin. In subject and form, Bresdin's engravings had a dark, otherworldly quality that anticipated surrealism. Other artists who influenced Redon during this period were Eugene Delacroix and Gustave Moreau. Redon shared with Moreau an interest in the mystical, and he admired Delacroix's use of color.

Two other interests had an even greater impact on the young Redon. His friend Armand Clavaud introduced him to the microscopic world of botany and to the "interior landscapes" found in the writings of Edgar Allen Poe and Gustave Flaubert. Redon drew much more from these influences than from his training at the École des Beaux Arts in Paris, where he remained for only a brief period. Reacting against the academic, realist approach to art—and exploring his fascination with the fantastic and macabre—Redon embarked on a period where he created many bizarre, mystical works of art. Working in charcoal and later in lithography, he eschewed color for the darker ambiguity he admired in Rembrandt's shadows and in enigmatic works like Albrecht Dürer's *Melancholia*.

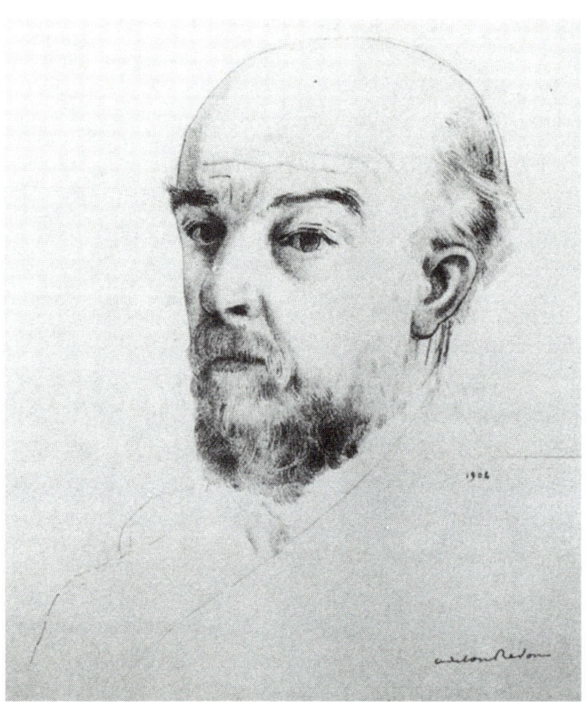

Odilon Redon, self-portrait

In a period that would last roughly two decades, Redon created a series of lithographs exploring subjects with a penchant for mystery. Many of these lithographs depicted the impact of the dream world on daily life or the origin and destiny of humanity as Redon saw it. Using nature as a reference point, he alternated finished with unfinished portions of the work, populating an ambiguous landscape with strange creatures, such as plants with human heads. Typical of this period is a lithograph entitled *The Balloon Eye* (1882) from his series *À Edgar Poe*. Instead of taking a literal approach to Poe, Redon attempted to recreate the mysterious, foreboding atmosphere of a Poe story. In the foreground is a dark, alien landscape with a balloon drifting over it. A large eyeball points skyward from the surface of the balloon amid a radiant sky fringed with dark clouds. These incongruous images are disturbing for the viewer. It is not hard to see why, a generation later, the surrealists cited Redon's work as a key influence.

"[I am] putting the logic of the visible in the service of the invisible."

Jean-Louis Ferrier in *Art of the Century*, 1988

Redon chose to work alone and did not closely associate with other artists. With his idiosyncratic approach, he, like so many other artists in similar circumstances, might easily have worked and died in obscurity. Redon's life departed from this familiar script only when, by quirk of chance at the age of 44, his work was brought to public attention by a most unlikely source—a scandalous novel. *A Rebours*, a popular novel by the symbolist J.K. Huysmans, revolved around a dissolute aristocrat who, incidentally, collected paintings by an obscure artist named Redon. With the publication of this novel, Redon became associated with symbolism. He sympathized with the symbolists' quest to bring together the spiritual world and the world of the senses. During the 1880s, Redon participated in discussions with other symbolist writers, such as Stéphane Mallarmé, and he exhibited with other symbolist painters. Though he found acceptance with them and had an important impact on younger symbolist painters such as Paul Gauguin, he re-

Symbolism

In symbolist literature, associated with late 19th-century France, writers convey their meaning indirectly, through symbols, in order to evoke and suggest rather than define. Among the many writers giving voice to symbolist ideas was Stéphane Mallarmé, in his 1897 *Divigations* (Ramblings). In art, too, symbolism denied that the purpose of painting and other media was simply to represent the subject as naturally as possible. Odilon Redon, moving beyond impressionism, celebrated the nonliteral, and in his charcoal drawings and lithographs used art to tap into the mythical, prereflective, imaginative, and emotional, attempting to let the unconscious speak in a way that, he believed, faithful reproduction of the surface appearance of things could not. Paul Gauguin and Émile Bernard, breaking from what they regarded as the analytic approach of impressionism, collaborated in the use of bright color and decorative patterns, a style they called symbolist. Gauguin saw art as a kind of language, indeed a more fundamental kind than words, and his art during this period, such as *Where Do We Come From? Who Are We? Where Are We Going?* (1897), reflects this view. Gauguin also helped mount the first symbolist exhibition, in Paris in 1889. Inspired by Gauguin and by Maurice Denis, a group called the Nabis (from the Hebrew *navi:* prophet) also rejected impressionism's adherence to nature and sought to take great freedom with color, believing that art is not a reporting of nature but a result of the way an artist converts nature into personally meaningful symbols. Key among the Nabis were Pierre Bonnard, Paul Ranson, Paul Sérusier, and Édouard Vuillard.

Despite that era's open discussions of the idea of symbolism and the fact that some artists adopted the name as their own, it is difficult to draw a line between symbolism, post-impressionism, and other movements of the late 19th century. Various artists such as Pierre Cécile Puvis de Chavannes, James Ensor, Ferdinand Hodler, and Edvard Munch may also be classified as symbolists. What connects these artists is not what they embrace but what they reject; not their precise use of symbols, but the general movement away from representation, including greater freedom with color and form. As such, symbolism is the forerunner of 20th-century styles such as fauvism, expressionism (especially through Munch), and surrealism.

mained a private figure—a "painter's painter"—largely unappreciated by critics and the general public.

This scenario would change around the turn of the century, when a newer generation of painters came to admire Redon. Meanwhile, Redon's work underwent a transformation. During the 1890s, Redon added vivid color and changed subject matter in his repertoire. Trading in charcoal and lithography for oils and pastels, he chose a wider array of subjects to depict, including flowers and scenes from mythology. Events in his personal life—overcoming a religious crisis and serious illness—fueled the happier outlook evident in his newer work. He did not abandon the ambiguous and fantastic nature of his earlier work, but in works such as *Flowers* (1903) he merged his earlier appreciation for shadow and mystery with new vitality, through imaginative use of color and radiant light.

The final two decades of Redon's life were filled with triumphs. The poet and painter Maurice Denis touted his influence and included him in his *Homage to Cezanne* alongside other leading artists. Henri Matisse cited him as inspiration for his flower paintings. Major modern art exhibitions, like New York City's groundbreaking Armory Show in 1913, devoted significant space to his paintings. In the end, although Redon never abandoned his preference for privacy, he gained acceptance with a public more accustomed to experimentation. Instead of fading into obscurity, his work found its way into major collections and found expression in the jarring images of the surrealists he influenced. Instead of dying an obscure artist, he lived to appreciate his success and the affirmation of his life's work. ◆

Rembrandt

July 15, 1606–October 4, 1669 ● Painter

Rembrandt van Rijn was born in Leiden, Holland, to a wealthy miller, the family's name, van Rijn, being derived from the proximity of their home to the Rijnmill malt mill. As a child he studied at the Leiden Latin School but as an adolescent was only briefly enrolled at the university as his parents soon realized that his painting skills were worthy of greater attention. At the age of 15 he was allowed to enter the workshop of the architectural painter Jacob Issacz van Swanenburgh, with whom he served a three-year apprenticeship, which gave him only an elementary technical training. The next six months spent with the painter Pieter Lastman were more beneficial and kindled in him an ambition to paint historical and biblical subjects. He also did numerous portraits of members of his family, and, somewhat unusually, often chose old people as models for his portraits.

In 1631 a desire for wider opportunities took him to Amsterdam, where he moved in with the dealer and painter Hendrik van Uylenburgh and began to establish a reputation as a

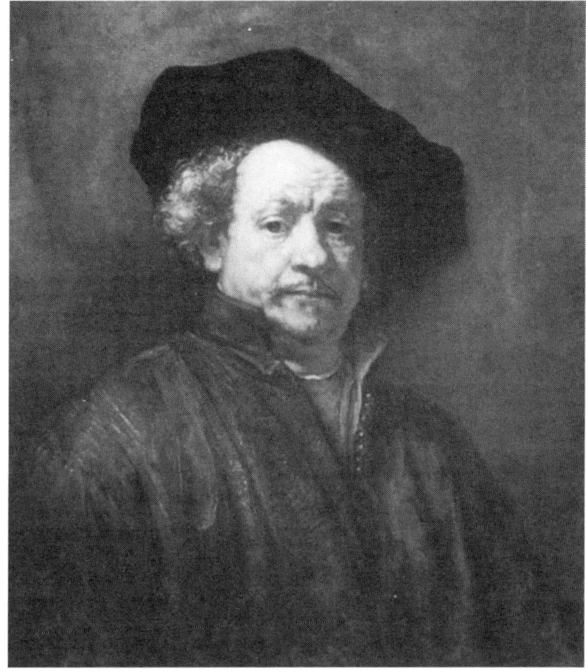

Rembrandt, self-portrait, 1660

portrait painter. His first large-scale group portrait, the famous *The Anatomy Lesson of Dr. Tulp,* which now hangs in the Mauritshuis in The Hague, was painted at the age of 26, and proved his ability to surpass all his contemporaries in Amsterdam in the dramatic vividness of his work. His fame increased steadily, climaxing at the end of the decade. Marriage to Saskia van Uylenburgh also served to improve his standing as he came into a substantial sum of money that helped him extend his contacts in the city. He greatly enjoyed his wealth and prestige and was apt to indulge his extravagant taste, impulsively collecting objects of art and curiosities. His wife, whom he adored, and whom he represented, sometimes somewhat raucously, in his paintings, seems to have encouraged his tendency to ostentatiousness.

In 1639 Rembrandt purchased a large house (now a museum of his etchings) that strained his financial resources to the limit and contributed to his eventual financial collapse. His personal life also took a turn for the worse. He painted many inhabitants of the Jewish ghetto, some of them incorporated into his biblical pictures. His mother died in 1640 and Saskia in 1642, just after the birth of their only surviving child, Titus. Rather than deterring his career, however, adversity seems to have purified and refined his outlook and infused his works with a heightened sensitivity to humanity, which was reflected in a move from baroque theatricality to more natural simplicity in his work. Titus, to whom he was devoted, appeared in many of the biblical paintings, while a frequent model for his perception of womanhood became Hendrickje Stoffles, who entered his home as a servant but remained with him as his companion for the rest of his life.

His financial situation deteriorated and in 1650 he transferred his house to Titus and pleaded insolvency. The liquidation of his property and the sale of his paintings at prices below their value did not relieve the strain. Titus and Hendrickje

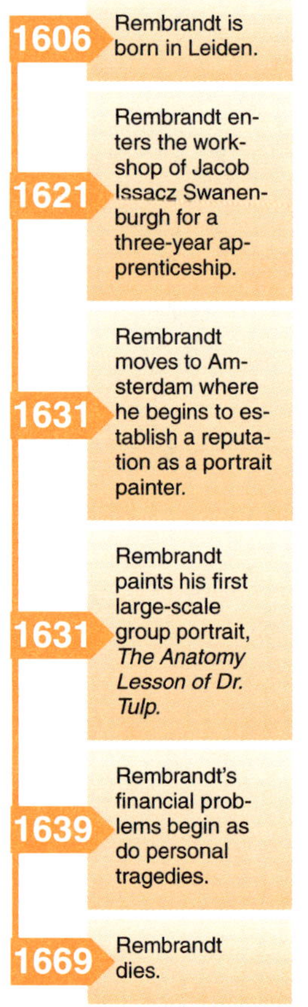

came to the rescue with a business relationship whereby they made Rembrandt their employee and they sold his works of art, allowing him to avoid the creditors while earning something from his own work.

Hendrickje did much to create a positive atmosphere in their home, but his previous wife's will, which stipulated termination of the small income from her estate if he remarried, prevented them from legalizing their union. Her death in 1663 was a further blow to him, and although Titus continued to care for him and manage the business, he too died several months after his own marriage, leaving Rembrandt alone with the young daughter he had fathered with Hendrickje. He was buried in an unknown rented grave.

Rembrandt was a temperamental man and a nonconformist who preferred the society of the common people to mingling with aristocrats and intellectuals. Unlike other painters of his generation who yearned for Italy, he preferred to remain close to home and fully explore his immediate surroundings. Considered the outstanding painter of the Dutch school, and one of the greatest of all time, he is famous for his treatment of light and shade, his portraits, particularly of the aged, and a gift for rendering common objects, ordinarily seen as ugly, with beauty. He is also admired for his etchings. His earliest pictures, *Saint Paul in Orison* and *Saint Jerome*, were painted in Leiden, but most of his work was done in Amsterdam after he settled there in 1631. His most famous works include *Presentation in the Temple*, *Anatomy Lesson*, *The Night Watch*, *Woman Taken in Adultery* and *The Good Samaritan* as well as self-portraits. ◆

Renoir, Pierre-Auguste

FEBRUARY 25, 1841–DECEMBER 3, 1919 ● PAINTER

Pierre-Auguste Renoir was born in Limoges, France, son of a tailor, Léonard Renoir, and a seamstress, Marguerite Merlet. Young Renoir would normally have been expected to follow in his parents' practical footsteps, but when he turned 13 he became an apprentice in a porcelain factory. It is not certain how long he remained at the factory, but already by 1860 he had decided to become a painter and was taking steps toward fulfilling his ambition. That year the 19-year-old Renoir

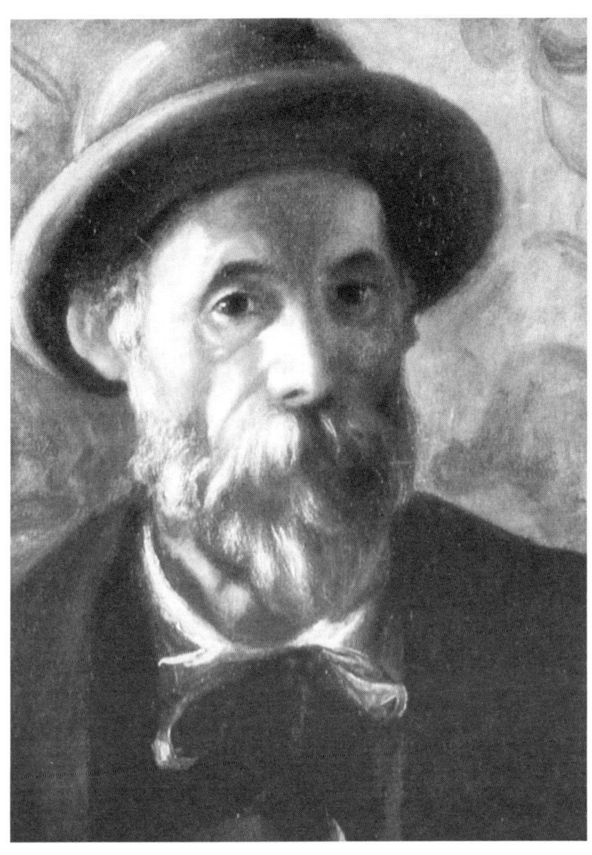

Pierre-Auguste Renoir, self-portrait, c. 1910

began visiting the Louvre museum to refine his skills and techniques in the time-honored manner of copying the paintings of the great masters on display there.

Although the young artist had the discipline to establish a private training regimen, he knew he would eventually need a formal teacher. In 1861 he began visiting the studio of the prominent Charles Gleyre and met another painter-in-training, Claude Monet. In 1862 he was accepted to the École des Beaux-Arts. The first major influences on Renoir's work were the landscape artists of the Barbizon School, so named because they routinely worked from nature in the Barbizon District in the north of France.

The young artists of Renoir's circle in the 1860s were fond of meeting at the Cafe Guerbois, where they shared their insights in technique and style. Members of this group included Monet, Alfred Sisley, and Frédéric Bazille, who together with Renoir are credited with founding the impressionist movement. This association proved inspirational to the young Renoir, and in 1864 he had his first painting accepted for Salon exhibition—a portrait of the character Esmeralda from Victor Hugo's *Notre Dame de Paris*. The next year the inspiration from his circle was even more direct, when he exhibited a portrait of Alfred Sisley's father.

Although Renoir and his circle favored landscapes, it was portraiture that paid the bills, and Renoir painted many of these throughout the 1860s and 1870s to maintain a secure income. At first both he and Monet struggled financially—so much so that in the late 1860s they had to sleep in the studio of their better-funded friend, Bazille. During this period, this circle of friends found themselves briefly out of favor with the established art world, when all three had their submissions rejected by the Salon of 1867. The following year brought Renoir better luck, however, when *Lise with a Parasol* (1867), which

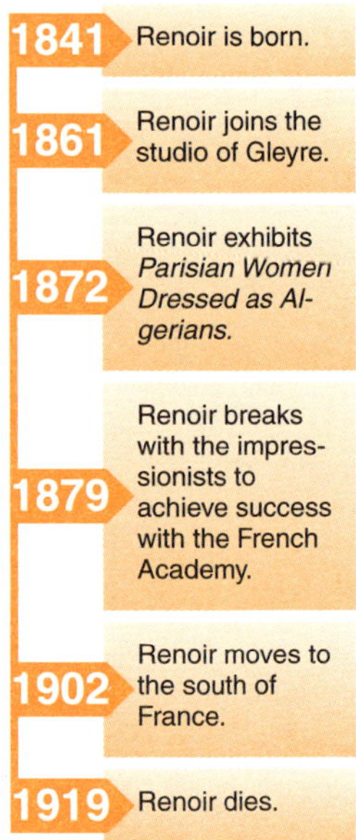

featured his mistress Lise Tréhot, won critical acclaim at the annual Salon exhibition. Riding the wave of success that followed, he succeeded in exhibiting paintings in the Salons of the next several years.

The Franco-Prussian War (1870–71) temporarily disrupted Renoir's artistic pursuits while he donned the uniform of the Tenth Cavalry, but immediately thereafter he returned to his creative pursuits. In 1872 he again submitted a work for exhibition. *Parisian Women Dressed as Algerians* was turned down by the official Salon, but it was exhibited that same year at the aptly-named Salon des Refusés, organized by painters who had run afoul of the Royal Academy of Art's admission standards for the regular Salon.

Renoir and the other members of the budding impressionist movement, tiring of their inability to gain the approval of the regular Salon's Academy judges, banded together to produce the first impressionist exhibition in 1874, which was repeated in 1876 and 1877. These independent exhibitions ensured that all the painters in the group would have a regular forum for presenting their works. Finally independent of the judgment of the mainstream art community, Renoir entered a highly productive period, boldly exploring new uses of color and new techniques in brushwork. He also began to gain the attention of collectors, and his dependence upon portrait commissions decreased.

"Renoir seems to have had the enviable ability to see anything as potentially of interest."
Wendy Beckett in *Sister Wendy's Story of Painting*, posted as part of *The Artchive* website

From 1864 to 1878, Renoir worked solidly within the impressionist style. In 1878, however, he broke decisively with this style, submitting a painting to the official Salon in that year and refusing to participate in the next two impressionist exhibitions (in 1879 and 1880). By this time Renoir felt he had explored impressionism as far as he could and began to look for a new style and form for expressing his artistic vision. In 1881, seeking new inspiration, he traveled to Italy, and on his return to France the following year he stopped in the south of France to work with Paul Cézanne, who, like Renoir, had exhibited with the impressionists before moving in a new direction.

Renoir had finally achieved some financial security, being sponsored by the prestigious art dealer Paul Durand-Ruel. This association had allowed the painter to take his first trip to Italy. It also freed him to make later journeys to the art museums of Amsterdam, Dresden, London, and Madrid, as well as to travel across the French countryside to draw inspiration from natural settings. His work increasingly won praise from the critics, and by the end of the century his reputation in France and abroad as an established artist was secure. In 1900 he was awarded the Legion d'honneur, and dealers clamored for his work.

Unfortunately, Renoir could not savor his success for long—in 1902 he began to suffer from rheumatism. To reduce the crippling pain in his joints, he moved to the gentler climate of Cagnes-sur-Mer. The change of climate did not alleviate his pain and stiffness, however, and by 1912 he was wheelchair-bound and remained so for the rest of his life. Still, he continued painting and began to explore the possibilities of sculpture as well. He achieved the fullest expression of his mature style in the last painting in his *Bathers* series, which he completed in 1919, the year of his death. ◆

Reynolds, Joshua

JULY 16, 1723–FEBRUARY 23, 1792 ● PAINTER

Joshua Reynolds was born in Plympton, England, son of a teacher and fellow at Balliol College, Oxford. Joshua's father, a clergyman, was a firm believer in education, so Joshua was exposed throughout his childhood to scholarship and the arts. Reynolds Senior wanted his son to become an apothecary, but Joshua had other plans. Upon leaving school in 1740 he went to London to begin formal painting apprenticeship with Thomas Hudson. He remained with Hudson's studio for three years but left to establish his own portrait studio in Devon in 1743.

Reynolds achieved some success right away, securing a number of valuable portrait commissions almost as soon as he set up his studio. His early paintings show a strong self-assurance and a willingness to experiment with the effects of light and dark on his canvases; this distinguishes his work from that of his mentor Hudson. By 1750, however, he was ready to expand his skills and, as was customary for artists of his day, set out for Italy to study the "great masters," among them Michelangelo, Raphael, Antonio Correggio, and Tintoretto. Reynolds learned much about style and technique from all these painters, but he was most influenced by Michelangelo, who is credited with inspiring the tradition of what he called the "Great Style" (or Grand Manner) in portraiture.

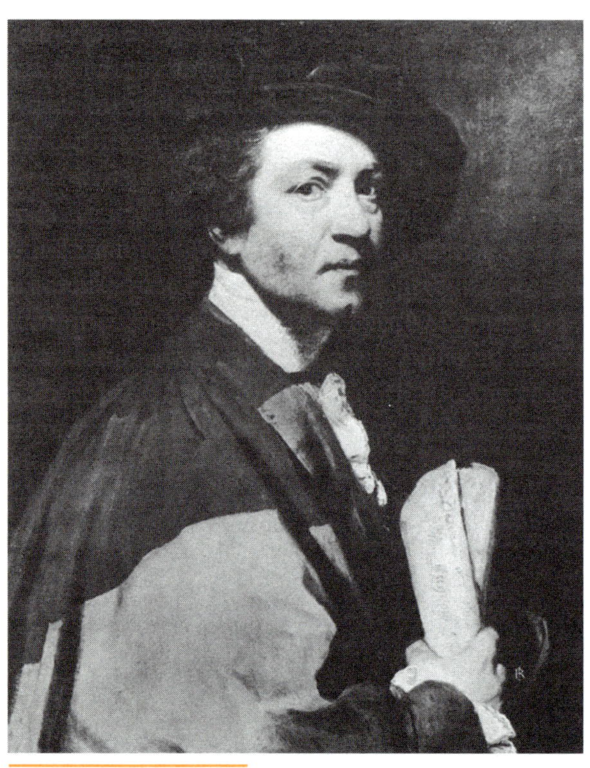

Joshua Reynolds, self-portrait, 1775

Reynolds remained in Italy for three years, visiting museums and private collections in Rome, Florence, Padua, and Venice. His notebooks of the trip show that he spent much time experimenting with poses and settings, as well as with practice sketches of how an arm or leg is articulated or the way fabric drapes on the human body. All of the paintings he made during this trip show his continued interest in manipulating light. Reynolds returned to England in 1753, and by 1758 he was in great demand as a portraitist, with as many as 150 sitters a year. His ability to convey animation and mood in an art form that was generally dismissed as "mere face painting" made him extremely popular, and he was considered to be the most innovative portraitist of the day.

For all portrait painters, success ultimately comes from securing the support of members of society's upper class. Reynolds courted royal patronage by painting the Prince of Wales, the Duke of Cumberland, and the Duke of York. While he failed to secure their patronage, he did gain the approval of the elites of his day. He was particularly popular among the literary types, and he produced portraits of the authors Laurence Sterne and Horace Walpole. He also drew sitters from the theater—his portrait of the great British actor David Garrick is considered one of his most outstanding efforts.

Reynolds was the Royal Academy's first president, and among his duties was to deliver a periodic lecture, called the *discourse,* to his fellow Academicians.

The year 1768 saw the founding of the Royal Academy of Arts, dedicated to establishing professional standards of training and to providing an annual forum for exhibiting works judged by its 40 members to represent the best in the nation. Reynolds was the Royal Academy's first president, and among his duties was to deliver a periodic lecture, called the *discourse*, to his fellow Academicians. In these speeches he presented his own philosophy about the discipline of painting and the other visual arts. For his service to the Royal Academy he was knighted by King George III in 1769, and he would remain its leader for the next 20 years, delivering 15 discourses during that time. It is in these lectures that Reynolds came to articulate the theory behind his "Grand Manner" style of painting.

By the late 1760s Reynolds was in such demand that he was driven to employ a small army of assistants to help him complete his paintings in return for the opportunity to develop their own skills and techniques. In 1771, James Northcote became one such assistant. He joined Reynolds's studio as an apprentice and went on to have a successful artistic career of his own, but perhaps his most important contribution to the arts is the biography he wrote about his mentor, *Memoirs of Sir Joshua Reynolds* (1813).

As Reynolds's gained ever greater favor within society and among the learned men of his time, so also did his local prestige grow. Though born to relatively humble parents, in 1773 he was made mayor of his hometown of Plympton. His success in politics is mirrored by his further success as an artist, as his reputation achieved international proportions—in 1775 he was elected to the academy of art in Florence. Ever the portraitist of the literary class, he actually joined their ranks in 1777 with his publication of the first seven of his *Discourses* to the Royal Academy.

The late 1770s mark the beginnings of Reynolds's declining health. In 1779 he suffered a stroke, which made it difficult for him to keep up his painting. He had another stroke in 1782, and by about this time his vision had begun to deteriorate. He continued to paint, although at a much reduced volume, for the remainder of the decade, and in fact in 1784 he completed one of his greatest portraits, a depiction of the actress Sarah Siddons in the role of the *Tragic Muse*. By 1790, however, he had largely ceased to work. He died in London in 1792. ◆

1723 Reynolds is born in Plympton, England.

1743 Reynolds establishes a portrait studio in Devon.

1750 Reynolds travels to Italy to study the great masters.

1769 King George III bestows knighthood on Reynolds.

1777 The first of Reynolds's *Discourses* are published.

1784 Reynolds completes the *Tragic Muse,* his portrait of Sarah Siddons.

1792 Reynolds dies in London.

Rodchenko, Alexander

NOVEMBER 23, 1891–DECEMBER 3, 1956 ● PAINTER AND SCULPTOR

Alexander Rodchenko was born in St. Petersburg, Russia, son of a prop designer and washerwoman. He studied art at the Kazan School (1910–14), then the Stroganov School. He was 23 when he returned to his native St. Petersburg from art school studies, and he joined Russia's

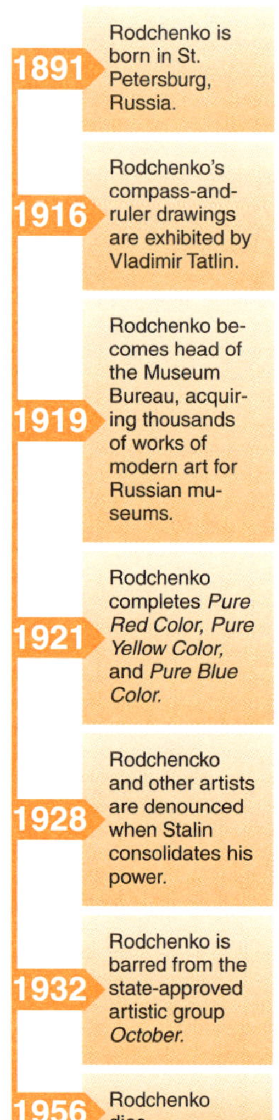

burgeoning avant-garde scene, establishing a close relationship with the futurist sculptor Vladimir Tatlin. Tatlin exhibited a series of 10 Rodchenko compass-and-ruler drawings in his show of 1916. These drawings showed Rodchenko's gift for technical detail and precision. World War I brought a pause in Rodchenko's artistic output after he was drafted as manager of a hospital train. Shortly before Rodchenko's discharge in December of 1917, revolution broke out in Russia, and the Bolsheviks seized power in the name of the proletariat (working class). The rhetoric of revolution favored new forms of art that would serve the goals of creating a new technology-based society for the common man, free of "bourgeois" values and aesthetics. The constructivists' shared goal was nothing short of transforming human beings through art.

Initially, Rodchenko continued experimenting with abstraction in painting and sculpture, with the goal of achieving a completely rational, objective mode of expression. His method was to isolate various visual elements—surface, texture, color, line—and explore variations in a series of similarly themed works. This exploration culminated in 1921 in a series of three monochrome paintings, *Pure Red Color, Pure Yellow Color,* and *Pure Blue Color.* Having taken abstraction to its logical conclusion—a flat, featureless plane of color—he turned to other forms of art, namely graphic art and photography, which he thought would more easily relate to revolutionary ideals. It is mostly this later work in graphic art, photography, and photo-collage for which he is remembered.

Rodchenko was among a circle of artists, writers, poets, and filmmakers searching for new ways to transform Russian society in the heady aftermath of revolution. He designed posters with revolutionary slogans, developed illustrations for leftist magazines, and originated a style of photo-collage that drew on current events and juxtaposition to give the art immediacy and impact. In *Revolutionary Manifesto* (1924), Rodchenko combined the photograph of a woman excitedly shouting with bold red, black, and white triangular elements and revolutionary slogans coming out of her mouth. The triangular graphics make it appear as though the woman is amplifying the slogans through a megaphone, giving the poster its dynamic appeal.

His work with photographs in graphic art and photo-collage stimulated Rodchenko's interest in developing his own photographic skills. He began taking pictures from dramatic angles of a wide array of subjects, from laborers to communist

Constructivism

The art movement known as constructivism began in Russia in the early 20th century. Influenced by cubism, futurism, and collage, and defined in works such as the "Realist Manifesto" (1920), authored by Vladimir Tatlin and sculptors Naum Gabo and Antoine Pevsner, the movement is marked by two broad goals. One was to achieve a perfect union between art and utility, while supporting communist, technological, and pro-worker ideas in the years following the Bolshevik revolution. Accordingly, media regarded as purely decorative or "bourgeois," such as canvas paintings, were often shunned. A second, related goal was to "construct" art, such as constructing abstract sculpture using plastic fragments, glass, wire, and sheet metal—elements associated with technology and industry. One example is Georgy Stenberg's *Spatial Construction/ KPS 51 NXI* (1921). While the artists associated with this movement would all emphasize space, form, and material, their aesthetic views differed somewhat: Tatlin would continue to insistent upon the need for art to contribute to human needs and practicality; Gabo affirmed art's spiritual essence regardless of its possible practical value. Other early constructivist adherents were El Lissitzky, an architect and engineer, and Aleksandr Rodchenko. Lissitsky openly embraced the use of art for state propaganda, as in his creation of posters with pro-worker messages. During the 1920s, Rodchenko moved away from painting toward practical ideas for furniture, photography, and poster and set design.

While constructivist goals were largely practical, its actual results outside of art were few. One example is Tatlin's gigantic model for a proposed "Monument to the Third International" (1920), a mammoth office building, which was architecturally unsound and so never built. Ideas for clothing and houseware also died on the drawing board.

Constructivism began to drift apart as its principal advocates faced a political environment less supportive of its work than in the utopian years immediately after the Bolshevik revolution. Many of its key figures traveled widely, however, spreading its influence to Germany, France, England, and the United States. Constructivist elements would endure in de Stijl and Bauhaus movements and in much 20th-century architecture and design, especially in the constructivists' desire to unite aesthetics and functionalism.

heroes such as the poet Mayakovsky. His goal was to present new, socially progressive perspectives. Mayakovsky shared these goals as a frequent collaborator on Rodchenko's projects. These included revolutionary posters, advertisements for state-run companies, covers for poetry books, and costumes and props for Mayakovsky's play *The Bedbug*.

Diverse artistic expression was characteristic of Rodchenko's work in the 1920s, when he undertook a number of different projects, from shooting films to designing a Worker's Club where people could spend leisure hours in a technologically sophisticated environment promoting collective values.

"Revolutionary art required the active participation of the viewer, who would be transformed by the effort of interpreting the work."
Alexander Rodchenko

Throughout this post-Revolution period, Rodchenko also occupied important administrative and teaching positions. Because of his close connections to key revolutionaries, he landed a position as head of the Museum Bureau in 1919. Through this influential position, he assembled a vast collection of modern art distributed throughout a network of museums. In 1920 Rodchenko was appointed as a teacher at the state art school. He was also a frequent contributor to constructivist magazines and a prominent member of artistic groups, like *October*, established to bridge gaps between artistic expression and a technology-centered, proletarian culture.

When Josef Stalin rose to power in the late 1920s, however, artistic expression underwent a rapid chill. As the initial euphoria of revolution faded, Soviet culture became increasingly conservative. Soviet politics, like art, was fiercely ideological and clique-oriented, with various circles accepted one year, then denounced as counter-revolutionary the next. Rodchenko, so recently a favorite of the government, first experienced this chill when in 1928 he was accused by the state-run newspapers of borrowing his photographic style from the "imperialist" West. In subsequent denunciations, his work was labeled "bourgeois formalism," an accusation that in the Soviet lexicon meant anything that was not in a state-approved style.

By 1932, Stalin had consolidated all artistic activity under the oversight of the Communist Party, which controlled everything from sales and commissions to exhibitions. Rodchenko was ejected from the *October* group and lost his income as a teacher when his school was closed. Forced to adapt to a state-sanctioned style or starve, Rodchenko made his peace with Stalin's regime by largely confining his work to photography in his last two decades. His most vital work behind him, Rodchenko spent his remaining years photographing circuses and parades and large state projects for the purposes of state propaganda. ◆

Rodin, Auguste

NOVEMBER 12, 1840–NOVEMBER 17, 1917 ● SCULPTOR

Auguste Rodin's father, Jean Baptiste Rodin, was a poorly paid clerk and an upright family man. Rodin had two older sisters, Clotilde from his father's first marriage who transgressed in some unknown way and was never mentioned after a certain point, and Marie, two years his elder, to whom he was devoted.

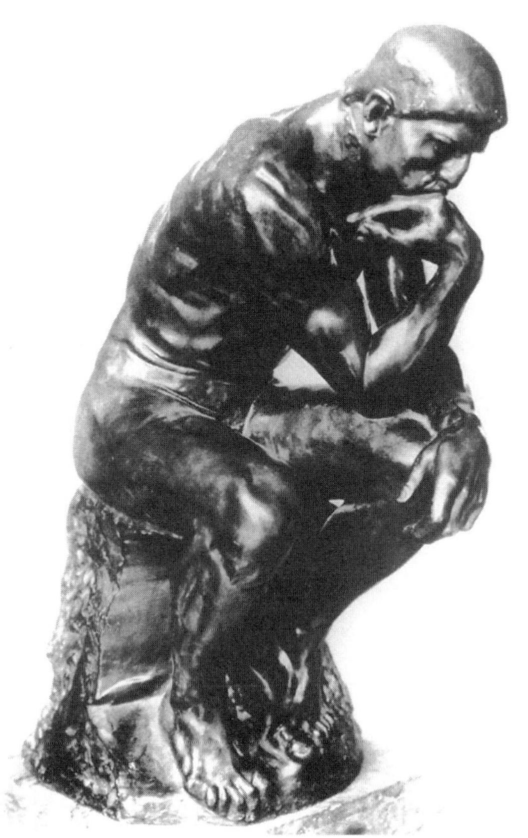

Rodin's *Thinker*, one of his masterworks.

Rodin was a poor student and at the age of nine was sent to a boarding school he described as akin to prison. There he spent most of his time drawing and was sent back home at 13, barely having learned to read and write. It was at this age that he discovered his passion. He wrote "I saw clay for the first time and I felt as if I were ascending into heaven." His father agreed to let him pursue sculpting as a profession and arranged an interview for him with a master who recognized the boy's talent and recommended he try to gain admittance to the state art school. While his talents were apparent, his style was too daringly naturalistic and not quite classical enough for the art establishment. He was rejected by the academy on three occasions.

Confident of his own abilities, Rodin continued sculpting and did whatever was necessary to support himself while at the same time attempting to continue his education on his own.

At the age of 20 Rodin faced a personal crisis. His sister Marie fell in love with a friend of his who paid her little attention and eventually announced his engagement to another woman. Marie teetered on the verge of insanity. She joined a nunnery for a short time and then underwent an unsuccessful operation and died. Rodin was heartbroken. He too attempted to escape by joining a monastery, but his basic unsuitability for such a life became apparent and he left before the end of two years.

Soon after he met Rose Beuret, who was to become his lifelong companion and who bore him an illegitimate son. A journey to Italy proved a turning point and his encounter with classical and baroque art brought a greater realism. He himself stated, "Michelangelo freed me from academicism."

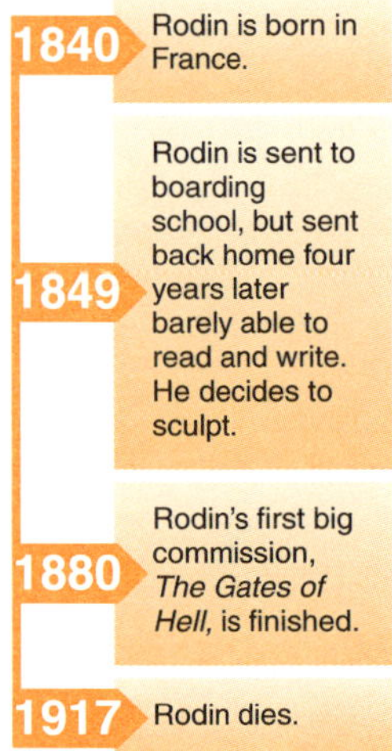

He worked for several years in Brussels with a partner and created the statue that brought him recognition. This statue, called *The Bronze Age*, depicted a Belgian soldier, so lifelike and human that the artist had to prove he had sculpted from a model rather than a mold. The sculpture is now in the Luxembourg Gardens in Paris.

Rodin's first big commission, *The Gates of Hell* (1880), was an all-consuming project that allowed him to unleash his imagination as never before. He worked quite prolifically at this period, turning out, among other works, his famed bust of poet Victor Hugo, and the Burghers of Calais, whose creation took so long that by the time it was completed the mayor of Calais could no longer afford to pay him.

By the 1880s his work was in great demand and buyers were willing to pay him high prices. His personal life became more involved as well, as he began a stormy and finally tragic relationship with a talented young sculptress named Camille Claudel. Around this period he began work on what is arguably his greatest piece, the brooding portrait of the author Honoré Balzac. This work was a particular challenge for the artist, as he had to work for the first time without a model and with little in the way of photographs. He continued with other portrait sculptures of famous figures including George Bernard Shaw, Georges Clemenceau, and Vaslav Nijinsky.

In his later years Rodin retired to the countryside with Rose, whom he eventually married, 25 days before her death. While still producing, his judgment in personal matters began to slip. He gained a reputation as a womanizer, succumbing to one woman, an American-born marquise who took advantage of the aging artist.

As he got older he grew more and more tyrannical toward his apprentices and at the same time increasingly childlike in his personal dealings. After his death, his coffin was draped in the French national colors, a rare tribute reserved for artists of his stature. Thanks to limited-edition bronze casting, many copies of his works are to be found throughout the world. Before his death he presented his own collection of his works to the French nation and they are housed in the Rodin Museum in Paris. ◆

Rossetti, Dante Gabriel

MAY 12, 1828–APRIL 9, 1882 ● PAINTER AND POET

Gabriel Charles Dante Rossetti was born in London to an Italian scholar father who taught at King's College, London. Already as a young man, he was passionately drawn to both writing and painting and would continue to pursue both loves for his entire life. He attended King's College School in London, then Henry Sass's Drawing Academy (1841). In 1845 he matriculated at the Antique School of the Royal Academy.

Rossetti had never been a particularly diligent student, and at the Academy he chafed at what he regarded as repetitious and boring training. Similarly, he did not last long working with Ford Madox Brown, although the two continued a long friendship and intellectual conversation. Again Rossetti moved on, to work with William Holman Hunt in 1848. With Hunt and several of his peers he formed the Pre-Raphaelite Brotherhood (PRB) in that same year.

Art critics note that Rossetti's ability as a painter was inferior to most of his fellow PRB members. Nevertheless, he became the group's leader, both by virtue of his charisma and inextinguishable ego, and by the fact that he not only practiced art and felt a youthful rebellion against established forms of art, but also was able to articulate an artistic vision that others could make their own. The members of the brotherhood preferred to take as their subject matter classical, biblical, or poetic themes, depicted in a more realistic manner that did not conform to the rules of the Academy of the day.

Dante Gabriel Rossetti, 1862

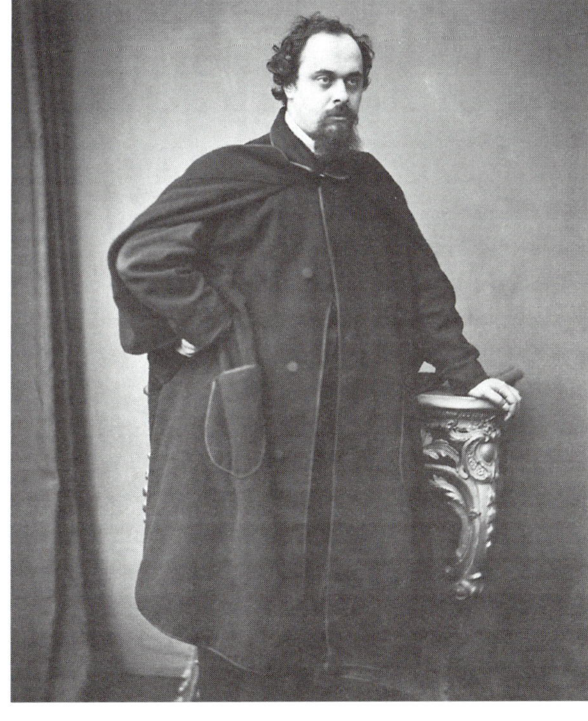

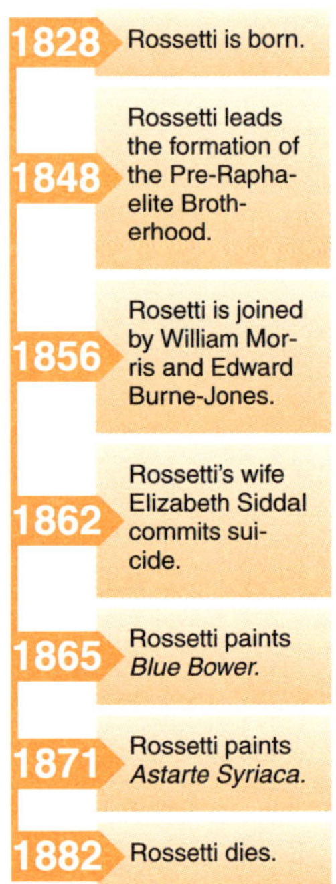

While the PRB name would make its mark in art history, many of its component pieces did not last much longer than Rossetti's earlier projects. The original members of the PRB disbanded within four years. Rossetti's magazine, the *Germ*, which was to be the organ for conveying his new vision for art, managed only four issues before ceasing publication.

Rossetti first exhibited his works in London—*The Girlhood of Mary Virgin* (1849) and *Ecce ancilla Domini!* (The Annunciation, 1850). Critics were merciless in their estimation, and unfortunately Rossetti possessed both a large ego and thin skin—he decided never again to participate in a public exhibition in London. Rossetti's style was almost naive, each figure imbued with great emotion and tension. In this sense his work can be seen as linked to later expressionism. He also introduced subtle symbolic touches in his work. While critics accustomed to greater technical skill were not immediately receptive to Rossetti, the prominent critic John Ruskin championed his work, in particular his watercolors. Ruskin convinced Rossetti to take a lectureship at London's Working Men's College, while introducing his work to influential art collectors.

Rossetti's earliest subject matter was largely drawn from well-known poets such as Shakespeare, Robert Browning, and his namesake, Dante. Later the Arthur legends appear more prominent. While detractors had scant praise for his compositional skills and formal technique, some came to recognize his keen ability with color. Rossetti's fame spread, and in 1856, William Morris and Edward Burne-Jones, two Oxford students, went to London to join Rossetti and study under him. These three and others soon had the opportunity to decorate the Oxford Union Building Debating Hall, and the style they developed in their renderings of Arthurian tales (as interpreted in Thomas Malory's *Morte d'Arthur*) led to a new and distinctive stage in the PRB style. The three would later join forces in a company that designed tapestries and furniture, as well as stained glass (as with Rossetti's 1861 *Parable of the Vineyard*).

Rossetti also continued to work in other media. The designs he contributed for a new edition of Lord Alfred Tennyson's *Poems* (1857) proved to be very popular, and many of his drawings show that, despite his tendency toward lack of discipline and rigor, he was capable of technically meticulous work. Despite these successes, Rossetti was about to face one of the greatest tragedies of his life. Anyone who views his paintings will quickly see the predominance of one face above all

The Pre-Raphaelite Brotherhood

In mid-19th-century England, the Italian artist Raphael was often held up as the ideal for young artists seeking formal training at the Royal Academy. The aspiring painter should follow certain rules about composition, light, and shadow in order to produce beautiful art. In the minds of a group of young Englishmen in the mid-1840s, this emphasis on static rules betrayed the innovative spirit and creativity of Raphael and other artistic geniuses. Also, emphasis on a single idea of beauty interfered with art's ability to represent truth, which for these men meant highly realistic depictions of earnest and significant themes. As a result, the members of this movement, the Pre-Raphaelite Brotherhood (PRB), turned away from common subjects such as still lifes and toward more lofty subjects, drawn especially from mythology, poetry, religion, and medieval folklore.

The PRB began in 1848 with young painters William Holman Hunt (*Valentine Rescuing Sylvia from Proteus,* 1851), John Everett Millais, and Dante Gabriel Rossetti at its core, along with painter James Collinson, critics William Michael Rossetti and Frederick George Stephens, and Thomas Woolner, a sculptor. For a short time they had their own journal, *The Germ,* which especially gave voice to D. G. Rossetti's poetry, and they exhibited their works as a group. At first, most critical reaction to them, as with their Royal Academy show in 1850, was unenthusiastic and even hostile. What the PRB considered natural, the critics often regarded as poorly composed, amateurish, and sentimental. Art critic John Ruskin's support of their work helped soften critical resistance, however. PRB paintings include Millais's *Isabella* (1849) and D. G. Rossetti's *The Meeting of Dante and Beatrice in Paradise* (1852) and the hauntingly lifelike *Il Ramoscello* (1865).

As a tightly-knit group, the first PRB lasted only about five years. Several other painters followed, however, including Edward Burne-Jones, Walter Howell Deverell, Arthur Hughes, and Frederick Sandys. PRB style influenced Gustave Moreau and symbolism, and later painters would adopt Rossetti's interest in medieval themes or the PRB interest in meticulous rendering of color and detail.

others, the beautiful Elizabeth Siddal, who was Rossetti's model throughout the 1850s and his wife as of 1860. In 1862, one year after giving birth to a still-born child, she committed suicide. Thereafter, Rossetti commemorated her with dozens of works, including *Beata Beatrix* (1864–70), the title referring to the blessed heavenly woman in the Italian poet Dante's *Divine Comedy*.

After this time, Rossetti continued a theme he had already begun—bust-length depictions, usually oil paintings, of individual voluptuous young women. Works in this style range from *Boca baciata* (1859) to *Blue Bower* (1865). These works proved popular, and as a result he became financially and socially secure.

"Rossetti ... never made a memorandum of anything in the world except the female face between 16 and 26."
William Bell Scott on Rosetti's favorite passion besides his art, in *Autobiographical Notes*, 1892, quoted on the *ArtMagick* website

Rossetti's personal charm and professional attainments ought to have signaled the end of his struggles for acceptance, but he was to face a crisis resulting from the other great love of his life, poetry. In 1870 his poetry was so strongly attacked that Rossetti—who had never learned to take criticism well—suffered a nervous breakdown, attempted suicide, and developed substance addiction. He then became much less prolific in his art. Toward the end of his life he continued to focus on women, pursuing his ideal of feminine beauty. His works in this vein included *Mariana* (1870) and *Astarte Syriaca* (1877). The model for this latter work was Jane Morris, in whose beauty Rossetti was as deeply engrossed as he had been, earlier, in Elizabeth Siddal's. Rossetti's art in this period also turned more introspective and somber. He died a mentally ill and broken man.

Rossetti's work was greatly admired by the French symbolists. He has also continued to be studied for his role as leader of the PRB and as a member of a family of extraordinary talent, including his brother, art critic William Michael Rossetti, and his sister, the brilliant poet Christina Rossetti. ◆

Rousseau, Henri

MAY 21, 1844–SEPTEMBER 2, 1910 ● PAINTER

Painter Henri Rousseau began his career at the end of an era in French art. Up to this time, to be taken seriously an artist was expected to follow the normal career path: early academic training and a period of apprenticeship with an accepted artist. If an artist wished to exhibit his works at the annual Salon, he first needed to submit his paintings for the approval of a jury of critics and established artists. Had Rousseau been forced to fulfill these requirements, his career would have ended before it began. Instead, Rousseau lived long enough to secure both critical and commercial success in the art world, despite being self-taught and working outside the formal academic paths.

Henri Rousseau was born in Laval, in northwestern France, to a solid, middle-class family. After conventional schooling, he served as a clarinet player in an army band. He spent his military years uneventfully, stationed in the western town of Angers and never seeing action. The lack of excitement then

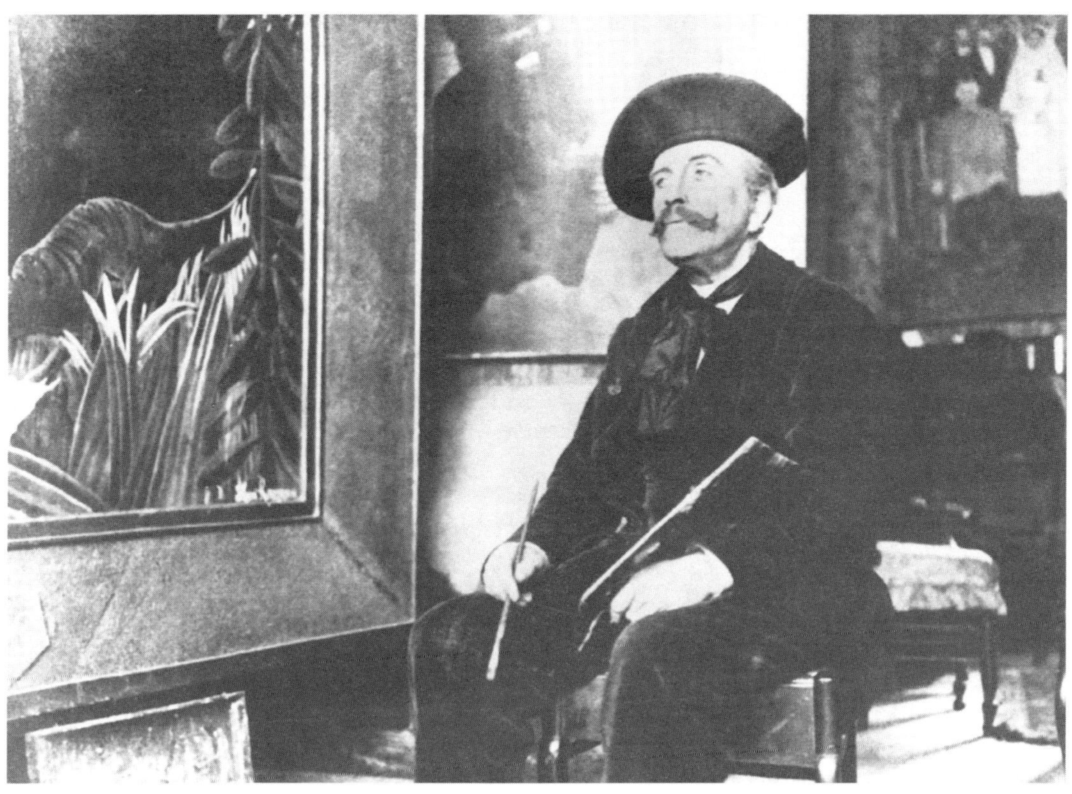

Henri Rousseau in his studio, 1904.

and later in his life, however, inspired Rousseau to make colorful claims of having been in the thick of military action in Mexico.

Rousseau left the army in 1869 and moved to Paris, where he eventually took a government job as a city gatekeeper, a minor position within the Customs Office. The job was not particularly interesting or challenging, and Rousseau may have turned to painting to relieve the long hours of tedium he spent at the city gates. In any case, he never received formal training in art, either as a schoolboy or by apprenticing himself to the studio of a recognized artist in the city.

The lure of the artistic life struck Rousseau somewhat late. In about 1884, while he was still working for the customs office, he secured a permit to work in the Louvre. He spent hours copying the famous paintings hanging there. Copying was, and still is, an important aspect of an artist's training—by attempting to master the styles and techniques of acknowledged masters, an aspiring artist learns to use these skills in his or her own work. Rousseau's lack of training earned him his reputa-

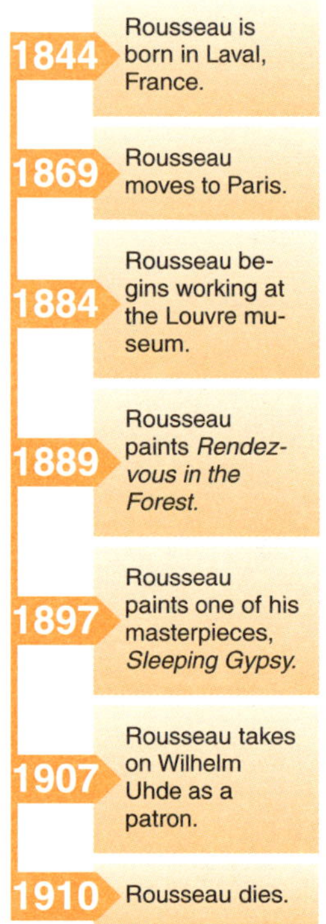

tion as the quintessential self-taught artist. However, the fact that he never formally studied art does not mean he failed to recognize the need to perfect his skill and his technique. From the very beginning, his work showed many of the elements that characterize his paintings throughout his career: a meticulous attention to detail, a fine if somewhat naive approach to composition, and a palette of bright, vibrant colors.

Rousseau took his own artistic efforts very seriously, and in 1885 he submitted his first paintings for public exhibition. He saw himself as working in the same tradition as such accepted painters as Paul Gauguin and Edgar Degas, but unfortunately the established artists and critics of the time were for the most part unimpressed with his efforts. His first exhibition submissions were shown at the newly founded Salon des Independants, which provided a free public forum for artists without requiring the prior approval of a jury. Although he attracted the attention of some avant-garde artists, his paintings were roundly ridiculed by the mainstream.

Undaunted by the critics, Rousseau insisted upon being taken seriously as an artist. He retired from his position with the Customs Office because it took too much time away from his painting, and he spent the next several years supporting himself by taking odd jobs. This was an extraordinary decision. At 41 years of age, he was no longer a young man, and to throw aside the security of a steady government job for the uncertain life of an independent painter demonstrates his profound commitment to his art.

Slowly he began to attract the attention and admiration of several of his more innovative contemporaries, including the popular Henri de Toulouse-Lautrec. Still, mainstream acceptance eluded him for many years, and even after he had left his job at the Customs House he was frequently dismissed as an amateur.

In 1893 Rousseau qualified for full retirement from employment, and from this time forward he lived almost entirely on the pension he had earned from his years as gatekeeper, supplementing his income by taking on occasional students. Finally free to devote himself entirely to his painting, he entered his most productive period. Over the next decade he exhibited his works regularly, and his perseverance finally began to pay off. By the turn of the century, on the strength of such works as *Rendezvous in the Forest* (1889), he had accumulated a following despite the disapproval of the established critics, and he could number among his supporters such fellow artists as Robert Delauney and Pablo Picasso. In 1907 his reputation was further strengthened through the efforts of his new patron, Wilhelm Uhde, a wealthy and respected collector and art critic.

Rousseau would have only a very few years to enjoy his newly enhanced reputation. Uhde's support brought the artist a substantial increase in the sales of his work, and public opinion of his paintings now became more positive. Sadly, in 1910 Rousseau contracted an infection, and he died later that same year.

While the old academic and peer-review system may have discriminated against self-taught artists, its judgments against Rousseau were not always wrong. Although Rousseau's paintings are powerfully affecting, they exhibit some technical problems the artist never overcame. Even his famous piece *Sleeping Gypsy* (1897) shows that Rousseau never fully mastered aspects of representation. But these shortcomings are offset by the artist's ability to infuse his canvases with a dreamy, allegorical quality through his use of composition and, especially, vibrant color. Picasso, for one, praised him as a forerunner of surrealism, while Wassily Kandinski credited Rousseau as the founder of an entirely new form of realism. ◆

"Rousseau tried to paint in the academic manner of such traditionalist artists as Bouguereau and Gérôme, but it was the innocence and charm of his work that won him the admiration of the avant-garde."

On Henri Rosseau's style, as quoted on the *WetCanvas* website

Rubens, Peter Paul

JUNE 28, 1577–MAY 30, 1640 ● PAINTER

Born in Siegen, Westphalia, Paul Rubens was taken as a child to Antwerp, where he received an education in the humanities and a knowledge of six languages. His mother was a widow and could not continue to provide for her children, forcing him to stop studying and enter the service of the countess of Lalaing. Very little detail is known about Rubens's personal life; he hid personal affairs from the public, and it is not known why he decided to become a painter, or when he began to study. His first two masters were Adam van Noort and Octave van Veen.

In 1599 Rubens earned the title of master of the Brotherhood of Saint Luke in Antwerp, which entitled him to sell his own works. He dreamed, however, of going to Italy to study

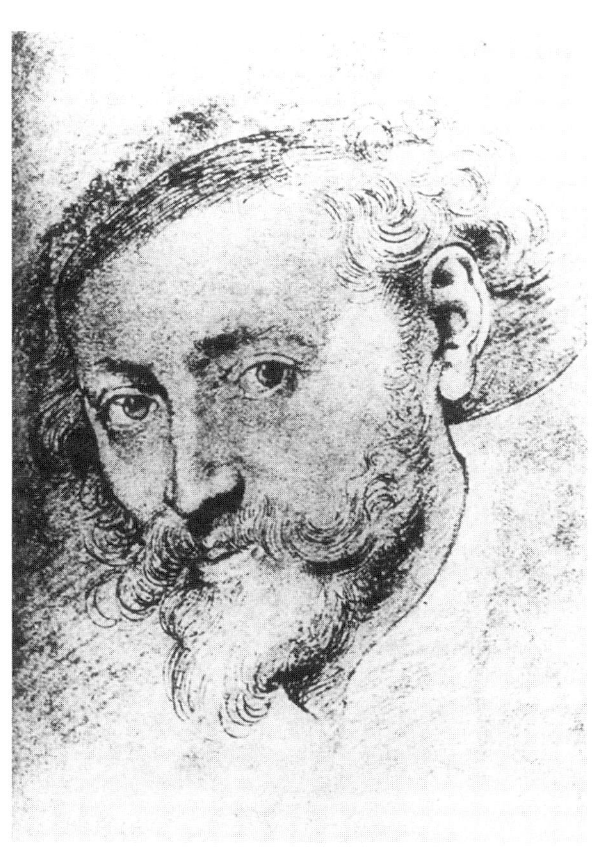

Paul Rubens, self-portrait

classical art and the work of the classical masters, and in 1600 he set out. He made his way to Venice to study the works of Titian and Veronese and almost immediately had the good fortune to enter the service of Vincento Gonzaga, the duke of Mantua. His duties as court painter and gentleman of the court for the duke required painting portraits of the prince and his family, copying famous works for the duke's gallery, and decorating various rooms in the palace.

In 1603 he was put in charge of a shipment of presents to the Spanish king and in 1605 sent on a mission to Philip II of Spain, thus establishing himself as a diplomat whose intellect, polish, and linguistic accomplishments suited him admirably to the task. His diplomatic assignments did not detract from his painting career and while in Madrid he painted many portraits of the Spanish nobility and several historical subjects. He settled in Antwerp and was appointed court painter in 1609 to Archduke Albert and his wife Isabella. His great triptych, the *Erection of the Cross*, in the cathedral of Antwerp, established him as the leader of the Flemish school of painting. It was followed by the equally impressive triptych *The Descent from the Cross*. In 1622 he was invited to France by Marie de Médicis, the queen mother, who was decorating the palace of the Luxembourg in Paris, for which he completed 21 large works (now in the Louvre). In 1628 he was sent by Isabella on a diplomatic mission to Philip IV of Spain and in 1629 appointed envoy to Charles I of England, his mission being a peace treaty. His negotiations were skillfully accomplished. While there he also completed the painting *Peace and War*, which hangs in the National Gallery in London, a portrait of the king and queen as Saint George and Cleolinde, which is on display in Windsor, and sketches for the apotheosis of James I for the banquet hall in Whitehall. He was knighted by both Charles I and Philip IV.

Baroque

The term baroque (perhaps from the Italian *barocco,* meaing illogical, bizarre) covers a vast number of various artists, from about 1600 to 1750, in a number of countries and media, including painting, architecture, and sculpture. Like fauvism, the term was originally intended as an insult, suggesting that certain kinds of art were bizarre outgrowths of the classical style. Baroque painting tends to be highly realistic. The people in baroque paintings seem vivid and real, because subjects are rendered with close attention to clothing, facial structure, and emotion. Caravaggio was a key baroque figure, depicting people from all areas of life in realistic ways, as in his *Martyrdom of Saint Matthew* (1600). Baroque architecture features strong contrasts of light and color, giving the viewer the sense of being in an emotion-filled and exciting space. Giovanni Lanfranco pioneered architectural illusionism, the sense that the viewer is not looking merely at a work of art but a boundless space, as in his *Assumption of the Virgin* at the dome of the church of Sant' Andrea della Valle in Rome. Much baroque art was commissioned by the Roman Catholic Church, especially in reaction to the earlier mannerist style that was regarded as too irreverent. The intense religious mysticism of baroque style is also seen in Lorenzo Bernini's *Ecstasy of Saint Theresa* (1652), a sexually charged depiction of the great Spanish Catholic mystic.

Baroque was centered in Italy but influenced several other countries. In Antwerp, now in Belgium, Peter Paul Rubens drew from Italian influences to produce several masterpieces; his series *The Life of Marie de Médicis* (1625) is one of his greatest works. These works show the baroque taste for realistic depiction, vivid color, and dramatic poses. Anthony van Dyck, his student, was also skilled at realistic depictions. The Dutch genius Rembrandt van Rijn is also important in baroque style.

Some historians attempt to organize baroque into three types. The first is classicism, as with the works of the Carracci family (Annibale Carracci painted the ceiling of the Farnese Palace Galleria). A second style, realism, is associated with figures such as Caravaggio. A third, baroque proper, is seen in Pietro da Cortona's ceiling at the Palazzo Barbeini. Whatever definition one uses, the movement signals a greater celebration of the intensity of human spirit, drama, vitality, and emotion than earlier classical styles enjoyed, but with greater realism than the mannerist movement.

Rubens continued to receive ambitious commissions from various parts of Europe although during the last decade of his life much of the actual painting was executed by his pupils. He is the outstanding representative of the baroque school of painting, and his work is marked by its dramatic power and structure filled with movement. He introduced the Flemish naturalist tradition into classic baroque, with its style, subject matter, and colors. His subjects were of the most varied, including portraits, biblical scenes, book illustrations, allegories, historial and mythological events, nudes, and everyday life of his times. His nude figures are particularly characteristic with their ample, voluptuous flesh. His landscapes paved the way for the 19th-century romantics. His influence on European art was great down to the end of the 19th century while in French art the dominant style at the end of the 17th century was known as "Rubensism." ◆

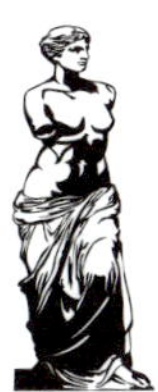

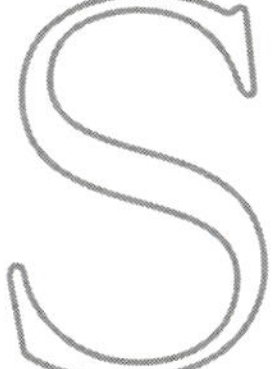

Schwitters, Kurt

JUNE 20, 1887–JANUARY 8, 1948 • ARTIST

Multi-media artist Kurt Schwitters was born in Hannover, Germany. He attended the prestigious Kunstacademie in Dresden from 1909 until 1914. While the First World War somewhat interrupted his art training, during which time he served as a clerical officer, he was able to find work as a draftsman. Schwitters was a prolific artist, and in the 1910s a variety of influences informed his work. Some pieces are naturalistic, others impressionistic, and still others move toward expressionism.

By 1918 Schwitters had aligned himself with the *Der Sturm* (The Storm) movement, contributing creative work to its magazine and exhibiting with other *Der Sturm* artists, such as Paul Klee. Both his early art and poetry showed his interest in taking pre-existing objects (seemingly random bits of conversation or printed matter, trash from the streets) and forming them into art. He saw this practice as a metaphor for the transformation of decayed German culture into something new and beautiful. Around this time, he began adopting the word "Merz" (randomly derived from the German *kommerz*) to refer to his art and the theory underpinning it.

In 1920 Schwitters began the first of three *Merz-bau* constructions. These were truly ambitious, if unwieldy, enterprises. He would take any trash he found interesting and add it to an ever-expanding construction located in his home. It ballooned to such a size that it outgrew the room in which it was located.

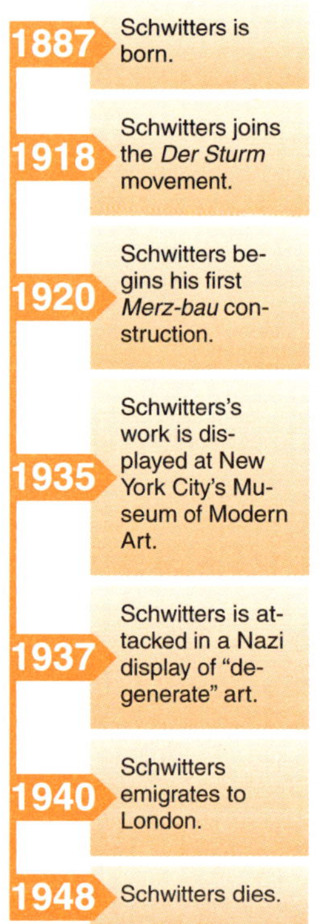

The *Merz-bau* are good examples of Schwitters's approach to art—incorporating the ordinary or discarded into the beautiful. *Merz* was also the name of Schwitters's magazine, which was published from 1923 to 1932 and served as a sounding board for artists from various modern movements, including de stijl and dada. Finally, he produced *Merz* collages on a much smaller scale than the constructions.

What is remarkable about Schwitters's art in this period is that, although he used highly modern and innovative styles—and even embraced elements of chaos and chance—he was regarded by many of his contemporaries as too conservative. Schwitters believed that art could be made from simple and everyday objects such as string, wire, and discarded newspapers, and that many people had the capacity to produce art—it was not the sole property of a privileged few. On the other hand, he had no intention of abandoning the idea of art and beauty. He was challenging received ideas about what was beautiful and artistic, but he strongly believed that his own work was art. Moreover, he was much less overtly involved in political disagreements than many of his more enthusiastic contemporaries. As a result, in a demonstration of political power more than artistic ideals, Richard Huelsenbeck, the head of the dada movement in Berlin, actually called for Schwitters to be excluded from dada activities in that city.

Fortunately, Schwitters was more interested in pursuing his own artistic vision than in seeking to destroy the competing visions of others, and he did not let this disagreement sour his relation to dada. His magazine continued to feature dada ideas, and he maintained close working relations with other prominent dada artists and teachers.

Throughout the 1920s, Schwitters experimented with a number of different styles and movements. From his association with Theo van Doesburg came de stijl influences in some of his *Merz* pictures of that period. He also joined with abstractionists and constructivists, including El Lissitzky, and in 1932 joined the *Abstraction-Création* movement based in Paris, continuing a gradual movement toward simpler, less chaotic arrangements.

Schwitters's work was gaining a wider audience, but not always to his benefit. While the Museum of Modern Art featured his work in 1935, just two years later another exhibition, the Nazi exhibition of "degenerate" art, included his art as a way of signaling that Schwitters was a threat to the ideals of the Third Reich. The rise of the Nazi party in Germany spelled trouble for Schwitters, as for so many other artists of his day, and accordingly in 1937 he fled Germany for Lysaker, Norway. With the German invasion of that country in 1940, he fled again to England. England did not immediately welcome him—he spent time in an internment camp, and according to some stories, he was so passionate about his need to create that he formed sculptures from leftover scraps of food. After this series of displacements, however, he was greeting warmly by the modern art community in London. He moved yet again, to Ambleside in the picturesque Lake District, and as he had done in Germany and Norway, again began to create a *Merz-bau*, which however was not completed before his death.

"Every form is the frozen instantaneous picture of a process."
Kurt Schwitters, quoted in the *Dictionary of Art*, Volume 30

Although Schwitters was constantly aligned with various modernist movements, his belief in nature was much stronger than that of many of his contemporaries. We see his clash with Huelsenbeck not only in Huelsenbeck's rejection of him, but also in Schwitters's own writings, such as *Die Zwiebel*, where Huelsenbeck's Marxist materialism is absent, in favor of the romantic idea of the artist as spiritual figure. Moreover, it cannot be said that Schwitters saw himself as outside or above the world of capitalist commerce. Throughout his life he turned to more conventional forms of art, such as portrait painting, as a source of reliable income. His advertising agency, formed in the 1920s, was a commercial success. Schwitters is best seen not as a rebel against traditional views of economics or art, but as one who tried through his writings and his many different artistic media to explore new possibilities in art for conveying the spontaneity and richness of the world. ◆

Seurat, Georges

DECEMBER 2, 1859–MARCH 29, 1891 ● PAINTER

Georges Seurat was born in Paris, son of a customs official. It appears that Seurat had little art training as a youth, though in his teens his uncle, Paul Haumonté, gave him a few basic lessons. In 1875 he began attending lessons with sculptor Justin Lequien, where he learned about the relation between drawing and sculpture. At that stage in his development, he was interested in the paintings of Jean-Auguste-Dominique Ingres; he pursued this interest in early

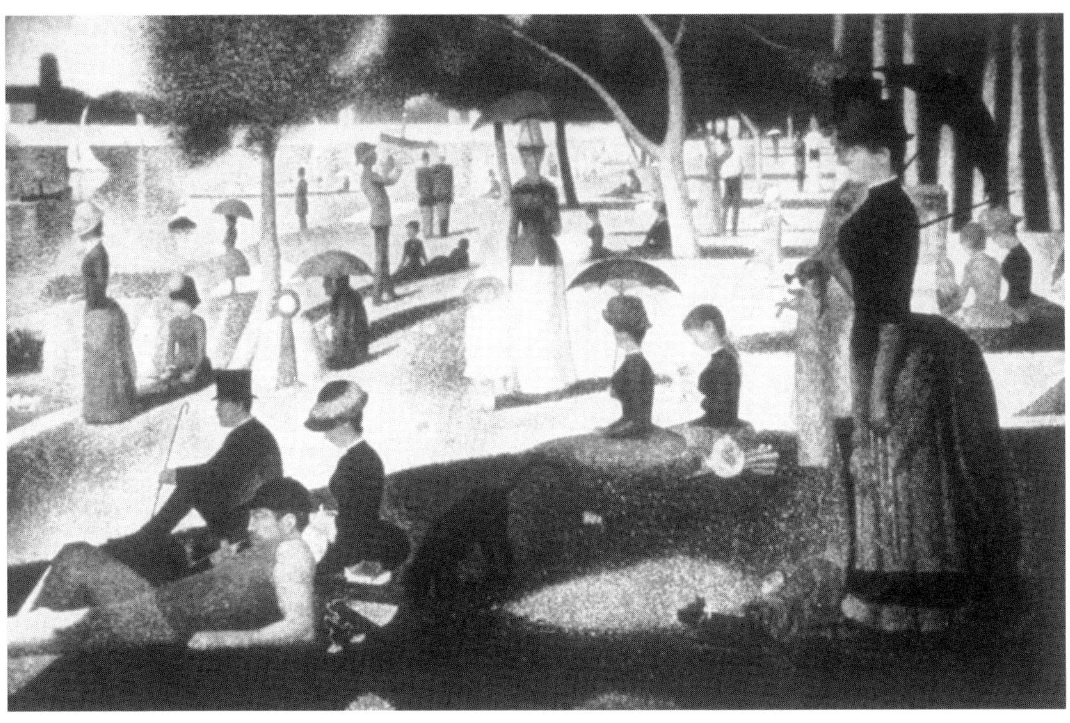

Georges Seurat's *A Sunday Afternoon on the Island of La Grande Jatte*, 1886.

1878 when he began training with former Ingres student Henri Lehmann, teacher at the École des Beaux-Arts. For all of Ingres's genius as a painter, however, he did not leave a legacy of great followers, and Lehmann proved to be the kind of derivative academic who was neither a first-rate painter nor an inspiring teacher. Seurat left the École by the end of 1879. He then turned for inspiration to Pierre Puvis de Chavannes, a renowned French muralist whose use of non-natural color and simplified forms would soon inspire French symbolist painters.

While Seurat was influenced by painters, including the works of Peter Paul Reubens and Bartolomé Esteban Murillo, his own artistic vision, based on rigorous reasoning about color, was also influenced by scholarly works on the nature of color and form. Early important treatises laying the groundwork for his original thinking include Michel Eugène Chevreul's *De la loi du contraste simultanée des couleurs* (*Of the law simultaneous contrast of colors*; 1839), David Sutter's comments on composition in "Les phénomènes de la vision" (1880), and Charles Blanc's *Grammaire des arts du dessin* (*Grammar of drawing arts*; 1867), from which Seurat derived ideas about color complementarity. Seurat also experienced a revelation when he at-

Pointillism

Nineteenth-century impressionist painters achieved remarkable results, but to some painters their approach seemed too relaxed, chaotic, and random in form and color. Neoimpressionism is the name given to artists who strove to use greater precision in various aspects of their art. Because of the prominence of neoimpressionist Georges Seurat, the movement is largely identified with one style he perfected—pointillism. In pointillism, the painter uses only small, distinct strokes or bits (points) of primary colors, meticulously arranged in contrasting clusters. When seen from a distance, the painting appears to the viewer as a brilliant display of a coherent picture, in a range of colors different from those perceived at close range. Such technique required careful attention to color theory and the process by which the human eye perceives color. "Divisionism," a term sometimes treated as identical to pointillism, applies to the color theory underlying this careful process; pointillism pertains most properly to the technique, the use of dots or points.

Seurat's *Bathing at Asnières* appeared at the Salon des Indépendants exhibition in Paris (1884), showing his use of pointillism and focus on the deliberate composition of the work's form. Another major work is his massive *Sunday Afternoon on the Island of La Grande Jatte* (1886). Pointillism remained primarily a French phenomenon, and for all its admirers it never attracted a large number of practitioners; other important figures are Henri-Edmond Cross, Camille Pissarro, Theodoor van Rysselberghe, and most significantly, Paul Signac. Pointillism's primary influence was on French fauvism and surrealism, especially in its shift away from realism.

tended an impressionist art exhibition in 1879, viewing the works of Claude Monet and Camille Pissarro. His artistic investigations took on new turns, and he continued working on pencil and crayon drawings even though he was drafted for military service.

Seurat's fellow artists saw in his work a greater interest in form than was found in impressionists, along with much more rigor in the use of color.

In 1881 Seurat closely studied another important influence, Eugène Delacroix's *Fanatics of Tangier* (1836–38). Delacroix had used colors in complementary pairs—to the viewer standing at a distance, the individual colors appeared as a mixture of the two colors, rather than as two distinct colors. Seurat was ready to apply these ideas to his own art. In 1882 he completed *Boy Seated on the Grass, Pontabert*. In 1883 he began work on *Bathers at Asnières*, the first of his paintings that would achieve great fame. The work failed to capture the imagination of the judges for the 1884 Salon, so he showed it at the Salon des Indépendants in the spring of 1884. While that work was beginning to attract attention, he was working on another painting, his masterpiece, *A Sunday Afternoon on the Island of La Grande Jatte* (1884–86). In some ways, this work appears quite ordinary

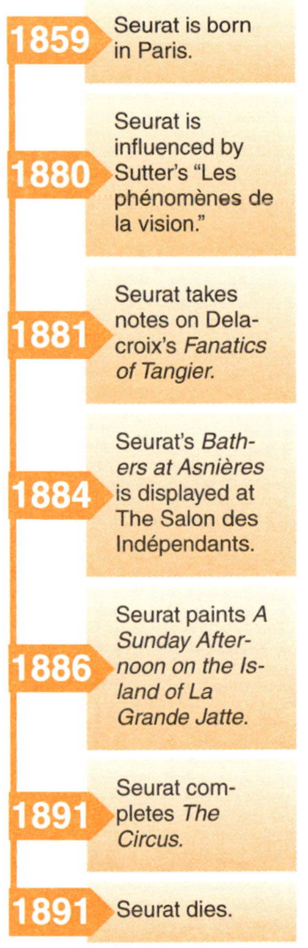

at first glance. In terms of setting, it depicts a number of sharply outlined people enjoying the sun and shade of a weekend outdoors. What makes the work more remarkable is that, like the paintings of the impressionists before Seurat, it conveys the outlines of form not through solid outlines but through distinct dabs or points of color. This use of points gives the work a kind of shimmering light, an effect quite appropriate for viewing people sitting outdoors in the afternoon sun. While the work's fame rests largely on the technique in which it was made, it is also interesting for its subject matter, when viewed alongside *Bathers at Asnières*. The relatively well-off people in the former work do not seem to be having much fun; the lower-class workers appear to be making the most of their chance to relax.

While *Bathers at Asnières* did not have an immediate impact on the audience, *Sunday Afternoon* did. Included in the impressionist exhibition in 1886, it caused a sensation among both popular audiences and Seurat's fellow artists, who acclaimed him a major new voice in the field. Critics saw in his work a greater interest in form than was found among the impressionists, along with much more rigor in the use of color. For these reasons, Seurat was considered the leader of neoimpressionism—or, to be more precise, he considered himself the leader. While others respected his work greatly, they did not necessarily share his assessment of his own singular genius. As a result, despite continued successful paintings such as the vivacious *Le Chahut* (1889–90), depicting dancing women, and *The Circus* (1890–91), featuring a woman in a circus ring balancing on the back of a horse, Seurat began to alienate his natural allies. At the time of his premature death in 1891, he was largely isolated from his former friends, including even Paul Signac, who would continue to explore some of Seurat's techniques for years to come. ◆

Sluter, Claus

c. 1360–c. 1405 ● Sculptor

Against the earlier preference in French sculpture for idealized figures, Claus Sluter introduced figures that were much more real and personal, and at the same time grander and more emotionally evocative. Sluter also moved away from the use of fluid, light drapery (the clothing of the sculpted figures) to heavier styles. His sculptural style was widely imitated not only in Burgundy where he worked, but also throughout northern Europe into the Renaissance.

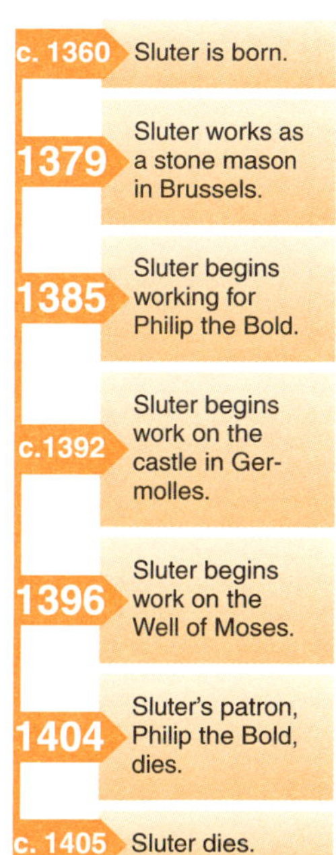

Very little is known about Sluter's life, least of all his early life. He was born some time between 1340 and 1360, perhaps in Haarlem, in the Netherlands. One conjecture is that he was born to a family of stonecutters, in whose workshop in Haarlem he spent his early years. He moved to Brussels, where he began formal training in his craft. By 1379 he was working as a stone mason in that city.

How quickly Sluter established his fame, we do not know, but it is difficult to imagine that his remarkable skills went unnoticed for long. In any case, by 1385 he began working for the Duke of Burgundy, also known as Philip the Bold, who had established a workshop to provide himself with high-quality sculpture. Sluter's overseer at the workshop, Jean de Marville, died four years later, and Sluter was the obvious choice to take over his role. Soon thereafter, Sluter began the first of a small number of large-scale projects on which his later fame would rest.

Philip the Bold had made plans for a portal for the Charterhouse (Chartreuse) at a Carthusian monastery in Champmol, near Dijon, Burgundy, France, but work on the project languished for years. Under Sluter's management, the project was given new life, and he breathed into it his own artistic vision. Figures for the portal included both his patrons and religious figures: with Philip the Bold and his wife appeared John the Baptist, Catherine of Alexandria, and the Virgin Mary with Jesus. Today it is difficult to determine how Sluter sought to integrate the portal into the rest of the Charterhouse, because so much of it was destroyed centuries later in the French Revolution. However, it is known that the freestanding figures of the duke and his wife were highly realistic, with natural poses.

Not long after producing these works, Sluter was involved in other related projects. In the early 1390s, Sluter was collaborating on the art for a castle in Germolles, near Chalon-sur-Saône. This involved not only producing new art but also transporting preexisting art and studying the work of other artists, including those working for Philip the Bold's brother, the Duc de Berry, who was equally renowned in his day as a wealthy patron for many artists. Much of Sluter's work from this period has been lost or destroyed, including his depiction

The sculpted faces were highly personalized, with their own expressions and even wrinkles, as though each person were reacting to the duke's death in his own way.

of the duke and duchess with sheep at the entrance to the castle. His contributions to the oratory at Champmol, which probably included figures of Antony the desert father, John the Baptist, and the Virgin Mary, also have not survived.

In 1396 Sluter began work on the sculptures that marked the pinnacle of his career. In the center of the Charterhouse cloister was to stand an enormous fountain. The work, only part of which survives, is a marvel. In the middle of the fountain was a pier, above which rose a cross. Figures evoking the crucifixion and Calvary were added. Six Hebrew prophets stood around the pier—David, Moses, Jeremiah, Zachariah, Daniel, and Isaiah, all carved in Asnières stone, and each one given a pose that evokes a trademark characteristic. Six angels graced the six corners. Besides the ambitious scale of the project, the fountain—now called the "Well of Moses"—is remarkable for the distinctive appearances of the prophets and the dramatic power of their poses and lifelike faces.

During this time, Sluter was also working on another project—the tomb for his patron, Philip the Bold. Such long term overlapping projects were much more common in sculpture than in painting. Many of the greatest paintings in European art have been completed within a year, but larger sculpture projects involving several individual pieces have often taken many years, both for the logistical challenge of assembling the raw material and the time needed to carve and install the works. The tomb took many years to execute. The site was commissioned as early as 1381. Sluter's early mentor, Jean de Marville, had designed the site, but most of the work languished until 1391, when alabaster was purchased for the angels and mourners ("weepers"). The duke's own figure was also to appear in alabaster, and the next year Sluter went to Paris to obtain it. For the most part, however, plans for the tomb did not move forward until the duke died in 1404, more than two decades after it was first commissioned. New plans for the tomb included about 100 angels and mourners. Sluter would die around 1405 or 1406, and it fell to his nephew, Claus de Werve, to complete the work.

The resulting tomb depicts a procession of figures with facial detail astonishing for that era—the sculpted faces were highly personalized, with their own expressions and even wrinkles, as though each person were reacting to the duke's death in his own way. It is this attention to detail that made Sluter's work so influential and highly respected. His works are also enjoying renewed popularity on the Internet, and can be viewed at a number of web sites. ◆

Soutine, Chaim

1893–August 9, 1943 ● Painter

Chaim Soutine was born in Smilovichi, Belorussia, the tenth among the 11 children of a poor Jewish tailor, who once locked Chaim in the cellar for two days because he took money to buy colored pencils. At the age of ten, he was apprenticed to a tailor, but in 1907 began working is a retoucher for a photographer in Minsk. Soutine one day asked the rabbi of his village to pose for a portrait, and the rabbi's son was so incensed that he gave Soutine a beating which sent him to hospital and cost the rabbi 25 rubles in damages. With this money, Soutine was able to go to Vilna to study art. There, he ate at a soup kitchen, and received some financial assistance from a doctor, whose daughter gave a benefit for Soutine, earning 50 rubles. This was enough for Soutine to go to Paris, where he enrolled at the Ecole des Beaux Arts. When World War I broke out in August 1914, Soutine obtained a residency permit. He also volunteered for the "workers' army" but was rejected because of poor health.

Chaim Soutine, self-portrait, 1918

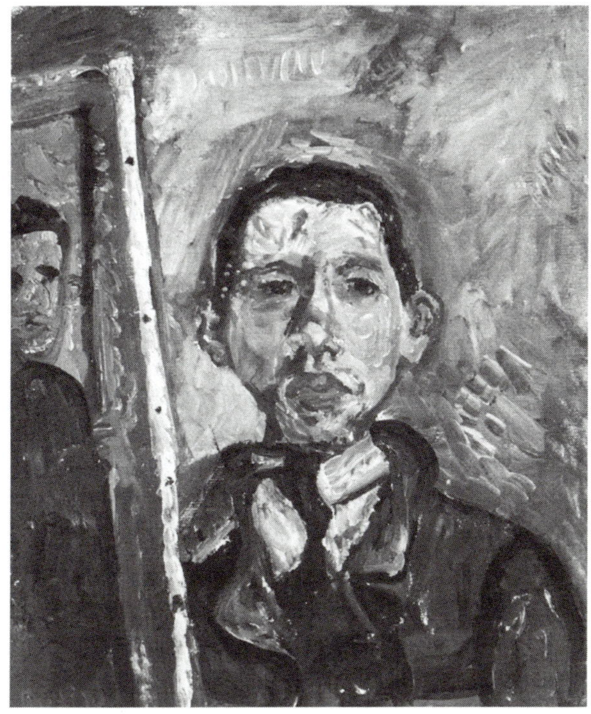

In Paris, Soutine lived in the Cité Falguière, where his studio adjoined that of Amedeo Modigliani and the two became drinking companions and close friends. Modigliani introduced Soutine to his art-dealer, the Polish poet Leopold Zborowski, who, enthusiastic about his work, gave Soutine a stipend of five francs a day. Soutine was very critical of his own paintings and destroyed many of them, but Zbo-

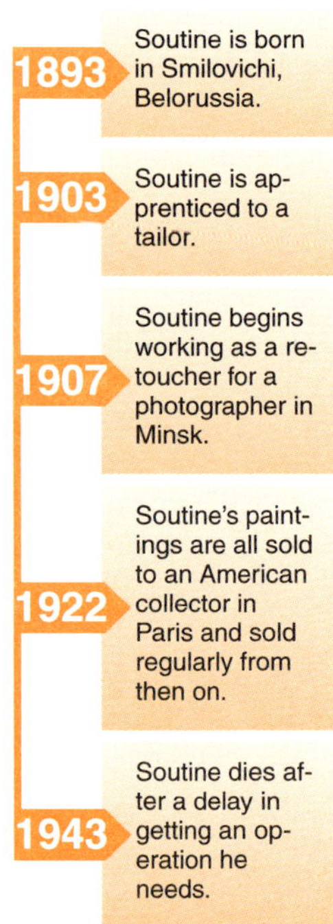

rowski managed to rescue some, on occasion even sending work to a restorer.

In 1922, an American collector, Albert C. Barnes, was so impressed by Soutine's work that he bought everything (more than 50 paintings) in Zborowski's possession, paying 60,000 francs. (The paintings now hang at the Barnes Foundation at Merion, near Philadelphia.) When Soutine came for his daily five francs, Zborowski increased his stipend to 25 francs a day. From then on, Zborowski sold Soutine's paintings regularly, for good prices.

For a while, Soutine moved frequently, but finally he took a large studio in the boulevard Saint Michel, near a slaughterhouse. Here he painted a series of paintings of carcasses of beef. Paulette Jourdain, who was his model, assisted him by going to the slaughterhouse every few days to get fresh blood to pour over the carcasses so that they would maintain their color. When inspectors from the health department came to remove the carcasses, Jourdain persuaded them to let the carcasses remain until Soutine finished his paintings, on the condition that they inject the beef with ammonia, as a deodorant.

In Montparnasse, Soutine met a German Jewish refugee. Gerda Groth, who moved into his apartment. In 1940, however, as the German army neared France, the government ordered a roundup of all German nationals and Gerda Groth was arrested and sent to an internment camp. Soutine himself received several invitations to take refuge in the United States, but refused.

He met Marie-Berthe Aurenche, the former wife of Max Ernst, in Paris. Believing that as a Jew Soutine was in danger, Aurenche took him to friends who agreed to hide them. They remained for three months, but fearing that the concièrge would report them to the Gestapo, fled to the unoccupied zone and settled in Champigny in Touraine.

In 1943, Aurench and Soutine were living in Chinon, when Soutine began to suffer terrible pain from stomach ulcers. At the hospital in Chinon, he was told that he needed an immediate operation. Aurenche arranged for an ambulance to take them to Paris, as the operation could be performed only there. In order to avoid the police, they were forced to detour, and the trip which should have taken five hours, took more than 24. When they arrived in Paris, Soutine was operated on immediately, but died the next day. Aurenche had Soutine buried in her family plot in the Christian cemetery in Montparnasse. Space in the grave was left for her, and when, in 1960, she committed suicide, she was buried beside him. A cross is engraved on the stone slab she had placed over the grave. Among the few friends who attended Soutine's funeral were Pablo Picasso, Jean Cocteau, Max Jacob, and Gerda Groth, who had recently been released from the internment camp.

Soutine was a painter in the expressionist tradition; his turbulent paintings and bright colors conveyed his own inner tumult. His portraits are often twisted and distorted and his work is always disturbing, but he has become recognized as an outstanding representative of the school of Paris. ◆

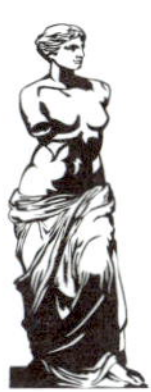

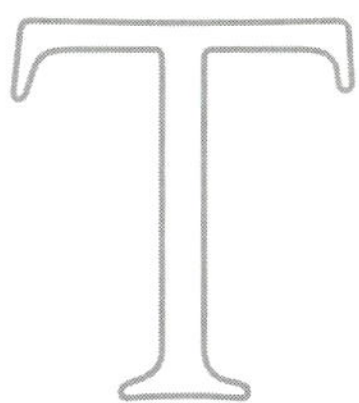

Tintoretto

1518–May 31, 1594 ● Painter

Tintoretto was the only one of the dominant Venetian painters of the 16th century who was actually born in Venice. More than those of Titian or Veronese, his career was essentially based in Venice, and his major works remain in the churches and confraternities of that city.

Tintoretto's sobriquet, meaning "little dyer," derives from his father's profession as a cloth dyer. Little is known of his training as a painter. One tradition places him briefly as an apprentice with Titian, who is said to have expelled the youngster, being jealous of his talent. Tintoretto's earliest paintings suggest study in the busy, conservative workshop of Bonifazio de' Pitati, whereas his more ambitious figural style may have found inspiration in the art of Pordenone. By 1539 he is recorded as an independent master, "mistro Giacomo depentor."

In 1548 he very publicly declared himself with a canvas for the meeting hall of the Scuola Grande di San Marco (a confraternity) representing *St. Mark Rescuing a Slave*. The painting caused a sensation; celebrated in a letter of the writer Pietro Aretino, it was initially rejected by the brothers of the *scuola*. In this composition acutely **foreshortened** figures define a dynamic spatial structure and break the tableau flatness of the canvas, a flatness that had been traditional in Venetian mural decoration. Possibly even more disturbing to contemporaries was the evident speed of execution, the rapid brushwork that disturbed even Aretino. Radical foreshortening and an ener-

foreshortened: made compact so that an illusion in space is created.

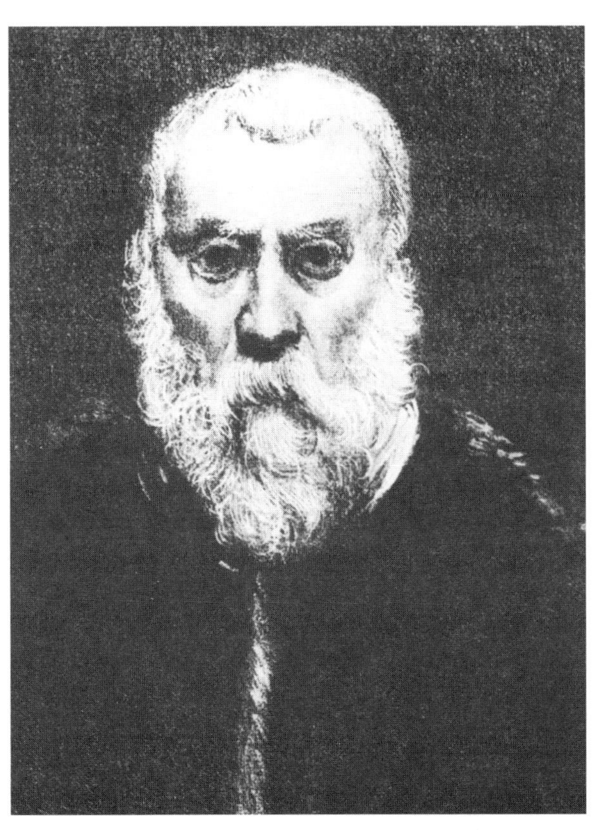

Tintoretto, self-portrait, c. 1585

getic brush remained two of the defining characteristics of Tintoretto's style. Indeed, the speed of his brush led critics like Giorgio Vasari to claim that Tintoretto made a mockery of the art of painting, passing off unfinished canvases as completed works of art.

Tintoretto was said to have painted a motto over the door to his studio: "The Drawing of Michelangelo and the Coloring of Titian." Tintoretto was an avid student of Michelangelo's art, drawing after small casts of the Florentine's sculpture and studying graphic copies of his pictorial inventions; he adapted those models to the active economies of his own compositions—for example, in *St. Mark Rescuing the Slave* and on the facade frescoes of Ca' Gussoni (lost, known through graphic copies).

Between 1562 and 1566 Tintoretto executed three more paintings for the Scuola di San Marco, further scenes of the life and miracles of the patron saint of Venice: *The Carrying of the Body, The Finding of the Body,* and *The Miraculous Rescue of the Saracen by St. Mark.* The first of these is quite thinly painted on a brownish toned canvas, with long strokes of white painting defining spectral figures and architecture in the background, just the kind of rapid execution that left doubt as to its state of finish. But the carping of central Italian critics did not hinder the painter's local success. Tintoretto set out to fill the available walls of Venice with his work, and his business strategies proved as unconventional as his art.

Thus, in 1564, did he gain the commission for the ceiling painting in the board room of the Scuola Grande di San Rocco. Rather than submit a small model to the competition, he had a quickly executed painting of *The Apostheosis of St. Roch* installed and presented it as a gift, an offering to the saint that could not be refused. Despite criticism of his tactics, he managed to extend his control of the decorations of the room, executing next a monumental *Crucifixion* (1565), generally considered his grandest painting, and in the following two years representations of Passion scenes leading up to that event. The radical foreshortening and precipitous spaces that mark Tintoretto's compositions are subject to more certain pictorial control by the larger chiaroscuro patterns—overall distribution of light and dark values—that establish a dominant pictorial organization. Such dynamic contrast is fundamental to Tintoretto's art.

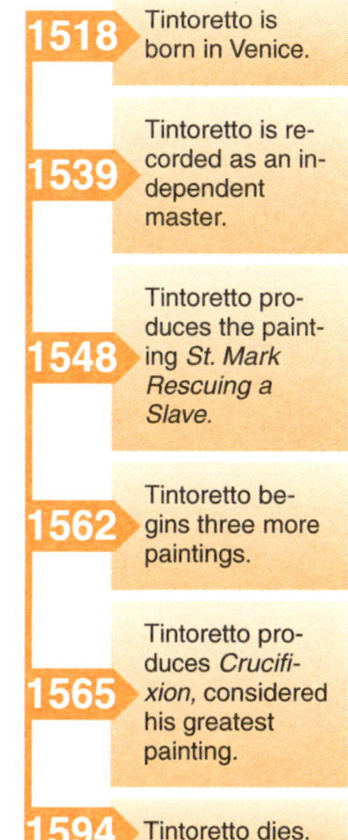

Tintoretto became a brother of the Scuola di San Rocco and arranged to continue his decorative efforts. In 1575–1576 he painted the central ceiling canvas of the large meeting hall of the *scuola*, representing *The Brazen Serpent*. In the following two years he completed the project with further Old Testament scenes: *Moses Striking Water from the Rock* and *The Gathering of Manna*, smaller ovals of *The Fall of Man and The Paschal Feast*, and flanking images of prophets. On the walls below he then painted a cycle dedicated to the life of Christ (1579–1581), continuing on the ground floor with scenes from the infancy (1583–1587). The pictorial decorations of the Scuola di San Rocco thus trace the development of Tintoretto's art over the course of two decades; the building itself stands as the most important monument to that art.

Although he did receive commissions from beyond the lagoon—such as the cycle celebrating the Gonzaga triumphs (1578–1580)—Tintoretto's primary patronage came from within Venice. His early work in the Sala del Maggior Consiglio (Hall of the Great Council) of the Ducal Palace was destroyed by fire in 1577. In the major campaign of redecoration, however, he and his workshop played a dominant role, including the central ceiling panel of a celestial Venice receiving Doge Nicolò da Ponte, the Signoria (1580–1584) and the enormous canvas, *Paradise*, behind the ducal throne (1588–1592), as well as many of the votive pictures of the doges and portraits of Venetian officials.

In addition to such state commissions and the patronage of the *scuole grandi*, the great confraternities, Tintoretto worked extensively for the lesser confraternities of Venice, the smaller *scuole*, many of which maintained chapels dedicated to the Holy Sacrament in churches throughout the city. For these groups he produced a number of representations of the Last Supper, often paired with a scene of the Washing of the Feet; the earliest of these are canvases for the church of San Marcuola (1547). His conception of the Last Supper, in contrast to

iconography: material in a pictorial form that illustrates a subject.

that of Paolo Veronese, is characterized by a modesty of setting and person. His **iconography** is essentially humble, appealing to a more popular congregation—although his last, most luminous rendition of the theme was for the Benedictines of San Giorgio Maggiore (1592–1594).

Many of these late canvases represent the collective work of the master and assistants. Tintoretto directed a family workshop; his chief assistant and heir was his son Domenico (1560–1635), after whom the Tintoretto shop continued for another generation. Such collective enterprise and professional continuity were typical of artistic production in Venice, sustained by a guild system that lasted well into the 18th century.

Tintoretto's bold brushwork did indeed effect a union of design and color; long, directional strokes of light paint over a darker ground charge the surface with a graphic energy. It is especially in the brilliance of his brush that Tintoretto brings to a climax an essential component of 16th-century Venetian painting. ◆

Titian

c. 1488–August 27, 1576 ● Painter

Titian was born in Pieve di Cadore in the Italian Alps and apprenticed to a Venetian mosaicist when only nine years old. Although there is no surviving documentation of his activities before 1508, it is accepted that in the early 1500s he worked as an apprentice in the workshops of Giovanni Bellini and Giorgione. In 1508 he was a junior assistant to Giorgione, who had been commissioned to paint the frescoes for the facade of the Fondaco dei Tedeschi in Venice. In 1511 he received payment for his first commissioned work, frescoes of Saint Anthony for the Scuola di San Antonio in Padua. On the death of Bellini in 1516 Titian was appointed official painter of the Venetian Republic.

The death of Bellini marked a significant stage in Titian's artistic development. Prior to Bellini's death Titian's work was heavily influenced by the style and form of his master, but subsequently he began to develop his own style, which ultimately gained international recognition. In 1518 he began a series of altarpieces, starting with the *Assumption of the Virgin* for the Church of Santa Maria Gloriosa dei Frari in Venice. Although this attracted a storm of criticism from the religious community for its size, it was soon recognized as an original masterpiece. Titian continued this phase of his work with the *Madonna* of the Pesaro Family (1519–1526), also in the Frari, and the *Death of Saint Peter the Martyr* (1528–1530) for the Church of Santi Giovanni e Paolo, Venice.

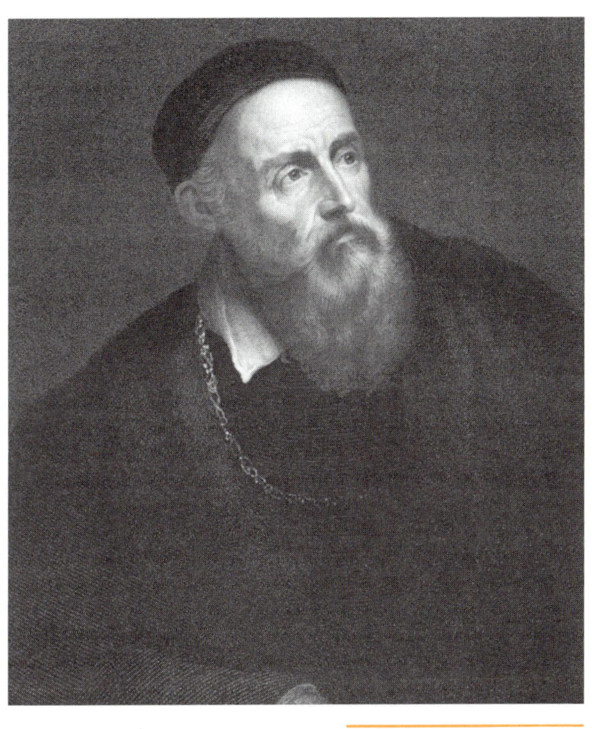

Titian

During the following decade Titian concentrated on painting more natural forms and executed such masterpieces as the *Presentation of the Virgin* (1534–1538) and *Venus of Urbino* (1538). In 1533 he was appointed court painter to the Holy Roman Emperor Charles V, who made him Count Palatine and conferred upon him the Order of the Golden Spur. Titian's fame spread and he was in great demand among the nobility for his portraits.

In 1545 Titian went to Rome as a celebrity and met with Michelangelo. On his return to Venice he was invited to the imperial court at Augsburg, where he completed his most important portrait, that of Charles V on horseback at the Battle of Mühlberg (1548). During this period he also developed what was to become a longstanding relationship with the emperor's son, the future Philip II of Spain. Between 1550 and 1560 he worked on a number of mythological paintings commissioned by Philip, which included the *Rape of Europa* (1559), *Venus and Adonis*, and the *Luteplayer* (1560). These mythological figures were based on classical texts from which Titian derived inspiration, while the models for his sensuous paintings were usually Venetian prostitutes.

Titian's final years were spent in Venice. Along with his friends the writer Pietro Aretino and the sculptor-architect Jacopo Sansovino, he formed the core of an elite that ruled Venice's cultural life. It was said that his home "was frequented by all the princes, learned men, and gallants of his time, for to genius he added also the most courtly manners."

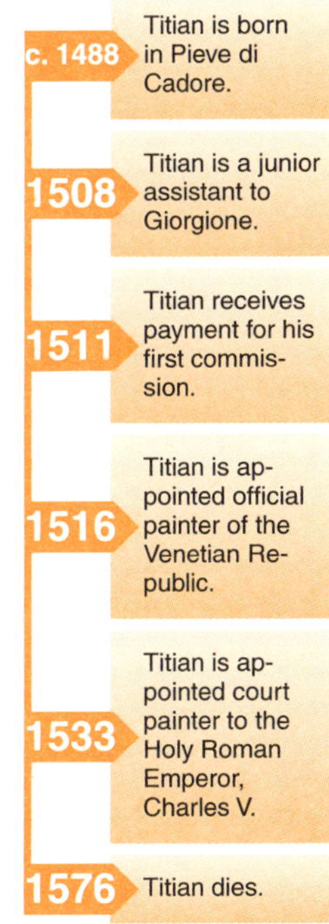

In the later part of his life Titian would begin a painting by sketching directly onto the canvas, outlining the basic form of the figures, and then turn the canvas to the wall, often for weeks on end, periodically making critical adjustments until he was satisfied that he had eradicated all faults. Finally, he would then complete the painting, using his fingers as frequently as his brush. He continued to paint almost to his death, by which time he was probably in his mid-eighties (his birthdate is uncertain).

When Titian died, a public funeral march was planned to glorify the painter who was the most renowned master of the Venetian school. However, these plans were thwarted by the plague that then ravaged Venice. Acknowledged during his lifetime as a creative genius, Titian leaves a legacy that both influenced and reflected the development of Italian art in the 16th century. ◆

Toulouse-Lautrec, Henri de

NOVEMBER 24, 1864–SEPTEMBER 9, 1901 ● PAINTER AND POSTER ARTIST

Descended from an aristocratic family, Henri de Toulouse-Lautrec was born in the town of Albi but moved with his family to Paris when he was nine years old. He attended the best of schools, as would be expected given his family's lofty station in French society, and his school records show him to have been an apt pupil. Unfortunately, Henri was not a robust child, and because of his frail health he was forced to leave school before completing his studies. Studying at home, he turned to drawing, at which he exhibited a marked talent.

"Toulouse-Lautrec's crippling illness forced him to become an observer rather than a participant in life."

From the *Artgardens* website, on why Henri de Toulouse-Lautrec became an artist

In 1878, he suffered the first of two major accidents that had a profound effect on his life, and ultimately on his art as well. At 14, Toulouse-Lautrec broke his left thigh bone, and a year later he did the same to his right one. Medical science of the day was advanced enough to save his legs, but the growth centers in the bones were destroyed. His legs never developed to their proper adult length and size. As the rest of his body matured, he became sensitive about his "grotesque" physical appearance and became increasingly withdrawn from society, retreating into his art.

By this time, Toulouse-Lautrec's parents had come to recognize their young son's talent, and they granted him permission to work with René Princeteau, a painter who specialized in equestrian subjects. Toulouse-Lautrec's earliest paintings reflect the influence of this mentor both in subject matter and in their somewhat impressionistic style. These early pieces showed great promise, but he had not yet developed his own distinctive approach to drawing and painting. That would soon change.

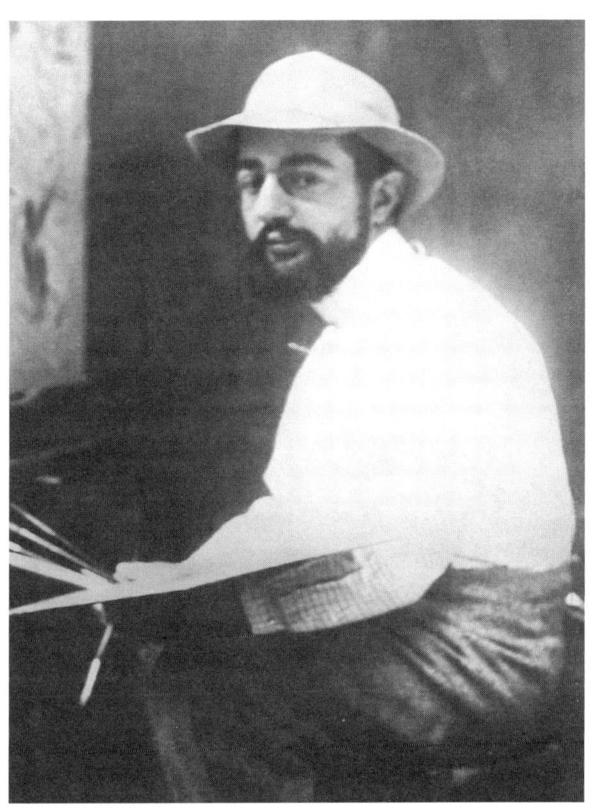

Henri de Toulouse-Lautrec working at his easel.

Toulouse-Lautrec's removal from formal schooling left him ill-equipped to face the state baccalaureate examination, required for admission into any of the more conventional professions. He failed his exams in 1881 and thereafter devoted himself to a career as an artist. With his parents' blessing, he gained admission into the studio of Léon Bonnat, who provided the young artist with a strong academic training in drawing and painting. Like all young artists of the day, Toulouse-Lautrec spent a great deal of time producing formal studies of the human figure. A year later he moved on to work with the artist Fernand Cormon, and soon he met Vincent van Gogh.

Toulouse-Lautrec's work in the early 1880s still retained a strong impressionistic sensibility, and he clearly showed the influence of a number of artists working in that school. His most profound admiration, however, was for the work of Edgar Degas, who is remembered today for his studies, on canvas and in sculpture, of ballet dancers. In his studio work, Toulouse-Lautrec had already begun to display a penchant for satire and caricature. He had also begun incorporating elements drawn from Japanese prints, which were highly popular in French art at the time.

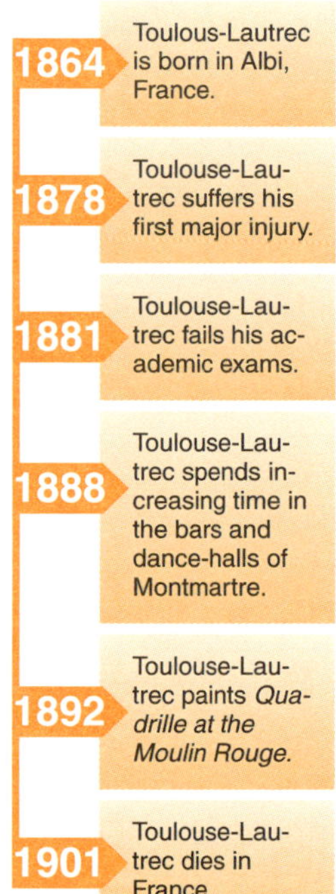

By 1888, the now 24-year-old artist had arrived at the mature expression of his style. He had also discovered what would be his signature subject matter. Living on his own in Paris, Toulouse-Lautrec took to visiting the bars and dance-halls of Montmartre, the dance-hall and brothel district of Paris. The stunted, crippled artist felt most at home there, among the prostitutes, dancers, and circus performers who lived and worked in the district. For the rest of his short life, he would devote himself to depicting the scenes and people of Paris's nightlife.

Among the works he produced over the next few years, Toulouse-Lautrec frequently featured the legendary Moulin Rouge, a popular nightclub in Montmartre. His paintings, as in the *Quadrille at the Moulin Rouge* (1892), clearly show that he viewed his subjects sympathetically, capturing the grace as well as the tawdriness of the nightlife. Fittingly, given his subjects, he used theatrical, even garish, colors for effect. He strove to capture movement and emotion in a very few strokes of the brush or pen. His style was perfectly suited for posters, and in 1891 he received his first commission from the Moulin Rouge to produce an advertisement for the nightclub's enormously popular dancers. He would ultimately produce 31 posters, and these are the works for which he is best remembered today.

With his posters and his paintings, Toulouse-Lautrec enjoyed great success. He began a series of paintings focusing on the prostitutes in the local brothels, and showed these—along with his dance-hall paintings and posters—at an exhibition in 1893. This exhibition earned him much attention and approval from his fellow artists, and brought him the praise of his idol, Degas.

In 1895, Toulouse-Lautrec received a portrait commission from Oscar Wilde, which led him to travel to London. He soon returned to Paris, however, to begin the most productive period of his artistic life. For the next two years he completed a great many paintings, posters, and lithographs. By 1897, however, his life in the cabarets was beginning to wear on him. He was plagued by sickness, exacerbated by his heavy drinking, and in 1899 he was forced to sign himself into a clinic in an attempt to regain his health. This provided only a temporary improvement in his condition, however, and in 1901, at the young age of 37, he died in Malromé, France. ◆

Turner, Joseph

1775–1851 • Painter

Joseph Turner was born in London to a barber who was delighted by his son's early interest in art and reportedly displayed young Joseph's works in his shop for purchase by curious clients. Turner's earliest formal training occurred in the Royal Academy school and with Thomas Malton, Jr., a topographer and teacher of watercolor and perspective. Already by 1790 the Royal Academy displayed Turner's own watercolor efforts, such as *The Archbishop's Palace, Lambeth.* The next year he traveled to Bristol, taking along his art supplies and sketching whatever caught his fancy. Such "sketching tours" would later become a regular part of Turner's life, as he traveled throughout England and Europe. In addition to sketching, Turner also investigated engraving. From the 1790s on, when he produced drawings for the *Copper Plate Magazine*, he would be remarkably prolific in this medium. Other works include the *History of Richmondshire* (1818) and the *Liber Studiorum*, which he worked on for many years but never completed.

For his engravings, he borrowed from his sketches, which were also the basis for many of his watercolors. Watercolors were the medium of Turner's earliest painterly training, but he grew more interested in oil painting: perhaps, as some have suggested, because he knew that this was the only "serious" paint medium for acceptance in academic circles; perhaps because his own creative interests were evolving in that direction. In any case, already in 1796 he completed his first oil painting, *Fishermen at Sea*, and by the time other seascape oils ap-

Joseph Turner

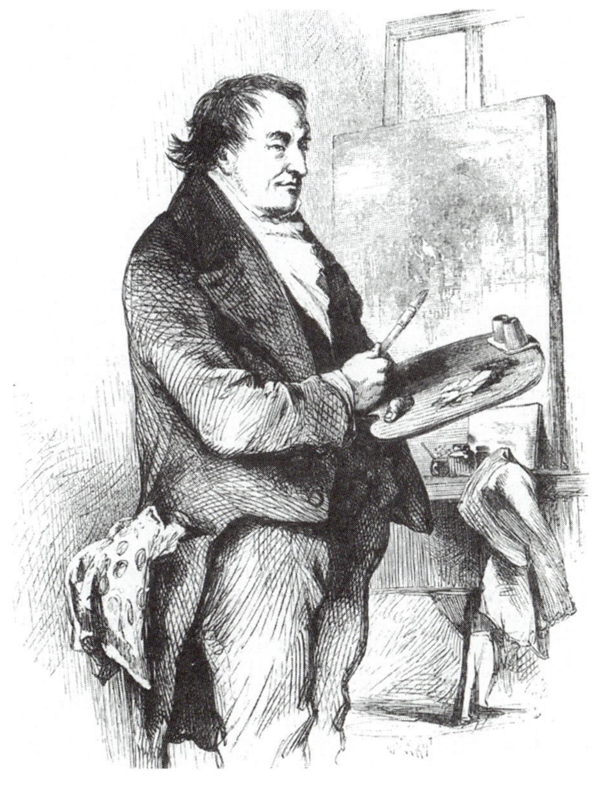

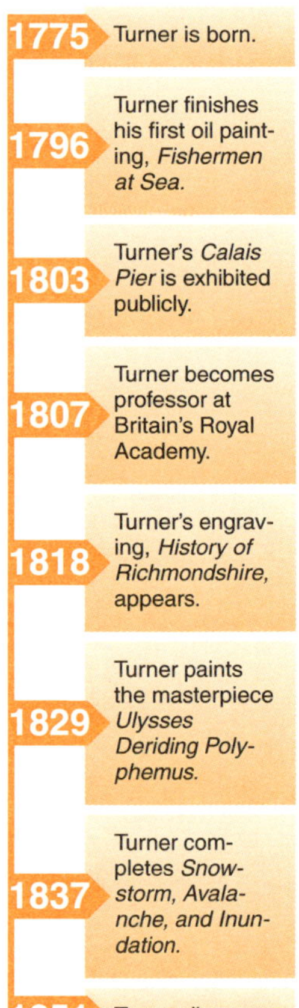

peared later that decade, he was breaking new ground in his subtle representation of light as it appeared in different weather conditions and times of day. This keen interest in the different appearances of light in different outdoor conditions shows a fascination Turner shared with the French impressionists several decades later. Turner's boldness also appears in his attempts to prove himself the peer of painters who came before him, as he incorporated epic biblical themes and sea storms into his work. For a time, many of his paintings were direct challenges to his predecessors, as he sought to illustrate his virtuosity by surpassing them. By 1803 his seapiece *Calais Pier* was shown publicly, and the public and critics alike responded strongly—the critics criticized, the public hungered for more. Flush with this greater popularity, he opened his own gallery in London and set about finding well-placed patrons. He went on to produce other major works such as *Snow Storm: Hannibal and his Army Crossing the Alps* (1812) and *Dido Building Carthage* (1815).

Fortune was smiling on Turner—he had been elected to full membership in the Academy in 1802 and received a professorship there in 1807. Turner was not without his detractors, however, including George Beaumont, a representative of the old guard who thought Turner's original ideas undermined venerable academic traditions. Moreover, as time went on and Turner mastered more and more kinds of subject matter, his creativity and drive for innovation only increased, leading to an increase in criticism and greater confusion—and apathy—from potential buyers and patrons.

One of the sources of criticism was his use of color. His paintings grew lighter and lighter in tone, to the point that they became dominated by yellows and whites. It may have been his visit to Italy that sealed his fascination with this "Mediterranean" light, and by the 1820s this style was firmly established. Although the brilliant results strike the viewer as anything but studious, they were the result of his sophisticated study of color and several experiments in different techniques for achieving the best lighting effects. In these studies he was influenced by a colleague, George Field.

Another example of Turner's shift is *Ulysses Deriding Polyphemus* (1829). The lighting effects are dazzling, with astonishing contrasts of dark and light, and rich vibrant color. Today the work is regarded as a masterpiece, because we recognize its originality—it combines influences from Venetian painters and Italian fresco with Turner's own contributions to watercolor and gouache work. At the time, however, critics were not so kind, as its nonrealistic style offended their taste. A few years after its appearance, Turner faced another setback, as one of his most stalwart patrons, Egremont, died. Happily, H. A. J. Munro was willing to help Turner continue to travel, and from their association came Turner's trips to the Lucerne and the Alps, resulting in paintings such as aptly titled *Snow-storm, Avalanche, and Inundation* (1837). Though he continued the traveling he so loved, by the early 1840s he began to reduce his traveling schedule because of ill health. However, he continued producing a number of watercolors to the end of his life. Also important in his later years was the renowned art critic John Ruskin, who championed Turner and introduced his work to a new group of patrons. Ruskin's view proved prophetic—today, because of his dazzling and dramatic technique and mastery of light and color, Turner is generally regarded as the greatest landscape painter in art history, as well as the greatest British painter. ◆

"[Turner is] the only perfect landscape painter the world has ever seen."

John Ruskin, in an essay on Joseph Turner in G. W. Chubb's *Sketches of Great Painters*

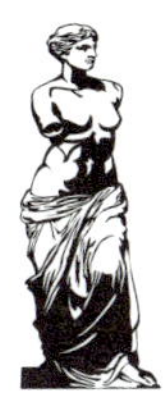

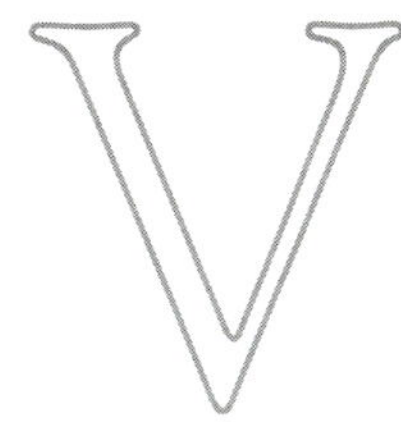

Van Dyck, Anthony

MARCH 22, 1599–DECEMBER 9, 1641 • PAINTER

Sir Anthony Van Dyck's professional eminence encompassed broad swaths of geography (present-day Belgium, Italy, and England) and expertise (religion, mythology, and portraiture). But it was in his portraits—almost exclusively of royalty and nobility—that Van Dyck established a formidable standard of expressive nuance and grace that placed him among the leading painters of his era. In the words of one critic, "His naturalistic portrait style and, more precisely, his loose, liquid handling of drapery were to inform English portraiture for 200 years."

Antoon Van Dyck (he changed it to Anthony after he moved to England) was born in Antwerp on March 22, 1599, the seventh of 12 children. His artistic lineage traces to his paternal grandfather, a leading painter in Antwerp who eventually forsook art for commerce, building the textile business that he passed on to his son Frans, Antoon's father. In this prosperous household young Antoon flourished into an artistic **prodigy** whose talent was encouraged by his mother, Maria. By the age of ten, Antoon had already become an apprentice of Hendrik van Balen, a leading Antwerp painter. He remained there for several years (variously estimated at three to eight years) before joining the studio of Peter Paul Rubens, one of Europe's most important artists of the day.

prodigy: a highly developed and talented child who excels in a particular area of academics or artisitic works.

Van Dyck's precocity leaps off one of his earliest surviving canvases, *Self-Portrait*, an astonishingly assured and expressive

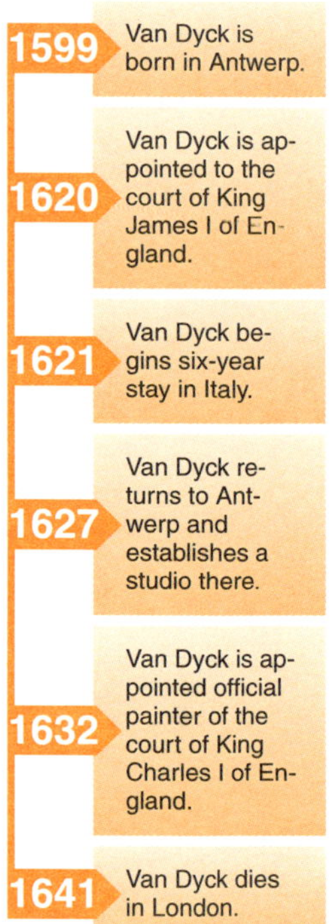

work that Van Dyke completed when he was only 14. Already an accomplished painter by the time he became Rubens's chief assistant—his associate, really—Van Dyck played a key role on several of the master's major projects, including the *Decius Mus* tapestry cycle and the painting *Coup de lance*.

At the age of 21, Van Dyck traveled to England, where Rubens's recommendation helped him to secure a position in the court of James I. While there he painted his masterly portrait of the Earl of Arundel and *Continence of Scipio*, but despite a generous salary of 100 pounds a year, Van Dyck left England after only five months. He stopped briefly in Antwerp in October 1621 on his way to Italy, where he remained for the next six years.

Van Dyck assimilated the artistic riches of Genoa, Rome, Venice, and Sicily, cultivating patrons for whom he produced a series of distinguished portraits, including *Sir Robert Shirley*, *Cardinal Bentivoglio*, and *Elena Grimaldi Cattaneo*. Van Dyke was inspired, according to one scholar, "by [the painter] Titian's skill in modeling in tone, rendering flesh and fabric in a subtle play of light and shadow." These virtues are evident in Van Dyck's altarpiece *Madonna of the Rosary* at the Dominican Oratorio del Rosario in Palermo, Sicily.

Preceded by his growing international reputation, in 1627 Van Dyck returned to Antwerp, where he established a studio and worked on a variety of projects—narrative paintings (such as *Rinaldo and Armida* and *The Arrest of Samson*), altarpieces, and portraits. His commissions were enhanced by the absence of Rubens from 1626 to 1630. Van Dyck became a small industry, hiring assistants to help him meet the unremitting demand for his exquisite canvases. His growing renown led to his appointment as court painter for Isabella, the Archduchess of Southern Netherlands, an honorific post that attested to his importance in the region's cultural life.

Van Dyck's career crested in 1632 with his appointment as official painter to the English royal court, or, in the words of the original proclamation, "principalle Paynter in ordinary to their Majesties," King Charles I and Queen Henrietta Maria. Upon his arrival in England, Van Dyck was knighted and given a golden chain, a princely annual income of 200 pounds, a summer residence in Kent, and an unending stream of commissions, almost all portraits. Charles's motives for importing Van Dyck were clear: in the words of Susan Fegley Osmond, "Charles I . . . was a man of educated tastes and was a real fan of

Titian, and he imported Van Dyck to bring new verve, grace, and sophistication to English painting. The artist succeeded so well in this revolution that his works became the model for English portraiture for the next 250 years. They profoundly influenced artists such as Reynolds, Gainsborough, and the American-born John Singer Sargent." In fact, on his deathbed Gainsborough supposedly whispered to Reynolds, "We are all going to Heaven, and Vandyke [sic] is one of the party."

"[Van Dyck] loved private character and painted the interplay between that character and the public mask with a sensitivity that few artists have rivaled since."

Art critic Robert Hughes on Anthony Van Dyck's painting style

The royals chiefly prized Van Dyck's knack for endowing mere mortals with an aura of lordly heroism and grace. Often the trick was as simple as a slight extension of the subject's height or a discreet elongation of the hands, complemented by exquisitely rendered fabrics and elegantly appointed surroundings, rendered in painstaking detail. The result was an enduring portrait of a social class's collective dream of itself, summarized by the critic Tom Lubbock as "the cool, sleepy-eyed ladies framed in curls, the lanky, droopy, dreamy knights with floppy hair, who fall so effortlessly into their poses, assume superiority so unassumingly, their fingers, tapering, hardly a hard edge among their features, and rendered with a correspondingly casual brilliance."

Outstanding examples of Van Dyck's English portraiture include *King Charles on Horseback*, *Archbishop Laud*, *Sir John Sucking*, and *The Countess of Southampton*. According to E.H. Gombrich, the portrait of King Charles, widely regarded as his masterpiece, "showed the Stuart monarch as he would have wished to live in history: a figure of matchless elegance, of unquestioned authority and high culture, the patron of the arts, and the upholder of the divine right of kings, a man who needed no outward trappings of power to enhance his natural dignity." It is easy enough to dismiss such paintings as a form of "spin doctoring," as one critic has. On the other hand, it was Van Dyck, as Gombrich put it, "more than anyone else, who helped to crystallize the ideals of blue-blooded nobility and gentlemanly ease which enrich our vision of man no less than do Rubens's robust and sturdy figures over-brimming with life."

Van Dyck's portraits of the king garnered such enthusiasm that soon all of England's leading aristocrats were in line for his services—Van Dyck's studio churned out the likenesses at an average rate of one per week, some 400 in seven years. To meet the clamorous demand, Van Dyck again took on a staff of assistants, who often executed the torsos and costumes of the subjects before Van Dyck painted the head, a procedure that some scholars have faulted for encouraging an impersonal, assembly-line approach to portraiture.

In 1640 the devoutly Catholic Van Dyck, anxious over the rising tide of Puritan opposition to the crown, decamped to Antwerp, perhaps in the hope of supplanting the recently deceased Rubens. Seemingly driven by uncertainty and anxiety, he traveled to Paris, returned briefly to England, and then dashed to Paris once again, seeking an appointment from Louis XIII. But by now illness was taking its toll, and he decided to return to London, where he died on December 9, 1641, at the age of 42. ◆

Velasquez, Diego

June 6, 1599–August 7, 1660 ● Painter

Born in Seville, Spain, Diego Velasquez was descended from Portuguese aristocracy. Already at an early age he was dedicated to the life of an artist, beginning his training at the age of 12 when he studied briefly under Francisco Herrera. He then became the student of Francisco Pacheco, training with him from 1611 to 1617. A year later he married his mentor's daughter, Juana. Velasquez's early works were in the established genres of the day, including religious paintings, portraits, and **genre paintings** (*bodegones*), in which the subjects are shown eating or preparing food. In 1622 he traveled to Madrid, where his work won him recognition and praise—especially popular was his portrait of Luis de Góngora. A year later he was back in Madrid with a lofty appointment: court painter to the king, Phillip IV. Over the course of his long association with the royal court, he would produce many portraits of the king and many of Spain's highest nobles.

genre paintings: paintings that depict scenes from ordinary everyday life, common citizens, and mundane activites; the height of popularity for genre painting came in seventeenth century Holland.

Velasquez's association with the court was a remarkable achievement for such a young man—he was only 23—but it had its drawbacks. For example, in 1627 he was elevated to the rank of gentleman usher, a position requiring many duties that took him away from his painting. Nonetheless, he remained highly productive, and in that same year he won an important painting competition securing his status as Spain's premier artist. His painting, *The Triumph of Bacchus*, triumphed over his competition. During this year, Velasquez also made the acquaintance of the painter Peter Paul Rubens, who came to the Spanish court to paint portraits of the king.

In 1629 Velasquez left his responsibilities at court to travel to the artistic capitals of Europe. Over the next three years he visited Venice, Rome, and Naples. During this trip he executed two of his most celebrated paintings: *Joseph's Coat* (1630) and *The Forge of Vulcan* (1630). This was a time of great development for the artist, as he refined his skills at landscapes and the depiction of nudes. Soon, however, this idyllic period of release from the demands of the Spanish court would end, and Velasquez returned to Madrid in 1631. On his return he acquired an assistant who later became his son-in-law, and to whom, in 1634, Velasquez was able to turn over his duties as usher.

The 1630s saw Velasquez once again painting numerous portraits of the nobility, but it also marked his turning to other, less exalted subjects. He did a series of paintings of dwarves and court jesters, deformed characters kept by the court for amusement. These paintings realistically showed the defects of their subjects, but they never sank to the level of caricature. On the other hand, he did several paintings of characters from Roman mythology, and in these he was quite willing to strip his subjects of any sense of majesty or even dignity, often treating them as laughable rustics.

Even though Velasquez had left his court appointment, he remained a favorite of the king, who was a frequent visitor to the artist's studio. He also did not remain free of courtly demands upon his time, for he was named "gentleman of the wardrobe" in 1636, and "gentleman of the bedchamber" seven years later. Nonetheless, he continued to produce a great many works during this period, including *The Fable of Arachne* (also known as "The Tapestry Weavers") and *The Toilet of Venus* (both 1644–48), both done for private patrons, as well as many more portraits of the king, the royal family, and important courtiers.

It was not until 1648 that Velasquez was again free to travel to Italy, and even then the reason for the trip was a royal assignment: he was sent to acquire artworks for the royal palace. He made good use of his freedom, however, executing several paintings of members of the court at the Vatican, including a portrait of Pope Innocent X. Velasquez returned to Madrid in 1651 and once again found his time in great demand by the king. He was named Chief Steward of the Palace in 1652, and

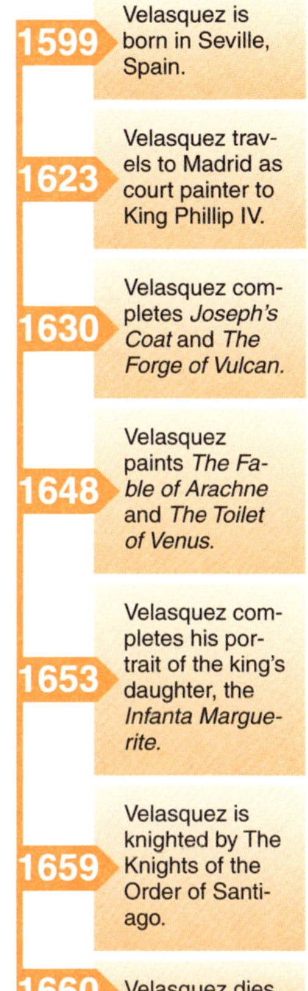

Velasquez's association with the royal court of Spain was a remarkable achievement for such a young man—he was only 23—but it had its drawbacks.

his new duties in this office seriously disrupted his painting. At a time when his skills and technique were at their peak, he had very little time to employ them.

Remarkably, however, he still completed several important and accomplished works during this time. Among the best paintings are a powerful portrait of the royal family and a charming portrait of the king's youngest daughter, the *Infanta Marguerite* (1653). The artist's success in these and other paintings earned him consideration for a singular honor: membership in the Knights of the Order of Santiago. After a grueling investigation, in which testimony was sought from some 100 witnesses, the knighthood was bestowed upon him in 1659. This honor, however, was ultimately the artist's undoing. The demands of knighthood were so great that Velasquez found it impossible to make time for his painting. He died the following year. ◆

Vermeer, Jan

OCTOBER 31, 1632–DECEMBER 16, 1675 ● PAINTER

Historians have offered conflicting stories about the early life of Dutch genre painter Jan (Johannes) Vermeer. His father was a skilled weaver and, later, art dealer. Jan Vermeer probably began his own formal art training in the late 1640s, perhaps under the well-known painter Leonard Bramer; some authorities also suggest the influence of Hendrick Terbrugghen. In April of 1653 Vermeer married, and later that year he attained the position of master in the Delft Guild of St. Luke. He later held leadership offices in the guild, enabling him to meet many other artists of his day. It appears that in those early years he earned little if anything as a painter, supporting his wife and his growing family primarily through his income as an art dealer.

Most of Vermeer's earliest surviving work suggests that he specialized in history paintings—works that take as their subject matter well-known stories, especially from Roman and Greek mythology and history, and the Bible. These interests are evident in the titles of some of his early pieces, such as *Christ in the House of Mary and Martha* and *Diana and her Companions* (1655). In these early works, Vermeer tended to use larger canvases and already showed his tremendous gift for subtle use of light.

Around 1656 began what historians call Vermeer's middle period, which would last for 11 years. In these paintings, he often depicted people in interior spaces. In a work such as *Woman with a Water Jug* (circa 1665), a woman holds a water jug in one hand while opening a window with the other. The arrangement of light is remarkable and beautiful—the area near the window on the left glows, and the tones grow quite dark further into the room, with extra radiance on the tray on the table. As Vermeer continued refining his technique with friends such as Pieter de Hooch, fewer people were shown in each painting, and they became more prominent in the works. Throughout this time, his works also grew more realistic, and the precision of many of the paintings is striking even today. His interest in realism may have fueled his interest in the camera obscura, a forerunner of the modern camera, in which the images of objects placed in bright light (usually sunlight) could be projected onto walls or paper, where they could be viewed or even traced. The effects of the **camera obscura** appear in some paintings where perspective is distorted as through a fish lens—objects in the foreground are exaggeratedly large, those in the background smaller, and several objects are out of focus, in contrast to his other style of precise and sharp representation.

As Vermeer's career progressed, his style grew more and more precise, even mathematical. He was less likely to use rough painted surfaces, moving toward smoother surfaces. In terms of style, he began using tone instead of lines to show the boundaries of objects and features. One example is his *Head of a Girl with a Pearl Earring* (1665), where the girl's features, such as nose and cheek, are defined by separate bits of paint ("**impasto,**" a feature also used by Rembrandt). Also astonishing is his *Love Letter* (1667). The viewer has the illusion of looking into an adjoining room, where a seated woman looks over her shoulder at her maid who, it appears, has just brought her (or is about to carry away) a letter held by the seated woman. Darker tones frame the margins, while the light glows in the center from the lit room where the realistically detailed women remain. In 1667, Vermeer also completed his *Allegory of Painting*, which some regard as his best use of light and space.

Around 1667 begins Vermeer's "late period," which lasted until his death in 1675. In this period, Vermeer continued to use bits of paint rather than outlines. Like his contemporaries

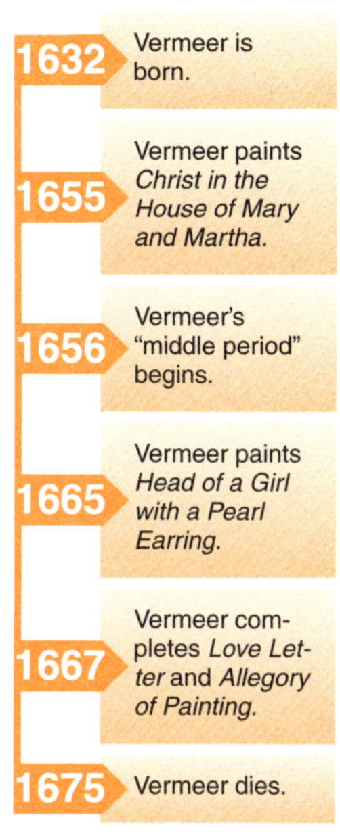

camera obscura: almost literally, the first camera; a darkened room with a tiny hole in a wall through which light would pass and transmit an inverted image of an outside scene on a screen.

impasto: a thick, lumpy application of paint, or deep brush marks.

As Vermeer's career progressed, his style grew more and more precise, even mathematical.

among Dutch painters, and like the French impressionists two centuries later, he became more interested in color than form. Some art historians include his *Love Letter* in this period; in any case, that work's strong contrast of light and dark, as opposed to the subtle shadings of light in earlier works, is typical of his later works.

Vermeer never enjoyed financial success as an artist, and in fact some doubt that he ever sold a painting in his own lifetime. As a result, we do not have much testimony about how his contemporaries viewed him. Moreover, because Vermeer was so precise in his work, laboring over each one and often reworking key elements of them, he did not produce many paintings. Only about 36 works survive—fewer than any other painter of similar fame. Clearly, however, he made the most of each work. Although he was virtually ignored after his death, his reputation began to be restored in the 19th century, especially under the influence of the French art critic T. Thoré. Today Vermeer is remembered for his genius in composing a painting, his technique in light, and his meticulous use of painting techniques. ◆

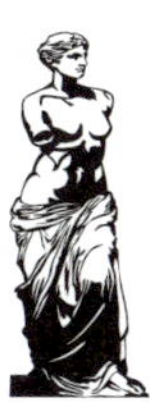

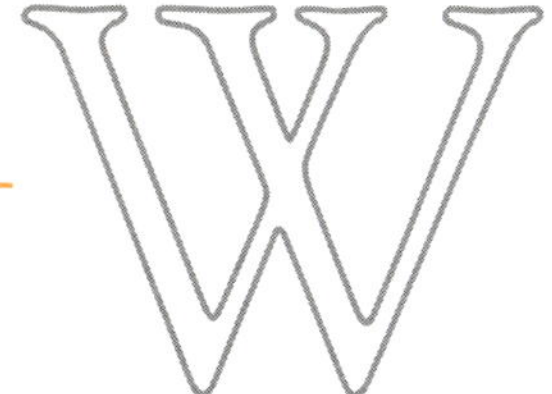

Watteau, Antoine

October 10, 1684–July 18, 1721 • Painter

Jean Antoine Watteau was born in Valenciennes, France (formerly a Flemish town), to a tilemaker. While little is known of Watteau's early life, he probably studied in Valenciennes with an artist of local renown, Jacques-Albert Gérin. Already at this early age Watteau was interested in depicting subjects of local color, including townspeople and clowns. He traveled to Paris in 1702 to make his way as an artist, beginning by producing piecework in devotional art. He trained with stage designer and engraver Claude Gillot, where he was exposed to Italian theater and began making drawings from the commedia dell'arte. These were recurring characters from an Italian comic troupe that took on a life of their own in Paris theaters and the popular cultural life of that day. In 1708 Watteau studied with Claude Audran III, who oversaw the art collections at the Luxembourg Palace in Paris. There, Watteau developed a fascination with one important part of the collection, Peter Paul Reubens's baroque paintings of scenes from the life of Marie de Medici (1622–25). From Audran he also learned about interior decoration and ornamentation. Audran gave his gifted protegé an unusual amount of freedom in the design of their decorations.

Still, Watteau yearned for greater artistic freedom. This young painter—who just a few years before had been making cheap mass-produced religious art—was on the verge of a meteoric rise in fame and prestige. He gained attention when he

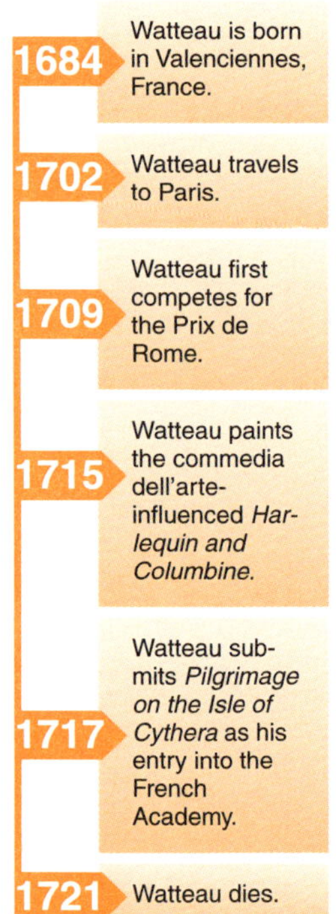

placed second in the Prix de Rome (1709), sponsored by the Académie Royale de Peinture et de Sculpture. While he was disappointed at not taking first prize, offers for commissions began pouring in. He revisited Valenciennes (1709–10) and soon completed several works depicting military scenes. These scenes were of interest because they showed soldiers not in grand poses or in the midst of famous battles, but as they appeared in their daily lives, such as relaxing and preparing food. In 1712, Watteau's entry in the Prix de Rome again gained him attention—again, he did not win, but the president of the French Academy in Paris was so taken with Watteau's work that he encouraged him to join the Académie de Peinture. In 1712 he was named an associate of the French Academy.

By 1715 Watteau had completed *Harlequin and Columbine*, an example of his interest in commedia dell'arte figures. Many of these works were innovative, because while they included commedia dell'arte figures, they did not depict identifiable scenes from known plays or stories—they were not part of a series of works pointing to a broader plot, but isolated settings with their own symbolism and drama. In *Harlequin and Columbine*, for example, part of the painting depicts Harlequin springing toward Columbine, the object of his extreme sexual lust, while the other part depicts a more sedate setting, as music—apparently tranquil, soothing music—is played for a group of people.

Around 1714 Watteau began painting the works for which he would be best remembered, the *fêtes galantes*. These were depictions of upper-class people of the court, usually in parks and outdoor settings, in various kinds of repose, recreation, and relaxation. Other painters had used the same subject matter, but Watteau introduced important innovations. First, somewhat like his commedia dell'arte works, these works were stripped of plot and narrative—it was never clear exactly how the people depicted came to be where they were. Second, this focused greater emphasis on the particularity of the settings, gestures, and so forth, and Watteau made the most of this shift by giving his characters intriguing elements of facial expression and gesture—subtle touches that suggested intimate connections and interactions among the people. Watteau's brilliant use of gesture and his ability to give dramatic form to his figures probably came from his familiarity with popular drama and comedy. Third, although his characters are realistically drawn, their dress is often unreal—some people might be dressed in street clothing, others in theatrical garb, suggesting that there was something very unreal or absurd about the scene, even though each individual looked completely real.

In the 1710s, Watteau also embarked on painting a subject to which he would return often—Cythera. Cythera is a mythical island of love, a place only lovers can go, and one at which seekers can never remain forever. His *Pilgrimage to [or, "on"] the Isle of Cythera* is one of his best-known treatments of the myth, and he used this work to accompany his formal entry ("reception piece") into the Académie de Peinture (1717), which he had put off for several years. While it is difficult to determine how Watteau interpreted the myth, in part because the titles of his works are not his own, the themes of longing and desire are certainly present. In style, too, such as the bright pink colors and the delicate ornamentation, the piece represented his use of rococo touches.

Watteau gave his characters intriguing elements of facial expression and gesture—subtle touches that suggested intimate connections and interactions among the people.

Not long after this period, however, Watteau, who had never been robust in health, grew quite ill, and he died of tuberculosis in Nogent-sur-Marne in 1721, at the peak of his fame and creative abilities. His *fêtes galantes* were enormously popular in his day, but their rococo style—their use of light decorative ornamentation for sensuous and playful themes—fell out of favor with the rise of French neoclassicism, which favored somber, austere settings with high moral purpose. Neoclassicists, who tended to paint in a fairly narrow spectrum of muted colors, also did not appreciate Watteau's great mastery of vivid colors. His reputation steadily increased in the 19th century, however, as romantics and impressionists saw in him a foreshadowing of their interest in emotion. Watteau's reputation as a draftsman has also survived, and his hundreds of studies, especially of the human body, are regarded as some of the most exciting of his period. ◆

Weyden, Rogier van der

c. 1399–June 16, 1464 ● Painter

Rogier van der Weyden, a cutler's son born at Tournai, is almost certainly the "Rogelet de le Pasture" who entered the workshop of the painter Robert Campin in 1427. However, he probably began his apprenticeship in his

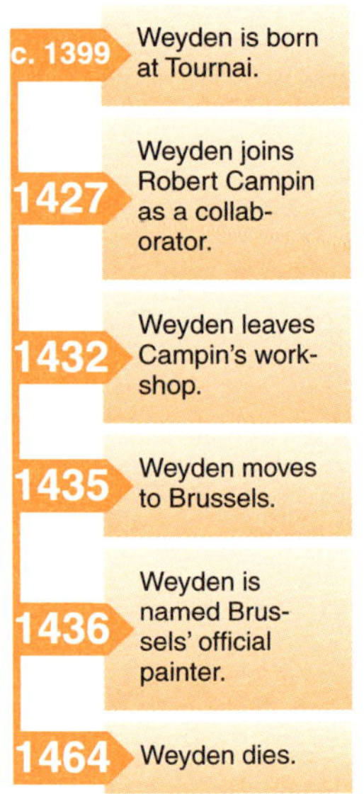

teens—as was common practice—and joined Campin in 1427 as a collaborator, not as a pupil as is generally believed. He may have trained at the workshop of the Master of Flémalle, upon whose style van der Weyden's was founded.

Van der Weyden left Campin's workshop in 1432, moved to Brussels by October 1435, and was named that city's official painter by May 1436, a position he retained for the rest of his life. He painted four large panels in the late 1430s and 1440s (now lost, with one panel reportedly dated 1439), representing the *Justice of Trajan* and the *Justice of Herkinbald* for the courtroom of the Brussels town hall.

Van der Weyden's surviving works are neither signed nor dated and are poorly documented. However, the Miraflores Triptych, given in 1445 to the Charterhouse of Miraflores near Burgos by King John II of Castile, is recorded in the donation as being painted by "the great and famous Fleming Rogel." The *Descent from the Cross*, obviously completed by the time it was copied in 1443, was reportedly acquired from the chapel of Our Lady Outside the Walls at Louvain by the regent of the Netherlands, Mary of Hungary. Mary passed the painting on to her nephew Philip II of Spain, who offered it to the Escorial in 1574. It is listed at the Escorial in the inventory of the gift, together with a *Crucifixion*, as by "Rogier." The inventory states that the *Crucifixion* came from the "Charterhouse of Brussels," almost certainly the Charterhouse of Scheut outside Brussels, to which van der Weyden made a gift of money and pictures. A number of works are attributed to van der Weyden on the basis of these three devotional paintings; they must thus form the point of departure for an assessment of his achievement.

The *Deposition* is influenced by the tradition of the *Schnitzaltar*, an altarpiece in which carved and painted figures were assembled inside boxes. Here, the actors are placed on a narrow stage inside a shallow gilded box, which both underlines the theatricality of this drama, acted out so close to the viewer and above the altar, and eliminates all superfluous detail, thus allowing for focused contemplation. As the dead Christ is lowered in the center of the composition, the Virgin swoons in the immediate foreground, echoing the arabesque of his pose. Van der Weyden's relief-like ensemble comes alive as a result of his superb rendering of movements, emotions, and textures.

Masterly synthesis and theatrical staging are likewise characteristic of the Miraflores Triptych, which includes the *Holy Family*, the *Pietà*, and the *Final Appearance of Christ to His*

Mother. These tableaux are placed just beyond painted arches, which simulate the **portals** of a Gothic cathedral and support carved saints and scenes from the *Life of the Virgin* on the archivolts.

portals: grand and imposing entrances, usually associated with cathedrals or other places of worship.

In the tall, austere, and perfectly symmetrical *Crucifixion*, van der Weyden draws the viewer's attention to the pathos of the Virgin and John at the foot of the cross. The cross is raised in front of an unfolded red drapery, which serves as a precious foil for the dead Christ and both mourners seen in dramatic close-up.

Van der Weyden was also an outstanding portrait painter. In his bust-length portraits *Francesco d'Este*, *Antoine, Grand Bâtard de Bourgogne*, and *Young Woman*, the heads and torsos are turned in three-quarter profile toward the left before a blank ground, and one or two hands are placed at the bottom of the configuration. Van der Weyden's intensely expressive art was in great demand, and his highly original compositions, exquisite draftsmanship, and abstracting tendencies—more easily assimilated than van Eyck's daunting illusionism—influenced artists in many areas of western Europe well into the 16th century. ◆

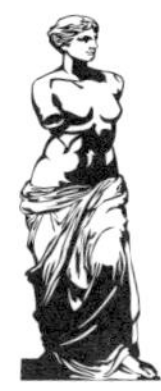

Time Line of Events in European Art History

1277

Nicola Pisano's Great Fountain at the main square of Perugia is erected; the basins include scenes from the Old Testament and classical mythology.

1334

Giotto is commissioned to manage the fabric and workshop of the cathedral of Florence and to design its new tower; the versatility Giotto displayed in being able to command such a wide range of talent was unrivaled at the time.

1385

Claus Sluter begins working for the Duke of Burgandy, known as Philip the Bold. The duke had established a workshop to provide himself with the highest quality sculptures, and Sluter works on the large-scale projects for which he would become famous.

1402

The Limbourg Brothers secure a commission to prepare an illuminated Bible for the Duke of Burgandy.

1419

The *Arte del Cambio* (guild of moneychangers) commissions Lorenzo Ghiberti to sculpt a bronze statute for the guild's niche on the facade of the Orsanmichele. Ghiberti creates *Saint Matthew* and displays a great awareness of the structure and movement of the body and an understanding of antique art.

1425

Philip the Good selects Jan van Eyck as court painter and valet. Van Eyck's work for Philip entitles the artist to travel extensively and ensures that his works will become much more popular, thanks to Philip's prestige.

Robert Campin's triptych of the Annunciation displays his pursuit of realism and use of three-dimensional human figures and perspective.

1426

Masaccio receives a commission to create an altarpiece for the chapel in the Carmine in Pisa by Ser Giuliano di Colino degli Scarsi da San Giusto.

1430

Fra Angelico completes *Coronation of the Virgin*, which he makes for San Domenico in Fisesole, demonstrating his strict adherence to gilding punchwork and brilliant pigments.

1436

Rogier van der Weyden is named the official painter of the city of Brussels, a position he holds for the remainder of his life.

1445

Pierro della Francesca secures his first known commission, the polyptych *Madonna della Misericordia*.

1476

Giovanni Bellini's *Coronation* is completed; it is a high altarpiece for the church of San Francisco in Pesaro that features a highly malleable form and a harmonious use of space.

1478

Sandro Botticelli completes a fresco of the Pazzi conspirators, who were hanged for the murder of Giuliano outside of the Palazzo della Signoria.

1481

Hugo van der Goes, who suffers from depression and fears damnation, is given an overabundance of commissions and lapses into madness, only briefly recovering before his death the next year.

1488

Andrea Mantegna goes to Rome to decorate a chapel in the Villa Belvedere for Pope Innocent VIII.

1497

Albrecht Dürer's woodcut *Men's Bath* explores different material surfaces—such as the use of the whiteness of the paper—to suggest solids and open passages and complex spatial constructs.

1501–04

Michelangelo completes work on *David,* a 15-foot- statue and an example of the heroic male figure, for which he is renowned.

1503–05

Leonardo da Vinci paints *La Gioconda,* known as the *Mona Lisa.* It becomes perhaps the best known painting in the world and is today displayed at The Louvre art museum in Paris, France.

1504

Hieronymus Bosch gains a commission from Duke Philip the Fair of Burgandy to paint *Last Judgment,* which is identified with the Vienna *Last Judgment.* Bosch's work attracts the interest and patronage of many European aristocrats.

1505

Louis Cranach the Elder moves to Wittenberg and becomes the court painter of the Saxon elector, Frederick the Wise, dominating the art of northern and eastern Germany for more than 50 years.

1513

Albrecht Dürer, the extraordinarily talented German painter, printmaker, and designer, produces *Knight, Death, and Devil.*

Raphael completes the most celebrated study of the theme of the Madonna and Child, *Sistine Madonna.*

1519

Matthias Grünewald completes the altarpiece dedicated to *The Virgin of the Snow* for a chapel in Aschaffenburg.

1521

Hans Holbein completes *Body of the Dead Christ* and displays his growing personal conviction that a new human form inhabits religious figures, which is reflected in this and future pieces.

1522

Corregio is commissioned to paint frescoes dedicated to Santa Maria Assunta throughout the cathedral of Parma in honor of the city's veneration of the Virgin.

1528

Baldassare Castiglione declares Giorgione as one of the greatest painters of his age. Giorgione is later dubbed the originator of the "modern style of painting in Venice.

1545

Titian paints *Portrait of Pope Paul III with His Grandsons* shortly after his arrival in Rome and his meeting with Michelangelo.

1553

Benvenuto Cellini completes *Perseus* and reaches the high point of his tumultuous career.

1565

Pieter Bruegel paints *The Peasant Wedding*, a theme he emphasizes continually in his work.

During work on the ceiling painting in the board room of the Scuola Grande di San Rocco (Grand School of San Rocco), Tintoretto completes *Crucifixion*, which is generally considered his greatest painting.

1568

Pieter Brugel the Elder's three emblematic pictures—*Parable of the Blind*, *Peasant and Bird Nester*, and *Misanthrope*—comment on the period leading up to the Eighty Years War.

1599

Caravaggio receives his first public commission, which is to paint the lateral canvases depicting the *Calling of St. Matthew* and the *Martyrdom of St. Matthew* in the Contarelli Chapel of San Luigi dei Francesi in Rome. This commission establishes Caravaggio's reputation.

1600

El Greco, a follower and admirer of Titian, completes *View of Toledo*.

1616

Artemesia Gentileschi enters the Accademia del Disegno (Academy of Design) and becomes the first female member of the famous academy in Florence, Italy.

1623

Peter Paul Rubens completes *Maria de Medici, Queen of France, Landing in Marseilles*, part of a series of portraits commissioned by the queen that now hang in The Louvre.

1624

Nicolas Poussin journeys to Rome and continues to be influenced by the mannerist style, as shown in his paintings *Battle of Gideon against the Midianites* and *Battle Scenes*.

1627

Anthony Van Dyke returns to Antwerp and establishes a studio to produce various projects, such as narrative paintings, altarpieces, and portraits.

1629

Gianlorenzo Bernini is named the chief architect of St. Peter's Basilica and the Palazzo Barberini, epitomizing the success he experiences as a result of the patronage of Pope Urban VIII.

1639

George de la Tour is named "Painter to the King" by Louis XIII of France.

1642

Rembrandt paints *The Night Watch* in the midst of personal adversity that lends an increased sensitivity to his work.

1656

Diego Velazquez completes *Las Meninas* (*Maids of Honor*).

1664

Frans Hals paints *Regents of the Haarlem Old Men's Alms House*, an example of how the artist changed the tone and tenor of his paintings to suit changing tastes and art consumers' preference for more somber art.

1667

Jan Vermeer completes *Allegory of Painting*, which many regard as his greatest use of space and light.

1715

Antoine Watteau completes *Harlequin and Columbine*.

1728

Jean-Baptiste-Simeon Chardin is admitted into the Royal Academy of Painting in France based on two works that hang in The Louvre to this day: *The Buffet* and *The Rayfish*.

1735

Francois Boucher earns his first royal commission, and paints four large cherubs depicting the four virtues of Plato; wisdom, courage, temperance, and justice. The work hangs in the palace of Versailles.

1735

William Hogarth completes *A Rake's Progress*, a pictorial morality tale, most likely the most well-known of his works and among the finest examples of English rococo art.

1748

Thomas Gainsborough receives an invitation to contribute to a painting at London Foundling Hospital; the piece exemplifies the rococo style he brought to his early work.

1761

Jean-Honore Fragonard completes *Corseus Sacrifices Himself to Save Callirhoe*; the painting is widely acclaimed by critics at the Paris Salon and sold to the royal court.

1764

Angelica Kauffmann completes two paintings based on classical literature, *Penelope at Her Loom* and *Bacchus and Ariadne*.

1768

Jean Antoine Houdon travels to Paris and is accepted into the Royal Academy on the strength of his sculpture *Morpheus*; Houdon's return to France marks the true beginning of his portrait sculpting career.

1769

Joshua Reynolds is knighted by King George III of England for his service as the first president of the Royal Academy of the Arts, which establishes professional training standards and an annual exhibition of art.

1773

After failing three times in a row, Jacques-Louis David again attempts suicide by starvation and fails for the fourth time; the next year he wins the Prix de Rome with *Anitochus and Stratonice*.

1787

Antonio Canova is commissioned to sculpt a papal tomb in St. Peter's Basilica in the Vatican. Canova's monument to Clement XIII was the first neoclassical sculpture to be placed in the basilica.

1801

Jean Ingres wins the Prix de Rome for his work *Envoys of Agamemnon*, which demonstrates his strength in the French modern style. Winning the Prix de Rome also brings Ingres his first portrait commissions.

1804

William Blake's one-man show in London is largely a failure, though following the show Blake finds limited fame as an artist by illustrating the works of Chaucer and Milton.

1814

Francisco Goya paints *Tres de Mayo, 1808* (*The Third of May, 1808*), which brilliantly depicts the bloody violence of the Napoleonic Wars.

The French drive their occupiers out of Dresden, and Caspar David Friedrich expresses every Frenchman's feeling of patriotism with his works *On the Sailing Ship* and *Two Men Contemplating the Moon*.

1817

Theodore Géricault embarks on his most ambitious project, a painting depicting a tragic ship wreck of the French frigate *Medusa*. Géricault's *Raft of the Medusa* blends the desperation of the dying crew, the heroic efforts of the living, and the peace of those who died. People either love or hate the stunning painting.

1824

John Constable exhibits three of his works at the Paris Salon and earns a gold medal and recognition from his contemporaries, including Eugène Delacroix.

1831

Honore de Daumier publishes a lithograph on the cover of a French magazine depicting Louis-Phillipe, the constitutional monarch of France, as the monster figure Gargantua, swallowing extorted bags of gold taken from the French people.

1834

Eugene Delacroix's unveils the first work from his journey to Morocco, *Women of Algiers in Their Apartment*, which is notable for its freedom of line, density of color, and poetic effect.

1842

J. M. W. Turner paints *Snowstorm: Steamer off a Harbour's Mouth*, which demonstrates his ability to capture varying forces of nature.

1847

John Everett Millais wins the gold prize from the Royal Academy in Great Britain for his painting *Benjamin Seizing the Daughters of Shiloh*.

1848

François Millet's painting *The Winnower* symbolizes the Barbizon School of drawing from historical scenery in an idealized fashion and portraying scenes from a rustic, humble life.

1849

Gustave Courbet completes *After Dinner at Ornans*, which is exhibited at the 1849 Paris Salon and makes an important stride in Courbet's attempts at portraying the lives of the poor and disenfranchised.

1857

Dante Gabriel Rossetti contributes illustrations for a new edition of Tennyson's *Poems;* the drawings are very popular and display a meticulous style not always seen in Rossetti's other works.

1863

Edouard Manet completes *Le Déjeuner sur l'herbe* (*Luncheon on the Grass*) while experimenting with different techniques based on the Old Masters.

1864

Jean-Baptiste-Camille Corot's *Vile d'Avaray* and *Memory of Mortefontaine* exemplify the Barbizon influence under which he had studied and had changed his painting style.

Gustave Moreau wins a medal at the 1864 Paris Salon for his piece *Oedipus and the Sphinx,* which depicts a theme Moreau painted often—the tension between good and evil, men and women, and spirituality and physicality.

1865

Edgar Degas abandons the historical themes with which he had established himself and begins to paint scenes from contemporary life.

1871

Camille Pissarro and his wife return to France following the Franco-Prussian War and find their home in tatters after Prussian troops destroyed it and 15 years worth of Pissarro's artwork.

1872

Claude Monet creates *Impression: Sunrise*, one of two painting considered to be Monet's first impressionist pieces.

1876

Pierre-Auguste Renoir executes *Le Moulin de la Galette*, which he finishes during his strictly impressionist period.

1877

Edward Burne-Jones has a highly successful exhibition at Grosvenor Gallery in London, and subsequent works and exhibitions cement his status as one of England's greatest painters.

1880

Auguste Rodin sculpts *The Thinker,* which leads to several other commissions during the same time period.

1885

Edvard Munch begins associating with "stiania Bohemia," a group of writers and artists committed to the bohemian lifestyle who produce subjective, inner-directed art. Munch's contribution to this genre includes paintings such as *The Sick Child*.

Georges Seurat paints his masterpiece, *A Sunday Afternoon on the Island of La Grand Jatte*.

Henri Rousseau retires from his steady job at the Customs Office to concentrate on his painting in his desire to be taken seriously as an artist; he supports himself by taking odd jobs.

1887

James Ensor paints the first in the series of religious paintings that reflect the artist's identification with internal torture and deepening religious spirituality.

1889

Vincent van Gogh completes *The Starry Night* shortly before his death.

1890

Pierre Bonnard and fellow artists attending the School of Fine Arts in Paris form a group of impressionists called the Nabis, from the Hebrew word for "prophets," to exchange ideas of impressionism and forge their dedication to it.

1893

Henri de Toulouse-Lautrec works on *At the Moulin Rouge*, which accompanies his portraits of dance-halls and brothels at an exhibition.

1897

Paul Gauguin completes his masterpiece *Where Do We Come From? What Are We? Where Are We Going?* shortly before he attempts to take his own life.

1898

Paul Cézanne creates *Mont Sainte-Victoire From Bibemus Quarry*, an example of his penchant for painting at the same site but from varying perspectives.

1903

Odilon Redon paints *Flowers*, in which he combines his early appreciation for shadowy and mysterious colors with a newly found vitality and interest in brighter colors.

1907

Georges Braque exhibits his *fauves* paintings at a Paris exhibition and sells them all; Braque then signs a contract with a Paris gallery owner, who introduces him to Pablo Picasso.

Pablo Picasso's *Les Demoiselles d'Avignon* is a revolutionary painting that expresses the influences of the artist's fascination with African sculpture.

1908

Henri Matisse paints *Harmony in Red* during the height of the fauvism period.

Gustave Klimt completes his best-known portrait, *The Kiss*, which depicts an embracing couple.

Fernand Léger establishes a studio in Montparnasse and makes the acquaintance of such artists as Guillaume Apollinaire, Blaise Cendrars, Marc Chagall, Robert Deluanay, and Jacques Lipchitz. His work during this period reflects a strong impressionist influence.

1910

Oskar Kokoschka moves to Berlin and joins the circle of artists known as *Der Sturm*, a vibrant group of German expressionist artists. Kokoschka's career takes flight as a result of the group's support and encouragement.

1911

Marc Chagall completes *I and the Village*.

Franz Marc and Vassily Kandinsky resign their membership from the Neue Künstlervereinigung M&umml;nchen (NKVM) when some members of the group reject Kandinsky's entry for an exhibition.

Umberto Boccionoi's *Forces of a Street* encapsulates the futurist artistic movement by utilizing "lines of force" and a gathering of colors and form.

Paul Klee is given his first opportunity to exhibit his work in shows when he is introduced to Wassily Kandinsky and other avant-garde artists who together form the art collective known as The Blue Rider group.

1912

Marcel Duchamp's *Nude Descending a Staircase, No. 2* is a bold step in transcending and challenging cubism and becomes a polarizing piece at the Armory Show in New York City the next year.

1912

Hans Arp meets Wassily Kandinsky, whose influence leads Arp to produce a series of expressionist woodcuts and paintings that are heavily outlined in black.

1913

The landmark New York Armory show is held in New York City, bringing the works of modernist European painters to America for the very first time. The event changes the face of art in both America and Europe, and its importance cannot be overstated.

1915

Ernst Ludwig Kirchner is called for army service during World War I. Assigned to the mounted artillery, he suffers a breakdown and is hospitalized for several months, although he manages to produce *Self-portrait as a Soldier* during that time.

1916

Juan Gris explores pointillism and produces still-life collages such as *Newspaper and Fruit Dish*, and *Fruit Dish, Glass, and Lemon*.

1917

Amedeo Modigliani has an exhibition of a series of reclining nude portraits at the Berthe Weill Gallery, but the police remove some of the paintings from the gallery window and from the walls.

1920

Giorgio de Chirico makes a break with modernism and returns to more traditional methods of painting and the techniques of the Old Masters.

1921

Leading figures in the dadaist movement in Germany collaborate to arrange for some of Max Ernst's collages to appear at a group show in Paris.

Alexander Rodchenko's exploration and experimentation with abstract painting and sculpting results in his series of three monochrome paintings, *Pure Red Color, Pure Yellow Color*, and *Pure Blue Color*.

1922

Albert C. Barnes, an American art collector, is so impressed by Chaim Soutine's work that he purchases the artist's entire collection from Leopold Zborowski (Soutin's patron) for 60,000 francs.

1922

Alberto Giacometti moves to Paris and begins five years of intermittent study under the sculptor Emile-Antoine Bourdelle.

1924

Kasimir Malevich is named the director of the Institute of Artistic Culture in Petrograd, Russia, but the Soviet government closes the institute two years later as a result of the modernistic works Malevich's students produced.

1928

Constantin Brancusi creates *Bird in Space*.

Joan Miró is inspired by a trip to the Netherlands and executes a series of paintings called *Dutch Interiors*, in which he transforms the literalism of the Dutch painting geniuses into surrealistic fantasies.

1931

Salvador Dali's unveils *Persistence de la mémoire* (*The Persistence of Memory*), which depicts melting wristwatches floating in an atmosphere of menacing calm; it later becomes perhaps the most widely reproduced surrealist work.

1933

Emil Nolde joins the Nazi Party—and supports its belief in racial purity and superiority—even though the Nazis looked upon Nolde's work as degenerate modern art.

Francis Bacon completes *Crucifixion*, his first successful work, earning him a place in a London art show entitled *Art Now*.

Hans Hofmann opens the Hans Hofmann School of fine Arts in New York City, where he teaches modernist theory for 25 years before closing the school to concentrate on his artistic work.

1937

The Nazi Party, which is in control in Germany, prominently features the works of Max Beckmann in the infamous "Degenerate Art" exhibition in Munich; Beckmann flees Germany shortly thereafter.

The Nazi Party declares the work of Kurt Schwitters as degenerate and a direct threat to the ideals and goals of the Third Reich; Schwitters leaves Germany for Norway.

1942

Piet Mondrian's *Broadway Boogie-Woogie* is an example of the artist's use of small colored rectangles in rhythm vertically and horizontally.

1943

Girl with Roses is the first portrait by Lucian Freud that crystallizes his early surrealist leanings with the odd juxtapositions of disparate images and objects that would characterize his best work.

1944

Jean Dubuffet makes his public debut with paintings of everyday subjects drawn in a somewhat childish manner, all of which are intended to provoke viewers.

1948

René Magritte signs a contract with influential New York City art dealer Alexandre Iolas, increasing the artist's popularity in North America.

1957–58

Henry Moore produces *UNESCO Reclining Figure*, which exemplifies the Yucatan influence on his work.

1966

Jean Arp dies.

1970

David Hockney produces one of the most well-known paintings in modern British art, *Mr. And Mrs. Clark Percy*, a portrait of a couple's profound distance and alienation set against a bright, clean background.

1975

Anselm Kiefer's fascination with recent German history leads him to study the Nibelung tales that had inspired the composer Richard Wagner; Keifer also incorporates his study of Hebrew scriptures and tales of the military conquests of Alexander the Great into his work.

1976

German painter Max Ernst dies.

1982

The Salvadore Dalí museum opens in St. Petersburg, Florida. The museum houses more than 200 of the famous surrealist's works.

1986

English sculptor Henry Moore dies.

1992

Francis Bacon dies.

1995

One of the largest exhibits of Claude Monet's work ever held is staged at the Art Institute of Chicago. The show encompasses Monet's entire career and fills 17 rooms of the museum.

1996

"David Hockney: A Print Retrospective" is held at the Museum of Contemporary Art in Tokyo to celebrate David Hockney's career.

1999

A major retrospective of Anselm Kiefer's work entitled "Anselm Kiefer: Works on Paper," is held at the Metropolitan Museum of Art in New York City.

2000

Author Jacob Baal-Teshuva publishes *Chagall: A Retrospective*, a new work offering a complete history of Russian painter Marc Chagall's life and work; Chagall died in 1985.

A major traveling exhibition called "Van Gogh: Face to Face" offers an opportunity to view more than 65 of Vincent van Gogh's portraits and self-portraits from museums and collections throughout the world. The show stops in Detroit, Boston, and Philadelphia.

Article Sources

The following authors contributed the new articles for **Macmillan Profiles:** *European Artists:*

Mary Carvlin
Nancy Gratton
John N. Jones
William Kaufman
Michael Levine

The following articles were adapted from the *Encyclopedia of the Renaissance*, published by Charles Scribner's Sons:

ARTICLE	AUTHOR
Angelico, Fra	William Hood
Bellini, Giovanni	Carolyn C. Wilson
Bosch, Hieronymus	Walter S. Gibson
Botticelli, Sandro	Michael J. Amy
Bruegel, Pieter (Elder)	Walter S. Gibson
Caravaggio, Michelangelo	Mario Pereira
Cellini, Benvenuto	Flavio Boggi
Corregio	Maureen Pelta
Cranach, Lucas the Elder	Joseph Leo Koerner
Donatello	Maureen Pelta
Durer, Albrecht	Jeffrey Chipps Smith
Eyck, Jan van	Marina Belozerskaya
Gentileschi, Artemesia	Mary D. Garrard
Ghiberti, Lorenzo	Flavio Boggi
Girogione	Carolyn C. Wilson
Giotto di Bondone	Matthew G. Shoaf
Goes, Hugo van der	Michael J. Amy

Grunewald, Matthias	Jane Tylus
Hobein, Hans (Younger)	Stephanie Leitch
Mantegna, Andrea	Francis Ames-Lewis
Masaccio	Marina Belozerskaya
Piero della Francesca	J.V. Field
Tintoretto	David Rossand
Weyden, Rogier van der	Michael J. Amy

The following article was adapted from *Ancient Greece and Rome*, published by Charles Scribner's Sons:

ARTICLE
Praxiteles

The following articles were adapted from the *Dictionary of Jewish Biography*, published by Macmillan Library Reference:

ARTICLE
Chagall, Mark
Modigliani, Amedeo
Pissarro, Camille
Soutine, Chaim

The following articles were adapted from *They Made History*, published by Macmillan Library Reference:

ARTICLE
Blake, William
Cezanne, Paul
da Vinci, Leonardo
Gogh, Vincent van
Goya
El Greco
Manet, Edouard
Michelangelo
Phidias
Picasso, Pablo
Raphael
Rembrandt
Rodin, Auguste
Titian

Photo Credits

Photographs appearing in *European Artists* are from the following sources:

Arp, Jean (Hans) (page 4): Archive Photos
Bacon, Francis (page 10): Corbis
Beckmann, Max (page 13):Corbis
Blake, William (page 22): Corbis
Brancusi, Constantin (page 41): Corbis
Braque, Georges (page 44): Archive Photo
Canova, Antonio (page 57): Corbis
Caravaggio (page 61): Library of Congress
Cellini, Benvenuto (page 65): Library of Congress
Cézanne, Paul (page 70): Corbis
Chagall, Marc (page 74): AP/Wide World
Chardin, Jean-Simeon (page 77): Archive Photo
De Chirico, Giorgio (page 80): Corbis
Corot, Jean-Baptiste Camille (page 86): Public Domain
Cranach, Lucas (page 96): Corbis
Dalí, Salvador (page 103): AP/Wide World
David, Jacques-Louis (page 110): Archive Photo
Degas, Edgar (page 113): Corbis
Delacroix, Eugene (page 116): Corbis
Donatello (page 119): Library of Congress
Duchamp, Marcel (page 126): Archive Photo
Durer, Albrecht (page 129): AP/Wide World
Ensor, James Sydney (page 138): Corbis
Ernst, Max (page 141):Corbis
Eyck, Jan van (page 144): Corbis
Freud, Lucian (page 156): Corbis

Friedrich, Casper David (page 158): Corbis
Gauguin, Paul (page 165): Corbis
Gericault, Theodore (page 171): Library of Congress
Giacometti, Alberto (page 176): Corbis
Giotto (page 182): Library of Congress
Gogh, Vincent van (page 188): Corbis
Goya (page 191): Corbis
Greco, El (page 194): Corbis
Gris, Juan (page 197): Corbis
Grunewald, Matthias (page 199): Corbis
Hockney, David (page 206): Archive Photo
Ingres, Jean-Auguste-Dominique (page 220): Library of Congress
Kandinsky, Wassily (page 226): Corbis
Klee, Paul (page 237): Corbis
Kokoschka, Oskar (page 242): Corbis
Leger, Fernand (page 248): Corbis
Malevich, Kasimir (page 258): Corbis
Manet, Edouard (page 261): Corbis
Marc, Franz (page 266): Corbis
Matisse, Henri (page 271): Corbis
Michelangelo (page 275): Library of Congress
Millais, John Everett (page 278): Corbis
Miró, Joan (page 284): AP/Wide World
Mondrian, Piet (page 289): Archive Photo
Monet, Claude (page 293): Library of Congress
Moore, Henry (page 297): AP/Wide World
Munch, Edvard (page 302): Corbis
Phidias (page 312): Corbis
Picasso. Pablo (page 314): AP/Wide World
Pissarro, Camille (page 320): Library of Congress
Poussin, Nicolas (page 325): Library of Congress
Praxiteles (page 327): Corbis
Raphael (page 330): Corbis
Redon, Odilon (page 332): Library of Congress
Rembrandt (page 335): Corbis
Renoir, Pierre-Auguste (page 337): Corbis
Reynolds, Joshua (page 340): Public Domain
Rodin, Auguste (page 345): Corbis
Rosetti, Dante Gabriel (page 347): Corbis
Rousseau, Henri (page 351): Corbis
Rubens, Peter Paul (page 354): Unknown Source
Seurat, Georges (page 360): AP/Wide World

Soutine, Chaim (page 365): Corbis
Tintoretto (page 370): Corbis
Titian (page 373): Corbis
Toulouse-Lautrec, Henri de (page 375): Corbis
Turner, Joseph (page 377): Corbis

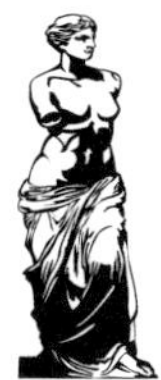

Additional Resources

GENERAL SOURCES

BOOKS

Chilvers, Ian, ed. *The Concise Oxford Dictionary of Art and Artists*. Oxford University Press, 1997.

Cliff, Stafford. *The French Archive of Design and Decoration*. Harry N. Abrams, 1999.

Craske, Matthew. *Art in Europe 1700-1830: A History of the Visual Arts in an Era of Unprecedented Urban Economic Growth*. Oxford University Press, 1997.

Fiedler, Jeannine and Peter Feierabend, eds. *Bauhaus*. Konemann, 2000.

Gowing, Sir Lawrence. *A Biographical Dictionary of Artists*. Checkmark Books, 1995.

Hale, J.R., ed. *A Concise Encyclopaedia of the Italian Renaissance*. W.W. Norton, 1981.

Herbert, Robert L. *Impressionism: Art, Leisure, and Parisian Society*. Yale University Press, 1991.

Jarrasse, Dominique. *18th Century French Painting*. Terrail, 1999.

Krystal, Barbara. *100 Artists Who Shaped World History*. Bluewood Books, 1997.

Lincoln, W. Bruce. *Between Heaven and Hell: The Story of a Thousand Years of Artistic Life in Russia*. Viking Press, 1998.

Murray, Chris, ed. *Dictionary of the Arts*. Checkmark Books, 1994.

Murry, Peter and Linda. *Penguin Dictionary of Art and Artists*. Penguin USA, 1998.

Osborne, Harold, ed. *The Oxford Companion to Art*. Oxford University Press, 1983.

Prettejohn, Elizabeth, ed. *After the Pre-Raphaelites: Art and Aestheticism in Victorian England*. Rutgers University Press, 1999.

Read, Herbert, ed. *The Thames and Hudson Dictionary of Art and Artists*. Thames & Hudson, 1994.

Romanelli, Giandomenico, ed. *Venice: Art & Architecture*. Konemann, 1999.

Rowland, Ingrid T. *The Culture of the High Renaissance: Ancients and Moderns in Sixteenth-Century Rome*. Cambridge University Press, 1998.

Saunders, Ann. *The Art and Architecture of London: An Illustrated Guide*. Phaidon Press, 1996.

Toman, Rolf, ed. *The Art of the Italian Renaissance: Architecture, Sculpture, Painting, Drawing*. Konemann, 1998.

Toman, Rolf, ed. *The Baroque: Architecture, Sculpture, Painting*. Konemann, 1998.

Turner, Jane Shoaf, ed. *The Dictionary of Art*. Grove's Dictionaries, Inc., 1996.

Vaughan, William H.T., ed. *Encyclopedia of Artists*. Oxford University Press, 2000.

Vaughan, William and Francoise Cachin. *Arts of the 19th Century: 1780-1850*. Harry N. Abrams, 1998.

VIDEORECORDINGS

Art of the Western World, 1994.

Arts & Splendor - Michelangelo and the Sistine Chapel, 1996.

Biography: Leonardo Da Vinci, 1997.

Biography: Michelangelo, 1999.

Biography: Pablo Picasso, 1999.

Biography: Vincent Van Gogh, 1999.

The Definitive Dali, 1986.

Francis Bacon: Portrait of an Artist, 1985.

Landmarks of Western Art, 1999.

The Life of Leonardo Da Vinci, 1990.

The Louvre, 1978.

Portrait of an Artist: Hockney, 1983.

Portrait of an Artist: Joan Miro, 1978.

Portrait of an Artist: Les Silences De Manet, 1989.

Portrait of an Artists: Magritte, 1978.

Portrait of an Artist: Matisse, 1987.

Portrait of an Artist: Monet, 1989.

Portrait of an Artist: Paul Cezanne, 1985.

Portrait of an Artist: Tintoretto, 1984.

Portrait of an Artist: Vermeer, 1996.

Sister Wendy's Story of Painting, 1997.

WEBSITES

Absolutearts, http://www.absolutearts.org

Addio Gallery, http://www.mcs.csuhayward.edu/~malek/Addio.html

Amore Gallery, http://www.mcs.csuhayward.edu/~malek/Amore.html

Art and Architecture of Venice, http://www.boglewood.com/cornaro/xcornaro.html

Artchive, http://www.artchive.com/

Artcyclopedia, http://www.artcyclopedia.com/

Artgardens, http://www.artgardens.com/

ARTnewsroom.com, http://artnewsroom.com/

ARTonline, http://www.myartonline.com/

Artpics, http://users.pandora.be/bernard/Artpics/

Bella Gallery, http://www.mcs.csuhayward.edu/~malek/Bella.html

CGFA, http://sunsite.auc.dk/cgfa/index.html

Loggia, http://www.loggia.com/

Mystudios.com, http://www.mystudios.com

OCAIW, http://www.ocaiw.com/index.htm

Olga's Gallery, http://www.abcgallery.com/index.html

The Printroom, http://www.ukans.edu/~sma/prints.html

Sohoart.com, http://www.sohoart.com/

Surrealism Gallery, http://www.mcs.csuhayward.edu/~malek/Surrealism/index.html

Tesoro Gallery, http://www.mcs.csuhayward.edu/~malck/Tesoro.html

Uffizi, http://www.televisual.net/uffizi/

Web Gallery of Art, http://www.kfki.hu/~arthp/welcome.html

WebMuseum, http://metalab.unc.edu/wm/

WetCanvas, http://www.wetcanvas.com/

INDIVIDUAL ARTISTS

ANGELICO, FRA

Artchive: Fra Angelico, http://www.artchive.com/artchive/ftptoc/fra_angelico_ext.html

CGFA: Fra Angelico, http://sunsite.auc.dk/cgfa/angelico/

Morachiello, Paolo. *Fra Angelico: The San Marco Frescoes*. Thames & Hudson, 1996.

Spike, John T. *Fra Angelico*. Abbeville Press, 1997.

WebMuseum: Fra Angelico, http://metalab.unc.edu/wm/paint/auth/angelico/

ARP, HANS (JEAN)

Artchive: Jean Arp, http://www.artchive.com/artchive/A/arp.html

ARTonline: Jean Arp, http://www.myartonline.com/artist/Arp.htm

Soby, James T. *Arp*. Ayer Co. Publishing, 1986.

BACON, FRANCIS

Artchive: Francis Bacon, http://www.artchive.com/artchive/ftptoc/bacon_ext.html

Farson, Daniel. *The Gilded Gutter Life of Francis Bacon*. Pantheon Books, 1993.

Francis Bacon Image Gallery, http://www.francis-bacon.cx/

Peppiatt, Michael. *Francis Bacon: Anatomy of an Enigma*. Farrar, Straus and Giroux, 1997.

Russell, John. *Francis Bacon*. Thames & Hudson, 1993.

Sinclair, Andrew. *Francis Bacon: His Life and Violent Times*. Crown, 1993.

UD Art: Francis Bacon, http://desires2.desires.com/2.4/Art/Bacon/bacon.html

BECKMANN, MAX

Artchive: Max Beckmann, http://www.artchive.com/artchive/ftptoc /beckmann_ext.html

Beckett, Wendy. *Max Beckmann and the Self*. International Book Import Service, Inc., 1997.

Beckmann, Max. *Max Beckmann*. Ayer Co. Publishing, 1987.

Beckmann, Max. *Max Beckmann: Self-Portrait in Words: Selected Writings and Statements, 1903-1950*. University of Chicago Press, 1999.

Sohoart.com: Max Beckmann, http://www.sohoart.com/beckmann.htm

BELLINI, GIOVANNI

Art and Architecture of Venice: Giovanni Bellini, http://www.boglewood.com /cornaro/xgbellini.html

Artchive: Giovanni Bellini, http://www.artchive.com/artchive/B/bellini.html

Goffen, Rona. *Giovanni Bellini*. Yale University Press, 1989.

Tempestini, Anchise. *Giovanni Bellini*. Abbeville Press, Inc., 1999.

WebMuseum: Giovanni Bellini, http://metalab.unc.edu/wm/paint/auth/bellini/

BERNINI, GIAN LORENZO

Artchive: Gianlorenzo Bernini, http://www.artchive.com/artchive/B/bernini.html

Scribner, Charles. *Gianlorenzo Bernini*. Harry N. Adams, 1991.

Web Gallery of Art: Gian Lorenzo Bernini, http://www.kfki.hu/~arthp/bio/b /bernini/gianlore/biograph.html

BLAKE, WILLIAM

The Blake Multimedia Project, http://cla.calpoly.edu/%7Esmarx/Blake /blakeproject.html

Blake, William, et al. *Blake's Poetry and Designs: Authoritative Texts, Illuminations in Color and Monochrome, Related Prose, Criticism*. W.W. Norton, 1980.

Gilchrist, Alexander. *The Life of William Blake*. Dover Publications, 1998.

Heppner, Christopher. *Reading Blake's Designs*. Cambridge University Press, 1995.

Norvig, Gerda S. *Dark Figures in the Desired Country: Blake's Illustrations to the Pilgrim's Progress*. University of California Press, 1993.

WebMuseum: William Blake, http://metalab.unc.edu/wm/paint/auth/blake/

The William Blake Archive, http://jefferson.village.virginia.edu/blake/

BOCCIONI, UMBERTO

Artchive: Umberto Boccioni, http://www.artchive.com/artchive/B/boccioni.html

BONNARD, PIERRE

Artchive: Pierre Bonnard, http://www.artchive.com/artchive/B/bonnard.html

Artgardens: Pierre Bonnard, http://www.artgardens.com/Artists/bonnard_pierre.htm

Hyman, Timothy. *Bonnard (The Word of Art)*. Thames & Hudson, 1998.

Watkins, Nicholas and Pierre Bonnard. *Bonnard*. Phaidon Press, 1994.

Whitfield, Sarah and John Elderfield. *Bonnard*. Harry N. Adams, 1998.

BOSCH, HIERONYMUS

Artchive: Hieornymus Bosch, http://www.artchive.com/artchive/ftptoc/bosch_ext.html

CGFA: Hieornymus Bosch, http://sunsite.auc.dk/cgfa/bosch/

Dixon, Laurinda S. *Alchemical Imagery in Bosch's Garden of Delights*. Umi Research Press, 1981.

Gibson, Walter S. *Hieronymus Bosch*. Thames & Hudson, 1985.

Lafond, Paul. *Prints of Hieronymus Bosch*. Alan Wofsy Fine Arts, 2000.

Linfert, Carl. *Hieronymus Bosch*. Harry N. Abrams, 1989.

University of Athens: Hieronymus Bosch, http://www.di.uoa.gr/~grad0146/

BOTTICELLI, SANDRO

Absolutearts: Botticelli, http://www.absolutearts.org/masters/names/Botticelli_Sandro.html

Artchive: Botticelli, http://artchive.com/artchive/B/botticelli.html

CGFA: Botticelli, http://sunsite.auc.dk/cgfa/botticel/

Lightbown, Ronald. *Botticelli: Life and Work*. Abbeville Press, Inc., 1989.

Santi, Bruno. *Botticelli*. Riverside Book Company, 1995.

WebMuseum: Botticelli, http://metalab.unc.edu/wm/paint/auth/botticelli/

Zollner, Frank. *Botticelli: Images of Love and Spring*. International Book Import Service, 1998.

BOUCHER, FRANCOIS

CGFA: Francois Boucher, http://btr0xw.rz.uni-bayreuth.de/cgfa/boucher/

OCIAW: Francois Boucher, http://www.ocaiw.com/boucher.htm

WebMuseum: Francois Boucher, http://metalab.unc.edu/wm/paint/auth/boucher/

BRANCUSI, CONSTANTIN

Artchive: Constantin Brancusi, http://www.artchive.com/artchive/B/brancusi.html

Bach, Friedrich Teja, et al. *Constantin Brancusi, 1876-1957*. Philadelphia Museum of Art, 1995.

Isamu Noguchi Museum: Constantin Brancusi, http://www.noguchi.org/brancusi.html

OCIAW: Constantin Brancusi, http://www.ocaiw.com/bracusi.htm

Romanian-American Forum: Brancusi, http://cpcug.org/user/stefan/brancus.html

Shanes, Eric. *Constantin Brancusi*. Abbeville Press, 1989.

BRAQUE, GEORGES

Artchive: Georges Braque, http://www.artchive.com/artchive/ftptoc/braque_ext.html

Golding, John, et al. *Braque: The Late Years*. Yale University Press, 1997.

Wilkin, Karen. *Georges Braque*. Abbeville Press, 1992.

BRUEGEL THE ELDER, PIETER

Artchive: Pieter Bruegel the Elder, http://www.artchive.com/artchive/ftptoc/bruegel_ext.html

CGFA: Pieter Bruegel the Elder, http://sunsite.auc.dk/cgfa/bruegel1/

Gibson, Walter S. *Bruegel*. Thames & Hudson, 1985.

Seipel, Wilfried, ed. *Pieter Bruegel the Elder at the Kunsthistorisches Museum in Vienna*. Skira, 1999.

Stechow, Wolfgang. *Pieter Bruegel: The Elder*. Harry N. Abrams, 1990.

WebMuseum: Pieter Bruegel the Elder, http://metalab.unc.edu/wm/paint/auth/bruegel/

BURNE-JONES, EDWARD COLEY

CGFA: Sir Edward Coley Burne-Jones, http://sunsite.auc.dk/cgfa/burne/

Mancoff, Debra N. *Burne-Jones*. Pomegranate, 2000.

OCAIW: Sir Edward Coley Burne-Jones, http://www.ocaiw.com/burne.htm

WebMuseum: Sir Edward Coley Burne-Jones, http://metalab.unc.edu/wm/paint/auth/burne-jones/

Wildman, Stephen and John Christian. *Edward Burne-Jones: Victorian Artist-Dreamer*. Harry N. Abrams, 1998.

Wood, Christopher. *Burne-Jones: The Life and Works of Sir Edward Burne-Jones (1833-1898)*. Stewart Tabori & Chang, 1998.

CAMPIN, ROBERT

Artpics: Robert Campin, http://users.pandora.be/bernard/Artpics/Campin.htm

WebMuseum: Master of Flémalle (Robert Campin), http://metalab.unc.edu/wm/paint/auth/flemalle/

CANOVA, ANTONIO

OCAIW: Antonio Canova, http://www.ocaiw.com/canova.htm

Johns, Christopher M.S. *Antonio Canova and the Politics of Patronage in Revolutionary and Napoleonic Europe*. Univeristy of California Press, 1998.

Loggia: Antonio Canova, http://www.loggia.com/art/artists/canova.html

CARAVAGGIO

Artchive: Caravaggio, http://www.artchive.com/artchive/C/caravaggio.html

CGFA: Caravaggio, http://sunsite.auc.dk/cgfa/caravagg/

Hibbard, Howard. *Caravaggio*. Icon (Harpe), 1985.

Puglisi, Catherine. *Caravaggio*. Phaidon Press, 2000.

Robb, Peter. M: *The Man Who Became Caravaggio*. Henry Holt & Company, 2000.

Seward, Desmond. *Caravaggio: A Passionate Life*. William Morrow & Co., 1998.

WebMuseum: Caravaggio, http://metalab.unc.edu/wm/paint/auth/caravaggio/

CELLINI, BENVENUTO

Cellini, Benvenuto. *The Autobiography of Benvenuto Cellini*. Penguis USA, 1999.

OCAIW: Benvenuto Cellini, http://www.ocaiw.com/1cellini.htm

Scalini, Mario. *Benvenuto Cellini*. Riverside Book Company, 1996.

Web Gallery of Art: Benvenuto Cellini, http://www.kfki.hu/~arthp/html/c/cellini/index.html

CEZANNE, PAUL

Artchive: Paul Cezanne, http://www.artchive.com/artchive/ftptoc/cezanne_ext.html

Cachin, Francoise, et al. *Cezanne*. Harry N. Abrams, 1996.

Callow, Philip. *Lost Earth: A Life of Cezanne*. Ivan R. Dee, Inc., 1995.

Fry, Roger Eliot. *Cezanne: A Study of His Development*. University of Chicago Press, 1989.

OCAIW: Paul Cezanne, http://www.ocaiw.com/cezanne.htm

Rewald, John. *Cezanne: A Biography*. Harry N. Abrams, 1996.

WebMuseum: Paul Cezanne, http://metalab.unc.edu/wm/paint/auth/cezanne/

CHAGALL, MARC

Artchive: Marc Chagall, http://www.artchive.com/artchive/ftptoc/chagall_ext.html

Bohm-Duchen, Monica. *Chagall*. Phaidon Press, 1998.

CGFA: Marc Chagall, http://sunsite.auc.dk/cgfa/chagall/

Chagall, Marc. *My Life*. Da Capo Press, 1994.

Conrad, Christopher and Ulrike Gauss, eds. *Chagall: The Lithographs*. Distributed Art Publishers, 1999.

Marchesseau, Daniel. *Chagall: The Art of Dreams*. Harry N. Adams, 1998.

OCAIW: Marc Chagall, http://www.ocaiw.com/1chagall.htm

CHARDIN, JEAN-SIMEON

Artchive: Jean Baptiste Simeon Chardin, http://www.artchive.com/artchive/C/chardin.html

ARTnewsroom.com: Jean-Baptiste Chardin, http://artnewsroom.com/ArtNewsHeadlines-03/chardin.html

Michel, Marianne Roland. *Chardin*. Harry N. Abrams, 1996.

Naughton, Gabriel. *Chardin*. Phaidon Press, 1996.

CHIRICO, GIORGIO DE

Artchive: Giorgio de Chirico, http://www.artchive.com/artchive/ftptoc/de_chirico_ext.html

Baldacci, Paolo. *De Chirico: The Metaphysical Period, 1888-1919*. Bullfinch Press, 1998.

Braun, Emily. *Girogio De Chirico and America*. Umberto Allemandi, 1997.

De Chirico, Giorgio. *The Memoirs of Giorgio De Chirico*. Da Capo Press, 1994.

The Giorgio De Chirico Metaphysical Gallery, http://www.geocities.com/Athens/6163/

CONSTABLE, JOHN

Artchive: John Constable, http://www.artchive.com/artchive/ftptoc/constable_ext.html

CFGA: John Constable, http://sunsite.auc.dk/cgfa/constabl/

Leslie, Charles Robert. *Memoirs of the Life of John Constable*. Phaidon Press, 1995.

Parkinson, Ronald. *John Constable: The Man and His Art*. Victoria & Albert Museum, 1998.

Rosenthal, Michael. *Constable: The Painter and His Landscape*. Yale University Press, 1986.

WebMuseum: John Constable, http://metalab.unc.edu/wm/paint/auth/constable/

COROT, JEAN-BAPTISTE CAMILLE

Artchive: Jean-Baptiste-Camille Corot, http://www.artchive.com/artchive/ftptoc/corot_ext.html

CGFA: Jean-Baptiste-Camille Corot, http://sunsite.auc.dk/cgfa/corot/

Hours, Madeleine. *Corot*. Harry N. Abrams, 1984.

WebMuseum: Jean-Baptiste-Camille Corot, http://metalab.unc.edu/wm/paint/auth/corot/

CORREGGIO

CGFA: Correggio, http://sunsite.auc.dk/cgfa/correggi/

Ekserdjian, David. *Correggio*. Yale University Press, 1998.

Smyth, Carolyn. *Correggio's Frescoes in Parma Cathedral*. Princeton University Press, 1997.

WebMuseum: Correggio, http://metalab.unc.edu/wm/paint/auth/correggio/

COURBET, GUSTAVE

Artchive: Gustave Courbet, http://www.artchive.com/artchive/ftptoc/courbet_ext.html

CGFA: Gustave Courbet, http://sunsite.auc.dk/cgfa/courbet/

Clark, T.J. *Image of the People: Gustave Courbet and the 1848 Revolution*. University of California Press, 1999.

Mack, Gerstle. *Gustave Courbet*. Da Capo Press, 1989.

OCAIW: Gustave Courbet, http://www.ocaiw.com/courbet.htm

Rubin, James Henry. *Courbet*. Phaidon Press, 1997.

WebMuseum: Gustave Courbet, http://metalab.unc.edu/wm/paint/auth/courbet/

CRANACH, LUCAS

CGFA: Lucas Cranach the Elder, http://sunsite.auc.dk/cgfa/cranach1/

OCAIW: Lucas Cranach the Elder, http://www.ocaiw.com/ncranach.htm

WebMuseum: Lucas Cranach the Elder, http://metalab.unc.edu/wm/paint/auth/cranach/

Stepanov, Alexander. *Lucas Cranach the Elder: 1472-1553*. Parkstone Press, 1997.

DA VINCI, LEONARDO

Artchive: Leonardo da Vinci, http://www.artchive.com/artchive/ftptoc/leonardo_ext.html

Bramly, Serge. *Leonardo: The Artist and the Man*. Penguin USA, 1995.

Brown, David Alan. *Leonardo Da Vinci: Origins of a Genius*. Yale University Press, 1998.

Clark, Kenneth. *Leonardo Da Vinci*. Penguin USA, 1993.

Leonardo da Vinci Museum, http://www.davinci-museum.com/

Turner, A. Richard. *Inventing Leonardo*. University of California Press, 1994.

WebMuseum: Leonardo da Vinci, http://metalab.unc.edu/wm/paint/auth/vinci/

DALÍ, SALVADOR

Ades, Dawn, ed. *Dali's Optical Illusions*. Yale University Press, 2000.

Dali, Salvador. *The Secret Life of Salvador Dali*. Dover Publications, 1993.

Descharnes, Robert and Gilles Neret. *Salvador Dali: 1904-1989*. TASCHEN America, 1998.

Goff, Robert. *The Essential Salvador Dali*. Andrews McMeel Publishing, 1998.

Gala-Salvador Dali Foundation, http://www.dali-estatc.org/

Salvador Dali Art Gallery, http://www.dali-gallery.com/

The Salvador Dali Museum, http://www.salvadordalimuseum.org/

DAUMIER, HONORE

Daumier Print Collection, http://www.umt.edu/partv/famus/print/daumier/Daumier.htm

Laughton, Bruce. *Honere Daumier*. Yale University Press, 1996.

Ramus, Charles, ed. *Daumier, 120 Great Lithographs*. Dover Publications, 1979.

WebMuseum: Honore Daumier, http://metalab.unc.edu/wm/paint/auth/daumier/

WetCanvas: Honore Daumier, http://www.wetcanvas.com/Museum/Artists/d/Honore_Daumier/

DAVID, JACQUES-LOUIS

CGFA: Jacques-Louis David, http://sunsite.auc.dk/cgfa/jdavid/

Lajer-Burcharth, Ewa. *Necklines: The Art of Jacques-Louis David After the Terror*. Yale University Press, 1999.

Lee, Simon. *David*. Phaidon Press, 1999.

OCAIW: Jacques-Louis David, http://www.ocaiw.com/david.htm

Roberts, Warren. *Jacques-Louis David and Jean-Louis Prieur, Revolutionary Artists: The Public, the Populace, and Images of the French Revolution*. State University of New York Press, 1999.

WebMuseum: Jacques-Louis David, http://metalab.unc.edu/wm/paint/auth/david/

DEGAS, EDGAR

Artchive: Edgar Degas, http://www.artchive.com/artchive/ftptoc/degas_ext.html

CGFA: Edgar Degas, http://pollux.bibl.u-szeged.hu/cgfa/degas/

Gordon, Robert. *Degas*. Harry N. Abrams, 1996.

Gruitrooy, Gerhard. *Degas: Impressions of a Great Master*. Todtri Productions, Ltd., 1998.

Kendall, Richard. *Degas Dancers*. Vendome Press, 1996.

Meyer, Susan E. *Edgar Degas*. Harry N. Abrams, 1994.

WebMuseum: Edgar Degas, http://metalab.unc.edu/wm/paint/auth/degas/

DELACROIX, EUGENE

Artchive: Eugene Delacroix, http://www.artchive.com/artchive/ftptoc/delacroix_ext.html

Artgardens: Eugene Delacroix, http://www.artgardens.com/Artists/delacroix_eugene.htm

Delacroix, Eugene. *The Journal of Eugene Delacroix: A Selection*. Phaidon Press, 1995.

Jobert, Barthelemy. *Delacroix*. Princeton University Press, 1998.

Neret, Gilles. *Eugene Delacroix 1798-1863: The Prince of Romanticism*. TASCHEN America, 1999.

OCAIW: Eugene Delacroix, http://www.ocaiw.com/1delacro.htm

DONATELLO

Artchive: Donatello, http://www.artchive.com/artchive/ftptoc/donatello_ext.html

OCAIW: Donatello, http://www.ocaiw.com/donate.htm

Bertela, Giovanna G. *Donatello*. Riverside Book Company, 1994.

Poeschke, Joachim. *Donatello and His World; Sculpture of the Italian Renaissance*. Harry N. Abrams, 1993.

Web Gallery of Art: Donatello, http://www.kfki.hu/~arthp/html/d/donatell/index.html

Wirtz, Rolf C. *Donatello*. Konemann, 1998.

DUBUFFET, JEAN

Artchive: Jean Dubuffet, http://www.artchive.com/artchive/D/dubuffet.html

Glimcher. *Jean Dubuffet Simulacres*. Pace Gallery Publications, 1969.

Selz, Pe. *Work of Jean Dubuffet*. Ayer Company Publishing, 1981.

DUCHAMP, MARCEL

Artchive: Marcel Duchamp, http://www.artchive.com/artchive/ftptoc/duchamp_ext.html

Cabanne, Pierre. *Dialogues with Marcel Duchamp*. Da Capo Press, 1988.

Encounter with Duchamp, http://www.marcelduchamp.org/

Joselit, David. *Infinite Regress: Marcel Duchamp 1910-1941*. MIT Press, 1998.

Naumann, Francis M. *Marcel Duchamp: The Art of Making Art in the Age of Mechanical Reproduction*. Harry N. Abrams, 1999.

Tomkins, Calvin. *Duchamp: A Biography*. Owl Books, 1998.

Tout-Fait, http://www.toutfait.com/

DURER, ALBRECHT

Artchive: Albrecht Durer, http://www.artchive.com/artchive/ftptoc/durer_ext.html

CGFA: Albrecht Durer, http://sunsite.auc.dk/cgfa/durer/

Durer, Albrecht. *The Complete Engravings, Etchings, and Drypoints of Albrecht Durer.* Dover Publications, 1972.

Hutchison, Jane Campbell. *Albrecht Durer.* Princeton University Press, 1992.

Panofsky, Erwin. *The Life and Art of Albrecht Durer.* Princeton University Press, 1971.

WebMuseum: Albrecht Durer, http://metalab.unc.edu/wm/paint/auth/durer/

ENSOR, JAMES SYDNEY

Becks-Malorny, Ulrike. *James Ensor, 1860-1949: Masks, Death, and the Sea.* TASCHEN America, 1999.

Lund Humphries Publishing Staff, ed. *James Ensor: Visionary Landscapes, Masqueraders, and a Taste for the Macabre.* Antique Collectors Club, 1997.

The Printroom: James Ensor, http://www.ukans.edu/~sma/ensor/ensor.htm

ERNST, MAX

Artchive: Max Ernst, http://www.artchive.com/artchive/ftptoc/ernst_ext.html

Bella Gallery: Max Ernst, http://www.mcs.csuhayward.edu/~malek/Ernst.html

Ernst, Max. *Une Semaine De Bonte: A Surrealistic Novel in Collage.* Dover Publications, 1976.

Quinn, Edward. *Max Ernst.* Konemann, 1999.

Turpin, Ian. *Ernst.* Phaidon Press, 1993.

EYCK, JAN VAN

Artchive: Jan van Eyck, http://www.artchive.com/artchive/ftptoc/van_eyck_ext.html

CGFA: Jan van Eyck, http://sunsite.auc.dk/cgfa/eyck/

Hall, Edwin. *The Arnolfini Betrothal: Medieval Marriage and the Enigma of Van Eyck's Double Portrait.* University of California Press, 1997.

Harbison, Craig. *Jan Van Eyck: The Play of Realism.* Reaktion Books, 1997.

WebMuseum: Jan van Eyck, http://metalab.unc.edu/wm/paint/auth/eyck/

FRAGONARD, JEAN-HONORE

Massengale, Jean Montague. *Jean-Honore Fragonard.* Harry N. Abrams, 1993.

Sheriff, Mary D. *Fragonard: Art and Eroticism.* University of Chicago Press, 1990.

Washington State: The European Enlightenment Gallery: Jean-Honore Fragonard, http://www.wsu.edu/~dee/ENLIGHT/FRAG.HTM

DELLA FRANCESCA, PIERO

Calvesi, Maurizio. *Piero Della Francesca.* Rizzoli International Publications, 1998.

Laskowski, Birgit. *Piero Della Francesca.* Konemann, 1998.

Longhi, Roberto. *Piero Della Francesca.* Sheep Meadow Press, 2000.

Uffizi: Piero della Francesca, http://www.televisual.net/uffizi/p_france.html

WebMuseum: Piero della Francesca, http://metalab.unc.edu/wm/paint/auth/piero/

FREUD, LUCIAN

Artchive: Lucian Freud, http://www.artchive.com/artchive/ftptoc/freud_ext.html

Cook, Angus and Leigh Bowery. *Lucian Freud: Recent Drawings and Etchings*. Matthew Marks, 1993.

Hughes, Robert. *Lucian Freud Paintings*. Unknown, 1997.

WebMuseum: Lucian Freud, http://metalab.unc.edu/wm/paint/auth/freud/

FRIEDRICH, CASPAR DAVID

CGFA: Caspar David Friedrich, http://sunsite.auc.dk/cgfa/friedric/

Hofmann, Werner. *Caspar David Friedrich*. Thames & Hudson, 2000.

Koerner, Joseph Leo. *Caspar David Friedrich and the Subject of Landscape*. Yale University Press, 1995.

OCAIW: Caspar David Friedrich, http://www.ocaiw.com/friedr.htm

Sala, Charles. *Caspar David Friedrich and Romantic Painting*. Terrail, 1997.

Schmied, Wieland. *Caspar David Friedrich*. Harry N. Abrams, 1995.

WebMuseum: Caspar David Friedrich, http://www.southern.com/wm/paint/auth /friedrich/

GAINSBOROUGH, THOMAS

CGFA: Thomas Gainsborough, http://sunsite.auc.dk/cgfa/gainsbor/index.html

Gainsborough's House, http://www.gainsborough.org/

Kalinsky, Nicola. *Gainsborough*. Phaidon Press, 1995.

Rosenthal, Michael. *The Art of Thomas Gainsborough*. Yale University Press, 2000.

WebMuseum: Thomas Gainsborough, http://metalab.unc.edu/wm/paint/auth /gainsborough/

GAUGUIN, PAUL

Artchive: Paul Gauguin, http://www.artchive.com/artchive/ftptoc/gauguin_ext.html

CGFA: Paul Gauguin, http://sunsite.auc.dk/cgfa/gauguin/Cachin, Francoise. *Gauguin: The Quest for Paradise*. Harry N. Abrams, 1992.

Gauguin, Paul. *Gauguin's Intimate Journals*. Dover Publications, 1997.

Goldwater, Robert. *Gauguin*. Harry N. Abrams, 1983.

Thomson, Belinda. *Gauguin*. Thames & Hudson, 1987.

WebMuseum: Paul Gauguin, http://metalab.unc.edu/wm/paint/auth/gauguin/

GENTILESCHI, ARTEMISIA

Artemisia Gentileschi and the Age of Baroque, http://rubens.anu.edu.au/student.projects/artemisia/Artemisia.html

Bissell, R. Ward. *Artemisia Gentileschi and the Authority of Art*. Pennsylvania State University Press, 1999.

Garrard, Mary D. *Artemisia Gentileschi*. Princeton University Press, 1991.

Great Women Artists: Artemesia Gentileschi, http://www.uwrf.edu/history/prints/women/artemesia.html

GERICAULT, THEODORE

Artchive: Theodore Gericault, http://www.artchive.com/artchive/G/gericault.html

Whitney, Wheelock. *Gericault in Italy*. Yale University Press, 1997.

GHIBERTI, LORENZO

Artchive: Lorenzo Ghiberti, http://www.artchive.com/artchive/G/ghiberti.html

OCAIW: Lorenzo Ghiberti, http://www.ocaiw.com/1ghibert.htm

Web Gallery of Art: Lorenzo Ghiberti, http://www.kfki.hu/~arthp/html/g/ghiberti/

GIACOMETTI, ALBERTO

Alberto Giacometti Page, http://www.electroasylum.com/giacometti/

Artchive: Alberto Giacometti, http://www.artchive.com/artchive/G/giacometti.html

Bonnefoy, Yves. *Alberto Giacometti: A Biography of His Work*. Abbeville Press, 1991.

Lord, James. *Giacometti Portrait*. Noonday Press, 1980.

Schneider, Angela, ed. *Alberto Giacometti: Sculptures, Paintings, Drawings*. International Book Import Service, 1997.

GIORGIONE

Anderson, Jaynie. *Giorgione: The Painter of "Poetic Brevity"*. Abbeville Press, 1997.

Artchive: Giorgione, http://www.artchive.com/artchive/G/giorgione.html

CGFA: Giorgione, http://sunsite.auc.dk/cgfa/giorgion/

Pignatti, Terisio and Filippo Pedrocco. *Giorgione*. Rizzoli Bookstore, 1999.

Settis, Salvatore. *Giorgione's Tempest: Interpreting the Hidden Subject*. University of Chicago Press, 1994.

GIOTTO

CGFA: Giotto, http://www.sai.msu.su/cjackson/giotto/index.html

Ladis, Andrew, ed. *The Arena Chapel and the Genius of Giotto: Padua*. Garland Publishing, 1998.

Mueller, Anne. *Giotto*. Konemann, 1998.

Steel, Susannah. *Giotto*. DK Publishing, 1999.

Web Gallery of Art: Giotto, http://www.kfki.hu/~arthp/tours/giotto/index.html

WebMuseum: Giotto, http://metalab.unc.edu/wm/paint/auth/giotto/

GOES, HUGO VAN DER

Uffizi: Hugo van der Goes, http://www.televisual.net/uffizi/h_goes.html

Web Gallery of Art: Hugo van der Goes, http://www.kfki.hu/~arthp/html/g/goes/index.html

WebMuseum: Hugo van der Goes, http://metalab.unc.edu/wm/paint/auth/goes/

GOGH, VINCENT VAN

Artchive: Vincent van Gogh, http://artchive.com/artchive/V/vangogh.html

De La Faille, J.B. *The Works of Vincent Van Gogh: His Paintings and Drawings*. Alan Wofsy Fine Arts, 1970.

De Leeuw, Ronald, ed. *The Letters of Vincent Van Gogh*. Penguin USA, 1998.

Erickson, Kathleen Powers. *At Eternity's Gate: The Spiritual Vision of Vincent Van Gogh*. Wm. B. Eerdmans Publishing, 1998.

Metzger, Rainer. *Vincent Van Gogh: 1853-1890*. TASCHEN America, 1996.

Van Gogh Museum, http://www.vangoghmuseum.nl/

Vincent van Gogh Information Gallery, http://www.vangoghgallery.com/

GOYA

Artchive: Francisco Goya, http://www.artchive.com/artchive/ftptoc/goya_ext.html

Baticle, Jeannine. *Goya: Painter of Terrible Splendor*. Harry N. Abrams, 1994.

Harris, Enriqueta. *Goya*. Phaidon Press, 1994.

InfoGoya, http://goya.unizar.es/

Tomlinson, Janis. *Francisco Goya y Lucientes: 1746-1828*. Phaidon Press, 1999.

Waldron, Ann. *Francisco Goya*. Harry N. Adams, 1992.

WebMuseum: Francisco Goya, http://metalab.unc.edu/wm/paint/auth/goya/

GRECO, EL

Artchive: El Greco, http://www.artchive.com/artchive/ftptoc/el_greco_ext.html

Bronstein, Leo. *El Greco*. Harry N. Abrams, 1990.

CGFA: El Greco, http://sunsite.auc.dk/cgfa/greco/

Lopera, Jose Alvarez. *El Greco: Identity and Transformation*. Skira, 1999.

Serraller, F. Calvo. *El Greco: The Burial of Count Orgaz*. Thames & Hudson, 1995.

WebMuseum: El Greco, http://metalab.unc.edu/wm/paint/auth/greco/

GRIS, JUAN

Artchive: Juan Gris, http://www.artchive.com/artchive/ftptoc/gris_ext.html

Green, Christopher. *Juan Gris*. Yale University Press, 1993.

Telefonica: Juan Gris, http://www.telefonica.es/fat/egrintro.html

WebMuseum: Juan Gris, http://metalab.unc.edu/wm/paint/auth/gris/

GRUNEWALD, MATTHIAS

Monick, Eugene. *Evil, Sexuality, and Disease in Grunewald's Body of Christ.* Spring Publications, 1993.

Olga's Gallery: Matthias Grunewald, http://www.abcgallery.com/G/grunewald /grunewald.html

Richter, Gottfried. *The Isenheim Altar: Suffering and Salvation in the Art of Grunewald.* Floris Books, 1999.

HALS, FRANS

Frans Hals: An Exploration in Painting and Fashion, http://www.nga.gov /collection/gallery/gg46/gg46-main1.html

National Gallery of Art: Frans Hals, http://www.nga.gov/collection/gallery/gg46 /gg46-main1.html

Slive, Seymour, ed. *Frans Hals.* Alan Wofsy Fine Arts, 1989.

Van Der Groot, Georg. *Frans Hals, His Life, His Paintings: A Critique of His Art.* Gloucester Art Press, 1979.

HOCKNEY, DAVID

Artchive: David Hockney, http://www.artchive.com/artchive/ftptoc /hockney_ext.html

Clothier, Peter. *David Hockney.* Abbeville Press, 1995.

Hockney, David. *That's the Way I See It.* Chronicle Books, 1996.

Melia, Paul. *David Hockney.* Manchester University Press, 1995.

WebMuseum: David Hockney, http://sunsite.sut.ac.jp/wm/paint/auth/hockney/

HOFMANN, HANS

Estate of Hans Hofmann, http://www.hanshofmann.org/

Friedel, Helmut, et al. *Hans Hofmann.* Hudson Hills Press.

Goodman, Cynthia. *Hans Hofmann.* Abbeville Press, 1994.

Hans Hofmann, http://www.hanshoffman.com/

HOGARTH, WILLIAM

Artchive: William Hogarth, http://www.artchive.com/artchive/H/hogarth.html

Bindman, David. *Hogarth.* Thames & Hudson, 1985.

CGFA: William Hogarth, http://sunsite.auc.dk/cgfa/hogarth/

Uglow, Jennifer S. *Hogarth: A Life and a World.* Farrar Straus & Giroux, 1997.

William Hogarth's Realm, http://www.hogarth.cjb.net

HOLBEIN THE YOUNGER, HANS

Batschmann, Oskar and Pascal Griener. *Hans Holbein*. Princeton University Press, 1999.

Buck, Stephanie. *Hans Holbein: Masters of German Art*. Konemann, 1999.

CGFA: Hans Holbein the Younger, http://sunsite.auc.dk/cgfa/hholbei2/

Langdon, Helen. *Holbein*. Phaidon Press, 1993.

Web Gallery of Art: Hans Holbein the Younger, http://gallery.euroweb.hu/html/h/holbein/hans_y/

WebMuseum: Hans Holbein the Younger, http://metalab.unc.edu/wm/paint/auth/holbein/

HOUDON, JEAN-ANTOINE

Artcyclopedia: Jean-Antoine Houdon, http://www.artcyclopedia.com/artists/houdon_jean-antoine.html

Catholic Encyclopedia: Jean-Antoine Houdon, http://www.newadvent.org/cathen/07499a.htm

INGRES, JEAN-AUGUSTE-DOMINIQUE

Artchive: Jean-Auguste-Dominique Ingres, http://www.artchive.com/artchive/ftptoc/ingres_ext.html

CGFA: Jean-Auguste-Dominique Ingres, http://sunsite.auc.dk/cgfa/ingres/

Ockman, Carol. *Ingres's Eroticized Bodies: Retracing the Serpentine Line*. Yale University Press, 1995.

The Regency Portraits: Jean-Auguste-Dominique Ingres, http://locutus.ucr.edu/~cathy/reg6in.html

Rosenblum, Robert. *Jean-Auguste-Dominique Ingres*. Harry N. Abrams, 1990.

KANDINSKY, WASSILY

Artchive: Wassily Kandinsky, http://www.artchive.com/artchive/ftptoc/kandinsky_ext.html

Becks-Malorny, Ulrike. *Wassily Kandinsky, 1866-1944: The Journey to Abstraction*. TASCHEN America, 1999.

CGFA: Wassily Kandinsky, http://sunsite.auc.dk/cgfa/kandinsky/

Faerna, Jose Maria, ed. *Kandinsky*. Abradale Press, 1996.

Kandinsky, Wassily. *Kandinsky, Complete Writings on Art*. Da Capo Press, 1994.

Messer, Thomas M. *Kandinsky*. Harry N. Abrams, 1997.

OCAIW: Wassily Kandinsky, http://www.ocaiw.com/kandisk.htm

KAUFFMANN, ANGELICA

Artcyclopedia: Angelica Kauffmann, http://www.artcyclopedia.com/artists/kauffmann_angelica.html

Mayer, Dorothy M. *Angelica Kauffmann, R.A. 1741-1807*. Dufour Editions.

Women in Art: Angelica Kauffmann, http://www.mystudios.com/women/klmno/kauffmann.html

KIEFER, ANSELM

Artchive: Anselm Kiefer, http://www.artchive.com/artchive/K/kiefer.html

The Broad Art Foundation: Anselm Kiefer, http://www.broadartfdn.org/bio-kiefer.html

Celant, Germano and Massimo Cacciari. *Anselm Kiefer*. Charta, 1997.

Rosenthal, Mark. *Anselm Kiefer*. International Book Import Service, 1989.

Saltzman, Lisa. *Anselm Kiefer and Art after Auschwitz*. Cambridge University Press, 1999.

WebMuseum: Anselm Kiefer, http://metalab.unc.edu/wm/paint/auth/kiefer/

KIRCHNER, ERNST

Artchive: Ernst Ludwig Kirchner, http://www.artchive.com/artchive/K/kirchner.html

Artcyclopedia: Ernst Ludwig Kirchner, http://www.artcyclopedia.com/artists/kirchner_ernst_ludwig.html

Grisebach, Lucius. *Ernst Ludwig Kirchner 1880-1938*. TASCHEN America, 1999.

KLEE, PAUL

Artchive: Paul Klee, http://www.artchive.com/artchive/ftptoc/klee_ext.html

CGFA: Paul Klee, http://sunsite.auc.dk/cgfa/klee/

Faerna, Jose Maria, ed. *Klee*. Abradale Press, 1996.

Franciscono, Marcel. *Paul Klee: His Work and Thought*. University of Chicago Press, 1991.

Klee, Paul. *The Diaries of Paul Klee, 1898-1918*. University of California Press, 1964.

Klee, Paul. *Paul Klee on Modern Art*. Faber & Faber, 1985.

WebMuseum: Paul Klee, http://metalab.unc.edu/wm/paint/auth/klee/

KLIMT, GUSTAVE

Artchive: Gustav Klimt, http://www.artchive.com/artchive/ftptoc/klimt_ext.html

CGFA: Gustav Klimt, http://sunsite.auc.dk/cgfa/klimt/

Costantino, Maria. *Klimt*. Knickerbocker Press, 1998.

Dean, Catherine. *Klimt*. Phaidon Press, 1996.

Gustav Klimt Museum, http://www.laks.com/deutsch/klimtmuseum.html

Fliedl, Gottfried. *Gustav Klimt 1862-1918: The World in Female Form*. TASCHEN America, 1998.

Neret, Gilles. *Gustav Klimt 1862-1918*. TASCHEN America, 1996.

KOKOSCHKA, OSKAR

Artchive: Oskar Kokoschka, http://www.artchive.com/artchive/K/kokoschka.html

Artcyclopedia: Oskar Kokoschka, http://www.artcyclopedia.com/artists/kokoschka_oskar.html

Faerna, Jose Maria, ed. *Kokoschka*. Abradale Press, 1995.

Kokoschka, Oskar. *Kokoschaka Portraits and Figure Drawings: 47 Works*. Dover Publications, 1996.

Schroder, Klaus A. and Johann Winkler, eds. *Oskar Kokoschka*. International Book Import Service, 1991.

DE LA TOUR, GEORGES

Artchive: Georges de La Tour, http://www.artchive.com/artchive/ftptoc/de_la_tour_ext.html

Conisbee, Philip. *Georges De La Tour and His World*. Yale University Press, 1996.

Thuillier, Jacques. *Georges De La Tour*. Abbeville Press, 1993.

Web Gallery of Art: Georges de La Tour, http://www.kfki.hu/~arthp/html/l/la_tour/georges/

LEGER, FERNAND

Artchive: Fernand Leger, http://www.artchive.com/artchive/L/leger.html

Faerna, Jose Maria, ed. *Leger*. Abradale Press, 1996.

Lancher, Carolyn. *Fernand Leger*. Harry N. Abrams, 1998.

LIMBOURG BROTHERS (POL, HERMAN, JEAN)

CGFA: Limbourg Brothers, http://sunsite.auc.dk/cgfa/limbourg/index.html

Meiss, Millard. *French Painting in the Time of Jean De Berry: The Limbourgs and Their Contemporaries*. George Braziller, 1982.

Web Gallery of Art: Limbourg Brothers, http://gallery.euroweb.hu/html/l/limbourg/

WebMuseum: Limbourg Brothers, http://www.sai.msu.su/wm/rh/glo/limburg.html

MAGRITTE, RENE

Artchive: Rene Magritte, http://www.artchive.com/artchive/ftptoc/magritte_ext.html

Alden, Todd. *The Essential Rene Magritte*. Andrews McMeel Publishing, 1999.

CGFA: Rene Magritte, http://sunsite.auc.dk/cgfa/magritte/index.html

Hammacher, Abraham Marie. *Rene Magritte*. Abradale Press, 1995.

Magritte.com, http://www.magritte.com/

OCAIW: Rene Magritte, http://www.ocaiw.com/1magrit.htm

Paquet, Marcel. *Rene Magritte 1898-1967: Thoughts Rendered Visible*. TASCHEN America, 2000.

MALEVICH, KASIMIR

Artchive: Kasimir Malevich, http://www.artchive.com/artchive/ftptoc/malevich_ext.html

Bella Gallery: Kasimir Malevich, http://www.mcs.csuhayward.edu/~malek/Malevik.html

Milner, John. *Kasimir Malevich and the Art of Geometry*. Yale University Press, 1996.

WebMuseum: Kasimir Malevich, http://metalab.unc.edu/wm/paint/auth/malevich/

MANET, EDOUARD

Artchive: Edouard Manet, http://www.artchive.com/artchive/ftptoc/manet_ext.html

Brombert, Beth Archer. *Edouard Manet: Rebel in a Frock Coat*. University of Chicago Press, 1997.

CGFA: Edouard Manet, http://sunsite.auc.dk/cgfa/manet/

Courthion, Pierre. *Edouard Manet*. Harry N. Abrams, 1984.

Duchting, Hajo. *Edouard Manet: Images of Parisian Life*. International Book Import Service, 1997.

Eyewitness Encyclopedia: Manet, http://eyewitness.dk.com/VolumeContents.asp?BkNo=94

Fried, Michael. *Manet's Modernism: Or, the Face of Painting in the 1860s*. University of Chicago Press, 1996.

MANTEGNA, ANDREA

Carr, Dawson W. *Andrea Mantegna: The Adoration of the Magi*. J. Paul Getty Museum Publications, 1998.

Christiansen, Keith. *Andrea Mantegna: Padua and Mantua*. George Braziller, 1994.

Greenstein, Jack M. *Mantegna and Painting as Historical Narrative*. University of Chicago Press, 1992.

Web Gallery of Art: Andrea Mantegna, http://gallery.euroweb.hu/html/m/mantegna/

WebMuseum: Andrea Mantegna, http://metalab.unc.edu/wm/paint/auth/mantegna/

MARC, FRANZ

Artchive: Franz Marc, http://www.artchive.com/artchive/M/marc.html

Rosenthal, Mark Lawrence. *Franz Marc*. International Book Import Service, 1989.

WebMuseum: Franz Marc, http://metalab.unc.edu/wm/paint/auth/marc/

MASACCIO

Artchive: Masaccio, http://www.artchive.com/artchive/M/masaccio.html

Casazza, Ornella. *Masaccio and the Brancacci Chapel*. Riverside Book Company, 1994.

Fremantle, Richard. *Masaccio*. Smithmark Publishing, 1998.

Spike, John T. *Masaccio*. Abbeville Press, 1996.

Web Gallery of Art: Masaccio, http://www.kfki.hu/~arthp/html/m/masaccio/index.html

MATISSE, HENRI

Artchive: Henri Matisse, http://www.artchive.com/artchive/ftptoc/matisse_ext.html

Clement, Russell T. *Henri Matisse*. Greenwood Publishing Group, 1993.

Henri Matisse Art Gallery, http://www.geocities.com/Paris/LeftBank/4208/

Neret, Gilles. *Henri Matisse*. TASCHEN America, 1999.

Schaffner, Ingrid. *The Essential Henri Matisse*. Andrews McMeel Publishing, 1999.

Spurling, Hilary. *The Unknown Matisse: A Life of Henri Matisse: The Early Years, 1869-1908*. Knopf, 1998.

WebMuseum: Henri Matisse, http://metalab.unc.edu/wm/paint/auth/matisse/

MICHELANGELO

CGFA: Michelangelo, http://sunsite.auc.dk/cgfa/michelan/

De Vecchi, Pierluigi. *Michelangelo: The Vatican Frescoes*. Abbeville Press, 1997.

The Digital Michelangelo Project, http://graphics.stanford.edu/projects/mich/

Goldscheider, Ludwig. *Michelangelo: Paintings, Sculpture, Architecture*. Phaidon Press, 1996.

Michelangelo Buonarroti, http://www.michelangelo.com/buonarroti.html

Stone, Irving. *The Agony and the Ecstasy: A Biographical Novel of Michelangelo*. New American Library, 1996.

Wallace, William E. *Michelangelo: The Complete Sculpture, Painting, Architecture*. Hugh Lauter Levin Associates, 1998.

MILLAIS, JOHN EVERETT

CGFA: Sir John Everett Millais, http://sunsite.auc.dk/cgfa/millais/

Ash, Russell. *Sir John Everett Millais*. Trafalgar Square, 1998.

Fleming, Gordon H. *John Everett Millais: A Biography*. Constable & Co., 1999.

OCAIW: Sir John Everett Millais, http://www.ocaiw.com/millais.htm

Olga's Gallery: Sir John Everett Millais, http://www.abcgallery.com/M/millais/millais.html

MILLET, JEAN-FRANCOIS

Artcyclopedia: Jean-Francois Millet, http://www.artcyclopedia.com/artists/millet_jean-francois.html

Murphy, Alexandra R., ed. *Drawn Into the Light: Jean-Francois Millet*. Yale University Press, 1999.

MIRÓ, JOAN

Artchive: Joan Miro, http://www.artchive.com/artchive/ftptoc/miro_ext.html

Bella Gallery: Joan Miro, http://www.mcs.csuhayward.edu/~malek/Miro.html

Erben, Walter. *Miro*. TASCHEN America, 1998.

Lanchner, Carolyn. *Joan Miro*. Museum of Modern Art, 1993.

Mink, Janis. *Joan Miro: 1893-1983*. TASCHEN America, 1996.

OCAIW: Joan Miro, http://www.ocaiw.com/1miro.htm

MODIGLIANI, AMEDEO

Artchive: Amedeo Modigliani, http://www.artchive.com/artchive/ftptoc/modigliani_ext.html

Kruszynski, Anette. *Amedeo Modigliani: Portraits and Nudes*. International Book Import Service, 1996.

Mann, Carol. *Modigliani*. W.W. Norton, 1985.

OCAIW: Amedeo Modigliani, http://www.ocaiw.com/modiglia.htm

WebMuseum: Amedeo Modigliani, http://metalab.unc.edu/wm/paint/auth/modigliani/

MONDRIAN, PIET

Artchive: Piet Mondrian, http://www.artchive.com/artchive/M/mondrian.html

Faerna, Jose Maria, ed. *Mondrian*. Abradale Press, 1997.

Milner, John. *Mondrian*. Phaidon Press, 1995.

Schapiro, Meyer. *Mondrian: On the Humanity of Abstract Painting*. George Braziller, 1995.

WebMuseuem: Piet Mondrian, http://metalab.unc.edu/wm/paint/auth/mondrian/

MONET, CLAUDE

Artchive: Claude Monet, http://www.artchive.com/artchive/ftptoc/monet_ext.html

CGFA: Claude Monet, http://sunsite.auc.dk/cgfa/monet/

House, John. *Monet*. Phaidon Press, 1993.

Monet at Giverny, http://www.mmfa.qc.ca/visite-vr/anglais/index.html

Murray, Elizabeth. *Monet's Passion: Ideas, Inspiration, and Insights from the Painter's Gardens*. Pomegranate, 1989.

Patin, Sylvie. *Monet: The Ultimate Impressionist*. Harry N. Abrams, 1993.

Russell, Vivian. *Monet's Garden: Through the Seasons at Giverny*. Stewart, Tabori & Chang, 1995.

MOORE, HENRY

Artchive: Henry Moore, http://www.artchive.com/artchive/ftptoc/moore_ext.html

Hedgecoe, John. *A Monumental Vision: The Sculpture of Henry Moore*. Stewart, Tabori & Chang, 1998.

Mitchinson, David, ed. *Celebrating Moore: Works from the Collection of the Henry Moore Foundation*. University of California Press, 1998.

Moore, Henry and John Hedgecoe. *Henry Moore: My Ideas, Inspiration, and Life as an Artist*. Collins & Brown, 1999.

Henry Moore Foundation, http://www.henry-moore-fdn.co.uk/hmf/

MOREAU, GUSTAVE

Artchive: Gustave Moreau, http://www.artchive.com/artchive/M/moreau.html

Lacambre, Genevieve. *Gustave Moreau*. Princeton University Press, 1999.

Lacambre, Genevieve. *Gustave Moreau: Magic and Symbols*. Harry N. Abrams, 1999.

WebMuseum: Gustave Moreau, http://metalab.unc.edu/wm/paint/auth/moreau/

MUNCH, EDVARD

Artchive: Edvard Munch, http://artchive.com/artchive/M/munch.html

CGFA: Edvard Munch, http://sunsite.auc.dk/cgfa/munch/

Faerna, Jose Maria, ed. *Munch*. Abradale Press, 1996.

Hodin, Josef Paul. *Edvard Munch*. Thames & Hudson, 1985.

Messer, Thomas M. *Edvard Munch*. Harry N. Abrmas, 1986.

Schneede, Uwe M. *Edvard Munch: The Early Masterpieces*. W.W. Norton, 1991.

WebMuseum: Edvard Munch, http://metalab.unc.edu/wm/paint/auth/munch/

NOLDE, EMIL

Artchive: Emil Nolde, http://www.artchive.com/artchive/ftptoc/nolde_ext.html

Artcyclopedia: Emil Nolde, http://www.artcyclopedia.com/artists/nolde_emil.html

Nolde, Emil. *Emil Nolde: Works from American Collections*. Pennsylvania State University, 1988.

PHIDIAS

Artcyclopedia: Phidias, http://www.artcyclopedia.com/artists/phidias.html

Britannica.com: Phidias, http://www.britannica.com/bcom/eb/article/2 /0,5716,61132+1+59633,00.html

PICASSO, PABLO

Artchive: Pablo Picasso, http://www.artchive.com/artchive/ftptoc/picasso_ext.html

Brassai. *Conversations with Picasso*. University of Chicago Press, 1999.

Picasso, http://www.clubinternet.com/picasso/

Picasso Biography and Directory, http://www.showgate.com/tots/picasso/piclink.html

Richardson, John. *A Life of Picasso, 1881-1906*. Random House, 1996.

Rosenblum, Robert. *Picasso and the War Years: 1937-1945*. Thames & Hudson, 1998.

Schaffner, Ingrid. *The Essential Pablo Picasso*. Andrews McMeel Publishing, 1999.

PISANO, NICOLA

Artcyclopedia: Nicola Pisano, http://www.artcyclopedia.com/artists/pisano_nicola.html

Moskowitz, Anita Federer. *Nicola Pisano's Arca Di San Domenico and Its Legacy*. Pennsylvania State University Press, 1994.

Web Gallery of Art: Nicola Pisano, http://www.kfki.hu/~arthp/html/p/pisano/nicola/

PISSARRO, CAMILLE

Artchive: Camille Pissarro, http://www.artchive.com/artchive/ftptoc/pissarro_ext.html

Brettell, Richard R. and Joachim Pissarro. *The Impressionist and the City: Pissarro's Series Paintings*. Yale University Press, 1992.

Camille Pissarro Page, http://www-personal.umich.edu/~macduffe/

Pissarro, Joachim. *Camille Pissarro*. Harry N. Abrams, 1993.

Ward, Martha. *Pissarro, Neo-Impressionism, and the Spaces of the Avant-Garde*. University of Chicago Press, 1996.

WebMuseum: Camille Pissarro, http://metalab.unc.edu/wm/paint/auth/pissarro/

POLYKLEITOS

Great Buildings Online: Polykleitos, http://www.greatbuildings.com/architects/Polykleitos.html

Moon, Warren G., ed. *Polykleitos, the Doryphoros, and Tradition*. University of Wisconsin Press, 1995.

POUSSIN, NICOLAS

Carrier, David. *Poussin's Paintings: A Study in Art-Historical Methodology*. Pennsylvania State University Press, 1993.

CGFA: Nicolas Poussin, http://sunsite.icm.edu.pl/cjackson/poussin/index.html

Cropper, Elizabeth and Charles Dempsey. *Nicolas Poussin*. Princeton University Press, 2000.

Marin, Louis. *Sublime Poussin*. Stanford University Press, 1999.

Web Gallery of Art: Nicolas Poussin, http://www.kfki.hu/~arthp/html/p/poussin/index.html

PRAXITELES

Artcyclopedia: Praxiteles, http://www.artcyclopedia.com/artists/praxiteles.html

RAPHAEL

Artchive: Raphael, http://www.artchive.com/artchive/R/raphael.html

Beck, James H. *Raphael*. Harry N. Abrams, 1994.

CGFA: Raphael, http://sunsite.auc.dk/cgfa/raphael/

Jones, Roger. *Raphael*. Yale University Press, 1987.

Hall, Marcia B., ed. *Raphael's School of Athens*. Cambridge University Press, 1997.

Oberhuber, Konrad. *Raphael: The Paintings*. International Book Import Service, 1999.

WebMuseum: Raphael, http://metalab.unc.edu/wm/paint/auth/raphael/

REDON, ODILON

Artchive: Odilon Redon, http://www.artchive.com/artchive/ftptoc/redon_ext.html

CGFA: Odilon Redon, http://sunsite.auc.dk/cgfa/redon/

Gibson, Michael. *Odilon Redon 1840-1916: The Prince of Dreams*. TASCHEN America, 1996.

Harrison, Sharon R. *Etchings of Odilon Redon*. Da Capo Press, 1986.

WebMuseum: Odilon Redon, http://metalab.unc.edu/wm/paint/auth/redon/

REMBRANDT

Artchive: Rembrandt, http://www.artchive.com/artchive/ftptoc/rembrandt_ext.html

Kitson, Michael. *Rembrandt*. Phaidon Press, 1993.

Munz, Ludwig and Bob Haak. *Rembrandt*. Harry N. Abrams, 1990.

Rembrandt Mania, http://www.rnw.nl/doubledutch/en/rembrandt/

Schama, Simon. *Rembrandt's Eyes*. Knopf, 1999.

Van de Wetering, Ernst. *Rembrandt: The Painter at Work*. Amsterdam University Press, 1997.

WebMuseum: Rembrandt, http://metalab.unc.edu/wm/paint/auth/rembrandt/

RENOIR, PIERRE-AUGUSTE

Artchive: Pierre-Auguste Renoir, http://www.artchive.com/artchive/ftptoc/renoir_ext.html

CGFA: Pierre-Auguste Renoir, http://pollux.bibl.u-szeged.hu/cgfa/renoir/

Copplestone, Trewin. *Pierre-Auguste Renoir*. Grammercy, 1998.

House, John. *Pierre-Auguste Renoir: La Promenade*. J. Paul Getty Museum Publications, 1998.

OCAIW: Pierre-Auguste Renoir, http://www.ocaiw.com/1renoir.htm

Pach, Walter. *Pierre-Auguste Renoir*. Harry N. Abrams, 1983.

Rayfield, Susan. *Pierre-Auguste Renoir*. Harry N. Abrams, 1998.

REYNOLDS, JOSHUA

Artcyclopedia: Sir Joshua Reynolds, http://www.artcyclopedia.com/artists/reynolds_sir_joshua.html

CGFA: Sir Joshua Reynolds, http://sunsite.auc.dk/cgfa/reynolds/index.html

Mannings, David. *Sir Joshua Reynolds: A Complete Catalogue of His Paintings*. Yale University Press, 2000.

Postle, Martin. *Sir Joshua Reynolds: The Subject Pictures*. Cambridge University Press, 1995.

Wendorf, Richard. *Sir Joshua Reynolds: The Painter in Society*. Harvard University Press, 1998.

RODCHENKO, ALEXANDER

Artnet.com: Alexander Rodchenko, http://www.artnet.com/Magazine/features/schjeldahl/schjeldahl7-16-98.asp

Lavrentiev, Alexander, ed. *Rodchenko: Photography 1924-1954*. Konemann, 1999.

MoMA: Alexander Rodchenko, http://www.moma.org/exhibitions/rodchenko/index.html

RODIN, AUGUSTE

Artchive: Auguste Rodin, http://www.artchive.com/artchive/ftptoc/rodin_ext.html

Champigneulle, Bernard. *Rodin*. Thames & Hudson, 1999.

Crone, Rainer and Siegfried Salzmann, eds. *Rodin: Eros and Creativity*. International Book Import Service, 1997.

Korn, Irene. *Auguste Rodin: Master of Sculpture*. Todtri Productions, 1998.

Lampert, Catherine. *Rodin: Sculpture & Drawings*. Yale University Press, 1987.

Musee Rodin, http://www.musee-rodin.fr/

WebMuseum: Auguste Rodin, http://metalab.unc.edu/wm/paint/auth/rodin/

ROSSETTI, DANTE GABRIEL

Ash, Russell. *Dante Gabriel Rossetti*. Harry N. Abrams, 1995.

CGFA: Dante Gabriel Rossetti, http://sunsite.auc.dk/cgfa/rossetti/index.html

Marsh, Jan. *Dante Gabriel Rossetti*. J.M. Dent & Sons, 1999.

OCAIW: Dante Gabriel Rossetti, http://www.ocaiw.com/rossetti.htm

Prettejohn, Elizabeth. *Rossetti and His Circle*. Stewart, Tabori & Chang, 1998.

The Rossetti Archive, http://jefferson.village.virginia.edu/rossetti/index.html

ROUSSEAU, HENRI

Artchive: Henri Rousseau, http://www.artchive.com/artchive/ftptoc/rousseau_ext.html

Bouret, Jean. *Henri Rousseau*. Wittenborn Art Books, 1961.

Schmalenbach, Werner. *Henri Rousseau: Dreams of the Jungle*. International Book Import Service. 1998.

RUBENS, PETER PAUL

Addio Gallery: Peter Paul Rubens, http://www.mcs.csuhayward.edu/~malek/Rubens.html

Alpers, Svetlana. *The Making of Rubens*. Yale University Press, 1995.

Artchive: Peter Paul Rubens, http://www.artchive.com/artchive/ftptoc/rubens_ext.html

Belkin, Kristin Lohse. *Rubens*. Phaidon Press, 1998.

CGFA: Peter Paul Rubens, http://sunsite.auc.dk/cgfa/rubens/

Scribner, Charles. *Peter Paul Rubens*. Harry N. Abrams, 1989.

SCHWITTERS, KURT

Dietrich, Dorothea. *The Collages of Kurt Schwitters: Tradition and Innovation*. Cambridge University Press, 1995.

Gamard, Elizabeth Burns. *Kurt Schwitters' Merzbau: The Cathedral of Erotic Misery*. Princeton Architectural Press, 2000.

The Kurt Schwitters Page, http://www.soroptimist.de/kshome.htm

SEURAT, GEORGES

Artchive: Georges Seurat, http://www.artchive.com/artchive/ftptoc/seurat_ext.html

CGFA: Georges Seurat, http://sunsite.auc.dk/cgfa/seurat/index.html

Courthion, Pierre. *Georges Seurat*. Harry N. Adams, 1988.

Rewald, John. *Seurat: A Biography*. Harry N. Abrams, 1992.

Russell, John. *Seurat*. Thames & Hudson, 1985.

WebMuseum: Georges Seurat, http://metalab.unc.edu/wm/paint/auth/seurat/

SLUTER, CLAUS

Artcyclopedia: Claus Sluter, http://www.artcyclopedia.com/artists/sluter_claus.html

Morand, Kathleen. *Claus Sluter: Artist at the Court of Burgundy*. University of Texas Press, 1991.

Web Gallery of Art: Clause Sluter, http://www.kfki.hu/~arthp/html/s/sluter/

SOUTINE, CHAIM

Artchive: Chaim Soutine, http://www.artchive.com/artchive/S/soutine.html

Artcyclopedia: Chaim Soutine, http://www.artcyclopedia.com/artists/soutine_chaim.html

Kleeblatt, Norman L. and Kenneth E. Silver. *Chaim Soutine: An Expressionist in Paris*. International Book Import Service, 1998.

TINTORETTO

Artchive: Tintoretto, http://www.artchive.com/artchive/ftptoc/tintoretto_ext.html

Artcyclopedia: Tintoretto, http://www.artcyclopedia.com/artists/tintoretto.html

Nichols, Tom. *Tintoretto*. Reaktion Books, 1999.

Pinakothek, Alte, ed. *Jacopo Tintoretto: The Gonzaga Cycle*. Hatje, 2000.

WebMuseum: Tintoretto, http://metalab.unc.edu/wm/paint/auth/tintoretto/

TITIAN

Artchive: Titian, http://www.artchive.com/artchive/ftptoc/titian_ext.html

Biadene, Susanna, et al. *Titian: Prince of Painters*. International Book Import Service, 1990.

CGFA: Titian, http://sunsite.auc.dk/cgfa/titian/

Cole, Bruce. *Titian and Venetian Painting, 1450-1590*. Westview Press, 1999.

Kaminski, Marion. *Titian*. Konemann, 1998.

OCAIW: Titian, http://www.ocaiw.com/1tiziano.htm

TOULOUSE-LAUTREC, HENRI DE

Archive: Henri de Toulouse-Lautrec, http://www.artchive.com/artchive/ftptoc/toulouse-lautrec_ext.html

Freches, Claire. *Toulouse-Lautrec: Scenes of the Night*. Harry N. Abrams, 1994.

Frey, Julia Bloch. *Toulouse-Lautrec: A Life*. Trafalfar Square, 1998.

Heller, Reinhold. *Toulouse-Lautrec: The Soul of Montmartre*. International Book Import Service, 1997.

Thomson, Richard. *Toulouse-Lautrec*. Yale University Press, 1992.

Tesoro Gallery: Henri de Toulouse-Lautrec, http://www.mcs.csuhayward.edu/~malek/Toulouse.html

WebMuseum: Henri de Toulouse-Lautrec, http://metalab.unc.edu/wm/paint/auth/toulouse-lautrec/

TURNER, JOSEPH

Artchive: Joseph Mallord William Turner, http://www.artchive.com/artchive/ftptoc/turner_ext.html

Brown, David Blayney. *The Art of J.M.W. Turner*. Knickerbocker Press, 1998.

CGFA: Joseph Mallord William Turner, http://sunsite.auc.dk/cgfa/turner/

Rodner, William S. *J.M.W. Turner: Romantic Painter of the Industrial Revolution*. University of California Press, 1998.

Townsend, Richard P. *J.M.W. Turner, "That Greatest of Landscape Painters": Watercolors from London Museums*. University of Washington Press, 1998.

WebMuseum: Joseph Mallord William Turner, http://metalab.unc.edu/wm/paint/auth/turner/

VAN DYCK, ANTHONY

Blake, Robin. *Anthony Van Dyck*. Ivan R. Dee, 2000.

Brown, Christopher, ed. *Van Dyck: 1599-1641*. Rizzoli International Publications, 1999.

CGFA: Anthony van Dyck, http://sunsite.icm.edu.pl/cjackson/dyck/index.html

Gritsai, Natalia. *Anthony Van Dyck*. Parkstone Press, 1997.

Anthony van Dyck, http://www.vandyck.co.uk/welcome.html

WebMuseum: Anthony van Dyck, http://metalab.unc.edu/wm/paint/auth/dyck/

VELASQUEZ, DIEGO

Artchive: Diego Velazquez, http://www.artchive.com/artchive/V/velazquez.html

CGFA: Diego Velazquez, http://sunsite.icm.edu.pl/cjackson/velazque/index.html

Kagane, Liudmila. *Diego Velasquez*. Parkstone Press, 1997.

Serullaz, Maurice and Christian Pouillon. *Velazquez*. Harry N. Abrams, 1987.

WebMuseum: Diego Velazquez, http://metalab.unc.edu/wm/paint/auth/velazquez/

VERMEER, JAN

CGFA: Jan Vermeer, http://sunsite.auc.dk/cgfa/vermeer/

Mystudios.com: Jan Vermeer, http://www.mystudios.com/vermeer/

OCAIW: Jan Vermeer, http://www.ocaiw.com/vermeer.htm

WebMuseum: Jan Vermeer, http://metalab.unc.edu/wm/paint/auth/vermeer/

Wheelock, Arthur P. *Jan Vermeer*. Abradale Press, 1998.

WATTEAU, ANTOINE

Artchive: Jean-Antoine Watteau, http://www.artchive.com/artchive/W/watteau.html

Posner, Donald. *Antoine Watteau*. Cornell University Press, 1984.

Wintermute, Alan and Colin B. Bailey. *Watteau and His World: French Drawing from 1700 to 1750*. Merrell Holberton, 1999.

Web Gallery of Art: Antoine Watteau, http://www.kfki.hu/~arthp/html/w/watteau/

WebMuseum: Jean-Antoine Watteau, http://metalab.unc.edu/wm/paint/auth/watteau/

WEYDEN, ROGIER VAN DER

Artchive: Rogier van der Weyden, http://www.artchive.com/artchive/W/weyden.html

CGFA: Rogier van der Weyden, http://mirror.tvd.be/cjackson/weyden/index.html

De Vos, Dirk. *Rogier Van Der Weyden: The Complete Works*. Harry N. Abrams, 2000.

Van der Weyden, Rogier. *Rogier Van Der Weyden: Masters of Dutch Art*. Konemann, 2000.

WebMuseum: Rogier van der Weyden, http://metalab.unc.edu/wm/paint/auth/weyden/

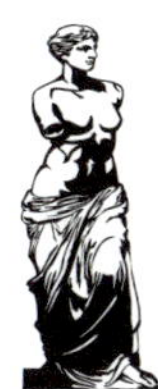

Glossary

abstract expressionism An artistic movement in painting characterized by the artist applying paint rapidly and with force onto giant canvases in an attempt to convey emotion and feeling.

abstractionism An artistic movement characterized by the artist's use of imagery that departs from traditional and representational accuracy, and the simplification or exaggeration of forms.

Acropolis The fortified hill of ancient Athens.

aesthetic Responding to or being enthusiastic over the appreciation of artistic endeavors.

allegorical Possessing veiled spiritual meaning transcending the literal interpretation of a sacred work.

allegory An expression by utilizing symbolic fictional characters and actions of truths or generalizations about the human condition.

altarpiece The work of art and ornamentation that decorates the space behind and above an altar in a church.

anachronism An individual or idea whose time has past and is considered severely and drastically outdated.

Annunciation A painting depicting Robert Campin's interpretation of the church festival celebrating the announcement of the Incarnation to the Virgin Mary.

anomalous Inconsistent with the normal or usual; irregular.

anti-Semite An individual or state of thought hostile towards Jews and the Jewish faith.

art nouveau French term for "new art"; a 19th and early 20th century style characterized by depicting flowers and leaves in undulating lines and flowing vines.

avant-garde French term for vanguard; symbolizes artists at the forefront of creative and original ideas that often oppose established tradition and methods.

Barbizon A philosophy of artistic work displayed by artists such as Bannister, Millet and Corot; Barbizon school emphasizes themes from nature and the natural world.

Baroque A style of art in which artists sought to convey movement, emotion, and variety in their pieces; this style was at its peak in the mid-17th century mainly in Catholic nations.

bas-relief A sculptural relief in which the projecting image from its surrounding surface is slight, and no part of the model is undercut.

benign Description of a gentle, unthreatening disposition.

bohemian Usually associated with artists characterized by living in an unconventional circumstance, such as in a colony with like-minded individuals.

Byzantine Relating to the Byzantine Empire and its architectural styles, particularly the fifth and sixth century domes carried on pendentives over a square, and marble veneers incrusted with mosaics on gold grounds.

camera obscura Almost literally, the first camera; a darkened room with a tiny hole in a wall through which light would pass and transmit an inverted image of an outside scene on a screen.

chiaroscuro The method painters use to depict light and shade by making them contrast drastically; the word chiaroscuro is taken from the Italian word for dark.

color field painting A form of painting in which a large canvas is covered with solid areas of color.

conceptualism A 20th century artistic movement characterized by the artist's own verbal interpretation of his or her work.

courtier An individual in the attendance of a royal court.

crescendo The peak of a gradual increase; usually associated with music.

cubism School of art popularized by the works of Pablo Picasso and characterized by squared-off images of many different objects, animals, and people.

cupola A small structure constructed on top of a roof or ceiling.

degenerate Description of a person or thing that has sunk below what would be considered the normal standards of decency and taste; term was applied by the Nazi Party in Germany to describe artists with whom the party disagreed.

drypoints A printing process in which burrs are left on a plate by a pointed needle that inscribes lines.

ducal Of or relating to a duke or dukedom.

embryology The branch of biology that examines the development of embryos.

emigrate To leave one's place of origin to live elsewhere.

encroaching Movement of an individual or group in a gradual or unwelcome fashion into an area where they are unwelcome.

ephemeral Lasting for a short period of time.

epitaph A short statement or expression honoring and summing up a dead person or past event or ceremony.

epitomized Described or characterized perfectly a situation or individual.

equanimity Attribute characterized by a balanced mind and sense of fairness and equity.

erudite Possessing a knowledge gleaned nearly exclusively from books and bookreading.

Etruscan Of or relating to citizens of the ancient nation of Etruria.

evocative Serving to evoke a particular spirit or emotion.

existentialism A 20th century philosophical movement centering on the study of the individual's existence in an endless universe and the acts of the individual who assumes responsibility for his acts without the knowledge of what is right and wrong.

expressionism A style of art in which the artist produces a work that conveys his or her emotions, expressed through abstractions and distortions; expressionist work can be found throughout many periods of art history.

fauvism A French style of painting during the early 20th century; the word *fauves* means "wild beast" in French, and was used to describe the artists of this style who reflected an uncontrolled and violent use of intense colors in their paintings.

francs French currency.

fresco A method of painting on either dry or wet plaster.

frieze Any ornamentally sculptured band on furniture, a gallery, or a wall.

futurism An early 20th century artistic movement with roots in Italy that emphasized an effort to give an expression to mechanical functions and processes.

genre paintings Paintings that depict scenes from ordinary everyday life, common citizens, and mundane activities; the height of popularity for genre painting came in 17th century Holland.

gouaches Heavy opaque watercolor paints that produce a strongly colored and less watered looking picture than regular watercolor.

Hellenic Relating to the ancient Greeks and their language.

hermetic Invulnerable to outside influences or beliefs; keeping to oneself.

humanist An individual who give priority in their life and work to the endeavors, works, and needs of human beings rather to religious gods, symbols, or any other non-human entities.

iconography Material in a pictorial form that illustrates a subject.

illegitimate Description of a child born out of wedlock.

illuminator An individual who worked as an illustrator of manuscripts and used silver, gold, and other bright colors with oftentimes elaborate decorations.

illusionism Style of art that distorts imagery to create an optical illusion to the viewer.

impasto A thick, lumpy application of paint, or deep brush marks.

impetus A driving force or stimuli resulting in an increase of activity.

impudence The state of being impudent, which is to lack modesty or to display brash and brazen boldness in attitude towards others.

inimical Being purposely belligerent due to hostility or malevolence.

intermittent The coming and going of a career or other happening; going in intervals.

internecine A confrontation characterized by bitter and conflict and mutual destruction.

juxtapositions Instances in which two or more objects or ideas are placed together.

languid Sluggish or lacking in forcefulness.

lithography The process of printing an image, which is to be printed in ink, from a plane surface.

macabre Dwelling on death or ghastly thoughts and occurrences.

maelstrom A powerful and violent whirlpool that envelops objects within a particular radius.

malaria Tropical disease caused by parasites in red blood cells and transmitted by mosquitoes; characterized by attacks of chills and fevers.

mannerism The style of art reflected in the works of European artists between 1520 and 1600 and characterized by emotion and distortion symbolizing the enormous tension in Europe during that time period.

mannerist An artist in the mannerism genre who composed pieces that made an effort to reflect the enormous amount of tension on the European continent between 1520 and 1600; mannerists specialized in reflecting emotion and distortion.

metaphysical school A movement in Italian art during the early 20th century that strove to present an alternative reality by utilizing ordinary subject material and expressing it in a stark fashion.

modernism A school of art incorporating innovative forms of expression, integrating previous methods and techniques, and utilizing new materials and types of paint and material in creating abstract pieces as opposed to realistic representations.

montages A single composition comprised of juxtaposed or superimposed images or designs.

mosaics Pictures or designs made up of small pieces of glass, colored stone, tile, or paper attached to a surface typically seen on walls, floors and ceilings.

motif A reoccurring or dominant, salient theme in a work of art.

myriad A wide array of activities or contents.

Napolenonic Wars Wars commenced by Napoleon I of France in his ambition to rule Europe.

naturalism An artistic style that attempts to portray an object in nature in its most realistic state on a canvass or paper.

neo-classicism An artistic style in 19th century France that responded to the Baroque school of artistic expression, and is characterized by the revival of ancient Roman and Greek ideals of classic form to express love of country, courage, and sacrifice.

neo-impressionism A painting movement composed of artists, led by Georges-Pierre, Seurat reacting to the impressionist school; Seurat perfected the pointillism technique, in which the artist brings together dots of pure color made by the paintbrush.

neoplastic An art movement advocating simplicity and abstraction reduced to the rectangle and colors to the primary colors and black and white.

nymph In classical mythology, the minor divinities represented as beautiful maidens who lived in nature.

oeuvre A French word meaning or representing a substantial body of work by an artist, composer, or writer.

one-point perspective A form of linear perspective wherein all lines in the piece seem to form a horizon and meet at a single point.

pagan An individual who adheres to little or no religion and who revels in sensual pleasures and material wealth.

paradigms Typical examples and patterns of behavior.

pariah An individual outcast from society for criminal or immoral actions as deemed by that society.

pastels Pigments mixed with gum that are pressed into a stick form and used as crayons; the works of art done with such a substance are called pastels.

pastoral Relating to shepherds, herdsmen, and countryside images in an idealized form.

patronage The financial, emotional, and professional support supplied to an artist by a patron.

pedestrian Description of mundane, common, and unexciting day-to-day activities or actions.

pendants An object hanging from another object, such as an ornament hanging from a necklace.

penury An extreme and crippling lack of financial resources or extreme frugality.

pergola A column-lined walkway supporting a roof of trellis work on which ivy and other plants grow.

perspective A technique used by artists to convey a three-dimensional illusion onto a two-dimensional surface.

pointillism Artistic technique in which the artist brings together dots of pure color made by the paintbrush.

polychrome Multicolored.

pop art An artistic style originating in the 1950s in England and the United States in the 1960s; characterized by vivid colors and the use of familiar commercial images and products.

portals Grand and imposing entrances, usually associated with cathedrals or other places of worship.

portraiture The art of creating portraits.

post impressionism An art movement originating in France that immediately followed the Impressionist and neo-Impressionist school; the artists of post-Impressionism emphasized structure, form, and expression more so than ever and rejected the emphasis of nature and the depiction of light.

primordial The earliest formed growth of an individual, movement, or society.

prodigy A highly developed and talented child who excels in a particular area of academics or artistic works.

protege An individual who is trained or apprenticed by a person of high prominence or experience in a particular field.

pulpit An elevated platform from which a member of the clergy conducts a worship service and or delivers a sermon.

reconcilliation A settlement or resolution of a conflict between two or more parties.

refraction The distorting of an image by looking at it through a medium.

Renaissance A period of time in Europe in which a cultural and intellectual rebirth took place during the 14th and 15th centuries, concentrated in Italy, Germany, and other European nations; the period was marked by a renewed interest in Greek and Roman art, design, and philosophy.

renditions Performances or interpretations.

renowned Well-known and recognized for a body of work in the arts or other area of life.

reveries daydreams.

Rococo A style of painting emerging in the 18th century that emphasized the leisurely lives of aristocrats as opposed to religious martyrs or heroes; the focus was on love and romance and was characterized by free flowing movement, use of line, and color.

rustic An individual who lives in a rural area or affects the behavior of an unsophisticated or coarse person.

satire A form of writing or speaking that utilizes wit, irony, and sarcasm to express commentary on human follies and foibles.

sloth inactivity or apathy of the spirit; insolent and lazy behavior; said to be one of the seven deadly sins.

spatial Occupying, related to, or having the character of space.

stipend A fixed amount of money disbursed periodically for services or work.

sui generis Making up a class or category that stands alone in uniqueness.

supplemented Added or completed.

surrealist movement A literary and art movement founded by writer André Breton in Paris in 1924 and practiced internationally into the 1930s. It was grounded in the psychoanalytic theories of Sigmund Freud, particularly those relating to the expression of the imagination as revealed in dreams. Using a range of styles, the surrealists, such as Salvador Dalí and René Magritte, filled their works with fantastic imagery and dream-inspired symbols.

tapestries Heavy handwoven textiles with pictorial designs that are utilized as curtains, hangings, and upholstery.

temerity Foolish or unwise casualness in the face of opposition or danger.

tempera A painting process that utilizes egg yolks to bind pigments; the artist must manufacture the substance by mixing pigment, water, and diluted egg yolk; this process was used before the availability of oil paints.

tepid Lukewarm in enthusiasm.

theorems Statements, formulas, or propositions in mathematics or logical deduction.

treatise A systematic written demonstration that includes examples of fact and principle, and a summation and presentation of a final conclusion.

triptych A painting that is made up of three different parts, canvases, or panels commonly found in altarpieces during the Middle Ages and the Renaissance period.

verdant Green in tint or color; green growing plants.

vespers Relating to the evening; the sixth of the canonical hours said or sung in the late afternoon.

vistas Distant views along or through an opening or avenue.

voluptuous Complete delight to the senses, especially as related to sensual gratification.

woodcuts A print fashioned by a cut design in the grain of a side of a block of wood; ink is transferred from the raised surfaces to the paper.

zodiac The imaginary belt in the heavens that is said to encompass the paths of each of the principal planets with the exception of Pluto, and is divided into 12 signs or constellations for astrological purposes.

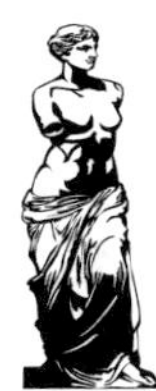

Index

T

U

V